INTERMEDIATE ACCOUNTING STEP BY STEP

with graded exercises

R. J. Thornhill

Edward Arnold
A division of Hodder & Stoughton
LONDON   NEW YORK   MELBOURNE   AUCKLAND

Acknowledgements

I would like to express my sincere thanks to many people who helped in writing this book. In particular I am grateful to my wife, Teresa, to whom this book is dedicated for her support, patience and forbearance. I would also like to thank Elaine Kavanagh and Paul Skehan who provided invaluable help in the preparation and correction of the material. I wish to thank my teaching colleague, Rory O'Sullivan, for his help with the chapter on Computers in Accounting. I would also like to express my thanks to my students for class-testing the graded exercise material.

I would also like to express my appreciation of the valuable suggestions made by D.E.O. Cox in the course of editing the text.

Questions from past examination papers are reproduced by kind permission of the following: the Association of Accounting Technicians, the Chartered Association of Certified Accountants, the London Chamber of Commerce and Industry, Pitman Examinations Institute and the Royal Society of Arts Examinations Board. The answers given are the responsibility of the author, not the examining body.

The extracts from SSAP 10 are reproduced by permission of the Accounting Standards Committee of the Consultative Committee of Accountancy Bodies.

© 1988 R. J. Thornhill

First published in Great Britain 1988

British Library Cataloguing in Publication Data

Thornhill, R.J.
   Intermediate accounting step by step
   1. Accounting
   I. Title
   657

ISBN 0 7131 7666 0

All rights reserved. No part of this publication may be reproduced or transmitted in any form or by any means, electronically or mechanically, including photocopying, recording or any information storage or retrieval system, without either prior permission in writing from the publisher or a licence permitting restricted copying. In the United Kingdom such licences are issued by the Copyright Licensing Agency, 33–34 Alfred Place, London WC1E 7DP.

Typeset in Linotron Plantin by
Wearside Tradespools, Fulwell, Sunderland
Printed and bound in Great Britain for
Edward Arnold, the educational, academic and medical publishing division of Hodder and Stoughton Limited, 41 Bedford Square, London WC1B 3DQ by Richard Clay plc, Bungay, Suffolk

Contents

Preface	page vii
1. Accounting concepts	1
Statements of Standard Accounting Practice	4
Exercises Set 1	5
2. Accounting records and documentation, VAT	10
Accounting records	10
Exercises Set 2A	14
Treatment of Value Added Tax	18
Exercises Set 2B	20
3. The trial balance and suspense accounts	25
The trial balance: location and correction of errors	25
Exercises Set 3A	32
Suspense accounts: effects of errors on net profit	33
Exercises Set 3B	38
4. Bank reconciliation statements	49
Exercises Set 4	57
5. Control accounts	69
Exercises Set 5	76
6. Capital and revenue expenditure and receipts	89
Exercises Set 6	92
7. Adjustments for accruals, prepayments and bad debts	95
Adjustments for accruals and prepayments	95
Exercises Set 7A	99
Adjustments for bad debts	103
Exercises Set 7B	109

8. Depreciation of fixed assets 112
Methods of calculating depreciation 114
Exercises Set 8 121

9. Final accounts of sole traders 131
Trading and Profit and Loss Accounts 132
The balance sheet (position statement) 136
Exercises Set 9 141

10. Partnership ledger and final accounts 153
Partners' accounts 153
Partnership Profit and Loss Appropriation Account 154
Partners' balance sheet 158
Exercises Set 10 159

11. Formation of partnership I: treatment of goodwill 173
Methods of valuing goodwill 174
Treatment of goodwill in the books 175
Revaluation of assets 176
Exercises Set 11 185

12. Formation of partnership II: amalgamations to form a partnership 196
Exercises Set 12 202

13. Dissolution of partnership 208
Exercises Set 13 213

14. Joint venture accounts 218
Exercises Set 14 221

15. Consignment accounts 225
Exercises Set 15 229

16. Bills of exchange 232
Parties to a bill of exchange 232
Advantages of a bill of exchange 233
Treatment of bills in books of account 234
Exercises Set 16 243

17. Branch accounts 247
Records kept at head office 248
Records kept at branch 254
Exercises Set 17 256

Contents v

18. Issue of shares and debentures, redemption and purchase of company's own shares	261
Shares	261
Debentures	266
Redemption and purchase of company's own shares	267
Exercises Set 18	271
19. Purchase of a business	276
Exercises Set 19	285
20. Manufacturing accounts	289
Exercises Set 20	294
21. Preparation and presentation of internal final accounts and balance sheets of companies	306
Exercises Set 21	328
22. Interpretation of financial statements	353
Ratio analysis	355
Ratio analysis: problems and remedies	364
Exercises Set 22	367
23. Accounts of non-commercial organisations	391
Receipts and payments accounts	391
Income and expenditure accounts	393
Exercises Set 23	401
24. Preparation of accounts from incomplete records	416
Exercises Set 24	431
25. Treatment of stock and stock valuation	447
Methods of stock valuation	447
Importance of stock valuation	452
Exercises Set 25	453
26. Hire purchase accounts and agreements to pay by instalments	456
Methods of dealing with interest	457
Hire purchase trading account	462
Exercises Set 26	463
27. Sources and applications of funds	465
Exercises Set 27	471

28. Computers in accounting	481
Abridged answers	490
Index	531

Preface

This is an accounting textbook based on the theory that proficiency in accounting and examination success are best gained by a particular combination of knowledge and application of theory. I believe that these dual aims are best achieved by combining a concise explanation of theory, demonstrated in graded worked examples, with a large quantity of graded exercise material. Each chapter in *Intermediate Accounting Step by Step* starts with a clear explanation of the accounting theory involved, followed by a detailed set of step-by-step instructions. These instructions are followed by one or two fully worked examples which implement the instructions. In order to provide the student with the practice vital to the complete understanding of the theory and to examination success a series of finely graded exercises is included with each chapter. These exercises start by testing the basic concepts and build up, point by point, to a complete revision and testing of all the theory and procedures. Each set of exercises is followed by suitable examination questions from various examining bodies. The student who has progressed through the various steps in the previous exercises should have no problem in answering all the examination questions.

The text covers the syllabuses of the Association of Accounting Technicians (Intermediate), the London Chamber of Commerce and Industry (Intermediate), Pitman (Intermediate) and the Royal Society of Arts (Stage II) as well as the core topics of the syllabuses of other examining bodies.

After a brief revision of basic theories and concepts the text fully covers the ledger and final accounts of sole traders, partnerships, and limited companies. A large section is devoted to the interpretation of accounts. Other subjects dealt with include Consignment, Joint Venture, Branch and Hire Purchase Accounts, issue and redemption of shares, sources and application of funds, accounts of non-commercial organisations and accounts for incomplete records. A chapter on computerised accounting is included.

Abridged answers, where appropriate, are provided at the end of the book. These aim, by giving key information, to help students check that they have followed the correct procedure.

1 *Accounting concepts*

Accounting has been defined by the American Institute of Certified Public Accountants as follows: 'Accounting is the art of recording, classifying and summarising in a significant manner and in terms of money, transactions and events which are, in part at least, of a financial character, and interpreting the results thereof.' The important words in this definition are 'recording', 'classifying', 'summarising', 'significant' and 'interpreting'.

Recording deals with the book-keeping aspect, the making of records. Correct recording is vital if proper and accurate books and records are to be kept. It is important that records are prepared in a consistent manner so that accurate comparisons can be made between one period and another. Records should be kept in such a way that information can be easily extracted from the books for presentation to interested parties.

Classifying means that figures are collected together, properly labelled under specified headings so that comparison can be made between different periods to enable greater control to be exercised by management. Classifying must be consistent so that like can be compared with like over a given period.

Summarising takes place for simplification and to make concise information available.

Interpreting takes the figures and information available and from them extracts ratios and percentages which enables management to make rational, well-informed judgements to make the control and use of resources more efficient. Information leads to control and action to rectify undesirable aspects and trends in the business.

The word *significant* means significant in content and significant to those who will be reading them. 'Significant' accounts and accounting procedures will be of prime concern to management. The definition also points out one of the main shortcomings of financial accounting in that it concerns itself only with transactions that can be expressed only in monetary terms (see the money measurement concept). It also assumes that the value of money will remain constant so that it does not directly take inflation into account. Non-monetary

2 Accounting concepts

but highly important other aspects of the business are not dealt with in the accounts, such as management–staff relationships, staff morale, the activity of competitors or the state of the economy.

All the aspects mentioned in the definition will be employed within a total or overall framework or theory, which will underpin the accounting treatment of all financial transactions. We call this body of theory or framework *accounting concepts*.

Accountants work within recognised broad outlines of accounting theory known as accounting principles or concepts. These principles are being continuously examined and analysed by accountants in their search for better ways and means of presenting and interpreting accounting data. It is important that students recognise and apply these principles to the accounts they prepare and recognise them in the accounts presented to them by others.

The generally accepted principles or concepts are:

1. The business entity concept
2. The money measurement concept
3. The double-entry concept
4. The realisation concept
5. The objectivity concept
6. The materiality concept
7. The going-concern concept
8. The accruals or matching concept
9. The concept of conservatism (or the prudence concept)
10. The concept of consistency.

1. The business entity concept sees the business as distinct from the owner or owners irrespective of the legal position. It means that the accounts are prepared from the point of view of the business and not from the point of view of the owners. For example, when a sole trader invests money in his business the business is seen as having that money as its own; the owner is just a creditor for capital. It does not matter that in law he is liable even to the extent of his private assets for the debts of the business. It is essential that only business transactions appear in the accounts.

2. The money measurement concept recognises that accounting is concerned only with those facts and transactions that can be expressed in monetary terms. The value of assets, liabilities, gains and losses is expressed in currency terms. This concept accepts that financial statements in themselves can never give a complete picture of the affairs of a firm. Such important factors as, for example, management–worker relationships, staff morale, the activity of competitors or the state of the economy are not revealed by the accounting procedures. This concept also has the disadvantage that it does not take inflation or deflation into account. It implies that the value of money remains stable.

3. The double-entry concept sees the twofold nature of each transaction, i.e. a giving by one party of some sort of wealth and a receiving of the same wealth by another party. The transaction is entered twice in the accounts: once on the debit side of one account and once on the credit side of another account. This is the reason for the well-worn phrase 'every debit must have a corresponding credit'.

4. The realisation concept assumes that profit is earned or realised at the time of sale to the customer even though payments may not be received until the next accounting period. This concept seems to clash with the concept of conservatism (see **9** below).

5. The objectivity concept holds that the figures the accountant uses should, as far as possible, be based on facts which can be verified by an outside observer. For example, accountants like to record the value of fixed assets at 'cost'. This figure is verifiable from invoices.

6. The materiality concept places the onus on the person preparing the accounts to use his common sense and integrity in including in the appropriate sections of the accounts items that are relevant or material.

For example, a wastepaper basket which costs £5 and will last for ten years is, strictly speaking, a capital item. Will the accountant depreciate its value each year by 50p? Of course he will not. He will use his common sense and write it off in the first year as a sundry expense. It is not a material item. However, if the firm were to buy a paper shredder for £5 000 with a life span of ten years it would be wrong to write it off in the year of purchase. It now *is* a material item. The decision as to what is 'material' will depend on the amount involved, the size of the firm and – mainly – on the accountant's judgement.

7. The going-concern concept means that accounts are prepared on the assumption that the business will continue in existence for the foreseeable future. Interpretation of accounts also takes place on this basis. However, banks and finance companies continue to value a company's assets at their 'break-up' or sale value in the event of the company ceasing to exist. They are mainly interested in making sure that the break-up values cover their loans.

If the accountant feels that the business will not be continuing in its present form accounts should *not* be prepared on a going-concern basis. The new basis (e.g. break-up value) should be explicitly stated, otherwise it will be assumed that the going-concern basis is used.

8. The accruals or matching concept requires that revenue income and expenditure are precisely matched over the period in question in the financial statements. It requires that all items of revenue expenditure that refer to a particular period are included in the accounts for that period. Similar treatment must be given to revenue receipts that apply to the particular period. Expenses and receipts for other accounting periods must be excluded from the financial statements of the current period. Income and expenditure must be precisely matched for the accounting period in question.

9. The concept of conservatism (or the prudence concept) means that the accountant should foresee and allow for all possible losses but that possible gains should not be anticipated. For this reason when the accountant is faced with a choice between two figures (for instance, over stock valuation) he will choose the figure which will tend to underestimate rather than overestimate the profits. Also, for this reason, the prudent trader will make provision for losses which are likely to occur, but will make no allowance for revenue receipts likely to occur in the future.

10. The concept of consistency means that the firm, having adopted one particular system of accounting, will use the same system year after year. It will not change the system of preparing and presenting accounting data without the deepest consideration. It is most important that accounts and statements should be shown consistently so that like can be compared with like in extracting financial ratios and making monetary judgements.

Statement of Standard Accounting Practice No. 2 (SSAP 2), Disclosure of Accounting Policies, gives added weight to the importance of the last four concepts, when it states that 'in the absence of a clear statement to the contrary there is a presumption that the four fundamental concepts have been observed.'

SSAP 2 also defines accounting bases and accounting policies. *Accounting bases* are defined as the methods developed for applying fundamental accounting concepts to financial transactions and items for the purpose of financial accounts and in particular (*a*) for determining the accounting periods in which revenue and costs should be recognised in the Profit and Loss Account, and (*b*) for determining the amounts at which material items should be stated in the balance sheet.

Accounting policies are the specific accounting bases selected and consistently followed by a business enterprise as being, in the opinion of the management, appropriate to its circumstances and best suited to present fairly its results and financial position.

Legal recognition has been given to these last five concepts in the Companies Act. The student should be constantly aware of these requirements and see the operation of these concepts right through the subject so that his practice will be built on a sound theoretical base.

Statements of Standard Accounting Practice

Consistency

Over the last twenty years consistency in the preparation and presentation of accounting data has been achieved by the introduction of Statements of Standard Accounting Practice (SSAPs).

An Accounting Standards Committee was set up in 1969 to propose definitive standards of financial accounting and reporting to which all accountants would be expected to conform.

These statements have been approved by the major professional accounting bodies for application to financial statements which purport to give a true and fair view of the financial position of the organisation or to statements of profit and loss.

Accountants who belong to the professional bodies must observe the requirements of these accounting standards or explain deviations from them.

The following is the list of Statements of Standard Accounting Practice in numerical order:

SSAP
1. Accounting for the Results of Associated Companies
2. Disclosure of Accounting Policies
3. Earnings per Share
4. The Accounting Treatment of Government Grants
5. Accounting for Value Added Tax
6. Extraordinary Items and Prior Year Adjustments
7. (Provisional) Accounting for Changes in the Purchasing Power of Money (withdrawn January 1978)
8. The Treatment of Taxation under the Imputation System in the Accounts of Companies
9. Stocks and Work-in-progress
10. Statements of Source and Application of Funds
11. Accounting for Deferred Taxation (withdrawn October 1979)
12. Accounting for Depreciation
13. Accounting for Research and Development
14. Group Accounts
15. Accounting for Deferred Taxation
16. Current Cost Accounting
17. Accounting for Post-Balance Sheet Events
18. Accounting for Contingencies
19. Accounting for Investment Properties
20. Foreign Currency Translation
21. Accounting for Leases and Hire Purchase Contracts
22. Accounting for Goodwill
23. Accounting for Acquisitions and Mergers.

Exercises Set 1

1 (a) Define the term 'accounting' so as to emphasise its more important functions.
  (b) Distinguish between 'accounting' and 'book-keeping'.

2 What are Statements of Standard Accounting Practice (SSAPs)?

3 How do Statements of Standard Accounting Practice help accountants when preparing financial statements?

6 Accounting concepts

4 Financial statements are normally prepared on the basis of a number of accounting concepts.

State what you understand by each of the following accounting concepts, and how they are applied in the preparation of financial statements: **a** entity; **b** going concern; **c** accruals (or matching); **d** conservatism (or prudence); **e** consistency.

[*Association of Accounting Technicians, June 1984*]

5 In preparing the accounts of your company, you are faced with a number of problems. These are summarised below:
1. The managing director wishes the company's good industrial relations to be reflected in the accounts.
2. The long-term future success of the company is extremely uncertain.
3. Although the sales have not yet actually taken place, some reliable customers of the company have placed several large orders that are likely to be extremely profitable.
4. One of the owners of the company has invested his drawings in some stocks and shares.
5. At the year end, an amount is outstanding for electricity that has been consumed during the accounting period.
6. All the fixed assets of the company would now cost a great deal more than they did when they were originally purchased.
7. During the year, the company purchased £10 worth of pencils; these had all been issued from stock and were still in use at the end of the year.
8. The company has had a poor trading year, and the owners believe that a more balanced result could be presented if a LIFO (last-in, first-out) stock valuation method was adopted, instead of the present FIFO (first-in, first-out) method.
9. A debtor who owes a large amount to the company is rumoured to be going into liquidation.
10. The company owns some shares in a quoted company which the accountant thinks are worthless.

a State which accounting rule the accountant should follow in dealing with each of the above problems.
b Explain briefly what each rule means.

[*Association of Accounting Technicians, June 1982*]

6 In preparing the accounts of Fruit and Nut for the year to 31 March 1985, a number of problems were encountered. These were as follows:
1. The partnership had paid both Fruit and Nut's personal income tax for the year to 5 April 1984.
2. Fruit and Nut employed an excellent manager who had worked for the firm for 25 years. He was regarded as just as valuable an asset as the premises in which he worked, and the partners are insisting that his worth be included on the balance sheet.
3. Specialist equipment had cost £10 000 to build, but if the partnership went into liquidation, it would probably have no value.
4. Certain stocks were valued on a FIFO (first-in, first-out) basis, but it was believed that less tax would be paid by the partners if the stocks were valued on a LIFO (last-in, first-out) basis.
5. At 31 May 1985, there were only two gallons of petrol in the firm's delivery van. The partners are not sure how this should be recorded in the books of account.
6. The partnership owed £2 000 for outstanding rates as at 31 March 1985.

7. It was believed that one of the firm's customers had gone into liquidation. The customer owed Fruit and Nut £500.
8. Although some goods had been sold to a customer, it was not expected that the cash for them would be received until the end of June 1985.

a State which accounting procedure you would adopt in dealing with each of the above problems, outlining briefly the reasons for your choice. (*Note.* Journal entries are NOT required.)
b Explain briefly how Statements of Standard Accounting Practice (SSAPs) help accountants prepare accounting statements.

[*Association of Accounting Technicians, June 1985*]

7 In preparing accounts, accountants adopt a set of accounting rules or *concepts*, as they are sometimes known. The following cases represent various situations where an accountant would have to decide which rule to adopt:
1. The managing director wants to change the method of stock valuation.
2. A customer is likely to go bankrupt owing the company £1 000.
3. A customer owes £3 000 for electricity consumed during the current financial year.
4. The company secretary wants to capitalise some small items of office equipment purchased during the year for £50.
5. Equipment used by the company and which had cost £100 000 to construct would be worthless if the company went into liquidation.
6. The advertising department has recruited a highly talented poster designer. The marketing director describes him as a very great asset to the company and he thinks that this fact should be recorded under the fixed assets section on the company's balance sheet.
7. The company chairman wants to capitalise laboratory operating expenses incurred in researching into a new drug.
8. The sales ledger manager takes a very gloomy view of the company's ability to recover some of its debts and he wants to double the provision for bad debts even though there is no evidence to support his view.

a State which *overriding* accounting rule an accountant should adopt in dealing with each of the above cases, briefly explaining the reasons for your choice.
b Distinguish between capital and revenue expenditure.

[*Association of Accounting Technicians, December 1985*]

8 Accounting concepts

8 The accounts of a small business have recently come into your possession and are reproduced below:

M. and A. Margan
Trading and Profit and Loss Account
for year ended 30 April 1985

	£	£
Sales		
Cash	72 010	
Credit	83 206	
		155 216
Less		
Cost of sales		
Opening stock	18 352	
Purchases	124 693	
	143 045	
Closing stock	(21 824)	
Goods used by owner	(640)	
COST OF SALES		120 581
GROSS PROFIT		34 635
Add Trade discounts received on purchases	16 530	
Value Added Tax included in purchases	14 500	
		31 030
		65 665
Less Wages and salaries	28 726	
Value Added Tax included in sales	16 000	
Goods used by owner	640	
Heating and lighting	6 127	
Depreciation	5 760	
Other expenses	4 036	
		61 289
NET PROFIT FOR YEAR		4 376

Explanatory notes

Sales. The figure shown comprises amounts actually received (including Value Added Tax) for both cash and credit sales after deducting cash discounts for prompt settlement of accounts. The Value Added Tax element is then charged as an expense.

Cost of sales. Opening stock has been valued at FIFO (first-in, first-out) purchase cost but during the year it has been thought appropriate to take account of storage and handling charges; consequently closing stock includes a surcharge of 5 per cent to cover this item.

Purchases are included at gross catalogue price (including Value Added Tax). Both reclaimable Value Added Tax and trade discounts on purchases are then shown as additional items of revenue.

M. and A. Margan
Balance sheet as at 30 April 1985

	£	£
Fixed assets		
Premises	44 000	
Vehicles	10 240	
		54 240
Current assets		
Stock	21 824	
Debtors	6 017	
Bank and cash	511	
	28 352	
Current liabilities		
Creditors	27 809	
		543
		54 783
Capital		
Opening	53 000	
Net profit for year	4 376	
	57 376	
Drawings	(6 000)	
		51 376
Unidentified difference in books		3 407
		54 783

Wages and salaries. This item comprises the amounts actually paid within the year, irrespective of the period in which they were earned.

Depreciation. Premises have been depreciated on a straight-line basis on cost, assuming a 50-year life.

Vehicles have been depreciated at the rate of 20 per cent per annum on a reducing balance basis.

Identify and comment upon the specific instances in which the accounts of the business have been prepared in apparent conflict with generally accepted accounting principles, practices and conventions.

[*Chartered Association of Certified Accountants, Level 1, June 1985*]

2 Accounting records and documentation, VAT

Accounting records

Carefully study the diagram which gives an overall view of the functioning of the book-keeping process from first entry to balance sheet.

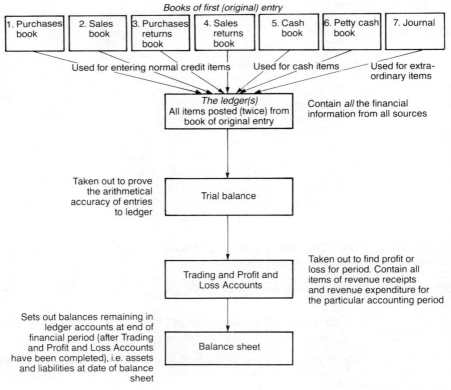

An overall view of book-keeping

Because accounting deals with transactions that have a monetary value it is both logical and necessary that records be kept.

Records should show the owners of the business clearly and accurately:

1. the amount of money owed *to* the business by others and the amount owed to others *by* the business;
2. the profit or loss made by the business over a given period of time;
3. the value of assets owned by the business and changes that take place in the value of them.

To achieve these aims the principle of double entry was invented which saw every transaction as having two sides: (*a*) a giving by one party of some form of wealth (e.g. money or goods); (*b*) a receiving of the same wealth by another party.

When an account receives wealth it is debited, i.e. the money value of the wealth is placed on the *debit* side or column of the account. At the same time the money value of the wealth is put on the *credit* side or column of the account that gives wealth. Because both aspects of the transfer of wealth are recorded at the same time it follows that every *debit must have a corresponding credit*.

The fundamental rule of double-entry book keeping is:

Debit the receiving account
Credit the giving account.

It is convenient to subdivide this rule into three rules according to the three different classes of account.

Class of account	What it records	Rules
1. Personal accounts	Transactions whereby persons become indebted to a business or it to them. Personal accounts include individuals, partnerships, limited companies (legal persons). Examples: Joseph Michael, The Rolling Stones, Products Ltd, Loan Account, Capital Account	Debit the receiver Credit the giver
	All these are legal 'persons' (the individual, group, and company). Loan and Capital Accounts record how the business becomes indebted to the lender (loans) or to the owner(s) (capital)	
	All other accounts are impersonal	
2. Real accounts	The values of assets such as land, buildings, plant and machinery, stock and changes in those values	Debit increases in value of assets Credit reductions in value of assets
3. Nominal accounts	Gains, losses or expenses. Gains arising from such items as sales, rents receivable, etc., expenses such as purchases, wages, rent payable and losses such as bad debts, discounts allowed, etc.	Debit losses and expenses Credit gains

A closer look at books of original entry

Name of the book	What the book should contain
1. Purchase book	A record of purchases on credit of goods for resale, i.e. credit purchases of goods in which the trader normally deals.
2. Sales book	A record of sales on credit of goods in which the trader normally deals.
3. Purchase returns or Returns outwards	A record of (*a*) purchases returned which had been previously bought on credit and entered in the purchases book, and (*b*) allowances received from suppliers in respect of damaged or soiled goods or for any other reason.
4. Sales returns or Returns inwards	A record of (*a*) goods returned to the trader which he had previously sold on credit and entered into his sales book, and (*b*) allowances made by the trader to his customers in respect of damaged or soiled goods or for any other reasons.
5. Cash book	*Debit side* A record of all cash received, cash banked and discount allowed. *Credit side* A record of all cash paid out, cheques issued and charges made by the bank.
6. Journal	A record of all transactions which cannot properly be entered in any of the other books of original entry, e.g. purchase and sale of items in which the trader does *not* normally deal, opening entries, correction of errors, transfers between ledger accounts, closing entries, etc.

Note. Discount Allowed and Discount Received: Cash book used only as memorandum. Double entry must be completed in ledger accounts. Discount Allowed: Debit Discount Allowed Account with total. Credit customer's account with individual amounts. Discount Received: Debit supplier's accounts with individual amount. Credit Discount Received Account with total.

Source of information	Rules for posting to the ledger accounts
Suppliers' invoices	(a) Debit Purchases Account with total for the period.
	(b) Credit supplier's personal accounts with individual amounts.
Copies of invoices sent to customers	(a) Debit customer's personal account with individual amounts.
	(b) Credit Sales Account with total for the period.
Credit notes received from suppliers	(a) Debit supplier's personal account with individual amounts.
	(b) Credit Purchases Returns Account with total for the period.
Copies of credit notes sent to customers	(a) Debit Sales Returns Account with total for period.
	(b) Credit customer's personal account with individual amounts.
Copies of cash receipts Copies of bank lodgements	Credit each item (except contras)* to the account named. (The debit is contained in the cash book itself.)
Cash receipts, cheque counterfoils, bank statements	Debit each item (except contras) to the account named. (The credit is contained in the cash book itself.)
Various	Debit items in debit column of journal to named account.
	Credit items in credit column of journal to named account.

---

*Contras (cash book) means transfers between the Cash and Bank Accounts.

14 Accounting records and documentation, VAT

In a business of any size it would be impossible to record transactions in the ledger as they arise, so *books of first* or *original entry* were invented so that full details of all transactions that take place could be entered and then more concise entries could be transferred from them to the ledger accounts.

It is vital to understand what each of these books of first entry contains (or should contain) and how they are correctly posted to the ledger. Students must understand the meaning of the terms used when deciding which is the appropriate book of original entry. No item is posted to the ledger account without first being entered in a book of first entry.

A concise resumé of the contents, source documents and rules for posting items contained in all the books of first entry to the various ledger accounts is set out in the table (pages 12–13).

Exercises Set 2A

1 Into which book of first entry of Woodcliffe Products (a general store) would each of the following items be posted?
   (a)   goods sold on credit to E. Phelan, £1 000
   (b)   goods returned by E. Phelan, £400
   (c)   goods purchased on credit for resale from T. Kite, £12 000
   (d)   goods bought for cash for resale from T. Kite, £500
   (e)   goods previously bought on credit from T. Kite returned to him, £3 000
   (f)   purchased office typewriter by cheque, £940
   (g)   bought goods on credit from R. Green, £9 000
   (h)   paid R. Green £4 000 on account
   (i)   received credit note from R. Green for goods returned to him which were damaged, £1 380
   (j)   bought shop fittings on credit from New Fitters Ltd, valued at £3 500
   (k)   invoiced goods to P. Lawford for £13 400

- (*l*) sold old lorry on credit to T. Hand for £2 760
- (*m*) M. Aspen bought goods on credit for £6 500
- (*n*) M. Aspen was given an allowance, £300, for goods damaged in transit
- (*o*) goods were purchased by cheque for resale for £1 160 from J. Oakes
- (*p*) received an invoice from A. Green for goods for resale, £18 400
- (*q*) sent debit note to A. Green for goods received damaged, £400
- (*r*) sold goods for cash to customer, £1 400
- (*s*) bought new lorry from Top Garages on credit, £24 000
- (*t*) bought items for resale for cash, £700
- (*u*) received invoice from A. Mann for stock, £7 800
- (*v*) received credit note for goods returned to him, £1 800
- (*w*) cash sales to customers, £650.

2 In each case in Question 1 indicate in which ledger accounts and on which sides the double entry would be made.

3 Tick the correct answer.
  1. The total of the purchase book is posted to:
     a the credit side of the Purchases Account □
     b the debit side of the Purchases Account □
     c the debit side of the Sales Account □
     d the debit side of the Sales Returns Account □
  2. The total of the sales book is posted to:
     a the debit side of the Sales Account □
     b the credit side of the Purchases Account □
     c the credit side of the Sales Account □
     d the debit side of the Purchases Account □
  3. The total of the sales returns (returns in) book is posted to:
     a the debit side of the Sales Returns Account □
     b the credit side of the Sales Account □
     c the debit side of the Sales Account □
     d the credit side of the Sales Returns Account □
  4. The total of the purchases returns (returns out) book is posted to:
     a the debit side of the Purchases Returns Account □
     b the debit side of the Purchases Account □
     c the credit side of the Purchases Account □
     d the credit side of the Purchases Returns Account □
  5. The usual source of information for the sales book is:
     a copies of invoices sent out □
     b credit notes received □
     c invoices received □
     d the cash register total □
  6. The usual source of information for the purchases returns book is:
     a invoices sent out □
     b invoices received □
     c credit notes sent out □
     d credit notes received □
  7. The usual source of information for the purchases book is:
     a invoices received □
     b credit notes received □
     c copies of invoices sent out □
     d debit notes sent out □

16 Accounting records and documentation, VAT

8. The usual source of information for the sales returns book is:
   a invoices received ☐
   b letters sent to customers ☐
   c credit notes received ☐
   d copies of credit notes sent to customers ☐
9. The journal is the correct book for entering one of the following:
   a sales of stock on credit ☐
   b cash sales ☐
   c buying of fixed assets on credit ☐
   d buying of fixed assets for cash ☐
10. The journal is the correct book for entering one of the following:
    a return of stock already recorded in sales book ☐
    b return of stock already recorded in purchases book ☐
    c correction of errors made in ledger accounts ☐
    d sale of stock for cash ☐

4 The following information is provided relating to transactions undertaken by D. Gooch in the first few days of 1985:
1 January: Sales on credit to G. Glyn £250.
2 January: Purchase of a machine on credit from R. Barlow for £1 500.
            Receipt of cash from G. Glyn £240. A discount of £10 was allowed for prompt settlement.
3 January: Loan received from J. McGregor £1 000.
            Purchase of investments for cash £700.

Record the above transactions in the form of journal entries. For each ledger account named in the journal entries, you should clearly indicate whether it is a real account or a nominal account or a personal account.

Note. Narratives need not be provided.

[*Royal Society of Arts, II, May 1985*]

5 James opens a shop on 1 July 1982, and during his first month in business, the following transactions occurred:
1982
1 July   James contributes £20 000 in cash to the business out of his private bank account.
2 July   He opens a business bank account by transferring £18 000 of his cash in hand.
5 July   Some premises are rented, the rent being £500 per quarter payable in advance in cash.
6 July   James buys some second-hand shop equipment for £300, paying by cheque.
9 July   He purchases some goods for resale for £1 000, paying for them in cash.
10 July Seddon supplies him with £2 000 of goods on credit.
20 July James returns £200 of the goods to Seddon.
23 July Cash sales for the week amount to £1 500.
26 July James sells goods on credit for £1 000 to Frodsham.
28 July Frodsham returns £500 of the goods to James.
31 July James settles his account with Seddon by cheque, and is able to claim a cash discount of 10 per cent.
31 July Frodsham sends James a cheque for £450 in settlement of his account, any balance remaining on his account being treated as a cash discount.

31 July   During his initial trading, James has discovered that some of his shop equipment is not suitable, but he is fortunate in being able to dispose of it for £50 in cash. There was no profit or loss on disposal.

31 July   He withdraws £150 in cash as part payment towards a holiday for his wife.

a   Enter the above transactions in James's ledger accounts, balance off the accounts and bring down the balances as at 1 August 1982.
b   Extract a trial balance as at 31 July 1982.

[*Association of Accounting Technicians, December 1982*]

*6 After the draft accounts had been prepared for the financial year ended 31 December 1983 the treasurer of an amateur football club discovered a batch of vouchers which had fallen down behind his desk, none of which had been processed.

The vouchers related to the following matters:
1. an invoice dated 23 January 1984 from Patchems Medical Supplies for a new first-aid kit for the club's trainer. The kit had cost £21.96 and had been supplied on 5 January 1984;
2. an invoice dated 11 January 1984 from Sports Equipment (1978) Ltd for £36.70, being the cost of a new goal net, corner flags and linesmen's flags, delivered to the club on 20 December 1983;
3. a cheque counterfoil, dated 15 December 1983, for £15, being the match fee for a match away from the home ground to be played on 4 February 1984;
4. a cheque counterfoil, dated 5 January 1984, for £20, being the match fee for a match away from the home ground to be played on 18 February 1984;
5. an invoice dated 6 January 1984 for £328.85 for work carried out at the club's home ground during November 1983 by Plumbing Services. The work consisted of the installation of two extra shower baths in the changing rooms (£268.30) and sundry repairs and renovations (£60.55);
6. a cheque counterfoil dated 17 January 1984 for £32.62 being the wages of the part-time groundsman, £11.21 of which had been earned up to 31 December 1983.

Other information
The club depreciates its equipment at the rate of 20 per cent per annum on a straight-line basis on gross cost at the year-end.

a   Journalise such of the above transactions as affect the 1983 final accounts.
b   State the individual items in the draft balance sheet affected by the journal entries in a and the respective amounts by which they would increase or decrease.

[*Association of Certified Accountants, Level 1, June 1984*]

*This question is more difficult than the others in this section and might be omitted at first reading.

Treatment of Value Added Tax

Value Added Tax (VAT), is a tax imposed by the government on the value of goods and services sold by persons and firms that are liable for it. It works as follows: each person in the chain of production charges VAT at the rate indicated by the government to the person or firm supplied with the goods or service.

EXAMPLE
Iron Foundries PLC sells tin to tin box manufacturers, Paul Ltd, to the value of £1 000 + VAT at 10 per cent. Paul Ltd makes up 500 tin boxes which it sells to Sardines Ltd, a canning firm, for £2 000 + VAT at 10 per cent. Sardines Ltd in turn sells 500 boxes of sardines to its customers at £3 per box + VAT at 10 per cent.

Calculate the VAT and show how it is paid.

VAT calculations	£	*VAT payments*
Iron Foundries PLC charges Paul Ltd 10% of £1 000	100	Iron Foundries PLC sends Customs and Excise cheque for £100
Paul Ltd charges Sardines Ltd 10% of £2 000	200	Paul Ltd sends Customs and Excise cheque for £100, i.e. £200 less £100 paid to Iron Foundries PLC
Sardines Ltd charges its customers 10% of £3 000	300	Sardines Ltd sends Customs and Excise cheque for £100, i.e. £300 less amount paid to Paul Ltd (£200) in respect of VAT
Customer pays £3 000 + 10% of £3 000	3 330	
Price to customer including VAT	3 330	

HM Customs and Excise collects £300 in tax which is finally paid by the consumer. Only the consumer gets no refund unless he/she happens to be either an exempted firm, or a zero-rated firm.

In the example Iron Foundries PLC, Paul Ltd and Sardines Ltd are all taxable firms.

Exempted firms. If a firm is an exempted firm it means that this firm is not obliged to charge VAT on its goods or services. Examples are banks and insurance companies who at present (1988) do not charge VAT on financial services. Small firms with a very small turnover in terms of income have the option to register or not register for VAT purposes (the limit varies from time to time).

Zero-rated firms for VAT purposes are firms who pay tax on their purchases but are not allowed to charge VAT specifically to their customers. For example, a manufacturing firm which exports its products will have paid VAT on its inputs (raw material, etc.) but because exports are not liable to VAT it will not be able to charge VAT to its customers abroad. It can, however, recover the

VAT and purchases

VAT paid to its suppliers from the Customs and Excise Department.

When a business is VAT registered VAT is added to sales invoices and must be shown separately as proof that it has been charged. It is important to note that VAT is added to the invoice after the trade discount has been deducted, in other words VAT is charged on the net invoice price.

VAT and purchases

VAT paid on the purchase of fixed assets (except motor cars) can be reclaimed by VAT-registered firms. A VAT-registered firm that charges VAT on its sales will be able to reclaim VAT on its purchases. It sometimes happens that due to a time lag the Customs and Excise records show a greater amount owed to the firm on purchases than the amount charged on sales. In such cases the excess will be refunded by the Customs and Excise Department. Normally the net difference is the amount paid by the firm to the Customs and Excise Department.

EXAMPLE

Thom Ltd sold the following goods during January 19–1:

Date	Customer	Net invoice value	Invoice value + VAT @ 10%
		£	£
1 Jan.	Iron Foundries Ltd	1 000	1 100
12 Jan.	M. Formby	2 000	2 200
20 Jan.	R. Locke	3 000	3 300

Post the sales book and ledger accounts and prepare trial balance.

Entries

The sales book is written up from the sales invoices. To record VAT an extra column is added to the sales book.

Sales book (page 1)

Date	Detail	Invoice No.	Folio	Total	Net	VAT
19–1				£	£	£
1 Jan.	Iron Foundries Ltd	452	DL/21	1 100	1 000	100
12 Jan.	M. Formby	453	DL/22	2 200	2 000	200
20 Jan.	R. Locke	454	DL/23	3 300	3 000	300
TOTAL				6 600	6 000	600
					GL12	GL13

Debtors ledger
Iron Foundries Ltd (21)

19–1		Fo.	£	
1 Jan.	Sales	SB01	1 100	

M. Formby (22)

19–1		Fo.	£	
12 Jan.	Sales	SB01	2 200	

R. Locke (23)

19–1		Fo.	£	
20 Jan.	Sales	SB01	3 300	

Sales Account (12)

		19–1		Fo.	£
		30 June	Sundry debtors	SB01	6 000

Value Added Tax (13)

		19–1		Fo.	£
		30 June	Sundry debtors	SB01	600

Thom Ltd
Trial balance at 31.1.19–1

Account name	Account No.	Dr. (£)	Cr. (£)
Iron Foundries Ltd	21	1 100	
M. Formby	22	2 200	
R. Locke	23	3 300	
Sales Account	12		6 000
Value Added Tax Account	13		600
		6 600	6 600

Exercises Set 2B

1 T. Madox, a VAT-registered firm, made the following credit sales during January 19–1:

Date	Buyer	Amount
19–1		£
6 January	R. Mason	420
10 January	T. Cummins	450
12 January	M. Lacey	430
15 January	M. Lacey	100
20 January	R. Black	200
25 January	R. Black	70

Write up Madox's sales book and make the double posting in the ledger. Charge a VAT rate of 20 per cent.

Exercises set 2B

2 N. Blake, a VAT-registered firm, made the following credit sales during February 19–2:

Date 19–2	Buyer	Amount £
4 February	B. Blue	80
7 February	P. Cox	30
8 February	F. Mason	40
16 February	B. Blue	75
19 February	F. Mason	30
25 February	P. Cox	5
29 February	F. Mason	30

Enter these transactions in Blake's sales book and then post to the ledger. Charge a VAT rate of 10 per cent.

3 Cantwell, a taxable firm, received the following goods on credit:

Date 19–1	Supplier	Amount £
1 March	A. Ansley	260
3 March	B. Blue	200
5 March	C. Crane	800
7 March	M. Moran	630
	B. Blue	140
17 March	A. Ansley	450
30 March	B. Blue	260

Enter the above transactions in Cantwell's purchases book and make the double posting in the ledger. Cantwell has been charged 10 per cent VAT by his suppliers.

4 S. Dillon, a taxable firm, made the following credit purchases during the month of April 19–4:

19–4		£
1 April	Purchased from P. Townsend	80
3 April	Purchased from R. Poole	150
5 April	Purchased from E. Polland	300
7 April	Purchased from P. Townsend	250
11 April	Purchased from R. Poole	60
15 April	Purchased from E. Polland	250
20 April	Purchased from P. Townsend	100
29 April	Purchased from R. Poole	420

Write up Dillon's purchases book and post to the ledger accounts. The rate of VAT charged is 20 per cent.

5 The sales of a firm, Joxer Ltd, inclusive of VAT, amounted to £220 000 for the month of March. The purchases for the same period were £132 000, inclusive of VAT. On 1 March, the firm owed £7 800 for VAT for the previous accounting period. During the month of March, the firm paid £8 400 VAT to the Customs and Excise. The rate of VAT applicable to sales and purchases during the period is 10 per cent.

Show the appropriate ledger accounts.

22 Accounting records and documentation, VAT

6 M. Richards, proprietor of a taxable firm, had the following transactions with creditors during the month of May 19–5:

19–5		£
1 May	Purchased goods from. M. Ryan	750
3 May	Purchased goods from R. Newman	850
6 May	Returned goods to R. Newman	130
8 May	Purchased goods from J. Steel	720
12 May	Purchased goods from R. Newman	600
15 May	Returned goods to J. Steel	150
22 May	Purchased goods from J. Steel	280
29 May	Returned goods to R. Newman	50
30 May	Purchased goods from R. Newman	400

Write up the day books. Post to the ledger. Suppliers have charged Richards a VAT rate of 10 per cent.

7 (*a*) C. Grey, a taxable firm, sent the following invoices to customers for June 19–6:

Date	Buyer	Invoice No.	Amount
19–6			£
1 June	A. Ansley	520	100
7 June	A. Ansley	521	210
10 June	T. Cummins	522	320
12 June	N. Noble	523	200
14 June	A. Damson	524	75
16 June	C. Green	525	120
18 June	T. Call	526	405
20 June	M. Morphy	527	45
22 June	B. Brief	528	320
24 June	T. Cummins	529	410
26 June	R. Eagle	530	20
28 June	C. Green	531	105
30 June	B. Brief	532	260

Write up Grey's sales book and post to the ledger. Grey must charge a VAT rate of 20 per cent to his customers.

(*b*) C. Grey sent credit notes to customers for goods they returned, as follows:

Date	Buyer	Credit note No.	Amount
19–6			£
14 June	N. Noble	CN 2	85
16 June	T. Cummins	CN 3	155
18 June	C. Green	CN 4	50
20 June	B. Brief	CN 5	160

Show these transactions in the sales returns book of Grey and post to the ledger. VAT is at the rate of 20 per cent.

8 During the quarter ended 31 May 1986, the raw materials purchased by John Henry Ltd, manufacturers of furniture, amounted to £181 590 before VAT at the standard rate of 15 per cent and, in addition, the following items of expenditure occurred:

		£	£
12 March	Highway Garage Ltd		
	Motor van C478 TBR	9 500.00	
	VAT @ 15%	1 425.00	
		10 925.00	
	Vehicle excise duty	100.00	
			11 025.00
19 March	Smith Motors Ltd		
	Motor car C379 KTA	8 000.00	
	VAT @ 15%	1 200.00	
		9 200.00	
	Vehicle excise duty	100.00	
			9 300.00
23 April	Super Machines Ltd		
	Used drilling machine		
	Number KXY54	8 200.00	
	VAT @ 15%	1 230.00	
			9 430.00
7 May	Highway Garage Ltd		
	Car repairs	210.00	
	VAT @ 15%	31.50	
			241.50
20 May	Machine Repairs Ltd		
	Renovation drilling machine		
	Number KXY54	500.00	
	VAT @ 15%	75.00	
			575.00

Note. This renovation was necessary before the drilling machine could be used in the factory.

The VAT due to the Customs and Excise Department on 28 February 1986 amounting to £84 000 was paid on 20 March 1986.

During the quarter ended 31 May 1986, the company's turnover, before VAT, amounted to 800 000 and analysed for VAT purposes was as follows:

	Turnover
	£
Taxable: standard rate	620 000
zero rated	120 000
Non-taxable: exempt	60 000
	800 000

24   Accounting records and documentation, VAT

The company maintains an analytical purchases day book.

a Prepare the analytical purchases day book for the three months ended 31 May 1986 of John Henry Ltd.

Note. Raw material purchases for the three months ended 31 May 1986 should be shown as one entry in the purchases day book.

b Prepare the account for HM Customs and Excise – VAT for the three months ended 31 May 1986 in the accounts of John Henry Ltd.

[*Association of Accounting Technicians, June 1986*]

9 Harold Peacock, a retailer, is registered for VAT purposes.

During September 1986, the following transactions took place in Harold Peacock's business:

18 September   Goods bought, on credit, from T. King and Sons Ltd, list price £640.00 subject to trade discount of 10 per cent and also a cash discount of 2½ per cent for payment within 30 days.

22 September   New car, for use in the business, bought from XL Garages Ltd at an agreed price of £8 000.00; payment to be effected on delivery.

25 September   Goods sold, on credit, to G. Siddle Ltd, list price £1 200.00 subject to trade discount of 15 per cent and cash discount of 2 per cent for payment within 30 days.

All the above transactions are subject to VAT at 15 per cent.

Record the above transactions in the ledger accounts of Harold Peacock.

Note. Harold Peacock does not maintain total or control accounts for debtors or creditors.

[*Association of Accounting Technicians, December 1986*]

3 The trial balance and suspense accounts

The trial balance: location and correction of errors

When all entries have been made in the ledger accounts the accounts are balanced and the accuracy of the postings are checked by taking out a *trial balance*. A trial balance is defined as a list of the balances of every account, classified into those that are debit and those that are credit. If all entries have been posted correctly it follows that the total of all the debit balances must be equal to the total of all the credit balances. If we set out the balances in the ledger accounts under two columns headed Debit and Credit, and total both columns, and if the totals of the two columns agree, there is prima-facie evidence that the accounts have been posted and balanced correctly. However, agreement of the trial balance is not conclusive proof of the accuracy of the books – it is only a test of the arithmetical accuracy of the ledger accounts.

Note. Horizontal and vertical rules are omitted from most accounts from now on.

EXAMPLE
From the following accounts taken from the balanced ledger accounts of Sid Jones prepare trial balance at 31 December 19–1.

Land and Buildings Account

19–1		£
31 Dec.	Balance b/d	50 000

Fixtures and Fittings Account

19–1		£
31 Dec.	Balance b/d	10 000

Cash Book

19–1		Cash	Bank
		£	£
31 Dec.	Balance b/d	500	2 000

26 The trial balance and suspense accounts

Stock Account

19–1		£	
31 Dec.	Balance b/d	5 000	

T. Doyle

19–1		£	
31 Dec.	Balance b/d	700	

A. Lyons

	19–1		£
	31 Dec.	Balance b/d	400

Insurance Account

19–1		£	
31 Dec.	Balance b/d	200	

Wages Account

19–1		£	
31 Dec.	Balance b/d	50 000	

Rent Payable Account

19–1		£	
31 Dec.	Balance b/d	800	

Discount Allowed Account

19–1		£	
31 Dec.	Balance b/d	100	

Discount Received Account

	19–1		£
	31 Dec.	Balance b/d	200

Carriage Outwards Account

19–1		£	
31 Dec.	Balance b/d	400	

Loan Account (to Brother)

19–1		£	
31 Dec.	Balance b/d	20 200	

Capital Account S. Jones

	19–1		£
	31 Dec.	Balance b/d	139 300

Solution

Sid Jones
Trial balance as at 31 December 19–1

	Dr. £	Cr. £
Land and buildings	50 000	
Fixtures and fittings	10 000	
Bank	2 000	
Cash	500	
Stock	5 000	
T. Doyle	700	
A. Lyons		400
Insurance	200	
Wages	50 000	
Rent payable	800	
Discount allowed	100	
Discounts received		200
Carriage outwards	400	
Loan Account (to Brother)	20 200	
Capital Account: Sid Jones		139 300
	139 900	139 900

Note:

1. That all assets, expenses and losses are on the debit side and that all gains and liabilities are on the credit side.
2. That the Capital Account of the proprietor (Sid Jones) is equal to the difference between the total of both sides.

   The losses and expenses are *nominal accounts* (Insurance, Wages, Rent, etc.).
   The assets are *real accounts* (Land, Buildings, Fixtures and Fittings, etc.).
   The *personal accounts* (Doyle and Loan Account) are debits in this instance. Lyons is a credit.
3. That both sides should always agree because the accounts are kept on double-entry principles.
4. That it is possible for the totals to agree whilst the individual accounts may be wrong in total or placed on the incorrect side of the trial balance.

Procedure to be followed if totals of the trial balance do not agree

1. Check for mistakes in addition by adding up both sides again.
2. Check that the debit column contains only accounts for assets, expenses and losses and that the credit column contains accounts for liabilities and gains.
3. If the mistake is not found find the differences between the two sides. Let us suppose the debit side is smaller by £108. Check that no account with a debit balance of £108 has been left out of the trial balance.
4. If the error is not found by this means divide the amount of the error by two, in this case £54. Is there an item for £54 on the wrong side of the trial balance?

5. Divide the error by 9. If 9 divides evenly into the number the error could be one of transposition, e.g. writing down 49 instead of 94 (the difference of 45 divides evenly by 9).
6. If control accounts are used, totalling the lists of balances against the control accounts will eliminate certain sections of the ledgers as sources of the error(s). See Chapter 5.
7. If all the above steps fail the only way left to find the error(s) is to check each double entry that has been entered in the books until the error(s) has/have been found.

Errors not revealed by the trial balance

There are six types of error not revealed by the trial balance:

errors of original entry,
errors of omission,
errors of commission,
errors of principle,
compensating errors,
complete reversal of entries.

It is essential to remember that *all* entries to the books of original entry should be *supported by a document* of one kind or another (see pp. 12 and 13). The books of original entry gather together the daily transactions dealing with either credit or cash items. These books are totalled and posted at regular intervals to the ledger accounts using double-entry principles.

1. Errors of original entry. These are errors in the books of original entry which have been posted to the ledger, e.g. sale on credit £1 000 to R. Peters entered in the sales book as £100 and posted as £100 to the debit side of R. Peters's account and to the credit side of the Sales Account.

It is obvious that both R. Peters's account and Sales Account will be incorrect. Both will be short by £900, but because the original error has been repeated in the ledger accounts, the trial balance will not disclose the errors as the trial balance still balances – the totals of the debit and credit columns will be the same even though the total of both columns will be incorrect.

2. Errors of omission. Here transactions are omitted *completely* from the books of original entry and therefore also omitted from the ledger accounts and the trial balance, e.g. goods sold on credit to G. Edwards, £900, were completely omitted from the books. Here again the trial balance will balance, but two accounts, Sales and G. Edwards, are wrong because of the omission.

3. Errors of commission. This means posting the correct amount to the correct side of the *wrong* account, e.g. £100 posted to the debit side of P. Long's account instead of to the debit side of J. Long's account. Here again two accounts are incorrect, whilst the trial balance balances.

4. *Errors of principle.* This means entering an item in the *wrong class* of account, e.g. entering the purchase of a capital item (such as a machine) in the Purchases Account. Suppose that a machine costing £50 000 was entered into the purchases book. This machine should have been debited by journal entry to Machinery Account; instead it was posted from the purchases book to the debit side of the Purchases Account. The trial balance will still balance, but both accounts (Purchases and Machinery) will be wrong until corrected.

5. *Compensating errors.* Two errors which cancel out one another, e.g. posting £100 instead of £150 to the debit side of R. Strong's account and at the same time posting £100 instead of £150 to the credit side of T. Lane's account. Both Strong's and Lane's accounts are incorrect, but the trial balance balances, because one error cancels out the other.

6. *Complete reversal of entries.* This occurs where the correct amounts are used but *both entries are made on the wrong sides of the accounts involved*, e.g. a credit purchase where the supplier's account is debited and the purchaser's account credited, e.g. goods bought from A. Wong for £1 000 were debited to Wong's account and credited to Purchases Account. Again, Wong's account, Purchases Account and trial balance are all incorrect until the error is corrected.

Correction of errors

All errors when found should be corrected immediately. The first thing to do is to recognise the mistake, see which accounts are involved and correct them by means of journal entry, paying particular attention to the narration. The narration explains to everybody involved what mistakes have been made and how they are being corrected. Students are advised, when they are asked to make a number of corrections, to take each one separately, think it out logically and then correct it by journal entry before attempting the next one. Students are also strongly advised to make simple 'T' accounts on a piece of paper, showing the error that has been made; once the error is seen clearly like this the correction is made much easier.

EXAMPLES OF CORRECTION OF ERRORS

1. *Errors of original entry*

e.g. On 1 January 19–1 a credit sale of £830 to A. Client was entered in the sales book as £380.

'T' accounts

Dr.	A. Client		Cr.	Dr.	Sales Account		Cr.
19–1		£			19–1		£
1 Jan.	Goods	380			1 Jan. Sundries		380

30   The trial balance and suspense accounts

It is obvious that A. Client's Account has been debited with £450 too little; similarly Sales Account has been credited with £450 too little. So the journal entry to correct the position is clear.

Error of original entry corrected

Journal

		Fo	Dr. £	Cr. £
19–1 1 Jan.	A. Client Sales Account Correction of error – sales to A. Client understated in sales book by £450	DL1 GL2	450	450

2. Errors of omission

e.g.   On 2 January 19–2 an invoice received from T. Black £500 was completely omitted from the books.

'T' accounts

Purchases Account		T. Black	
19–1 2 Jan.	?	19–2 2 Jan.	?

Purchases Account is short a debit of £500
T. Black's account is short a credit of £500

Error of omission corrected

Journal

		Fo	Dr. £	Cr. £
19–1 2 Jan.	Purchases Account T. Black Correction of error – purchases on credit from T. Black Invoice No. . . omitted from the books.	GL1 DL2	500	500

3. Errors of commission

On 3 January 19–1 credit sales of £700 to B. White were posted to C. White's Account.

'T' accounts

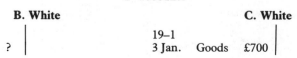

Error of commission corrected

Journal

19–1		Fo	Dr. £	Cr. £
2 Jan.	B. White	DL3	700	
	C. White	DL4		700
	Correction of error – sale of goods to B. White debited to C. White's account.			

4. Errors of principle

e.g. On January 19–1 a purchase of machinery on credit £100 000 was debited to Purchases Account. Here the purchase of a fixed asset has been charged to a revenue account.

Purchases Account has been over-debited by £100 000.
Machinery Account has been under-debited by £100 000.

So by journal entry we add £100 000 to Machinery Account and reduce Purchases Account by £100 000.

Error of principle corrected

Journal

19–1		Fo	Dr. £	Cr. £
4 Jan.	Machinery Account	GL2	100 000	
	Purchases Account			100 000
	Correction of error – purchase of fixed asset debited to revenue account.			

5. Compensating errors

e.g. On 5 January 19–1 both the purchases and sales books had been overcast by £4 000.

As a result of this error Purchases Account and Sales Account will be under-debited and under-credited respectively by £4 000.

Compensating errors corrected

Journal

19–1		Fo	Dr. £	Cr. £
5 Jan.	Sales Account	GL5	4 000	
	Purchases Account	GL1		4 000
	Correction of error Sales and purchases book overcast by £4 000 each.			

6. Complete reversal of entries

e.g. On 6 January 19–1 a cheque for £1 800 received from P. Lane was entered on the credit side of the cash book (bank column) and posted to the debit side of Lane's account.

'T' accounts

P. Lane

Dr.			
19–1			£
6 Jan.	Bank		1 800

Cash book

				Cash	Cr. Bank
	19–1			£	£
	6 Jan.	P. Lane			1 800

A glance at the above 'T' accounts will show that the amount necessary to correct the error is *twice* the amount of the error, i.e. £3 600.

Complete reversal of entries corrected

19–1		Fo.	£	£
6 Jan.	Bank Account	CB	3 600	
	P. Lane			3 600
	Correction of error – cheque received from P. Lane debited to Lane and credited to bank.			

Exercises Set 3A

1 Prepare complete journal entries to correct errors given as examples of errors not revealed by the trial balance on pages 28–9.

2 Show ledger accounts after correction of errors given in the worked examples on pages 29–32.

3 Prepare journal entries to correct the following errors:
   (a) Goods sold to M. Hayes, £300, were entered in T. Hayes's account.
   (b) A computer bought for office use for £6 000 was charged to the Purchases Account.
   (c) Goods bought on credit for resale from B. Memory, £500, were completely omitted from the books.
   (d) Goods returned by B. Taaffe, £300, were entered in the sales returns book as £100.
   (e) Both the purchases returns books and sales returns books were undercast by £200.

(f) A payment of £340 to P. Dunne was entered on the debit side of the cash book and on the credit side of Dunne's account.
(g) A purchase of goods from J. Clarkin of £1 340 was entered in the purchases book as £1 520.
(h) A payment of £290 made by R. Gray was credited to the account of R. Day.
(i) Goods returned by J. Hayes, £580, were not recorded in the books.
(j) An office machine sold for £700 was included in the sales book.
(k) Discount allowed to T. Kenny, £300, was debited to Kenny's account and credited to Discount Allowed Account.
(l) The purchases and purchases returns books were overcast by £100.

Suspense Accounts: effects of errors on net profit

Suspense Accounts are used when errors are made that affect the balancing of the trial balance, i.e. prevent it from balancing. Due to one or more errors the totals of the debit and credit sides of the trial balance do not agree.

In order not to delay the preparation of final accounts and balance sheet, an account called a Suspense Account is opened for the difference and put on the side of the trial balance with the smaller total. The totals will now agree, but as soon as possible the books must be examined carefully and the errors that caused the trial balance not to balance corrected through the journal. When the journal entries are posted, there is now a completely correct set of accounts and accurate final accounts can be prepared. The Suspense Account is then cleared.

Errors that *do* affect the balancing of the trial balance are:

errors in figures or additions,
posting only one side of the double entry.

Procedure

1. Open a Suspense Account and enter the trial balance difference if given.*
2. Correct all errors found by means of the journal, using the Suspense Account where errors affect the balancing of the trial balance.
3. Post the journal entries. When posted, there will be no balance left on the Suspense Account. It will be closed.

*In real life the opening difference is always known. In examinations sometimes the difference is not given but it is the balancing figure for the Suspense Account.

A Simple Example
On 1 January 19–1 J. Lang's trial balance will not agree – the debit total is £4 100 less than the credit total. The difference is placed in a Suspense Account. Subsequently, the following errors were discovered:

(a) The purchases book was under-totted by £10 000.
(b) Goods sold to M. Lane at £1 800 were included in the Sales Account but not posted to Lane's account.
(c) Discount received from P. Jason of £1 300 was entered in the Discount Received Account but omitted from Jason's account.

(d) A typewriter bought for £700 for use in the office was posted to the Purchases Account.
(e) Goods bought on credit from A. Flynn at £4 500 were debited to his account.

a Show the journal entries to correct these errors.
b Show the Suspense Account after the corrections have been completed.

SOLUTION
a

Journal

19–1				Dr. £	Cr. £
1 Jan.	(a)	Purchases Account		10 000	
		Suspense Account			10 000
		Correction of error – Purchases book under-totted by £10 000			
	(b)	M. Lane		1 800	
		Suspense Account			1 800
		Correction of error – Goods £1 800 not posted to Lane's account			
	(c)	P. Jason		1 300	
		Suspense Account			1 300
		Correction of error – Discount received not posted to Jason's account			
	(d)	Office Equipment Account		700	
		Purchases Account			700
		Correction of error – Typewriter charged to Purchases Account			
	(e)	Suspense Account		9 000	
		A. Flynn			9 000
		Correction of error – Goods £4 500 bought from A. Flynn debited to his account			

b

Suspense Account

Dr.					Cr.
19–1		£	19–1		£
1 Jan.	Difference in books	4 100	1 Jan.	(a) Purchases Account	10 000
	(e) A. Flynn	9 000		(b) M. Lane	1 800
				(c) P. Jason	1 300
		13 100			13 100

Notes

1. Notice that item (d) was not included in the Suspense Account as it did not upset the balancing of the trial balance – error of principle.
2. Item (e) required double the amount to correct the error (importance of using 'T' accounts).

Effects of errors on net profit

A More Difficult Example

John Blake's trial balance failed to agree on 31.12.19–1 and he entered the difference in a Suspense Account. On examination of the books the following errors were revealed:

(a) Goods sold on credit to A. Mann, valued at £400, had been credited to his account.
(b) A photocopier, purchased for £1 800, had been debited to the Purchases Account.
(c) Blake had received a credit note for £550 from a creditor, T. Willis, for goods returned. No entry had been made in the books.
(d) A payment for rates, £950, was entered on the credit side of the Rates Account as £590.
(e) Bank charges of £600 were entered in the cash book but not posted to the ledger.
(f) R. Owens, a debtor, was declared bankrupt and was only able to pay 25p in the pound on a debt of £1 000. No entry had been made in the books in respect of the bad debt.

The correcting of the above errors enabled the books to be balanced.

a Journalise the necessary corrections.
b Show the Suspense Account.

Solution

a

J. Blake
Journal

19–1			Dr. £	Cr. £
31 Dec.	(a)	A. Mann	800	
		Suspense Account		800
		Correction of error – Sales to A. Mann £400 credited to his account		
	(b)	Office Equipment	1 800	
		Purchases Account		1 800
		Correction of error – Photocopier charged to Purchases Account		
	(c)	T. Willis	550	
		Purchases Returns Account		550
		Correction of error – No entry made for goods returned to T. Willis		
	(d)	Rates Account	1 540	
		Suspense Account		1 540
		Correction of error – Rates paid £950, credited to Rates Account as £590		
	(e)	Bank Charges Account	600	
		Suspense Account		600
		Correction of error – Bank charges not posted to ledger account		
	(f)	Bad Debts Account	750	
		Bank Account	250	
		R. Owens		1 000
		Being write-off of £750 as bad debt due to bankruptcy of R. Owens who paid 25p in the pound on a debt of £1 000		

b
Dr.   **Suspense Account**   Cr.

19–1		£	19–1		£
31 Dec.	Difference in books*	2 940	31 Dec.	A. Mann (a)	800
				Rates Account (d)	1 540
				Bank Charges Account (e)	600
		2 940			2 940

*In this question the amount of the original difference was not given. It must be the amount necessary to balance the Suspense Account when all errors involving the Suspense Account have been corrected and posted.

Effects of errors on net profit

Any error made in the posting of ledger accounts will affect either the net profit or the balance sheet. Generally speaking an error made in a nominal account will affect the net profit and errors made in real and personal accounts will affect the balance sheet. Errors in net profit arise from *errors in items that go to make up net profit*, i.e. errors in entries in the Trading and/or Profit and Loss Accounts. So the question to be asked in the case of each error is:

Does this error affect any item in the Trading or Profit and Loss Account?

If it does, it affects the accuracy of the net profit. (Of course, an error in the Profit and Loss Account which is a nominal account will always affect the balance sheet.) If mistakes are discovered after the final accounts and balance sheets have been prepared, they should be corrected immediately and a new Profit and Loss Account and balance sheet drafted.

In examinations students are often asked both to correct errors and to show a statement of corrected profit. Corrections should be made by journal entry with a full narration. Any statement you are asked for in accounting examinations should be drawn up in a clear, neat, methodical manner. It is no use adding and subtracting figures at random, even though the figure arrived at may be correct. Unless the statement is properly presented and explained it is almost worthless.

The student should also remember when asked to show both a Suspense Account and a corrected statement of net profit that *while all errors in nominal accounts affect the net profit, the only errors that appear on the Suspense Account are those that affect the balancing of the trial balance.*

To summarise

1. All errors must be corrected through the journal.
2. All errors in Trading and Profit and Loss Accounts affect the net profit.
3. Only errors affecting the balance of the trial balance are put in the Suspense Account.
4. Errors in real and personal accounts affect the balance sheet.

EXAMPLE

A trial balance extracted from the books of Careless Ltd as on 31 December 19–1 did not agree and the amount of the difference was entered in a Suspense Account. A Trading and Profit and Loss Account was prepared on the basis of this trial balance and showed a net profit of £30 000. The following errors were afterwards discovered and the difference eliminated:

(a) A sales invoice for £940 had been completely omitted from the books.
(b) A bank overdraft of £376 which appeared as a credit balance in the cash book on 31 December 19–1 had been omitted from the trial balance.
(c) A payment of £216 to James Callaghan, a trade creditor, correctly entered in the cash book had been debited to his personal account as £360.
(d) The debit side of Wages Account had been undercast by £120.
(e) A provision of £64 for rent outstanding at 31 December 19–1 debited to Rent Account at that date, had not been brought forward to the credit of the account in the following period and no credit entry had been made in any other account.
(f) Discounts received from suppliers, £704, had been entered on the wrong side of the Discount Account.

a Show the entries in the Suspense Account.
b Show your calculation of the corrected net profit.

SOLUTION

a

Suspense Account

Dr.					Cr.
19–1		£	19–1		£
31 Dec.	Trial balance error (b)	376	31 Dec.	Difference in books	1 872
	Callaghan (c)	144		Wages (d)	120
	Rent (e)	64			
	Discount received (f)	1 408			
		1 992			1 992

Careless Ltd

b **Statement of Corrected Profit for year ended 31 Dec. 19–1**

	£	£
Net profit as per accounts		30 000
Add Sales understated (a)	940	
Add Discount received understated (f)	1 408	
		2 348
		32 358
Less Wages undercast (d)		120
Corrected net profit for year		32 228

Notes

1. When final accounts and balance sheet are prepared before errors are discovered and corrected, the balance on the Suspense Account will be shown on the balance sheet.

38   The trial balance and suspense accounts

If the balance is a debit balance it is shown on the asset side; if a credit balance it is shown on the liability side.
2. A statement of corrected net profit can also be shown in account form by re-opening the Profit and Loss Account and making adjustments as necessary, thus producing a corrected net profit.

Exercises Set 3B

1 There are six types of error which the trial balance does not reveal. List them and give examples of each type.

2 The following errors were discovered in the books of a trader. Taking each item separately, state which column of the trial balance, debit or credit, would be greater as a result and by how much.
   (a) Sales on credit to T. Crowe, £850, were debited to the account of Crowe Ltd.
   (b) The sales book had been undercast by £1 000.
   (c) A payment of £500 in respect of insurance had been charged to Sundry Expenses Account as £150.

3 From the following balances taken from the ledger accounts on 31 December 19-2 of C. Keenan prepare a trial balance at that date.

	£		£
Stock	7 000	Sales	35 000
Buildings	12 000	Purchases	17 000
Discount received	1 000	Rent payable	900
Discount allowed	1 500	Rent receivable	1 100
Rates	2 100	Dividends received	2 500
Insurance	750	Light and heat	1 200
A. Flynn (debtor)	2 500	C. Grant (creditor)	6 400
Loan (received)	15 000	Salaries	25 000
Commission received	2 400	Commission paid	1 200
Loan given to customer	7 000	Postage	800
Carriage in	300	Carriage out	700
Advertising	750	Interest paid	250
Bank overdraft	1 900	Cash in till	50
Purchases returns	5 000	Sales returns	6 000

4 The following trial balance was taken out by an inexperienced clerk at 31 December 19-3, from the books of James Careless. You are asked to prepare a corrected trial balance at this date.

	Dr. £	Cr. £
Stock at 1.1.19-3	3 500	
Buildings	56 000	
Carriage in	150	
Carriage out		350
Discount received	500	
Discount allowed		750
Rates	1 050	

	Dr. £	Cr. £
Purchases		85 000
Sales	125 000	
Rent payable		4 500
Rent received	5 500	
Bank	9 500	
Cash in hand		250
Commission paid	600	
Commission received		1 200
Insurance	3 750	
Loan received		7 500
Loan given to wife	3 500	
Advertising	3 750	
Trade creditors		35 000
Trade debtors	70 000	
Salaries		25 000
Dividends received		3 000
Commission received	4 800	
Light and heat	2 400	
Postage	1 600	
Interest paid		500
Carriage out	1 400	
Capital		91 050
	293 000	254 100

5   On 31 December 19–3 Edward Fox's trial balance failed to agree, the debit side being £5 600 greater than the credit side. He opened a Suspense Account for the amount of the difference. He subsequently discovered the following errors:
   (a)   A debtor, T. Downs, had paid his account in full, £8 200, but this had not been credited to his account.
   (b)   The total of the discount received for the year, £800, had not been posted to the Discount Received Account.
   (c)   The purchases book had been undercast by £3 400.

   Show:
   a   the journal entries to correct these errors
   b   the Suspense Account after the corrections had been completed.

6   On 31 March 19–4 John Gains extracted a trial balance from his ledger accounts. The trial balance totals did not agree, and he opened a Suspense Account which he debited with £3 620. A further check revealed the following errors:
   (a)   The Discount Received Account had been debited with £2 620.
   (b)   The Discount Allowed Account had been credited with £3 600.
   (c)   A cheque was paid to H. Noone in full settlement of his account, £4 000, less 5 per cent cash discount. This was correctly entered in the cash book but no entry for the cash discount appeared in Noone's account.
   (d)   A cheque paid for rent, £480, had been entered correctly in the cash book but posted to the ledger as £840.
   (e)   A credit sale to W. Cross, £1 820, had been correctly entered in the sales book but had not been posted to Cross's account.

   Show the Suspense Account after these errors have been corrected.

40 The trial balance and suspense accounts

7 The trial balance of Tom Moran, a car dealer, failed to agree on 31.12.19–9, and he entered the difference in a Suspense Account. On examination of the books the following errors were revealed:
(a) A car purchased for £6 000 was debited to the Equipment Account.
(b) A credit note for £178 received from a creditor, M. Walsh, had been debited in Walsh's account as £196.
(c) A payment of £190 for repairs to machinery had been entered in the Plant and Machinery Account.
(d) Discount received, £700, had been posted to the incorrect side of the Discount Account.
(e) Capital introduced in cash during the year by the owner, £2 000, had been entered correctly in the Capital Account but the double entry had not been completed.
(f) Cash received, £400, from a debtor, R. Spade, had been entered correctly in Spade's account but no entry had been made in the cash book.

a Journalise the necessary corrections.
b Show the Suspense Account.

8 John Clegg's trial balance failed to agree on 31.3.19–1 and he entered the difference, a credit balance of £4 030, in a Suspense Account. On examination of the books the following errors were revealed:
(a) Interest received, £840, had been entered on the incorrect side of the Interest Account.
(b) James Taylor, a debtor, was declared bankrupt and had made a first and final payment of 20p in the pound in respect of the original debt of £1 500. No entry had been made in the books in respect of the bad debt.
(c) Shop equipment costing £2 500 purchased on credit from J. Drake had been entered in the purchases book and posted to the debit of Drake's account.
(d) A payment of £790 to a creditor, R. Poole, had been credited to his account as £970.
(e) The total of the sales book, £18 990, had been posted to the Sales Account as £19 880.
(f) A car, costing £30 000, purchased by Clegg for his wife, had been posted to the Motors Expenses Account.

a Journalise the necessary corrections.
b Show the Suspense Account.

9 James Sweeney's trial balance failed to agree on 31.12.19–2, and he entered the difference in a Suspense Account. On examination of the books the following errors were revealed:
(a) Interest paid by Sweeney, £1 000, had been entered on the incorrect side of the Interest Account.
(b) Bank charges, £150, entered correctly in the cash book had not been posted to the ledger.
(c) A payment of £1 400 for repairs to motor vehicles had been debited to the Motor Vehicles Account.
(d) A cheque for £960 received from a debtor, M. Grace, had been entered correctly in the cash book but credited to the Debtors Account as £690.
(e) Goods sold on credit for £1 800 had not been entered in the books.
(f) The purchases day book had been over-totted by £250.

a Journalise the necessary corrections.

b Show the Suspense Account.
c Calculate the correct net profit if the original figure was £98 000.

10 The book-keeper of Newfield Ltd, having been unable to balance the trial balance at 30 September 19–6, raised a Suspense Account on which he entered the amount he was out of balance. The following errors were subsequently discovered and rectified, thus balancing the books:
(a) Goods bought on credit by A. Clott, value £2 400, had been debited to the account of A. Clott Ltd.
(b) Purchases book overcast by £1 000.
(c) Fixtures and fittings, £800, bought on credit and charged to Purchases Account.
(d) Sales book overcast by £500.
(e) A credit note received from R. Shine for £250 had been entered twice on his account.
(f) Two payments of £4 000 each on succeeding days to R. Bowen had been entered correctly in the cash book, but only one had been entered in Bowen's account.
(g) Bank charges, £200, had been entered in the cash book but not posted to the ledger.
(h) A credit balance on the Rent Receivable Account, £1 800, had been entered in the trial balance as £8 000.

a Show the journal entries correcting these errors.
b Show the complete Suspense Account.
c Prepare a statement showing the corrected net profit after the errors had been corrected. The net profit prior to correction was £252 810.

11 F. Tobin's trial balance at 31 October 19–7 failed to agree. He opened a Suspense Account for the difference, prepared a Trading and Profit and Loss Account and the following balance sheet:

F. Tobin
Balance sheet as at 31 October 19–7

	£	£		£	£
Fixed assets					
Buildings	80 000		Capital (1 Nov. 19– 6)	80 000	
Fixtures and fittings	20 000		*Add* Net profit	14 500	
		100 000		94 500	
Current assets				4 500	
Stock	8 000		*Less* Drawings		90 000
Debtors	12 000		*Current liabilities*		
Bank	5 000		Creditors		34 900
		25 000	Suspense Account		100
		125 000			125 000

The following errors, which accounted for the difference in the trial balance, were subsequently discovered:
(a) Bank charges, £200, entered in the cash book had not been posted to the ledger.

(b) Sales book undercast by £2 000.
(c) Rates Account was under-debited by £100.
(d) New desks for the office bought on credit from Office Supplies Ltd, value £1 200, had been entered in the purchases book.
(e) A sale of goods to M. Malone, £1 840, had been posted to his account as £1 480.
(f) The totals of the discount allowed and discount received columns, £1 940 and £700 respectively in the cash book, had not been posted to the ledger.

a Make the journal entries necessary to correct the above errors.
b Draw up a statement showing corrected net profit.
c Prepare a corrected balance sheet.

12 Alan Rafter's trial balance failed to agree on 31.12.19–9. He opened a Suspense Account for the difference and prepared a Trading and Profit and Loss Account and the following balance sheet. He included the original difference on the Suspense Account with bills payable in the balance sheet.

Balance sheet as at 31.12.19–9

	Cost £	Depreciation to date £	Net £	Total £
Fixed assets				
Equipment	50 000		50 000	
Motor vehicles	90 000		90 000	
	140 000		140 000	140 000
Current assets				
Stock		38 000		
Debtors		27 000		
Bank		14 000		
		79 000		
Less Current liabilities				
Creditors	21 000			
Bills payable (including suspense)	19 000			
		40 000		
Working capital				39 000
TOTAL NET ASSETS				179 000
Financed by:				
Capital 1 Jan. 19–9		110 000		
Add Net profit		69 000		
CAPITAL EMPLOYED				179 000

On examination of the books the following errors were revealed:
(a) On 31 December 19–9 goods with a sales value of £2 000 were returned by N. Corr, a debtor. The returns, which had cost £1 600, had not been included in stocks entered in the books.

(b) Equipment purchased on credit from A. Lyons for £8 600 was entered correctly in the Equipment Account but debited to Lyons's account as £6 800.
(c) Bank overdraft of £2 900 at the beginning of the year had been brought down on the debit side of the Bank Account in the ledger.
(d) Discount allowed, £2 400, had been entered on the incorrect side of the Discount Account.
(e) Bank interest, £250, paid to the bank had been entered in the cash book but had not been posted to the ledger.

a Show the Suspense Account.
b Prepare a statement showing the correct net profit.
c Prepare a corrected balance sheet.

13 R. Hood's trial balance failed to agree on 31.12.19–8, and he entered the difference in a Suspense Account. On examination of the books the following errors were revealed:
(a) The sales day book was incorrectly totalled and therefore incorrectly posted to the Sales Account as £20 480 instead of £20 840.
(b) A payment of £790 to T. Dobson had been posted to the credit of Dobson's account as £970.
(c) Furniture and fittings purchased on credit from R. Patton for £350 had been entered in the purchases book and posted to the debit of Patton's account.
(d) R. Hood, the proprietor, won a trip to Spain worth £400. He gave the ticket for the trip to one of his salesmen as part-payment of the salesman's commission for the year. No entry had been made in the books.
(e) A receipt of £60 for the sale of an old desk (book value £50) had not been shown in the books.
(f) A debit note received from M. Edwards for £85 had been entered correctly in the subsidiary book but not posted to Edwards's account.

a Journalise the necessary corrections.
b Show the Suspense Account.
c Prepare a statement showing the true profit if the profit before the correction of the above errors was £20 000.

14 The trial balance of Smart Ltd, a pop record store, failed to agree and the difference was entered in a Suspense Account. The Trading and Profit and Loss Account was prepared on the basis of the figures in the trial balance and showed a net profit of £28 462 at 31.12.19–7.

The following errors were afterwards discovered:

(a) Discounts amounting to £194 on the debit side of the cash book had been posted to the incorrect side of the Discount Account.
(b) The sales day book had been over-totted by £34.
(c) £62 received from B. White, a customer, had been entered correctly in the cash book, but debited to his personal account as £36.
(d) A debit balance of £90 on the personal account of C. Larkin in the purchases ledger had been omitted from the trial balance.
(e) The purchase of a motor car on credit from M. Tierney for £1 600 had been posted from the purchases day book to the debit of Tierney's account in the creditors ledger.

44 The trial balance and suspense accounts

(f) A payment of £130 for the repairs to a motor van had been debited to the Motor Vans Account.

After discovery of these errors the Suspense Account was closed and the Profit and Loss Account re-drafted.

a Show the Suspense Account.
b Calculate the amount of the net profit as it would appear in the re-drafted Profit and Loss Account.

15 Joan White owned a retail and wholesale grocery business and her trial balance failed to agree on 31.12.19–1. She opened a Suspense Account for the difference and prepared a Trading and Profit and Loss Account and the following balance sheet. She included the original difference on the Suspense Account with cash in the balance sheet.

Balance sheet as at 31.12.19–1

	Cost	Depreciation to date	Net	Total
	£	£	£	£
Fixed assets				
Motor vehicles	80 000		80 000	
Shop furniture and equipment	20 000		20 000	
	100 000		100 000	100 000
Current assets				
Stock			46 000	
Debtors			29 000	
Cash (incl. Suspense Account balance)			33 930	
			108 930	
Less Current liabilities				
Creditors	22 500			
Bank	43 730			
Rent due	1 400			
			67 630	
Working capital				41 300
TOTAL NET ASSETS				141 300
Financed by:				
Capital 1 Jan. 19–1			110 000	
Add Net profit for the year 19–1			31 300	
CAPITAL EMPLOYED				141 300

On examination of the books the following errors were revealed:
(a) A credit note for £450 received from a creditor had been entered correctly in the appropriate day book but on the incorrect side of the personal account.
(b) A delivery van sold on credit for £14 000 had been entered in the sales book and posted to the incorrect side of the debtor's account.
(c) Rent, £600, due on 1.1.19–1 had been paid during the year. The amount was entered correctly in the cash book but had not been posted to the Rent Account.

(d) A payment of £850 for repairs to equipment had been entered on the credit side of the Furniture and Equipment Account as £580.
(e) Cash, £1 500, and stock valued at £2 000 taken by the owner during December and given to his wife had not been entered in the books.

a   Journalise the necessary corrections.
b   Show the Suspense Account.
c   Prepare a statement showing the correct net profit.
d   Prepare a corrected balance sheet.

16   A. Fryer, a tyre distributor, has extracted the following trial balance from his books of account as at 30 April 1984. He has not been able to balance the trial balance and so he posted the difference to a Suspense Account.

When Fryer's books of account were examined in more detail, the following errors were discovered:
1. The sales day book had been undercast by £500.
2. Purchases had been debited with a motor van costing £5 000.
3. Discounts allowed of £1 500 had been completely omitted from the books of account.
4. Goods worth £3 000 received from Cook had been included in the closing stock, although the invoice for them was not received until 10 May 1984.
5. Archer's debtor's account balance of £750 had been omitted from the list of sales ledger balances.
6. Fryer had forgotten to accrue £400 for the cost of electricity consumed during the month to 30 April 1984 supplied by the Mercia Electricity Board.
7. The bad debts provision account should have been increased by £500 because of a greater amount of trade debtors.
8. The bank overdraft of £4 000 had been included as a debit balance in the trial balance.
9. Discounts received of £200 had not been entered in Lee's personal account.
10. Fryer had not depreciated his workshop fittings. These should have been depreciated at a rate of 50 per cent per annum on the reduced balance. The fittings had originally cost £15 000 and the accumulated depreciation at 1 May 1983 was £7 000.

Show wherever possible the journal entries necessary to correct the above errors, and where this is not required, state how the errors that cannot be journalised would be corrected.

[*Association of Accounting Technicians, June 1984*]

17 The following balance sheet was prepared for Broadbridge Ltd at 31 December 1984:

	£	£		£	£
Share capital		200 000	Fixed assets at cost		75 000
Retained profit			*Less* Depreciation		22 500
at 1.1.1984	37 500				52 500
Net profit for 1984	26 900				
		64 400			
		264 400			
Current liabilities			*Current assets*		
Proposed dividend	50 000		Stocks	137 600	
Creditors and			Debtors	194 300	
accruals	71 100		Bank	1 100	
		121 100			333 000
		385 500			385 500

After the above balance sheet was prepared, the following errors and omissions were discovered:
1. An invoice for £3 750 relating to goods sold and despatched on 30 December 1984 had been omitted from the books.
2. The bank statement for December was received which showed bank charges of £80.
3. The stock-take sheets had been undercast by £4 500.
4. Insurances of £400 paid on 1 April 1984, for the forthcoming twelve months, had been debited to the Profit and Loss Account.
5. A machine costing £10 000 was delivered to the company's premises on 20 December 1984 and the invoice arrived on the same day. The machine was first used on 1 January 1985 and the invoice was paid on 10 January. Nothing had been entered in the books in respect of these transactions at 31 December 1984.

Required:
a The journal entries to correct the above errors and omissions. Narratives are not required.
b A statement showing the corrected net profit.
c The revised balance sheet of Broadbridge Ltd after making the necessary adjustments.

[*Royal Society of Arts, II, November 1985*]

18 A trial balance was extracted from the books of Armitage, a sole trader and it was found that the debit side exceeded the credit side by £106. This amount was entered in the Suspense Account. The following errors were then discovered and corrected:
  (i) The total of sales was understated by £33.
  (ii) An amount of £75 received from Baker had been credited to his account as £57.
  (iii) Purchase returns totalling £60 for the month of May had been posted to the debit side of the Sales Returns Account.
  (iv) £105 paid to a supplier named Cook had not been posted to his account.

(v) An amount of £40 in the sales returns book had not been posted to the debtors' account.

You are required to show the entries in the Suspense Account arising from the correction of the above and to close off the accounts.

[*Pitman Intermediate*]

19 Allan Smith, an inexperienced accounts clerk, extracted the following trial balance, as at 31 March 1986, from the books of John Bold, a small trader.

	£	£
Purchases	75 950	
Sales		94 650
Trade debtors	7 170	
Trade creditors		4 730
Salaries	9 310	
Light and heat	760	
Printing and stationery	376	
Stock at 1 April 1985	5 100	
Stock at 31 March 1986		9 500
Provision for doubtful debts		110
Balance at bank	2 300	
Cash in hand	360	
Freehold premises:		
At cost	22 000	
Provision for depreciation		8 800
Motor vehicles:		
At cost	16 000	
Provision for depreciation		12 000
Capital at 1 April 1985		23 096
Drawings	6 500	
Suspense		21 760
	160 236	160 236

In the course of preparing the final accounts for the year ended 31 March 1986, the following discoveries were made:

1. No entries have been made in the books for the following entries in the bank statements of John Bold:

1986	Payments	£
26 March	Bank charges	16
31 March	Cheque dishonoured	25

Note. The cheque dishonoured had been received earlier in March from Peter Good, debtor.

2. In arriving at the figure of £7 170 for trade debtors in the above trial balance, a trade creditor (Lionel White £70) was included as a debtor.
3. No entries have been made in the books for a credit sale to Mary Black on 29 March 1986 of goods of £160.
4. No entries have been made in the books for goods costing £800 withdrawn from the business by John Bold for his own use.
5. Cash sales of £700 in June 1985 have been posted to the credit of trade debtors' accounts.

48 The trial balance and suspense accounts

6. Discounts received of £400 during the year under review have not been posted to the appropriate nominal ledger account.
7. The remaining balance of the Suspense Account is due to cash sales for January and February 1986 being posted from the cash book to the debit of the Purchases Account.

a Make the journal entry necessary to correct for item 7 above.
   Note. A narrative should be included.
b Prepare a corrected trial balance as at 31 March 1986.
[*Association of Accounting Technicians, June 1986*]

20 The following draft balance sheet of Minton Stoke Ltd, roadworks contractor, was prepared at 31 December 1985:

	£		£
Ordinary share capital: 100 000 Ordinary shares of £1 each fully paid (authorised capital £100 000)	100 000	Freehold property	85 000
		Machinery	40 000
		Motor vehicles	30 000
			155 000
Profit and Loss Account balance 31.12.85	61 190	Stock in trade	48 000
Creditors	50 000	Debtors	38 000
Accruals	5 000	Cash in hand	570
Bank overdraft	25 000		
Suspense	380		
	241 570		241 570

Subsequently a note was made of the following items which might or might not eliminate the £380 suspense item.
1. An item of £237 in the purchases journal had been posted in the purchases ledger incorrectly as £277.
2. An examination of the bank pass book revealed that a cheque for £400 dated 29.12.85, of which Minton Stoke was the drawer, had not been presented for payment.
3. A long-term loan of £1 500 from a director had been treated in error as a cash sale.
4. An accounting machine (purchase price £500) had been received on 20.12.85 and was used immediately. No invoice had been received and the terms of payment were one month after receipt of invoice. The cost had been included in the balance sheet.
5. A trade discount of £80 on a purchase invoice for a mechanical digger, list price £480, had been posted to the Discount Received Account and the balance of £400 had been posted to the Asset Account.

Using the relevant information from the above:
a prepare journal entries (without narrations but including dates)
b prepare a Suspense Account
c state the working capital of Minton Stoke Ltd as at 31 December 1985, giving details of its make-up.
[*London Chamber of Commerce and Industry, autumn 1986*]

4 Bank reconciliation statements

When asked to prepare a bank reconciliation statement we must be quite clear about what we are attempting to do. In this context the word 'reconcile' means to make the same or show that the record kept by the trader (the bank column in the cash book, or Bank Account in the ledger) is the same as the record kept by the bank (the bank statement) when the necessary adjustments have been made.

The bank column in the cash book or Bank Account in the ledger should agree with the bank statement because *both sets of books deal with precisely the same transactions.*

What items appear in the trader's cash book (bank column)?

Debit side
1. Cheques received and lodged in the bank
2. Cash lodged in the bank
3. Amounts lodged in the bank on behalf of the trader by others (e.g. credit transfers)

Credit side
1. Cheques paid out
2. Cash withdrawn from the bank
3. Charges made by the bank (e.g. interest, bank charges, dishonoured cheques, etc.)
4. Payments made by the bank on the trader's behalf (e.g. standing orders, direct debits)

This is the Bank Account as kept by the trader, and the balance on it shows either the amount the trader has in the bank (debit balance) or the amount the trader owes the bank (credit balance).

At the same time the bank keeps an account in the name of the trader (customer) in its books. What does this account show?

What items appear in the bank statement of the trader?

Debit side (column)
1. Cheques paid out on behalf of the trader by the bank
2. Cash withdrawn by the trader from the bank
3. Charges made by the bank to the trader (e.g. bank interest, bank charges)
4. Payments made by the bank on the trader's behalf (e.g. standing orders, direct debits)

Credit side (column)
1. Lodgements of cash or cheques received from the trader
2. Lodgements of cash or cheques received on behalf of the trader from others (e.g. by bank giro)
3. Amounts collected by the bank on behalf of the trader (e.g. interest, dividends, etc.)

50 Bank reconciliation statements

The bank statement acts as a check on the entries made in the trader's books. Similarly the Bank Account in the trader's books checks on the accuracy of the bank statement.

The important point to note is that both sets of books deal with *precisely* the same transactions.

The trader receives from the bank at regular intervals (daily, in some cases) a statement of account which is an exact copy of his account in the bank's books. This he compares with his own Bank Account in either cash book or ledger. If the balance as shown by the bank statement disagrees with the balance as shown by the trader's books, he immediately sets about finding the reasons for the difference, corrects any mistakes or omissions in his own records and sets out the reasons for the remaining differences in a bank reconciliation statement. The bank reconciliation statement always bears a date.

A Simple Example

From the following transactions prepare the cash book of Peter Hill (bank columns only) and compare with the bank statement for the month of January 19–1.

19–1		£
1 Jan.	Balance at bank	4 000
5 Jan.	Received and lodged cheque from P. Drake	3 000
8 Jan.	Paid M. Hely by cheque	1 500
10 Jan.	Cash sales lodged in bank	10 000
13 Jan.	Paid rent by cheque	500
14 Jan.	Paid G. Hall (wages) by cheque	250
17 Jan.	Cash sales lodged in bank	5 000
20 Jan.	Paid insurance by cheque	400
21 Jan.	Paid J. Gold (creditor) by cheque	3 500
22 Jan.	Bank charges for keeping account	200
24 Jan.	Cash sales lodged in bank	6 000
26 Jan.	Paid J. King (creditor) by cheque	5 400
29 Jan.	Received and lodged cheque from A. Bard (debtor)	3 600
30 Jan.	Paid G. Hall (wages) by cheque)	250
31 Jan.	Cash sales lodged	8 000

Barclays Bank PLC – any branch
Bank statement

Mr Peter Hill		Dr. £	Cr. £	Balance £
1 Jan.	Balance b/f			4 000
5 Jan.	Lodgement (P. Drake)		3 000	7 000
10 Jan.	M. Hely (Cheque No. 1)	1 500		5 500
	Lodgement (Cash sales)		10 000	15 500
15 Jan.	Rent (Cheque No. 2)	500		15 000
17 Jan.	G. Hall (Cheque No. 3)	250		14 750
17 Jan.	Lodgement (Cash sales)		5 000	19 750
22 Jan.	Insurance (Cheque No. 4)	400		19 350
24 Jan.	J. Gold (Cheque No. 5)	3 500		15 850
	Bank charges	200		15 650

Bank reconciliation statements

		Dr. £	Cr. £	Balance £
	Lodgement (Cash sales)		6 000	21 650
28 Jan.	J. King (Cheque No. 6)	5 400		16 250
29 Jan.	Lodgement (A. Bard)		3 600	19 850
31 Jan.	G. Hall (Cheque No. 7)	250		19 600
	Lodgement		8 000	27 600

This statement indicates that Barclays Bank owes Peter Hill £27 600 on 31 January 19–1.

Check for yourself that all the items on the debit side of the cash book appear in the credit column of the bank statement and items appearing on the credit side of the cash book are entered in the debit column of the bank statement. (Tick off each entry in both records.)

SOLUTION

Step 1

Peter Hill
Cash book (bank columns only)

Dr. Date		£	Date		Cr. £
1 Jan.	Balance b/d	4 000	8 Jan.	M. Hely	1 500
5 Jan.	P. Drake	3 000	13 Jan.	Rent	500
10 Jan.	Cash sales	10 000	14 Jan.	G. Hall (wages)	250
17 Jan.	Cash sales	5 000	20 Jan.	Insurance	400
24 Jan.	Cash sales	6 000	21 Jan.	J. Gold	3 500
29 Jan.	A. Bard	3 600	22 Jan.	Bank charges	200
31 Jan.	Cash sales	8 000	26 Jan.	J. King	5 400
			30 Jan.	G. Hall (wages)	250
			31 Jan.	Balance c/d	27 600
		39 600			39 600
31 Jan.	Balance b/d	27 600			

This account also indicates that Peter Hill has a balance in his account at Barclays Bank PLC of £27 600.

Step 2

Bank statement

When Peter Hill gets his statement from the bank, he ticks off all items against his cash book and knows that both accounts are correct and agree.

But the balances will not always agree on a particular date because of:
1. A time-lag in recording transactions by either party, e.g.
   (a) When a cheque is paid out (issued by the trader), he immediately enters it on the credit side of his Bank Account, thereby reducing the balance. The bank, on the other hand, will not record the transaction until the cheque is presented for payment.
   (b) When the trader lodges money in the bank, he immediately debits his Bank Account in his own books, thereby increasing it; this entry will not be made by the bank for at least a few days after receiving the lodgement.

Bank reconciliation statements

(c) When the bank receives a direct lodgement on behalf of the trader, it credits the trader's account, while the trader has to wait until he is notified before debiting his Bank Account.
2. Lack of knowledge by one party of an entry made by the other party which results in an omission by that party, e.g.
   (a) bank dishonours a cheque but trader is unaware of dishonour,
   (b) bank debits trader's account with bank charges or interest and trader is unaware of it until he receives the statement.
3. Errors by either party, e.g.
   (a) entering wrong amounts,
   (b) entering amounts on wrong side of the account,
   (c) errors in arithmetic.

So the obvious and practical thing for the trader to do is first to find the errors and omissions in his own books and correct them, then to account for the remaining differences in a bank reconciliation statement. This is the procedure that is carried out in practice – in fact, the cash book is reopened and the necessary adjustments are made immediately.

In brief the procedure is to:
1. correct the cash book or Bank Account in the ledger,
2. reconcile this corrected figure with the bank statement.

In correcting the cash book enter items missing from it on the appropriate side. Errors in figures are corrected by entering the correcting figure on the appropriate side.

ANOTHER EXAMPLE

M. Hilman
Cash book (bank columns only)

Dr.						Cheque No.	Cr. £
19–2		£	19–2				
1 July	Balance b/d	960	4 July	Wages		001	548
3 July	J. Lane	1 280		T. Kitt		002	220
5 July	M. Kirk	256	9 July	W. Cod		003	248
7 July	T. Butler	108	12 July	B. Good		004	1 300
11 July	M. James	676	14 July	Petty cash		005	80
14 July	S. Torrance	328	17 July	Wages		006	580
19 July	V. Hill	316	26 July	J. Blake		007	668
25 July	D. Eaton	1 200		C. Cotter		008	188
30 July	E. Geary	840	30 July	M. Moran		009	336
31 July	R. Burns	1 800	31 July	Balance c/d			3 596
		7 764					7 764
31 July	Balance b/d	3 596					

Mr M. Hilman
19–2

Bank of Scotland – Dundee Branch
Bank statement

		Dr. £	Cr. £	Balance £
1 July	Balance			960
3 July	Lodgement		1 280	2 240
5 July	Cheque 001	548		1 692
	Lodgement		256	1 948
	Cheque 002	220		1 728
7 July	Lodgement		108	1 836
10 July	Cheque 003	248		1 588
11 July	Lodgement		678	2 264
13 July	Cheque 004	1 300		964
14 July	Cheque 005	80		884
15 July	Lodgement		328	1 212
18 July	Cheque 006	580		632
19 July	Lodgement		316	948
25 July	Lodgement		1 200	2 148
27 July	Cheque 007	668		1 480
	Cheque 008	188		1 292
	Credit transfer		800	2 092
28 July	Standing order	200		1 892
29 July	Bank charges	80		1 812

In this example we see that the balance on the cash book is £3 596 and the balance on the bank statement is £1 812.

On ticking off the items against each other, we find three items in the bank statement that are not in the cash book, namely:
1. Credit transfer, £800.
2. Standing order, £200.
3. Bank charges, £80.

We also find three items in the cash book that do not appear in the bank statement, namely:
1. E. Geary (lodgement), £840.
2. R. Burns (lodgement), £1 800.
3. M. Moran (cheque 009), £336.

Procedure

Step 1

Correct the cash book by reopening it and entering the items missing from it; bring down the correct balance.

Dr.		Cash book (bank columns only)			Cr.
19–2		£	19–2		£
31 July	Balance b/d	3 596	31 July	Standing order	200
	Credit transfer	800		Bank charges	80
				Balance c/d	4 116
		4 396			4 396
	Balance b/d	4 116			

Step 2

Reconcile the bank statement balance with the *corrected* cash book or Bank Account balance in trader's books, starting either with the bank statement balance (A) or cash book balance (B).

M. Hilman
Bank reconciliation statement as at 31 July 19–2

		£
(A)	Balance as per bank statement	1 812
	Add Lodgements not credited (by bank) (£840+£1 800)	2 640
		4 452
	Deduct Cheques paid not presented (to bank for payment)	336
	Balance as per corrected cash book	4 116

or

		£
(B)	Balance as per corrected cash book	4 116
	Add Cheques paid not presented	336
		4 452
	Deduct Lodgements not credited	2 640
	Balance as per bank statement	1 812

Where an error is made by the bank, e.g. lodging a customer's personal lodgement to the business Bank Account, two things can be done:
1. The bank statement can be adjusted to the correct figure (usually after telephoning the bank and agreeing that an error has been made).
   or
2. Adjustment can take place in the reconciliation statement itself (see example below). This is the more usual way of making the adjustment for examination purposes.

EXAMPLE
On 31.12.1985 the bank column of John Archer's cash book showed a debit balance of £1 120. His bank statement on that date showed a credit balance of £2 064. On examination of the cash book and bank statement you find that:
(a) cheques issued by Archer amounting to £1 720 had not yet been presented for payment
(b) a cheque for £392 received by Archer had been entered on the incorrect side of the cash book
(c) lodgements, amounting to £2 080, had not yet been credited by the bank
(d) a cheque for £320 lodged by Archer and correctly entered in the cash book had been dishonoured by the bank (Archer had not adjusted this item in his books)
(e) bank charges, £40, and credit transfers received, £260, had not been entered in Archer's books
(f) Archer had given £400 out of his private funds to his secretary to lodge to his personal account, but in error she lodged the money to the business account
(g) an amount of £220 lodged by a *David* Archer had been entered in error by the bank on the correct side of John Archer's account.

a   Adjust Archer's cash book and bring down the correct balance.
b   Prepare a statement on 31.12.1985 reconciling the adjusted cash book balance with the bank statement balance.

Procedure

SOLUTION
a *Adjust the cash book*

Cash book

Dr.		Bank £			Bank £	Cr.
1985			1985			
31 Dec.	Balance b/d	1 120	31 Dec.	Dishonoured cheque	320	
	Error	784		Bank charges	40	
	Credit transfers	260		Balance c/d	1 804	
		2 164			2 164	
31 Dec.	Balance b/d	1 804				

b *Prepare bank reconciliation statement*

John Archer
Bank reconciliation statement as at 31 December 1985

		£
Balance as per bank statement		2 064
Add Lodgement not credited		2 080
		4 144
Less Cheques paid not presented		1 720
		2 424
Less Errors made by bank	400	
(lodged to wrong accounts)	220	
Balance as per corrected cash book		620
		1 804

A MORE DIFFICULT EXAMPLE

R. Mason's cash book showed a balance of £23 665 at the bank on 31 December 19–1. His bank statement on the same date showed that his balance at the bank amounted to £7 065. On investigation he found that

1. Standing order payments amounting to £620 had not been entered in his cash book.
2. He had brought down his opening balance in the cash book of £3 293 as a debit balance instead of a credit balance.
3. A debtor's cheque for £150 had been dishonoured by the bank but the dishonour had not been recorded in the cash book.
4. Bank charges of £30 had not been entered in the cash book.
5. Lodgements made by Mason, £985, on 31 December had not been credited by the bank.
6. Some of Mason's customers had agreed to settle their accounts by direct debit. The bank had credited direct debits amounting to £8 325 to another customer's account.
7. A cheque drawn by Mason for £230 had been entered in his cash book as £275.
8. Cheques drawn by Mason for £226 had not been presented for payment.
9. An old cheque for £440 had been written back in the cash book but the bank had already honoured it.
10. Mason had not entered receipts of £265 in his cash book.

a Adjust Mason's cash book as necessary.
b Prepare a bank reconciliation statement as at 31 December 19–1.

56 Bank reconciliation statements

SOLUTION
a *Adjust Mason's cash book*

Cash book (bank columns)

19–1		£	19–1		£
31 Dec.	Balance b/d	23 665	31 Dec.	Standing order (1)	620
	Error (transposition) (7)	45		Error in opening	
	Receipt omitted (10)	265		balance (2)	6 586
				Dishonoured cheque (3)	150
				Bank charges (4)	30
				Old cheque presented (9)	440
				Balance c/d	16 149
		23 975			23 975
31 Dec.	Balance b/d	16 149			

b *Prepare bank reconciliation statement*

R. Mason
Bank reconciliation statement as at 31 December 19–1

	£
Balance as per bank statement	7 065
Add Lodgement not credited by bank	985
Add Direct debits incorrectly posted to another customer's account	8 325
	16 375
Less Cheques paid not presented	226
Balance as per corrected cash book	16 149

Note

Sometimes in examination questions the bank statement balance is not given. In this case the cash book or Bank Account in the ledger is first corrected. Then, starting with this figure:
Add cheques paid not presented
Deduct lodgements not credited.

The result must be: (Correct) balance as per bank statement.

Exercises Set 4

1 The bank columns of T. Barker's cash book were as follows:

Dr. 19–1			£	19–1			£
1 Jan.	Balance b/d		1 680	4 Jan.	L. Coles		320
10 Jan.	M. Evans		200	10 Jan.	W. Dodge		160
16 Jan.	B. Easy		880	12 Jan.	Wages		520
29 Jan.	C. Franks		720	24 Jan.	J. Pryer		480
30 Jan.	A. Denis		180	29 Jan.	Petty cash		160
				30 Jan.	T. Mee		320
				31 Jan.	Balance c/d		1 700
			3 660				3 660
31 Jan.	Balance b/d		1 700				

Cr.

Barker's bank statement was as follows:

		Dr. £	Cr. £	Balance £
19–1				
1 Jan.	Balance			1 680
7 Jan.	Cheque	320		1 360
10 Jan.	Lodgement		200	1 560
12 Jan.	Cheque	160		1 400
14 Jan.	Cheque	520		880
19 Jan.	Lodgement		880	1 760
20 Jan.	Standing order	1 600		160
30 Jan.	Bank charges	10		150

a Correct the cash book as necessary.
b Prepare the bank reconciliation statement as at 31 January 19–1.

2 The bank columns of R. Stokes's cash book showed the following entries for March 19–2:

Dr. 19–2			£	**Cash book** 19–2			Cr. £
1 Mar.	Balance b/d		2 964	2 Mar.	Petty cash		40
4 Mar.	S. Davis		676	6 Mar.	G. Banks		334
6 Mar.	B. Jones		180	7 Mar.	Wages		348
10 Mar.	N. Grace		1 840	14 Mar.	Wages		368
11 Mar.	N. Davies		304	15 Mar.	L. Timony		580
16 Mar.	T. Doyle		64	21 Mar.	Wages		352
18 Mar.	P. Dobson		60	28 Mar.	B. Harty		1 480
22 Mar.	B. Good		520	28 Mar.	Wages		360
25 Mar.	D. Duck		2 960	29 Mar.	M. Hall		484
29 Mar.	S. Green		924	30 Mar.	T. Jacobs		248
30 Mar.	R. Coote		360	31 Mar.	N. Drumm		924
					Balance b/d		5 352
			10 852				10 852
31 Mar.	Balance b/d		5 352				

Bank statement

19–2		Dr. £	Cr. £	Balance £
1 Mar.	Balance			2 964
2 Mar.	Cheque	40		2 924
4 Mar.	Lodgement		676	3 600
6 Mar.	Lodgement		180	3 780
9 Mar.	Cheque	336		3 444
10 Mar.	Cheque	348		3 096
	Lodgement		1 840	4 936
11 Mar.	Lodgement		304	5 240
16 Mar.	Cheque	368		4 872
	Lodgement		64	4 936
17 Mar.	Cheque	560		4 376
18 Mar.	Lodgement		60	4 436
22 Mar.	Lodgement		520	4 956
23 Mar.	Cheque	352		4 604
25 Mar.	Lodgement		2 960	7 564
29 Mar.	Cheque	360		7 204
31 Mar.	Cheque	248		6 956
	Bank charges	40		6 916
	Standing order	100		6 816
	Credit transfer		200	7 016
	Dishonoured cheque	64		6 952

a Correct the cash book as necessary.
b Prepare the bank reconciliation statement as at 31 March 19–2.

3 On 28 February 19–2 T. Moore's cash book (bank columns) showed a debit balance of £2 241.32. His bank statement on the same date showed a credit balance of £2 568.98. On comparing the cash book and bank statement he found:
   (a) £519.08 had been paid by Moore into the bank on 28 February but did not appear in the bank statement.
   (b) Bank charges, £30, had not been entered in the cash book.
   (c) A cheque drawn on 3 February in favour of R. Cole, £988.84, had not yet been presented for payment.
   (d) On 26 February the bank had paid a standing order for £62.10 but this had not been entered in the cash book.
   (e) On 28 February the bank had dishonoured a cheque, £50, which formed part of a lodgement made by Moore on 26 February. No entry relating to the dishonour was made in Moore's books.

   a Prepare a statement showing the balance which should appear in the cash book on 28 February after all necessary corrections had been made.
   b Prepare a statement reconciling the corrected cash book balance with the bank statement.

4 William Tell's cash book (bank columns) for April 19–3 was as follows:

Dr. 19–3		£	19–3		Cr. £
1 April	Balance b/d	1 000	2 April	B. Wary	150
6	D. Jones	474	5	Wages	250
9	T. Dore	246	10	M. Laing	850
14	R. Stokes	76	15	Drawings	120
20	P. McIntosh	176	21	Rent	90
28	D. Brook	46	22	E. Cross	136
29	C. Cooke	530	24	P. Woodman	30
			27	Rates	274
			28	Cheque book	4

His bank statement on 30 April 19–3 showed:

		Dr. £	Cr. £	Balance £
1 April	Balance b/d			1 280
3	Wary	150		1 130
6	Wages	250		880
7	Jones		474	1 354
8	Dividends		100	1 454
9	Dore		246	1 700
11	Laing	850		850
15	Stokes		76	926
15	Murphy	110		816
16	Drawings	120		696
20	McIntosh		176	872
23	Cross	136		736
28	Cheque book	4		732
29	Flanagan	170		562
29	S/O	40		522
30	Bank charges	30		492

Balance the cash book, make any adjustments necessary and reconcile the adjusted cash book balance with the balance according to the bank statement.

5 On 31 March 1986 the bank columns of M. Smith's cash book showed a debit balance of £32 000. On examination of the cash book and bank statement you find that:
  (a) A cheque book costing £8 had been entered in the cash book on the debit side.
  (b) Cheques received amounting to £1 734 were recorded in the cash book as having been lodged in the bank on 30 March 1986, but were entered in the bank statement on 4 April 1986.
  (c) R. Lord's cheque received for £400 had been dishonoured, and had been corrected by debiting the cash book.
  (d) The following items had been omitted entirely from the cash book:
     (i) a standing order payable by Smith on 18 March 1986 for £1 200
     (ii) bank interest charged by the bank amounting to £540
     (iii) a dividend receivable of £82 had been paid direct to the bank.
  (e) A cheque for £164 drawn by Elm Ltd had been charged to Smith's Bank Account in error.

60 Bank reconciliation statements

(f) Cheques issued, amounting to £15 000, had not yet been presented by creditors.

a Make appropriate adjustments in the cash book, bringing down the correct balance.
b Prepare a statement, reconciling the adjusted balance in the cash book with the balance in the bank statement.

6   Set out below are the cash book (bank columns only) and bank statement of Richard Douglas for the month of March 1986:

Cash book (bank columns)

Dr. 1986			£	1986		Cr. £
1 Mar.	Balance b/d		1 500	3 Mar.	T. Mason	280
8	Sales lodged		1 040	5	N. Oakes	320
20	Lodgement		1 760	7	Rates	148
28	Lodgement		1 260	9	Wages	160
				16	B. Enfield	252
				20	Wages	160
				25	G. Ward	540
				28	J. Cross	1 300
				31	Balance c/d	2 400
			5 560			5 560
Balance b/d			2 400			

Bank statement on 31 March 1986

1986		Dr. £	Cr. £	Balance £
1 Mar.	Balance b/d			1 500
4	Interest received		360	1 860
8	Lodgement		1 040	2 900
9	T. Mason	280		2 620
12	Wages	160		2 460
13	Insurance standing order	380		2 080
15	Dividends received		1 620	3 700
18	Bank charges	40		3 660
19	Credit transfer		180	3 840
20	B. Enfield	252		3 588
20	Lodgement		1 760	5 348
26	G. Ward	540		4 808
28	A. Muggins's R/D (dishonoured)	300		4 508

The £180 entered in the bank statement on 19 March 1986 was credited in error by the bank to R. Douglas's account instead of R. Dugdale's account.

a Show the adjusted cash book of Richard Douglas and bring down the correct balance.
b Prepare a statement on 31.3.1986 reconciling the adjusted cash book balance with the bank statement balance.

7   On 30 June 19–6 the cash book of Thomas Lally showed a debit balance of £1 248. You are given the following information:
   (a) Lally discovered that he had overcast the debit side of his cash book (bank column) by £200.
   (b) He also found that a cheque received by him for £196 had been entered in the cash book as £178.
   (c) Interest on a deposit account amounting to £56 had been credited by the bank but did not appear in the cash book.
   (d) A cheque received by him for £120 and lodged in the bank had been dishonoured by the bank but no entry referring to the dishonour appeared in the cash book.
   (e) Cheques drawn during the month amounting to £276 had not been presented for payment.
   (f) A lodgement of cheques valued at £480 made by him on 29 June did not appear on the bank statement.

   a   Correct his cash book.
   b   Reconcile it with the amount that would have appeared on the bank statement.

8   The cash book of Pat Smyth, a trader, showed that at 31 January 19–7 his account at the bank was overdrawn by £741.88. After comparing his bank statement as of that date with his cash book, he found that the entries in both agreed except in regard to the following matters:
   (a) Cheques drawn and entered in the cash book amounting to £1 057.64 had not been presented to the bank.
   (b) A lodgement made on 31 January 19–7 for £58.34 did not appear in the bank statement.
   (c) A charge of £23.88 for interest on overdraft appearing in the bank statement had not been entered in the cash book.
   (d) Smyth had discounted with the bank a promissory note received from a customer for £600, but in error this amount had been entered in his cash book. The net proceeds as shown in the bank statement were £576.90.

   Prepare a statement showing: **a** what balance the bank statement showed on 31 January 19–7, and **b** what the balance in Smyth's cash book would be after making the necessary additional entries.

9   From the following data prepare a bank reconciliation statement:

	£
Balance at credit of Bank Account in nominal ledger	2 495.34
Overdraft as per bank statements	1 782.22
Cheques issued but not yet presented at the bank for payment	1 084.68
Lodgement not yet credited by bank	384.92
Debits on bank statements which do not appear in the company's books:	
Bank charges £8.40	
Bank interest £62.68	71.08
Credit in bank statement which does not appear in the company's books:	
Investment income	84.44

10 When T. Brown received his bank statement for the half-year ended 31 December 1985, the balance was not in agreement with that shown in the cash book, namely £2 972 in favour of Brown. On investigation it was found that:
   (a) White, who received a cash discount of 2½ per cent on his account of £200, had

sent a cheque on 10 December 1985 for the net amount due. In error the gross amount had been entered in the bank column of the cash book.

(b) A lodgement of £492 made on 31 December 1985 was not credited by the bank until 2 January 1986.

(c) Bank charges, £17, had not been entered in the cash book.

(d) A debit of £42 appears in the bank statement for an unpaid cheque, which had been returned marked 'out of date'. The cheque was re-dated by the drawer and relodged to Brown's account on 6 January 1986.

(e) Cheques issued amounting to £4 672 were not presented to the bank until after 31 December 1985.

(f) On 29 December 1985 a customer had paid direct to the firm's Bank Account in payment for goods supplied, £656. The advice was not received by Brown until 2 January 1986 and entered into the cash book under that date.

(g) £364 paid into the bank had been entered twice in the cash book.

(h) On 24 December 1985 Brown had given the cashier £100 to be lodged to his personal account. By mistake the cashier had paid it into Brown's business account.

(i) On 28 November 1985 the bank had advised that a cheque for £78 drawn by B. Smart had been returned 'unpaid'. No entry was made in the cash book.

After making the adjustments required by the foregoing, the bank statement agreed with the balance in the cash book.

a Show the necessary adjustments in the cash book of T. Brown, bringing down the correct balance on 31 December 1985.

b Draw up a bank reconciliation statement as on that date.

11 The bank column of T. Fox's cash book showed a credit balance of £104 on 31 March 1986. On examination of the cash book and bank statement you find that:

(a) Fox had lodged £150 in a night safe in the bank on 30.3.1986. This did not appear in his bank statement.

(b) Bank charges, £24, had been debited to his cash book as £42.

(c) A cheque for £1 040 drawn by T. Fox had been entered in another customer's account by the bank.

(d) Dividends, £110, received by the bank on behalf of T. Fox had been debited in error to his account by the bank. No entry had been made in the cash book.

(e) T. Fox had debited his cash book with £800 in respect of a 6-month bill receivable which he lodged to the bank. The bank statement, however, had shown this item discounted at the rate of 10 per cent per annum.

(f) A payment of £50 by the bank on behalf of T. Fox had not been entered in the cash book.

(g) A cheque for £146 lodged by T. Fox had been returned by the bank marked R/D. The bank had adjusted Fox's account, but no entry had been made in the cash book.

(h) T. Fox lost a cheque which he himself had signed. He immediately notified the bank, but in spite of this the cheque for £320 was cashed by a bank branch. The bank accepted responsibility for this amount, but no adjustment had been made in the bank statement by 31.3.1986.

a Adjust Fox's cash book.

b Prepare a statement on 31.3.1986 reconciling the adjusted cash book balance with the bank statement balance.

12 Hay has received his bank pass sheets for the year to 31 October 1983. At that date, his balance at the bank amounted to £14 130 whereas his own cash book showed a balance of £47 330. His accountant investigated the matter, and discovered the following discrepancies:
1. Bank charges of £60 had not been entered in the cash book.
2. Cheques drawn by Hay and totalling £450 had not yet been presented to the bank.
3. Hay had not entered receipts of £530 in his cash book.
4. The bank had not credited Hay with receipts of £1 970 paid in to the bank on 31 October 1983.
5. Standing order payments amounting to £1 240 had not been entered in the cash book.
6. Hay had entered a payment of £560 in his cash book as £650.
7. A cheque received for £300 from a debtor had been returned by the bank marked 'refer to drawer', but this had not been written back in the cash book.
8. Hay had brought down his opening cash book balance of £6 585 as a debit balance instead of as a credit balance.
9. An old cheque payment amounting to £880 had been written back in the cash book, but the bank had already honoured it.
10. Some of Hay's customers had agreed to settle their debts by direct debit. Unfortunately, the bank had credited some direct debits amounting to £16 650 to another customer's account.

a   Prepare a statement showing Hay's adjusted cash book balance as at 31 October 1983.
b   Prepare a bank reconciliation statement as at 31 October 1983.
c   State briefly the main reasons for preparing a bank reconciliation statement.
[*Association of Accounting Technicians, December 1983*]

13 The treasurer of the Camford School Fund is attempting to reconcile the balance shown in the cash book with that appearing on the bank pass sheets. According to the cash book, the balance at the bank as at 31 May 1982 was £1 900, whilst the bank pass sheets disclosed an overdrawn amount of £470. Upon investigation, the treasurer discovers the following errors:
1. A cheque paid to Summer Ltd for £340 had been entered in the cash book as £430.
2. Cash paid into the bank for £100 had been entered in the cash book as £90.
3. A transfer of £1 500 to the Midlands Savings Bank had not been entered in the cash book.
4. A receipt of £10 shown on the bank statement had not been entered in the cash book.
5. Cheques drawn amounting to £40 had not been paid into the bank.
6. The cash book balance had been incorrectly brought down at 1 June 1981 as a debit balance of £1 200 instead of a debit balance of £1 100.
7. Bank charges of £20 do not appear in the cash book.
8. Receipts of £900 paid into the bank on 31 May 1982 do not appear on the bank pass sheets until 1 June 1982.
9. A standing order payment of £30 had not been entered in the cash book.
10. A cheque for £50 previously received and paid into the bank had been returned by the subscriber's bank marked 'account closed'.
11. The bank received a direct debit of £100 from an anonymous subscriber.

64 Bank reconciliation statements

12. Cheques paid into the bank had been incorrectly totalled. The total amount should have been £170 instead of £150.

Draw up a bank reconciliation statement as at 31 May 1982.

[*Association of Accounting Technicians, June 1982*]

14 The following information relates to the Bywater School Fund for the month of March 1984:

Cash book (Bank Account extract)

		£			Cheque	£
29.2.84	Total receipts	2 200	29.2.84	Total		
	Balance c/d	400		payments		2 600
		2 600				2 600
1.3.84	Balance b/d	400	2.3.84	Flyn	123	10
5.3.84	Tote money	150	5.3.84	Ned	124	20
9.3.84	Sponsored walk	400	6.3.84	Hay	125	50
12.3.84	Tote money	325	7.3.84	Bedford	126	100
14.3.84	Donation	1 000	9.3.84	Smith Press	127	500
19.3.84	Tote money	100	14.3.84	Joy	128	40
23.3.84	Coffee evening	175	15.3.84	Morris Ltd	129	150
26.3.84	Tote money	250	19.3.84	Henley	130	60
31.3.84	Staff dance	200	20.3.84	Waters	131	25
			21.3.84	Richey	132	5
			23.3.84	Oxford Ltd	133	250
			30.3.84	Petty cash	134	30
			31.3.84	Balance c/d		1 420
		3 010				3 010
1.4.84	Balance b/d	1 420				

Notes
1. The Bank Account extract was compiled by the treasurer from his own records. It contains some arithmetical errors, and no adjustments have been made to it.
2. As at 29 February 1984, a cheque for £550 (cheque number 122) had not been credited by the bank.

A copy of the bank statement is shown below:

Bank statement (copy)

Details	Payments	Receipts	Date	Balance
			1.3.84	150
Counter credit		150	5.3.84	300
Bank charges	10			290
Counter credit		400	9.3.84	690
	124	20	12.3.84	
Counter credit		325		995
	127	500	13.3.84	495
Counter credit		1 000	14.3.84	1 495
Standing order	45		15.3.84	1 450
Counter credit		100	19.3.84	
Returned cheque	15			1 535
	126	100	21.3.84	1 435
Direct debit	120		22.3.84	1 315
Counter credit		175	23.3.84	1 490
	131	25	24.3.84	
	130	60		1 405
Counter credit		250	26.3.84	1 655
	132	5	27.3.84	
	123	10		1 640
Transfer to deposit	75		30.3.84	1 565
	128	40	31.3.84	
	122	550		
	129	150		
Refund of bank charges		10		835

a Calculate the correct cash book balance as at 31 March 1984.
b Prepare a bank reconciliation statement as at that date.

[*Association of Accounting Technicians, June 1984*]

15 The cash book, bank columns, for January 1984, of S. Simpson, sole trader is as follows:

1984			£	1984			£
1 Jan.	Balance		1 507.71	2 Jan.	Electricity Board		43.10
9 Jan.	Sales		1 370.00	2 Jan.	John Jones Ltd		149.10
17 Jan.	Sales		168.54	4 Jan.	Printers' Supplies Ltd		29.30
23 Jan.	T. White Ltd		310.00	5 Jan.	Kingsway Products		37.08
24 Jan.	Sales		150.00	12 Jan.	Harold Smith Ltd		138.32
30 Jan.	Sales		44.70	17 Jan.	Gray's Machines Ltd		645.10
31 Jan.	Sales		210.00	24 Jan.	Giant Displays		70.56
				26 Jan.	P. Swann		124.64
				30 Jan.	Deposit account		2 000.00
				30 Jan.	Wages		320.40
				31 Jan.	Balance		203.35
			3 760.95				3 760.95

On 6 February 1984, S. Simpson received his bank statement for the previous month; the bank statement was as follows:

Mr S. Simpson – Statement of account with North Bank PLC, Main Street Branch, Westford

Date 1984	Particulars	Payments £	Receipts £	Balance £
1 Jan.	Balance			1 468.21
3 Jan.	Bank giro credit		100.00	1 568.21
4 Jan.	145688	149.10		1 419.11
5 Jan.	145686	60.50		1 358.61
6 Jan.	Charges	15.40		1 343.21
9 Jan.	Standing order	12.00		1 331.21
10 Jan.	Bank giro credit		1 370.00	2 701.21
11 Jan.	145687	43.10		2 658.11
13 Jan.	145690	37.08		2 621.03
17 Jan.	Sundry credit		168.54	2 789.57
18 Jan.	145691	138.32		2 651.25
20 Jan.	145689	29.30		2 621.95
23 Jan.	Sundry credit		310.00	2 931.95
26 Jan.	Standing order	44.00		2 887.95
27 Jan.	Bank giro credit		150.00	3 037.95
30 Jan.	Deposit account	2 000.00		1 037.95
30 Jan.	Sundry credit		44.70	1 082.65
31 Jan.	145693	70.56		1 012.09

On 8 February 1984, S. Simpson discovers that the sales debited in the cash book on 31 January 1984 should read £230.00 not £210.00 and is advised by the bank that the standing order charge of £44.00 on 26 January was made in error and that the bank account has now been credited with £44.00.

Prepare a bank reconciliation statement as at 31 January 1984.

[*Association of Accounting Technicians, pilot, 1985*]

16 The head cashier of a factory making jam found that the balance of money at the bank according to his cash book at the close of business on 30 June was £29 760.

When he received his bank statement early in July he found the balance at 30 June shown by the bank to be a different figure, for the following reasons:
- (*a*) The bank had paid a standing order for £12 subscription renewal on 25 June but this had not been entered in the cash book.
- (*b*) The following cheques had been received by the cashier on 30 June but had not been paid into the bank until 1 July:
  Webster £1 890   Walker £639   Williams £830.
- (*c*) A cheque for £704, paid into the bank on 20 June had been dishonoured and debited in the bank statement on 29 June. This cheque was re-presented and paid on 7 July.

(d) A dividend for £1 500 had been received direct by the bank on 29 June but had not been recorded in the cash book.
(e) Cheques totalling £6 410 drawn in June were not presented for payment until July.

You are required to prepare a reconciliation of the balance shown by the cash book with that shown in the bank statement at 30 June.

[*Pitman Intermediate*]

17 The bank reconciliation statement as at 19 September 1986 for the account number 0439567 of John Henry Ltd with Industrious Bank PLC showed that the difference between the cash book and bank statement was due entirely to four unpresented cheques, numbers 765417 to 765420 inclusive.

The cash book (bank columns) for the period from 19 September to 30 September 1986, of John Henry Ltd is as follows:

1986		£	1986		Cheque	£
23 Sept.	B. Main	692.30	19 Sept.	Balance b/fd		21.00
23 Sept.	T. Patrick	27.24	22 Sept.	S. Salter Ltd	765421	25.67
25 Sept.	S. Saunders	410.00	22 Sept.	Sway District Council	765422	275.10
26 Sept.	P. King	400.00	23 Sept.	North South Electricity Authority	Direct debit	316.50
26 Sept.	K. Plunket	39.60	23 Sept.	J. Peters Ltd	765423	18.34
28 Sept.	J. Lim	324.92	24 Sept.	Furniture Trade Assoc.	Standing order	45.00
30 Sept.	S. Balk	220.39	24 Sept.	K. Patel	765424	19.04
			25 Sept.	Cash (petty cash)	765425	50.00
			26 Sept.	J. Green Ltd	765426	45.00
			26 Sept.	G. Glinker	765427	174.00
			29 Sept.	Deposit account		600.00
			29 Sept.	Wages	Transfer	390.00
			30 Sept.	Balance c/d		134.80
		2 114.45				2 114.45
1 Oct.	Balance b/fd	134.80				

68 Bank reconciliation statements

Early in October 1986, John Henry Ltd received the following statement from Industrious Bank PLC:

John Henry Ltd – Statement of account with Industrious Bank PLC, East Road, Streamly

Account number 0439567

Date	Particulars	Payments	Receipts	Balance
1986		£	£	£
19 Sept.	Balance			453.26
22 Sept.	765419	138.35		314.91
23 Sept.	Sundry credits		719.54	1 034.45
23 Sept.	Direct debit	316.50		717.95
24 Sept.	765421	25.67		692.28
24 Sept.	Standing order	45.00		647.28
25 Sept.	765420	160.04		487.24
26 Sept.	765422	275.10		212.14
26 Sept.	Sundry credits		400.00	612.14
26 Sept.	Bank giro credit		410.00	1 022.14
29 Sept.	Bank giro credit		334.92	1 357.06
29 Sept.	765418	21.69		1 335.37
29 Sept.	765424	19.04		1 316.33
29 Sept.	Transfer to deposit account	600.00		716.33
29 Sept.	Transfer	390.00		326.33
29 Sept.	765425	50.00		276.33
29 Sept.	As advised		65.00	341.33
29 Sept.	Bank giro credit		39.60	380.93
30 Sept.	Loan account interest	41.25		339.68
30 Sept.	Bank charges	16.70		322.98

The following additional information is given:
1. The amount received from J. Lim on 28 September 1986 was £334.92 not £324.92.
2. The amount credited in the bank statement on 29 September 1986 and shown as 'As advised £65.00' concerned dividends received.
3. John Henry Ltd has written to the bank complaining concerning the bank charges of £16.70; the company's view is that no charges should arise for the month of September. The bank has a reputation for not cancelling bank charges.

a   Prepare a bank reconciliation statement as at 30 September 1986.
   Note. Indicate the amount which should be included in the balance sheet as at 30 September 1986 of John Henry Ltd for the company's account number 0439567 with Industrious Bank PLC.
b   What are the major uses of a bank reconciliation statement?
[*Association of Accounting Technicians, December 1986*]

5 Control accounts

When a business expands and numerous transactions have to be recorded in ledger accounts, it becomes impracticable and wasteful to have all ledger accounts in one ledger. The ledger must be subdivided. Generally, the ledger will already have been subdivided into:
1. A sales or debtors ledger – containing debtors' accounts only.
2. A purchases or creditors ledger – containing creditors' accounts only.
3. A general or nominal ledger – containing accounts for assets, nominal accounts, etc.
4. A private ledger – in which are kept Capital, Drawings, Profit and Loss Accounts, etc.

As business expands, these ledgers may have to be subdivided further, e.g. the sales ledger may be divided on a territorial basis, e.g. north ledger and south ledger, or alphabetically, e.g. A–F, G–R, S–Z. The subdivision will be geared to the particular type of business.

To facilitate postings to these ledgers the subsidiary books will carry additional columns corresponding to the ledger subdivisions, e.g.

Sales book

Date	Particulars	Fo.	Detail	Total	Analysis columns		
					Ledger A–F	Ledger G–R	Ledger S–Z
				£	£	£	£
1 Jan.	S. Mackey, Goods	DL3		100		100	
2 Jan.	T. Banks, Goods	DL4		200	200		
3 Jan.	P. Roche, Goods	DL5		300			300
	Total			600	200	100	300

These items will be posted in the usual way, e.g. for sales: individual accounts will be debited with individual amounts; Sales Account will be credited with the total.

But note that in addition, for each section of the ledger an account will be raised in the general ledger called Sales (Sold) Ledger Control Account or

Debtors Ledger Control Account. Into this account, in total, will go the amounts that have been debited or credited to the individual accounts and on the same side as on the individual accounts. The same will apply to all subsidiary books. The purchases ledger will have a Purchases (Bought) or Creditors Control Account.

The key to doing control accounts is to ask yourself the simple question: *on which side of the individual account did this item appear? It will appear on the same side of the control account.*

Remember that *all items appearing in the control accounts come from totals in the books of first entry.*

Advantages of control accounts

Control accounts have the following uses and advantages.
1. They act as a check on the posting of the individual ledger accounts and on their totals.
2. They enable errors to be localised and therefore found more speedily.
3. They also identify the individuals making the errors, if an individual is responsible for posting a particular section or subsection.
4. The totals owed by debtors and to creditors can be ascertained quickly by simply balancing the control account; the alternative would be to balance each individual account and add up the balances. The last procedure is known as *listing* the balances. It is done to double-check the accuracy of the entries and the balance on the control account. Remember that the list total and control account balance *must* always agree as they are dealing with precisely the same figures.
5. Knowledge of control accounts is very important for preparing accounts from incomplete records.

The balance in the control account in the general ledger will be equal to the total of all the balances in the individual accounts. The following items might appear on the Sales Ledger Control Account and on the Creditors Ledger Control Account.

Dr.		Sales/Sold/Debtors Ledger Control Account		Cr.
1 Jan.	Balances due by debtors at start of period		31 Dec.	Sales returns, or allowances to debtors during period
	Credit sales to debtors during period			Cash paid by debtors during period
	Carriage charged to debtors during period			Discount allowed to debtors during period
	Debtors' cheques dishonoured during period			Bad debts written off during period
	Discount disallowed during period			Bills receivable accepted during period
	Interest charged to debtors during period			Balance c/d (at end of period)
	Bills receivable dishonoured during period			
	Balance b/d			

Dr.	Creditors/Purchases/Bought Ledger Control Account		Cr.
31 Dec. Purchases returns Cash paid to creditors Discount received from creditors Bills payable accepted Balance c/d (at end of period)		1 Jan. 31 Dec.	Balance due to trade creditors Credit purchases Carriage charged on purchases Discount received disallowed Interest charged by creditors Bills payable dishonoured Balance b/d

The account is balanced and the balance is brought down to the first day of the new period. The balance brought down (b/d) on the debit side of the Debtors (Sales) Ledger Control Account is *total* amount *owed* to the *firm* by trade debtors on the date.

Similarly with creditors the balance brought down on the credit side is the total owing to trade creditors on that date. Cash sales or cash purchases will not be entered in the control accounts – they will be dealt with directly in the cash book and individual ledger accounts.

Opening and closing balances

A control account may have both a debit and a credit opening and closing balance. For example, most debtors' accounts will be showing debit balances, but one or more may have a credit balance. Consider the case where a customer returns goods after his account has been settled or a creditor grants an additional discount after he has been paid in full. In both of these cases the control account will have both debit and credit opening and closing balances.

Contra accounts

An individual may be both a debtor and a creditor to a business, i.e. he will have an account in both the debtors and creditors ledgers. He may wish to set off one balance against another, e.g. if the balance owed by him (in the debtors ledger) is greater than the balance due to him (in the creditors ledger), he may wish to set off the amount due to him against the amount owed by him. This will be done by debiting his account in the creditors ledger and crediting that amount in the debtors ledger. These transfers must also be recorded in the two control accounts in exactly the same way as in the individual accounts.

Self-balancing ledgers

Sometimes in order to maintain complete double entry, an additional account called General Ledger Adjustment Account is kept in the debtors ledger and creditors ledger. The entries are all on the opposite side to those in the general ledger. For example:

Dr.	General Ledger Adjustment Account in sales ledger	Cr.
Cash paid by debtors Discount allowed to debtors Bad debts written off etc.		Balance due by debtors Sales to debtors Carriage charged to debtors etc.

Thus each ledger is self-balancing.

A Simple Example

From the following figures prepare a Debtors Ledger Control Account and a Creditors Ledger Control Account for December 1985:

	£
Creditors ledger balance 1.12.85 Cr.	4 800
Creditors ledger balance 1.12.85 Dr.	200
Debtors ledger balance 1.12.85 Dr.	3 800
Debtors ledger balance 1.12.85 Cr.	160
Bad debts written off	240
Debtor's cheque dishonoured	80
Payments to creditors	7 320
Credit purchases	8 460
Discounts allowed	560
Discounts received	380
Credit sales	10 580
Returns out	220
Returns in	320
Cash received from debtors	8 400
Interest charged on overdue debtors accounts	70
Bills payable	880
Debtors ledger balance transferred to creditors ledger	460
Creditors ledger balance 31.12.85 Dr.	190
Debtors ledger balance 31.12.85 Cr.	150

Solution (for Explanation see opposite)

Dr.			Debtors Ledger Control Account			Cr.
1985		£	1985			£
1 Dec.	Balance b/d	3 800	1 Dec.	Balance b/d		160
31 Dec.	Debtors' cheque dishonoured	80	31 Dec.	Bad debt written off		240
	Credit sales	10 580		Discount allowed		560
	Interest on overdue accounts	70		Returns in		332
	Balance c/d	150		Cash received from debtors		8 400
				Contra		460
				Balance c/d		4 528
		14 680				14 680
31 Dec.	Balance b/d	4 528	31 Dec.	Balance b/d		150

Note

Another good way of remembering the side on which an entry goes in the Debtors Control Account – *if the item increases the amount owed by debtors, it goes on the debit side; if it reduces the amount owed by debtors, it goes on the credit side.*

EXPLANATION

Entry		Source of entries	£	Which control account?	Which side?
Creditors ledger balance 1.12.85	Cr.	Creditors Ledger Control Account	4 800	Creditors	Credit
Creditors ledger balance 1.12.85	Dr.	Creditors Ledger Control Account	200	Creditors	Debit
Debtors ledger balance 1.12.85	Dr.	Debtors Ledger Control Account	3 800	Debtors	Debit
Debtors ledger balance 1.12.85	Cr.	Debtors Ledger Control account	160	Debtors	Credit
Bad debts written off		Journal – debit Bad Debts Account credit Customers Account	240	Debtors	Credit
Payments to creditors		Total of payments to creditors from analysed cash book	7 320	Creditors	Debit
Credit purchases		Total of purchases book	8 460	Creditors	Credit
Discounts allowed		Total of discount allowed column in cash book	560	Debtors	Credit
Discounts received		Total of discount received column in cash book	380	Creditors	Debit
Credit sales		Total of sales book	10 580	Debtors	Debit
Returns out (purchases returns)		Total of purchases returns book	220	Creditors	Debit
Returns in (sales returns)		Total of sales returns book	332	Debtors	Credit
Cash received from debtors		Total of payments by debtors from analysed cash book	8 400	Debtors	Credit
Interest charged on overdue accounts		Journal – debit customers' accounts credit Interest Account	70	Debtors	Debit
Bills payable		Total of bills payable book	880	Creditors	Debit
Debtors ledger balance transferred to creditors ledger		Journal – debit Creditors Account credit Debtors Account } for same person	460	Creditors Debtors	Debit Credit
Creditors ledger balance 31.12.85	Dr.	Put on *credit* side of creditors ledger so that it will come down on debit side when account is balanced.	£190		
Debtors ledger balance 31.12.85	Cr.	Put on *debit* side of debtors ledger so that it will come down on credit side when account is balanced.	£150		

74 Control accounts

Dr.		Creditors Ledger Control Account			Cr.
1985		£	1985		£
1 Dec.	Balance b/d	200	1 Dec.	Balance b/d	4 800
31 Dec.	Payments to creditors	7 320	31 Dec.	Credit purchases	8 460
	Discounts received	380		Balance c/d	190
	Returns out	220			
	Bills payable	880			
	Contra	460			
	Balance c/d	3 990			
		13 450			13 450
31 Dec.	Balance b/d	190	31 Dec.	Balance b/d	3 990

Students should attempt Exercises 1–7 before considering the next example.

A More Difficult Example

On 31 December 1984 the Debtors Ledger Control Account of Michael Lyons showed a debit balance of £18 740. This figure did not agree with the schedule (list) of debtor balances drawn up on the same date. An examination of the books revealed:

(a) sales book had been over-totted by £164;
(b) goods returned, valued at £260, had not been recorded in the books;
(c) bad debts written off, £90, had not been entered in the Debtors Account in the personal ledger;
(d) a contra item of £226 representing the balance due to him in the creditors ledger had been transferred to T. Barnes's account in the debtors ledger but was not shown in the control account;
(e) a personal account in the debtors ledger had been debited with sales of £172 instead of the correct figure of £136;
(f) a credit balance of £268 in the debtors ledger had not been brought down and was therefore omitted;
(g) a cheque for £124 received from a customer had been dishonoured, but this fact had not been recorded in the books;
(h) discount disallowed of £106 had only been entered in the customer's personal account – no other entry had been made in the books.

a Show the adjusted Debtors Ledger Control Account.
b Show the adjusted schedule of debtors showing the original balance.

Procedure

1. Reopen Debtors Ledger Control Account and post corrections as necessary.
2. Show list as per accounts and add and subtract items that affect list as necessary.

Solution

Dr.			Debtors Ledger Control Account			Cr.
1984		£	1984			£
31 Dec.	Balance b/d	18 740	31 Dec.	Error – sales over-totted (a)		164
	Dishonoured cheque (g)	124		Sales returns (b)		260
	Discount disallowed (h)	106		Bad debts written off (c)		90
				Contra (d)		226
				Balance c/d		18 230
		18 970				18 970
	Balance b/d	18 230				

List of balances

		£	£
Balance as per list*			18 760
Add Dishonoured cheque (g)			124
			18 884
Less Sales returns (b)		260	
Bad debts written off (c)		90	
Debtor's account overcharged (e)		36	
Credit balance omitted (f)		268	654
Balance as per control account			18 230

*Balance at 31.12.84 as per list is arrived at by working backwards from correct balance as per control account. In practice, this would not occur as both balances would be known.

Note

It is assumed that bad debts written off were omitted from Debtors Ledger Control Account.

Reasoning

Item

(a) Involves Control Account only as only total is wrong.
(b) Involves both Control Account and list.
(c) Involves both Control Account and list.
(d) Involves Control Account only.
(e) Involves list only. Error in Personal Account not in total.
(f) Involves list only – failure to complete balancing.
(g) Involves both Control Account and list.
(h) Involves Control Account only.

76 Control accounts

Exercises Set 5

1 The following details are in the books of J. Moss at 31 January 19–1:

		£
1 Jan.	Balance due by debtors	4 000
31 Jan.	Credit sales for month	16 000
	Cash received from debtors	10 000
	Sales returns	400
	Discount allowed	100

Prepare and balance Debtors Ledger Control Account in the general ledger.

2 From the following prepare and balance Ray Flood's Creditors Control Account in the general ledger at 28 February 19–2:

		£
1 Feb.	Balance due to suppliers	3 200
28 Feb.	Credit purchases	8 800
	Purchases returns	400
	Cash paid to creditors	7 000
	Discount received	200

3 From the following details prepare and balance: **a** Sales Ledger Control Account, **b** Purchases Ledger Control Account in the general ledger of J. Feely, a trader, at 31 March 19–3:

		£	
1 March	Balances: purchases ledger	16 500	Cr.
	sales ledger	19 000	Dr.
31 March	Cash received from debtors	16 000	
	Credit purchases	9 500	
	Purchases returns	500	
	Credit sales	13 400	
	Cash paid to creditors	15 000	
	Discount received	750	
	Sales returns	600	
	Bad debts written off	300	
	Debtor's cheque dishonoured	160	

4 From the following figures prepare and balance J. Clarkin's Bought Ledger Control Account and Sold Ledger Control Account at 30 April 19–4:

	£	
Sold ledger balances at 1 April	10 300	Dr.
	600	Cr.
Bought ledger balances at 1 April	300	Dr.
	8 400	Cr.
Payments to creditors	6 000	
Cash received from debtors	17 400	
Credit sales	13 000	
Credit purchases	9 600	
Discounts received	500	
Discounts allowed	400	
Returns in	800	
Returns out	1 400	
Bills receivable accepted	2 000	

	£	
Debtor's cheque dishonoured	100	
Bad debts written off	180	
Bills payable accepted	4 000	
Sold ledger balance at 30 April	420	Cr.
Bought ledger balance at 30 April	200	Dr.

5 The following details were extracted from the books of N. Palmer for the year ended 31 December 19–5:

	£	
Debtors ledger balances at 1 January 19–5	80 000	Dr.
	760	Cr.
Creditors ledger balances at 1 January 19–5	320	Dr.
	50 000	Cr.
Credit sales	171 400	
Credit purchases	101 800	
Cash paid to creditors	90 500	
Amounts received from debtors	180 514	
Allowances received from creditors	1 500	
Discount allowed to debtors	1 440	
Bills payable accepted	13 000	
Interest charged to debtors	150	
Discount disallowed by creditors	440	
Bills receivable accepted	10 000	
Bad debts written off	400	
Debtors ledger debits transferred to creditors ledger	260	
Creditors ledger balance at 31 December	480	Dr.
Debtors ledger balance at 31 December	560	Cr.

Draw up and balance the Debtors and Creditors Control Accounts at 31 December 19–5.

6 A London firm prepares Sales Ledger Control Accounts for each of three sections of the sales ledger which it has divided on a geographical basis, namely North, South and West.

From the following details prepare a Sales Ledger Adjustment Account for each of the three sections and bring down the balances as at 31 December 19–6.

		North £	South £	West £
Balances at 1 January 19–6	Dr.	15 000	21 600	8 400
	Cr.	560	350	—
Credit sales		25 800	30 550	18 764
Cash received from debtors		29 136	38 572	17 096
Returns in		4 840	3 304	1 480
Discount allowed		1 456	1 798	858
Interest charged to debtors		150	230	48
Bad debts written off		—	474	104
Credit balances at 31 December		—	450	178

It was discovered when taking out the balances that a payment made by a Tom O'Dea of North area for £100 was included in error in the South section.

Also included in cash received from debtors was an amount of £1 200 in payment of a bill of £1 380 by Michael Tobin of South area. He had set off an amount of £180 due to him by the firm against his bill when settling his account.

7   P. Devlin keeps a Debtors Ledger Control Account. On 31 December 19–7 the balance after recording the year's transactions was £11 340. However, when he totalled the list of balances taken from the debtors' personal accounts, he arrived at a figure of £10 740. On investigation he discovered that:
   (a)   the sales book had been undercast by £200;
   (b)   a customer's account having a debit balance of £560 had been omitted from the list of balances taken from the ledger accounts;
   (c)   the sales returns book had been overcast by £20;
   (d)   a debtor's cheque for £80 had been recently dishonoured, but this had not been recorded;
   (e)   an invoice for £500 sent to a customer had been entered correctly in the sales book, but had not been posted to the personal account in the ledger;
   (f)   a debtor's account for £240 had been entered twice in the list of balances extracted from the ledger accounts.

Show the adjusted Debtors Ledger Control Account and the corrected total for list of balances.

8   From the following figures in the books of T. Watson prepare a Debtors Ledger Control Account and a Creditors Ledger Control Account for December 1984.

	£
Creditors ledger balance 1.12.84 Cr.	4 800
Creditors ledger balance 1.12.84 Dr.	200
Debtors ledger balance 1.12.84 Dr.	3 800
Debtors ledger balance 1.12.84 Cr.	160
Bad debts written off	240
Debtor's cheque dishonoured	80
Payments to creditors	7 320
Credit purchases	8 460
Discounts allowed	560
Discounts received	380
Credit sales	10 580
Returns out	220
Returns in	320
Cash received from debtors	8 400
Interest charged on overdue debtors' accounts	70
Bills receivable	880
Debtors ledger balance transferred to creditors ledger	460
Creditors ledger balance 31.12.84 Dr.	190
Debtors ledger balance 31.12.84 Cr.	150

9   From the following figures in the books of James Player prepare a Debtors Ledger Control Account and a Creditors Ledger Control Account for December 1985:

	£
Creditors ledger balance 1.12.85 Dr.	160
Debtors ledger balance 1.12.85 Cr.	130
Creditors ledger balance 1.12.85 Cr.	4 200
Debtors ledger balance 1.12.85 Dr.	3 200

	£
Bills receivable	800
Returns in	420
Returns out	240
Discount received	580
Discount allowed	260
Cash received from customers	7 400
Interest charged by Player on overdue accounts	80
Credit sales	12 240
Credit purchases	9 800
Payments to creditors	8 600
Cheques received from customers dishonoured	200
Bad debts written off	120
Balance transferred from debtors ledger to creditors ledger	250
Creditors ledger balance 31.12.85 Dr.	140
Debtors ledger balance 31.12.85 Cr.	110

10 John Richards prepared a Debtors Ledger Control Account on 31.12.1985. His control account showed that he was owed £11 316 by his debtors, but this figure did not agree with the schedule (list) of debtors drawn up on the same date. An examination of his books revealed the following:
  (a) the sales day book was over-totted by £220;
  (b) P. O'Neill's personal account was under-debited by £140;
  (c) discounts allowed, £76, had been credited to the customer's account but had not been entered in the Discount Account;
  (d) goods sold on credit to P. Condon for £108 had not been entered in the books;
  (e) a credit balance of £30 in E. O'Donnell's personal account had not been brought down and had therefore been omitted from the schedule of debtors;
  (f) bad debt written off, £96, was shown in the debtor's account but not in the Bad Debts Account;
  (g) a contra item of £114 representing the balance due to him in the creditors ledger had been entered in P. O'Grady's Debtors Ledger Account but was not shown in the control account;
  (h) interest on overdue accounts, £50, was shown in the Interest Account but not in the personal accounts.

  a Show the adjusted Debtors Ledger Control Account.
  b Show the adjusted schedule of debtors showing the original balance.

11 A Creditors Ledger Control Account which was prepared by Thomas Harvey on 31.12.1980 showed that he owed £15 720 to his creditors. However, this figure did not agree with the schedule (list) of creditors' balances drawn up on the same date. An examination of the books revealed the following:
  (a) interest amounting to £36 charged by a creditor on an overdue debt had been entered in the personal account but not in the Interest Account;
  (b) a debit balance of £320 in J. Flynn's account had not been brought down in the account and therefore had not been included in the schedule of creditors' balances;
  (c) goods to the value of £190, returned to N. Hely, had not been entered in the books;
  (d) the purchases day book had been under-totted by £500;
  (e) an invoice for £1 340 received from R. Conway had been completely omitted from the books;

(f) a contra item of £324 representing the balance owed by N. Finn in the debtors ledger had been entered in Finn's account in the creditors ledger but had not been shown in the control account;
(g) discounts received, £482, had been entered in the Discount Account but had not been entered in the creditors' accounts;
(h) the personal account of T. Enfield had been over-credited, because the correct figure, £58, in the purchases book had been posted to the personal account as £184.

    a   Show the adjusted Creditors Ledger Control Account.
    b   Show the adjusted schedule of creditors showing the original balance.

*12 The following balances were extracted from the books of F. Nolan on 31 October 1985:

	£
Total debtors per sales ledger on 1 November 1984	2 476
Total of cash from debtors column of cash book	27 868
Sales per sales day book	31 142
Bills received from debtors during year, per bill book	1 500
Discount allowed	306
Returns per returns inwards book	158
Bad debts written off during year	552
Total debtors on 31 October 1985 as listed from sales ledger	3 286

You are given the following additional information:
(a) Examination of the sales ledger balances on 31 October 1985 reveals that:
   (i) the account of Mr Green had been debited with £350, representing goods sent to him on a sale or return basis. Mr Green did not intimate acceptance of the goods until November 1985, and they were included in stocks in hand on 31 October 1985;
   (ii) a balance of £412 at credit of Mr Trant represents the recovery of a bad debt written off in the previous year. This sum has been entered in the cash from debtors column of the cash book in error and posted to the sales ledger;
   (iii) Mr Larkin is a bankrupt, and the trustee of his estate is to pay a first and final dividend of $27\frac{1}{2}$p per pound. The balance due by Mr Larkin on 31 October 1985 was £240 and it was decided to write off the irrecoverable part as a bad debt.
(b) The remaining difference in the Sales Ledger Control Account is due to cash sales entered in error in the cash from debtors column of the cash book.

Prepare the following:
a journal entries (omitting narratives) for all necessary corrections
b a statement showing the adjustments which have to be made to the sales ledger balances on 31 October 1985
c the Sales Ledger Control Account for the year ended 31 October 1985.

* This question is more difficult than the others in this section and might be omitted at first reading.

13 April Showers sells goods on credit to most of its customers. In order to control its debtor collection system, the company maintains a Sales Ledger Control Account. In preparing the accounts for the year to 30 October 1983, the accountant discovers that the total of all the personal accounts in the sales ledger amounts to £12 802, whereas the Sales Ledger Control Account balance discloses a balance of £12 550.

Upon investigating the matter, the following errors were discovered:
1. sales for the week ending 27 March 1983 amounting to £850 had been omitted from the control account;
2. a debtor's account balance of £300 had not been included in the list of balances;
3. cash received of £750 had been entered in a personal account as £570;
4. discounts allowed totalling £100 had not been entered in the control account;
5. a personal account balance had been undercast by £200;
6. a contra item of £400 with the purchase ledger had not been entered in the control account;
7. a bad debt of £500 had not been entered in the control account;
8. cash received of £250 had been debited to a personal account;
9. discounts received of £50 had been debited to Bell's Sales Ledger Account;
10. returns inwards valued at £200 had not been included in the control account;
11. cash received of £80 had been credited to a personal account as £8;
12. a cheque for £300 received from a customer had been dishonoured by the bank, but no adjustment had been made in the control account.

a Prepare a corrected Sales Ledger Control Account, bringing down the amended balance as at 1 November 1983.
b Prepare a statement showing the adjustments that are necessary to the list of personal account balances so that it reconciles with the amended Sales Ledger Control Account balance.

[*Association of Accounting Technicians, December 1983*]

14 In preparing the accounts for the year to 31 October 1982, the chief accountant of Cecil Ltd had ascertained that the Purchases Ledger Control Account balance of £71 900 does not agree with the balances as extracted from the purchases ledger of £68 700. Upon investigation, the following errors were discovered:
1. a vehicle bought on credit for £5 000 had been credited to the Purchases Ledger Control Account;
2. returns outwards of £1 500 had been omitted from the Purchases Ledger Control Account;
3. a cheque for £2 000 payable to Lean had not been debited to his account in the purchases ledger;
4. discounts received of £300 had been entered twice in the Purchases Ledger Control Account;
5. a contra arrangement of £1 000 with a trade debtor had not been set off in the purchases ledger;
6. an account with a balance of £7 500 had been omitted from the purchases ledger balances;
7. purchases of £8 000 for January had not been credited to the Purchases Ledger Control Account;
8. Scott's account in the purchases ledger had been undercast by £500.

Show the adjustments necessary to:
a the schedule of balances as extracted from the purchases ledger
b the balance in the Purchases Ledger Control Account.
[*Association of Accounting Technicians, December 1982*]

15 The following information relates to Roxy Ltd for the year to 31 May 1983:

Extract from the Purchases Ledger Control Account at 31 May 1983

	£
Trade creditors as at 1 June 1982	20 000
Credit purchases	240 000
Payments made to trade creditors	232 000
Discounts received	6 000

The accountant has extracted a list of credit balances which total £23 800. There were no debit balances.

In checking these credit balances the following errors were discovered:
1. Goods costing £1 500 had been omitted from Collin's account.
2. Discounts received for January 1983 amounting to £500 had not been entered in any of the personal accounts.
3. The credit side of Brown's account had been undercast by £1 000.
4. A cash payment of £200 to Almond had been credited to his account.
5. A bank payment to Martin of £750 had been omitted from his account.
6. Ashton's balance of £2 000 had not been included in the list of balances.
7. The entry for a motor car purchased from Gill, and costing £5 000 should not have appeared in the purchases ledger.
8. Discounts allowed totalling £350 had been debited to Crosby's account.

a Prepare the Purchases Ledger Control Account for the year to 31 May 1983.
b Prepare a statement showing the necessary corrections to the list of purchase ledger balances as originally extracted at 31 May 1983.
[*Association of Accounting Technicians, June 1983*]

16 The following information for the year ended 31 March 1984 has been extracted from the accounting records of Loner Ltd:

	£
Sales Ledger Control Account as at 1 April 1983:	
Debit balance	25 684
Credit balance	748
Credit sales	194 710
Goods returned from trade debtors	1 420
Payments received from trade debtors	188 176*
Discounts allowed to trade debtors	6 710

* This figure includes cheques totalling £304 which were dishonoured before 31 March 1984, the debts in respect of which remained outstanding at 31 March 1984. The only sales ledger account with a credit balance at 31 March 1984 was that of T. Stones with a balance of £532.

After the preparation of the Sales Ledger Control Account for the year ended 31 March 1984, from the information given above, the following errors were discovered:
1. the sales day book for November 1983 had been undercast by £1 400;

2. in July 1983, a debt due of £160 from Peter Smith had been written off as bad. Whilst the correct entries have been made in Peter Smith's personal account, no reference to the debt being written off has been made in the Sales Ledger Control Account;
3. cash sales of £5 600 in September 1983 have been included in the 'Payments received from trade debtors £188 176';
4. no entries have been made in the personal accounts for goods returned from trade debtors of £1 420;
5. the debit side of L. Brown's personal account has been overcast by £140;
6. 'Credit sales £194 710' includes goods costing £5 000 returned to suppliers by Loner Ltd;
7. no entry has been made in the company's books of account for the set-off of a debt due from G. Kelly of £300 against an amount due to him of £1 200 in the purchases ledger.

a Prepare the Sales Ledger Control Account for the year ended 31 March 1984 as it would have been before the various accounting errors outlined above were discovered.
b Prepare a computation of the amount arising from the sales ledger to be shown as trade debtors in the balance sheet as at 31 March 1984 of Loner Ltd.

[*Association of Accounting Technicians, pilot, 1985*]

17 Stream Ltd maintains control accounts for its sales and purchases ledgers. Balances at 31 December 1982 were:

	Debit £	Credit £
Sales ledger	45 862	348
Purchases ledger	619	36 941

Details of transactions during 1983 were as follows:

	£
Sales	422 987
Purchases	284 142
Receipts from credit customers	394 281
Cash sales	241 652
Payments to suppliers for goods purchased on credit	276 110
Cash purchases	560
Returns inwards	3 048
Returns outwards	2 361
Bad debts written off	4 668
Debts settled by contra between ledgers	1 862
Increase in provision for bad debts	1 150

At 31 December 1983 credit balances on the sales ledger were £384 and debit balances on the purchases ledger were £450.

Prepare the Sales Ledger Control Account and Purchases Ledger Control Account for Stream Ltd for 1983.

[*Royal Society of Arts, II, June 1984*]

Control accounts

18 From the following information you are required to prepare Trade Debtors and Trade Creditors Control (or Total) Accounts for that year ended 31 December.

	£
Balance of trade debtors at 1 January	28 490
Balance of trade creditors at 1 January	45 670
Cash paid	189 460
Sales returns	2 216
Discount received	1 392
Purchases	205 126
Bad debt written off	920
Cash received	211 315
Credit sales	232 417
Discount allowed	804
Debit balance on debtors' account transferred to creditors	2 411
Purchase returns	2 381
Debtors' cheques dishonoured	903

[*Pitman Intermediate*]

19 From the following information you are required to prepare Debtors and Creditors Control Accounts for the year ended 31 December, bringing down the balances at that date.

On 1 January the sales ledger balances were £8 000 debit and £32 credit and the bought ledger balances at the same date £29 debit and £4 380 credit.

During the year to 31 December sales amounted to £23 500; purchases to £19 170; cash received from debtors £21 120; cash paid to creditors £19 776; discounts received £824; discounts allowed £880; returns inwards £425; returns outwards £310; bad debts written off £160; credit balance in the sales ledger transferred to the bought ledger £77; credit sales ledger balances at 31 December £19; debit bought ledger balances at 31 December £91.

[*Pitman Intermediate*]

Sales Ledger Control Account

20 The Sales Ledger Control Account of a trading business for the month of November 1983 was prepared by the accountant, as shown below:

Sales Ledger Control

	£		£
Opening debit balance b/d	27 684.07	Opening credit balance b/d	210.74
Credit sales	31 220.86	Allowances to customers	1 984.18
Purchase ledger contras	763.70	Cash received	1 030.62
		Cheques received	28 456.07
Discounts allowed	1 414.28	Cash received (on an account previously	
Closing credit balance c/d	171.08	written off as a bad debt)	161.20
		Closing debit balance c/d (balancing figure)	30 416.18
	61 253.99		61 258.99
Opening debit balance b/d	30 416.18	Opening credit balance b/d	171.08

The book-keeper balanced the individual customers' accounts and prepared a debtors' schedule of the closing balances which totalled £25 586.83 (net of credit balances).

Unfortunately both the accountant and the book-keeper had been careless, and in addition to the errors which the accountant had made in the Control Account above, it was subsequently discovered that:
1. in an individual debtor's account, a debt previously written off but now recovered (£161.20) had been correctly credited and re-debited but the corresponding debit had not been posted in the Control Account;
2. discounts allowed had been correctly posted to individual debtors' accounts but had been under-added by £100 in the memorandum column in the combined bank and cash book;
3. allowances to customers shown in the control account included sums totalling £341.27 which had not been posted to individual debtors' accounts;
4. a cheque for £2 567.10 received from a customer had been posted to his account as £2 576.10;
5. the credit side of one debtor's account had been over-added by £10 prior to the derivation of the closing balance;
6. a closing credit balance of £63.27 on one debtor's account had been included in the debtors' schedule among the debit balances;
7. the purchase ledger contras, representing the settlement by contra transfer of amounts owed to credit suppliers, had not been posted to individual debtors' accounts at all;
8. the balance on one debtor's account, £571.02, had been completely omitted from the debtors' schedule.

Identify and effect the adjustments to the Sales Ledger Control Account and debtors' schedule, as appropriate, so that the net balances agree at 30 December 1983.

[*Association of Certified Accountants, Level 1, June 1984*]

21 The book-keeper of Excel Stores Ltd prepared a schedule of balances of individual suppliers' accounts from the creditors ledger at 30 June 1984 and arrived at a total of £86 538.28.

He passed the schedule over to the accountant who compared this total with the closing balance on the Creditors Ledger Control Account reproduced below:

Creditors Ledger Control Account

1984		£	1984		£
30 June	Purchases returns	560.18	1 June	Balance b/d	89 271.13
	Bank	96 312.70	30 June	Purchases	100 483.49
	Balance c/d	84 688.31		Discount received	2 656.82
				Debtors ledger control (contras)	3 049.75
		192 561.19			195 261.19
			1 July	Balance b/d	84 688.31

During his investigation into the discrepancy between the two figures, the accountant discovered a number of errors in the control account and the individual ledger accounts and schedule. You may assume that the total of each item posted to the

control account is correct except to the extent that they are dealt with in the list below:
1. one supplier had been paid £10.22 out of petty cash. This had been correctly posted to his personal account but has been omitted from the control account;
2. the credit side of one supplier's personal account had been under-added by £30.00;
3. a credit balance on a supplier's account had been transposed from £548.14 to £584.41 when extracted on to the schedule;
4. the balance on one supplier's account of £674.32 had been completely omitted from the schedule;
5. discounts received of £12.56 and £8.13 had been posted to the wrong side of two individual creditors' accounts;
6. goods costing £39.60 had been returned to the supplier but this transaction had been completely omitted from the returns day book.

a Prepare a statement starting with the original closing balance on the Creditors Ledger Control Account, then identifying and correcting the errors in that account and concluding with an amended closing balance.
b Prepare a statement starting with the original total of the schedule of individual creditors, then identifying and correcting errors in that schedule and concluding with an amended total.

[*Chartered Association of Certified Accountants, Level 1, December 1984*]

22 You are required to prepare a Sales Ledger Control Account from the following for the month of October inserting the missing balance.

		£
1 October	Sales ledger – debit balances	8 850
	Sales ledger – credit balances	76
31 October	Transactions for the month:	
	Credit sales	9 120
	Cash sales	3 200
	Bad debts	296
	Discounts allowed	305
	Returns inwards	614
	Refund in respect of overpayment	65
	Cheques and cash received from credit customers	8 170
	Dishonoured cheques	49
31 October	Sales ledger – debit balances	?
	Sales ledger – credit balances	215

[*Royal Society of Arts, II, November 1986*]

*23 Mainway Dealers Ltd maintains a debtors (sales) ledger and a creditors (purchases) ledger.

The monthly accounts of the company for May 1986 are now being prepared and the following information is now available:

		£
Debtors ledger as at 1 May 1986:	Debit balances	16 720
	Credit balances	1 146

* This question is more difficult than the others in the section and might be omitted at first reading.

		£
Creditors ledger as at 1 May 1986: Debit balances		280
Credit balances		7 470
Credit sales May 1986		19 380
Credit purchases May 1986		6 700
Cash and cheques received May 1986: Debtors ledger		15 497
Creditors ledger		130
Cheques paid May 1986: Debtors ledger		470
Creditors ledger		6 320
Credit note issued May 1986 for goods returned by customers		1 198
Credit note received from suppliers May 1986 for goods returned by Mainway Dealers Ltd		240
†Cheques received and subsequently dishonoured May 1986: Debtors ledger		320
Discounts allowed May 1986		430
Discounts received May 1986		338
Bad debts written off May 1986		131
†Bad debt written off in December 1985 but recovered in May 1986 (R. Bell)		142
Debtors ledger as at 31 May 1986: Debit balances	To be determined	
Credit balances		670
Creditors ledger as at 31 May 1986: Debit balances		365
Credit balances	To be determined	

† Included in cash and cheques received May 1986 £15 497.

It has been decided to set off a debt due from a customer, L. Green, of £300 against a debt due to L. Green of £1 200 in the creditors ledger.

The company has decided to create a provision for doubtful debts of 2½ per cent of the amount due to Mainway Dealers Ltd on 31 May 1986 according to the Debtors Ledger Control Account.

a Prepare the Debtors Ledger Control Account and the Creditors Ledger Control Account for May 1986 in the books of Mainway Dealers Ltd.
b An extract of the balance sheet as at 31 May 1986 of Mainway Dealers Ltd relating to the company's trade debtors and trade creditors.
[*Association of Accounting Technicians, June 1986*]

*24 The balances at 31 October 1986 of the Sales Ledger Control Account of Timber Products Ltd according to the draft final accounts were:

	£
Debit	21 700.00
Credit	700.00

The account of T. Bean in the sales ledger was closed in September 1985 when the debit balance of £400.00 was written off as a bad debt. In August 1986, T. Bean unexpectedly received a legacy from the estate of a distant relative. T. Bean's improved circumstances enabled him to pay Timber Products Ltd a cheque for £400.00 in early September 1986; this receipt was credited to an account for T. Bean in the sales ledger.

Note. T. Bean will not be trading with Timber Products Ltd in the future.

★This question is more difficult than the others in this section and might be omitted at first reading.

The company's finance director has now decided that:
1. the following balances due to the company should be written off as bad:
   K. Milson   £250.00
   T. Longdon   £150.00
2. the provision for doubtful debts at 31 October 1986 should be 3 per cent of the amount due to the company at that date according to the sales ledger.

   Note. The balance of the Provision for Doubtful Debts Account brought forward at 1 November 1985 was £890.00.

a Prepare a computation of the corrected Sales Ledger Account balances at 31 October 1986.
b Write up the Provision for Doubtful Debts Account for the year ended 31 October 1986.

[*Association of Accounting Technicians, December 1986*]

6 *Capital and revenue expenditure and receipts*

The distinction between capital and revenue expenditure

When an individual, a group of individuals (e.g. a club) or a business pays out money for a good or a service, the benefit derived from the expenditure will vary in duration. If the benefit derived from the expenditure lasts a long time and permanently increases the earning capacity of the business, it is regarded as capital expenditure. If the benefit derived from the expenditure is of a temporary nature or only *temporarily* increases the earning capacity of the business, then this type of expenditure is regarded as revenue expenditure.

Capital expenditure is expenditure incurred in the purchase of fixed assets, or that which adds to the value of fixed assets, which permanently increases the earning capacity of the business.

Revenue expenditure is expenditure which does *not* add to the value of fixed assets or permanently increase the earning capacity of the business but represents the costs incurred in running the business during the accounting period.

The main difference between capital and revenue expenditure is one of *time*, i.e. the length of time the expenditure is of benefit to the business.

For our purposes we will regard expenditure, the benefit of which is used up during the accounting period (usually a year) as *revenue expenditure*. Expenditure, the value of which lasts longer than the accounting period and adds to the earning capacity of the business we will regard as *capital expenditure*.

The importance of the distinction between capital and revenue expenditure

The distinction is very important particularly when preparing final accounts, because mistakes in their allocation will affect both the calculation of profit and loss and the presentation of the correct value for fixed assets in the balance sheet.

Expenditure of a revenue nature is a charge against profits.

Expenditure of a capital nature is reflected in an increase in value of fixed assets in the balance sheet, e.g.

(a) If capital expenditure is treated as revenue expenditure (e.g. purchase of

fixtures debited to Profit and Loss Account), profits will be *understated* as also will the value of fixed assets in the balance sheet.
(b) If revenue expenditure is treated as capital expenditure (e.g. maintenance of machinery debited to Machinery Account), profits will be *overstated* as will the value of fixed assets in the balance sheet.

EXAMPLES OF CAPITAL AND REVENUE EXPENDITURE

Capital	*Revenue*
Purchase of premises	Cost of heating premises
Purchase of fixtures and fittings	Repairs to fixtures and fittings
Purchase of machinery	Depreciation of machinery
Cost of installing machinery	Cost of lubricating oil for machinery
Building of showroom	Cost of stock for showroom

Note

It is always necessary to know the type of business involved. Items which are revenue to one business may be capital items in another, e.g. cars and vans are normally capital items but to a garage owner they are revenue because they are bought for resale.

Capital and revenue receipts

When an organisation receives wealth the receipt can be of two kinds:

1. A *capital receipt*, for instance money or fixed assets supplied by a sole trader to start a business or a legacy received by a club has the effect of increasing the funds available to the enterprise.
2. *Revenue receipts* arise as a result of the normal day-to-day transactions, for example rent received, discount received, sales, etc.

When the revenue receipts and expenditure are compared, the difference is the profit or loss made by the enterprise.

Names given to Revenue Receipts and Expenditure Accounts

The names given to the accounts which deal with revenue expenditure and receipts vary with the type of enterprise:

Type of enterprise	*Names given to Revenue Account*	*Net result*
Traders	Trading and Profit and Loss Account	Net profit/loss
Clubs, societies, etc.	Income and Expenditure Account	Excess of income or expenditure
Manufacturers	Manufacturing, Trading and Profit and Loss Accounts	Net profit/loss

General rules for posting Revenue Accounts (matching costs and revenues)

Debit side must contain *every item* of revenue expenditure *applicable* to the enterprise during *the accounting period* and only that amount. (See Chapter 7 dealing with accruals, prepayments, etc.)

Credit side must be credited with *all revenue receipts applicable to the account period* and only that amount.

EXAMPLES

(a) **Sole trader's account**

	£
Rent paid during the year	1 000
Quarter's rent due at end of year	250
Total chargeable to Profit and Loss Account	1 250

(b) **Club accounts**

Subscriptions received during the year, £20 000, which included £1 000 due from members for last year and £1 500 paid in advance by members for next year.

The amount to be credited to Income and Expenditure Account would be arrived at thus:

	£
Subscriptions received	20 000
Less subscriptions due at beginning	1 000
	19 000
Less subscriptions prepaid	1 500
Credit to Income and Expenditure Account	17 500

Capitalisation of revenue expenditure

This simply means that some items of expenditure that are normally revenue expenditure must sometimes be treated as capital expenditure because they increase the value of a particular asset. For example, a trader buys a new machine and pays his own workers £100 to install the machine and get it fit for service. Now, wages of employees are normally a revenue expense but because the wages have been expended in installing a fixed asset they are regarded as increasing its value and are therefore charged to the Asset Account.

Revenue expenses not directly charged to the Revenue Account

This is the type of loss such as breakage or pilferage that affects stocks. For example, if £1 000 of stock is stolen during the year, this loss is *not* debited to the Profit and Loss Account but will show up in a reduced closing stock which will automatically reduce gross profit by that amount.

Exercises Set 6

1 Write a note on the distinction between capital and revenue expenditure. Give examples.

2 Mark James, a butcher, started business on 1 January 19–1. His expenses for the month of January were:
(a) wages paid to staff, £1 000; (b) paid suppliers for goods for resale, £12 000; (c) bought weighing scales for shop, £650; (d) rent of premises for month, £300; (e) postage, £30; (f) paid for repairs to window, £10; (g) purchased shop fittings on credit from W. Malon, £2 500.

State which items are revenue and which items are capital expenditure and why.

3 Tom Ford is a garage owner. The following items appear in his ledger accounts during the year:

		£
(a)	bought cars for resale	240 000
(b)	bought cars for use of salesmen	35 000
(c)	purchased new air compressor for garage	6 500
(d)	paid wages to install new compressor	290
(e)	cost of petrol used by salesmen	1 200
(f)	sales of petrol to customers	48 600
(g)	cost of annual painting of petrol pumps	250

a State which items are capital expenditure and which revenue expenditure and give reasons for your answers.
b What effect would it have on profits if the capital items above were treated as revenue?
c How would the value of fixed assets in the balance sheet be affected?

4 Jim Slye bought Jack Charleton's premises, a public house, which was valued by an independent valuer at £150 000 for £200 000. He carried out during the first month the following transactions:
(a) solititor's fees in connection with the purchase, £2 500;
(b) auctioneer's fees, £10 000;
(c) stamp duty, £6 000;
(d) to suppliers for whiskey, beer and wines, £12 000;
(e) alterations to premises to provide new lounge bar, £20 000;
(f) win in prize bonds which he lodged in Business Bank Account, £10 000;
(g) a cheque received from a customer, £35, was dishonoured by the bank and he was unable to collect from the customer;
(h) paid licence fee for bar (annual), £100;
(i) paid for repairs to beer dispenser, £40;
(j) bar takings for the month amounted to £15 760;
(k) discovered at month-end stock-taking that 5 bottles of whiskey @ £12 each were missing.

Using the headings capital expenditure, revenue expenditure, capital receipts and revenue receipts, list each of the above items under the appropriate heading, adding any comment you think necessary to justify your classification.

5 Timber Products Ltd had the following expenses for the year 19-4. Copy them out and put a tick in the appropriate columns.

Expenses	£	Type of expense		Position in final accounts		
		Capital	Revenue	Trading	P and L	Bal. sheet
(a) New lathe	52 500					
(b) Building of new workshop	60 000					
(c) Wages of sawmill workers	70 000					
(d) Wages of workers building workshop	20 000					
(e) Carriage out	2 500					
(f) Carriage in	1 000					
(g) Repairs to lorries	3 450					
(h) Typewriter for office	350					
(i) Hire of fork-lift trucks	1 800					

6 When T. Black, a coal merchant, examined his books at the end of 19-5, he found his Wages Account £62 500 greater than for 19-4, despite the fact that no additional men had been employed during 19-5 and that wages per man had remained at the 19-4 level. On investigation he discovered that during January 19-5, owing to heavy snow the men were unable to deliver coal and he had employed them erecting a new coal shed, the value of which was not shown in his books. He found out that invoices totalling £50 500 in respect of raw materials for the coal shed had been passed through purchases book and that the wages of the men for January (£12 000) had been debited in the usual way to Wages Account.

    a Show the journal entries necessary to correct the books and capitalise these expenses.
    b How would his 19-5 profits have been affected if these entries had been ignored?

7 Explain, with examples, how you would distinguish between capital and revenue expenditure. Describe the manner in which each of these types of expenditure is dealt with when preparing annual accounts.
[*Royal Society of Arts, II, March 1983*]

8 Explain how to distinguish between capital expenditure and revenue expenditure. What is the effect on capital employed and reported profit of the wrong allocation of revenue expenditure to capital expenditure?

Indicate whether each of the following items is capital or revenue expenditure:
    (a) legal expenses incurred when acquiring a new building
    (b) repairing the engine in a delivery van
    (c) building an extension to an existing factory
    (d) annual repainting of factory.
[*Royal Society of Arts, II, June 1984*]

94 Capital and revenue expenditure and receipts

9 Define the terms 'capital expenditure' and 'revenue expenditure'. Explain to which category each of the following items belongs and describe how each would be treated in the final accounts of a company:
   (a)   the purchase for resale of a car by a garage
   (b)   the purchase of a delivery van by a retail grocer
   (c)   the addition of an automatic paper feed to a printing press.

[*Royal Society of Arts, II, March 1985*]

7 Adjustments for accruals, prepayments and bad debts

Adjustment for accruals and prepayments

We have already stated that Revenue Accounts (i.e. Trading and Profit and Loss Accounts) should show exactly the losses, expenses and gains applicable to the accounting period and not a penny more or less (accruals or matching concept).

In actual practice, however, it would be a miracle if, at the date final accounts were being prepared, the books showed just the amount of revenue receipts and expenditure applicable to the period and nothing more or less. It just does not happen. No matter how well the business is run, some expense items will be due but not paid (accruals), and other items will have been paid in advance (prepayments), e.g. some rent payable, wages or electricity charges referring to the period may be due but unpaid, while such items as rates and insurance will generally have been paid in advance (i.e. covering part of the next accounting period). Similarly revenue receipts like rent or commission receivable may be in arrears or advance at the end of the accounting period.

If we are to prepare an accurate Trading and Profit and Loss Account these items must be catered for. Otherwise the profit will either be understated or overstated. It will be wrong. The balance sheet will also be wrong as assets and liabilities will not be shown as they really are. So all items that refer to the accounting period must be included in the final accounts and all items not referring to this particular accounting period must be excluded.

As a general rule, *all expense or loss or expense items due but unpaid and referring to the period* must be added to the expenses or losses already in the books. All items referring to previous or subsequent periods must be excluded. Also all revenue items referring to the period must be included.

Adjustments may have to be made for some or all of the following items:
1. amounts due by the firm but unpaid (accruals);
2. amounts paid in advance by the firm (prepayments);
3. amounts due to the firm but unpaid (accrued receipts);
4. amounts paid in advance to the firm (prepaid receipts).

Provision may also be required for:
5. bad or doubtful debts;
6. cash discounts on debtors and creditors;

96   Adjustments for accruals, prepayments and bad debts

It may also be required for depreciation of fixed assets – this is dealt with in Chapter 8.

If adjustments are to be provided properly a thorough understanding of ledger accounts is necessary. If ledger accounts are properly understood, adjustments, no matter how complicated, can be worked out logically and correctly.

Note

In the following examples we assume that the accounting period covers one year, 1 January to 31 December.

1. Amounts due by the firm but unpaid (accruals)

Let us suppose that the rent payable in respect of premises is £1 000 p.a., and is payable on 31 March, 30 June, 30 September and 31 December in arrears, and that all payments except the payment due on 31 December have been made when the final accounts are being prepared. The ledger account for rent will look like this:

Stage 1

Dr.		Rent Account		Cr.
19–1			£	
31 Mar.	Bank		250	
30 June	Bank		250	
30 Sept.	Bank		250	

Now we know that the correct amount to charge against the profits in the Profit and Loss Account is one full year's rent, i.e. £1 000. The correct way to charge the correct amount to the Profit and Loss Account is to transfer this amount (£1 000) by means of journal entry.

Journal

		Fo.	Dr.	Cr.
			£	£
31 Dec.	Profit and Loss Account		1 000	
	Rent Account			1 000
	Being rent for year transferred			

When this journal entry is posted the Rent Account will now look like this:

Stage 2

Dr.		Rent Account				Cr.
19–1			£	19–1		£
31 Mar.	Bank		250	31 Dec.	Profit and Loss	1 000
30 June	Bank		250			
30 Sept.	Bank		250			

Adjustments for accruals and prepayments 97

All that is left to do now is balance the Rent Account and bring down the balance on the credit side for next year. This shows that we still owe £250. It is a liability and like all other liabilities will appear on the liability side of the balance sheet.

When completed the Rent Account will be as below:

			Rent Account			Stage 3
Dr.						Cr.
19–1		£	19–1			£
31 Mar.	Bank	250	31 Dec.	Profit and Loss Account		1 000
30 June	Bank	250				
30 Sept.	Bank	250				
31 Dec.	Balance c/d (rent due)	250				
		1 000				1 000
			31 Dec.	Balance b/d		250

If we had been asked to make this adjustment without showing the ledger account our Profit and Loss Account would look like this:

Dr.	Profit and Loss Account for the year ended 31.12.19–1			Cr.
	£	£		
Rent paid	750			
Add Rent due	250	1 000		

This item will appear on the balance sheet among the current liabilities:

Balance sheet as at 31 December 19–1

Current liabilities	£
Rent due	250

Note

To show adjustments in final accounts more professionally, put in the correct figure on the Profit and Loss Account, indicate that it contains an adjustment by putting a reference (e.g. Note 1) in the Profit and Loss Account. Then outside of the Profit and Loss Account under the heading Note 1, show the ledger account concerned.

2. Amounts paid in advance by the firm (prepayments)

Suppose we have paid a yearly insurance premium, £160, on 30 June 19–1, to cover the year 1 July 19–1 to 30 June 19–2.

When preparing our final accounts at 31 December 19–1, it is evident that half of the amount we paid in June relates to next year and it would be wrong to charge the total amount to this year's Profit and Loss Account.

So again we charge the correct amount, £80, to the Profit and Loss Account through the journal:

Journal

	Dr. £	Cr. £
Profit and Loss Account	80	
Insurance Account		80
Being insurance premiums for year transferred		

and balance the account, bringing down the balance on the debit side.

Dr.			**Insurance Account**			Cr.
19–1		£	19–1			£
30 June	Bank	160.00	31 Dec.	Profit and Loss Account		80.00
				Balance c/d (prepaid)		80.00
		160.00				160.00
31 Dec.	Balance c/d	80.00				

The balance b/d is a temporary asset (the insurance company owes us cover up to this amount) and must appear as a current asset in the balance sheet.

Note

Some firms add prepayments to the figure for debtors and show one figure for debtors and prepayments.

3. Amounts due to the firm but unpaid (accrued receipts)

A firm has sublet part of its premises at a rent of £1 200 p.a. payable on the first day of each quarter in arrears. The firm has received only three payments by 31 December 19–1. The Rent Receivable Account will be like this:

Cr.		**Rent Receivable Account**				Dr.
19–1		£	19–1			£
31 Dec.	Profit and Loss Account	1 200	31 Mar.	Bank		300
			30 June	Bank		300
			30 Sept.	Bank		300
			31 Dec.	Balance c/d		300
		1 200				1 200
31 Dec.	Balance b/d	300				

Here again we transfer the correct amount to the Profit and Loss Account (credit side this time) by journal entry on 31 December.

Journal

	Dr. £	Cr. £
31 Dec. Rent Receivable Account	1 200	
Profit and Loss Account		1 200
Being transfer of rent receivable for year		

We balance the account and bring down the balance on the debit side and show this amount as an asset in the balance sheet.

4. Amounts paid in advance to the firm (prepaid receipts)

Suppose that in the above example the September payment had been £900 instead of £300. At 31 December 19–1 we would have received £300 in respect of 19–2.

Dr.		**Rent Receivable Account**			Cr.
19–1		£	19–1		£
31 Dec.	Profit and Loss Account	1 200	31 Mar.	Bank	300
	Balance c/d	300	30 June	Bank	300
	(advance payment)		30 Sept.	Bank	900
		1 500			1 500
			31 Dec.	Balance b/d	300

The balance brought down in this case is on the credit side showing that it is a liability of the firm (it owes the tenant this amount) and it must appear as a current liability in the balance sheet.

Exercises Set 7A

1 The following table gives some information relating to the accounts named in the table at 31 December 19–1, the date on which final accounts are prepared.

Complete the table and show the ledger accounts.

Account	Amount due on 1 Jan.	Total paid during year	Amount due on 31 Dec.	Charge to P and L Account
	£	£	£	£
(a) Rent (payable)	—	800	200	?
(b) Electricity	370	2 000	?	3 040
(c) Fees	—	?	350	1 850
(d) Salaries	2 750	104 000	3 000	?
(e) Interest (payable)	?	450	90	480

100 Adjustments for accruals, prepayments and bad debts

2 From the following information prepare the Telephone Account in the books of Peter Brown, a trader, transferring the correct amount to his Profit and Loss Account at 31 December 19–2.

19–2	£
1 Jan. Balance due	145.00
Payments	
15 Jan.	145.00
24 Apr.	163.00
18 July	147.50
14 Oct.	182.00

The telephone bill for the quarter ended 31 December 19–2 was £192.50, but was not paid until 8 January 19–3.

3 On 1 January 19–3 A. Tenant owed two months' rent, £300, in respect of premises occupied by him. During 19–3 he paid by cheque £300 on each of the following dates: 9 January, 3 March, 6 May, 15 July, 10 September, 16 November.

Prepare Tenant's account as it would appear in his ledger after his Profit and Loss Account for the year ended 31 December 19–3 had been prepared.

What entry would appear on his balance sheet at that date?

4 On 1 January 19–4 the Rates Account of B. Wise showed a prepayment of £225. His payments for the year were:

13 Apr. (half-year to 30 September 19–4)	£480
16 Oct. (half-year to 30 March 19–5)	£480

Show Wise's Rates Account after the preparation of the Profit and Loss Account at 31 December 19–4.

5 Mark McCormick pays his fire insurance once yearly on 1 May. On 1 January 19–7 his Fire Insurance Account showed a prepayment of £120. During 19–7 and 19–8 he made the following cheque payments:

1 May 19–7	£540
1 May 19–8	£600

Show the Fire Insurance Account for the two years ended 31.12.19–7 and 31.12.19–8.

6 K. Lawlor pays his car tax twice yearly on 1 April and on 1 October.

On 1 January 1984 his Car Tax Account showed a prepayment of £144. During 1984 and 1985 he made the following payments by cheque:

1 April 1984	£336
1 October 1984	£336
1 April 1985	£420
1 October 1985	£420

You are required to show the Car Tax Account for the two years ended 31.12.1984 and 31.12.1985.

7 The following payments were made in respect of insurance by A. Broker, a trader, during the year 19–5. All are annual premiums.

		£
31 Mar.	Fire insurance	180
30 June	Motor vehicle	2 000
30 Sept.	Public liability	120
1 Dec.	Cash in transit	720

a Show his Insurance Account after the preparation of his Profit and Loss Account on 31 December 19–5.

b Show proof that your charge to Profit and Loss Account is correct.

8 British Products Ltd keeps a combined Rent and Rates Account. The firm prepares its final accounts on 30 June each year. The account on 1 July 19–6 was as shown below.

Dr.			**Rent and Rates Account**			Cr.
19–6		Rent	Rates	19–6	Rent	Rates
1 July	Rates prepaid to 30 September		£320	1 July Rent due to 30 June	£800	

Copy the above opening balances and complete and balance the account on 30 June 19–7 after final accounts have been prepared.

(a) Quarter's rent due on 30 June was paid on 4 July.
(b) Rent due on 30 September was paid on 1 October.
(c) Rates for the half year from 1 October, £640, were paid on 10 October.
(d) Rent due on 31 December was paid on that date.
(e) Rent due on 31 March 19–7 was paid on 5 April 19–7.
(f) Rates for the half-year 1 April to 1 October, £720, were paid on 15 April.
(g) Six months' rent was paid on 25 June 19–7.

9 In the books of T. Spain, a grocer, there is a combined Rent and Insurance Account. After the final accounts for year ended 31 October 1976 had been prepared, the following balances remained on the account:
(a) insurance prepaid to 30 June 1977   £80
(b) rent accrued due from 1 October 1976   £20

During the following three years, payments were made as follows:

			£
1977	1 January	Rent	60
	1 April	Rent	60
	1 July	Insurance Y/E 30.6.78	120
	1 July	Rent	60
	1 October	Rent	60
	1 December	Rent	60
1978	1 March	Rent	60
	1 July	Insurance Y/E 30.6.79	180
	1 August	Rent	90
	1 October	Rent	90
		Additional insurance premium Y/E 30.6.79	60
	1 November	Rent	90

Adjustments for accruals, prepayments and bad debts

				£
1979	1 January	Rent		90
	1 April	Rent		90
	1 July	Rent		90
	1 September	Insurance Y/E 30.6.80		240
	1 October	Rent		90

The rent was increased to £360 per annum with effect from 1 April 1978. You are required to write up the Rent and Insurance Account for each of the three years ended 31 October 1979 as it would appear in the nominal ledger of T. Spain.

10 B. Brief, a trader, rents three lock-up garages to D, E and F.

At 31 December 1977 D had paid rent, £25, for the two months ended 28 February 1978 in advance; E owed rent, £30, for the three months ended 31 December 1977 and F owed rent, £15, for the month of December 1977.

During the year ended 31 December 1978 the following amounts were received by B. Brief in respect of rent:
(a) £100 for 8 months to 31 October from D
(b) £160 for 16 months to January 1979 from E
(c) £180 for 12 months to 30 November 1978 from F.

You are required to show the Rent Receivable Account as it would appear in the books of B. Brief for the year ended 31 December 1978, showing the transfer to Profit and Loss Account at the end of the year and the balance brought down on 1 January 1979, indicating clearly the individual amounts due or paid in advance, by D, E and F.

11 Traders Ltd lease their premises at an annual rent of £8 000, payable quarterly in advance on 1 February, 1 May, 1 August and 1 November.

On 1 December 1979 part of the premises were sublet to Black Ltd at an annual rent of £1 200, payable quarterly in arrears on 28 February, 31 May, 31 August and 30 November.

The following transactions took place during the year 1980:
(a) 2 February, paid rent for quarter year to 30.4.1980.
(b) 3 March, received rent for quarter year to 28.2.1980.
(c) 5 May, paid rent for quarter to 31.7.1980.
(d) 4 June, received rent for quarter to 31.5.1980.
(e) 2 August, paid rent for quarter to 31.10.1980.
(f) 1 September, received rent for quarter to 31.8.1980.
(g) 1 November, paid rent for quarter to 31.1.1981.
(h) 30 November, received rent for quarter to 30.11.1980.

You are required to write up the combined Rent Receivable and Payable Account in the company's ledger for the year 1980.

12 1. The Spinola Restaurant commenced business on 1 June Year 4. Its financial year ends on 31 March, though the first trading period was shorter. The management pays fire insurance annually in advance on 1 June each year, as follows:

	£
1 June Year 4	600
1 June Year 5	660
1 June Year 6	720

a Show the Fire Insurance Account in Spinola Restaurant's books for the years ending 31 March Year 6 and 31 March Year 7.

b Show the relevant extract from Spinola Restaurant's balance sheet as at 31 March Year 6 and as at 31 March Year 7.

2. The Rent and Rates Account in the ledger of F. Stannerton, a sole trader, showed that on 31 December Year 5 the rent for the three months to 31 December was outstanding and that the rates for the half-year ended 31 March Year 6, amounting to £256, had been paid. During the year to 31 December Year 6, the following payments relating to rent and rates were made by cheque:

Year 6		Rent £	Rates £
12 Jan.	3 months ended 31.12. Year 5	420	
21 Mar.	3 months ended 31.3. Year 6	420	
27 May	6 months ended 30.9. Year 6		284
12 July	3 months ended 30.6. Year 6	420	
23 Sept.	3 months ended 30.9. Year 6	480	
21 Dec.	3 months ended 31.12. Year 6	480	
Year 7			
18 Jan.	6 months ended 31.3. Year 7		284

a Prepare the Rent and Rates Account as it would appear after the books have been balanced on 31 December Year 6.
b Show how the balance sheet would appear in respect of rent and rates as at 31 December Year 5.
[*London Chamber of Commerce and Industry, Intermediate, March 1987*]

Adjustments for bad debts

5. Bad or doubtful debts

a. *The nature of bad debts.* Bad debts are debts which are irrecoverable, i.e. the customer who owes money is unwilling or unable to pay the amount owed by him. Unless this amount is written off as soon as the firm becomes certain of the non-payment, this account will continue to be treated as good. The value of debtors in the balance sheet should show only those debtors who are expected to pay amounts owed by them.

Immediately the firm becomes aware that a particular debt is bad, the customer's account must be closed. This is done by journal entry. Suppose the amount is £500 on 31 December 19–1 owed by H. Jackson.

Journal

	Dr. £	Cr. £
Bad Debts Account	500	
H. Jackson		500
Being bad debt written off		

At the end of the accounting period, Bad Debts Account is closed to the Profit and Loss Account.
    Debit Profit and Loss Account.
    Credit Bad Debts Account.

H. Jackson

Dr.						Cr.
19–1		£	19–1			£
31 Dec.	Balance b/d	500	31 Dec.	Bad Debts Account		500

Bad Debts Account

Dr.						Cr.
19–1		£	19–1			£
31 Dec.	H. Jackson	500	31 Dec.	Profit and Loss Account		500

Profit and Loss Account (extract)

	£
Bad debts	500

Bad debts in the next accounting period can be transferred from individual customers' accounts to the Bad Debts Account and from there the total bad debts for the year are transferred to the Profit and Loss Account as in the example given above.

Another method of treating bad debts is shown below where bad debts are transferred from the customers' accounts to a Provision for Bad Debts Account and from there to the Profit and Loss Account.

Both methods are equally acceptable from the point of view of examinations.

b. *Provision for bad and doubtful debts.* The trader knows from bitter experience that some of his debtors will not pay him but, unfortunately, he normally does not know who these individuals will be. He will go on his experience in former years. He will have learned what percentage of his total debtors did not pay and if he is prudent he will create a provision for bad and doubtful debts equal to this amount. He will open a Provision for Bad and Doubtful Debts Account and set aside a provision (say 5 per cent) of total debtors out of his profits. This is done by:

    debiting Profit and Loss Account.
    crediting Provision for Bad Debts Account.

This amount will be there to cover possible bad debts in the next accounting period.

Note

As provision for bad debts is a credit balance, you would expect to find it on the liability side of the balance sheet. Instead it is shown as a deduction from debtors on the asset side, thereby giving a clearer picture of the debtors' position.

c. *How to treat bad debts where a provision exists.* Where a provision for bad debts exists, bad debts in the next accounting period can be written off the Provision Account by closing the Bad Debts Account to the Provision for Bad Debts Account, and any charges for a new provision will be made against the Profit and Loss Account. (Remember, the figure for debtors will change from year to year.) An example will clarify the matter.

EXAMPLE

At 31 December 19–1 X, a trader whose debtors totalled £25 000, decided to make a 5 per cent provision for bad debts for 19–2. During 19–2 bad debts amounted to £800. His debtors at 31 December 19–2 were £30 000, and he wished to retain a 5 per cent provision.

Show the accounts.

SOLUTION

Dr.		**Bad Debts Account**				Cr.
19–2			£	19–2		£
	Sundry customers		800	31 Dec.	Provision for Bad Debts Account	800
			800			800

Dr.		**Provision for Bad Debts Account**				Cr.
19–2			£	19–2		£
31 Dec.	Bad Debts Account		800	1 Jan.	Balance c/d	1 250
31 Dec.	Balance c/d		1 500	31 Dec.	P and L Account	1 050
			2 300			2 300
				31 Dec.	Balance b/d	1 500

Dr.		**Profit and Loss Account**		Cr.
19–2			£	
	Provision for Bad Debts Account		1050	

Adjustments for accruals, prepayments and bad debts

Balance sheet (extract)

	£	£
Trade debtors	30 000	
Less Provision for bad debts	1 500	
		28 500

EXPLANATION IN WORDS

X had a provision of £1 250 at 1 January 19–2. He used up £800 of it on actual bad debts. This left him a balance of £450. He needed £1 500 to carry forward to 19–2. Therefore he charged the difference (£1 500−450), £1 050, to Profit and Loss Account at 31.12.19–2.

An alternative method is to use *only* the Bad Debts Provision Account and to use it for both bad debts written off and bad debts provision. Using this method the solution would read:

Bad Debts Provision Account

19–2		£	19–2		£
31 Dec.	Sundry debtors	800	1 Jan.	Balance b/d	1 250
31 Dec.	Balance c/d		31 Dec.	Profit and Loss Account	1 050
	(5% of 30 000)	1 500			
		2 300			2 300
			31 Dec.	Balance b/d	1 500

e. Reducing the provision. Suppose that in the previous example none of the debts proved bad during 19–2 and X decided to reduce the provision to 3 per cent of £30 000 for 19–3. He would reduce the provision by journal entry.

Journal	Dr.	Cr.
	£	£
Bad Debts Provision Account	350	
Profit and Loss Account		350

This would leave a balance on the Provision Account of £900 (3 per cent of £30 000).

f. Bad debts recovered. It sometimes happens that a debtor whose debt has been written off as bad subsequently pays the amount. A problem now arises. His account has been closed by the writing off of the original debt as bad, so it would be incorrect to debit bank and credit customer's account and leave it at that. If that were done the customer's account would be showing a credit balance.

There are two ways of treating bad debts recovered when the money is received from the customer:

Method I
Entries:
    Debit bank or cash
    Credit Bad Debts Provision Account } with amount received

thus by-passing the customer's account
or
Method II
Entries:
(i) Debit customer's account
   Credit Bad Debts Provision
       Account or Bad Debts
       Recovered Account
} with the amount of the debt previously written off

then
(ii) Debit bank or cash
    Credit customer's account
} with money received.

The second method has the advantage that it shows that, even though the debt was written off originally, it was subsequently paid. This may be a very important factor in deciding whether or not to give the customer further credit.

6. Cash discounts on debtors and creditors

Some firms make a provision for cash discounts they allow to debtors who pay their bills promptly. If debtors are going to pay promptly, then in order to show debtors at their true value on the balance sheet, discounts allowable to debtors should be subtracted. The amount of the provision is normally arrived at in the same manner as provision for bad debts but discount will be provided for 'good' debtors only. This means in effect that the provision for bad debts must be deducted from debtors before provision for discount can be calculated, for example:

	£
Debtors	5 000
Provision for bad debts (5%)	250
	4 750
Provision for discount, e.g.	
$2\frac{1}{2}$% of £4 750	118.75

The journal entry is simple:

Journal

	Fo.	Dr. £	Cr. £
Profit and Loss Account		118.75	
Provision for discount on debtor's account			118.75

Being provision of $2\frac{1}{2}$ per cent of net debtors to cover discounts.

108 Adjustments for accruals, prepayments and bad debts

The balance sheet will look like this:

	£	£
Debtors	5 000.00	
Less Provision for bad debts	250.00	
	4 750.00	
Less Provision for discount on debtors	118.75	
		4 631.25

Discounts on creditors. Some firms also provide for discount on creditors (i.e. discount the firm will receive when it pays its creditors). This is generally regarded as bad accounting practice as accountants hold that gains should never be anticipated (the concept of conservatism).

However, if required for examination purposes, discounts on creditors will be shown on the credit side of the Profit and Loss Account and deducted from creditors on the balance sheet. The journal entry is:

Debit provision for discount on creditor's account.
Credit Profit and Loss Account.

Exercises Set 7B

1. At 31 December 19–1 a firm's debtors totalled £50 000 and its provision for bad debts stood at £2 000. During 19–2 debts amounting to £600 were written off as bad. At 31 December 19–2 debtors stood at £60 000 and it was decided to carry forward a provision of 5 per cent for 19–3.

   Show:
   a the Bad Debts Account
   b the Bad Debts Provision Account
   c the relevant sections of Profit and Loss Account and balance sheet.

2. The Bad Debts Provision Account of J. Stain, a trader, showed a balance of £1 800 on 1 January 19–2. During the year bad debts amounted to £1 200. The debtors at 31 December 19–2 were £40 000 and Stain decided to make a new provision of 5 per cent.

   Show journal and ledger, Profit and Loss and balance sheet entries.

3. On 1 January 19–3 the balance on the Provision for Bad Debts Account in the books of A. Strange stood at £1 000. Bad debts during the year amounted to £1 620. The debtors at 31 December 19–3 were £38 000 and a new provision of 5 per cent is required.

   Show the necessary journal, ledger, Profit and Loss and balance sheet entries.

4 On 1 January 19–4 M. Mullen's provision for bad debts was £5 000. During the year actual bad debts written off amounted to £590. The debtors at 31 December 19–4 amounted to £54 000. The trader carried forward to 19–5 a 5 per cent provision for bad and doubtful debts.

Make the necessary journal and ledger entries and show also the Profit and Loss Account and balance sheet.

5 On 1 July 19–7 the provision for bad and doubtful debts in the books of A. Roche amounted to £3 500.

During the year ended 30 June 19–8 the following transactions occurred:
(a) On 1 September 19–7 the following debts were written off as irrecoverable:

	£	£
A. Black	120	
C. Donovan	280	
E. Forbes	460	
M. Hill	1 010	
		1 870

(b) A first and final dividend of 15p in the pound was received from P. Morris, whose debt of £2 000 had been written off as irrecoverable some years ago. On 30 June 19–8 the total risk for bad and doubtful debts is estimated as follows:
  (i) B. Smart has disappeared without trace leaving a balance due to the firm of £600.
  (ii) M. Moore is expected to pay a dividend of 40p in the pound on £1 000.
  (iii) It is considered that a provision equal to 5 per cent of the remaining sundry debtors on 30 June 19–8, £62 000, be made to cover all other contingencies.

You are required to show the Bad and Doubtful Debts Account for the year ended 30 June 19–8.

6 On 1 January 19–8 R. Smith had a balance of £4 000 on his Provision for Bad Debts Account. On 1 July 19–8 a debtor, J. Sweeney, who owed him £3 000 since 19–6, was declared bankrupt and paid 40p in the pound. On 31 December 19–8 Smith was owed £86 400 by his debtors. He decided to write off as a bad debt £400 owed by a debtor, P. Hickson, and to maintain a provision for bad debts at 5 per cent of the remaining debtors.

Show:
a J. Sweeney's account
b Provision for Bad Debts Account
c Bad Debts Account.

7 M. Carr had a balance of £6 200 on his Provision for Bad Debts Account on 1 January 19–2. On 1 October 19–2 A. Truck, a debtor, who owed him £4 400 since 19–0, was declared bankrupt and paid a first and final dividend of 25p in the pound. The balance on this account was written off as a bad debt. On 31 December 19–2 Carr was owed £141 000 by his debtors. He decided to write off as a bad debt £1 000 owed by a debtor, T. Owens, and to make a provision for 19–3 at 5 per cent of the remaining debtors.

110   Adjustments for accruals, prepayments and bad debts

You are required to show the following accounts in M. Carr's books:
a   A. Truck's account
b   Bad Debts Account
c   Provision for Bad Debts Account.

8   J. Royal commenced business on 1 April 1981. The following information relates to the first three years that he is in business:

Year to 31 March	1982 £	1983 £	1984 £
Sales (all credit)	458 400	567 600	537 200
Cash received	355 300	512 700	481 200
Discounts allowed	45 800	47 300	48 600
Specific bad debts at 31 March (to be written off)	2 200	4 900	2 500
	%	%	%
Provision to be made for bad debts	5	10	$7\frac{1}{2}$
Provision to be made for discounts on trade debtors	10	$12\frac{1}{2}$	15

Write-up the following accounts for each of the three years to 31 March 1982, 1983 and 1984 respectively:
a   Trade Debtors
b   Bad Debts
c   Bad Debts Provision
d   Discounts Allowed Provision.

[*Association of Accounting Technicians, June 1984*]

9   Docks Ltd, a window replacement company, offers fairly generous credit terms to its high-risk customers. Provision is made for bad debts at a varying percentage based on the level of outstanding trade debtors, and an assessment of general economic circumstances, resulting in the following data for the last three accounting periods:

Year to 31 March	1980 £	1981 £	1982 £
Trade debtors at the year end (before allowing for any bad debts)	186 680	141 200	206 200
Estimated bad debts (companies in liquidation)	1 680	1 200	6 200
Provision for bad debts	10%	12.5%	15%

The provision for bad debts at 1 April 1979 amounted to £13 000.

a   Prepare the Provision for Bad Debts Account for each of the three years to 31 March 1980, 1981 and 1982 respectively, showing how the balances would appear on the balance sheets as at these dates.
b   Assuming that a debt of £1 000 written off as bad in 1980 was subsequently recovered in cash in 1981, state briefly how this would have affected the profit for the year to 31 March 1980, and also how it would be treated in the accounts for the year to 31 March 1981.

[*Association of Accounting Technicians, June 1982*]

10 a Define provisions and reserves and give an example of each.
   b Describe how provisions and reserves are accounted for in the Profit and Loss Account and reported in the balance sheet.

   [Royal Society of Arts, II, June 1986]

8 Depreciation of fixed assets

Fixed assets, as we have seen, are assets that are used over a long period of time in the business, and are not primarily for resale or conversion into cash. All fixed assets (except perhaps land), no matter how well constructed or maintained, wear out gradually over the years until eventually they are only of scrap value. This wearing out process we call *depreciation*.

Depreciation has been defined as 'the reduction in value of an asset as a result of fair wear and tear or the passage of time'. It is obvious that fixed assets will have to be replaced sooner or later. What is not so obvious to students, perhaps, is that this loss in value is a cost to the business and should be charged against the profits of the business. If depreciation is not charged, the profits will be overstated and the 'true' value of the assets will not be shown on the balance sheet. A simple example may help to clarify the matter. If I buy a motor car for £10 000 and five years later that same car is worth £2 000 then the cost to me of the use of the car for the five years is £8 000. Of course the only time I can calculate the depreciation accurately is when I dispose of the car.

Causes of depreciation

1. Wear and tear or loss of value through use.
2. Passage of time. Generally speaking, as assets get older they get less valuable.
3. Obsolescence or becoming out of date as a result of new inventions.
4. Inadequacy, which means that the asset for some reason is no longer adequate for the purposes for which it was originally bought.

How is depreciation assessed or estimated?

As already mentioned, depreciation cannot be accurately calculated until the asset is disposed of. However, an estimate of depreciation must be made each year so that it can be charged against the profits of the year or accounting period. To calculate the charge to be made against the profits, three factors are involved:

1. the original cost of the asset which is known;
2. the estimated life of the asset;
3. the estimated residual, scrap or break-up value.

Treatment of depreciation in the accounts

There are two fundamental methods of treating depreciation: treat depreciation in the Asset Account or leave the Asset Account alone and treat depreciation in a special Provision for Depreciation Account.

Method I using the Asset Account – by journal entry
Entries:
 (a) Debit Depreciation Account } with amount written
     Credit Asset Account   off each year
 (b) Debit Profit and Loss Account } with total written
     Credit Depreciation Account   off all assets

Method II
Entries:
 (a) (i) Leave the Asset Account showing the original cost
     (ii) Open Provision for Depreciation Account for each asset
 (b) Debit Profit and Loss Account   } with amount provided
     Credit Provision for Depreciation   for the year
       Account for each asset

Note

When depreciation is charged to the Manufacturing Account, the Manufacturing Account is debited instead of the Profit and Loss Account.

Because of the requirements of the Companies Acts the second method is becoming more widespread.

Depreciation of assets bought and sold

When assets are bought or sold during an accounting period, depreciation on the assets bought or sold can be calculated in two ways:
1. *By ignoring the dates of purchase or sale.* This means that assets bought at any time during the accounting period will have a full year's provision for depreciation and assets sold will have no provision made for them for that period.

EXAMPLE
Accounting period 1 January to 31 December:
Assets bought on 1 October – full year's depreciation.
Assets sold on 28 December – no depreciation.

2. *Proportional depreciation.* Here assets bought, say, on 1 April will be written down at 31 December by three-quarters of the annual rate. Assets sold will be treated similarly.

Notes

1. When precise dates are given assume, unless otherwise stated, that depreciation is to be calculated on a monthly basis, i.e. a month's depreciation for a month's ownership.
2. Always show depreciation to the nearest pound; it is only an estimate and should not be given an implied accuracy by using pence.

Methods of calculating depreciation

There are many methods of calculating depreciation. The ones we will deal with are:
1. The straight-line or fixed or equal instalment method.
2. The diminishing balance method.
3. The revaluation method.

1. Straight-line or equal instalment method

In this method a fixed amount is set aside each year out of the profits over the estimated useful life of the asset. At the end of this period the value will be reduced to nil or scrap value.

EXAMPLE
A machine which costs £5 000 is estimated to have a useful life of four years and to have a scrap value of £1 000 at the end of this period.

Calculation of annual charge:

$$\text{Annual charge} = \frac{\text{Original cost less scrap value}}{\text{Estimated lifetime in years}} = \frac{£5\ 000 - £1\ 000}{4} = £1\ 000$$

Journal

Method I If depreciation is charged to Asset Account:
Entries:
- (a) Debit Depreciation Account } £1 000 each year
  Credit Machinery Account
- (b) Debit Profit and Loss Account } £1 000 each year
  Credit Depreciation Account

Method II If Provision for Depreciation Account is used:
Entries:
- (a) Debit Profit and Loss Account
- (b) Credit Provision for Depreciation } £1 000 each year
  on Machinery Account

Methods of calculating depreciation

Method I

Ledger accounts

Dr.   **Machinery Account**   Cr.

		£			£
Year 1	Bank	5 000	Year 1	Depreciation Account	1 000
				Balance c/d	4 000
		5 000			5 000
Year 2	Balance b/d	4 000	Year 2	Depreciation Account	1 000
				Balance c/d	3 000
		4 000			4 000
Year 3	Balance b/d	3 000	Year 3	Depreciation Account	1 000
				Balance c/d	2 000
		3 000			3 000
Year 4	Balance b/d	2 000	Year 4	Depreciation Account	1 000
				Balance c/d	1 000
		2 000			2 000
Year 5	Balance b/d	1 000			

Dr.   **Depreciation Account**   Cr.

		£			£
Year 1	Machinery Account	1 000	Year 1	Profit and Loss Account	1 000
Year 2	Machinery Account	1 000	Year 2	Profit and Loss Account	1 000
Year 3	Machinery Account	1 000	Year 3	Profit and Loss Account	1 000
Year 4	Machinery Account	1 000	Year 4	Profit and Loss Account	1 000

Dr.   **Profit and Loss Account**   Cr.

		£
Year 1	Depreciation: machinery	1 000
Year 2	Depreciation: machinery	1 000
Year 3	Depreciation: machinery	1 000
Year 4	Depreciation: machinery	1 000

Balance sheet (extracts)
as at 31 December Year 1

		£	£
Fixed assets			
Machinery		5 000	
Less Depreciation		1 000	
			4 000

as at 31 December Year 4

		£	£
Fixed assets			
Machinery		2 000	
Less Depreciation		1 000	
			1 000

Method II
Ledger accounts

Dr.   **Machinery Account**   **Cr.**

		£
Year 1	Bank	5 000

Dr.   **Provision for Depreciation on Machinery Account**   **Cr.**

		£			£
Year 1	Balance c/d	1 000	Year 1	Profit and Loss Account	1 000
		1 000			1 000
Year 2	Balance c/d	2 000	Year 2	Balance b/d	1 000
				Profit and Loss Account	1 000
		2 000			2 000
Year 3	Balance c/d	3 000	Year 3	Balance b/d	2 000
				Profit and Loss Account	1 000
		3 000			3 000
Year 4	Balance c/d	4 000	Year 4	Balance b/d	3 000
				Profit and Loss Account	1 000
		4 000			4 000
				Balance b/d	4 000

Dr.   **Profit and Loss Account**   **Cr.**

		£
Year 1	Provision for depreciation machinery	1 000
Year 2	Provision for depreciation machinery	1 000
Year 3	Provision for depreciation machinery	1 000
Year 4	Provision for depreciation machinery	1 000

Balance sheet (extracts)
as at 31 December Year 1

	Cost	Depreciation to date	Net
	£	£	£
Fixed assets			
Machinery	5 000	1 000	4 000

as at 31 December Year 4

	Cost	Depreciation to date	Net
	£	£	£
Fixed assets			
Machinery	5 000	4 000	1 000

It is obvious that the second method gives more information as regards the age of the assets and the depreciation policy in operation. It is recommended that students use the second method once they understand that the amount of depreciation charged will be exactly the same.

SSAP 12 adds weight to the desirability of using this method.

2. The diminishing balance method

Under this method the asset is depreciated by a fixed percentage every year on the diminishing balance of the Asset Account. For the mathematically-minded student the rate of depreciation is calculated by either of the following formulae:

$$R = P \times \left(\frac{100 - R}{100}\right)^n \quad \text{or} \quad R = 1 - \sqrt[n]{\frac{S}{C}}$$

R = rate of depreciation.
P = original cost.
n = number of years.

R = rate of depreciation.
n = number of years.
C = original cost.
S = residual value.

EXAMPLE
A firm's depreciation policy is to write 25 per cent p.a. off the diminishing balance of the asset. Show the Motor Van Account for three years on a motor van which cost £8 000.

SOLUTION

Dr. **Motor Van Account** Cr.

		£			£
Year 1	Bank (cost)	8 000	Year 1	Depreciation (25% of £8 000)	2 000
				Balance c/d	6 000
		8 000			8 000
Year 2	Balance b/d	6 000	Year 2	Depreciation (25% of £6 000)	1 500
				Balance c/d	4 500
		6 000			6 000
Year 3	Balance b/d	4 500	Year 3	Depreciation (25% of £4 500)	1 125
				Balance c/d	3 375
		4 500			4 500
Year 4	Balance b/d	3 375			

Advantages and disadvantages of straight-line and diminishing balance methods of depreciation

(a) Straight-line method

Advantages
1. It is straightforward and easily understood.
2. At the end of the predicted useful life the asset appears in the books at exactly the scrap or residual value.

Disadvantages
1. The charge against profit is low when the asset is new and higher as the asset gets older (due to fixed depreciation) plus an increasing charge for maintenance and repairs.
2. When new assets are bought or old assets sold the depreciation must be recalculated.

(b) Diminishing balance method

Advantages
1. It is straightforward.
2. The charge against the profit is more evenly spread – high when the asset is new and low when repairs and maintenance charges increase.
3. It is not affected by purchase or sale of assets.

Disadvantages
1. The asset is never completely written off.
2. Where the asset has a very short life the rate of depreciation is ridiculously high.

Sale or disposal of assets

When assets are sold there will usually be a profit or loss on sale. To determine the amount of the profit or loss we need to know (a) the original cost, (b) depreciation to date, (c) amount received for the asset.

Procedure

Open Disposal of Asset Account.

Entries:
1. Debit Disposal of Asset Account
   Credit Asset Account } with original cost price
2. Debit Provision for Depreciation on Asset Account
   Credit Disposal of Asset Account } with aggregate depreciation to date
3. Debit bank
   Credit Disposal of Asset Account } with money received on sale of the asset.

The difference will be either a profit or a loss on sale.

If a loss (small):
Entries:
   Debit Profit and Loss Account
   Credit Disposal of Asset Account.

If a profit: Reverse the above entry.

Methods of calculating depreciation 119

Note
If loss is a significant amount this should be debited to a special Loss on Sale of Assets Account.

EXAMPLE
1 January, Year 1: bought 2 lorries at £12 000 each (Nos. 1 and 2).
1 January, Year 2: bought lorry No. 3 at £13 000.
1 January, Year 3: sold lorry No. 1 for £7 000 and bought lorry No. 4 for £14 000.

Depreciation is calculated at the rate of 20 per cent p.a. on cost which is credited to a Provision for Depreciation on Lorries Account each year.

Show:
a the ledger accounts for Years 1, 2 and 3
b your calculations of depreciation and transfers to Disposal of Asset Account.

SOLUTION

a   **Ledger accounts**

Dr.   **Lorries Account**   Cr.

Year 1		£	Year 3		£
1 Jan.	Bank (Lorry No. 1)	12 000	1 Jan.	Disposal Account	
	Bank (Lorry No. 2)	12 000		(Lorry No. 1)	12 000
Year 2				Balance c/d	39 000
1 Jan.	Bank (Lorry No. 3)	13 000			
Year 3					
1 Jan.	Bank (Lorry No. 4)	14 000			
		51 000			51 000
Year 3					
1 Jan.	Balance b/d	39 000			

Dr.   **Provision for Depreciation (Lorries) Account**   Cr.

Year 3		£	Year 1		£
1 Jan.	Disposal Account	4 800	31 Dec.	Profit and Loss	
31 Dec.	Balance c/d	15 200		Account	4 800
			Year 2		
			31 Dec.	Profit and Loss	
				Account	7 400
			Year 3		
			31 Dec.	Profit and Loss	
				Account	7 800
		20 000			20 000
				Balance b/d	15 200

120   Depreciation of fixed assets

Dr. **Disposal of Asset Account** Cr.

Year 3		£	Year 3		£
1 Jan.	Lorries Account (Lorry No. 1)	12 000	1 Jan.	Provision for Depreciation Account	4 800
				Bank	7 000
				Profit and Loss Account (loss on sale)	200
		12 000			12 000

b Calculations

Depreciation
Year 1: 20% × 24 000 = 4 800
Year 2: 20% × 37 000 = 7 400
Year 3: 20% × 39 000 = 7 800

Transfer of provision to Disposal Account
Date bought: 1 January, Year 1
Date sold: 1 January, Year 3
Cost: £12 000
Therefore, years of ownership = 2 years
Provision transferred = 2 × 20% × 12 000
 = £ 4 800

3. The revaluation method

The revaluation method of calculating depreciation is used where it is either too difficult or too costly or inappropriate to use the other methods of depreciation. Examples would include such items as loose tools (screwdrivers, spanners, etc.), bottles, crates, or other containers, items such as cattle, sheep and pigs, etc.

The method is simple:

The items are valued collectively (denoted by a) at the beginning of the period. Any additions (b) made during the period are added to this figure.

The items are again valued at the end of the period and this figure (c) is subtracted from $a + b$. If an increase in value occurs the calculation is $c - (a + b)$.

The resultant figure is the amount by which the asset has depreciated or appreciated. This is the figure that is transferred to the final accounts.

EXAMPLE

On 1 January 19–1 the Fizzo Mineral Water Co. Ltd had a stock of 10 000 bottles valued at 2p each. On 1 July bottles were purchased costing £150. On 31 December the stock of bottles was valued at £280.

Show the Bottles Account for the year ended 31 December 19–1.

SOLUTION

Dr. **Bottles Account** Cr.

19–1		£	19–1		£
1 Jan.	Balance b/d	200	31 Dec.	Manufacturing Account*	70
1 July	Bank	150		Balance c/d	280
		350			350

*Calculation: 200 + 150 − 280 = 70

Appreciation of fixed assets

Some fixed assets (e.g. land) increase in value over the years particularly if the site is in a 'prime' location. In this case the increase in value should be recorded to give a true and fair picture of the affairs of the business and also to discourage takeover bids.

The journal entry would be as follows:
Suppose land is revalued upwards e.g. £25 000

Journal

		Dr. £	Cr. £
19–1			
1 Jan.	Land Account	25 000	
	Revaluation of Land Account		25 000
	Revaluation to take account of increasing site value		

Revaluation increases shareholders' funds but revaluations must normally be treated as a capital reserve not as a revenue reserve. (See Chapter 21.)

Exercises Set 8

1. On 1 January 19–1 R. Dolan bought a machine for £12 000. Its estimated working life was five years and its probable scrap value at the end of that time was £2 000.

   Using the fixed instalment method show the Machinery Account for the five years.

2. On 1 January 19–2 Tom Forbes bought a machine for £5 000; the scrap value in ten years' time is expected to be £500. Depreciation is to be written off by equal instalments on 31 December each year.

   Show the Machinery Account for the first three years.

3. A lease is purchased for a term of five years for £10 000. Show how the Lease Account would appear in the ledger during this period, depreciation being written off in equal instalments each year. Show also the entries on the balance sheet for each year.

4. Madox Ltd purchased a motor van on 1 January 19–2 for £5 000. It was estimated that the van would have a useful life of five years and be worth £200 at the end of that period. The company's financial year ends on 31 December in each year. At that date depreciation is credited to a Provision for Depreciation Account. The company depreciates on a straight-line basis.

   Show the journal and ledger entries for each of the three years ended 31 December 19–4.

Depreciation of fixed assets

5   Jason Ltd bought a lorry on 1 January 19–1 for £15 000 and another on 1 January 19–4 costing £18 000. It was estimated that the lorry would have a life of three years, with no residual value at the end of that period. The straight-line method of depreciation is operated by the company.

At the end of each financial year, depreciation is credited to a Provision for Depreciation Account, and the accumulated depreciation is deducted from the cost of the lorry in the balance sheet.

Show:
a   entries in the journal and ledger for the three years to 31 December 19–4, and also
b   the entry in the balance sheet at the end of 19–4.

6   On 1 January 19–5 Dex Ltd started a delivery business and on that date bought two lorries and a pick-up truck for £4 800, £3 600 and £3 000 respectively. It was decided to write off depreciation at 20 per cent p.a. using the reducing balance system and accumulating the depreciation in a Provision for Depreciation Account.

Show the accounts relating to depreciation for the first three years of business.

7   The following information is provided relating to A. Dealer who makes up his accounts on the calendar year basis:
1.   Purchased two new motor vehicles for £10 000 each on 1 January 19–2.
2.   Sold one of the motor vehicles, purchased on 1 January 19–2, for £1 300 on 23 June 19–4.
3.   Purchased an additional motor vehicle for £12 000 on 25 June 19–4.
4.   It is the company's policy to charge depreciation on the reducing balance basis at 40 per cent on motor vehicles owned at the end of each accounting period.

a   Explain why companies charge depreciation on fixed assets.
b   Prepare the Motor Vehicles Account, Provision for Depreciation Account and Disposals Account recording the above transactions.
c   Give the relevant balance sheet figures for fixed assets at 31 December 19–4.

8   You are required to record, in ledger accounts of Baxter Ltd, the following transactions for the year ended 31 March 19–5:

	£
Cost of plant in use at 1 April 19–4	166 000
Depreciation provision at 1 April 19–4	138 000
Original cost of plant sold for £5 400 on 31 March 19–5	38 000
Cost of plant installed 1 October 19–4	128 000

Assume depreciation to be at the rate of 25 per cent per annum on original cost from date of purchase.

The plant sold at 31 March 19–5 consisted of two items which were bought on 1 April 19–0 for £24 000 and 1 April 19–2 for £14 000 respectively.

9   New Firm Ltd commenced business on 1 January 19–4 and purchased equipment as follows:

1 January 19–4	£9 600
5 May 19–5	£12 000
20 December 19–6	£8 400

Depreciation on original cost is accumulated in a Provision for Depreciation Account. Each piece of equipment is estimated to last six years and to have a scrap value of one-tenth of its original cost.

Show the account for the first three years and the entries on the balance sheet on the 31 December in each year.

Note. The company's practice is to charge a full year's depreciation each year on the fixed instalment basis, irrespective of the date of purchase.

10 On 1 July 19–6 Mex Ltd purchased lorry No. 1 for £20 000 and lorry No. 2 for £22 000. On 30 September 19–8 lorry No. 1 was sold for £13 000 and replaced by lorry No. 3 costing £25 000. Depreciation calculated at 20 per cent on cost price is credited each year to a Provision for Depreciation Account. The financial year ends on 30 June each year and depreciation is calculated on additions from the date of purchase and on disposal to date of sale.

Show the accounts for the year ended 30 June 19–7, 19–8, 19–9.

11 The following is an extract from the plant register of Concrete Ltd, who debit all purchases of plant and machinery to a Plant and Machinery Account.

Year	Date	Number	Cost	Estimated life (years)	Scrap value
			£		£
19–1	1 Jan.	1	10 000	8	2 000
19–2	1 April	2	6 000	5	1 000
19–3	30 Sept.	3	2 000	3	200
19–4	1 Dec.	4	14 400	10	Nil

On 30 June 19–5 machine No. 2 was sold for £500 and replaced by machine No. 5 costing £9 000 with an estimated life of four years and a scrap value of £1 000.

The company's financial year ends on 31 December each year and depreciation is written off by fixed instalments from each asset to a Provision for Depreciation Account. Depreciation is calculated proportionately on each item of plant and machinery in the years of purchase and disposal.

You are required to show the entries from 1 January 19–1 to 31 December 19–5, in the following accounts:
a   the Plant and Machinery Account
b   the Provision for Depreciation Account
c   the Plant and Machinery Disposal Account.

Note. Show all calculations.

124 Depreciation of fixed assets

12 Happy Transport Ltd, whose final accounts are prepared on 31 December each year, maintains its fixed assets at cost and depreciation is accumulated in a Provision for Depreciation Account. On 1 January 19–8 the following balances appeared in the firm's books.
Buses at cost £160 000
Provision for depreciation £50 000
The following details relate to the years 19–8 and 19–9:
1.7.19–8   Purchased bus for £50 000 by cheque.
31.12.19–8   Depreciation charge to Profit and Loss Account £20 000.
1.1.19–9   Sold for £14 000 cash a bus which had cost £40 000.
       The depreciation to date on this bus was £25 000.
31.12.19–9   Depreciation charge to Profit and Loss Account £17 000.

Show for the two years 19–8 and 19–9:
a the Bus Account
b the Provision for Depreciation Account
c the Bus Disposal Account.

13 On 1 April 1969 Home Providers owned the following vehicles:

Vehicle	Original cost	Date of purchase
A	£900	1 July 1967
B	£1 200	1 October 1967
C	£700	1 February 1968
D	£1 500	1 May 1968
E	£2 200	1 November 1968

During the year ended 31 March 1970 the following transactions took place.
(a)   1 May 1969 – Vehicle B sold for £400.
(b)   1 June 1969 – Vehicle F purchased for £1 100.
(c)   1 September 1969 – Vehicle C sold for £600.
(d)   1 December 1969 – Vehicle G purchased for £800.
(e)   1 March 1970 – Vehicle H purchased for £1 600.

Home Providers, which came into existence on 1 April 1967, depreciates its motor vehicles using the straight-line method, at the rate of 20 per cent per annum.

You are required to write up the Motor Vehicles Account for each of the three years ended 31 March 1970, showing the transfer to the Profit and Loss Account in each year. (All calculations to be made to the nearest pound.)

14 Europa Bus Hire Ltd commenced business on 1.1.19–4 and prepares its final accounts on 31 December each year. The firm estimates that each bus will have a useful life of eight years and at the end of this period its scrap value will be one-tenth of its original cost. Depreciation is calculated from the date of purchase to the date of disposal and is accumulated in a Provision for Depreciation Account.

On 1.1.19–6 the following balances appeared in the firm's books:
Buses at cost £160 000
Provision for depreciation £25 200

During the years 19–6 and 19–7 the following transactions took place:
30.6.19–6   Sold bus which cost £32 000 for £22 000.

30.9.19–6 Bought bus for £64 000.
30.4.19–7 Bus which cost £48 000 was traded in against another bus which cost £72 000. The firm was allowed £36 000 for the old bus.

The bus which was sold on 30.6.19–6 was bought on 1.1.19–4 and the bus traded in on 30.4.19–7 was bought on 1.1.19–5.

Show for the two years 19–6 and 19–7:
a   the Bus Account
b   the Provision for Depreciation Account
c   the Bus Disposal Account.

15   Welsh Hauliers Ltd, whose final accounts are prepared on 31 December each year, depreciates its lorries at the rate of 10 per cent of cost per annum, calculated from the date of purchase to the date of disposal. The company commenced business on 1.1.19–6 and on that date purchased three lorries for cash for £40 000, £48 000 and £60 000 respectively.

During the years 19–8 and 19–9 the following transactions took place:
1.6.19–8   Purchased lorry for £56 000 by cheque.
1.10.19–8 Sold the lorry which had cost £40 000 for £28 000 cash.
1.5.19–9   During March 19–9, the lorry which had cost £60 000 was damaged in an accident and during April, the insurance company paid £7 200 to Welsh Hauliers Ltd in settlement of their subsequent claim. Instead of repairing the lorry Welsh Hauliers Ltd decided to trade it in and they received an allowance of £36 000 against a new lorry costing £96 000.

You are required to show for the two years 19–8 and 19–9:
a   the Lorry Account
b   the Provision for Depreciation Account
c   the Lorry Disposal Account
d   the relevant entries in the Company's Profit and Loss Account and balance sheet.

16   What is depreciation, and why is it charged when preparing the Profit and Loss Account?

Describe two methods by which the depreciation charge may be calculated.

[*Royal Society of Arts, II, June 1984*]

17   Plant Ltd was established and started trading on 1 January 1980, and its purchases and disposals of fixed assets over the subsequent three years were as follows:

Asset	Date of purchase	Cost £	Date of disposal	Proceeds on disposal £
A	1 January 1980	2 500	—	—
B	1 January 1980	1 250	1 January 1982	450
C	1 January 1982	3 500	—	—

a   Prepare the following accounts as they would appear in the books of Plant Ltd for the years 1980, 1981 and 1982 on the assumption that the company charges depreciation of *20 per cent per annum calculated on the straight-line basis*:
  (i)   Fixed Assets at Cost Account
  (ii) Provision for Depreciation Account

126 Depreciation of fixed assets

(iii) Disposal of Fixed Assets Account.
b Show your calculation of the depreciation charge for the years 1980, 1981 and 1982 and the profit or loss on the disposal of asset B which would result from calculating depreciation at the rate of *30 per cent per annum on the reducing balance basis.*
c Discuss the purpose of charging depreciation when preparing a set of accounts and indicate on what basis the choice of method should be made.

[*Royal Society of Arts, II, June 1983*]

18 Brown is in business as a building contractor. At 1 May 1982 he had three lorries, details of which are as follows:

Lorry registration number	Date purchased	Cost £	Accumulated depreciation to date £
BAB 1	1 July 1979	16 000	9 000
CAB 2	1 January 1981	21 000	8 000
DAB 3	1 April 1982	31 000	6 000

During the year to 30 April 1983, the following lorry transactions took place:
1. BAB 1 was sold on 31 July 1982 for £3 000 on cash terms. On 1 August 1982 Brown replaced it with a new lorry, registration number FAB 4 for which he paid £35 000 in cash.
2. On 15 December 1982, the new lorry (FAB 4) was involved in a major accident, and as a result was completely written off. Brown was able to agree a claim with his insurance company, and on 31 December 1982 he received £30 000 from the company. On 1 January 1983 he bought another new lorry (registration number HAB 6) for £41 000.
3. During March 1983, Brown decided to replace the lorry bought on 1 April 1982 (registration number DAB 3) with a new lorry. It was delivered on 1 April 1983 (registration number JAB 6). He agreed a purchase price of £26 000 for the new lorry, the terms of which were £20 000 in part exchange for the old lorry and the balance to be paid immediately in cash.

Notes
(i) Brown uses the straight-line method of depreciation based on year end figures.
(ii) The lorries are depreciated over a five-year period by which time they are assumed to have an exchange value of £1 000 each.
(iii) A full year's depreciation is charged in the year of acquisition, but no depreciation is charged if a lorry is bought and sold or otherwise disposed of within the same financial year.
(iv) No depreciation is charged in the year of disposal.
(v) Brown does not keep separate accounts for each lorry.

a Write up the following accounts for the year to 30 April 1983:
(i) Lorries Account
(ii) Lorries Disposal Account
(iii) Provision for Depreciation on Lorries Account.
b Show how the Lorries Account and the Provision for Depreciation Account would be presented in Brown's balance sheet as at 30 April 1983.

[*Association of Accounting Technicians, June 1983*]

19 You are provided with the following information relating to Speed, a firm of delivery merchants, for the year to 31 October 1983:

1. Balance sheet (extract) at 31 October 1982:

	£
Vans at cost	14 000
Less Depreciation to date	6 000
Net book value	8 000

2. Purchases of vans:

Date	Registration number	Cost £
1.1.79	AAT 10	2 000
1.5.80	BAT 20	3 000
1.12.80	CAT 30	4 000
1.8.82	DAT 40	5 000
1.12.82	EAT 50	6 000
1.8.83	FAT 60	9 000

3. Sales of vans:

Date	Registration number	Sale proceeds £
30.11.82	AAT 10	500
31.7.83	CAT 30	2 000
30.9.83	DAT 40	4 000

4. Vans are depreciated at a rate of 20 per cent per annum on cost. A full year's depreciation is charged in the year of purchase, but no depreciation is charged in the year of disposal.

a Enter the above transactions in the following accounts for the year to 31 October 1983, being careful to bring down the balances as at 1 November 1983: (i) Vans Account; (ii) Vans Depreciation Provision Account; and (iii) Vans Disposal Account.

b State briefly whether you think that the reducing balance method of depreciation would be a more appropriate method of depreciating delivery vans.

[*Association of Accounting Technicians, December 1983*]

20 Shown below is an extract from the balance sheet of Disposals Ltd as at 31 March 1981:

	£
Lorries at cost	67 500
Less Provision for depreciation	30 900
Net book value at 31 March 1981	36 600

During the year to 31 March 1982, the following transactions took place, the lorries being identified by their registration numbers:

1. Two lorries were sold. DV 100 had originally cost £7 000 in 1978 and was sold for £2 000 on 30 June 1981, whilst EV 200 had cost £15 000 in 1979 and was sold for £5 000 on 31 January 1981.
2. Three new lorries were purchased: IV 600 on 1 July 1981 at a cost of £15 000 and IV 800 on 1 February 1982 at a cost of £25 000. However, IV 600 proved to be too small, and was replaced with IV 700 on 1 December 1981. This would

have cost £30 000, but £20 000 was accepted by the supplier in part exchange for IV 600.

The company uses the straight-line method of depreciation at a rate of 20 per cent per annum on original cost. A full year's depreciation is charged in the year of acquisition, but no depreciation is charged in the year of disposal.

Write up the Lorries Account, the Provision for Depreciation Account, and the Lorry Disposal Account for the year to 31 March 1982.

[*Association of Accounting Technicians, June 1982*]

21 Kirkpatrick Ltd, sellers and repairers of motor vehicles, commenced business on 1 January 1982.

The company's balance sheet as at 31 December 1983 included the following items in the fixed assets section:

	At cost	Aggregate depreciation	Net
	£	£	£
Motor vehicles	21 000	7 560	13 440

All the motor vehicles included above were acquired when the company commenced business, the vehicles were XYZ 123 costing £10 000, ABC 456 costing £7 000 and PQR 789 costing £4 000. The company's policy up to 31 December 1983 has been to provide depreciation at the rate of 20 per cent per annum using the reducing balance method. However, it has now been decided to adopt the straight-line method of providing for depreciation and to adjust the motor vehicles provision for depreciation at 1 January 1984 in accordance with the new policy. In future, depreciation will be provided annually at the rate of 20 per cent of the original cost of motor vehicles held at each accounting year end.

During 1984, the following transactions took place involving motor vehicles (fixed assets):

31 March	Vehicle XYZ 123 was badly damaged in a road accident. The insurance company decided that the vehicle was beyond repair and therefore paid Kirkpatrick Ltd £7 100 in full settlement.
30 June	Vehicle RST 765 bought for cash from Express Traders Ltd. Kirkpatrick Ltd paid a cheque for £8 000 in full settlement of the amount due which included the insurance of the vehicle for the year commencing 30 June 1984 of £500.
30 September	Kirkpatrick Ltd exchanged vehicle PQR 789 for a new vehicle DEF 432 and paid a cheque for £3 000 in full settlement. The list price of the new vehicle was £5 000.
10 October	Paid Quickspray Ltd £200 for repainting DEF 432 in the company's colours before it was used by Kirkpatrick Ltd.

a Prepare the journal entries (or entry) required for the transaction of 30 September 1984.

Note. Narratives are required.

b Prepare the following accounts in the books of the company for the year ended 31 December 1984: Motor Vehicles – at Cost; Motor Vehicles – Provision for Depreciation; Motor Vehicles Disposals.

Note. A separate account is opened for each vehicle disposal.

[*Association of Accounting Technicians, pilot, 1985*]

22 JPR Haulage Ltd specialises in long-distance haulage of raw materials. On 1 January 1985, the company had three lorries which had been purchased for cash as follows:

Lorry	Purchase date	Purchase cost £
A	1 January 1983	16 500
B	1 October 1983	18 100
C	1 January 1984	19 400

The company depreciates its lorries on a straight-line basis over five years with no residual value. The company's financial year ends on 31 December each year.

A full year's depreciation is charged in the year of acquisition, but no depreciation is charged in the year of disposal.

The following transactions took place in the year ended 31 December 1985:

Lorry
D Purchased 5 April 1985 for £20 200 cash.
B Sold on 30 June 1985 for £4 720 cash.
E Purchased 8 August 1985 on hire purchase terms. The cash price was £18 000. The hire purchase terms provided for a deposit of £7 200 and 24 monthly instalments of £560.
F Purchased 9 September 1985 for £16 900 cash.

a Prepare a depreciation schedule in the following format:

Year ended 31 December	1983	1984	1985	Total
Lorry				
A				
B				
C				
D				
E				
F				
Total				

b Prepare *total* accounts for the year ended 31 December 1985 for:
(i) Motor lorries
(ii) Accumulated depreciation on motor lorries.

Note. Individual lorry details should not appear in these total accounts.

[*London Chamber of Commerce and Industry, Intermediate, spring 1986*]

23 The accounting year of Truck Ltd ends on 31 December. On 1 January 1985 the following balances were brought down in the Motor Vehicles at Cost Account and Provision for Depreciation of Motor Vehicles Account.

	£
Motor vehicles at cost	127 000 (debit)
Provision for Depreciation of Motor Vehicles Account	52 000 (credit)

The company calculates depreciation on vehicles on the straight-line basis, assuming a five-year life and a zero scrap value. A full year's charge is made in the year in which a vehicle is acquired, and no charge is made in the year of disposal.

On 1 January 1985 none of the vehicles owned by Truck Ltd was more than five years old.

130 Depreciation of fixed assets

During 1985 the following transactions involving vehicles took place:
(a) Bought from Van Ltd, on credit, a new vehicle for £15 000.
(b) Sold, for £4 500 cash, a vehicle purchased in 1983 for £8 000.

a   Prepare journal entries (including that for cash) to record the vehicle acquisition and disposal which took place in 1985. Narratives are not required, but all transfers related to the disposal should be included.

b   Write up the following accounts for 1985 and carry down their balances at 31 December 1985: Motor Vehicles at Cost; Provision for Depreciation of Motor Vehicles; Disposal of Motor Vehicles Account.

[*Royal Society of Arts, II, June 1986*]

24 The following information has been extracted from the motor lorry records of Express Transport Ltd:

Lorry	Date bought	Cost £	Method of payment
B393 KPQ	1 October 1983	22 000	Cash transaction
B219 BXY	1 January 1984	25 000	Cash transaction
C198 TKL	1 October 1985	34 000	Cash transaction
C437 FGA	1 April 1986	28 000	B393 KPQ given in part exchange plus cheque for £18 000

Express Transport Ltd, which was incorporated in 1983, has only owned the vehicles mentioned above during its existence.

Up to 30 September 1985, the company used the reducing balance method for depreciating its motor lorries; the rate of depreciation being 25 per cent per annum.

However, as from 1 October 1985 it has been decided to change to the straight-line method for depreciating the motor lorries; the rate of depreciation to be used is 20 per cent per annum and it is assumed that all vehicles will have a nil residual value. As a result of this decision, it will be necessary for appropriate adjustments to be made in the company's accounts so that the balance of the Motor Lorries Provision for Depreciation Account at 1 October 1985 will be on the basis of the straight-line method.

a   Prepare the journal entry (or entries) necessitated by the change of depreciation policy on 1 October 1985 from the reducing balance method to the straight-line method.
Note. Journal entries should include narratives.

b   Prepare the following accounts for the year ended 30 September 1986 in the books of Express Transport Ltd: Motor Lorries at Cost; Motor Lorries Provision for Depreciation; Motor Lorry B393 KPQ Disposal.

[*Association of Accounting Technicians, December 1986*]

9 Final accounts of sole traders

The sole trader like all other forms of business enterprise should keep correct ledger accounts for all financial transactions that take place in the business during the course of the financial year. From these ledger accounts the trader will transfer the correct amount to either Manufacturing, Trading or Profit and Loss Accounts as appropriate.

The outcome of the Profit and Loss Account will reveal either a net trading profit or loss for the period. In the case of the sole trader this profit or loss will be transferred directly to his capital account as he is not obliged to share profits or losses with anybody else.

Appropriations of profits or losses take place only in the case of Partnership and Company Accounts because in these cases either by legal arrangements or by law the profits or losses must be shared by two or more people. In the case of partnerships the appropriation of profits or losses will be dealt with in the partnership agreement or by the Partnership Act. In the case of public limited companies the appropriation of profits and losses will be proposed by the directors to the shareholders with voting powers at the annual general meeting of the company each year.

In all types of business organisation Trading and Profit and Loss Accounts will be prepared in the same way each year. In the case of a public limited company the law will require the production of final accounts and balance sheets to show clearly certain figures required by the country's legislation. Individuals or companies that manufacture goods will also prepare a Manufacturing Account so that the cost of manufacture can be ascertained and included with the cost of finished goods in the Trading Account.

The format of Manufacturing, Trading and Profit and Loss Accounts will be the same for all types of business up to and including the finding of the net trading profit for the year. The balance sheets of all types of business unit will consist of the accounts with balances left on them in the ledger accounts after the Trading and Profit and Loss Accounts have been completed. These represent the assets and liabilities of the business at the end of the financial period.

We will deal in this chapter firstly with the Trading and Profit and Loss Accounts and secondly with balance sheets of sole traders. After that the appropriations necessary for partnerships and company accounts can be dealt with

(Chapters 10 and 21). Manufacturing accounts will also be discussed as the content and style of the Manufacturing Account is common to all types of business enterprise (see Chapter 20).

Trading and Profit and Loss Accounts

The *Trading Account* compares net sales with the cost of sales so that gross trading profit or loss for the period is ascertained.

The *Profit and Loss Account* adjusts the gross profit for all selling expenses and losses and revenue gains for the period.

So, in short, the Trading and Profit and Loss Accounts compare the revenue gains of the period with the revenue expenses and losses for the period and the result is either a net profit or net loss.

(Net) sales less cost of sales = Gross profit
Gross profit + revenue gains, less selling expenses and losses = Net profit

EXPLANATION
When asked to prepare a Trading and Profit and Loss Account at the end of a trading period we are being asked to provide a statement showing the revenue receivable from normal trading against the cost incurred in obtaining that revenue.

The revenue involved in the Trading Account arises from sales; the expenditure to match this revenue is called 'Cost of sales'.

The difference between the two figures arrived at is called *gross profit* (i.e. profit before selling expenses and trading losses are deducted). When these expenses are deducted the resultant figure is *net profit* (i.e. profit net of expenses) or true profit.

It is very easy to understand Trading and Profit and Loss Accounts if we thoroughly understand the ingredients of (*a*) sales; (*b*) cost of sales; (*c*) revenue expenses.

SALES mean all cash and credit sales (net of returns inwards) of goods in which the trader normally deals.

Less
COST OF SALES comprising the basic costs incurred in making these sales. It must include:
    Opening stock of goods for resale
    Add   Purchases (cash and credit) of goods for resale
    +   Carriage on purchases
    +   Customs duties on purchases
    =   (Cost of) goods available for sale
    Less Closing stock of goods for resale
    =   COST OF SALES made during the period
So:
Sales
Less Cost of sales   = Gross profit

Gross profit
Less Selling expenses and losses attributable directly and indirectly to the same volume of sales   = Net profit (true profit) for the year

This is one aspect of the exercise ('The income statement') the result of which is the finding of the profit or loss on operations.

The second half of the exercise is to produce 'The position statement', usually called a balance sheet, at the end of the operating period.

The balance sheet sets out:

The ASSETS – What the firm *owns* plus what is owing to it at that date.
The LIABILITIES – What the firm *owes* at that date.

It sets them out in the most informative way showing:
FIXED ASSETS at cost
Less Depreciation to date   (giving) Net (book) value

To the total for fixed assets is added the value of NET CURRENT ASSETS or WORKING CAPITAL, which is found by deducting CURRENT LIABILITIES from CURRENT ASSETS.

The total arrived at is equal to TOTAL NET ASSETS. In short

Fixed assets + Working capital = Total net assets

These assets are funded or financed by:
   CAPITAL (supplied by proprietors)
+ RETAINED PROFITS
+ LONG-TERM DEBT (borrowed from outside the firm)
= TOTAL NET ASSETS = CAPITAL EMPLOYED

Fixed assets + Working capital (net current assets)
          = Capital + Retained profits + Long-term liabilities

The Trading and Profit and Loss Accounts must show *all* the gains, losses and expenses (whether realised or not) for the period in question and not a penny more. This, we know, is the reason for adjustments such as accruals, prepayments, depreciations and bad debts provision, etc. We must have the precise figures for all entries so that the final result will be accurate.

In transferring the entries necessary to prepare the Trading and Profit and Loss Accounts we will, in effect, be closing the ledger accounts concerned except those that have a balance coming down at the end of the year such as:

Fixed assets
Personal accounts (debtors and creditors)
Closing stocks
Accruals and prepayments
Capital
Loans
Bank and cash

134 Final accounts of sole traders

The ledger accounts with balances on them represent the assets and liabilities of the business at the end of the period and are set out in the form of a balance sheet on the last day of the period in question.

In examination questions on final accounts, ledger accounts by themselves are generally not shown. Instead, all balances taken from the ledger accounts are presented in the form of a trial balance from which, with given closing stock and other adjustments, the student is usually asked to prepare a Trading and Profit and Loss Account for the year ended on a certain date and also a balance sheet on that same date.

Note

All assets, losses and expenses are *debits*
All liabilities and gains are *credits* } on trial balance

Up to a few years ago it was usual to divide up the Trading and Profit and Loss Accounts into two separate accounts using ledger accounts in format 'T' accounts. This is still quite legitimate and has the advantage of emphasising that these accounts are ledger accounts. However, nowadays a slightly different format (removing the division between the debit and credit sides in the 'T' style accounts) is generally used and is more readily understood by readers. It is called the vertical style.

A Simple Example

From the following trial balance taken from the books of Trevor Jones, prepare a Trading and Profit and Loss Account for the year ended 31 December 19–1, and a balance sheet on that date.

Trevor Jones
Trial balance at 31 December 19–1

	Dr. £	Cr. £
Sales		110 000
Returns in (Sales returns)	10 000	
Stock at 1 January 19–1	10 000	
Purchases	58 000	
Returns out (Purchases returns)		8 200
Carriage in (Carriage on purchases)	200	
Discount received		2 000
Rent payable	720	
Rates	400	
Insurance	400	
Wages	20 000	
Carriage out (Carriage on sales)	400	
Buildings at cost	40 000	
Fixtures at cost	10 000	
Trade debtors	16 000	
Provision for bad debts		2 000
Cash at bank	1 380	
Cash	120	
Creditors		10 420

	Dr. £	Cr. £
Drawings	4 000	
Long-term loan		8 000
Capital		31 000
	171 620	171 620

The following information is given:
Stock at 31 December 19–1, £12 000
Rent due, £180
Insurance prepaid, £100

Depreciation:
Buildings 5% } on cost
Fixtures 10% }

SOLUTION

Trading and Profit and Loss Account of Trevor Jones (operating statement) for year ended 31 December 19–1

	£	£	£
Sales	110 000		
Less Returns in	10 000		
			100 000
Less			
Cost of sales			
Stock as at 1 January 19–1		10 000	
Add Purchases	58 000		
Less Returns out	8 200		
		49 800	
Add Carriage in		200	
Stock available for sale		60 000	
Less Stock 31 December 19–1		12 000	
COST OF SALES			48 000
GROSS PROFIT TO PROFIT AND LOSS ACCOUNT			52 000
Add Discount received			2 000
			54 000
Less			
Selling expenses and losses			
Rent	720		
Add Rent due	180		
		900	
Rates		400	
Insurance	400		
Less Insurance prepaid	100		

[cont. over

	£	£	£
		300	
Wages		20 000	
Carriage out		400	
Depreciation			
Buildings (5% of £40 000)	2 000		
Fixtures (10% of £10 000)	1 000		
		3 000	
TOTAL EXPENSES			25 000
NET PROFIT TO CAPITAL ACCOUNT			29 000

Adjustments

It is more modern and more informative to show adjustments in the form of notes. In the example above the notes would be as follows:

Notes

1. *Rent payable*   £
   Rent paid   720
   Add Rent due   180

   Charge to Profit and Loss Account   900

2. *Insurance*   £
   Insurance paid   400
   Less Insurance prepaid   100

   Charge to Profit and Loss Account   300

3. *Depreciation*
   (a) Buildings (at 5%)
      Charge to Profit and Loss Account 5% of £40 000 = £2 000
   (b) Fixtures (at 10%)
      Charge to Profit and Loss Account 10% of £10 000 = £1 000

The balance sheet (position statement)

The balance sheet is not an account. It is a list of balances which remain in the ledger accounts after final accounts have been prepared. It is a list of assets and liabilities on the date of the balance sheet. It can be looked at in *two ways*:

1. A statement showing on a particular date
   (a) what the business *owns* and what is owing to it } its assets
   (b) what the business *owes*
      (i) to the proprietor(s)
      (ii) to others } its liabilities.

2. The balance sheet can also be seen as showing:
   (a) How the business is using its finance – (net) assets.
   (b) Where the finance is coming from – liabilities.
   This is a more modern and informative way of looking at balance sheets.

The example below (taken from the trial balance on pp. 134–5) sets out the proper method of laying out a balance sheet in the most informative way.

Balance sheet of Trevor Jones as at 31 December 19–1

	Cost	Depreciation to date	Net	Total
Fixed assets	£	£	£	£
Buildings	40 000	2 000	38 000	
Fixtures	10 000	1 000	9 000	
	50 000	3 000	47 000	47 000
Current assets	£		£	
Trade debtors	16 000			
Less Provision for bad debts	2 000			
			14 000	
Stock			12 000	
Cash at bank			1 380	
Cash			120	
Prepayments			100	
			27 600	
Less Current liabilities				
Creditors	10 420			
Accruals	180			
			10 600	
Working capital				17 000
TOTAL NET ASSETS				64 000
Financed by:				
Capital				
Balance at 1 January 19–1			31 000	
Add Net profit			29 000	
			60 000	
Less Drawings			4 000	
				56 000
Long-term liabilities				
Term loan				8 000
CAPITAL EMPLOYED				64 000

The balance sheet above is shown in the *order of permanence*. Fixed assets (most permanent) come first, followed by current assets. Similarly, the liabilities are shown with capital liabilities (most permanent) coming first, followed by long-term liabilities (less permanent).

138 Final accounts of sole traders

Balance sheets can also be shown in the *order of liquidity*, showing less permanent (current) assets before fixed assets and long-term liabilities before capital. It is a complete reverse of the order of permanence. It is used by firms such as banks which have a greater proportion of their assets and liabilities in liquid form.

A More Complete Example

The following trial balance was extracted from the books of A. Boles, a shopkeeper, on 31 December 19–2:

	Dr. £	Cr. £
Stock at 1 January 19–2	16 000	
Sales		160 000
Purchases	80 000	
Returns out		2 000
Returns in	4 000	
Carriage on purchases	1 400	
Carriage on sales	600	
Premises (cost £200 000)	160 000	
Fixtures and fittings (cost £60 000)	44 000	
Motor van (cost £40 000)	20 000	
Trade debtors	14 000	
Provision for bad debts at 1.1.19–2		1 400
Bad debts	3 000	
Creditors		30 000
Drawings	10 000	
Discount allowed	3 000	
Discount received		30 000
Wages	28 000	
Rent	5 000	
Rates	7 000	
Insurance	1 000	
Office expenses	4 400	
Telephone	1 600	
Bank loan		18 000
Cash at bank	2 400	
Cash in hand	600	
Bank interest	1 400	
Capital at 1 January 19–2		192 800
	407 400	407 400

The following additional information is given:
(a) Stock at 31 December 19–2 was valued at £18 000
(b) Wages due, £1 200
(c) Rent prepaid, £1 000
(d) Bank interest due, £400
(e) Maintain bad debts provision at 5 per cent of trade debtors
(f) Depreciation:
   Premises 2 per cent
   Fixtures and fittings 10 per cent } on cost
   Motor van 20 per cent

Prepare Trading and Profit and Loss Account for year ended 31 December 19–2 and a balance sheet at that date.

SOLUTION

A. Boles
Trading and Profit and Loss Account for year ended 31 December 19–2

	£	£	£
Sales	160 000		
Less Returns in	4 000		
			156 000
Less			
Cost of sales			
Stock at 1.1.19–2		16 000	
Add Purchases	80 000		
Less Returns out	2 000		
		78 000	
Add Carriage on purchases		1 400	
		95 400	
Less Stock at 31.12.19–2		18 000	
COST OF SALES			77 400
Gross profit to Profit and Loss Account			78 600
Add Discount received			3 200
			81 800
Less			
Selling expenses and losses			
Carriage on sales		600	
Bad debts provision (Note 1)		2 300	
Discount allowed		3 000	
Wages (Note 2)		29 200	
Rent (Note 3)		4 000	
Rates		7 000	
Insurance		1 000	
Office expenses		4 400	
Telephone		1 600	
Bank interest (Note 4)		1 800	
Depreciation (Note 5)			
Premises	4 000		
Fixtures and fittings	6 000		
Motor van	8 000		
		18 000	
Total expenses			72 900
NET PROFIT TO CAPITAL ACCOUNT			8 900

A. Boles
Balance sheet as at 31 December 19–2

	Cost	Depreciation to date	Net	Total
Fixed assets	£	£	£	£
Premises	200 000	44 000	156 000	
Fixtures and fittings	60 000	22 000	38 000	
Motor vans	40 000	28 000	12 000	
	300 000	94 000	206 000	206 000

Add			
Current assets	£	£	£
Stock at 31.12.19–2		18 000	
Trade debtors	14 000		
Less Provision for bad debts	700	13 300	
Cash at bank		2 400	
Cash in hand		600	
Prepayment (Note 3)		1 000	
			35 300

Less Current liabilities			
Creditors		30 000	
Accruals (Notes 2 and 4)		1 600	
			31 600

Working capital	3 700
TOTAL NET ASSETS	209 700
Financed by:	
Capital Account (Note 6)	191 700
Long-term liability	
Bank loan	18 000
CAPITAL EMPLOYED	209 700

Notes

1.

Dr.	**Bad Debts Provision Account**			Cr.
19–2		£	19–2	£
31 Dec.	Bad Debts Account	3 000	1 Jan. Balance b/d	1 400
	Balance c/d	700	31 Dec. Profit and Loss Account	2 300
		3 700		3 700
			31 Dec. Balance b/d	700

2. *Wages*		£
Wages paid		28 000
Add Wages due		1 200
Profit and Loss Account		29 200

3. *Rent* | £
Rent paid | 5 000
Less Rent prepaid | 1 000
Profit and Loss Account | 4 000

3.	*Rent*	£
Rent paid	5 000
Less Rent prepaid	1 000
Profit and Loss Account	4 000
4.	*Bank interest*	£
Bank interest paid	1 400
Add Bank interest due	400
Profit and Loss Account	1 800
5.	*Depreciation*	£
Premises 2% of £200 000	4 000
Fixtures and fittings 10% of £60 000	6 000
Motor van 20% of £40 000	8 000
Profit and Loss Account	18 000
6.	*Capital Account*	£
Balance at 1.1.19–2	192 800
Add Net profit	8 900
	201 700
Less Drawings	10 000
Balance at 31.12.19–2	191 700

Exercises Set 9

1 Tick the correct answer.
   1. Gross profit equals:
      a sales plus cost of sales ☐
      b sales minus purchases ☐
      c opening stock plus purchases minus sales ☐
      d sales minus cost of sales ☐
   2. Stock at start, £1 000; Purchases, £3 000; Sales, £5 600; Stock at end, £600. The cost of sales is:
      a £5 000 ☐
      b £3 400 ☐
      c £2 600 ☐
      d £4 600 ☐
   3. In Question 2 above the gross profit is:
      a £2 200 ☐
      b £2 600 ☐
      c £3 400 ☐
      d £6 000 ☐
   4. Net profit is equal to:
      a gross profit plus expenses ☐
      b gross profit minus expenses ☐
      c cost of sales plus gross profit ☐
      d sales minus cost of sales ☐

142 Final accounts of sole traders

5. The gross profit was £20 000 and the following payments were made: Rent, £2 000; Rates, £1 000; Fixtures and fittings, £4 000; Wages, £10 000.
   The net profit is:
   a £3 000 □
   b £16 000 □
   c £13 000 □
   d £7 000 □
6. Net profit plus expenses equals:
   a cost of sales □
   b sales □
   c gross profit □
   d capital □
7. A balance sheet is:
   a a list of debtors and creditors □
   b a statement of receipts and payments for year □
   c a statement of income and expenditure for year □
   d a statement showing a firm's assets and liabilities on a certain date □
8. Total net assets are the same as:
   a working capital □
   b fixed assets minus current liabilities □
   c capital employed □
   d capital minus current liabilities □
9. Which of the following is a current asset for a garage?
   a the managing director's Mercedes □
   b the salesman's Audi □
   c the Ford Orion in the salesroom □
   d a customer's Volkswagen in the repair shop □
10. Which of the following is a fixed asset for a newsagent?
    a the magazines on the shelves □
    b cash in the cash register □
    c the cash register □
    d debtors for newspapers □
11. Which of the following is a current liability?
    a rates prepaid □
    b term loan □
    c capital □
    d accrual □

Look at the following balance sheet and answer Questions 12 to 17.

Balance sheet as at 31 December 19–1

	Cost	Depreciation to date	Net	Total
	£	£	£	£
Fixed assets				
Freehold buildings	100 000	—	100 000	
Fixtures and fittings	80 000	40 000	40 000	
Motor vans	40 000	10 000	30 000	
	220 000	50 000	170 000	170 000
Goodwill				30 000
				200 000

	£	£	£
Current assets			
Stock	30 000		
Trade debtors	10 000		
Bank	2 500		
Rent prepaid (3 months)	1 000		
		43 500	
Less Current liabilities			
Trade creditors	20 000		
Rates due (½ year)	800		
Interest due on mortgage loan	2 500		
		23 300	
			20 200
			220 200
Financed by:			
Capital			
Balance at 1 January 19–1	160 400		
Add Net profit	39 800		
	200 200		
Long-term liability			
12½% mortgage loan	20 000		
			220 200

12. Capital employed at 31 December 19–1 was:
    a £12 200 ☐
    b £200 000 ☐
    c £220 200 ☐
    d £43 500 ☐
13. Book value of fixed assets was:
    a £170 000 ☐
    b £50 000 ☐
    c £220 000 ☐
    d £200 000 ☐
14. The total net assets figure was:
    a £200 000 ☐
    b £23 300 ☐
    c £243 500 ☐
    d £220 200 ☐
15. The annual rent payable is:
    a £1 000 ☐
    b £2 000 ☐
    c £4 000 ☐
    d £250 ☐
16. Tangible assets at 31 December 19–1 were:
    a £200 000 ☐
    b £213 500 ☐
    c £220 000 ☐
    d £170 000 ☐

Final accounts of sole traders

17. The working capital at 31 December 19–1 was:
    - a £23 300 ☐
    - b £220 200 ☐
    - c £159 800 ☐
    - d £20 200 ☐

2 a Using your own figures prepare a trial balance containing at least:
   Three fixed assets   One long-term liability
   Four current assets   Eight nominal accounts
   Two current liabilities   One capital account
   b Using this trial balance and adding at least three adjustments, prepare a Trading and Profit and Loss Account for the period and a balance sheet on the last day of the period you have chosen.

3 The following trial balance was extracted from the books of W. Tate on 31 March 19–5:

	Dr. £	Cr. £
Capital account – 1 April 19–5		6 370
Stock – 1 April 19–5	10 372	
Sales		260 932
Purchases	231 900	
Returns inwards	402	
Returns outwards		1 198
Goodwill – at cost	2 000	
Loan		2 000
Office furniture (cost £2 400)	1 950	
Salaries	8 618	
Drawings – W. Tate	2 800	
Rent and rates	1 536	
Discount allowed	3 734	
Discount received		3 860
Motor vehicle (cost £6 000)	4 800	
Sundry creditors		8 276
Insurance	420	
Office expenses	1 924	
Lighting and heating	276	
Telephone	242	
Motor vehicle expenses	2 592	
Interest on loan	120	
Sundry debtors	8 350	
Balance at bank	600	
	282 276	282 636

You are given the following information:
- (a) The office furniture is to be depreciated at the rate of 10 per cent per annum on cost.
- (b) The motor vehicles are to be depreciated at the rate of 20 per cent per annum on cost.
- (c) Insurance paid in advance on 31 March 19–6 amounted to £132.
- (d) £124 is to be provided for telephone charges accrued on 31 March 19–6.
- (e) Stock on 31 March 19–6 amounted to £8 542.

Prepare a Trading and Profit and Loss Account for the year ended 31 March 19–6 together with balance sheet as on that date.

4 On 31 March 19–4 the following balances were extracted from the books of D. Frame, a general merchant:

	£
Land and buildings (cost £130 000)	120 000
Motor vehicle (cost £12 000)	10 000
Bank overdraft	7 600
Cash in hand	200
Sundry debtors	61 600
Purchases	131 800
Selling expenses	8 000
Carriage outwards	7 800
Stationery	1 600
Wages	44 400
Discount allowed	5 600
Rates	2 800
Stock on 1 April 19–3	64 000
Sundry creditors	13 200
Bank interest paid	400
Sales	249 600
Capital on 1 April 19–3	187 800

The following additional information is given:
(a) Stock on 31 March 19–4 amounted to £75 000.
(b) The following outstanding amounts have to be provided for:

Rates	£2 800
Bank interest	£200

(c) Depreciation has to be provided on the original cost of the assets at the following rates:

Land and buildings	5%
Motor vehicles	20%

You are required to prepare a Trading and Profit and Loss Account for the year ended 31 March 19–4, together with balance sheet as on that date.

5 The following trial balance was extracted from the books of P. Spencer on 31 January 19–9:

	Dr. £	Cr. £
Capital Account – 1 February 19–8		480
Stock in trade – 1 February 19–8	12 840	
Sales		210 726
Purchases	175 380	
Purchases returns		880
Sales returns	1 480	
Goodwill (at cost)	4 000	
Loan from brother		3 000
Interest on loan	150	
Wages and salaries	6 400	
Rent and rates	1 800	
Discount allowed	884	

146   Final accounts of sole traders

	Dr. £	Cr. £
Discount received		428
Office equipment (cost £4 000)	3 200	
Motor vehicles (cost £6 000)	4 800	
Sundry debtors	15 200	
Sundry creditors		13 840
Insurance	480	
Sundry expenses	1 620	
Cash on hand	120	
Bank overdraft		3 440
Drawings – P. Spencer	3 880	
Provision for bad debts – 1 February 19–8		400
	232 714	232 714

You are given the following information:
(a) Stock in trade on 31 January 19–9 had cost the business £12 200. Of this, £640 is considered to be valueless.
(b) Depreciation is to be provided on the original cost of the assets as follows:
    Office equipment   10%
    Motor vehicles   20%
(c) Bad debts amounting to £600 are to be written off and the provision made equal to 5 per cent of the sundry debtors.
(d) The loan from the proprietor's brother carries interest at the rate of 10 per cent per annum. (Income tax to be ignored.)
(e) The Insurance Account includes a payment of £240 in respect of the year ended 30 June 19–9.
(f) The following amounts were due and unpaid on 31 January 19–9:
    Rates   £120
    Sundry expenses   £200

You are required to prepare a Trading and Profit and Loss Account for year ended 31 January 19–9 together with balance sheet as on that date.

6 The following trial balance was extracted from the books of K. Crossan on 30 November 19–1:

	Dr. £	Cr. £
Leasehold premises (cost £20 000)	15 000	
Plant and machinery (cost £7 200)	4 400	
Office equipment (cost £2 000)	1 200	
Motor vehicle (cost £5 000)	3 600	
Bank balance		23 700
Provision for bad debts, 1 December 19–0		600
Sundry debtors	36 000	
Sundry creditors		26 600
Goodwill	3 000	
Stock, 1 December 19–0	7 500	
Sales		130 000
Purchases	97 600	
Wages	13 800	
Salaries	6 400	
Rent	800	

	Dr. £	Cr. £
Rates	224	
Electricity	156	
Telephone	126	
Stationery	112	
Advertising	300	
Repairs and renewals	1 252	
Motor expenses	1 146	
Bank interest	1 552	
General expenses	56	
Drawings	3 700	
Capital Account		7 024
	187 924	187 924

The following additional information is given:
(a) The undernoted accounts were due and unpaid on 30 November 19–1:

		£
(i)	Wages	200
(ii)	Rent	200
(iii)	Electricity	24
(iv)	Telephone	34
(v)	Stationery	28
(vi)	Repairs and renewals	48
(vii)	Audit fee	200

(b) Rates, £24, had been paid in advance.
(c) The stock in hand on 30 November 19–1 was £9 100.
(d) Depreciation is to be provided on the original cost of the assets as follows:
    (i) Leasehold premises   10%   (iii) Office equipment   10%
    (ii) Plant and machinery   20%   (iv) Motor vehicles   20%
(e) Bad debts amounting to £1 000 have been written off and the provision for bad debts is to remain at £600.

You are required to prepare a Trading and Profit and Loss Account for the year ended 30 November 19–1, together with a balance sheet as on that date.

7 The following trial balance was extracted from the books of M. Holt, a trader, as on 31 December 19–7:

	Dr. £	Cr. £
Stock, 1 January 19–7	7 460	
Fixtures and fittings at cost	1 200	
Purchases	27 600	
Sales		41 250
Returns inwards	520	
Returns outwards		310
Rent and rates	1 270	
Discount received		120
Discount allowed	290	
Trade debtors	7 290	
Trade creditors		3 630
Motor van – at cost	800	
Wages and salaries	3 700	

	Dr. £	Cr. £
Bad debts provision at 1 January 19–7		380
Bank overdraft		2 130
Cash in hand	20	
M. Holt, capital		7 780
M. Holt, drawings	1 800	
Administration expenses	4 210	
Depreciation to 1 January 19–7:		
Fixtures and fittings		240
Motor van		320
	56 160	56 160

You are required to prepare a Trading and Profit and Loss Account for the year ended 31 December 19–7, together with a balance sheet as on that date, after taking into account the following matters:
(a) Stock at 31 December 19–7, £8 640.
(b) Rent unpaid, 31 December 19–7, £210.
(c) Bad debts amounting to £90 have to be written off and the bad debts provision maintained at 5 per cent of the sundry debtors.

8 The following trial balance was extracted from the books of T. Port, a retail wine merchant, on 31 December 19–8:

	Dr. £	Cr. £
Cash in hand	56	
Bank overdraft		2 400
Capital		8 000
Drawings	1 700	
Buildings	4 000	
Goodwill	2 000	
Motor delivery vans	1 600	
Fixtures and fittings	900	
Stock: 1 January 19–8	5 700	
Sales		63 030
Purchases	51 400	
Returns inwards	266	
Returns outwards		316
Wages and salaries	2 842	
Discount allowed	654	
Discount received		788
Trade debtors	3 946	
Trade creditors		2 760
Rent received		500
Rent and rates	1 550	
Heating and lighting	642	
Insurance	204	
Bank charges	84	
Advertising	250	
	77 794	77 794

You are required to prepare a Trading and Profit and Loss Account for the year ended 31 December 19–8, together with a balance sheet as on that date, after taking into consideration the following:
(a) The value of stock in trade on 31 December 19–8 was £6 100
(b) Depreciation is to be written off:
    Buildings 5%
    Motor delivery vans 25%
    Fixtures and fittings 10%
(c) Advertising expenditure of £150 is to be written off, the balance to be carried forward as prepaid expenditure.

9 The following balances have been extracted from the books of Berry, a sole trader, as at 30 September 1982:

	Dr. £	Cr. £
Bank	1 850	
Capital		10 000
Cash in hand	100	
Creditors		400
Debtors	7 000	
Drawings	5 000	
Electricity	200	
Furniture, at cost	1 500	
General expenses	1 300	
Insurance	250	
Provision for depreciation on furniture (at 1 October 1981)		300
Purchases	53 500	
Rent	2 000	
Sales		70 000
Stock (at 1 October 1981)	5 000	
Wages	3 000	
	80 700	80 700

Notes
1. Stock at 30 September 1982 was valued at £6 000.
2. At 30 September 1982, an amount of £150 was outstanding for electricity, insurance was prepaid by £50, and there was a bad debt of £100. These items had not been entered in the books of account.
3. Depreciation is to be provided on furniture at a rate of 10 per cent per annum on cost.

Prepare Berry's Trading, Profit and Loss Account for the year to 30 September 1982, and a balance sheet as at that date.

[*Association of Accounting Technicians, December 1982*]

150 Final accounts of sole traders

10 B. Norris is in business as a wholesale supplier of motor equipment. The following is his trial balance as at 31 March 1983:

	Dr. £	Cr. £
Accumulated van depreciation (at 1 April 1982)		15 000
Capital (at 1 April 1982)		8 400
Creditors		10 000
Cash at bank	200	
Debtors	16 700	
Drawings	11 000	
Office expenses	12 600	
Opening stock	5 000	
Provision for doubtful debts (at 1 April 1982)		600
Purchases	62 000	
Rates	1 500	
Sales		100 000
Vans, at cost	25 000	
	134 000	134 000

You are provided with the following additional information:
1. The value of closing stock at 31 March 1983 was £6 000.
2. Debtors include a certain bad debt of £500.
3. The provision for doubtful debts is to be made equal to 5 per cent of outstanding debtors as at 31 March 1983.
4. At 31 March 1983, Norris owed £300 for rates.
5. Insurance prepaid at 31 March 1983 amounted to £100.
6. Norris uses the reducing balance method of depreciation at a rate of 60 per cent per annum. There were no purchases or sales of vans during the year.
7. Stock withdrawn for personal use during the year was estimated to be worth £1 000.
8. No entry had been made in the books of account for a cheque received from a debtor on 15 March 1983 made payable to Norris for £200.

Prepare B. Norris's Trading and Profit and Loss Account for the year to 31 March 1983 and a balance sheet as at that date.
[*Association of Accounting Technicians, June 1983*]

*11 John Lane runs a shop known as the John Lane Emporium, and on 1 January 1983 his total assets and liabilities, including both personal and business items, were, at historical cost less depreciation where appropriate:

Assets	£
Business premises	30 000
House	20 000
Delivery van	3 500
Cash float in till	100
Trading stock	14 250
Personal bank account	700
Business bank account	2 300

* This question is more difficult than the others in this section and might be omitted at first reading.

	£
Shop fittings	5 000
House furniture	2 840
Personal clothes	740
Premium bonds	550
Garden greenhouse	450
Garden shed	150
Personal car	2 000
Watch	40
Liabilities	
Creditors for stock purchases	1 500
Domestic electricity	70
Business electricity	85

The business bank account for the year to 31 December 1983 is:

	£		£
Balance brought down	2 300	Wages	11 500
Sales	75 350	Electricity	250
		Motor expenses	750
		Purchases	52 200
		Drawings	10 000
		Additional shop fittings	1 600
		Balance carried down	1 350
	77 650		77 650

You are given the following information:
1. At 31 December 1983 creditors for stock purchases were £2 000 and £100 was owed for business electricity.
2. The value of shop fittings at 31 December 1983 was £5 940 and the van was valued at £2 500.
3. At 31 December 1983 a float of £100 was held in the till, and trading stock was valued at £15 850.

a Prepare the balance sheet of the John Lane Emporium at 1 January 1983 to show clearly the capital which John Lane has invested in his business.
b Prepare the Trading and Profit and Loss Account of the John Lane Emporium for the year to 31 December 1983 and a balance sheet at that date. The cost of goods sold and gross profit should be identified in the Trading Account.

[*Royal Society of Arts, II, March 1984*]

12 You are presented with the following balance sheet:

Rawe
Balance sheet at 30 September 1983

	Cost	Depreciation	Net book value
Fixed assets	£	£	£
Plant	150 000	60 000	90 000
Vehicles	20 000	10 000	10 000
	170 000	70 000	100 000

	£	
Current assets		
Stock	10 000	
Trade debtors	20 000	
Bank	500	
	30 500	
Less Current liability		
Trade creditors	12 000	
		18 500
		118 500

Financed by:	
Capital	20 000
Net profit for the year	53 600
Suspense Account	44 900
	118 500

Upon investigation, you discover the following errors:
1. The balance on the Bad Debts Provision Account as at 1 October 1982 had been credited to the Profit and Loss Account. The balance of the account as at that date was £1 800.
2. The Bad Debts Provision Account should have been made equal to 10 per cent of trade debtors as at 30 September 1983.
3. Depreciation is charged on plant at a rate of 20 per cent per annum on cost, and on vehicles at a rate of 50 per cent per annum on the reduced balance. The depreciation for the year to 30 September 1983 has been correctly charged to the Profit and Loss Account for that year, but no adjustments have been made elsewhere.
4. The closing stock amounted to £12 000, but the amount shown on the balance sheet was the opening stock.
5. A transpositional error had understated sales by £900.
6. A new motor vehicle costing £5 000 had been included in motor expenses. It is the company's policy not to charge any depreciation in the year of acquisition.
7. Drawings amounting to £10 000 had been debited to the Profit and Loss Account.
8. Discounts allowed of £1 000 had been credited to the Profit and Loss Account, and discounts received amounting to £1 500 had been debited to the Profit and Loss Account.
9. A loan of £5 000 had been credited to the Profit and Loss Account.
10. Trade creditors had been understated by £10 000.

Prepare Rawe's corrected balance sheet as at 30 September 1983.

[*Association of Accounting Technicians, December 1983*]

10 Partnership ledger and final accounts

The Partnership Act 1890 defines a partnership as 'the relationship which subsists between persons carrying on a business in common with a view of profit'.

When two or more persons come together to form a partnership it is usual for them to draw up a legal document called a *deed of partnership* or *partnership agreement*. This agreement will set out the rights, duties and obligations of each partner and the rules governing the partnership as a whole. In the absence of such an agreement between the partners, or where the agreement is silent, all partners are bound by the Partnership Act of 1890 (Section 24), the main provisions of which are:

1. All profits and losses must be shared equally.
2. All partners have the right to take part in the business.
3. No interest is to be allowed on capital.
4. All partners have the right to prevent the introduction of new partners.
5. No interest is to be charged on drawings.
6. All partners have the right to examine the books of the partnership.
7. No partner is allowed a salary.
8. All the partners have the right to receive interest at 5 per cent p.a. on loans and advances made to the firm in excess of their capital subscription.
9. Differences of opinion shall be settled by the majority of the partners but the nature of the business cannot be changed without the consent of all.
10. A true account of all partnership business must be made by all partners.

Partners' accounts

The minimum number of accounts that must be kept in the absence of any indication to the contrary is a Capital Account for each partner. However, it is usual, particularly where partners' capitals are fixed, to have a Current Account for each partner.

Partners' Capital Accounts will contain details of the original amount introduced into the business by the partner either in money or other assets and any additions or reductions to that figure.

Partners' Current Accounts will record the monetary transactions that take place between the partner and the business. They will record on the *credit side* amounts due to the partner by the business such as interest on capital, interest on Current Account credit balance, share of profits and any other amounts due to partners out of the normal running of the firm. On the *debit side* will be recorded amounts owing to the firm such as interest on Current Account debit balance, drawings and interest thereon.

Note that interest on partners' *loans* must be debited to the Profit and Loss Account proper as this is a charge against the profit, not an appropriation.

Partners' Drawings Accounts. Sometimes, in addition to a Current Account, a Drawings Account is kept for each partner into which drawings in cash or goods plus interest on drawings are debited as they occur. This account is closed to each partner's Current or Capital Account at the end of each financial period. The entry is:

Debit partner's Current Account (or Capital Account if he has no Current Account)
Credit Drawings Account.

Partnership Profit and Loss Appropriation Account

The final accounts of a partnership are similar to those of a sole trader. All charges attributable to the running of the business, including interest on partners' loans, are debited to the Partnership Profit and Loss Account. All revenue receipts are credited. The net profit or loss is transferred to the Partnership Profit and Loss Appropriation Account or more correctly to the appropriation section of the Profit and Loss Account.

Appropriation of profit or loss

When the net profit or loss has been ascertained in the normal way, it is appropriated or distributed in accordance with the terms of the partnership agreement. When the appropriation is complete the profit or loss will have been shared between the partners and will appear with any other item due to, or by, them on their Current (or Capital) Accounts.

Appropriations usually take the form of:
(a) Interest allowed on partners' Capital Accounts.
(b) Interest allowed on partners' Current Account credit balances.
(c) Partners' salaries.
(d) Partners' commissions.
(e) Any other financial allowance made to partners.
When all appropriations have been deducted from net profit (or added to net loss), the final appropriation will always be
(f) Partners' share of profit or loss.

Note that all these items (except share of loss) must be credited to partners' Current or Capital Accounts as appropriate – share of loss will be debited to Current or Capital Accounts.

Items added to net profit before it is appropriated or divided are *items that increase net profit:*

(a) Interest on partners' drawings.
(b) Interest on partners' Current Account debit balances must be added to net profit before appropriation takes place. These items increase the profit available for distribution. They must be debited to partners' Current Accounts or Drawings Accounts as appropriate because they increase the amount owed to the firm by the individual partners.

An example will help to illustrate these points.

EXAMPLE

Jean, Jack and Rose are in partnership. The partnership agreement states:

1. Capitals are fixed at £40 000, £30 000 and £10 000 respectively.
2. Profits and losses are to be shared in the ratio 5:4:1.
3. Interest is allowed on Capital and Current Account credit balances at the beginning of each year at the rate of 10 per cent p.a.
4. Interest is charged on Current Account debit balances as at the beginning of each year at 5 per cent p.a.
5. Rose is entitled to a salary of £16 000 p.a.
6. Jack is entitled to commission of £4 000 p.a.
7. Interest is charged on partners' drawings at 10 per cent p.a.

The Current Account balances at 1 January 19–1 were:
Jean, £2 400 (Dr.); Jack, £3 500 (Cr.); Rose, £100 (Dr.).

Drawings during the year were as follows:

Date	Jean £	Jack £	Rose £
30 June	1 600	800	400
30 Sept.	800	1 600	800
31 Dec.	400	200	400

The profit for the year, before allowing for the above, was £64 000.

Show:
a Profit and Loss (appropriation section) for the year ended 31 December 19–1.
b Partners' Capital Accounts.
c Partners' Current Accounts.
d Partners' Drawings Accounts.
e Appropriate balance sheet extracts as at 31 December 19–1.

Show all workings.

SOLUTION
a   **Profit and Loss Account (appropriation section)**
                for year ended 31.12.19–1

	£	£	£
Net profit b/d			64 000
Add Interest on partners' drawings (Note 1)			220
Interest on Current Account debit balances (Note 2)			130
			64 350
Less Appropriations as under			
Interest on capital			
Jean (10% of £40 000)	4 000		
Jack (10% of £30 000)	3 000		
Rose (10% of £10 000)	1 000		
		8 000	
Interest on Current Accounts (Cr.)			
Jean (10% of £3 500)		350	
Salary – Rose		16 000	
Commission – Jack		4 000	
Share of profit (£36 000)			
Current Account – Jean $\tfrac{5}{10}$	18 000		
Current Account – Jack $\tfrac{4}{10}$	14 400		
Current Account – Rose $\tfrac{1}{10}$	3 600		
		36 000	
			64 350

Notes
1. *Interest on drawings* is calculated as follows:

   Jean
       £1 600 (principal) × $\tfrac{10}{100}$ (10% interest) × $\tfrac{1}{2}$ (half year June–Dec.) = £80
       £800 × $\tfrac{10}{100}$ × $\tfrac{1}{4}$ (quarter year Sept.–Dec.) = £20
       Total = £100

   Jack
       £800 × $\tfrac{10}{100}$ × $\tfrac{1}{2}$ (half year June–Dec.) = £40
       £1 600 × $\tfrac{10}{100}$ × $\tfrac{1}{4}$ (quarter year Sept.–Dec.) = £40
       Total = £80

   Rose
       £400 × $\tfrac{10}{100}$ × $\tfrac{1}{2}$ (half year June–Dec.) = £20
       £800 × $\tfrac{10}{100}$ × $\tfrac{1}{4}$ (quarter year Sept.–Dec.) = £20
       Total = £40

   Total interest (£100 + £80 + £40) = £220

2. *Interest on Current Acount debit balances*
                    £
     Jean 5% of £2 400 = 120
     Rose 5% of £200 = 10
            Total   = 130

b

Capital Accounts

Dr.								Cr.
	Jean	Jack	Rose			Jean £	Jack £	Rose £
				19–1				
				1 Jan	Balance b/d	40 000	30 000	10 000

Current Accounts

Dr.								Cr.
		Jean £	Jack £	Rose £		Jean £	Jack £	Rose £
19–1					19–1			
1 Jan.	Balance b/d	2 400	—	200	1 Jan	Balance b/d	—	3 500	—
31 Dec.	Interest on Current Accounts	120		10	31 Dec.	Interest on Capital	4 000	3 000	1 000
	Drawings a/c	2 900	2 680	1 640		Salary	—	350	—
	Balance c/d	16 580	22 570	18 750		Commission	—	—	16 000
						Share of profit	18 000	14 400	3 600
		22 000	25 250	20 600			22 000	25 250	20 600
					31 Dec.	Balance b/d	16 580	22 570	18 750

d

Drawings Accounts

Dr.								Cr.
		Jean £	Jack £	Rose £		Jean £	Jack £	Rose £
19–1					19–1			
30 Jun.	Bank	1 600	800	400	31 Dec.	Current Accounts	2 900	2 680	1 640
30 Sept.	Bank	800	1 600	800					
31 Dec.	Bank	400	200	400					
	Interest (Note 1)	100	80	40					
		2 900	2 680	1 640			2 900	2 680	1 640

e

Jean, Jack and Rose
Balance sheet (extract) as at 31 December 19–1

	£	£
TOTAL NET ASSETS		137 900*
Financed by:		
Capital Accounts		
Jean	40 000	
Jack	30 000	
Rose	10 000	
		80 000
Current Accounts		
Jean	16 580	
Jack	22 570	
Rose	18 750	
		57 900
CAPITAL EMPLOYED		137 900

* Total net assets must always equal capital employed.

Note
Sometimes one partner is guaranteed a minimum share of profits from the partnership. In this case the guaranteed amount is deducted from the profit after the other deductions have been made and the balance is then divided among the other partners in their respective profit-sharing ratios.

If, in the above example, Jack was guaranteed a minimum share of the profits amounting to £18 000, there would only be £18 000 left to share between Jean and Rose in the ratio of 5:1.

Therefore Jean would get $\frac{5}{6}$ of £18 000 = £15 000
Rose would get $\frac{1}{6}$ of £18 000 = £3 000

Partners' balance sheet

The partners' balance sheet will be very like the sole trader's balance sheet except that there will be separate Capital Accounts and Current Accounts for each partner.

Complete pro-forma partnership balance sheet of A, B, C

	Cost	Depreciation to date	Net	Total
	£	£	£	£
Fixed assets				
1. _____				
2. _____				
3. _____				
4. _____				

Add
Current assets   £   £
1. _____
2. _____
3. _____
4. _____
                                                      _____
Less
Current liabilities
1. _____
2. _____
                                                      _____   _____
Working capital
TOTAL NET ASSETS   ═══════
Financed by:
Capital Accounts
A   _____
B   _____
C   _____   _____
Current Accounts (if Credit)
A   _____
B   _____
C   _____   _____
Long-term liabilities
1.   _____
2.   _____   _____
CAPITAL EMPLOYED   ═══════

Exercises Set 10

1. Adam and Bob are in partnership. The partnership agreement states that:
   (a) capitals are fixed at £50 000 and £30 000 respectively
   (b) interest on capitals is to be allowed at 5 per cent p.a.
   (c) partners share profits: A, $\frac{5}{8}$; B, $\frac{3}{8}$.

   Net profit for the year, before allowing interest on capital, was £84 000.

   Prepare the Partnership Profit and Loss Appropriation Account and each partner's Capital and Current Account.

2. Carol, Dolores and Evelyn are in partnership sharing profits and losses 3:2:1. On 1 January their Capital Accounts showed balances of £30 000, £20 000 and £10 000 respectively. Interest on capital is allowed at 5 per cent p.a. Dolores is to get a salary of £5 000 p.a. and Evelyn, the sales manager, is to get a commission of £2 000 p.a. Profits as determined in the Profit and Loss Account amounted to £37 000 for the year ended 31 December. Show the Profit and Loss Appropriation Account and partners' Capital and Current Accounts as at 31 December.

3. Tom, Dick and Harry are partners sharing profits and losses in proportion to their capitals which at 1 January 19–1 were £60 000, £40 000 and £20 000 respectively. Interest on capital is allowed at 5 per cent p.a. and on Current Account credit balances at the same rate. Harry is manager of the firm and as such has a salary of £10 000 p.a. and is guaranteed a minimum share of the profits of £15 000 each year,

the shortage, if any, to be made up by Tom and Dick in their profit-sharing ratios. The Current Account balances at 1 January 19–1 were: Tom, £5 000 (Cr.); Dick, £3 000 (Cr.); Harry, nil. The profit for the year, before allowing for the above, amounted to £76 400.

Show Profit and Loss Appropriation Account for the year ended 31 December 19–1 and each partners' Current Account at that date.

4 Dermot, Erick and Frank are partners sharing profits and losses 2:2:1. On 1 January 19–1 their Capital Accounts showed £20 000, £20 000 and £10 000 respectively. On the same date their Current Accounts showed the following balances: Dermot, £1 800 (Cr.); Erick, £800 (Dr.); Frank, £1 200 (Cr.).

The partnership agreement states:
(a) capitals are fixed
(b) interest on capital is allowed at 10 per cent per annum
(c) interest at 5 per cent per annum is charged and allowed on Current Account balances at 1 January each year
(d) Frank is entitled to a salary of £12 450.

The accounts for the year, before allowing for the above, showed a loss of £40 000.

Show:
a Profit and Loss Account (appropriation section) for year ended 31 December 19–1
b partners' Capital Accounts
c partners' Current Accounts.

5 Karl, Lester and Morgan are partners sharing profits and losses 3:2:1. Their capitals are £30 000, £20 000 and £10 000 respectively. The partnership agreement states
(a) 'that partners are entitled to interest on capital at 5 per cent p.a.',
(b) 'that interest at 5 per cent p.a. shall be charged on drawings made by the partners in anticipation of profits',
(c) 'that no interest is to be allowed or charged on partners' Current Account balances',
(d) 'that final accounts be prepared at 31 December in each year'.

The Current Account balances at 1 January 19–5 were: Karl, £7 000 (Cr.); Lester, £5 000 (Cr.); Morgan, £2 000 (Dr.).

Drawings for the year were:

	Karl £	Lester £	Morgan £
31 March	4 000	2 000	2 000
30 June	2 000	1 000	1 000
30 September	3 000	2 000	3 000

Profits before adjustments amounted to £60 040 for the year.

Show Profit and Loss Appropriation Account for year ended 31 December 19–5, and partners' Capital, Current and Drawings Accounts.

6 Ann, Bill and Carl are in partnership sharing profits and losses in the ratio 3:2:1 respectively.

Note the following:
(a) Capital Account balances, which are fixed at 1 January 19-6, were:
Ann £40 000
Bill £20 000
Carl £10 000
(b) Current Account balances on the same date were:
Ann £4 000 (Cr.)
Bill £2 000 (Cr.)
Carl £6 000 (Dr.)
(c) Interest is to be charged at 10 per cent per annum on drawings which were as follows:

	Ann	Bill	Carl
30 June	£2 000	£1 000	£1 000
30 September	£4 000	£4 000	£2 000

(d) Carl is to get a salary of £10 000 per annum.
(e) Ann is entitled to a commission of £2 500.
(f) Bill is entitled to a guaranteed income of £20 000.
(g) Partners are entitled to 10 per cent interest on capital.
(h) Net profit for the year, before appropriations, amounted to £55 000.

Show:
a Profit and Loss Appropriation Account for year ended 31 December 19-6
b partners' Capital, Current and Drawings Accounts for the year.

7 Pen and Ink are in partnership, and in 1983 their firm made a profit of £25 000. The partners have agreed to share profits as follows:
(a) Each partner is to receive 10 per cent interest on the balance on his Capital Account at 1 January.
(b) A salary of £3 000 per annum is to be paid to Pen, and one of £9 000 to Ink.
(c) During 1983 Pen withdrew £10 000 and Ink £12 000. Interest is to be charged on drawings; the charges for 1983 are Pen £300 and Ink £350.
(d) Any residue of profit is to be shared: Pen, three-fifths and Ink, two-fifths.
At 1 January 1983 the balances shown in the firm's books were:

	Pen £	Ink £
Capital Account	50 000	15 000
Current Account (credit balances)	3 000	4 500

The Capital Account balances are to remain unchanged.

Prepare the firm's Appropriation Account and the separate Current Account of each partner for 1983.

[*Royal Society of Arts, II, March 1985*]

8 The following information is provided in respect of Brief, Court and Deane who have been in business together for many years:
1. The partnership agreement includes the following provisions:
   (a) Interest on loans at 13 per cent per annum.
   (b) Interest on fixed capital at 10 per cent per annum.
   (c) No interest allowed on Current Account balances.
   (d) Interest charged at 5 per cent on drawings for the year.

(e) Deane is to receive a salary of £3 000 to compensate him for the fact that he works weekends.
(f) The balance of profit to be shared equally.

2. Balances at 1 January 1984 on:

	Fixed Capital Account £	Current Account £	Loan Account £
Brief	20 000	70	—
Court	15 000	30	10 000
Deane	5 000	50	—

3. Net profit for 1984 before interest charges, £28 100.

4. Drawings during 1984:
   Brief £8 000
   Court £10 000
   Deane £6 000

5. Interest charged on drawings:
   Brief £400
   Court £500
   Deane £300

Required:
a the firm's Profit and Loss Appropriation Account for 1984, taking account of the provisions of the partnership agreement
b a revised Profit and Loss Appropriation Account for 1984, assuming that the partners had failed to enter into a partnership agreement, so that the relevant provisions of the Partnership Act 1890 apply.

[*Association of Accounting Technicians, March 1983*]

9 Smith and Jones trade in partnership and agree to share profits in the ratio 3:2 respectively after allowing:
   (i) 10 per cent interest on Capital Account balances.
   (ii) Annual salaries of £7 000 for Smith and £10 000 for Jones.
All entries are to be made in the Current Accounts; the Capital Account balances are to remain unchanged.

The partners' Capital and Current Account balances at 1 January 1985 and their drawings for 1985 are:

	Capital Account £	Current Account £	Drawings £
Smith	75 000	6 250 (Cr.)	9 150
Jones	50 000	8 500 (Cr.)	12 500

a Prepare the Appropriation and Current Accounts of the partnership based on a trading profit for 1985 of £38 500.
b Show how an anticipated profit for 1986 of £20 000 would be shared between the partners.

[*Royal Society of Arts, II, March 1986*]

10 The following is the trial balance of Jack and Jill, who trade in partnership, at 31 March 1983:

	£	£
Capital Account balances 1 April 1982:		
Jack		15 000
Jill		5 000
Current Account balances 1 April 1982:		
Jack		1 500
Jill		2 500
Sales		75 000
Stock 1 April 1982	15 000	
Wages	7 250	
Rent	2 500	
Expenses	1 500	
Heat and light	600	
Debtors/creditors	7 000	5 750
Delivery costs	2 650	
Drawings:		
Jack	3 500	
Jill	4 500	
Cash	2 250	
Fixed assets	3 000	
Purchases	55 000	
	104 750	104 750

Notes
1. Stock at 31 March 1983 was valued at £20 000.
2. Depreciation of £750 is to be written off the fixed assets for the year to 31 March 1983.
3. At 31 March 1983 wages accrued amounted to £250, and rent of £500 was prepaid.
4. On 1 February 1983 the partnership ordered and paid for goods costing £350. These were recorded as purchases but were never received as they were lost by the carrier responsible for their delivery. The carrier accepted liability for the loss during March 1983 and paid full compensation of £350 in April 1983. No entries had been made in the books in respect of the loss or claim.
5. Jack took goods which had cost the firm £170 for his own use during the year. No entry has been made in the books to record this.
6. The partnership agreement provided that profits and losses should be shared equally between the partners after:
   (a) allowing annual salaries of £1 000 to Jack and £2 000 to Jill;
   (b) allowing interest of 5 per cent per annum on the balance of each partner's Capital Account; and
   (c) charging Jack £100 and Jill £150 interest on drawings.
7. The balances on the Capital Accounts shall remain unchanged, all adjustments being recorded in the Current Accounts.

Prepare the Trading, Profit and Loss and Appropriation Accounts for the Jack and Jill Partnership for the year to 31 March 1983 and the balance sheet as at that date.

[*Royal Society of Arts, II, June 1983*]

11 Ben, Ken and Len are in partnership sharing profits and losses in the ratio 3:2:1. The following is the trial balance of the partnership as at 30 September 1983:

	£	£
Bad debts provision (at 1 October 1982)		1 000
Bank and cash in hand	2 500	
Capital Accounts:		
Ben		18 000
Ken		12 000
Len		6 000
Current Accounts:		
Ben		700
Ken	500	
Len		300
Debtors and creditors	23 000	35 000
Depreciation (at 1 October 1982)		
Land and buildings		12 000
Motor vehicles		8 000
Drawings:		
Ben	4 000	
Ken	3 000	
Len	3 000	
Land and buildings, at cost	60 000	
Motor vehicles, at cost	20 000	
Office expenses	4 000	
Purchases	85 000	
Rates	4 000	
Sales		150 000
Selling expenses	14 000	
Stock (at 1 October 1982)	20 000	
	243 000	243 000

You are provided with the following additional information:
1. Stock at 30 September 1983 was valued at £30 000.
2. Fixed assets are written off at the following rates:
   Land and buildings   5% per annum on cost
   Motor vehicles   20% per annum on cost
3. At 30 September 1983 an amount of £1 775 was owing for selling expenses.
4. Rates were prepaid by £2 000 as at 30 September 1983.
5. A certain bad debt of £500 is to be written off.
6. The bad debts provision is to be made equal to 5 per cent of outstanding debtors as at 30 September 1983.
7. The partnership agreement covers the following appropriations:
   (a) Len is to be allowed a salary of £6 000 per annum.
   (b) Interest of 10 per cent per annum is allowed on the partners' Capital Account balances.
   (c) No interest is allowed on the partners' Current Accounts.
   (d) No interest is charged on the partners' drawings.

a Prepare the partners' Trading, Profit and Loss and Profit and Loss Appropriation Accounts for the year to 30 September 1983.
b Write up the partners' Current Accounts for the year to 30 September 1983, and bring down the balances as at 1 October 1983.
c Prepare the partnership balance sheet at 30 September 1983.

[*Association of Accounting Technicians, December 1983*]

12 Ray and Mond are in partnership sharing profits and losses in the ratio 2:1. The following trial balance has been extracted from the books of the partnership as at 31 May 1983:

	Dr. £	Cr. £
Cash at bank	400	
Accumulated depreciation on furniture (at 1 June 1982)		2 000
Furniture, at cost	4 000	
Gross profit for the year		35 000
Office expenses	10 000	
Partners' Capital Accounts (at 1 June 1982):		
Ray		20 000
Mond		10 000
Partners' Current Accounts (at 1 June 1982):		
Ray		5 000
Mond		2 000
Partners' drawings for the year:		
Ray	10 000	
Mond	9 000	
Premises, at cost	28 000	
Provision for doubtful debts		400
Rates	5 000	
Stock (at 31 May 1983)	1 500	
Trade creditors		6 000
Trade debtors	12 500	
	80 400	80 400

Notes
1. Mond is entitled to a salary of £6 000 per annum; no interest is payable or chargeable on either the partners' Capital or Current Accounts.
2. Depreciation is to be charged on the furniture at a rate of 10 per cent per annum on cost.
3. A bad debt of £500 is to be written off.
4. The provision for doubtful debts is to be made equal to 5 per cent of trade debtors as at 31 May 1983.

a Prepare the Profit and Loss, and the Profit and Loss Appropriation Accounts for the year to 31 May 1983.
b Compile the partners' Current Accounts for the year to 31 May 1983.
c Prepare the partnership balance sheet as at 31 May 1983.
[*Association of Accounting Technicians, June 1983*]

13 James White, who has been in business as a baker for several years, was joined in partnership by his former manager, David Green, as from 1 April 1983.

Under the partnership agreement, White's business is valued at £60 000 and was transferred to the partnership as his initial capital; at the same time Green paid £20 000 into the partnership for the credit of his Capital Account.

The partnership agreement also included the following items:
1. A Goodwill Account is not to be maintained in the partnership books of account.

2. Interest on partners' capital will be credited to partners at the rate of 10 per cent per annum.
3. Green is to be credited with a salary of £5 000 per annum.
4. The balance of profits and losses will be shared between White and Green in the ratio of 3:2.
5. A Capital and a Current Account is to be maintained for each partner.

The summarised balance sheet as at 31 March 1983 of James White was as follows:

	£	£
Fixed assets – Buildings, plant and machinery:		
At cost less depreciation to date		30 000
Net current assets:		
Stock	5 000	
Debtors	6 000	
Balance at bank	2 000	
	13 000	
Less Creditors	4 000	
		9 000
		39 000
Capital Account – at 31 March 1983		39 000

The following information for the year ended 31 March 1984 has been extracted from the partnership accounting records:

	£
Net profit	18 000
Cash drawings:	
James White	10 000
David Green	6 000

Write up the following accounts for the year ended 31 March 1984: Profit and Loss Appropriation Account; Capital Account for each partner; and Current Account for each partner.

[*Association of Accounting Technicians, pilot, 1985*]

14 Red, Amber and Green are partners in a commercial business. They share profits and losses 3:2:1 respectively. The partnership agreement allows them interest on capital at 6 per cent whilst interest of 10 per cent is allowed or charged on current account balances at the beginning of the year.

Amber is allowed an annual salary of £4 655.

Agency commission of 5 per cent of the net profit of the year, before charging the commission, is to be provided.

The following balances appeared in the books at 31 December:

	£
Debtors	11 840
Fixtures and fittings at cost	4 800
Sales	105 929
Operating expenses	19 989
Capital 1 January:	
Red	20 000
Amber	16 000

	£
Green	8 000
Purchases	62 460
Drawings:	
Red	1 886
Green	3 274
Premises at cost	32 000
Stock 1 January	10 880
Provision for doubtful debts	700
Current Account balances 1 January:	
Red (Dr.)	1 000
Amber (Cr.)	5 400
Green (Dr.)	2 200
Vehicles at cost	7 600
Creditors	3 980
Bank	2 080

The partners agree to depreciate vehicles at 15 per cent per annum.

Stock at 31 December is valued at £12 240.

You are required to prepare the partners' Current Accounts and the Trading and Profit and Loss Accounts for the year to 31 December and a balance sheet at that date.

[Pitman Intermediate]

15 Oak, Ash and Thorn were in partnership carrying on a retail business. The partnership agreement stated:
(a) Salaries to be credited at the end of each year:
Oak £1 500; Ash £900; Thorn £600
(b) Interest of 6 per cent per annum to be allowed on the balances at the credit of their respective Capital Accounts at the beginning of the year.
(c) No interest to be charged on drawings.
(d) After charging partnership salaries and interest on capital, profit and losses to be divided in the proportion: Oak 50 per cent, Ash 30 per cent, Thorn 20 per cent, with the proviso that Thorn's share in any year (exclusive of salary and interest) should not be less than £1 378, any deficiency to be borne in profit-sharing ratio by the other two partners.

At 31 December, the end of the trading year, the trial balance of the firm included the following:

	£
Drawings:	
Oak	2 550
Ash	1 650
Thorn	1 350
Partners' Capital Accounts at 1 January:	
Oak	12 000
Ash	7 500
Thorn	4 500
Partners' Current Accounts at 1 January:	
Oak	2 400 Cr.
Ash	1 800 Cr.
Thorn	1 200 Cr.

Net profit (before partners' salaries and interest on capital) is £9 930.

168 Partnership ledger and final accounts

You are required to show the partners' Current Accounts in columnar form for the year ended 31 December and the Appropriation Account for the year showing the distribution of profit.

[Pitman Intermediate]

16 Ray Dyo, Harry Ull and Val Vez are in partnership, trading under the name of Radtel Services, as radio and television suppliers and repairers, sharing profits and losses in the ratio one-half, one-third and one-sixth, respectively. Val Vez works full-time in the business with responsibility for general administration for which she receives a partnership salary of £4 000 per annum.

All partners receive interest on capital at 5 per cent per annum and interest on any loans made to the firm, also at 5 per cent per annum.

It has also been agreed that Val Vez should receive not less than £4 000 per annum in addition to her salary. Any deficiency between this guaranteed figure and her actual aggregate of interest on capital, plus residual profit (or less residual loss) less interest on drawings, is to be borne by Dyo and Ull in the ratio in which they share profits and losses; such deficiency can be recouped by Dyo and Ull at the earliest opportunity during the next two consecutive years provided that Val Vez does not receive less than the guaranteed minimum described above. During the year ended 30 September 1983, Dyo and Ull had jointly contributed a deficiency of £1 500.

Radtel Services rents two sets of premises – one, a workshop where repairs are carried out, the other, a shop from which radio and television sets are sold. The offices are situated above the shop and are accounted for as part of the shop.

The workshop and shop are regarded as separate departments and managed, respectively, by Phughes and Sokkitt who are each remunerated by a basic salary plus a commission of one-ninth of their departments' profits *after* charging their commission.

On 30 September 1984, the trial balance of the firm was:

	£	£
Stocks at 1 October 1983:		
shop (radio and television sets)	19 750	
workshop (spares, components, etc.)	8 470	
Purchases:		
radio and television sets	155 430	
spares, components, etc.	72 100	
Turnover:		
sales of radio and television sets		232 600
repair charges		127 000
Wages and salaries (employees):		
shop and offices	54 640	
workshop	18 210	
Prepaid expenses (at 30 September 1984)	640	
Accrued expenses (at 30 September 1984)		3 160
Provision for doubtful debts at 1 October 1983		920
Rent and rates:		
shop and offices	7 710	
workshop	8 450	
Stationery, telephones, insurance		
shop and offices	2 980	
workshop	1 020	

	£	£
Heating and lighting:		
shop and offices	4 640	
workshop	3 950	
Debtors	4 460	
Creditors		15 260
Bank	48 540	
Cash	960	
Other general expenses:		
shop and offices	3 030	
workshop	2 830	
Depreciation:		
shop and offices (including vehicles)	2 400	
workshop	2 580	
Shop fittings (cost)	17 060	
Workshop tools and equipment (cost)	55 340	
Vehicles (cost)	27 210	
Discount received:		
shop		420
workshop		390
Bank loan (repayable in 1988)		15 000
Loan from Harry Ull		10 000
Capital Accounts:		
R. Dyo		40 000
H. Ull		40 000
V. Vez		20 000
Current Accounts (after drawings have been debited):		
R. Dyo	290	
H. Ull		1 040
V. Vez		920
Loan interest:		
bank loan	2 400	
loan from H. Ull	500	
Provision for depreciation:		
shop fittings		3 190
workshop tools and equipment		10 020
vehicles		5 670
	525 590	525 590

The following matters are to be taken into account:
1. Manager's commissions.
2. Partnership salary (Vez).
3. Interest on partners' Capital Accounts (these have not altered during the year).
4. Interest on partners' drawings: Dyo £70; Ull £30; Vez £20.
5. Closing stocks: shop £31 080; workshop £10 220.
6. Provision for doubtful debts at 30 September 1984, £540.
7. Residual profits/losses.

Note. Loan interest and the movement in the provision for bad debts are regarded as 'shop' items.

a   Prepare columnar departmental Trading and Profit and Loss Accounts and a Partnership Appropriation Account for the year ended 30 September 1984 and the partnership balance sheet at that date.
b   Complete the posting of the partners' Current Accounts for the year.
[*Association of Certified Accountants, Level 1, December 1984*]

17 Nail, Tack and Rivet entered into partnership as electrical contractors on 1 January 1985. A formal partnership agreement was drawn up which included the following provisions:
A   Interest on fixed capital to be allowed at 10 per cent per annum.
B   Partnership salaries to be allowed as follows:

Nail	£8 000 per annum
Tack	£5 000 per annum
Rivet	£5 000 per annum

C   Any partner's loan will carry interest at 8 per cent per annum.
D   Nail, Tack and Rivet are to share profits and losses in the ratio 2:1:1 respectively.

At the commencement of the partnership, the following assets were introduced, all amounts to be regarded as fixed capital.

	Cash £	Premises £	Equipment £
Nail	15 000	—	—
Tack	6 000	14 000	2 000
Rivet	10 000	—	1 000

In addition, on 1 January 1985, Rivet made a loan of £8 000 to the partnership, repayable at the end of 1988.

The records kept for the first year were incomplete but, at the year end, the following information is obtained:
1. Cash received during the year from the settlement of customers' accounts: £159 200.
2. During the year a customer had gone into liquidation, and the entire balance of the account, £1 620, had been written off.
3. In July 1985 an electrical installation (value £285) had been made by the partnership at Tack's private residence. No payment has been made by Tack.
4. Cash sums paid by the partnership during the year were:

		£
(a)	To suppliers for materials	74 200
(b)	To employees for wages and salaries	29 300
(c)	For rates and insurances	5 980
(d)	For other costs	9 174
(e)	To Rivet: 6 months' loan interest	320

The following should also be taken into account:
(i)   Equipment is to be depreciated at 10 per cent per annum.
(ii) £1 090 is owed to suppliers at 31 December 1985 for materials purchased.
(iii) At 31 December 1985, £835 of unused materials remain in stock.
(iv) Nail paid £450 staff wages from his own pocket in the last week of the financial year. This sum has not yet been reimbursed.
(v)   £986 is owed by customers.

Prepare the Trading and Profit and Loss Account (including appropriation section) of Nail, Tack and Rivet for the year ended 31 December 1985.
[*London Chamber of Commerce and Industry, Intermediate, spring 1986*]

18 The following information is provided in respect of Able, Baker and Charles who have been in business together for many years:
1. Their partnership agreement includes the following provisions:
   (a) Partners will be paid interest on fixed capital at 10 per cent per annum.
   (b) Able is to receive a commission of 2 per cent of the net trading profit remaining after interest on capital has been deducted but before any other appropriations have been made.
   (c) Baker receives a salary of £8 000 p.a. and Charles receives a salary of £6 000 p.a.
   (d) On partners' drawings interest is to be charged as follows:

Able	£400
Baker	£300
Charles	£300

   (e) The balance of profits and losses is to be shared as follows: Able one-half, Baker one-third, and Charles one-sixth.
2. On the 31 October 1986 the balances on the partners' Capital Accounts were as follows:

Able	£40 000
Baker	£30 000
Charles	£30 000

   Drawings during the year were:

Able	£10 000
Baker	£8 000
Charles	£8 000

   Net trading profit for the year ended 31 October 1986 was £30 000.

a Prepare the firm's Profit and Loss Appropriation Account for the year ended 31 October 1986 taking account of the provisions of the partnership agreement.

b Prepare a Profit and Loss Appropriation Account for the same period assuming that no agreement existed and the conditions of the Partnership Act 1890 apply.

[*Royal Society of Arts, II, November 1986*]

19 The following list of balances as at 30 September 1986 has been extracted from the books of Peter James and Angus Victor who are trading in partnership:

	£
Freehold property:	
at cost at 30 September 1985	30 000
provision for depreciation at 30 September 1985	6 000
Fixtures and fittings:	
at cost at 30 September 1985	18 000
provision for depreciation at 30 September 1985	9 600
Stock at 30 September 1986	11 000
Debtors	4 600
Creditors	5 800
Balance at bank	2 700
Gross profit	39 000
Establishment and administrative expenses	9 100
Sales and distribution expenses	13 000
Capital Accounts at 30 September 1985:	
Peter James	25 000
Angus Victor	15 000

	£
Current Accounts at 30 September 1985:	
Peter James	6 000 credit
Angus Victor	2 300 debit
Loan from Peter James	10 000
Drawings:	
Peter James	15 700
Angus Victor	10 000

Additional information for the year ended 30 September 1986:
1. Interest at the rate of 10 per cent per annum is payable annually in arrears on the loan from Peter James; the loan was received on 1 April 1986.
2. All sales produce a uniform rate of gross profit.
3. Provision is to be made for depreciation as follows:
   Freehold property   5 per cent per annum on cost
   Fixtures and fittings   10 per cent per annum on cost
4. Electricity charges accrued due at 30 September 1986 amounted to £360.
   Note. The electricity charges are included in establishment and administrative expenses.
5. Two-thirds of sales took place in the second half of the year.
6. No provision has been made in the accounts for a sales commission of 2 per cent of gross profit payable to sales staff as from 1 April 1986.
7. Provision is to be made for a salary of £10 000 per annum to be credited to Angus Victor as from 1 April 1986.
8. Partners are to be credited with interest on the balances of their Capital Accounts at the rate of 5 per cent per annum.

a   Prepare the Partnership Profit and Loss Account and Profit and Loss Appreciation Account for the year ended 30 September 1986.
b   Prepare the balance sheet as at 30 September 1986.
c   Indicate one significant matter revealed in the accounting statements prepared which should be brought to the attention of the partners.

[*Association of Accounting Technicians, December 1986*]

11 Formation of partnership I: treatment of goodwill

Reasons for bringing in a new partner include the following:
(a) The existing partners may wish to expand the business and may need extra capital.
(b) As well as the additional capital, the new partner may have something to offer, such as expertise or business connections.
(c) The new partner may already be a valuable employee of the business, and the existing partners may invite him to become a partner to reward him for past services or to ensure he stays with the partnership.

When a new partner is introduced changes will have to be made in the partnership agreement. Very often, at this time, the existing partners will value the goodwill of the existing business and insist on the incoming partner paying for his share of it. Existing partners may also revalue the assets of the old firm at this time. All these changes will affect the capitals of the existing partners.

Goodwill

Goodwill has been defined as 'nothing more than the probability that the old customers will resort to the old place.' It may be due to:
(a) The personality of the proprietor.
(b) The good name of the product or service.
(c) The existence of trade marks or patents.
(d) The advantages accruing to the location of the business.
(e) The possession of a monopoly in the supply of a particular commodity.

Goodwill is an asset, even though an intangible one, as shown by the fact that when buying a business the purchaser very often has to pay an amount in excess of the net book value of the assets (i.e. book value of assets less liabilities taken over).

EXAMPLE

A business with assets valued at	£200 000
and liabilities valued at	£40 000
is bought for £240 000. The net (book) value is	£160 000
The purchase price is	£240 000
The goodwill has cost the buyer	£80 000

Formation of partnership I: treatment of goodwill

In this case it will be recorded as an asset in the ledger accounts and shown as an asset in the balance sheet. It is called an *intangible* asset to distinguish it from both the fixed and current assets. It is shown on the balance sheet after the tangible fixed assets and is added to them.

Methods of valuing goodwill

Method I   Average net profit

In this method the *average* net profit over a given number of years is found by adding up the net profits and dividing that figure by the given number of years. This figure is then multiplied by an agreed figure (called 'number of years' purchase') to find the value of goodwill.

EXAMPLE

Let us suppose that goodwill is to be valued at three years' purchase of the average profits over the past four years. Profits for the past four years were £10 000, £12 000, £16 000 and £22 000.

£10 000 + £12 000 + £16 000 + £22 000 = £60 000
Divide by 4   = £15 000 average
Multiply by 3   = £45 000 (value of goodwill)

Method II   Return on capital

Another method of calculating goodwill is to deduct from the average net profit the proprietor's remuneration in a similar business. This is regarded as the return on capital invested by him. Calculate what investment will produce this amount each year as a minimum rate of return on capital, say 15 per cent p.a. (i.e. 5 per cent for risk element at 10 per cent for pure interest).

To find the value of goodwill deduct from the figure obtained the value of net assets.

EXAMPLE

Average net profit	£24 000
Less Remuneration in similar business	£6 000
Return on capital	£18 000

£120 000 invested at 15 per cent p.a. will produce £18 000.
Assume the net assets are worth £112 000 then
Value of goodwill = £120 000 − £112 000 = £8 000.

Method III   Super profit

Deduct from average net profit:

(a)   owner's salary in a similar business and
(b)   interest on capital invested (at, for example, 15 per cent p.a.) in assets.

The balance will be super profit.

Now calculate what investment will produce this amount yearly at a given percentage per annum (say 15 per cent p.a.). The figure arrived at will be the value of goodwill.

EXAMPLE

Average net profit		£48 000
Less Salary in similar business	£12 000	
Less Interest on capital invested in assets (say £224 000) at 15 per cent p.a.	£33 600	£45 600
Super profit		£2 400

Calculate how much invested at 15 per cent p.a. will provide a yearly sum of £2 400. The answer is £16 000.

∴ Value of goodwill = £16 000.

Treatment of goodwill in the books

Method I
A Goodwill Account is opened for the agreed amount and the old partners' Capital Accounts are credited in their old profit-sharing ratios.

Entries:
Debit Goodwill Account with agreed value of goodwill.
Credit old partners' Capital Accounts in old profit-sharing ratios.

Method II
The old partners withdraw an agreed amount of cash which is charged to a Goodwill Account.

Entries:
Debit Goodwill Account.
Credit Bank Account.

Methods which do not involve a Goodwill Account

Method III
The incoming partner pays a cash premium for his share of the goodwill. This amount is drawn out by the old partners in their old profit-sharing ratios.

Entries:
1. Debit Bank Account } with the amount paid
   Credit Capital Accounts of old partners } as premium in old profit-sharing rates

2. Debit old partners' Capital Accounts } with amount drawn out by
   Credit Bank Account } existing partners

The only value this method has is that the premium for goodwill is seen going through the books.

Method IV
The incoming partner pays a premium for his share of the goodwill. The cash is retained in the business and is credited to the old partners' Capital Accounts in their old profit-sharing ratios.

Entries:
Debit Bank Account.
Credit old partners' Capital Accounts.

Method V
The premium for goodwill, payable by the new partner, is paid direct to the old partners and no entries are made in the partnership books.

Note. Method IV is the more usual method, as it has the advantage of retaining the additional cash in the business while at the same time compensating the existing partners.

Revaluation of assets

As already mentioned, when additional partners are being brought in, the existing partners take the opportunity to revise the value of individual assets either upwards or downwards.

To record a revaluation it is easier to open up a Revaluation Account in the books.

For items whose value has increased

Entries:
Debit each Asset Account } with the increase in its value.
Credit Revaluation Account

Debit Revaluation Account } with profit on revaluation
Credit old partners' Capital Accounts } shared in old profit-sharing ratios.

For items whose value is reduced

Entries:
Debit Revaluation Account } with the reduction in its value.
Credit each Asset Account

Debit old partners' Capital Accounts } with loss on revaluation
Credit Revaluation Account } shared in old profit-sharing ratios.

Procedure for tackling an examination question of this nature

Examination questions usually ask for journal, ledger accounts and new balance sheet.

Step 1

Open all accounts as per last balance sheet.

Deal with revaluation of assets (if required). Open Revaluation Account (if required), crediting or debiting old partners' accounts in their *old* profit-sharing ratios with net increases or decreases in value of existing assets – see above for entries.

Step 2

Deal with introduction of the new partner by means of journal entries in accordance with *new* agreement among all the partners. This will involve:

(a) The assets (including cash) brought in as capital.
    Debit (appropriate) Asset Accounts.
    Credit new partner's Capital Account.
(b) Goodwill – this will involve one of the methods of treatment specified above.
(c) Post journal entries to appropriate accounts.
(d) Balance the accounts as necessary.
(e) Prepare opening balance sheet of new partnership from ledger accounts.

A SIMPLE EXAMPLE (involving all the steps)
Ashley and Bell are partners sharing profits and losses equally. Their balance sheet on 1 January 19–1 was as follows:

Ashley and Bell
Balance sheet as at 1 January 19–1

	Cost	Depreciation to date	Net	Total
Fixed assets	£	£	£	£
Land and buildings	100 000		100 000	
Plant and machinery	50 000		50 000	
Fixtures and fittings	20 000		20 000	
Office equipment	10 000		10 000	
Motor vehicles	40 000		40 000	
	220 000		220 000	220 000
Current assets	£	£		
Stock	18 000			
Trade debtors	12 000			
Cash at bank	3 000	33 000		
Less Current liabilities				
Creditors		23 000		
Working capital				10 000
TOTAL NET ASSETS				230 000
Financed by:				
Capital Accounts				
Ashley		115 000		
Bell		115 000		
CAPITAL EMPLOYED				230 000

178 Formation of partnership I: treatment of goodwill

On 2 January they agree to admit Charles as a partner on the following conditions:
(a) Prior to the admission of Charles, the assets of Ashley and Bell are to be revalued as follows:

Land and buildings	£200 000	Plant and machinery	£45 000
Fixtures and fittings	£18 000	Office equipment	£9 000
Motor vehicles	£30 000	Stock	£20 000

(b) Charles is to contribute capital of £50 000 consisting of:
cash, £25 000; vehicles, £15 000; stock, £10 000.
(c) Charles is to pay a cash premium of £20 000 for his share of the goodwill, the cash to be retained in the business.
(d) In future, profits and losses are to be shared:
Ashley $\frac{2}{5}$ Bell $\frac{2}{5}$ Charles $\frac{1}{5}$

a   Record these transactions in the books of the new firm.
b   Show the opening balance sheet of the new partnership.

Solution
a   **Journal entries**

19–1			Dr. £	Cr. £
1 Jan.	Revaluation Account		18 000	
		Plant and Machinery Account		5 000
		Fixtures and Fittings Account		2 000
		Office Equipment Account		1 000
		Motor Vehicles Account		10 000
	(Being reduction in value of assets on revaluation)			
	Land and Buildings Account		100 000	
	Stock Account		2 000	
		Revaluation Account		102 000
	(Being increase in value of assets on revaluation)			
	Revaluation Account		84 000	
		Capital Account: Ashley		42 000
		Capital Account: Bell		42 000
	(Being profit on revaluation shared by existing partners)			
2 Jan.	Bank Account		25 000	
	Vehicles Account		15 000	
	Stock Account		10 000	
		Capital Account: Charles		50 000
	(Being capital contributed by new partner: Charles)			
	Bank Account		20 000	
		Capital Account: Ashley		10 000
		Capital Account: Bell		10 000
	(Being cash premium paid by Charles for his share of the goodwill – the cash to be retained in the business)			

Revaluation of assets

Dr.		Land and Buildings Account			Cr.
19–1		£	19–1		£
1 Jan.	Balance b/d	100 000	2 Jan.	Balance c/d	200 000
	Revaluation Account	100 000			
		200 000			200 000
2 Jan.	Balance b/d	200 000			

Dr.		Plant and Machinery Account			Cr.
19–1		£	19–1		£
1 Jan.	Balance b/d	50 000	1 Jan.	Revaluation Account	5 000
			2 Jan.	Balance c/d	45 000
		50 000			50 000
2 Jan.	Balance b/d	45 000			

Dr.		Fixtures and Fittings Account			Cr.
19–1		£	19–1		£
1 Jan.	Balance b/d	20 000	1 Jan.	Revaluation Account	2 000
			2 Jan.	Balance c/d	18 000
		20 000			20 000
2 Jan.	Balance b/d	18 000			

Dr.		Office Equipment Account			Cr.
19–1		£	19–1		£
1 Jan.	Balance b/d	10 000	1 Jan.	Revaluation Account	1 000
			2 Jan.	Balance c/d	9 000
		10 000			10 000
2 Jan.	Balance b/d	9 000			

Dr.		Motor Vehicles Account			Cr.
19–1		£	19–1		£
1 Jan.	Balance b/d	40 000	1 Jan.	Revaluation Account	10 000
2 Jan.	Capital Account: Charles	15 000	2 Jan.	Balance c/d	45 000
		55 000			55 000
2 Jan.	Balance b/d	45 000			

Dr.		Stock Account			Cr.
19–1		£	19–1		£
1 Jan.	Balance b/d	18 000	2 Jan.	Balance c/d	30 000
	Revaluation Account	2 000			
2 Jan.	Capital Account: Charles	10 000			
		30 000			30 000
2 Jan.	Balance b/d	30 000			

180 Formation of partnership I: treatment of goodwill

Dr.	Trade Debtors Account			Cr.
19–1		£		
1 Jan. Balance b/d		12 000		

Dr.		Bank Account			Cr.
19–1		£	19–1		£
1 Jan. Balance b/d		3 000	2 Jan. Balance c/d		48 000
2 Jan. Capital Account: Charles		25 000			
Premium: Charles (£20 000)					
Capital Account: Ashley		10 000			
Capital Account: Bell		10 000			
		48 000			48 000
2 Jan. Balance b/d		48 000			

Dr.	Creditors Account		Cr.
		19–1	£
		1 Jan. Balance b/d	23 000

Dr.			Capital Accounts					Cr.
19–1	Ashley	Bell	Charles	19–1		Ashley	Bell	Charles
	£	£	£			£	£	£
2 Jan. Balance c/d	167 000	167 000	50 000	1 Jan. Balance b/d		115 000	115 000	—
				Revaluation a/c		42 000	42 000	—
				Premium:				
				Charles		10 000	10 000	—
				2 Jan. Bank				25 000
				Vehicles a/c				15 000
				Stock a/c				10 000
	167 000	167 000	50 000			167 000	167 000	50 000
				2 Jan Balance b/d		167 000	167 000	50 000

Dr.	Revaluation Account			Cr.
19–1		£	19–1	£
1 Jan. Plant and Machinery Account		5 000	1 Jan. Land and Buildings Account	100 000
Fixtures and Fittings Account		2 000	Stock Account	2 000
Office Equipment Account		1 000		
Motor Vehicles Account		10 000		
Profit on revaluation (£84 000)				
Capital Account:				
Ashley (½)		42 000		
Bell (½)		42 000		
		102 000		102 000

b

Ashley, Bell and Charles
Balance sheet as at 2 January 19–1

	Cost	Depreciation to date	Net	Total
Fixed assets	£	£	£	£
Land and buildings	200 000		200 000	
Plant and machinery	45 000		45 000	
Fixtures and fittings	18 000		18 000	
Office equipment	9 000		9 000	
Motor vehicles	45 000		45 000	
	317 000		317 000	317 000
Add Current assets		£	£	
Stock at 2 January		30 000		
Trade debtors		12 000		
Cash at bank		48 000		
			90 000	
Less Current liabilities				
Creditors			23 000	
Working capital				67 000
TOTAL NET ASSETS				384 000
Financed by:				
Capital Accounts				
Ashley	167 000			
Bell	167 000			
Charles	50 000			
CAPITAL EMPLOYED				384 000

A MORE DIFFICULT EXAMPLE

John and Paul were in partnership sharing profits and losses in the ratio of 3:2. On 1 January 19–1 their balance sheet was as follows:

Balance sheet as at 1.1.19–1

	Cost	Depreciation to date	Net	Total
Fixed assets	£	£	£	£
Premises	14 000		14 000	14 000
Current assets		£	£	
Stock		8 000		
Debtors		4 200		
Bank		3 300		
			15 500	
Less Current liabilities				
Creditors			4 500	

[*cont. over*

182 Formation of partnership I: treatment of goodwill

	£	£	£	£
Working capital				11 000
TOTAL NET ASSETS				25 000
Financed by:				
Capital				
John			16 000	
Paul			9 000	
CAPITAL EMPLOYED				25 000

On 1.1.19–1 they agreed to admit Moses as a partner on the following conditions:

(a) Moses was to bring in a capital of £6 000 consisting of premises, £4 000, stock, £1 500 and the balance in cash.
(b) Future profits and losses to be shared: Paul, one-half; John, one-third; Moses, one-sixth.
(c) The assets of the old partnership were to be revalued as follows:
Premises, £18 800; Stock, £7 500; Debtors, £3 900.
(d) Goodwill was valued at two years' purchase of the average profits in excess of £3 000 per annum over the last three years. The profits for the last three years were £3 500, £3 400 and £3 900. Moses was to pay a cash premium for his share of the goodwill. This cash was retained in the business.
(e) The capital for the new partnership was fixed at £36 000. John and Paul were to introduce, or withdraw, cash so that the capitals of all three partners would be in the same proportions as their new profit-sharing ratios.

You are required to show:
a the ledger accounts necessary to record the admission of Moses
b the balance sheet of the new partnership.

SOLUTION
a   **Ledger accounts**

Dr.			**Premises Account**			Cr.
19–1		£	19–1			£
1 Jan.	Balance b/d	14 000	1 Jan.	Balance c/d		22 800
	Revaluation Account	4 800				
	Capital Account:					
	Moses	4 000				
		22 800				22 800
1 Jan.	Balance b/d	22 800				

Dr.			**Stock Account**			Cr.
19–1		£	19–1			£
1 Jan.	Balance b/d	8 000	1 Jan.	Revaluation Account		500
	Capital Account:			Balance c/d		9 000
	Moses	1 500				
		9 500				9 500
1 Jan.	Balance b/d	9 000				

Revaluation of assets

Dr.		Debtors Account			Cr.
19–1		£	19–1		£
1 Jan.	Balance b/d	4 200	1 Jan.	Revaluation Account	300
				Balance c/d	3 900
		4 200			4 200
1 Jan.	Balance b/d	3 900			

Dr.		Revaluation Account			Cr.
19–1		£	19–1		£
1 Jan.	Stock Account	500	1 Jan.	Premises Account	4 800
	Debtors Account	300			
	Profit on revaluation (£4 000)				
	Capital Account: John (⅗)	2 400			
	Capital Account: Paul (⅖)	1 600			
		4 800			4 800

Dr.		Capital Account: John			Cr.
19–1		£	19–1		£
1 Jan.	Bank	520	1 Jan.	Balance b/d	16 000
	Balance c/d	18 000		Revaluation Account	2 400
				Bank – goodwill premium	120
		18 520			18 520
			1 Jan.	Balance b/d	18 000

Dr.		Capital Account: Paul			Cr.
19–1		£	19–1		£
1 Jan.	Balance c/d	12 000	1 Jan.	Balance b/d	9 000
				Revaluation Account	1 600
				Bank – goodwill premium	80
				Bank	1 320
		12 000			12 000
			1 Jan.	Balance b/d	12 000

Dr.		Capital Account: Moses			Cr.
19–1		£	19–1		£
1 Jan.	Balance c/d	6 000	1 Jan.	Premises Account	4 000
				Stock Account	1 500
				Bank	500
		6 000			6 000
			1 Jan.	Balance b/d	6 000

184 Formation of partnership I: treatment of goodwill

Dr.		Bank Account			Cr.
19–1		£	19–1		£
1 Jan.	Balance b/d	3 300	1 Jan.	Capital Account: John	520
	Moses – Premium for goodwill	200		Balance c/d	4 800
	Capital Account: Moses	500			
	Capital Account: Paul	1 320			
		5 320			5 320
1 Jan.	Balance b/d	4 800			

Notice that Paul has to bring in an additional £1 320 and Moses an additional £500 to bring their capitals up to £12 000 and £6 000 respectively, while John withdraws £520.

Calculation of goodwill

	£
	3 500
	3 400
	3 900
	3)10 800
Average profits	3 600
Excess over	3 000
	$600 \times 2 = £1\ 200$

Moses' share of goodwill: $\frac{1}{6} \times 1\ 200 = £200$

b   **Balance sheet of John, Paul and Moses as at 1 January 19–1**

	Cost	Depreciation to date	Net	Total
Fixed assets	£	£	£	£
Premises	22 800		22 800	22 800
Current assets		£	£	
Stock		9 000		
Debtors		3 900		
Bank		4 800		
			17 700	
Less Current liabilities				
Creditors			4 500	
Working capital				13 200
TOTAL NET ASSETS				36 000
Financed by:				
Capital Accounts				
John			18 000	
Paul			12 000	
Moses			6 000	
CAPITAL EMPLOYED				36 000

Exercises Set 11

1. Tom and James are partners sharing profits and losses equally. Their balance sheet at 31 December 19–1 read:

	£		£
Buildings	10 000	Capital Accounts:	
Plant	5 000	Tom	12 000
Fixtures and fittings	2 000	James	12 000
Stock	3 600	Creditors	4 000
Debtors	4 400		
Cash at bank	3 000		
	28 000		28 000

   On 1 January 19–2 they agreed to admit Gary as a partner on the following conditions:
   (a) Gary is to bring in capital of £6 000 in cash.
   (b) Goodwill is to be valued at £4 000 and an Account for Goodwill is to be raised in the partnership books.
   (c) Future profits and losses are to be shared: Tom, two-fifths; James, two-fifths; Gary, one-fifth.

   Show:
   a the journal entries to record the above
   b the opening balance sheet of the new partnership.

2. Ann and Brian are partners sharing profits and losses in proportion to their capitals. The balance sheet of the business on 31 January 19–1 was:

	£		£
Premises	13 000	Capital Accounts:	
Fixtures and fittings	5 000	Ann	12 000
Stock	9 000	Brian	6 000
Debtors	2 800	Current Accounts:	
Cash	200	Ann	1 200
		Brian	800
		Creditors	6 000
		Bank overdraft	4 000
	30 000		30 000

   In order to obtain additional finance, they agree to admit Clem as a partner on 1 February 19–1 with a right to one-third of future profits and losses on the following conditions:
   (a) Clem is to bring in £10 000 in cash as his capital.
   (b) A Goodwill Account is to be raised in the books of the partnership. Goodwill is to be valued at two years' purchase of the average net profits of the previous four years which were: £3 000, £3 600, £4 400 and £1 000 respectively.
   (c) Ann and Brian are to share future profits and losses, after Clem has had his share, in the same ratio as before the admission of Clem.

   a Prepare journal entries (including cash) to record these transactions in the books of the partnership.
   b If profits for the following year amounted to £19 332, how much would each partner receive?

3 Acton and Bryant are partners in a firm of auctioneers sharing profits and losses 2:1. Their Capital Accounts show balances of £10 000 and £6 000 respectively. On 1 July 19–3 they admit Crowe as a partner on condition that he brings capital of £10 000 consisting of premises valued at £6 000 and the balance in cash. In addition, he is to pay a cash premium, £1 800, for his share of the goodwill to Acton and Bryant which is drawn out by the old partners.

Show journal and ledger entries to record these transactions.

4 C and D are partners sharing profits and losses 3:1. On 1 February 19–1 their balance sheet was as follows:

Balance sheet as at 1 February 19–1

	£	£		£	£
Land and buildings	16 000		Capital Accounts		
Plant and equipment	6 000		C	24 000	
			D	8 000	
		22 000			32 000
Stock	4 000		Creditors		2 000
Debtors	2 600				
Bank	5 400				
		12 000			
		34 000			34 000

On 2 February 19–1 they agree to admit E on the following conditions:
(a) E is to introduce £8 000 as capital consisting of premises worth £7 200 and the balance in cash. In addition, E is to pay a premium for goodwill of £600 which is to be retained in the business.
(b) Future profits are to be shared: C three-fifths; D one-fifth; E one-fifth.

Record these transactions in the books of the firm and show the opening balance sheet of the new partnership.

5   Kate and Susan were partners sharing profits and losses in the ratio of 3:2. On 1.1.19–1 their balance sheet was as follows:

	Cost £	Depreciation to date £	Net £	Total £
Fixed assets				
Buildings	36 000		36 000	
Furniture and fittings	1 960		1 960	
	37 960		37 960	37 960
Current assets		£	£	
Stock		6 200		
Debtors		9 040		
Cash		400		
			15 640	
Less Current liabilities				
Creditors		6 800		
Bank		2 800		
			9 600	
Working capital				6 040
TOTAL NET ASSETS				44 000
Financed by:				
Capital				
Kate			32 000	
Susan			12 000	
CAPITAL EMPLOYED				44 000

On that date they agreed to admit Joan as a partner on the following conditions:
(a) Joan was to introduce as her capital the following: Buildings, £8 000; Stock, £2 000; Furniture, £1 600; Cash, £400.
(b) Joan was also to pay a cash premium of £2 500 for goodwill which was to be retained in the business.

Show:
a the ledger accounts necessary to record the admission of Joan
b the opening balance sheet of the new partnership.

6   Tardy and Glynn are partners sharing profits and losses in the ratio 2;1. Their balance sheet on 1 March 19–3 was as follows:

Tardy and Glynn
Balance sheet as at 1 March 19–3

	Cost	Depreciation to date	Net	Total
Fixed assets	£	£	£	£
Buildings	40 000		40 000	
Plant and machinery	15 000		15 000	
Fixtures and fittings	5 000		5 000	
Office equipment	2 500		2 500	
Motor vehicles	22 500		22 500	
	85 000		85 000	85 000
Current assets		£	£	
Stock		8 000		
Trade debtors		4 500		
Cash at bank		7 500		
			20 000	
Less Current liabilities				
Trade creditors		4 500		
Rent due		500		
			5 000	
Working capital				15 000
TOTAL NET ASSETS				100 000
Financed by:				
Capital Accounts				
Tardy			75 000	
Glynn			25 000	
CAPITAL EMPLOYED				100 000

On 2 March they agree to admit Gray into the partnership on the following terms:
(*a*)   Gray is to bring in £30 000 as his capital comprising: Motor vehicles, £9 000; Stock, £3 500, and the balance in cash.
(*b*)   Tardy and Glynn are to withdraw £6 000 in their old profit-sharing ratios. This amount is to be charged to a Goodwill Account.
(*c*)   Gray is to receive one-quarter of all future profits. Tardy and Glynn are to share the remaining profits in the same ratio as before.

You are required to:
a   show journal and ledger entries to record these transactions
b   show the opening balance sheet of the new partnership as at 2 March 19–3
c   calculate the new profit-sharing ratios.

7 Hale and Hearty are in partnership sharing profits and losses in proportion to their capitals. On 1 April 19–4 their balance sheet was as follows:

Hale and Hearty
Balance sheet as at 1 April 19–4

	Cost	Depreciation to date	Net	Total
Fixed assets	£	£	£	£
Premises	94 000		94 000	
Equipment	46 000		46 000	
Fixtures and fittings	14 000		14 000	
Motor vans	36 000		36 000	
	190 000		190 000	190 000
Current assets		£	£	
Stock		51 000		
Trade debtors		16 600		
Rates prepaid		400		
			68 000	
Less Current liabilities				
Trade creditors		14 000		
Bank overdraft		4 000		
			18 000	
Working capital				50 000
TOTAL NET ASSETS				240 000
Financed by:				
Capital Accounts				
Hale		160 000		
Hearty		80 000		
CAPITAL EMPLOYED				240 000

They agree to admit Jacobs into the partnership on the following terms:
(a) Jacobs is to introduce capital of £140 000 comprising: Equipment, £14 000; Stock, £26 000 and the balance in cash.
(b) In addition, Jacobs is to pay a premium in cash of £6 000 for his share of the goodwill, the premium to be retained in the business.
(c) Jacobs is to get one-quarter of all future profits. Hale and Hearty are to share the remaining profits in the same ratio as before.
(d) Prior to the admission of Jacobs the assets are to be revalued as follows:
  Premises   £136 000
  Equipment £34 000
  Motor vans £24 000
  Stock   £48 000

You are required to show:
a journal entries recording the above transactions
b the relevant ledger accounts
c the opening balance sheet of the new partnership.

8 Eve and Patrick are partners in a business sharing profits and losses equally. On 31 December 19–6 the balance sheet of the business was as follows:

Balance sheet as at 31 December 19–6

	£	£		£	£
Goodwill	2 000		Capital Accounts:		
Premises	3 800		Eve	7 800	
Fixtures and fittings	1 400		Patrick	6 800	
Delivery van	1 800				14 600
		9 000			
Stock	3 000		Creditors		1 160
Debtors	3 500		Wages due		240
Cash at bank	500				
		7 000			
		16 000			16 000

On 1 January 19–7 they admit Thomas into partnership on the following terms:
(a) Future profits and losses are to be shared: Eve, two-fifths; Patrick, two-fifths; Thomas, one-fifth.
(b) Goodwill is to be revalued at £4 000 but is to be shown in the books at the old figure, and Thomas is to pay cash in addition to his capital for his share of the undisclosed goodwill. This cash is to be retained in the business.
(c) Thomas is to introduce capital of £4 000, consisting of stock, £1 700, and the balance in cash.
(d) Eve and Patrick are to introduce or withdraw cash so that the capitals of all three partners will be in exactly the same proportions as their new profit-sharing ratios.

Show:
a the journal and ledger entries (including cash) to implement this agreement
b the opening balance sheet of the new partnership as at 1 January 19–7.

9 Tim and Gerard had been in partnership together for a number of years. They decided to invite Jack to join the business and to become a partner in it. The following ledger accounts reflect adjustments made in the partnership's books to account for the new circumstances.

Dr.		**Premises Account**		Cr.
		£		
1 Dec.	Balance	50 000		
	Revaluation	10 000		
	Capital: Jack	28 000		

Dr.		**Furniture and Equipment Account**			Cr.
		£			£
1 Dec.	Balance	3 800	1 Dec.	Revaluation	300

Dr.		**Stock Account**			Cr.
		£			£
1 Dec.	Balance	9 400	1 Dec.	Revaluation	900

Dr.		**Cash Account**			Cr.
		£			£
1 Dec.	Balance	1 600	1 Dec.	Capital: Tim	400
	Capital: Jack	2 000			
	Goodwill – Capital: Tim	1 800			
	Goodwill – Capital: Gerard	600			
	Capital: Gerard	5 200			

Dr.		**Capital: Tim**			Cr.
		£			£
1 Dec.	Cash	400	1 Dec.	Balance	52 000
				Revaluation	6 600
				Cash – Goodwill	1 800

Dr.		**Capital: Gerard**			Cr.
					£
			1 Dec.	Balance	32 000
				Revaluation	2 200
				Cash – Goodwill	600
				Cash	5 200

Dr.		**Capital: Jack**			Cr.
					£
			1 Dec.	Premises	28 000
				Cash	2 000

You are required to:
a state the partnership agreement of the firm of Tim and Gerard before the introduction of Jack
b state the conditions attached to the introduction of Jack as a partner.

10 Bull and Bear traded in partnership and shared profits and losses in the ratio 2:1 respectively. Their balance sheet as at 31 December 1985 was as follows:

Bull and Bear
Balance sheet as at 31 December 1985

	£	£
Goodwill		3 800
Tangible fixed assets at cost	22 400	
Accumulated depreciation	3 910	
		18 490
		22 290
Stocks	3 325	
Debtors	8 937	
Prepayments	86	
Cash in hand	365	
	12 713	
Creditors	1 720	
Bank overdraft	983	
Interest due on Bear's loan	320	
	3 023	
		9 690
		31 980
Capital accounts:		
Bull		12 400
Bear		15 600
		28 000
Current accounts:		
Bull	180	
Bear	(200)	
		(20)
		27 980
Loan from Bear – repayable after five years		4 000
		31 980

On 31 March 1986, Bull retires.

For the purpose of deciding the amount due to Bull, the following information should be taken into account:
  (a) tangible fixed assets at net book value were revalued at £18 100 on 31 March 1986;
  (b) on 31 March 1986 goodwill was valued at £5 900;
  (c) in the three months to 31 March 1986, the partnership profit was £10 200, after charging depreciation of £2 100. Bull's drawings in the same period amounted to £6 275.

On 1 April 1986, Bison joins Bear in partnership, sharing profits equally.

Bison paid in £12 000 as capital, but made no payment for goodwill.

Bull was paid £10 500, and the balance of the sum due to him was placed on a loan account.

Goodwill was not to appear in the ledger following the admission of Bison.

Prepare a columnar Capital Account to record the entries necessary upon the retirement of Bull and the admission of Bison.

[*London Chamber of Commerce and Industry, spring 1986*]

11 On 1 January Year 2, M. Stockton, a sole trader, admitted C. Brook as a partner on the following terms: Brook to bring in £50 000 cash as capital, to have a salary of £4 000 per annum and to be entitled to a one-third share of the net profit. Stockton valued the goodwill at £25 000 and it was agreed that this amount should be credited to Stockton's Capital Account. The entries for the goodwill had not been made in the books of the firm but you are required to deal with it in the final account. The trial balance of the partnership at 31 December Year 2 is given below:

Trial balance at 31 December Year 2

	£	£
Stockton capital		25 000
Brook capital		50 000
Cash in hand	860	
Bank	21 760	
Bills payable		28 970
Freehold property	50 000	
Machinery and plant	27 000	
Stock – 1 January Year 2	39 260	
Sales		278 440
Purchases	192 870	
Rates, taxes and insurance	8 400	
Carriage outwards	9 760	
Debtors	73 000	
Creditors		69 780
Returns inwards	2 890	
General office expenses	9 800	
Repairs to machinery	4 100	
Stockton drawings	5 000	
Brook drawings	3 000	
Provision for bad debts:		
1 January Year 2		2 000
Bad debts written off	3 120	
Discounts allowed	3 370	
	454 190	454 190

The following additional information is available:
1. Stock in hand 31 December Year 2 – £12 530.
2. Provision for bad debts to be increased to 5 per cent on debtors.
3. Interest to be allowed on capital (not drawings) at 5 per cent per annum.

4. Depreciation to be charged at 5 per cent per annum on the stated value of machinery and plant.
5. Brook's salary has not been paid.

Given that the residue of the net profit after appropriating Brook's salary and interest on capital is £5 400, prepare the balance sheet of Stockton and Brook as at 31 December Year 2.

[*London Chamber of Commerce and Industry, Intermediate, March 1987*]

12 The following trial balance as at 31 March 1986 has been extracted from the books of John Brown, trading as Strongcolour Fabrics:

	£	£
John Brown: Capital Account, at 1 April 1985		61 000
John Brown: drawings	22 600	
Freehold property:		
At cost	40 000	
Provision for depreciation		6 000
Fixtures and fittings:		
At cost	30 000	
Provision for depreciation		5 400
Motor vehicles:		
At cost	12 000	
Provision for depreciation		5 000
Debtors	14 000	
Creditors		9 000
Balance at bank	5 700	
Sales		240 000
Cost of sales	168 000	
Stock at 31 March 1986	5 100	
Establishment and distribution expenses	29 000	
	326 400	326 400

On 1 January 1986, Peter Grey, a senior employee, joined John Brown in partnership, trading as Allcolour Cloths.

The goodwill of Strongcolour Fabrics was valued at 31 December 1985 at £12 000, but it has been agreed that a Goodwill Account will not be opened. A John Brown Loan Account is to be opened as from 1 January 1986 with a transfer of £20 000 from John Brown's Capital Account. A Capital Account and a Current Account are to be maintained for each partner.

Peter Grey has not been paid his salary of £12 000 per annum as administrative manager since 1 April 1985 and no adjustment has been made yet in the books for such salary in view of the impending partnership. However, it has now been agreed that the amount due to Peter Grey as an employee will form the basis of his capital as a partner of Allcolour Cloths.

It has been agreed that all assets and liabilities recorded in the books of Strongcolour Fabrics will be carried forward to Allcolour Cloths at their book values with the exception of freehold property which has been revalued at 1 January 1986 at £50 000.

The following additional information has been given for the year ended 31 March 1986:
1. All sales have produced a uniform rate of gross profit;
2. One-eighth of the turnover took place in the last quarter of the year;
3. Establishment and distribution expenses accrued due at 31 March 1986 amounted to £1 000;
4. Establishment and distribution expenses are to be apportioned uniformly throughout the year;
5. Depreciation, apportioned uniformly throughout the year, is to be provided at the following rates on the original cost of fixed assets held at the year end:

                Fixtures and fittings   12%
                Motor vehicles   25%

No depreciation is to be provided on the freehold property for the year.

a   Prepare a Trading and Profit and Loss Account for the nine months ended 31 December 1985 for Strongcolour Fabrics.
b   Prepare a Trading and Profit and Loss Account for the three months ended 31 March 1986 for Allcolour Cloths.
c   Prepare a balance sheet as at 31 March 1986 for Allcolour Cloths.

[*Association of Accounting Technicians, June 1986*]

12 Formation of partnership II: amalgamations to form a partnership

When two or more sole traders join together to form a partnership, they are in fact pooling their individual resources and talents to form a bigger and a better unit. They combine their respective assets, liabilities and capital into a single unit. This merger will be covered by a *partnership agreement* or *deed of partnership* which will set out the rights, duties and obligations of each individual.

The set of books kept by each individual, up to now, will be replaced by a single set of partnership books. Before the partnership agreement is signed, the prospective partners will meet, examine each other's books, and reach agreement as to the real value of each other's assets and liabilities. They will decide what assets and liabilities are to be taken over by the partnership and what value is to be placed on them. Each individual will try to have as high a value as possible accepted for his assets as this will increase his share (capital) in the new business and strengthen his claim to a larger share of future profit.

When a revaluation of the assets and liabilities of each individual takes place, it is better to adjust them separately before combining them. The easiest way to do this is to show a revised balance sheet for each individual incorporating the agreed changes and only the assets and liabilities taken over. Combine and enter these, by means of journal entries, in the partnership books.

The journal entries are:

Debit each Asset Account with combined values of the particular assets.
Credit each Liability Account with combined values of the particular liabilities.

Note that each partner will, of course, have a separate Capital Account.

Procedure

1. Prepare revised draft balance sheets for each individual incorporating agreed changes.
2. Prepare opening journal entries of new partnership by combining similar assets and liabilities from revised draft balance sheets.
3. Open ledger accounts in new partnership books from journal entries (No. 2 above) if required to do so.
4. Prepare opening balance sheets of new partnership if required.

Key thought
Two sets of accounts are to be combined into one set in accordance with the agreement made between the new partners.

A SIMPLE EXAMPLE
A and B, sole traders, agree to amalgamate their businesses on 1 January 19–3. Their balance sheets on 31 December 19–2 were as follows (all assets and liabilities are to be taken over by the partnership):

					A £	B £
Fixed assets						
Premises					40 000	20 000
Machinery					10 000	6 000
Fixtures and fittings					4 000	2 000
Vehicles					—	8 000
					54 000	36 000
	A		B			
	£	£	£	£		
Current assets						
Stock	5 000		3 000			
Debtors	5 400		2 600			
Bank	1 600		—			
Cash	—		400			
		12 000		6 000		
Less Current liabilities						
Creditors	2 800		1 600			
Bank overdraft	—		1 400			
		2 800		3 000		
Working capital					9 200	3 000
TOTAL NET ASSETS					63 200	39 000
Financed by:						
Capital Accounts						
					A £	B £
CAPITAL EMPLOYED					63 200	39 000

Show:
a journal and ledger accounts required to open the books of the partnership
b the opening balance sheet of the partnership.

Formation of partnership II: amalgamations to form a partnership

SOLUTION

a

<h3 style="text-align:center">Journal</h3>

	Dr. £	Cr. £
Premises Account	60 000	
Machinery Account	16 000	
Fixtures and Fittings Account	6 000	
Vehicles Account	8 000	
Stock Account	8 000	
Debtors Account(s)	8 000	
Bank Account	200	
Cash Account	400	
Creditors		4 400
Capital Accounts:		
A		63 200
B		39 000
	106 600	106 600

Being assets and liabilities taken over as per partnership agreement.

<h3 style="text-align:center">Ledger accounts</h3>

Dr.   **Premises Account**   Cr.

19–3   £
1 Jan.   Balance b/d   GJ   60 000

Dr.   **Machinery Account**   Cr.

19–3   £
1 Jan.   Balance b/d   GJ   16 000

Dr.   **Fixtures and Fittings Account**   Cr.

19–3   £
1 Jan.   Balance b/d   GJ   6 000

Dr.   **Vehicles Account**   Cr.

19–3   £
1 Jan.   Balance b/d   GJ   8 000

Dr.   **Stock Account**   Cr.

19–3   £
1 Jan.   Balance b/d   GJ   8 000

Dr.			**Debtors Account**			Cr.
19–3			£			
1 Jan.	Balance b/d	GJ	8 000			

Dr.			**Cash Book**			Cr.
			Cash	Bank		
19–3			£	£		
1 Jan.	Balance b/d	GJ	400	200		

Dr.			**Creditors Account**			Cr.
			19–3			£
			1 Jan.	Balance b/d	GJ	4 400

Dr.			**Capital Accounts**			Cr.
					A	B
			19–3		£	£
			1 Jan.	Balance b/d GJ	63 200	39 000

b   Balance sheet of A and B as at 1 January 19–3

	Cost	Depreciation to date	Net	Total
Fixed assets	£	£	£	£
Premises	60 000		60 000	
Machinery	16 000		16 000	
Fixtures and fittings	6 000		6 000	
Vehicles	8 000		8 000	
	90 000		90 000	90 000
Current assets	£	£		
Stock	8 000			
Debtors	8 000			
Bank	200			
Cash	400			
		16 600		
Less Current liabilities				
Creditors		4 400		
Working capital				12 200
TOTAL NET ASSETS				102 200
Financed by:				
Capital Accounts				
A		63 200		
B		39 000		
CAPITAL EMPLOYED				102 200

A More Difficult Example

Murphy and White are sole traders, both carrying on a drapery business. They decide to amalgamate on 1 January 19–2. Their respective balance sheets on 31 December 19–1 were as follows:

Balance sheets as at 31 December 19–1

	Murphy £	White £		Murphy £	White £
Premises	600	—	Capital	8 380	6 530
Equipment	500	700	Loan	3 000	—
Motor vehicles	3 450	2 000	Bank overdraft	—	500
Stock	2 750	3 550	Creditors	1 100	900
Debtors	2 270	1 230	Accruals (rent)	90	50
Bank	2 000	500			
Investment	1 000	—			
	12 570	7 980		12 570	7 980

(a) It was agreed that the new firm was to take over all the assets and liabilities except that Murphy should retain the investment and also pay off the loan out of his private resources. It was also agreed that White should pay off her bank overdraft.
(b) Future profits and losses were to be shared: Murphy, 75 per cent; White, 25 per cent.
(c) The capital of the new firm is to be £16 500 and is to be provided: Murphy £10 000, White £6 500. Adjustments are to be made in cash.
(d) Revaluations were to be made as follows:

	Murphy £	White £
Premises	800	—
Equipment	400	500
Motor vehicles	2 450	1 500
Stock	2 700	3 500
Debtors	2 500	1 300

Prepare the opening balance sheet of the new firm.

Solution

Revised draft balance sheets

	Murphy £	White £		Murphy £	White £
Premises	800	—	Capital	10 000	6 500
Equipment	400	500	Creditors	1 100	900
Motor vehicles	2 450	1 500	Accruals	90	50
Stock	2 700	3 500			
Debtors	2 500	1 300			
Bank	2 000	500			
Cash	340	150			
	11 190	7 450		11 190	7 450

Journal

	Dr. £	Cr. £
Premises Account	800	
Equipment Account	900	
Motor Vehicles Account	3 950	
Stock Account	6 200	
Debtors Accounts	3 800	
Bank Account	2 500	
Cash Account	490	
Capital Accounts:		
Murphy		10 000
White		6 500
Creditors Accounts		2 000
Rent Account		140
Being assets and liabilities of partnership, 1 January 19–2	18 640	18 640

Balance sheet of Murphy and White as at 1.1.19–2

	Cost £	Depreciation to date £	Net £	Total £
Fixed assets				
Premises	800		800	
Equipment	900		900	
Motor vehicles	3 950		3 950	
	5 650		5 650	5 650
Add Current assets	£	£		
Stock	6 200			
Debtors	3 800			
Bank	2 500			
Cash	490			
		12 990		
Less Current liabilities				
Creditors	2 000			
Accruals	140			
		2 140		
Working capital				10 850
TOTAL NET ASSETS				16 500
Financed by:				
Capital Accounts				
Murphy		10 000		
White		6 500		
CAPITAL EMPLOYED				16 500

Exercises Set 12

1. X and Y, two sole traders, decided to amalgamate their businesses on 1 January 19–2. Their balance sheets at 31 December 19–1 were as follows:

X's balance sheet as at 31 December 19–1

	£		£
Premises	10 00	Capital	16 000
Fixtures and fittings	2 000	Creditors	1 900
Stock	3 000		
Debtors	1 000		
Bank balance	1 900		
	17 900		17 900

Y's balance sheet as at 31 December 19–1

	£		£
Premises	20 000	Capital	32 000
Fixtures and fittings	4 000	Creditors	1 000
Motor vehicles	2 500		
Stock	1 400		
Debtors	3 600		
Bank balance	1 500		
	33 000		33 000

The partnership was to take over all the assets and liabilities of the two businesses at book value. Future profits were to be shared: X, two-thirds; Y, one-third.

Show the journal entries necessary to open the books of the partnership, the partnership ledger accounts and the opening balance sheet of the partnership.

2. Con and Dave are sole traders. They agree to amalgamate on 1 February 19–2 and to share future profits and losses: Con, three-fifths; Dave, two-fifths. The new business will be known as the C & D Stores.

Their respective balance sheets were as follows on 31 January 19–2:

	Con	Dave		Con	Dave
	£	£		£	£
Premises	4 000	5 000	Capital	10 000	6 000
Fixtures and fittings	1 800	1 200	Creditors	2 200	1 800
Stock	2 400	1 800	Bank overdraft		1 000
Debtors	1 000	600			
Investment	2 000	—			
Bank	900	—			
Cash	100	200			
	12 200	8 800		12 200	8 800

It was agreed that Con should retain the investment and that Dave should pay off his bank overdraft. All the other assets and liabilities were to be taken over by the new firm at book value.

Show the journal and ledger entries required to open the books of the partnership and the opening balance sheet of C & D Stores.

3 Early and Late, two grocers, agree to amalgamate their businesses on 1 March 19–3. Their respective balance sheets on 28 February 19–3 were as follows:

	Early	Late		Early	Late
	£	£		£	£
Premises	12 000	10 000	Capital	22 000	24 000
Equipment	1 600	1 200	Mortgage loan	—	2 800
Fixtures and fittings	500	800	Creditors	1 160	600
Vehicles	1 900	2 500	Wages due	200	—
Stock	7 400	9 000	Bank overdraft	2 800	—
Debtors	2 760	2 520			
Bank	—	1 380			
	26 160	27 400		26 160	27 400

The amalgamation agreement provided as follows:
(a) Late was to retain his bank balance and pay off his mortgage loan. Early was to pay off his overdraft out of his own resources. The other liabilities were to be taken over at book value.
(b) The following revaluations were to be made:

	Early	Late
	£	£
Premises	16 000	13 000
Equipment	1 000	600
Fixtures and fittings	400	700
Vehicles	1 600	2 200
Stock	7 300	8 900
Debtors	2 600	2 400

(c) Each partner was to bring in £1 000 to provide working capital.
(d) Profits and losses were to be shared equally.

Show the journal entries opening the partnership books and opening balance sheet of the partnership.

4 Morphy and Richards, sole traders, enter into a partnership on 1 January 19–1. Their respective balance sheets at 31 December 19–0 were as follows:

	Morphy	Richards		Morphy	Richards
	£	£		£	£
Premises	10 000	6 000	Capital	18 000	12 000
Equipment	1 000	600	Creditors	6 100	6 000
Motor vans	3 000	5 000	Accruals	1 900	700
Stock	4 000	3 000			
Debtors	5 000	2 900			
Bank	3 000	1 200			
	26 000	18 700		26 000	18 700

(a) It was agreed that the new firm would take over all the assets and liabilities.
(b) The goodwill of Morphy's business would be valued at £4 000 and that of Richards at £2 000.
(c) Future profits and losses would be shared: Morphy, 60 per cent; Richards, 40 per cent.
(d) The capital of the new firm would be £44 000 and would be provided in their profit-sharing ratios. Adjustments to be made in cash.
(e) Revaluations were to be made as follows:

	Morphy £	Richards £
Premises	16 000	10 000
Equipment	600	400
Motor vans	2 200	4 600
Stock	3 000	2 600
Debtors	4 600	2 400

Show a revised balance sheet for each partner, the journal entries necessary to open the books of the partnership and the opening balance sheet of the partnership.

5 A and B, sole traders, decided to amalgamate their businesses on 1 June 19–1. The balance sheets of the two businesses on 31 May 19–1 were as follows:

	A £	B £		A £	B £
Premises	8 640	4 360	Capital	28 000	18 000
Equipment	900	680	Mortgage loan	—	2 200
Motor vans	2 000	—	Creditors	1 900	1 600
Fixtures and fittings	1 820	180	Accruals	300	—
Stock	4 420	3 580	Bank overdraft	2 400	—
Debtors	10 220	9 600			
Bank	4 600	3 400			
	32 600	21 800		32 600	21 800

(a) It was agreed that A pay off his bank overdraft. B was to repay his mortgage loan out of private funds. All other assets and liabilities should be taken over by the new firm at book value.
(b) The goodwill of A's business should be valued at £4 000 and that of B's at £2 000.
(c) Future profits and losses should be shared: A, three-fifths; B, two-fifths.
(d) The capital of the new firm should be £60 000 and should be provided in their profit-sharing ratios. Adjustments to be made in cash.
Revaluations to be made as follows:

	A £	B £
Premises	12 640	8 360
Equipment	700	480
Fixtures and fittings	1 620	160
Stock	4 020	2 180
Debtors	10 000	9 000

a Show the entries necessary to open the books of the partnership.
b Show the opening balance sheet of the new firm.

6 Smyth and Harvey, sole traders, enter into partnership on 1 April 19–4. Their respective balance sheets at 31 March 19–4 were as follows:

	Smyth	Harvey		Smyth	Harvey
	£	£		£	£
Premises	16 000	—	Capital	28 000	10 000
Equipment	1 500	1 000	Loan from X	2 000	—
Motor vans	3 260	5 140	Creditors	5 060	1 940
Stock	7 000	2 400	Accruals	140	60
Debtors	5 440	2 640			
Bank	2 000	820			
	35 200	12 000		35 200	12 000

(a) It was agreed that the new firm was to take over all the assets and liabilities except the loan which Smyth was to pay off out of his private resources.
(b) The goodwill of Smyth's business was to be valued at £4 000 and that of Harvey at £2 000.
(c) Future profits and losses were to be shared: Smyth, 75 per cent; Harvey, 25 per cent.
(d) The capital of the new firm was to be £48 000 and was to be provided in their profit-sharing ratios. Adjustments to be made in cash.
(e) Revaluations were to be as follows:

	Smyth	Harvey
	£	£
Premises	20 000	—
Equipment	1 000	800
Motor vans	2 400	5 600
Stock	6 600	2 000
Debtors	5 040	2 540

Prepare the opening balance sheet of the new firm.

7 Morris and Newton were in partnership trading as M & N Products and sharing profits 2:1. They agreed to amalgamate with Oatfield, a sole trader in the same line of business as from 1 May 19–5. The balance sheets of the two firms on 30 April 19–5 were as follows:

	M & N	Oatfield		M & N	Oatfield
	£	£		£	£
			Capital:		
Premises	16 000	8 000	Morris	16 000	—
Plant	6 000	3 000	Newton	8 000	—
Furniture	1 500	400	Oatfield	—	12 000
Stock	2 500	1 200	Term loan	—	1 000
Debtors	1 800	900	Creditors	4 500	940
Bank	1 100	500	Accruals	400	60
	28 900	14 000		28 900	14 000

All the assets and liabilities were to be taken over by the new firm except the term loan which Oatfield was to repay out of private funds. A revaluation was agreed as follows:

	M & N £	Oatfield £
Premises	22 000	12 000
Plant	4 200	2 400
Furniture	1 380	320
Stock	2 200	1 000
Debtors	1 620	840

The profits and losses of the new firm are to be shared: Morris, 50 per cent; Newton, 25 per cent; Oatfield, 25 per cent. The value of Morris's and Newton's goodwill was agreed at £8 000 and that of Oatfield at £2 000. A Goodwill Account is to be raised equal to the excess of Morris's and Newton's over Oatfield's and Morris's and Newton's Capital Accounts are to be credited accordingly. The capital of the new firm is to be £52 000 and is to be provided in their new profit-sharing ratios. Any balance due to or by the partners is to be paid in cash.

Show the opening balance sheet of the new firm.

8 On 31 August the respective balance sheets of A and B who own and operate adjacent retail shops in the town of Stapley are as follows:

Balance sheet of A at 31 August

	£	£		£
Fixed assets			*Capital*	16 170
Freehold premises		6 000	*Current liabilities*	
Fixtures		7 140	Trade creditors	26 701
Vehicles		4 225		
		17 365		
Current assets				
Stock	12 621			
Debtors	9 450			
Cash at bank	3 435			
		25 506		
		42 871		42 871

Balance sheet of B at 31 August

	£	£		£
Fixed assets			*Capital*	23 770
Freehold premises		2 125	*Current liabilities*	
Fixtures		2 470	Trade creditors	1 405
Vehicle		700		
		5 295		
Current assets				
Stock	6 840			
Debtors	7 150			
Cash at bank	5 890			
		19 880		
		25 175		25 175

They decide it will be to their mutual advantage to amalgamate their businesses on 1 September and trade from that date under the firm name of Quality Assured.

The partnership agreement states that B is to be credited with goodwill of £5 000 and B's vehicle is to be decreased in value by £600, that all stocks are to be reduced by one-third, that a provision for bad debts of 8 per cent is to be made on all debtors and that A's vehicles are to be retained by him and not transferred to the partnership.

You are required to give the journal entries in both sets of books at 31 August to effect the above, and to show the opening balance sheet of Quality Assured on 1 September.

[*Pitman Intermediate*]

13 Dissolution of partnership

Subject to any agreement between the partners, the partnership may be dissolved for one of many reasons, for example:
(a) on the expiration of the term of partnership if fixed;
(b) by the assent of all partners;
(c) by the death, bankruptcy or insanity of one of the partners, etc.

When speaking of dissolution of partnership we are dealing with the winding up of the partnership which, for examination purposes, is taken to mean the sale or disposal of all the assets and the settlement of liabilities. It is important to visualise the end result – all the accounts in the partnership books will be closed. The assets are sold and the money received from the sale of assets must be used in the following order:
1. to pay debts and liabilities of the firm to outsiders;
2. to pay partners' loans;
3. to pay partners' capitals.

Key thought

Close all accounts in order indicated. When finished, all accounts will be closed.

Procedure

(a) Open accounts for all assets and liabilities as per last balance sheet.
(b) Open a Realisation Account

Step 1

Close the Asset Accounts except Bank by transferring assets to Realisation Account.

Entries:
 Debit Realisation Account
 Credit each Asset Account.

Step 2

Deal with money received from sale of assets.

Entries:
Debit Bank Account } with money received.
Credit Realisation Account

Note

| If a partner takes over a particular asset | Debit partner's Capital Account
Credit Realisation Account | with agreed value of assets taken over |

Step 3

Pay dissolution expenses.

Entries:
Debit Realisation Account
Credit Bank Account.

Step 4

Pay creditors (close Creditors Account).

Entries:
Debit Creditors Account } with amount paid to creditors.
Credit Bank Account

Note
If discount is received from creditors:

Entries:
Debit Creditors Account
Credit Realisation Account.

Step 5

Pay partners' loans (if any).
Entries:
Debit partner's Loan Account
Credit Bank Account.

Note
Where a partner's Capital Account is in debit, repayment of the partner's loan is not made but set off against (credited to) his Capital Account.

Entries:
Debit partner's Loan Account } with the amount of the loan.
Credit partner's Capital Account

Step 6

Close the Realisation Account by transferring the profit or loss (the difference between the two sides) to the partners' Capital Accounts.

If there is a profit on realisation:
Entries:
    Debit Realisation Account
    Credit partners' Capital Accounts

If there is a loss on realisation: } in their profit-sharing ratios.
Entries:
    Debit partners' Capital Accounts
    Credit Realisation Account

Step 7

If partners have Current Accounts, transfer balance on them to partners' Capital Accounts.

Step 8

Close the Bank Account and partners' Capital Accounts simultaneously.

Entries:
    Debit each partner's Capital Account } with amount due to
    Credit Bank   each partner.

Notes

(a) If all partners' accounts show credit balances there will be exactly enough cash left to clear them. All accounts will now be closed and the dissolution is complete.

(b) If one or more of the partners' Capital Accounts shows a debit balance after Step **6** (this means that his share of the loss is greater than his capital), he is obliged to bring in sufficient cash to make up the deficiency. Debit Cash, credit partner's Capital Account. Then proceed with Step **7** to pay off the other partners.

(c) *Garner* v. *Murray*
Should any partner be unable through bankruptcy or otherwise to pay up his deficiency and where the partnership agreement does not expressly provide for this contingency, that partner's deficiency must be borne by the other partners in proportion to their last agreed capitals. 'Last agreed capitals' is taken to mean capitals at date of last balance sheet. This ruling, known as '*Garner* v. *Murray*', is generally accepted by accountants.

EXAMPLE

John, Paul and Michael, who share profits and losses in proportion to their capitals, agreed to dissolve their partnership on 1.1.1982. Their balance sheet on that date was as follows:

	Cost £	Depreciation to date £	Net £	Total £
Fixed assets				
Buildings	96 000		96 000	
Motor vehicles	40 000		40 000	
Goodwill	22 000		22 000	
	158 000		158 000	158 000

	£	£
Current assets		
Stocks	21 600	
Debtors	16 600	
Bills receivable	5 800	
		44 000
Less Current liabilities		
Creditors	7 000	
Bank	1 800	
Wages due	1 200	
		10 000

	£
Working capital	34 000
TOTAL NET ASSETS	192 000
Financed by:	
Capital	
John	96 000
Paul	48 000
Michael	48 000
CAPITAL EMPLOYED	192 000

The following details relate to the dissolution:
(a) Buildings were sold for £120 000 and £5 600 was received for the bills.
(b) Michael took over some of the vehicles at a valuation of £24 000 and the remaining vehicles were sold for £15 000.
(c) John took over the stock at book value and Paul accepted responsibility for the payment of creditors.
(d) £16 300 was received from debtors in full settlement.
(e) Realisation expenses were £1 300.

You are required to record the dissolution in the books of the partnership showing all relevant ledger accounts.

Dissolution of partnership

SOLUTION **Ledger accounts**

Dr.	**Buildings Account**			Cr.
1982		£	1982	£
1 Jan. Balance b/d		96 000	1 Jan. Realisation Account	96 000

Dr.	**Motor Vehicles Account**			Cr.
1982		£	1982	£
1 Jan. Balance b/d		40 000	1 Jan. Realisation Account	40 000

Dr.	**Goodwill Account**			Cr.
1982		£	1982	£
1 Jan. Balance b/d		22 000	1 Jan. Realisation Account	22 000

Dr.	**Stock Account**			Cr.
1982		£	1982	£
1 Jan. Balance b/d		21 600	1 Jan. Realisation Account	21 600

Dr.	**Debtors Account**			Cr.
1982		£	1982	£
1 Jan. Balance b/d		16 600	1 Jan. Realisation Account	16 600

Dr.	**Bills Receivable Account**			Cr.
1982		£	1982	£
1 Jan. Balance b/d		5 800	1 Jan. Realisation Account	5 800

Dr.	**Creditors Account**			Cr.
1982		£	1982	£
1 Jan. Capital Account: Paul		7 000	1 Jan. Balance b/d	7 000

Dr.	**Wages Account**			Cr.
1982		£	1982	£
1 Jan. Bank		1 200	1 Jan. Balance b/d	1 200

Dr.	**Bank Account**			Cr.
1982		£	1982	£
1 Jan.	Realisation Account:		1 Jan. Balance b/d	1 800
	Buildings	120 000	Realisation Expenses	1 300
	Realisation Account:		Wages	1 200
	Bills Receivable	5 600	*Final settlement*	
	Realisation Account:		Capital Accounts:	
	Motor Vehicles	15 000	John	74 000
	Realisation Account:		Paul	54 800
	Debtors	16 300	Michael	23 800
		156 900		156 900

Dr.				**Capital Accounts**				Cr.
1982		John £	Paul £	Michael £	1982		John £	Paul £	Michael £

	John £	Paul £	Michael £		John £	Paul £	Michael £
1982				1982			
1 Jan. Realisation Account: Motor Vehicles			24 000	1 Jan. Balance b/d	96 000	48 000	48 000
Realisation Account: Stock	21 600			Creditors Account		7 000	
Share of loss	400	200	200				
Bank	74 000	54 800	23 800				
	96 000	55 000	48 000		96 000	55 000	48 000

Dr.		**Realisation Account**		Cr.
1982	£	1982		£
1 Jan. Buildings Account	96 000	1 Jan. Capital Account: Michael		
Motor Vehicles Account	40 000	Vehicles		24 000
Goodwill Account	22 000	Bank: Buildings		120 000
Stock Account	21 600	Bills Receivable		5 600
Bills Receivable	5 800	Vehicles		15 000
Debtors Account	16 600	Capital Account: John		
Bank – Realisation expenses	1 300	Stock		21 600
		Bank – Debtors		16 300
		Share of loss (£800)		
		Capital Account: John ($\frac{1}{2}$)		400
		Capital Account: Paul ($\frac{1}{4}$)		200
		Capital Account: Michael ($\frac{1}{4}$)		200
	203 300			203 300

Exercises Set 13

1 X and Y are in partnership sharing profits and losses equally. They decide on 31 December 19–1 to dissolve the partnership and realise the assets. Their balance sheet at that date was as follows:

	£		£
Freehold premises	10 000	Capital Accounts:	
Plant and machinery	6 000	X	10 000
Stock	4 000	Y	10 000
Debtors	3 000	Creditors	4 000
Cash at bank	1 000		
	24 000		24 000

The assets realised the following amounts: freehold premises, £9 000; plant and machinery, £5 000; stock, £3 600; debtors, £2 900. Creditors were paid in full. Expenses of realisation amounted to £200.

Record the dissolution in the books of the partnership showing all the relevant ledger accounts.

214 Dissolution of partnership

2 Bonnie and Clyde who had been in partnership for a number of years sharing profits and losses 2:1 agreed to dissolve the partnership on 31 January 19–2. Their balance sheet at that date read:

	£		£
Premises	24 000	Capital Accounts:	
Fixtures and fittings	5 000	Bonnie	28 000
Stock	11 000	Clyde	14 000
Debtors	9 400	Loan from X	2 000
Bank	2 600	Creditors	8 000
	52 000		52 000

Premises were sold for £36 000; fixtures and fittings realised £4 000; stock realised £10 000. Debtors paid £9 000. Creditors and the loan to X were paid in full. Dissolution expenses came to £600.

You are required to show the entries relating to the realisation of the assets and the distribution of the proceeds in the books of the partnership.

3 Dan, Erich and Frank, partners sharing profits and losses in proportion to their capitals, terminated their partnership by mutual agreement on 1 March 19–3. The balance sheet of the firm on that date was as follows:

	£		£
Premises	17 000	Capital Accounts:	
Fittings	6 500	Dan	18 000
Vehicles	5 040	Erich	12 000
Stock	6 560	Frank	6 000
Debtors	5 340	Loan Account: Erich	2 000
Bank	4 400	Creditors	6 840
	44 840		44 840

The assets realised the following amounts:

Premises	18 000
Fittings	6 200
Stock	5 840
Debtors	4 980

The vehicles were taken over by Frank at a valuation of £4 200. The Loan Account was paid and creditors accepted £6 580 in full settlement. Realisation expenses were £960.

Prepare the Realisation Account, Bank Account and partners' Capital Accounts.

4   The balance sheet of George, Harry and Irene at 1 April 19–4 was as follows:

	£		£
Premises	21 000	Capital Accounts:	
Plant and machinery	13 400	George	20 000
Fixtures and fittings	6 800	Harry	20 000
Stock	11 300	Irene	10 000
Debtors	5 940	Current Accounts:	
Bank	3 120	George	1 560
		Harry	1 280
		Irene	1 160
		Loan Account: Irene	2 000
		Creditors	5 560
	61 560		61 560

They shared profits and losses in proportion to their capitals. They agreed to dissolve partnership on 2 April 19–4. Details of dissolution were as follows:
(a)   Premises were sold for £24 000 and plant and machinery for £12 000.
(b)   George took over the fixtures and fittings at a valuation of £6 000.
(c)   Stock realised £10 800, debtors paid £5 400, the balance due from them being regarded as irrecoverable.
(d)   Expenses of realisation amounted to £750.
(e)   Creditors were paid less a discount of £80.

Prepare the main ledger accounts recording the dissolution.

5   The following is the balance sheet at 1 June 19–6 of Moran, Nelson and Nogood, who share profits and losses in the ratio 5:4:1.

	£		£
Freehold premises	6 500	Capital Accounts:	
Plant and equipment	3 874	Moran	10 000
Lorries	5 276	Nelson	8 000
Stock	5 126	Nogood	2 000
Debtors	3 504	Current Accounts:	
Bank	698	Moran	170
Current Account: Nelson	1 560	Creditors	8 170
Current Account: Nogood	1 802		
	28 340		28 340

The partners decided to dissolve the partnership on the date of the balance sheet. Details of dissolution were:
(a)   Freehold premises were sold for £7 000. Plant and equipment made £3 514.
(b)   Stock was sold for £3 176. Debtors paid £2 604 and the balance was irrecoverable.
(c)   Moran retained one lorry at a valuation of £1 800; the others were sold for £2 616.
(d)   Creditors were paid less a discount of £350.
(e)   Dissolution expenses were £280.

Nogood was unable to contribute anything towards his deficiency.

a Prepare Realisation Account, Bank Account and each partner's Current and Capital Accounts.
b What would the final payment to each partner have been using the *Garner* v. *Murray* rule?

6 The partnership of A, B and C, who shared profits 3:2:1, was dissolved on 1 August 19–7. At that date a balance sheet was made up and agreed which showed that A's capital was £5 500, B's £5 500, but that C was overdrawn to the extent of £350. The assets were: plant and machinery, £3 500; debtors, £6 730; bills receivable, £950; stock, £3 500. The liabilities were: bills payable, £805; creditors, £1 650; bank overdraft, £1 575. The assets realised the following amounts: plant and machinery, £3 000; debtors, £6 500; bills receivable, £925; stock, £3 300. Realisation expenses were £185. C was unable to contribute anything towards his deficiency.

Prepare the necessary ledger accounts to record the dissolution, showing
a the amount due to each partner, applying the *Garner* v. *Murray* rule
b the amount due to each partner if this rule is not applied.

7 X, Y and Z decided to dissolve their partnership. The position at 30 November 19–0, the date of dissolution, was as follows:

	£	£
Office furniture	1 000	
Stock	35 000	
Debtors	48 000	
Bills receivable	6 000	
Bank and cash	2 000	
Creditors		55 000
Loan Account X		6 000
Capital Accounts:		
X		20 000
Y		11 000
Z		nil
	92 000	92 000

They share profits and losses equally.

£400 of the debtors proved bad; bills receivable were paid in full; stock realised £34 000; office furniture was taken over by Y at book value; the expenses of realisation were £400, and a discount of £160 was obtained from the creditors.

Close the books of the partnership and show the Realisation Account.

8 Allen, Bond and Castles were in partnership sharing profits and losses in the ratio 3:3:2 respectively. They dissolved their partnership on 1 January 1986. At that date their balance sheet was:

	£	£		£	£	£
Fixed assets			*Capital Accounts*			
Freehold premises at cost	20 000		Allen		12 000	
Fixtures and fittings at cost less			Bond		8 000	
depreciation	3 000		Castles	2 000		
		23 000	*Less* Current			
Goodwill at cost		6 000	Account	340	1 660	21 660
Current assets			*Current Accounts*			
Stock		6 480	Allen		400	
Sundry debtors	4 800		Bond		600	1 000
Less Provision for bad			Sundry creditors			9 640
debts	400	4 400	Bank overdraft			7 600
Cash in hand		20				
		10 900				
		39 900				39 900

Fixtures and fittings were sold for £500 and freehold premises for book value. Stock was sold for £4 800 and goodwill was written off. Book debts were collected at ledger balances less £540 discounts, totalling £4 260. The costs of realisation – £720 – were paid by cheque. From the proceeds of realisation, creditors and bank overdraft were paid in full.

Draw up the Realisation Account and the partners' Capital Accounts (in columnar form) to show the distribution of the cash balance, bearing in mind that Castles was unable to bring in cash to cover his deficiency.

[*London Chamber of Commerce and Industry, autumn 1986*]

14 Joint venture accounts

Joint ventures are partnerships entered into by two or more persons for a definite business speculation or period of time usually until the venture has been completed. Joint ventures usually combine the marketing ability of one partner with the backing, financial or otherwise, of the other partner. A partnership agreement is signed by both parties setting out the terms and conditions applicable to the venture including the sharing of profits or losses. In the absence of a written agreement the terms of the Partnership Act 1890 apply. Each partner usually keeps his/her own set of books but to finalise the venture and settle accounts a Memorandum Joint Venture Account is drawn up to compile all the gains on the credit side and the expenses and losses on the debit side.

The memorandum is sent from one partner to the other. When checked and agreed the accounts are settled by payment in cash or by cheque of the amount owed by one partner to the other.

Step 1

Each partner opens in his own books an account named *Joint Venture Account with (name of other party)*.

Into this account must go all the transactions performed by the individual concerning the joint venture.

All purchases
All expenses } paid or due to each individual are
All allowances } *debited* to each Joint Venture Account.
Returns by customers

All sales (cash and credit) } by each individual are *credited* to
Property taken over } each Joint Venture Account.

Step 2

When all entries are completed open up a *Memorandum Joint Venture Account* for the partnership amalgamating all the sales (gains) on the credit side and all the expenses and losses on the debit side. The difference between the sides will in our example be £13 600 (Cr.) which means that a profit of £13 600 has been made on the venture. The accounts are completed by debiting Memorandum Joint Venture Account with £13 600 and *debiting* each of the partners with £6 800 (his share of the profit).

It is important to note that the Memorandum Joint Venture Account is *not* part of the double-entry system.

Step 3

Balance each partner's account and bring down the balance. Students are always surprised to find that the resultant debit balance on one partner's account is always exactly the same as the credit balance on the other partner's account. The partner with the debit balance on his account is owed that amount by the other partner who usually pays immediately by cash or cheque to finish the venture.

Note that *items retained* by a partner are treated as a sale by him. The Joint Venture Account in that particular partner's books is credited with the agreed value of the goods retained as also is the Memorandum Joint Venture Account.

EXAMPLE

On 1 January 19–1 James and Shirley enter into a joint venture to buy and sell antique silver. Sales will be made by both, but James is entitled to a rent of £1 000 for a shop supplied by him while Shirley is entitled to travelling expenses of £700. Profits and losses to be divided equally among the partners. The following transactions took place during the month of January 19–1:

	James	£		*Shirley*	£
4 Jan.	Bought silver at auction	5 000	5 Jan.	Sold silver (cheque)	3 000
6	Sold silver for cash	3 000	6	Paid carriage (cheque)	200
	Paid for repolishing (cash)	100	7	Bought silver (cheque)	7 000
8	Sold silver on credit	10 000	12	Sold silver on credit	12 000
27	Paid electricity charges – cheque	200	31	Kept remaining silver for agreed value of	600
	Paid rates (cheque)	500			
	Paid carriage out (cheque)	300			

Accounts were settled on 2 February 19–1 by cheque.

Show ledger accounts to cater for these transactions in each partner's books.

Solution

James's books

Joint Venture Account with Shirley

19–1			£	19–1		£
1 Jan.	Rent		1 000	6 Jan.	Sales (cash)	3 000
4	Cash:	Purchases	5 000	8	Sales (credit)	10 000
6	Cash:	Repolishing	100	31	Balance c/d	900
27	Bank:	Electricity	200			
		Rates	500			
		Carriage	300			
	Share of profit		6 800			
			13 900			13 900
31 Jan.	Balance b/d		900	2 Feb.	Bank	900

Shirley's books

Joint Venture Account with James

19–1			£	19–1		£
1 Jan.	Travelling expenses		700	5 Jan.	Sales (cheque)	3 000
6	Carriage		200	12	Sales (Cr.)	12 000
7	Cash:	Purchases	7 000	31	Silver retained	600
31	Share of profit		6 800			
	Balance c/d		900			
			15 600			15 600
2 Feb.	Bank		900		Balance b/d	900

James and Shirley

Memorandum Joint Venture Account for January 19–1

	£		£
Rent	1 000	Sales (3 000 + 10 000 + 3 000 +	
Purchases (5 000 + 7 000)	12 000	12 000)	28 000
Repolishing	100	Silver retained	600
Travelling expenses	700		
Electricity	200		
Rates	500		
Carriage (300 + 200)	500		
Profit on sale (£13 600)			
James ($\frac{1}{2}$)	6 800		
Shirley ($\frac{1}{2}$)	6 800		
	28 600		28 600

Exercises Set 14

1. Ann and Brian enter into a joint venture to buy and sell old silver and share profits and losses equally. The following transactions took place:

	Ann	£		Brian	£
1 Jan.	Bought goods	8 000	2 Jan.	Bought goods	10 000
	Paid carriage	300	3	Paid for repairs	700
7	Paid advertising charges	150	7	Paid travelling	
9	Sold goods – cash	4 400		expenses	190
10	Sold balance of goods	5 600	8	Sold goods – cash	7 600
11	Sent statement to Brian		9	Sold balance of goods – credit	5 400
			11	Sent statement to Ann	

   The joint venture was terminated on 12 January 19–1.

   Record these transactions in the books of both Ann and Brian and show the Memorandum Joint Venture Account assuming settlement was made in cash.

2. Derek and Peter enter into a joint venture to buy and sell second-hand televisions.

   They agreed to share profits and losses equally.

   The following transactions took place during the month of February 19–2:

	Derek	£		Peter	£
1 Feb.	Bought 50 televisions (cheque)	1 000	2 Feb.	Bought 30 televisions (cheque)	600
6	Paid for repairs (cash)	600	8	Sold 40 televisions (cash)	3 000
18	Sold 30 televisions on credit	2 800	12	Paid for spare parts (cash)	800
			20	Sold remainder on credit for	1 200

   On 28 February the partners settled their accounts by cheque.

   Show these transactions in the books of each partner and prepare a Memorandum Joint Venture Account.

3. X and Y entered into a joint venture to buy and sell a manufacturer's surplus stock, profits and losses to be shared 3:2. The transactions were as follows:

1 Jan.	X paid £10 000 and Y paid £15 000 at the auction of the stock.
2	X paid carriage charges, £800; Y paid carriage charges, £1 200.
2	X paid rent of warehouse, £400; Y paid fire insurance, £100.
4	Y paid advertising charges, £50; X paid wages, £200.
6	X sold part of the stock for £4 000 and lodged the money to his own account.
8	Y sold stock for £8 000 and lodged the money to his own account.
10	X sold balance of stock for £5 000; Y sold balance of stock for £7 000.
11	X and Y exchanged statements and settled in cash.

   Show:
   a the Joint Venture Account with Y in X's books
   b the Joint Venture Account with X in Y's books
   c the Memorandum Joint Venture Account showing the profit or loss on the venture.

4 On 1 Jan. 19–0 M and S entered into a joint venture to buy and sell antiques. The terms of the joint venture were as follows:
   (a) Profits and losses to be shared: M, ⅔ and S, ⅓.
   (b) An allowance of £1 800 travelling expenses to be paid to M.
   (c) £3 600 to be paid to S for the use of his store.
   (d) Each partner to receive a commission of 5 per cent on his net sales.
   (e) Each partner was to keep a record of his own transactions.

   Details of the transactions were as follows:
   2 Jan. M purchased antiques for £50 000 and paid expenses, £1 100.
   4   S purchased antiques for £80 000 and paid for repairs, £2 000.
   6   M paid advertising, £300.
   8   M sold antiques for £68 000.
   10   M refunded £8 000 for antiques returned.
   11   S paid delivery charges, £400.
   14   S sold antiques for £11 000.

   On 30 January 19–0 they agreed to terminate the joint venture and S agreed to take over the unsold antiques for £4 100. On this date a final settlement was made by cheque.

   You are required to show:
   a the Joint Venture Account in both M's and S's books
   b the Memorandum Joint Venture Account showing profit or loss on the venture.

5 Black and Green entered into a joint venture to buy and sell second-hand cars. Profits and losses were to be shared: Black, three-fifths; Green, two-fifths. On 15 August 19–9 Black purchased two cars for £3 600 and £6 400 respectively. He had the cars overhauled at a cost of £2 500 and on 5 September 19–9 he sold one of the cars for £5 000 and on 11 September the other car for £9 500. On 12 September 19–9 he purchased a further car for £7 500, which was sold two days later for £8 250 by Green who lodged the proceeds to his own account.

   On 12 August 19–9 Green bought a car for £4 000 which he sold for £5 000 on 18 August 19–9, after spending £500 on it for repairs. The car was returned by the customer on 1 September 19–9 as unsuitable, and he was allowed £4 750 thereon. This car remained unsold on 30 September 19–9 and it was agreed it should be taken over by Black at a valuation of £4 500. On 30 September 19–9 the sum required in full settlement as between Black and Green was paid by the party accountable.

   You are required to prepare:
   a the Joint Venture Account as it would appear in the books of Black, recording his transactions with the joint venture
   b a Memorandum Account for the joint venture showing the net profit.

6 A and B were partners in a venture for the buying and selling, for cash, of second-hand agricultural machinery. A Joint Bank Account was not opened, but A and B each passed his transactions through his own separate business accounts. The partners agreed that the profits and losses should be divided equally.

   The following transactions took place during the period 1 October to 31 December 19–7:
   A purchased on 5 October machinery for £6 200 (lot 1).
   B sold on 7 November portion of lot 1 for £9 100; A sold on 10 November the balance for £750.

B purchased on 17 November machinery for £16 900 (lot 2).
A sold on 22 December portion of lot 2 for £8 500.

As it was decided to terminate the venture, B agreed to take over on 30 December the balance of lot 2 at a valuation of £13 500.

Bearing in mind that travelling and total expenses, the costs of cleaning and repairing the machinery were paid by A, £1 610, and by B, £2 500, you are required to prepare a statement giving the result of the venture as a whole and show how the above transactions should be recorded in the Joint Account with A, in B's books and in the Joint Account with B, in A's books. A final settlement was effected by cheque on 30 December 19–7.

7   Tom and Ann entered into a joint venture to buy and sell second-hand machinery. Profits and losses were to be shared: Tom, three-fifths; Ann, two-fifths.

On 1 November 19–3 Tom purchased two machines for £3 600 and £7 400. He paid £1 800 for repairs to these machines and on 3 December 19–3 sold one of the machines for £5 600, and on 5 December sold the other machine for £8 000. In each case the proceeds were retained by Tom.

On 2 November 19–3 Ann purchased a machine for £10 000 and paid for repairs, £1 250. She sold the machine for £9 500 on 15 November, paying the proceeds into her Bank Account. The machine was returned by the purchaser on 7 December 19–3, and Ann paid £9 000 on the return of the machine. As the machine was unsold on 31 December 19–3, it was agreed that Ann should retain the machine at an agreed price of £9 250.

Other expenses paid by the parties were as follows:

	Tom £	Ann £
Carriage on machines	200	100
Insurance	150	50

On 31 December 19–3 the party concerned paid the full sum outstanding as between Tom and Ann in their final settlement of the Joint Venture Account.

You are required to prepare:
a   the Joint Venture Account with Tom as it would appear in the books of Ann
b   the Memorandum Joint Venture Account.

8   Jane and Rose decided to buy antiques on a Joint Venture Account. Profits and losses were to be divided equally.

On 1 August 19–6 Jane made purchases amounting to £10 900 and expenses were £700. On 7 August she purchased items for £9 380 plus expenses, £280. The items costing £9 380 were to be delivered direct to Rose.

On 3 August 19–6 Rose spent £17 380 including expenses on items, and on 12 August 19–6 she made further purchases amounting to £21 340.

Jane retained items amounting to an agreed value of £2 300 for her personal use and sold the remainder in her possession for £13 180. Jane retained items for herself to an agreed value of £4 380 and disposed of the remainder for £53 060. She paid for furniture repairs amounting to £1 360.

It was mutually agreed that Jane should be allowed a credit of £1 000 for travelling

224 Joint venture accounts

expenses and £1 500 for rent of storage premises owned by her. All sales were completed and payment received by the parties concerned on 26 August 19–6.

On 31 August 19–6 settlement in cash was made by the party accountable as between Jane and Rose.

You are required to prepare:
a the Joint Venture Account as it would appear in the books of Jane, recording her transactions with the joint venture
b the Memorandum Joint Venture Account showing the profit or loss.

9 Gary and John entered into a joint venture to buy and sell second-hand cars. Profits and losses were to be shared: Gary, two-fifths; John, three-fifths.

On 1 August 19–7 Gary purchased cars for £20 340 and paid delivery charges of £300. On 7 August 19–7 he bought cars to a total value of £38 400 and paid expenses, £580. On 6 August 19–7 John purchased cars for £29 800, expenses, £600, and on 18 August 19–7 he bought cars to a total value of £19 800 and paid expenses, £400. Gary sold all the cars purchased by him for £67 080 with the exception of one car which John sold for £2 000. John collected the £2 000 due. John retained one car for himself at an agreed value of £8 000 and sold the cars purchased by him for £51 000.

Gary paid selling expenses of £760 and John paid £600 expenses. All transactions were completed by 15 September 19–7 and on that date the sum required in full settlement as between Gary and John was paid by the party accountable.

You are required to prepare:
a the Joint Venture Account as it would appear in the books of John, recording his transactions with the joint venture
b the Memorandum Joint Venture Account showing profit or loss.

10 Josh and Tosh agreed to enter into a joint venture arrangement to buy and sell rare stamps under the following terms:
(*a*) Josh will bear all bad debts.
(*b*) Josh will receive 2 per cent commission on *all* sales.
(*c*) Profits and losses will be shared equally.

Details of transactions are as follows:
1 June   Josh purchased 12 collections of German stamps for £151 800. He paid £10 000 in cash and accepted a bill of exchange for the balance.
8 June   Josh sent Tosh stamps to the value of £60 000.
9 June   Tosh paid in £40 000 and purchased stamps for £14 000.
12 Aug. Tosh paid the bill of exchange which Josh had accepted.

By 20 August 19–3 all stamps purchased had been disposed of, Josh's sales being £150 000 and Tosh's, £80 000. Bad debts on the venture were £900.

During September goods sold by Josh for £5 000 were returned, the buyer claiming £2 000 damages in addition to the purchase price.

It was agreed by Josh and Tosh that the returned goods had no value, and that the loss would be borne by the venture, but that Josh would pay the damages and receive no commission on the sale.

Prepare:
a the Memorandum Joint Venture Account
b Josh's Joint Venture Account with Tosh.

15 Consignment accounts

Traders are always keen to sell their products as widely as possible both at home and abroad. One problem, however, is that customers and local conditions being far from the home base are not as well known as might be desired. Manufacturers and wholesalers get over this problem by appointing local agents who will sell the products on a commission basis. The goods are forwarded to the agent who stores them and sells them in his own area. He pays any necessary charges to get the goods to his customers but *at no stage does he own the goods*. It is not a debtor/creditor relationship.

The agent is not responsible for the bad debts of his customers *unless* he works on the basis of a *del credere* commission. This is an extra commission he becomes entitled to when he accepts responsibility for the bad debts of his customers. The agent is also called a *consignee* and the principal or sender of the goods is also called a *consignor*.

When the principal sends the goods outside the country he sends two items to his agent: (*a*) a copy of a bill of lading which enables the agent to collect the goods when they arrive at their destination, and (*b*) a pro-forma invoice indicating the price the principal (consignor) expects to get for the goods.

Step 1

On despatch of the goods the principal (consignor) opens two accounts in his books:
(i) Consignment Account to (the named agent)
(ii) Goods on Consignment Account.

Entries:
  Debit   Consignment Account with all expenses incurred by consignor
  Credit Bank or Cash Account as appropriate.

Step 2

Nothing further happens until a document called an *account sales* is received from the agent (consignee).

226 Consignment accounts

Then an account is opened in the agent's name.

The entries are Debit the Agent's Account } with gross sales as per account sales
Credit the Consignment Account

Debit the Consignment Account } with expenses incurred by the agent plus his commission.
Credit the Agent's Account

If the agent sends a cheque or bank draft { Debit Bank Account
Credit Agent's Account.

The value of the closing stock (i.e. stock unsold by the agent) is put on the credit side of the Consignment Account.

The student should now be able to see that once again the account is looking like a Trading and Profit and Loss Account – which it really is. To find out the consignor's profit or loss on the consignment the next step is:

Balance the Consignment Account – the balance represents the profit or loss on consignment which is transferred to his own Profit and Loss Account. The Goods on Consignment Account is closed off to his Trading Account.

Value of closing stock. A difficulty arises as to what value to place on stock unsold by the agent. It would be inaccurate to put it in at cost because charges such as lading fees, insurance, carriage, etc. have also been paid on the stock unsold so the formula for arriving at the value of closing stock is:

$$\text{Cost plus } \frac{\text{Value of unsold stock at cost}}{\text{Total value of consignment at cost}} \times All \text{ non-recurring expenses paid to date } excluding \text{ commission}$$

EXAMPLE

On 1 March 19–3 Dixon, a Birmingham manufacturer, sent the following goods on board the SS *Pirate* to his agent Archimedes in Cyprus:

> 40 pedal cycles which cost £50 each to make.

Dixon agreed to a commission of 10 per cent on all goods sold and a special 2 per cent del credere Commission. Dixon paid carriage of £200, insurance £100 and transport charges of £400.

On 17 March Dixon received from Archimedes an Account Sales indicating that he had sold 30 of the cycles @ £100 each. He had paid customs duties of £80, storage charges of £160, and he had deducted these and his commissions from the amount due by him. He enclosed a bank draft for the balance due by him on that date.

On 30 March Dixon received a further Account Sales indicating that Archimedes had sold the balance of the cycles at a price of £95 each. He enclosed a cheque for the amount due less commissions.

Show:
a the account sales dated 17 March
b the appropriate accounts in Dixon's books.

Solution

Dixon's books

a
Account Sales (Archimedes Cyprus)

Consignment on board SS *Pirate* of 40 pedal cycles Nos 1–40

Sold		£	£
30 cycles @ £100 each			3 000
Less Expenses as under			
	Customs duties	80	
	Storage charges	160	
	Commission (10% of £3 000)	300	
	Del credere commission –		
	(2% of £3 000)	60	600
Bank draft herewith			2 400
Cyprus 17 March 19–3		(Signed) Archimedes	

b
Consignment Account (Archimedes Cyprus)

		£			£
1 Mar.	Goods on consignment	2 000	17 Mar.	Account Sales Archimedes (No. 1)	3 000
	Bank: Carriage	200		*Balance c/d (Note 1)	735
	Insurance	100			
	Transport	400			
17 Mar.	Archimedes: Customs duties	80			
	Storage	160			
	10% commission	300			
	2% del credere commission	60			
	Profit on consignment to Profit and Loss Account	435			
		3 735			3 735
17 Mar.	Balance b/d	735	30 Mar.	Account Sales (No. 2)	950
31	Commission (95 + 19)	114			
	Profit on consignment to Profit and Loss Account	101			
		950			950

*Calculation of value of closing stock (Balance c/d £735)

Cost 10 items @ £50 each = £500

Add expenses $\dfrac{940 \times 500}{2\,000}$ = 235

Value of closing stock   735

Goods on Consignment Account

19–3		£	19–3		£
30 Mar.	Trading Account	3 000	1 Mar.	Consignment Account	3 000

Consignment accounts

Archimedes (Cyprus) Account

19–3		£	19–3			£
17 Mar.	Account Sales (No. 1)	3 000	17 Mar.	Bank:	Customs duty	80
					Storage	160
					Commission (10%)	300
					del credere commission (2%)	60
					Bank draft	2 400
		3 000				3 000
30 Mar.	Account Sales (No. 2)	950	30 Mar.	Bank: cheque		950

Procedure in agent's books

Open account for principal (consignor)
Open account for Bank and/or Bills Payable Account
Open account for commission

Entries:
1. On receipt of goods – no entry
2. On payment of expenses — Debit principal's (consignor's) account / Credit bank (cash)
3. On sale of goods — Debit bank or customer's account with value of goods sold. / Credit principal's (consignor's) account
4. Commission — Debit principal's (consignor's) account / Credit Commission Account
5. Payment made by cheque or bill to principal (consignor) — Debit principal's account / Credit bank or Bills Payable Account } with amount sent to principal

Agent's books in example above:

Archimedes' books

Dixon (Birmingham)

19–3			£	19–3		£
5 Mar.	Bank:	Customs dues	80	17 Mar.	Sales	3 000
		Storage	160	30	Sales	950
17		Commission	360			
30		Commission	114			
	Bank draft		2 400			
	Bank draft		836			
			3 950			3 950

Bank Account

19–3		£	19–3			£
17 Mar.	Sales (Account Sales 1)	3 000	5 Mar.	Expenses:	Customs	80
	Sales (Account Sales 2)	950			Storage	160
			17	Draft		2 400
			30	Cheque		836
				Balance c/d		474
		3 950				3 950
30 Mar.	Balance b/d	474				

Commission Account

19–3		£	19–3		£
30 Mar.	Balance c/d	474	17 Mar.	Account Sales Dixon (No. 1)	360
			30 Mar.	Account Sales Dixon (No. 2)	114
		474			474
			30 Mar.	Balance b/d	474

Exercises Set 15

1. On 1 January 19–1 Lords Ltd, Swansea, consigned to Aristocrates, their agent in Athens, goods valued at cost price, £5 000. They paid freight charges, £500, and insurance, £100. On 5 April 19–1 they received an Account Sales showing that all the goods had been sold for £8 000 and that the agent had paid landing charges, £200, and storage, £100. He deducted 5 per cent of gross proceeds as his commission and enclosed a bank draft for the amount due by him.

    Show the Account Sales and the entries in respect of these transactions in the principal's ledger.

2. On 1 February 19–2 a Glasgow firm, Celtic Sticks Ltd, sent a consignment of 7 000 hockey sticks costing £35 000 to O'Brien, who agreed to act as its Irish agent, getting $7\frac{1}{2}$ per cent of gross sales as his commission. The principal paid insurance charges, £250, and freight charges, £350. On 5 May 19–2 an Account Sales was received from O'Brien showing that he had sold 4 000 of the hockey sticks at £10 each and had paid landing charges, £130, customs duty, £100, and delivery charges, £500. He enclosed a bank draft for the amount due to date. On 3 June 19–2 a second Account Sales was received from O'Brien showing that the agent had sold the balance of the consignment at £9 each. He enclosed a bank draft in settlement.

    Record these transactions in the books of Celtic Sticks Ltd.

3. Rose, a Welsh fashion designer, shipped fashion goods to her Paris agent, Mme Sophie, on 1 April 19–4 and sent therewith a pro-forma invoice for £5 780 (goods, £5 000, insurance, £180, and freight, £600). On 4 July Mme Sophie sent an Account Sales showing that a portion of the goods had realised £4 600; from this she had deducted expenses, £100, and commission, £250. She enclosed a bank draft for the

amount due. On 25 August Rose received another Account Sales which showed that the balance of the consignment had been sold for £3 200 which, less £80 expenses and £100 commission, was remitted by bank draft.

Show how these transactions would appear in Rose's books.

4 Show the ledger accounts in the books of British Silk Ltd, Cawley, to record the following transactions (their financial year ends on 31 March):

15 November 19–2: Sent consignment of 2 000 British Silk dresses per SS *Never Die* to High Fashion Inc., New York, to be sold at £50 each.

The cost price of the goods was £40 000. Commission was agreed at $7\frac{1}{2}$ per cent of gross sales. Paid freight and insurance, £2 000.

3 January 19–3: Account Sales received accompanied by a bank draft, showing sale of 800 dresses @ £50 each and payments of dock dues, cartage and storage charges, £1 200. Commission was also deducted.

5 March 19–3: Account Sales received for sale of 100 dresses @ £50 each. Bank draft enclosed for sales less commission.

5 On 23 April 19–1 Robson Ltd, Leeds, consigned to their agent Camasaki in Toyko, 1 000 lorry tyres costing £50 each. Robson Ltd paid shipping charges, £2 000, and insurance, £8 000. On 10 May they received an Account Sales from Camasaki showing the sale of 800 tyres at £75 each. He had paid dock dues, £1 900, and delivery expenses, £400. He enclosed a bank draft for the amount due after he deducted 5 per cent commission on sales and a further 2 per cent del credere commission.

    a Explain the term 'del credere commission'.
    b Show the Consignment Account.
    c Prepare Camasaki's account in Robson Ltd's books.
    d Complete Robson's Bank Account.

6 Show the agent's ledger accounts in Question 1.

7 Show the consignee's ledger accounts in Question 2.

8 Show the agent's ledger accounts in Question 3.

9 Show the consignee's ledger accounts in Question 4.

10 (*a*) A British company wishing to sell their products in France have appointed agents to whom they will send the goods on consignment.
How would you advise them to arrange their book-keeping records with regard to the consignments?
    (*b*) Explain what is meant by 'Account Sales'.
    (*c*) B. Small of Norwich received 20 bales of fabric from his French principal, M. Jacques. He paid the following expenses:

	£
Dock and landing charges	400
Warehouse expenses	220
Insurance	370
Cartage	210

On 1 March 19–7 he sold 15 bales at £1 040 per bale less $7\frac{1}{2}$ per cent discount and on 30 April 19–7 he sold the balance for £5 770 net.

Small was entitled to $2\frac{1}{2}$ per cent commission and 1 per cent del credere commission on the proceeds of all sales. He remitted the account due to M. Jacques on 15 May 19–7.

You are required to prepare the Account Sales sent by Small to M. Jacques.

*11 Heath consigned goods to Stott on 1 October 19–8, their value at cost amounting to £150 000. It was agreed that Stott should receive 5 per cent commission on gross sales and should not be responsible for bad debts. Expenses of freight, insurance and handling, totalling £8 400, were paid by Heath.

Heath's financial year ended on 31 March 19–9, at which date an Account Sales was received from Stott giving the following details. Sixty per cent of the goods were sold for £120 000, but on 31 March 19–9 only £96 000 had been received in respect of these sales. Expenses in connection with the consignment, paid by Stott, were shown as £7 200 and selling expenses incurred amounted to £3 300. A sight draft was remitted with the Account Sales for the balance shown to be due and this was cashed in the bank on 6 April 19–9, when charges of £120 were incurred.

Heath received on 30 June 19–9 a further Account Sales which showed that the remainder of the goods had been sold for £80 000. Selling expenses of £2 400 were incurred. All cash had been received in respect of the sales with the exception of £800, a debt which proved to be irrecoverable. A sight draft for the balance due as shown on the Account Sales was received and this was cashed on 12 July 19–9, the bank charge for doing so being £100.

You are required to write up the necessary accounts in Heath's books to record the above transactions.

* This question is more difficult than the others in this section and might be omitted at first reading.

16 Bills of exchange

A *bill of exchange* is defined as 'an unconditional order in writing addressed by one person to another, signed by the person giving it, requiring the person to whom it is addressed to pay on demand, or at a fixed or determinable future time, a sum certain in money to, or to the order of, a specified person or to bearer' (Bills of Exchange Act 1882).

Parties to a bill of exchange

There are usually *two* persons but there are always *four* parties to a bill:
1. the *drawer* who writes out (draws up) the bill, i.e. the creditor,
2. the *drawee* to whom the bill is addressed, i.e. the debtor,
3. the *payee* to whom the money is to be paid (usually the creditor),
4. the *acceptor* – after acceptance the drawee becomes the acceptor – the debtor (i.e. he accepts legal responsibility to pay the amount).

EXAMPLE

No. 20 £100   London
                                                   1 January 19–1

Stamp   Three Months after Date   Pay me or order ......
        The Sum of One Hundred Pounds Sterling, value
        received

To: Simon Templar
    8 Patrick Street, Kenton   *James Bond*

This is a *draft bill* and does not become a bill of exchange until accepted by the drawer.

Acceptance

The drawee signifies his acceptance of the terms and conditions of the draft by writing the word 'ACCEPTED' on the face of the bill over his usual signature. The word 'accepted' is usual but not essential.

For example, on the above:

ACCEPTED

Simon Templar

This signature now makes Templar liable in law for the bill.

Advantages of a bill of exchange

(a) It is legal evidence of the debt – the creditor can sue on the bill itself.
(b) It fixes the date of payment.
(c) It is a negotiable instrument, i.e. it may be passed to another person in payment of a debt.
(d) It can be turned into cash by 'discounting' it at a bank or with a bill broker.
(e) It helps the creditor increase his credit sales and at the same time ensures payment.
(f) It gives the debtor time to sell the goods before having to pay for them.

All bills are:
Bills receivable – to those to whom the money is payable, i.e. the creditors. They are a current asset on the balance sheet.
Bills payable – to those who accept them, i.e. the debtors. They are a current liability on the balance sheet.

So a bill of exchange is an unconditional order, i.e. a definite instruction by the person writing out the bill (the creditor) addressed to the drawee (the debtor) to pay a certain sum of money at a certain time to the drawer or to somebody named by him or to the bearer of the bill.

A great deal of confusion can be avoided if one simple fact is remembered, i.e. a bill of exchange is just another way of paying a debt. If the bill follows its normal course the net effect will be exactly the same as payment of the debt by cash or cheque.

EXAMPLE
On 1 January B sells £100 worth of goods to A on credit. B draws up a bill of exchange for £100 which he sends to A. The bill is a three-month bill. A accepts the bill and sends it back to B.

B's books

Dr.	A's Account			Cr.
	£			£
1 Jan. Goods	100	1 Jan.	Bill receivable (No.)	100

Dr.	Bills Receivable Account		Cr.
	£		
1 Jan. A: Bill (No.)	100		

234 Bills of exchange

A's books

Dr.		B's Account			Cr.
		£			£
1 Jan.	Bill payable (No.)	100	1 Jan.	Goods	100

Dr.		Bills Payable Account		Cr.
				£
		1 Jan.	B: Bill payable (No.)	100

Maturity

The above bill will mature or become payable on 1 April, i.e. three months from 1 January. By 1 April at the latest A must send B the money due on the bill.

When B receives the money he } debits Bank.
credits Bills Receivable Account.

When A sends the money he } debits Bills Payable Account.
credits Bank.

So we can see that the bill is an intermediate step in the settlement of a debt.

Treatment of bills in books of account

Where a large number of bills are either drawn or accepted, a special subsidiary book called the bills receivable book or bills payable book is kept.

Bills receivable book

Date	No. of bill	From whom received	Drawer	Acceptor	Where payable	Term	Due	Ledger folio	Amount £	Remarks

Bills payable book

Date	No. of bill	To whom given	Drawer	Where payable	Term	Due	Ledger folio	Amount £	Remarks

Where the number of bills is small the general journal is used as a posting medium.

Posting bills receivable book or journal for bills receivable
(when a bill is received)

Entries:
  Debit Bills Receivable Account
  Credit debtor's account

Posting bills payable book or journal for bills payable
(when a bill is accepted)

Entries:
  Debit creditor's account
  Credit Bills Payable Account

Treatment of bills receivable/payable

When a creditor receives an 'accepted' bill from his debtor he can do one of three things with it.

1. Hold it to maturity and then present it to the debtor for payment. (Remember, it will be on the debit side of Bills Receivable Account in creditor's books and on the credit side of Bills Payable Account in debtor's books.)

Entries in creditor's (drawee's) books:
  Debit Bank Account ⎫
  Credit Bills Receivable Account ⎬ with amount of bill

Entries in debtor's (drawee's) books:
  Debit Bills Payable
  Credit Bank

2. Discount it with the bank or bill broker. This means he sells the bill to the bank or broker for less than its face value. The difference between the face value of the bill and the amount received for it is called *discount*.

Entries in creditor's books:
  (a) Debit Bank Account ⎫
      Credit Bills Receivable Account ⎬ with full amount of bill
  (b) Debit Bank Charges or ⎫
        Discounting Charges Account ⎬ with amount of discount
      Credit Bank Account ⎭

3. Negotiate the bill to a creditor. This means pass it in payment of a debt.

Entries:
  Debit creditor's Personal Account
  Credit Bills Receivable Account

Dishonour of a bill

A bill is dishonoured when the acceptor fails to make payment on the maturity of the bill. The guideline here is to restore all accounts to the position they were in before the bill was received – in other words, reverse the entries as far as possible.

1. Dishonour of bill held to maturity

Entries:
    Debit debtor's account
    Credit Bills Receivable Account

2. Dishonour of discounted bill

Entries:
    Debit debtor's account
    Credit Bank Account or broker's account

3. *Noting charges* are charges made by a *notary public* for recording the dishonour of the bill.

Entries:
    Debit debtor's account } with amount of the charge
    Credit Bank Account

4. Dishonour of negotiated bill

Entries:
    Debit acceptor's (debtor's) Personal Account
    Credit creditor's account (to whom bill has been given)

5. **When bill is dishonoured but debtor pays portion of the debt** (for example, composition of 40p in the pound)

Entries:
    (*a*) Debit debtor's account } with full amount of bill
          Credit Bills Receivable Account
    (*b*) Debit Bank Account with money received
          Debit Bad Debts account with amount not paid
          Credit debtor's account with full amount of the bill

Renewal of bill receivable (with interest)

A bill may be renewed by agreement between the drawer and drawee either (*a*) before the old bill reaches maturity or (*b*) after the old bill has been dishonoured. Renewal simply means replacing the old bill with a new one. Of course the drawer will naturally charge interest (he has to wait longer for his money) and this interest is included in the amount of the new bill.

Entries:
- (a) Debit Personal Account of debtor } with old bill
  Credit Bills Receivable Account
- (b) Debit Personal Account } with interest charged
  Credit Interest Account
- (c) Debit Bills Receivable Account } with value of new bill
  Credit debtor's account

Retiral of a bill

This means that the acceptor buys back the bill before date of maturity usually at a discount.

Entries:
Debit Bank Account with amount received
Debit Discount Account with discount allowed
Credit Bills Receivable Account with full amount of bill

Bills payable

These are bills looked at from the point of view of the acceptor or debtor. They are simpler in so far as they are not affected by discounting or negotiation by the drawer. Unless they are dishonoured, renewed or retired they remain in the Bills Payable Account (credit side) until met at maturity.

Details of entries are given in summary in tabular form.

Summary of treatment of bills of exchange

Transaction	Account to be debited	Account to be credited
Bills Receivable		
Receipt of acceptance	Bills Receivable	Debtor's Personal
Duly met at maturity	Bank	Bills Receivable
Discounted	(a) Bank (with amount received) (b) Bank Charges with discount	(a) Bills Receivable with full amount of bill (b) Bank with discount
Dishonoured at maturity	Debtor's Personal	Bills Receivable
Dishonoured after discounting	Debtor's Personal	Bank or bill broker
Dishonoured after negotiation	Debtor's Personal	Creditor's Personal
Renewal (with interest)	(a) Debtor's Personal (old bill) (b) Debtor's Personal (interest) (c) Bills Receivable	(a) Bills Receivable (old bill) (b) Interest (c) Debtor's Personal (new bill)
Noting charges	Debtor's Personal	Bank
Retiral under discount	Bank with amount received Discount with discount allowed	Bills Receivable with full value of bill

238 Bills of exchange

Summary of treatment of bills of exchange *contd*

Transaction	Account to be debited	Account to be credited
Bills payable		
Acceptance of draft	Creditor's Personal	Bills Payable
Duly met at maturity	Bills Payable	Bank
Dishonoured	Bills Payable	Creditor's Personal
Renewal (with interest)	(a) Bills Payable (old bill) (b) Interest (c) Creditor's Personal (new bill)	(a) Creditor's Personal (old bill) (b) Creditor's Personal (c) Bills Payable (new bill)
Retiral under discount	Bills Payable (total)	Bank with amount paid Discount with discount received

A Simple Example

On 1 August 19–3 P. Towser bought goods from A. Skelton valued at £2 500. He paid £400 by cheque and accepted the three bills of £1 000, £600 and £500 for three months, six months and eight months respectively. Skelton immediately discounted the first bill with his bank for £970 and transferred the other bill to A. Mann to whom he owed £600.

All bills were met at maturity. Record these transactions in the ledger accounts of both parties.

Note
In this question P. Towser is the debtor and drawee of the bills.
        A. Skelton is the creditor and drawer of the bills.
        For A. Skelton the bills are bills receivable.
        For P. Towser the bills are bills payable.

Solution

Books of A. Skelton – the creditor

Dr.			P. Towser				Cr.
19–3			£	19–3			£
1 Aug.	Goods		2 500	1 Aug.	Bank		400
					Bill receivable (No. 1)		1 000
					Bill receivable (No. 2)		600
					Bill receivable (No. 3)		500
			2 500				2 500

Dr.		**Bills Receivable Account**				Cr.
19–3		£	19–3			£
1 Aug.	P. Towser (Bill No. 1)	1 000	1 Aug.	Bank (Bill No. 1)		970
	P. Towser (Bill No. 2)	600		Discount		30
	P. Towser (Bill No. 3)	500		A. Mann (Bill No. 2)		600
			1 April	Bank		500
		2 100				2 100

Dr.	A. Mann			Cr.
19–3		£	19–3	£
1 Aug. Bill receivable (No. 2)		600	1 Aug. Balance due	600

Dr.	Discount Account		Cr.
19–3		£	
1 Aug. Bill receivable (No. 1)		30	

Dr.	Bank Account		Cr.
19–3		£	
1 Aug. P. Towser		400	
Bills receivable Discounted No. 1		970	
19–4			
1 April Bills receivable No. 3 honoured		500	

Note

Bill No. 1 matured on 1 November 19–3 (three months) and would be presented to P. Towser for payment by the bank who would collect the full £1 000.

Bill No. 2 matured on 1 February 19–4 and would be presented to P. Towser for payment in full by A. Mann.

Bill No. 3 matured on 1 April 19–4 and would be presented to P. Towser for payment by A. Skelton.

Books of P. Towser – the debtor

Dr.	A. Skelton			Cr.
19–3		£	19–3	£
1 Aug. Bank		400	1 Aug. Goods	2 500
Bill payable (No. 1)		1 000		
Bill payable (No. 2)		600		
Bill payable (No. 3)		500		
		2 500		2 500

Dr.	Bank Account			Cr.
		19–3		£
		1 Aug.	A. Skelton	400
		1 Nov.	Bills payable (No. 1) matured	1 000
		19–4		
		1 Feb.	Bills payable (No. 2) matured	600
		1 Apr.	Bills Payable (No. 3) Matured	500

240 Bills of exchange

Dr.		Bills Payable Account				Cr.
19–3			£	19–3		£
1 Nov.	Bank		1 000	1 Aug.	A. Skelton (Bill No. 1)	1 000
19–4					A. Skelton (Bill No. 2)	600
1 Feb.	Bank		600		A. Skelton (Bill No. 3)	500
1 Apr.	Bank		500			
			2 100			2 100

Note that no entries are made on Towser's books for the discounting of Bill No. 1 or the transfer of Bill No. 2.

Try questions **1** to **8**, then study the following example.

A MORE DIFFICULT EXAMPLE

On 1 January 19–4 J. Twine bought goods from D. Rope valued at £1 800. Twine accepted two bills of £1 100 and £700 at three months and six months respectively. Rope immediately discounted the first bill for £1 000 and passed the second bill on to P. Mills to whom he owed £700. Both bills were dishonoured at maturity. Twine paid the amount due in cash in respect of the first bill and Rope agreed to take another bill for one month, provided it included £50 interest and £5 noting charges. This bill was met at maturity.

Show journal and ledger entries in the books of both Rope and Twine.

SOLUTION

Rope's books – the creditor

	Journal	Dr.	Cr.
19–4		£	£
1 Jan.	J. Twine	1 800	
	Sales Account		1 800
	(goods sold on credit to Twine)		
	Bills Receivable Account	1 800	
	J. Twine		1 800
	(2 bills of £1 100 and £700 accepted by Twine at three months and six months respectively)		
	Bank	1 000	
	Discount	100	
	Bills Receivable Account		1 100
	(discounting of Bill No. 1 (for £1 000))		
	P. Mills	700	
	Bills Receivable Account		700
	(transfer of Bill No. 2 (£700) to creditor P. Mills)		
1 Apr.	J. Twine	1 100	
	Bank		1 100
	(Bill No. 1 dishonoured at maturity)		
	Bank	1 100	
	J. Twine		1 100
	(being payment in cash due on dishonoured bill)		

			Dr.	Cr.
19–4			£	£
1 July	J. Twine		700	
	P. Mills			700
	(being dishonour of bill negotiated to P. Mills)			
	Bills Receivable account		755	
	J. Twine			700
	Interest and Noting Charges Account			55
	(Bill accepted by Twine for one month – interest £50, noting charges £5)			
1 Aug.	Bank		755	
	Bills Receivable Account			755
	(Bill No. 3 honoured at maturity)			

Ledger accounts

Dr.		J. Twine			Cr.
19–4		£	19–4		£
1 Jan.	Goods	1 800	1 Jan.	Bills receivable	1 800
1 Apr.	Bank (dishonoured bill)	1 100	1 Apr.	Cash (bank)	1 100
1 July	P. Mills (dishonoured bill)	700	1 July	Bills receivable	700
		3 600			3 600

Dr.		Bills Receivable Account			Cr.
19–4		£	19–4		£
1 Jan.	J. Twine (Bill No. 1)	1 100	1 Jan.	Bank	1 000
	J. Twine (Bill No. 2)	700		Discount Account	100
1 July	J. Twine (Bill No. 3)	755	1 July	P. Mills	700
			1 Aug.	Bank	755
		2 555			2 555

Dr.		Bank Account			Cr.
19–4		£	19–4		£
1 Jan.	Bill receivable (No. 1)	1 000	1 Apr.	J. Twine (dishonoured bill)	1 100
1 Apr.	J. Twine (Cash)	1 100			
1 Aug.	Bill receivable (No. 3)	755			

Dr.		P. Mills			Cr.
19–4		£	19–4		£
1 Jan.	Bill receivable	700	1 Jan.	Balance b/d	700
			1 July	J. Twine	700

Dr.		Discount Account			Cr.
19–4		£			
1 Jan.	Bill receivable	100			

242 Bills of exchange

Dr.	Interest and Noting Charges Account		Cr.
	19–4		£
	1 July	Bills receivable	55

Twine's books

Journal

		Dr.	Cr.
19–4		£	£
1 Jan.	Purchases Account	1 800	
	D. Rope		1 800
	(purchase of goods on credit)		
	D. Rope	1 800	
	Bills Payable Account		1 800
	(two bills accepted for £1 100 and £700 at 3 and 6 months respectively)		
1 Apr.	Bills Payable Account	1 100	
	D. Rope		1 100
	(dishonour of bill No. 1 at maturity)		
	D. Rope	1 100	
	Bank		1 100
	(payment in cash of dishonoured bill)		
1 July	Bills Payable Account	700	
	D. Rope		700
	(dishonour of bill No. 2 at maturity)		
	D. Rope	755	
	Bills Payable Account		755
	(new bill accepted including interest and noting charges £55)		
1 Aug.	Bills Payable Account	755	
	Bank		755
	(new bill met at maturity)		

Ledger accounts

Dr.			D. Rope			Cr.
19–4		£	19–4			£
1 Jan.	Bills payable	1 800	1 Jan.	Goods		1 800
1 Apr.	Bank	1 100	1 Apr.	Dishonoured bill (No. 1)		1 100
1 July	Bills payable (No. 3)	755	1 July	Dishonoured bill (No. 2)		700
				Interest and noting charges		55
		3 655				3 655

Dr.			Bills Payable Account				Cr.
19–4			£	19–4			£
1 Apr.	D. Rope		1 100	1 Jan.	D. Rope (bill No. 1)		1 100
1 July	D. Rope		700		D. Rope (bill No. 2)		700
1 Aug.	Bank		755	1 July	D. Rope (bill No. 3)		755
			2 555				2 555

Dr.		Bank Account			Cr.
			19–4		£
			1 Apr.	D. Rope	1 100
			1 Aug.	Bills payable	755

Dr.		Interest and Noting Charges Account		Cr.
19–4		£		
1 July	D. Rope	55		

Exercises Set 16

1 From the following details show: **a** the bills receivable book and **b** the postings to the ledger in the books of A. Merchant.

19–2
15 Jan. from D. Falls, Luton £400 at 3 months
18 Feb. from G. Hicks, Cardiff £800 at 6 months
13 Mar. from G. Fritz, London £300 at 4 months
5 May from A. Heaney, Dublin £1 000 at 3 months
15 Aug. from J. Call, Munich £450 at 2 months
4 Oct. from W. Orr, Wembley £720 at 4 months

2 Jack Bradbury, a trader, accepted the following bills during March 19–3 for goods supplied to him.

3 March to M. Michaels, London £600 at 1 month
8 March to A. Scram, Rostrevor £320 at 3 months
11 March to M. Gospel, Watford £750 at 5 months
16 March to R. Poole, Exeter £1 000 at 6 months
25 March to S. Price, Leicester £240 at 3 months

Record these transactions in Bradbury's bills payable book and post to his ledger accounts.

3 On 1 January 19–1 Sydney Moss sold goods valued at £600 to John Lannon. Moss drew a bill on that date on Lannon for that amount at three months. Lannon accepted the bill which was duly met at maturity.

Show the journal and ledger entries for these transactions
a in Moss's books
b in Lannon's books.

4   On 5 March 19–4 D. Foster sold goods to D. Grumley valued at £1 600. Grumley paid £400 by cheque and accepted two bills drawn on him by Foster for £800 and £400 at three months and six months respectively. Both bills were honoured at maturity.

Show journal and ledger entries
a   in Foster's books
b   in Grumley's books.

5   On 13 May 19–5 T. Kane received two bills from P. Doon duly accepted in respect of goods supplied by him, value £850. The bills were for £550 and £300 at three months and six months respectively. He immediately discounted the £550 bill with his bank for £539 and held the other bill to maturity. Both bills were duly met at maturity.

Show the journal, cash book and ledger entries in the books of both parties.

6   On 1 June 19–6 T. Kelly accepted a bill of exchange drawn on him by J. Carr for £200 at four months for goods supplied on 26 May 19–5. The bill was dishonoured at maturity.

Record these transactions in
a   Kelly's books
b   Carr's books.

7   On 4 July 19–7 A. Peters accepted a draft drawn on him by J. Dee for £2 500 at three months. Dee transferred the bill to S. Short, his creditor, to whom he owed £3 000. The bill was duly met at maturity.

Record these transactions
a   in the books of Dee
b   in the books of Peters
c   in the books of Short.

8   On 8 July 19–7 T. Barnet accepted a bill of exchange drawn on him for £400 at four months by J. Doakes for goods supplied on 5 July. Doakes discounted the bill with his bank for £391. When the bill fell due for payment the bank informed Doakes that the bill had been dishonoured by Barnet.

Record these transactions in both Barnet's and Doakes's books.

9   J. Burke owed P. Collins £3 000 for goods supplied on 1 August 19–7. Collins drew two bills on Burke for £1 200 and £1 800 at one month and three months respectively. The bills were accepted by Burke. Collins immediately discounted the first bill (£1 200) with his bank for £1 193 and negotiated the other bill to a creditor. Both bills were dishonoured at maturity.

Show journal, cash book and ledger entries in both sets of books.

10   T. Monks owed N. Hicks £800. On 1 September 19–7 Hicks received a three months' acceptance for the amount owed. That day Hicks discounted the bill at his bank at 8 per cent p.a. The bill was dishonoured at maturity. On 4 December Hicks agreed to take a second bill for one month provided it included an additional £20 as interest and £2 for noting charges. The second bill was met at maturity.

Record these transactions in the books of both parties.

11 On 1 October D. Nestle accepted a bill drawn on him for £200 by T. Drennan at two months. On 1 November Nestle approached Drennan and asked him to retire the bill. This Drennan agreed to do and allowed Nestle a discount of £5.

Record these transactions in the books of both Drennan and Nestle.

12 On 18 September 19–7 George Ltd purchased machinery from the British Engineering Co. Ltd, valued at £10 000. On the same day the company drew on George Ltd a bill of exchange for £5 000 due in two months and one for £5 000 due in three months, both of which were accepted by George Ltd. The first bill was met on the due date. George Ltd was unable to meet the second bill when it became due, the British Engineering Co. Ltd agreed to renew it for a further period of one month, on George Ltd consenting to pay interest of £45 and also charges of £5 in connection with the dishonoured bill which the company had paid.

On 22 December 19–7 a new bill for £550 payable in one month was accepted by George Ltd and duly honoured at maturity.

Show by means of the following ledger accounts how the above transactions would be recorded in the books of George Ltd: **a** machinery; **b** British Engineering Co. Ltd; **c** bills payable; **d** interest and charges.

*13 M. Stone commenced business on 1 January 19–9. The following transactions took place during the period ended 28 February 19–9:

1 Jan.	Goods bought from A. Green, £5 400.
2 Jan.	Sent Green a cheque for £1 000 and accepted a bill drawn by him at one month for £2 000.
3 Jan.	Sold goods to D. Grey, £1 800.
10 Jan.	Bill drawn on Grey for amount due which was accepted and discounted forthwith at the bank for £1 780.
13 Jan.	Bought goods from H. Ford, £1 000, paid him by cheque, £400, on account.
16 Jan.	Sold goods to T. Cinders, £1 200, for cash, £500, and a promissory note at one month for the balance.
24 Jan.	Settled open balance on Green's account by endorsing to him Cinders' promissory note together with a cheque for the balance.
3 Feb.	Withdrew Green's bill for £2 000 by sending him a cheque for £1 000 and accepting another bill for £1 000 payable in one month.
14 Feb.	D. Grey's bill for £1 800 dishonoured.
17 Feb.	As D. Grey was in financial difficulties, it was agreed that he should return goods to the value of £200 and pay, by cheque dated 20 February 19–9, 80 per cent of the balance in full settlement.
19 Feb.	Cinders' promissory note duly met.
24 Feb.	Grey's cheque was honoured.

You are required to show in Stone's books the entries recording the above transactions as they appear in the personal accounts, and in the Bills Receivable Account and the Bills Payable Account in the general ledger bringing down any balances as on 28 February 19–9.

*This question is more difficult than the others in this section and might be omitted at first reading.

246 Bills of exchange

14 With regard to a bill of exchange, explain briefly what is meant by the following operations: **a** discounting, **b** dishonouring.

On 1 January 19–1 White owed Smythe £17 500 and accepted bills of £7 500 and £10 000 each, due respectively in two and three months. On the same day Smythe handed Green the bill for £7 500 in settlement of an account due by him. This bill was duly met. On 11 February Smythe discounted the second bill, incurring charges of £50. At due date the bill was dishonoured, noting charges amounting to £20. White agreed to pay £2 020 immediately and agreed to accept a further bill due in three months for the balance with interest at 8 per cent per annum, Smythe retaining this bill until maturity when it was duly met.

You are required to show, by means of journal entries, how Smythe would have recorded the above transactions in his books (omit narrations).

15 Show by means of journal entries how the following matters would be recorded in the accounts of A. Whitcombe:
   a A. Reardon's promissory note for £3 000 was renewed for four months with interest at 8 per cent p.a.
   b A. Whitcombe's acceptance of T. Thumb's bill for £10 000 was renewed for six months with interest at 8 per cent p.a.
   c B. Hill retired his acceptance for £13 000 by cheque for £7 000 and the acceptance of a new bill by Whitcombe at three months for the balance, interest at 9 per cent p.a. being paid in cash.
   d Goldsmith's acceptance for £10 000, which had been discounted by Whitcombe with his bankers, was dishonoured. Charges and expenses were debited to Whitcombe by his bankers, £20. A promissory note payable in three months with interest at 8 per cent p.a. was given by Goldsmith. Charges and expenses were repaid in cash.
   e Whitcombe's promissory note in favour of A. Mastik for £6 000 was dishonoured through the omission to give the bank instructions to pay. Charges incurred by A. Mastik, £20. Whitcombe discharged his liability by cheque.

16 On 1 February 1985, A purchased goods from B for £1 600 and, on 10 February 1985, A accepted a bill of exchange from B at three months for that amount. On 20 February 1985, A returned to B goods which had been damaged, invoice value £60. On 10 March 1985, B discounted his bill of exchange at Town Bank, Fenton, the discount charges being £5. On maturity, this bill was dishonoured, noting charges being £5. On 12 May 1985, B drew another bill of exchange on A at one month for the balance of A's account, including noting charges plus £12 for the extension of credit. The bill was accepted by A on 16 May 1985 and paid on maturity.

Prepare the following accounts, paying particular attention to dates and narrations (i.e. the name of the other account):

   a in A's ledger:
      (i) Bills Payable
      (ii) B's account
   b in B's ledger:
      (i) Bills Receivable
      (ii) A's account.

[*London Chamber of Commerce and Industry, summer 1986*]

17 Branch accounts

When a firm opens a branch which is situated at a distance from its head office a system of accounting has to be devised so that head office can:

(a) control and supervise the operations of the branch;
(b) find out at any time the trading results of the branch for incorporation into its own final accounts and for comparison with other branches.

Much will depend on the type of product sold. It is easy to supervise and control a branch selling, for example, heavy machinery whereas a branch selling perhaps 100 different grocery lines would require greater control and supervision to avoid thefts, wastage, misappropriation of funds, etc.

Accounting records are usually kept in either of two ways:

(a) all accounting records for the branch are kept at head office except those absolutely necessary at branch level (e.g. debtors ledger, petty cash book).
(b) the branch itself maintains its own accounting records, and only transfers its gross profit or loss at the end of the trading period.

Goods will usually be bought by head office on behalf of the branch and cash received by the branch will be remitted regularly to head office or lodged daily in the local bank to the credit of Head Office Account. When the books are kept at head office, branch salaries, wages and expenses are paid directly by head office.

It is important and helpful to remember that basically, as far as the financial records are concerned, the branch is treated as a customer of head office. For example, goods sent to the branch by head office are debited to Branch Stock Account and credited to Goods Sent to Branches Account.

Goods are invoiced to branch at either: (a) cost price; (b) cost price and fixed percentage; or (c) selling price.

Records kept at head office

Goods invoiced at cost price

Procedure

Open the following accounts in the ledger:
(a) Branch Stock Account for each branch.
(b) Goods Sent to Branches Account.
(c) Branch Expenses Account ⎱ where branch expenses
(d) Branch Profit and Loss Account ⎰ are paid by head office.

Entries:
1. Debit Branch Stock Account
   Credit Goods Sent to Branches Account
   } with value of goods sent to branch at cost price
2. Debit Goods Sent to Branches Account
   Credit Branch Stock Account
   } with any returns made by branch
   Reverse entries for returns by debtors to branch.
3. Debit Cash or Debtors Accounts
   Credit Branch Stock Account
   } with cash or summary of credit sales sent to head office
4. Enter closing stock at branch on credit side of Branch Stock Account. (This will be the opening stock of the next period.)
5. The difference between the two sides of the Branch Stock Account is the gross profit which is transferred to Branch Profit and Loss Account.
6. Debit Branch Expenses Account
   Credit Bank
   } with any branch expenses paid by head office
7. Debit Branch Profit and Loss Account.
   Credit Branch Expenses Account
   } with balance on Branch Expenses Account
   (This closes Branch Expenses Account.)
8. Balance the Branch Profit and Loss Account
9. Debit Branch Profit and Loss Account
   Credit Head Office Profit and Loss Account
   } with net profit of branch
10. Debit Goods Sent to Branches Account
    Credit Head Office Purchases Account
    } with balance on Goods Sent to Branches Account

A SIMPLE EXAMPLE: goods invoiced at cost
Len Dawson has a retail sales branch in Watford. All goods are invoiced to branch at cost price from head office. Branch sales are on a cash and credit basis. All cash received by the branch, together with a summary of credit sales, is sent daily to head office. All branch transactions are recorded in the books of the head office. The following transactions relate to the Watford branch for the year ended 31.12.19–1:

	£
Branch stock 1.1.19–1	18 100
Branch debtors 1.1.19–1	2 700
Goods invoiced to branch	30 200
Cash sales by branch	32 500
Credit sales by branch	16 100
Returns by debtors	700
Rent and rates of branch	2 400
Wages of branch	15 200
Returns by branch	1 200
Discounts allowed to debtors	450
Bad debts	130
Cash received from debtors	14 600
Branch stock 31.12.19–1	20 300

You are required to show:
a Watford Branch Stock Account
b Debtors Control Account
c Branch Profit and Loss Account.

SOLUTION

Head office books

a

Dr.   **Watford Branch Stock Account**   Cr.

19–1		£	19–1		£
1 Jan.	Balance b/d	18 100	31 Dec.	Cash sales	32 500
31 Dec.	Goods sent to branch	30 200		Credit sales	16 100
	Returns by debtors	700		Returns by branch	1 200
	Gross profit to branch Profit and Loss Account	21 100		Balance c/d (branch stock)	20 300
		70 100			70 100
31 Dec.	Balance b/d	20 300			

b

Dr.		Watford Branch Debtors Control Account			Cr.
19–1		£	19–1		£
1 Jan.	Balance b/d	2 700	31 Dec.	Returns by debtors	700
	Credit sales	16 100		Discounts allowed	450
				Bad debts	130
				Cash received from debtors	14 600
				Balance c/d	2 920
		18 800			18 800
31 Dec.	Balance b/d	2 920			

c

Dr.	Watford Branch Profit and Loss Account for year ended 31.12.19–1				Cr.
19–1		£	19–1		£
31 Dec.	Branch rent and rates	2 400	31 Dec.	Gross profit from Branch Stock Account	21 100
	Wages	15 200			
	Discounts allowed	450			
	Bad debts	130			
	Net profit to Head Office Profit and Loss Account	2 920			
		21 100			21 100

Goods invoiced at selling price or cost plus fixed percentage

Control of the branch becomes easier when goods are invoiced to branch at selling price or at cost plus fixed percentage, because if all items in the Branch Stock Account are recorded at invoice price then

opening stock at selling price + goods sent to branch at selling price must be equal to returns at selling price + sales + closing stock at selling price.

If not, something has gone wrong at the branch which will show itself in the Branch Stock Account. Some level of deficiency is normally tolerable particularly where goods sold are of a perishable nature. Deficiencies may be due to, for example, loss of weight in breaking bulk, items going stale or loss by evaporation. However, if the deficiency or shortage exceeds 'normal' levels it may have far more serious causes, e.g. pilferage, theft or misappropriation by staff or customers and this type of shortage must be investigated immediately. There are two main ways for treating goods invoiced to branch at selling price or at cost plus fixed percentage. Both systems have two things in mind:

1. Control of the branch and its operations.
2. Obtaining the trading results of the branch as was done for goods invoiced at cost.

Goods invoiced at selling price or cost plus fixed percentage

Remember that both will show the same results. The only difference is that the first way shown here uses memoranda columns which are not part of the double-entry system while the second system uses an extra account in the ledger (Adjustment Account) so that the double-entry system can be maintained.

Branch Stock Account with memoranda columns

Procedure:
Open Branch Stock Account but allow two columns headed 'Invoice price', one on each side of the account like this:

Dr.		**Branch Stock Account**		Cr.
Invoice price	Cost price		Invoice price	Cost price

All entries relating to opening stock, goods received from head office, returns to head office and closing stock will be recorded both at cost and invoice price. (It will be necessary to reduce these items to cost price because they will be appearing on the invoices at selling price.)

The columns headed 'Cost price' when balanced will give the gross profit or loss as for goods invoiced at cost. The columns headed 'Invoice price' should balance; if they do not, there is either a surplus or deficiency for the amount of the balance.

Branch Stock Account with additional Branch Stock Adjustment Account

Procedure:
Open Branch Stock Account
Open Branch Stock Adjustment Account
Open Goods Sent to Branches Account

Entries:
   Debit Branch Stock Account with invoice price of goods
   Credit { Goods Sent to Branches Account with cost price of goods
           Branch Stock Adjustment Account with difference (i.e. profit element)

Returns:
   Debit { Goods Sent to Branches Account with cost price of goods returned to head office
           Branch Stock Adjustment Account with profit element on goods returned
   Credit Branch Stock Account with returns at invoice price

Sales:
  (a) Cash Sales: Debit Bank   } with
                    Credit Branch Stock Account   } cash sales
  (b) Credit Sales: Debit Debtors Control Account }
                      or debtors' accounts   } with
                    Credit Branch Stock Account   } credit sales

Opening and closing stock. Opening and closing stock must be entered on Branch Stock Account at selling price but the unrealised profit element on both must appear on the Branch Stock Adjustment Account.

The unrealised profit on opening stock will appear on the credit side of Branch Stock Adjustment Account.

The unrealised profit on closing stock will appear on the debit side of the Branch Stock Adjustment Account.

Balance the Branch Stock Account and transfer the balance (which is either a surplus or shortage).

If a surplus: Debit Branch Stock Account
Credit Branch Stock Adjustment Account.

If a shortage, entries are reversed.

Balance the Branch Stock Adjustment Account. The balance will be the gross profit or loss which is transferred to Branch Profit and Loss Account.

A MORE DIFFICULT EXAMPLE: goods invoiced at selling price

A. Dore Ltd, retail traders, have a branch in Exeter. All goods are purchased by the head office and invoiced to the branch at selling price which is cost price plus 50 per cent. The head office keeps a record of all branch transactions. On 1 January 19–1 the stock at the Exeter branch, at selling price, was £9 000 and the amount owed by debtors was £1 460. The following particulars relating to the Exeter branch were extracted from the head office books for the year ended 31.12.19–1:

	£
Cash sales	58 000
Goods to branch at selling price	60 000
Goods returned by branch	300
Bad debts written off	60
Goods returned by credit customers	150
Branch expenses	5 640
Discount to debtors	180
Cash and cheques paid by debtors	3 720
Customers' cheques dishonoured	140
Stock at branch 31.12.19–1	7 200
Branch debtors 31.12.19–1	1 050

It had been agreed to allow authorised reductions of 1 per cent of total gross sales and if there was a surplus or deficiency it was to be treated as a bonus *or* a charge to the manager.

You are required to show:
a Branch Debtors Control Account
b (i) Branch Stock Account with memoranda columns
   or
   (ii) Branch Stock Account *and* Branch Stock Adjustment Account
c Branch Profit and Loss Account

Solution

Head office books

a

Dr.		Exeter Branch Debtors Control Account			Cr.
19–1		£	19–1		£
1 Jan.	Balance b/d	1 460	31 Dec.	Bad debts written off	60
31 Dec.	Dishonoured cheques	140		Sales returns	150
	Credit sales*	3 560		Discount allowed	180
				Payments by debtors	3 720
				Balance c/d	1 050
		5 160			5 160
31 Dec.	Balance b/d	1 050			

*It was necessary to compile the Debtors Control Account in this question as credit sales were not given.

b (i) Branch Stock Account with memoranda columns

Dr.				Exeter Branch Stock Account				Cr.
		Invoice Price	Cost Price				Invoice Price	Cost Price
19–1		£	£	19–1		£	£	£
1 Jan.	Balance b/d	9 000	6 000					
31 Dec.	Goods to Branches Account	60 000	40 000	31 Dec.	Credit sales Less returns	3 560 150		
	Surplus	525	—				3 410	3 410
	Gross profit to Branch Profit and Loss Account		20 410		Cash sales Returns by branch Reduction in selling price Balance c/d (stock)		58 000 300 615 7 200	58 000 200 — 4 800
		69 525	66 410				69 525	66 410
31 Dec.	Balance b/d	7 200	4 800					

(ii) Branch Stock Account and Branch Stock Adjustment Account

Dr.		Exeter Branch Stock Account				Cr.
19–1		£	19–1		£	£
1 Jan.	Balance b/d	9 000	31 Dec.	Credit sales Less returns	3 560 150	
31 Dec.	Goods to Branches Account	60 000				3 410
	Surplus	525		Cash sales		58 000
				Returns to head office		300
				Reductions in selling price		615
				Balance c/d		7 200
		69 525				69 525
31 Dec.	Balance b/d	7 200				

Dr.	Exeter Branch Stock Adjustment Account				Cr.
19–1		£	19–1		£
31 Dec.	Returns	100	1 Jan.	Balance b/d	3 000
	Reduction in selling		31 Dec.	Goods to branches	20 000
	price	615		Branch stock – surplus	525
	Branch Profit and Loss				
	Account	20 410			
	Balance c/d	2 400			
		23 525			23 525
			31 Dec.	Balance b/d	2 400

c

Dr.	Exeter Branch Profit and Loss Account for year ended 31.12.19–1				Cr.
19–1		£	19–1		£
31 Dec.	Bad debts	60	31 Dec.	Gross profit – Branch	
	Branch expenses	5 640		Stock Account	20 410
	Discount allowed	180			
	Manager's bonus	525			
	Net profit to head office				
	Profit and Loss				
	Account	14 005			
		20 410			20 410

Records kept at branch

When a branch is large enough, it may be preferable for a full set of books to be kept at the branch. The branch then keeps the same books as if it were an independent unit, the only difference being that the branch would *not* have a Capital Account. This Capital Account is replaced in the branch books by a Head Office Current Account (head office keeps a Branch Office Current Account with identical entries in both except, of course, on opposite sides). The branch has a debtor/creditor relationship with head office. The Head Office Current Account in the branch books contains records of transactions concerned with supplying of resources both of a capital and a revenue nature to the branch and the return of such resources from the branch to head office.

EXAMPLES
1. Head office buys premises for the branch.
   Branch books   Debit Premises Account
                           Credit Head Office Current Account
   Head office books   Debit Branch Current Account
                           Credit Bank Account
2. Branch remits cash to head office.
   Branch books   Debit Head Office Current Account
                           Credit (Branch) Bank Account

Head office books   Debit Head Office Bank Account
                      Credit Branch Current Account

So, everything received from head office is *credited* to Head Office Current Account in the branch books while everything sent to head office from the branch is *debited* to Head Office Current Account in the branch books. The reverse entries are made in the Branch Current Account in head office books.

The branch continues trading in the normal way during the year and prepares its own Trading and Profit and Loss Account. It transfers its net profit to the credit of Head Office Current Account.

It then submits its trial balance to head office for incorporation in the Head Office final accounts and balance sheet. On the branch trial balance will appear a credit balance for Head Office Current Account. This will be offset by a debit balance on head office trial balance for Branch Current Account.

Items in transit at end of accounting period

Some items, either cash or goods, may be in transit, i.e. on the way between head office and branch at the end of the accounting period. For example, cash remitted by branch on 31 December will not have arrived at head office on that date. The branch will have credited its cash book and debited Head Office Current Account with this amount but this item will not have been posted in head office books. If it were left like this, the balances on Head Office and Branch Current Accounts would not agree; they would be out of balance by the amounts in transit. But both accounts *must* agree so one party must make an adjustment. Normally head office will do it. In the example given, the Branch Current Account in head office would be credited with cash in transit and this amount would be brought down on the debit side of the Branch Current Account as a balance. This balance would be cleared when head office received the remittance.

Inter-branch transactions

Where branches of the same firm have credit dealings with each other, both branches will keep Current Accounts for each other. When the trial balances for each branch are submitted to head office, the balances on these accounts will cancel each other out. If goods are transferred between branches at selling price, the 'sending' branch will be showing a profit on these goods which the organisation as a whole does not realise until the goods are sold. A provision is made for unrealised profit on unsold stock at branches at the end of the accounting period. This provision is debited in Head Office Profit and Loss Account and deducted from stock in the combined balance sheet.

Exercises Set 17

1 A London firm, Dock Ltd, operates a branch in Crewe. All purchases are made by head office on behalf of the branch and invoiced to the branch at cost price. The branch sells on a cash only basis and remits all its takings directly to head office. The following transactions took place during the year 19–1:

	£
Goods sent to branch by head office	500 000
Goods returned by branch to head office	10 000
Branch cash sales during the year	650 000
Stock of goods at branch on 31 December 19–1	20 000

Record these transactions in head office books.

2 A company with its head office in Coventry maintains a branch in Leeds. All purchases for the branch are made by head office and charged to the branch at cost. No credit is allowed by the branch to its customers and the daily takings are lodged in the local bank to the credit of Head Office Account at the end of each day. The following details refer to the branch for the year 19–2:

	£
Stock at branch 1 January	26 000
Goods sent to branch by head office	380 000
Goods returned by branch	34 000
Cash lodged by branch to credit of Head Office Account	482 680
Stock of goods held at branch on 31 December 19–2	25 280

Prepare:
a   Goods Sent to Branches Account
b   Leeds Branch Stock Account in head office books.

3 Universal Supplies Ltd of Glasgow maintains a branch in St Andrew's. Head office invoices the goods to branch at cost price. The branch sells goods both for cash and on credit terms. The branch remits its daily cash takings by means of bank giro to the credit of Head Office Account. The branch office keeps a sales ledger and regularly sends a summary of its credit sales to head office. All other branch records are kept at head office. The following details relate to the branch for the year 19–3:

	£
Stock at branch at 1 January	36 000
Goods invoiced to branch	85 000
Cash sales	48 000
Credit sales	54 000
Goods returned by branch to head office	8 500
Returns by credit customers to branch	500
Stock at branch on 31 December 19–3	34 000

Write up the Branch Accounts in head office books.

4 United Kingdom Stores, whose head office is in Oxford, invoices its goods at cost to its Kettering branch. All branch records except debtors ledger are kept at head office. Both cash and credit sales are transacted by the branch and all cash received, together with a summary of credit sales, is remitted regularly to head office. Head office pays all branch expenses. The following are details of branch transactions for six months ended 30 June 19–4:

		£
1 Jan.	Stock at branch	6 700
30 June	Goods invoiced to branch	57 800
	Cash sales	21 430
	Credit sales	58 350
	Branch wages paid	12 500
	Branch expenses paid	2 300
	Goods returned by branch to head office	1 500
	Goods returned by credit customers to branch	700
	Branch rent and rates paid	1 200
	Stock at branch	12 650

Prepare the following accounts in head office books:
a Kettering Branch Stock Account
b Goods Sent to Branches Account
c Branch Expenses Account
d Branch Profit and Loss Account.

5 Welsh Products of Cardiff invoices goods to its Swansea branch at cost price. Swansea branch sells both on cash and credit terms. All cash received at the branch, together with a summary of credit sales, is sent daily to head office. The branch keeps a debtors ledger but all other branch records including a Debtors Control Account is kept by head office. All branch expenses are paid by head office. The following transactions relate to the Swansea branch for the month of January 19–5:

	£
Branch stock at 1.1.19–5	4 500
Branch debtors balance at 1.1.19–5	6 500
Goods invoiced to branch for month	21 750
Goods returned by branch	1 250
Branch salaries paid by head office	2 200
Credit sales	14 600
Goods returned to branch by debtors	600
Cash sales	19 200
Payment by branch debtors	9 800
Branch expenses paid by head office	460
Discount allowed to debtors	250
Stock at branch 31 January 19–5	3 760

Prepare:
a Swansea Branch Stock Account
b Goods to Branches Account
c Branch Expenses Account
d Branch Profit and Loss Account
e Debtors Control Account.

6 A London firm operates a Leicester branch. All purchases are made by head office and invoiced to branch at selling price which is cost plus 25 per cent. The branch sells on a cash only basis and remits all takings directly to head office. The following transactions took place for the month of July 19–7:

	£
Goods sent to branch	20 000
Branch returns to head office	2 000
Branch cash sales	17 000
Stock at branch on 31 July 19–7	1 000

Record these transactions of Leicester branch in head office books using Branch Stock Account with memoranda columns.

7 A firm invoiced goods to its branch at 125 per cent of cost. The branch sells both for cash and on credit terms. The following transactions relate to the branch for the month of February 19–8.

		£
1 Feb.	Stock at branch at selling price	80 000
28 Feb.	Goods invoiced to branch for month	160 000
	Cash sales by branch remitted to head office	126 000
	Goods returned by branch to head office	4 000
	Credit sales by branch	68 000
	Stock at branch	40 000

Show two ways of recording these transactions in head office's books.

8 From the following prepare: **a** Branch Stock Account, **b** Branch Stock Adjustment Account, in the books of a Lincolnshire firm which invoices goods to its London branch at cost price plus $33\frac{1}{3}$ per cent for the month of March 19–9.

	£
Stock at branch at invoice price, 1 March	40 000
Goods sent to branch	88 000
Goods returned by branch to head office	4 000
Goods returned to London branch by credit customers	2 000
Cash sales by branch	32 500
Credit sales by branch	30 000
Stock of goods at branch on 31 March at invoice price	36 000

9 Royal Products, whose head office is in Kensington, invoiced its goods to its Cambridge branch at $133\frac{1}{3}$ per cent of cost price. All records are kept at head office except a debtors ledger (head office keeps a Debtors Control Account). All receipts are banked daily to the credit of Head Office Account.

From the following figures show head office accounts for:
  a   Branch Stock Account with memoranda columns or Branch Stock Account and Branch Stock Adjustment Account
  b   Branch Expenses Account
  c   Branch Profit and Loss Account
  d   Branch Debtors Control Account for the month of October 19–1.

			£
1 Oct.	Stock at branch (invoice price)		42 000
	Branch debtors: balance		26 000
31 Oct.	Goods sent to branch		72 000
	Branch sales: cash		23 600
	credit		51 600
	Goods returned to branch by credit customers		2 000
	Returns to head office at invoice price		4 800
	Branch wages paid by head office		3 860
	Branch expenses paid by head office		1 330
	Cash received from branch debtors		45 240
	Discount allowed to branch debtors		760
	Branch rent paid by head office		800
	Stock at branch 31 October at invoice price		35 200

*10 Mark James carries on a retail business in two shops, one in Birmingham and the other in Manchester. Each shop keeps complete double-entry books, but all accounts relating to capital and fixed assets are kept in the Birmingham books.

The following trial balances were extracted from Mr James's books on 30 September 19–8.

	Birmingham		Manchester	
	Dr.	Cr.	Dr.	Cr.
	£	£	£	£
Capital Account Mr James				
On 1 October 19–7		268 460		
Drawings during year	20 780		8 400	
Freehold property at cost 1.10.19–7				
Birmingham	76 000			
Manchester	42 500			
Furniture and fittings at cost 1.10.19–7				
Birmingham	8 200			
Manchester	5 600			
Additions during year			800	
Stock in trade 1.10.19–7	52 360		48 100	
Purchases	125 120		32 070	
Sales		127 830		92 560
Purchases ledger balances	150	3 070		1 380
Sales ledger balances	21 300		14 230	260
Wages and National Insurance	9 130		6 480	
General expenses	7 620		5 630	
Birmingham Account 1.10.19–7	58 540			
Manchester Account 1.10.19–7				58 540
Remittances during year		34 250	35 550	
Cash in hand and at bank	6 310		1 480	
	433 610	433 610	152 740	152 740

* This question is more difficult than the others in this section and might be omitted at first reading.

You are given the following additional information:
(a) During the year goods costing £26 250 were forwarded from Birmingham to Manchester, but no entry has been made in the books for these.
(b) A remittance of £1 300 was in transit from Manchester to Birmingham on 30 September 19–8.
(c) Stock on 30 September 19–8 was valued as follows:
   Manchester   £61 550
   Birmingham   £33 620

You are required to prepare:
a the Profit and Loss Account for the year ended 30 September 19–8 showing the Manchester and Birmingham figures separately
b the balance sheet as on 30 September 19–8.

18 Issue of shares and debentures, redemption and purchase of company's own shares

Shares

Public limited companies can raise capital by the issue of shares and debentures provided they act in accordance with the Companies Acts. Each company must act in accordance with two documents: (*a*) its memorandum of association, and (*b*) its articles of association.

The memorandum of association is the document that, among other things, discloses the amount and type(s) of shares the company is authorised to issue.

Types of share

There are many types of shares, the more usual being:
1. *Preference shares.* The holder is entitled to a fixed dividend out of profits (if any) before any dividend is paid to ordinary shareholders, e.g. 10% preference shares.
2. *Cumulative preference shares.* These are similar to preference shares except that, if dividend is not paid in any one year due to the company not making a profit, the dividend accumulates until such time as the company makes a profit and can pay all arrears of dividend, e.g. 8% cumulative preference shares.
3. *Redeemable preference shares.* The company reserves the right to redeem them on or after a certain date. The redemption date should be shown on the balance sheet, e.g. 11% redeemable preference shares.
4. *Ordinary shares.* The dividend is not fixed on these shares. They share the distributed profits only after the preference shareholders have been paid. Ordinary shares, sometimes called equity shares, are the most important shares in a company as they carry voting rights unless these rights are specifically excluded. In effect, the ordinary shareholders own and control the company.

Types of share capital

(*a*) *Authorised or nominal or registered*, i.e. the full amount which the memoran-

dum of association authorised the company to issue, on which stamp duty has been paid.
(b) *Issued* is that portion of the authorised capital allotted for subscription.
(c) *Called-up* is that part of issued capital which the company has asked shareholders to pay for.
(d) *Paid-up* is the amount of called-up capital actually received by the company.
(e) *Uncalled* is the amount not called up on shares issued.

Prices at which shares are issued

(a) At par, i.e. at a price equal to nominal value (e.g. £1 for a £1 share).
(b) At a premium, i.e. at a price above nominal value (£1.50 for a £1 share).

Payment for shares issued

When issuing shares the company may ask for payment: (a) in full with application or in instalments, or it may ask for (b) part-payment with application, part-payment on allotment, or for the balance on call(s) by directors.

From the accounting point of view, shares are a liability of the company (the amount it owes to shareholders). A separate account should be kept for each class of share.

The important thing to remember and visualise is that when all the steps have been gone through, all the shares to be issued will have been issued (the full amount of nominal value of issued share capital will be on the credit side of the Share Capital Account and the corresponding money received will be on the debit side of the Bank Account).

Journal

1. Shares issued at par payable in full with application

Entries:
(a) Debit Shareholders Account } with full value of shares
    Credit Share Capital Account
(b) Debit Bank } with cash received from shareholders
    Credit Shareholders Account

2. Shares issued at par payable in instalments

Entries:
(a) Debit Application/Allotment/Call Account } with amount called up at each stage
    Credit Share Capital Account
(b) Debit Bank } with cash actually paid by shareholders at each stage
    Credit Application/Allotment/Call Account

3. Shares over-subscribed

Entries:
- (a) Debit Application Account / Credit Bank — if cash is returned to applicants for shares
- (b) Debit Application Account / Credit Allotment Account — if money over-subscribed is held against allotment

4. Shares under-subscribed

In this case only the number of shares applied for can be issued.

5. Unpaid calls

Entries:
    Debit Calls in Arrear Account
    Credit the appropriate Call Account

Alternatively, bring down unpaid calls as a debit balance on the appropriate account

6. Shares issued at a premium (assuming premium is due with allotment money)

Entries:
- (a) Debit Application Account / Credit Share Capital Account — with amount due on application
- (b) Debit Bank / Credit Application Account — with cash received on application
- (c) Debit Allotment Account with amount due on allotment including premium
    Credit Share Capital Account with amount due excluding premium
    Credit Share Premium Account with amount of premium

Continue in the usual manner with Call Accounts

7. Forfeiture of shares

Entries:
- (a) Debit Share Capital Account / Credit Forfeited Shares Account — with total amount *called-up* to date on shares forfeited
- (b) Debit Forfeited Shares Account / Credit Call Account — with value of calls in arrears

The credit balance on Forfeited Shares Account will represent the actual cash received in respect of the forfeited shares and would be shown as capital reserve on the balance sheet.

Reissue of forfeited shares

Note that the new shareholder must pay at least the amount due by the shareholder whose shares have been forfeited; he may be asked to pay more.

264 Issue of shares and debentures

Entries:
- (a) Debit new shareholder's account with amount payable in cash by him
- (b) Debit Forfeited Shares Account with difference between amount payable by new shareholder and nominal value of share
- (c) Credit Share Capital Account with nominal value of shares

EXAMPLE

The authorised capital of Brand PLC is £300 000 made up of 200 000 ordinary shares at £1 each and 100 000 10% preference shares at £1 each. On 1 January 19–1 all the preference shares and 150 000 of the ordinary shares were already issued. On that date the directors decided to offer the remaining ordinary shares for public subscription at a premium of 20p per share payable as follows:

40p on application
70p on allotment (including premium)
10p on first and final call.

Applications and cash were received for the shares on 11 February. The shares were allotted on 25 February and money due on allotment was received on 1 March. The first and final call was made on 10 April and all money due was received on 15 April, except for one shareholder who failed to pay the money due on 1 000 shares.

You are required to show:
a the ledger accounts to record the above transactions
b the appropriate sections of the balance sheet on 30.4.19–1.

SOLUTION

Note that the number of shares to be issued is 50 000.

a   **Ledger accounts**

Dr.			**Applications Account**				Cr.
19–1			£	19–1			£
1 Jan.	Ordinary Share Capital Account		20 000	1 Feb.	Bank		20 000

Dr.			**Allotment Account**				Cr.
19–1			£	19–1			£
25 Feb.	Ordinary share Capital Account		25 000	1 Mar.	Bank		35 000
	Share Premium		10 000				
			35 000				35 000

Dr.			**Share Premium Account**				Cr.
				19–1			£
				25 Feb.	Allotment Account		10 000

Dr.		First and Final Call Account				Cr.
19–1			£	19–1		£
10 Apr.	Ordinary Share Capital Account		5 000	15 Apr.	Bank Calls in Arrear Account	4 900 100
			5 000			5 000

Dr.		10% Preference Share Capital Account			Cr.
			19–1		£
			1 Jan.	Balance b/d	100 000

Dr.		Ordinary Share Capital Account				Cr.
19–1		£	19–1			£
30 Apr.	Balance c/d	200 000	1 Jan.	Balance b/d		150 000
				Application Account		20 000
			1 Mar.	Allotment Account		25 000
			1 Apr.	First and Final Call Account		5 000
		200 000				200 000
			30 Apr.	Balance b/d		200 000

Dr.		Calls in Arrear Account		Cr.
19–1		£		
15 Apr.	First and Final Call Account	100		

Dr.		Bank Account (extract)		Cr.
19–1		£		
11 Feb.	Application Account	20 000		
1 Mar.	Allotment Account	35 000		
15 Apr.	First and Final Call Account	4 900		

Note that it is not necessary to balance Bank Account as it is only an extract.

b

Brand PLC
Balance sheet as at 30.4.19–1 (extract)

	£	£
Sundry assets (Note 1)	250 000	
Bank	59 900	
		309 900

Financed by: *Share capital*	Authorised £	Issued £	Paid £	Total £
100 000 10% preference shares of £1 each	100 000	100 000	100 000	
200 000 ordinary shares of £1 each	200 000	200 000	199 900	
				299 900

Capital reserve		
Share premium		10 000
		309 900

Notes
1. *Sundry assets*. It is assumed that capital already issued has been used for purchase of various assets.
2. *Issued capital*. Ordinary shares could have been shown as follows:

	Issued £	£
	200 000	
Less Calls in arrears	100	
		199 900

Then the 'Paid' column would be omitted.

Debentures

Debentures are long-term loans to the company for a specified period. They earn a fixed rate of interest which must be paid whether the company makes a profit or not. They do not form part of company share capital.

1. Issue at par

Entries:
    Debit Bank Account
    Credit Debentures Account } with cash received

2. Issue at discount

Entries:
    Debit Bank Account with cash received
    Debit Debenture Discount Account with discount
    Credit Debentures Account with full amount

3. *Issue at premium*

Entries:
    Debit Bank Account with cash received
    Credit Debentures Account with nominal value
    Credit Debenture Premium Account with premium

Redemption and purchase of company's own shares

We have noted that a company can issue redeemable shares, i.e. shares that the company is legally entitled to buy back because they were sold to shareholders on that basis, e.g. 10% redeemable preference shares (1976–92). This means that at a date no earlier than a specified date in 1992 the company is empowered to buy back its redeemable shares at a price advised to the shareholder when buying the shares.

The price would also be stated on notes accompanying the company's balance sheet, e.g. 'the redeemable preference shares are redeemable at par in November 1992.'

Up to the Companies Act 1981 a company could not buy back its own shares unless they were specifically redeemable. Before 1981 companies outside Great Britain could buy back their own shares, even ordinary shares. The precise reasons why a British company was not allowed to buy back its own shares were probably tied up with the law's wish to preserve the rights of creditors and others owed money by the company. If a company were to buy back its own shares there would be less cash available for them in the event of company failure. Since the 1981 Act a company may buy back any class of its own shares if it is authorised to do so by its memorandum of association. There is one important safeguard built into the 1981 Act and it is that a company cannot issue redeemable shares unless it has also issued shares which are not redeemable. Otherwise a company would be put into a position whereby it could buy back all of its share capital thus getting rid altogether of its shareholders.

The company is also forbidden to 'purchase' its own shares unless there remain other shares issued which are not redeemable.

Additionally after purchasing its own shares the company must have at least two members.

All shares redeemed or purchased must be cancelled immediately. No further trading in them is allowed and they must not appear on the company balance sheet.

Advantages of company redeeming and purchasing its own shares

1. A public company with surplus cash and too high a current asset and liquid asset ratio might be anxious to get rid of some of its surplus cash by buying back or redeeming its shares rather than expanding the business.
2. The company might be anxious to increase the profits available to its equity shareholders and thereby be enabled to increase its dividends and improve the price of its shares on the stock exchange.

3. The company might wish to redeem shares to avoid the danger of a takeover bid. Too much liquidity is often a sign that the company is undertrading and companies undertrading are targets for takeover bids and asset stripping.
4. In private companies it encourages people to invest in them if they know that the company is willing to buy back its shares. Shares then have far more liquidity.
5. In family owned companies on the death of one of the main shareholders cash may be required to pay death duties or taxes. It may also help family companies retain ownership of their particular company.
6. 'Difficult' shareholders (e.g. shareholders who disrupt annual general meetings) can now be eliminated by the purchase of their shares. If you can't beat them buy them out!
7. It would encourage employees to accept shares as part of their overall wage settlement in the knowledge that they could be converted into cash at short notice.

The reasoning behind the Companies Act 1981 was that, while allowing a company to purchase or redeem its own shares, the capital invested in the company should not decrease when shares were purchased or redeemed.

The Act stipulates that only shares that are fully paid up can be redeemed or bought back by the company.

Redemption or purchase of shares by public companies

Sections 45 and 46 of the Act require for public companies that in respect of the nominal value of the shares to be redeemed or purchased there must be either:
(a) a new issue of shares to provide finance for the redemption or purchase of these shares
or
(b) a balance large enough to the credit of the Profit and Loss Appropriation Account to be used for the purpose of redeeming or purchasing the shares
or
(c) a combination of both

Three examples using the same company will help to illustrate the procedure to be followed in each case and the effects will be shown on a revised balance sheet after the transactions have been completed.

Let us suppose that the original capital structure of a company was as follows:

	£	£
Share capital		
Ordinary shares of £1 each	500 000	
10% preference shares of £1 each	50 000	
		550 000
Reserves		
Profit and Loss Appropriation Account (balance)		80 000
		630 000

Example 1

The preference shares are to be redeemed/purchased at par by the issue of 50 000 ordinary shares of £1 each. The issue is fully subscribed.

Journal

		Dr. £	Cr. £
(a)	New Ordinary Share Applicants Account Ordinary Share Capital Account	50 000	50 000
(b)	Bank Account New Ordinary Share Applicants Account Being allotment and receipt of cash for new issue of 50 000 ordinary shares of £1 each	50 000	50 000
(c)	10% Preference Share Capital Account 10% Preference Share Purchase Account	50 000	50 000
(d)	10% Preference Share Purchase Account Bank Account Being redemption/purchase of 50 000 10% preference shares of £1 each and cash payment made therefor	50 000	50 000

Revised balance sheet (extract)

	£
Share capital	
Ordinary shares £1 each	550 000
Reserves	
Profit and Loss Appropriation Account	80 000
	630 000

Example 2

The preference shares are to be redeemed/purchased at par with no new issue of shares to provide finance. The redemption/purchase is to be made out of the Profit and Loss Appropriation Account.

Journal

		Dr. £	Cr. £
(a)	10% Preference Share Capital Account 10% Preference Share Purchase Account	50 000	50 000
(b)	Preference Share Purchase Account Bank Account Being redemption/purchase of 50 000 10% preference shares and payment therefor	50 000	50 000
(c)	Profit and Loss Appropriation Account Capital Redemption Reserve Account Being transfer as per Section 45 of Companies Act 1981	50 000	50 000

Revised balance sheet (extract)

	£
Share capital	
Ordinary shares £1 each	500 000
Capital redemption reserve	50 000
	550 000
Profit and Loss Appropriation Account	30 000
	580 000

EXAMPLE 3

The preference shares are to be redeemed/purchased at par partly from the issue of 40 000 £1 ordinary shares at par and partly out of the Profit and Loss Appropriation Account.

Journal

		Dr. £	Cr. £
(a)	New Ordinary Share Applicants Account	40 000	
	Ordinary Share Capital Account		40 000
(b)	Bank Account	40 000	
	Ordinary Share Applicants Account		40 000
	Being new issue of 40 000 ordinary shares of £1 each at par and receipt of payment for same		
(c)	Profit and Loss Appropriation Account	10 000	
	Capital Redemption Reserve Account		10 000
	Being transfer to comply with Section 45, Companies Act 1981, where new issue does not cover all shares redeemed/purchased		
(d)	10% Preference Share Capital Account	10 000	
	10% Preference Share Purchase Account		10 000
(e)	10% Preference Share Purchase Account	10 000	
	Bank Account		10 000
	Being redemption/purchase of 10 000 10% preference shares and payment therefor		

Revised balance sheet (extract)

	£	£
Share capital		
Ordinary shares £1 each	540 000	
Capital redemption reserve	10 000	
		550 000
Profit and Loss Appropriation Account		70 000
		620 000

Notice that in Examples 2 and 3 the new share capital plus the capital redemption reserve is equal to the old share capital.

Redemption or purchase of shares by private companies out of capital

Since the 1981 Companies Act a private company which is unable to raise funds for redemption or purchase of its own shares by a new issue or out of its own distributable profits is empowered (by Section 54) to make payments out of capital reserves (permissible capital payments) on condition that

- it is authorised to do so by its memorandum of association
- the auditors make a satisfactory report
- the directors certify that the company will be able to pay its debts immediately after the payment for shares has been made and still be viable twelve months after the payment date.

Payments out of capital cannot be made until the company has used up

- the proceeds of any new share issues plus
- the balance of the company's distributable profits.

Exercises Set 18

1. On 1 January 19–1 ABC PLC offers 50 000 ordinary £1 shares to the public, payable in full with application. On 10 January all the shares are applied for and all the cash is received with the applications.

    Show journal, ledger and cash book entries.

2. On 1 February 19–2 Abacus PLC, whose authorised capital is 40 000 6% preference shares of £5 each and 120 000 ordinary shares of £1 each, invited application from the public for all the preference shares and half the ordinary shares, both payable in full with application. All money due was received on 12 February.

    Show journal and ledger (including cash book) entries and the appropriate section of the balance sheet.

3. Mere PLC, with registered capital of £100 000 divided into 30 000 10% cumulative preference shares of £1 each and 70 000 ordinary shares of £1 each, on 1 January 19–3 offers 50 000 ordinary shares to the public payable as follows:
    25p on application
    75p on allotment.

    Applications were received for 50 000 shares on 7 January and the shares were allotted on 9 January. All allotment money due was received on 15 January.

    a Prepare journal and ledger entries (including cash book) to record the issue of the shares in the company's books.
    b Show the effects of the issue on the company's balance sheet.

4. Parks PLC is registered with a nominal capital of £200 000 consisting of 20 000 8% preference shares of £5 each and 200 000 ordinary shares of 50p each. All the preference shares have been issued and are fully paid-up. On 1 June 19–4 the directors decide to issue 100 000 of the ordinary shares for public subscription, payable as follows:
    10p on application
    10p on allotment
    30p on first and final call.

Applications were received for 100 000 shares on 5 June and the shares were allotted on 12 June. Money due on allotment was received on 19 June. The first and final call was made on 1 August and by 31 August the money due had been received.

Prepare journal and ledger entries recording the above transactions and show the relevant entries on the company's balance sheet at 31 August.

5 Sunshine PLC, whose registered capital was £120 000 consisting of 120 000 £1 ordinary shares, invited applications on 1 March 19–5 for all of its registered capital payable as follows:
   20p on application
   30p on allotment
   30p on first call
   20p on final call.

The application list was closed on 8 March and by that time applications had been received for 150 000 shares. The directors decided to allot the shares to the applicants whose applications were received first and to remit the application money with a letter of regret to the unsuccessful applicants. The shares were allotted on 20 March. First call was made on 20 April and the final call one month later. All monies due were received within a month of being asked for.

Prepare the ledger accounts (including cash) to record the above transactions.

6 Assume that in Question 5 the directors decided to accept each applicant as a shareholder but scaled down the number of shares allotted to each shareholder and retained the surplus application money against allotment.

Show either journal or ledger entries and balance sheet.

7 Craft PLC, which was incorporated with a registered capital of £200 000 consisting of 8 000 8% preference shares of £5 each and 160 000 ordinary shares of £1 each, offered all the preference shares and 100 000 of the ordinary shares to the public on 1 October 19–8 payable as follows:
   preference shares payable in full with application
   ordinary shares 35p on application
   ordinary shares 45p on allotment
   balance on first and final call.

On 7 October applications were received for 42 000 preference shares and 120 000 ordinary shares. The directors decided to allot the preference shares to the first applications received and to return the application money to the unsuccessful applicants. They also decided to scale down the number of shares allotted to the applicants for ordinary shares and retain the excess application money against allotment.
   15 October   All shares were allotted.
   20 October   All money due on allotment received.
   1 November   First and final call was made.
   8 November   All money due on the first and final call was received except from one shareholder who had been allotted 600 shares.

Show journal and cash book, ledger entries and balance sheet.

8   Goodfirm PLC was registered a number of years ago with an authorised capital of £450 000 divided into 50 000 5% preference shares of £1 each and 400 000 ordinary shares of £1 each.

All the preference shares and 250 000 of the ordinary shares have already been issued and fully paid-up. The ordinary shares are at present being quoted on the Stock Exchange at £1.50. The company therefore decides to issue the balance of the ordinary shares at a premium of 25p per share payable as follows:
   20p on application
   50p on allotment (including premium)
   55p on first and final call.
All monies due are received.

Show journal, cash book and ledger entries and appropriate sections of balance sheet.

9   On 31 December 19–0 the balance sheet of Scottish Brandy PLC contains the following item:

	Authorised	Issued	Paid
200 000 ordinary shares of £1 each	£200 000	£120 000	£120 000

On 6 January 19–1 the directors decided to offer the un-issued shares to the public at a price of £1.35 payable as follows:
   75p on application
   45p on allotment (including premium)
   15p on first and final call.

Applications were received for 140 000 shares on 10 January. The directors decided to send letters of regret and refund application money to applicants for 20 000 shares. They also decided to scale down the applications of the other applicants and to retain the excess application money against allotment. Shares were allotted on 18 January and money due on allotment was received by 25 March. The first and final call was made on 8 June. All money due on first and final call was received, except from one shareholder, Ian Baker, who had been allotted 100 shares.

Show either ledger accounts and balance sheet, or journal entries and balance sheet.

10 On 1 July Home Stores Ltd offered 30 000 ordinary £1 shares for public subscription payable as follows:
   30p on application
   50p on allotment
   20p on first and final call.

Applications were received for 30 000 shares on 10 July. Allotment was made on 28 July and all cash due on allotment was received on 7 August. The first and final call was made on 1 September. All call money was received by 20 September, except the amount due from one shareholder who had been allotted 200 shares. After giving proper notice to the defaulting shareholder, the company declared the shares forfeit on 15 October.

Show these transactions in the company's ledger.

How would the balance on Forfeited Shares Account appear on the company's balance sheet?

274 Issue of shares and debentures

11 Joe Bloggs was allotted 300 ordinary shares (£1 each) in Venus PLC. He paid 40p per share on application and 30p per share on allotment. He failed to pay the amount due on first and final call and by resolution of the directors the shares were declared forfeited.

Prepare the journal entries to record these transactions.

12 The shares referred to in Question 11 were reissued to an employee of the company, A. Wren, on 31 October at 40p per share fully paid, cash due received 6 November.

Show ledger and cash book entries and the company's balance sheet as at 7 November.

13 Zeta PLC had an authorised capital of £400 000 divided equally into 12% preference shares and £1 ordinary shares. All the preference shares and half the ordinary shares have already been issued.

On 1 January 19–1 the company decided to issue the balance of the ordinary shares at a premium of 25p per share payable as follows:
40p on application
50p on allotment (including premium)
35p on first and final call.

Applications were received on 10 January for 120 000 shares. The directors declined the applications for 5 000 shares and returned application money the same day. The other applications for 115 000 shares were reduced proportionately and the excess application money held against allotment. Allotment was made on 31 January and all money due on allotment received by 20 February. First and final call was made on 31 March and all money due on call was received by 15 April, except the amount due from one shareholder who had been allotted 600 shares. These shares were declared forfeit by resolution of the board dated 15 May. They were reissued to Peter Fry on 22 May as fully paid at 50p per share.

a Record the above transactions in the appropriate ledger accounts.
b Show how the balances on these accounts should appear on the company's balance sheet as on 31 May.

14 The following summarised balance sheet shows the financial position of Rosemount Ltd as at 31 December 19–1:

Rosemount Ltd
Balance sheet as at 31 December 19–1

	£
Sundry assets	80 000
Bank	20 000
	100 000
Financed by:	
Share capital	
60 000 ordinary shares £1 each	60 000
15 000 8% preference shares £1 each	15 000
	75 000
Reserves	
Profit and Loss Appropriation Account	25 000
	100 000

The company wishes to redeem its preference shares at par. The funds required are to be raised by the issue of ordinary shares of £1 each at par.

Show the journal entries necessary to complete these transactions and the balance sheet when the transactions have been completed.

15 Rosemount Ltd (see balance sheet for Question **14**), wishes to purchase its preference shares at par by using the company's undistributed profits.

Show journal entries and revised balance sheet.

16 Rosemount Ltd (see balance sheet for Question **14**) wishes to redeem its preference shares at par. To finance the redemption it is proposed to issue 10 000 new ordinary shares of £1 each at par with the balance being provided out of the Profit and Loss Appropriation Account.

Show journal entries and revised balance sheet.

17 The Newstead Trading Estate Co. Ltd had an authorised capital of 400 000 shares of £1 each, divided equally between ordinary shares and 8% redeemable cumulative preference shares. The issued capital was 150 000 ordinary shares and 100 000 preference shares.

It was decided to:
1. issue the remainder of the ordinary shares at a premium of 25 per cent;
2. issue 50 000 8% debentures of £1 each at a discount of 5 per cent redeemable at par in 1996;
3. use the proceeds of the above two issues to redeem all the preference shares.

The ordinary shares were applied for with full cash on 25 February 1985 and allotted on 1 March 1985, as were the debentures, the dates being 25 March and 1 April 1985, respectively. The preference shares were redeemed in cash at par on 1 May 1985. On 1 September 1985 the company paid an interim dividend of two pence per share on the whole of its ordinary share capital. On 1 October 1985 the company paid the first half-yearly instalment of its debenture interest.

 a Show by means of journal entries (including cash items) how you would record the above in the books of the Newstead Trading Co. Ltd.
 b Indicate whether the debenture interest should be a charge against profits or an appropriation of profits.

[London Chamber of Commerce and Industry, summer 1986]

19 Purchase of a business

When considering the purchase of an existing business we will be preparing the accounts of the buyer. The same principles will apply whether the buyer is a sole trader, a partnership or a limited company.

The buyer will be taking over existing assets and liabilities at a price agreed between the buyer and seller. This price is sometimes called the purchase consideration.

The buyer and the seller agree on three things:
(a) what assets and liabilities are to be taken over
(b) what value is to be placed on these assets and liabilities
(c) the purchase price and how it is to be paid.

It is assumed that a business is sold as a going concern and it is usual to use the most recent balance sheet as a basis for valuation and negotiation. The book value of a business to its owner is the net book value, i.e. the value of the assets less liabilities as contained in the ledger accounts. For example

if the total value of the assets is £100 000
and the total value of the liabilities is £ 20 000

the net book value of the business is £ 80 000

If the buyer has to pay more than the net book value, say £90 000, the amount paid in excess of the net book value is £10 000 and is called goodwill. It must appear as an asset in the books of the buyer.

Having agreed on the assets and liabilities to be taken over and on the price to be paid, all that remains to be agreed is the way in which the purchase price is to be paid.

The purchase price can be paid in a number of ways:
(a) in cash (cheque)
(b) partly in cash, the balance due being loaned by the seller
(c) partly in cash, the balance being given to the seller by means of shares or debentures in the purchasing firm.

Procedure

Open a business Purchase Account.
Open an account for each asset taken over (including goodwill).

Open an account for each liability taken over.
Open an account for vendor (seller).

Entries:
1. Debit Business Purchase Account } with purchase price
   Credit seller's account
2. Debit individual Asset Accounts with agreed value of assets taken over
   Credit Business Purchase Account with total agreed value of assets taken over
3. Debit Business Purchase Account with total liabilities taken over
   Credit individual Liability Accounts with value of liabilities taken over
4. Debit seller's account } with amounts paid by cheque
   Credit Bank Account   to the vendor
5. Debit seller's account } with shares or debentures
   Credit Share Capital/Debenture given to seller in part
   Account   payment of purchase price

If the buyer has to bring in cash to pay the seller:

Entries:
  Debit Bank
  Credit buyer's Capital Account

A SIMPLE EXAMPLE

On 1 January 19–1 Ann and John entered into partnership by lodging £20 000 in equal amounts to their Partnership Bank Account. On that date they decided to take over the business of Richard Steel whose balance sheet was as follows:

Balance sheet as at 1 January 19–1

	Cost	Depreciation to date	Net	Total
Fixed assets	£	£	£	£
Premises	150 000		150 000	
Motor vehicles	40 000		40 000	
	190 000		190 000	190 000
Current assets	£		£	£
Stock		75 000		
Debtors	47 000			
Less Provision for bad debts	2 000			
		45 000		
		120 000		
Less Current liabilities				
Creditors	32 000			
Bank	8 000			
		40 000		
Working capital				80 000
TOTAL NET ASSETS				270 000

278 Purchase of a business

Financed by:
Capital Account		200 000
Mortgage loan		70 000
CAPITAL EMPLOYED		270 000

The terms of the purchase agreement were:
(a) Premises were to be revalued at £220 000 and stock at £72 000.
(b) The remaining assets were to be taken over at book value.
(c) All the liabilities except the bank overdraft were to be taken over by the partnership.
(d) The purchase price was agreed at £300 000 half of which was to be paid in cash. Steel agreed that the balance was to be loaned to the partnership.

You are required to show:
a   the ledger accounts necessary to open the books of the new firm
b   the opening balance sheet of the partnership.

SOLUTION
a   **Ann and John: ledger accounts**

Dr.   **(Partnership) Bank Account**   Cr.

19–1		£	19–1		£
1 Jan.	Capital Account: Ann	100 000	1 Jan.	R. Steel	150 000
	Capital Account: John	100 000		Balance c/d	50 000
		200 000			200 000
1 Jan.	Balance b/d	50 000			

Dr.   **Business Purchase Account**   Cr.

19–1		£	19–1		£
1 Jan.	R. Steel (purchase price)	300 000	1 Jan.	Premises Account	220 000
	Provision for Bad Debts Account	2 000		Motor Vehicles Account	40 000
	Sundry Creditors Account	32 000		Stock Account	72 000
	Mortgage Loan Account	70 000		Sundry Debtors Account	47 000
				Goodwill Account (Note)	25 000
		404 000			404 000

Dr.   **R. Steel (seller)**   Cr.

19–1		£	19–1		£
1 Jan.	Bank	150 000	1 Jan.	Business Purchase Account	300 000
	Loan Account	150 000			
		300 000			300 000

Purchase of a business

Dr.	Premises Account		Cr.
19–1		£	
1 Jan.	Business Purchase Account	220 000	

Dr.	Motor Vehicles Account		Cr.
19–1		£	
1 Jan.	Business Purchase Account	40 000	

Dr.	Stock Account		Cr.
19–1		£	
1 Jan.	Business Purchase Account	72 000	

Dr.	Sundry Debtors Account		Cr.
19–1		£	
1 Jan.	Business Purchase Account	47 000	

Dr.	Goodwill Account		Cr.
19–1		£	
1 Jan.	Business Purchase Account	25 000	

Dr.	Provision for Bad Debts Account		Cr.
	19–1		£
	1 Jan.	Business Purchase Account	2 000

Dr.	Sundry Creditors Account		Cr.
	19–1		£
	1 Jan.	Business Purchase Account	32 000

Dr.	Capital Accounts			Cr.
			Ann	John
	19–1		£	£
	1 Jan.	Bank	100 000	100 000

Dr.	Mortgage Loan Account		Cr.
	19–1		£
	1 Jan.	Business Purchase Account	70 000

Dr.	Loan Account – R. Steel		Cr.
		19–1	£
		1 Jan. R. Steel	150 000

Note on value of goodwill:
Value of assets taken over

	£	£
Premises	220 000	
Motor vehicles	40 000	
Stock	72 000	
Debtors	47 000	
Total		379 000
Less Value of liabilities taken over		
Provision for bad debts	2 000	
Creditors	32 000	
Mortgage loan	70 000	
		104 000
Net book value		275 000
Purchase price		300 000
Goodwill		25 000

b

Ann and John
Balance sheet as at 1 January 19–1

	Cost	Depreciation to date	Net	Total
Fixed assets	£	£	£	£
Premises	220 000		220 000	
Motor vehicles	40 000		40 000	
	260 000		260 000	
Goodwill	25 000		25 000	
	285 000		285 000	285 000
Current assets	£	£	£	
Stock		72 000		
Trade debtors	47 000			
Less Bad debts provision	2 000			
		45 000		
Bank		50 000		
			167 000	
Less Current liabilities				
Trade Creditors			32 000	
Working capital				135 000
TOTAL NET ASSETS				420 000
Financed by:				
Capital Accounts				
Ann	100 000			
John	100 000			200 000

Long-term liabilities
Mortgage loan	70 000	
Loan – R. Steel	150 000	
		220 000
CAPITAL EMPLOYED		420 000

A MORE DIFFICULT EXAMPLE
Wilson and Abel are in partnership sharing profits and losses equally. The following is their balance sheet at 31 December 19–2:

	Cost	Depreciation to date	Net	Total
Fixed assets	£	£	£	£
Buildings	50 000		50 000	
Plant and machinery	20 000		20 000	
Fixtures and fittings	15 000		15 000	
Motor vehicles	12 000		12 000	
	97 000		97 000	97 000
Current assets	£	£		
Stock		14 000		
Trade debtors	7 000			
Less Bad debts provision	700			
		6 300		
Rates prepaid		200		
		20 500		
Less Current liabilities				
Trade creditors	6 000			
Accruals	500			
Bank overdraft	2 000			
		8 500		
Working capital				12 000
TOTAL NET ASSETS				109 000
Financed by:				
Capital Accounts				
Wilson		65 000		
Abel		44 000		
CAPITAL EMPLOYED				109 000

On 1 January 19–3 the business was purchased by Vintners Ltd with an authorised capital of £200 000 on the following terms:
(*a*) Buildings and plant and machinery to be revalued at £70 000 and £30 000 respectively.
(*b*) Stock to be valued at £10 000.
(*c*) Accruals and bank overdraft to be paid off by the partners.
(*d*) All other assets and liabilities were to be taken over at book value.
(*e*) The purchase price was agreed at £150 000 and was to be paid half in cash and the balance in £1 ordinary shares in Vintners Ltd. Cash was to be made available by the issue to the public of the ordinary shares at par.

282 Purchase of a business

Show the journal and ledger entries in the books of Vintners Ltd and the balance sheet when entries were completed.

SOLUTION

Journal

		Dr. £	Cr. £
(a)	Business Purchase Account	150 000	
	Wilson and Abel		150 000
	Being agreed purchase price		
(b)	Building Account	70 000	
	Plant and Machinery Account	30 000	
	Fixtures and Fittings Account	15 000	
	Motor Vehicles Account	12 000	
	Stock Account	10 000	
	Trade Debtors Account	7 000	
	Rates (Prepaid) Account	200	
	Goodwill Account	12 500	
	Business Purchase Account		156 700
	Being value of assets taken over from Wilson and Abel at 1 Jan. 19–3		
(c)	Business Purchase Account	6 700	
	Trade Creditors Account		6 000
	Bad Debts Provision Account		700
	Being liabilities taken over from Wilson and Abel		
(d)	Wilson and Abel	75 000	
	Bank		75 000
	Being payment of half purchase price in cash		
(e)	Wilson and Abel	75 000	
	Ordinary Share Capital Account		75 000
	Being payment of half purchase price in £1 ordinary shares		
(f)	Sundry Shareholders Account	125 000	
	Ordinary Share Capital Account		125 000
	Being issue of 125 000 £1 ordinary shares at par		
(g)	Bank Account	125 000	
	Sundry shareholders		125 000
	Being cash received in respect of 125 000 shares issued at £1 each		

Ledger accounts

Dr.	Business Purchase Account			Cr.
19–3		£	19–3	£
1 Jan.	Wilson and Abel (purchase price)	150 000	1 Jan. Sundry assets	156 700
	Trade creditors	6 000		
	Bad Debts Provision Account	700		
		156 700		156 700

Dr.			Wilson and Abel			Cr.
19–3			£	19–3		£
1 Jan.	Bank		75 000	1 Jan.	Business Purchase Account	150 000
	Ordinary share capital		75 000			
			150 000			150 000

Dr.		Buildings Account		Cr.
19–3			£	
1 Jan.	Business Purchase Account		70 000	

Dr.		Plant and Machinery Account		Cr.
19–3			£	
1 Jan.	Business Purchase Account		30 000	

Dr.		Fixtures and Fittings Account		Cr.
19–3			£	
1 Jan.	Business Purchase Account		15 000	

Dr.		Motor Vehicles Account		Cr.
19–3			£	
1 Jan.	Business Purchase Account		12 000	

Dr.		Stock Account		Cr.
19–3			£	
1 Jan.	Business Purchase Account		10 000	

Dr.		Trade Debtors Account		Cr.
19–3			£	
1 Jan.	Business Purchase Account		7 000	

Dr.		Rates Account		Cr.
19–3			£	
1 Jan.	Business Purchase Account		200	

284 Purchase of a business

Dr.		Goodwill Account			Cr.
19–3		£			
1 Jan.	Business Purchase Account	12 500			

Dr.		Trade Creditors Account			Cr.
			19–3		£
			1 Jan.	Business Purchase Account	6 000

Dr.		Provision for Bad Debts Account			Cr.
			19–3		£
			1 Jan.	Business Purchase Account	700

Dr.		Bank Account			Cr.
19–3		£	19–3		£
1 Jan.	Sundry Shareholders Account	125 000	1 Jan.	Wilson and Abel	75 000
				Balance c/d	50 000
		125 000			125 000
1 Jan.	Balance b/d	50 000			

Dr.		Ordinary Share Capital Account			Cr.
19–3		£	19–3		£
1 Jan.	Balance c/d	200 000	1 Jan.	Wilson and Abel	75 000
				Sundry shareholders	125 000
		200 000			200 000
			1 Jan.	Balance b/d	200 000

Dr.		Sundry Shareholders Account			Cr.
19–3		£	19–3		£
1 Jan.	Ordinary Share Capital Account	125 000	1 Jan.	Bank	125 000
		125 000			125 000

Vintners Ltd
Balance sheet as at 1 January 19-3

	Cost	Depreciation to date	Net	Total
Fixed assets	£	£	£	£
Buildings	70 000		70 000	
Plant and machinery	30 000		30 000	
Fixtures and fittings	15 000		15 000	
Motor vehicles	12 000		12 000	
	127 000		127 000	
Goodwill at cost	12 500		12 500	
	139 500		139 500	139 500
Current assets	£	£	£	
Stock		10 000		
Trade debtors	7 000			
Less Provision for bad debts	700	6 300		
Rates prepaid		200		
Bank		50 000		
			66 500	
Less Current liabilities				
Trade creditors			6 000	
Working capital				60 500
TOTAL NET ASSETS				200 000
Financed by:				
Share capital	Authorised and issued			Paid
£1 ordinary shares	200 000			200 000
CAPITAL EMPLOYED				200 000

Exercises Set 19

1 On 1 January 19–1 Tom Jones purchased for £72 000 all the assets of John Peel, a trader. At that date the value of the assets as shown by Peel's balance sheet was:

	£
Freehold premises	40 000
Fixtures and fittings	10 000
Stock	12 000
Debtors	4 000

It was agreed that these figures represented a fair valuation. Jones brought in £80 000 as his capital and Peel was paid by cheque.

Show the journal and ledger entries (including cash) in Jones's books and also his opening balance sheet.

2 The following is the balance sheet of M. Pratt, a trader, on 31 July 19–2:

	£		£
Premises	72 500	Capital	100 000
Fixtures and fittings	7 500	Creditors	20 000
Motor van	5 000		
Stock	17 000		
Debtors	7 000		
Cash at bank	11 000		
	120 000		120 000

On this date J. Kitson purchased the business, taking over all the assets and liabilities except cash at bank at the values shown. The purchase price was agreed at £99 000. Kitson lodged £115 000 in the firm's Bank Account and paid Pratt by cheque.

Draft the journal, ledger and cash book entries and also Kitson's opening balance sheet.

3 On 1 January 19–3 George Powell decided to sell his business as a going concern to James Flavin for a consideration of £80 000 which Flavin agreed to pay by cheque.

Balance sheet of George Powell as at 31 December 19–2

	£		£
Premises	50 000	Capital	55 000
Fixtures and fittings	10 000	Creditors	20 000
Stock	20 000	Bank overdraft	25 000
Debtors	15 000		
Cash	5 000		
	100 000		100 000

It was agreed that:
(a) Flavin was to take over all the assets except cash at book value and also the creditors.
(b) Powell must pay off the bank overdraft out of private funds. Flavin brought in sufficient capital to pay Powell the purchase price in cash and have a cash balance of £10 000 for working capital.

Show journal and ledger entries in Flavin's books and also his opening balance sheet.

4 The following are the balance sheets of Allan and Ball, two sole traders, as at 31 December 19–3:

Allan's balance sheet

	£		£
Fixtures and fittings	12 000	Capital	13 000
Stock	17 400	Creditors	19 500
Debtors	16 000	Wages due	500
Insurance prepaid	600	Bank overdraft	14 000
Cash	1 000		
	47 000		47 000

Ball's balance sheet

	£		£
Buildings	130 000	Capital	200 000
Fixtures and fittings	24 000	Bank term loan	80 000
Stock	75 400	Creditors	54 000
Debtors	84 600		
Bank	20 000		
	334 000		334 000

On 1 January 19–4 Ball buys Allan's business on the following terms:
(a) Allan is to pay off his bank overdraft and wages due.
(b) Ball should take over the remaining assets and liabilities except cash at the following valuations:
  Fixtures and fittings £10 000
  Stock £16 000
  Debtors at book value less 5 per cent provision for bad debts. Insurance prepaid at book value.
(c) The agreed purchase price was £40 000 which Ball was to raise by way of a mortgage on buildings and pay in cash to Allan.

Show the transactions in Ball's books and Ball's balance sheet after these transactions have been completed.

5 On 1 July 19–3 Charles Cooke and John Banks formed a partnership to take over the old-established grocery business of James Logan on the basis of the following balance sheet:

Balance sheet of James Logan as at 30 June 19–4

	£		£
Premises	250 000	Capital	425 000
Fixtures and fittings	80 000	Mortgage loan	50 000
Delivery vans	45 000	Trade creditors	35 000
Stock	68 000		
Trade debtors	52 000		
Bank	15 000		
	510 000		510 000

It was agreed as follows:
(a) Premises were to be revalued at £280 000; fixtures and fittings at £72 000; stock at £60 000; debtors at book value less a provision of 5 per cent for bad debts.
(b) Logan was to retain the bank balance.
(c) The mortgage and creditors were to be taken over by the partnership.
(d) The purchase price was agreed at £480 000, half of which was to be paid by cheque on 5 July, the balance to be loaned to the partnership bearing interest at 10 per cent p.a.
(e) Cooke and Banks were to contribute sufficient capital in equal proportions to pay Logan the amount due to him on 5 July and were to lodge an additional amount of £40 000 to the credit of a bank account in the name of the partnership.
(f) Cooke and Banks were to share future profits and losses equally.

288 Purchase of a business

Record these transactions in the books of the partnership and show the partnership balance sheet as at 5 July 19–5.

6 A limited company, Gavin Ltd, was registered on 1 February 19–6 with a nominal capital of £400 000 divided into 400 000 ordinary shares of £1 each. The object of the company was to purchase the business of T. Holt, a sole trader, for a consideration of £300 000. T. Holt's balance sheet as at 31 January 19–6 was:

	£		£
Freehold premises	150 000	Capital	220 000
Plant and machinery	50 000	Loan from hire purchase co.	20 000
Delivery vans	10 000	Creditors	24 000
Stock	25 000		
Debtors	18 000		
Bank	10 700		
Cash	300		
	264 000		264 000

All the assets and liabilities were taken over at book value and the purchase price was to be paid as follows:

250 000 ordinary shares £1 each in Gavin Ltd and the balance in cash.

To make cash available to pay the seller, the company decided to offer the balance of the shares to the public at par and the money in respect of the issue was duly received on 25 February.

Show the entries recording these transactions in the books of Gavin Ltd and show the company's opening balance sheet.

20 Manufacturing accounts

Manufacturing Accounts are kept by firms engaged in converting raw materials of one sort or another into finished goods. The aim of the Manufacturing Account is to ascertain accurately the cost of the goods that have been manufactured or, more specifically, the cost of manufacture per unit. So the Manufacturing Account gathers together all the costs associated with the production of goods. The costs of manufacture can be broken down into two main constituents:
(*a*) prime costs (direct costs)
(*b*) factory overhead expenses (indirect costs).

Prime costs

These are costs that can be *directly* identified with a particular set of manufactured goods. They are:
1. *Direct materials*. All costs related to getting *raw materials* on to the factory floor, e.g. cost of raw materials, carriage on raw materials, customs duties on raw materials.
2. *Direct labour*. Cost of labour *directly* related to manufacture, e.g. manufacturing wages.
3. *Direct expenses*. Expenses that can be directly identified with a particular batch of goods, e.g. royalties for use of patents or licences (usually so much per unit), or hire of special plant or equipment necessary for manufacture.

Factory overhead expenses

These consist of all expenses that are incurred in the factory which can be seen to be costs of manufacture but *cannot* be specifically allocated to units being manufactured. They are the expenses of running the factory that cannot properly be included in prime costs. Factory overheads include:
1. Factory rent, rates and insurance.
2. Factory lighting, heating, cleaning and power.
3. Repair, maintenance and depreciation of machinery or tools.
4. Wages and salaries of factory managers, foremen, crane drivers, etc.

Work in progress or partly finished goods

It is highly unlikely that at the end of the accounting period all of the raw materials will have been turned into finished goods. There will be a certain amount of partly finished goods both at the beginning and end of the accounting period. These partly finished articles must be valued and the value included in the Manufacturing Account.

The formula is:

Add work in progress at the beginning

Deduct work in progress at the end.

This adjustment is made either to the prime cost figure or to the cost of production figure.

Note

In examinations you should be told at which stage to make the adjustment. In the absence of any instruction make adjustments to the cost of production figure.

The Manufacturing Account is a very important part of the final accounts of a manufacturer and should be set out so as to give as much information as possible, both for ease of understanding and for use later in the interpretation of final accounts. The layout, therefore, is very important and should be as clear and informative as possible.

A SIMPLE EXAMPLE

From the following figures prepare a Manufacturing Account for A. Coleman for the year ended 31 December 19–1:

	£
Stock of raw materials at 1.1.19–1	20 000
Purchases of raw materials during year	100 000
Carriage on raw materials	10 000
Customs duties on raw materials	8 000
Manufacturing wages	400 000
Royalties payment for use of patents	4 000
Hire of special equipment	6 000
Factory light, heat and power	50 000
Factory rent	18 000
Factory rates	8 000
Factory insurance	2 000
Machinery repairs and maintenance	16 000
Depreciation of machinery	30 000
Factory manager's salary	40 000
Stock of raw materials at 31.12.19–1	14 000
Work in progress (valued at factory cost) on 1.1.19–1	8 000
Work in progress (valued at factory cost) on 31.12.19–1	6 000

Work in progress or partly finished goods

SOLUTION

A. Coleman
Manufacturing Account for year ended 31 December 19–1

	£	£
Raw materials		
Stock at 1.1.19–1	20 000	
Add Purchases of raw materials for year	100 000	
Carriage on raw materials	10 000	
Customs duties on raw materials	16 000	
	146 000	
Less Stock of raw materials at 31.12.19–1	14 000	
Cost of raw materials consumed		132 000
Add		
Direct costs		
Manufacturing wages	400 000	
Royalties for use of patent	4 000	
Hire of special equipment	6 000	
		410 000
PRIME COST		542 000
Add		
Factory overheads		
Factory light, heat and power	50 000	
Factory rent	18 000	
Factory rates	8 000	
Factory insurance	2 000	
Repair and maintenance of machines	16 000	
Factory manager's salary	40 000	
Depreciation on factory machinery	30 000	
		164 000
		706 000
Add Work in progress at 1.1.19–1		8 000
		714 000
Less Work in progress at 31.12.19–1		6 000
COST OF MANUFACTURE		708 000

Cost of manufacture is then transferred to the Trading Account where COST OF FINISHED GOODS is added to arrive at COST OF SALES.

So, Cost of sales (for manufacturer)
= Cost of manufactured goods + Cost of finished goods

The cost of production (cost of manufacture) is transferred to the Trading Account at either:
(a) Cost of production value as in the previous example, *or*
(b) Current market prices, i.e. what they cost if brought in from outside the firm. In this case, the Manufacturing Account will show a MANUFACTURING PROFIT (difference between cost of manufacture and current market price).

This manufacturing profit is transferred from the Manufacturing Account to the Profit and Loss Account where it is shown as manufacturing profit in addition to the normal gross profit from Trading Account.

A more comprehensive example will help to clarify this point and also show the follow-through to the Trading and Profit and Loss Accounts.

A More Difficult Example

The following figures were taken from the books of M. Asprey, a manufacturer, on 31.12.19–2:

	£
Advertising	6 000
Sales	700 000
Purchase of raw materials	240 000
Purchase of finished goods	20 000
Stocks at 1.1.19–2:	
Raw materials	10 000
Work in progress	6 000
Finished goods	4 000
Light and heat	8 000
Purchase of finished goods	24 000
Carriage on raw materials	2 000
Customs duties on finished goods	3 000
Insurance	1 000
Hire of special equipment	14 000
Factory foreman's salary	19 200
Rent and rates	7 000
Factory buildings (cost £200 000)	140 000
Office buildings (cost £100 000)	80 000
Machinery (cost £30 000)	24 000
Office equipment (cost £8 000)	4 000
Delivery vans (cost £80 000)	20 000
Manufacturing wages	90 000
Office salaries	24 000
Travellers' commissions	5 000
Carriage on sales	3 000
Discount received	1 000
Postage, stationery and telephones	7 000
Sale of scrap materials	2 800

Notes
1. Stocks at 31.12.19–2:
   Raw materials   £12 000
   Work in progress   £8 000
   Finished goods   £11 000
2. Work in progress is to be valued at prime cost.
3. Goods are to be transferred from the factory at current market value of £400 000.
4. Rent and rates, light and heat and insurance are to be apportioned ⅗ to factory and ⅖ to office.
5. Depreciation:
   Buildings   10%
   Machinery   20%

Office equipment 25%
Delivery vans 20%

Prepare Manufacturing, Trading and Profit and Loss Accounts for year ended 31 December 19–2.

SOLUTION

M. Asprey
Manufacturing, Trading and Profit and Loss Accounts for year ended 31.12.19–2

	£	£	£
Sales			700 000
Less			
Cost of sales			
Raw materials:			
Stock at 1.1.19–2		10 000	
Add Purchases for year		240 000	
Carriage on raw materials		2 000	
		252 000	
Less Stock raw materials at 31.12.19–2		12 000	
Cost of raw materials consumed			240 000
Add			
Direct costs:			
Manufacturing wages		90 000	
Hire of special equipment		14 000	
		104 000	
Add Work in progress at 1.1.19–2		6 000	
		350 000	
Less Work in progress at 31.12.19–2		8 000	
PRIME COST			342 000
Factory overheads:			
Light and heat ($\frac{3}{5}$ of £8 000)		4 800	
Rent and rates ($\frac{3}{5}$ of £7 000)		4 200	
Insurance ($\frac{3}{5}$ of £1 000)		600	
Factory foreman's salary		19 200	
Depreciation:			
Factory buildings (10% of £200 000)		20 000	
Machinery (20% of £30 000)		6 000	
			54 800
			396 800
Less Sales of scrap materials			2 800
COST OF MANUFACTURE			394 000
Profit on manufacture to Profit and Loss Account			6 000

[cont. over

	£	£	£
COST OF MANUFACTURE AT CURRENT MARKET VALUE TO TRADING ACCOUNT		400 000	
Add Cost of finished goods:			
Stock at 1.1.19–2	4 000		
Add Purchases of finished goods	24 000		
Add Customs duties on finished goods	3 000		
	31 000		
Less Stock at 31.12.19–2	11 000		
Cost of finished goods		20 000	
COST OF SALES			420 000
GROSS PROFIT TO PROFIT AND LOSS ACCOUNT			280 000
Add Profit on manufacture			6 000
Add Discount received			1 000
			287 000
Less			
Selling expenses and losses			
Advertising		6 000	
Light and heat ($\frac{2}{5}$ of £8 000)		3 200	
Rent and rates ($\frac{2}{5}$ of £7 000)		2 800	
Insurance ($\frac{2}{5}$ of £1 000)		400	
Office salaries		24 000	
Travellers' commissions		5 000	
Carriage on sales		3 000	
Postage, stationery and telephones		7 000	
Depreciation			
Office buildings (10% of £100 000)		10 000	
Office equipment (25% of £8 000)		2 000	
Delivery vans (20% of £80 000)		16 000	
TOTAL EXPENSES			79 400
NET PROFIT TO CAPITAL ACCOUNT			207 600

Note. Sales of by-products or scrap materials are deducted from costs of manufacture.

Exercises Set 20

In the following questions prepare Manufacturing Accounts to show clearly:
a cost of raw materials consumed
b prime cost
c factory cost of production or cost of manufacture
d manufacturing profit (if any) and, where applicable, Trading and Profit and Loss Accounts to show:
  (i) cost of goods sold
  (ii) gross profit/loss
  (iii) net profit/loss.

		£
1	Stock of raw materials at 1 January 19–1	10 000
	Purchases of raw materials during the year	50 000
	Carriage on raw materials	2 000
	Manufacturing wages	13 000
	Rent and rates of factory	1 000
	Factory heating and lighting	500
	Wages of factory supervisor	2 500
	Stock of raw materials at 31 December 19–1	6 000

Note. Finished goods are to be valued at cost of production.

		£
2	Stock of raw materials at 1 January 19–2	30 350
	Purchases of raw materials	71 650
	Customs duties on raw materials	1 400
	Carriage on raw materials	600
	Factory wages	29 658
	Repairs to machinery	1 022
	Depreciation on machinery	1 120
	Factory lighting and heating	2 840
	Factory rent and rates	860
	Factory cleaning	550
	Stock of raw materials at 31 December 19–2	27 400
	Wages due at 31 December 19–2	480
	Rates prepaid at 31 December 19–2	160

Note. Finished goods are transferred to Trading Account at factory costs.

		£
3	Stock of raw materials at 1 January 19–3	73 654
	Work in progress at 1 January 19–3 (factory cost)	17 082
	Purchases of raw materials	289 258
	Carriage on raw materials	13 120
	Factory fuel and power	16 950
	Production wages	173 846
	Plant depreciation	29 000
	Factory insurance	194
	Factory rent and rates	5 072
	General factory expenses	2 900
	Stock of raw materials at 31 December 19–3	77 288
	Work in progress at 31 December 19–3 (factory cost)	19 564
	Insurance prepaid	74
	Rates due	1 650

Note. Goods are transferred to Trading Account at cost of manufacture.

296 Manufacturing accounts

4

	£
Stock of raw materials at 1 April 19–4	22 400
Stock of finished goods at 1 April 19–4	18 800
Stock of work in progress at 1 April 19–4 (prime cost)	11 200
Sales	550 000
Purchases:	
Raw materials	170 800
Finished goods	17 200
Carriage in:	
Raw materials	7 500
Finished goods	500
Supervisor's salary	3 920
Manufacturing wages	197 080
Rent and rates	13 200
Depreciation of plant	6 920
General factory expenses	1 880

At 31 March 19–5	£
Stocks:	
Raw materials	21 400
Finished goods	21 840
Work in progress (prime cost)	13 400

Note

Allocate rent and rates two-thirds to factory, one-third to office. Manufacturing wages due, £200. Only half of supervisor's salary is attributable to factory. Finished goods are to be transferred at current market value of £500 000.

5

	1 July 19–4	30 June 19–5
	£	£
Stocks:		
Raw materials	3 340	3 840
Work in progress (factory cost)	1 700	1 940
Finished goods	3 640	3 560
Loose tools	1 040	800
Purchases:		
Raw materials		35 200
Finished goods		8 800
Carriage on raw materials		2 680
Carriage on purchases of finished goods		400
Returns in		1 780
Returns out (finished goods)		1 960
Direct wages		21 400
Hire of special equipment for factory		4 800
Royalties on patent used in factory		1 200
Rent and rates		1 000
Insurance		300
Depreciation 5 per cent on factory premises valued at £40 000		
Depreciation 10 per cent on factory plant valued at £16 000		
Repairs to factory buildings		440
Repairs to machinery		280
Office salaries and wages		5 600
Sales		150 000
Bad debts		250

	£
Advertising	920
Lighting, heating and power	7 500
Office expenses	550
Sale of scrap materials	360
Depreciation of office machines	50
Depreciation of delivery vans	440
Discounts allowed	410
Discounts received	650
Bank charges	50
Salesmen's salaries	13 000
Salesmen's commission	3 000

Notes

1. Rent and rates, insurance, lighting and heating are to be allocated between factory and general office in the ratio 4:1.
2. Accruals:
Direct wages	£600
Lighting, heating and power	£500

   Prepayments:
Rates	£200
Insurance	£100
Advertising	£320
3. Goods are transferred from the factory at current market value of £129 000.

6 The following set of accounts was prepared by a willing but inexperienced clerk at 31 December 19–6. Re-draft them as you think fit.

Dr.			Manufacturing Account			Cr.
19–6			£	19–6		£
31 Dec.	*Opening stocks*			31 Dec.	*Closing stocks*	
	Raw materials		13 000		Raw materials	11 200
	Finished goods		5 000		Finished goods	6 800
	Carriage out		700		Returns out	400
	Purchases:				Balance to Trading	
	Raw materials		37 300		Account	61 600
	Finished goods		12 240			
	Salesmen's salaries		7 760			
			80 000			80 000

Dr.			Trading Account			Cr.
19–6			£	19–6		£
31 Dec.	Balance b/d		61 600	31 Dec.	Rates paid in advance	100
	Carriage in		720		Commission paid to	
	Factory rent and rates		900		salesmen	1 950
	Opening work in				Discount received	450
	progress		2 730		Closing work in	
	Advertising		470		progress	2 400
	Returns in		860		Sales	112 500
	Gross profit		50 120			
			117 400			117 400

Dr.		Profit and Loss Account			Cr.
19–6		£	19–6		£
31 Dec.	Factory manager's salary	8 000	31 Dec.	Balance from Trading Account	50 120
	Factory wages	15 704		Sale of by-products	480
	Discount allowed	460			
	Bad debts	50			
	Depreciation				
	Machinery	1 520			
	Office equipment	84			
	Office wages	4 494			
	Office expenses	370			
	Net profit	19 858			
		50 600			50 600

7 The following information has been extracted from the books of account of the Marsden Manufacturing Company for the year to 30 September 1984:

	£
Advertising	2 000
Depreciation for the year to 30 September 1984:	
Factory equipment	7 000
Office equipment	4 000
Direct wages	40 000
Factory:	
Insurance	1 000
Heat	15 000
Indirect materials	5 000
Power	20 000
Salaries	25 000
Finished goods (at 1 October 1983)	24 000
Office:	
Electricity	15 000
General expenses	9 000
Postage and telephones	2 900
Salaries	70 000
Raw material purchases	202 000
Raw material stock (at 1 October 1983)	8 000
Sales	512 400
Work-in-progress (at 1 October 1983)	12 000

Notes

1. At 30 September 1984, the following stocks were on hand:

	£
Raw materials	10 000
Work-in-progress	9 000
Finished goods	30 000

2. At 30 September 1984, there was an accrual for advertising of £1 000, and it was estimated that £1 500 had been paid in advance for electricity. These items had not been included in the books of account for the year to 30 September 1984.
3. The finished goods are transferred from the factory at the manufacturing cost of production plus an addition of 10 per cent for factory profit.

Prepare in the vertical columnar format Marsden's Manufacturing, Trading and Profit and Loss Account for the year to 30 September 1984.

[*Association of Accounting Technicians, December 1984*]

8 The summarised Manufacturing and Profit and Loss Account of Garden Ltd for 1982 was as follows:

	£
Raw materials used	100 000
Manufacturing wages	80 000
Factory rent	15 000
Depreciation of plant	30 000
Factory administration	20 000
General administration	25 000
	270 000
Net profit	30 000
Sales (30 000 units at £10 each)	300 000

From 1 January 1983 the selling price of each unit was reduced by 10 per cent, and this caused the volume of sales to increase by 50 per cent. To meet this additional demand, extra accommodation and plant was acquired. The additional rent was £8 000 per annum, and the annual depreciation charge for the new plant was £15 000. The expansion increased factory administration costs by £8 000 and general administration costs by £5 000. Wage rates were the same as in 1982, and the cost of raw materials and labour time for the production of each unit remained unchanged.

a Calculate for *1982* (that is, the year prior to the expansion):
   (i) The prime cost of production
   (ii) The total cost of production
   (iii) The total cost of Garden Ltd's operations
   (iv) The total direct cost of production
   (v) The total indirect cost of production
b Prepare a statement to show Garden Ltd's profit for *1983*.
c Comment on whether the expansion was worthwhile. Would your conclusion differ if the additional sales could have been achieved without reducing the selling price per unit?

[*Royal Society of Arts, II, March 1984*]

9 Cabinet Ltd was established on 1 January 1984 and manufactures three different products, designated W, X and Y. The following information is available about its first two years of trading:
1. Revenue and production cost for 1984:

Product	Sales	Manufacturing cost of goods sold	
		Variable	Fixed
	£	£	£
W	50 000	39 000	5 000
X	40 000	24 500	5 000
Y	110 000	69 250	10 000

2. Other costs for 1984 and 1985 were:

	1984	1985
	£	£
Advertising	5 000	16 750
Delivery	6 300	12 000
Administration	8 000	10 000
Sundry	2 300	3 800

3. Dividends for 1984 and 1985 were £10 000 and £20 000 respectively.
4. The company doubled its sales of each product in 1985 compared with 1984 without changing the selling price per unit.

Required:
a   Trading Accounts for 1984 in columnar form, showing the results for each product separately and in total, and the Profit and Loss Account and Appropriation Account for 1984.
b   Trading Accounts for 1985 in columnar form, showing the results for each product separately and in total, and the Profit and Loss Account and Appropriation Account for 1985. Show clearly the total profit carried forward to 1986.
c   Explain, with examples, the difference between fixed costs and variable costs.

[*Royal Society of Arts, II, March 1986*]

10 You are required to prepare a Manufacturing, Trading and Profit and Loss Account for the year ended 31 December and a balance sheet at that date for the firm of Precision Manufacture from the following balances and information:

	£
Furniture at cost	1 800
Discounts received	824
Proprietor's capital	70 000
Proprietor's drawings	16 000
Factory power	7 228
Bad debts written off	1 210
Bad debt provision at 1 January	2 000
Bank charges	240
Advertising	1 660
Cash at bank and in hand	8 202
Factory wages	41 400
Sales	158 348
Repairs to plant	1 570
Purchases of raw materials	69 506
Plant and machinery at cost	34 000
General expenses:	
Factory	410
Office	692
Insurance	1 804
Light and heat	964
Debtors	21 120
Stock at 1 January:	
Raw materials	10 460
Finished goods	18 100
Rent and rates	5 142
Office salaries	7 380
Creditors	17 716

The following liabilities are to be provided for:
    Light and heat   £320
    Rent and rates   £774
Advertising paid in advance is £340.
Five-sixths of rent and rates is to be allocated to the factory and one-sixth to the office.

Stocks at 31 December were:
Raw materials   £7120
Finished goods   £22 780

Provide depreciation at 12 per cent per annum on plant and machinery.

Increase the bad debt provision to 10 per cent of debtors at the year end.

[*Pitman Intermediate*]

11 The accountant of Acme Manufacturers closed off his books at 31 December, the end of the trading year.

From the following balances and information you are required to prepare Manufacturing Trading and Profit and Loss Accounts for the year ended 31 December and a balance sheet at that date.

	£
Factory machinery at cost	10 000
Stock of finished goods 1 January	10 682
Capital at 1 January	31 506
Furniture at cost (purchased 1 April)	2 400
Trade debtors	37 200
Manufacturing expenses	1 250
Factory salaries	4 400
Office salaries	7 500
Office wages	6 350
Factory power	18 862
Work in progress 1 January	1 172
Sales	206 254
Purchases of raw materials	60 374
Trade creditors	23 000
Stock of raw materials 1 January	4 474
Manufacturing wages	43 968
Rent and rates	1 112
Legal charges	1 434
General expenses	5 082
Cash at bank	44 500

Legal charges to be provided £1 760
Rates paid in advance £62
Bad debt to be written off £460
Provision of 5 per cent on balance of trade debtors
Depreciation to be provided:
    Factory machinery 12½ per cent per annum
    Furniture   10 per cent per annum
Stocks at 31 December:
    Raw materials   £6 144
    Work in progress   £634
    Finished goods   £12 190

[*Pitman Intermediate*]

12 The following trial balance was extracted from the books of G. Ashcroft at 31 October 1986:

Trial balance at 31 October 1986

	£	£
Capital		251 990
Drawings	25 700	
Trade debtors and creditors	42 800	14 600
Purchase of raw materials	208 000	
Manufacturing wages	150 600	
Factory expenses (excluding depreciation)	42 440	
Selling and distribution expenses	12 800	
Administration expenses	42 000	
Sales		630 000
Stocks at 1 November 1985:		
Raw materials	18 000	
Finished goods	48 500	
Work in progress	2 700	
Bad debts	1 900	
Provision for bad debts		2 350
Plant and machinery at cost	190 000	
Office furniture and equipment at cost	28 000	
Premises at cost	150 000	
Bank	18 500	
Provision for depreciation:		
Plant and machinery		76 000
Office furniture and equipment		7 000
	981 940	981 940

You are given the following additional information:
(i) Stocks at 31 October 1986:
    Raw materials   £17 800
    Finished goods   £41 900
    Work in progress   £3 200
(ii) Depreciation is written off fixed assets as follows:
    Plant and machinery: 25 per cent per annum using the reducing balance. Office furniture and equipment: 10 per cent per annum using the straight-line basis.
(iii) Part of the premises consist of a small flat which Ashcroft occupies privately. It was decided to charge £2 000 of the administration expenses to Ashcroft's drawings to allow for this.
(iv) The provision for bad debts is to be reduced to 5 per cent of debtors outstanding on 31 October 1986.

Prepare Ashcroft's Manufacturing, Trading and Profit and Loss Account for the year ended 31 October 1986 and his balance sheet as at that date. Your accounts should be in vertical form and should clearly show:
a prime cost
b cost of manufacture
c cost of goods sold.

[*Royal Society of Arts, II, autumn 1986*]

13 The following were some of the ledger balances in the books of Oven to Oven Ware Ltd, Stoke-on-Trent, on 31 December Year 7:

	£
Work in progress 1 January Year 7	34 000
Stock of finished goods 1 January Year 7	31 600
Raw materials stocks 1 January Year 7	23 000
Bank overdraft	15 000
Provisions for depreciation:	
Leasehold buildings	12 000
Plant and machinery	28 700
Fixtures and fittings	2 800
Repairs to buildings	4 800
Carriage outwards	7 300
Materials purchases	125 300
Factory rates	7 900
Direct wages	110 000
Sales	478 000
Leasehold buildings at cost	60 000
Factory power	9 900
Plant and machinery at cost	75 200
Indirect wages	97 300
Directors' fees	3 500
Returns inwards	2 000
Carriage inwards	6 800
Reserved for increased replacement costs of fixed assets	15 000

Notes
(i) The factory buildings are held on a 30 year lease.
(ii) Stocks at 31 December Year 7 were:
Raw materials £26 000; Work in progress £36 000; Finished goods £29 000.
(iii) Depreciate plant and machinery at $12\frac{1}{2}$ per cent using the straight-line method and fixtures and fittings at 10 per cent using the reducing balance method.
(iv) The factory production was charged to the finished goods warehouse at a standard cost of £380 000.

Prepare a Manufacturing Account for Oven to Oven Ware Ltd for the year ended 31 December Year 7, selecting from the list of balances only those you will require for this purpose.

[*London Chamber of Commerce and Industry, March 1987*]

14 The following balances as at 31 December 1985 have been extracted from the books of William Speed, a small manufacturer:

	£
Stocks at 1 January 1985:	
Raw materials	7 000
Work in progress	5 000
Finished goods	6 900
Purchases of raw materials	38 000
Direct labour	28 000
Factory overheads:	
Variable	16 000
Fixed	9 000
Administrative expenses:	
Rent and rates	19 000
Heat and light	6 000
Stationery and postages	2 000
Staff salaries	19 380
Sales	192 000
Plant and machinery:	
At cost	30 000
Provision for depreciation	12 000
Motor vehicles (for sales deliveries):	
At cost	16 000
Provision for depreciation	4 000
Creditors	5 500
Debtors	28 000
Drawings	11 500
Balance at bank	16 600
Capital at 1 January 1985	48 000
Provision for unrealised profit at 1 January 1985	1 380
Motor vehicle running costs	4 500

Additional information:
1. Stocks at 31 December 1985 were as follows:

	£
Raw materials	9 000
Work in progress	8 000
Finished goods	10 350

2. The factory output is transferred to the Trading Account at factory cost plus 25 per cent for factory profit. The finished goods stock is valued on the basis of amounts transferred to the debit of the Trading Account.
3. Depreciation is provided annually at the following percentages of the original cost of fixed assets held at the end of each financial year:

Plant and machinery	10 per cent
Motor vehicles	25 per cent

4. Amounts accrued due at 31 December 1985 for direct labour amounted to £3 000 and rent and rates prepaid at 31 December 1985 amounted to £2 000.

Prepare a Manufacturing, Trading and Profit and Loss Account for the year ended 31 December 1985 and a balance sheet as at that date.

Note. The prime cost and total factory cost should be clearly shown.

[*Association of Accounting Technicians, June 1986*]

15 The following list of balances as at 31 July 1986 has been extracted from the books of Jane Seymour who commenced business on 1 August 1985 as a designer and manufacturer of kitchen furniture:

	£
Plant and machinery, at cost on 1 August 1985	60 000
Motor vehicles, at cost on 1 August 1985	30 000
Loose tools, at cost	9 000
Sales	170 000
Raw materials purchased	43 000
Direct factory wages	39 000
Light and power	5 000
Indirect factory wages	8 000
Machinery repairs	1 600
Motor vehicle running expenses	12 000
Rent and insurances	11 600
Administrative staff salaries	31 000
Administrative expenses	9 000
Sales and distribution staff salaries	13 000
Capital at 1 August 1985	122 000
Sundry debtors	16 500
Sundry creditors	11 200
Balance at bank	8 500
Drawings	6 000

Additional information for the year ended 31 July 1986:
1. It is estimated that the plant and machinery will be used in the business for 10 years and the motor vehicles used for 4 years; in both cases it is estimated that the residual value will be nil. The straight-line method of providing for depreciation is to be used.
2. Light and power charges accrued due at 31 July 1986 amounted to £1 000 and insurances prepaid at 31 July 1986 totalled £800.
3. Stocks were valued at cost at 31 July 1986 as follows:
   Raw materials   £7 000
   Finished goods   £10 000
4. The valuation of work in progress at 31 July 1986 included variable and fixed factory overheads and amounted to £12 300.
5. Two-thirds of the light and power and rent and insurance costs are to be allocated to the factory costs and one-third to general administration costs.
6. Motor vehicle costs are to be allocated equally to factory costs and general administration costs.
7. Goods manufactured during the year are to be transferred to the Trading Account at £95 000.
8. Loose tools in hand on 31 July 1986 were valued at £5 000.

a Prepare a Manufacturing, Trading and Profit and Loss Account for the year ended 31 July 1986 of Jane Seymour.
b Give an explanation of how each of the following accounting concepts have affected the preparation of the above accounts: conservatism, matching, going concern.

[*Association of Accounting Technicians, December 1986*]

21 Preparation and presentation of internal final accounts and balance sheets of companies

Sole traders or partnerships are free to present final accounts (i.e. Trading and Profit and Loss Accounts) in any form they wish. Limited companies, however, must comply with the legal requirements of the country in which they are situated and are required to publish accounts containing minimum information for the public. The legal requirements in this respect vary from country to country, some requiring more information to be published than others. The reason for compelling companies to publish extracts from their accounts is mainly to protect the people who have an interest in the workings of the company, such as shareholders, employees, creditors and the general public.

The company will keep its final accounts in such a way as to combine:
(a) the maximum information, for internal use and for comparison with previous years, with
(b) the legal requirements of the country in which it operates, preferably in accordance with the recommendations and guidelines of the accountancy profession.

The accounts themselves, even though they record past financial transactions, nevertheless can be used for the future management and control of the business. They can be used in decision-making in respect of finance for expansion and development.

A Simple Example using vertical layout

Castle Industries Ltd
Manufacturing, Trading and Profit and Loss Accounts
for year ended 31 December 19-2

	£	£	£	£
Sales	403 000			
Less Returns	3 000			
				400 000
Less				
Cost of sales				
Raw materials consumed:				
Stock at 1 January 19-2	10 000			
Add Purchases for year	64 000			
	74 000			
Less Stock at 31 December 19-2	14 000			
Cost of raw materials used	60 000			
Add				
Direct costs:				
Factory wages	78 000			
Royalties on patent used	2 000			
PRIME COST	140 000			
Add				
Factory overheads:				
Factory manager's salary	10 000			
Factory rent and rates	2 000			
Heat, light and power	6 000			
Depreciation of machinery	2 000			
	20 000			
COST OF MANUFACTURE		160 000		
Add				
Cost of finished goods:				
Stock at 1 January 19-2		4 000		
Add Purchases for year	44 000			
Less Returns	2 000			
		42 000		
		46 000		
Less Stock at 31 December 19-2		6 000		
			40 000	
COST OF SALES				200 000
GROSS PROFIT TO PROFIT AND LOSS ACCOUNT				200 000
Add Discount received				4 000

Manufacturing brackets the raw materials through cost of manufacture section; *Trading* brackets the finished goods section.

[cont. over

Profit and Loss

		£	£	£	£
					204 000
Less					
Expenses					
Administration:					
	Office salaries	40 000			
	Postage	2 000			
	Stationery and printing	3 000			
	Telephones (+£600 due)	1 000			
	General expenses	500			
	Directors' fees	19 500			
			66 000		
Establishment:					
	Rent and rates (*less* prepaid £250)	13 000			
	Insurance (general)	1 500			
	Office heating and lighting	2 500			
Depreciation:					
	Office buildings (5% of £100 000)	5 000			
	Fixtures and fittings				
	(10% of £20 000)	2 000			
	Office machines	1 000			
		8 000			
			25 000		
Financial:					
	Bad debts and bad debts provision	2 000			
	Discount allowed	4 000			
	Audit fees	5 000			
	Legal fees	500			
	Bank interest and charges	1 500			
	Debenture interest (+ £400 due)	2 400			
	Mortgage interest	1 600			
			17 000		

Profit and Loss

Selling and distribution:					
	Salaries: sales staff	33 000			
	Commission: sales staff	6 000			
	Advertising and publicity	12 000			
	Showroom expenses	2 000			
	Carriage outwards	5 000			
	Delivery expenses	2 500			
	Packing materials	1 500			
Depreciation:					
	Delivery vehicles				
	(20% of £40 000)	8 000			
			70 000		
Research and development:					
	Research expenses	2 000	2 000		
TOTAL EXPENSES					180 000
NET PROFIT FOR YEAR					24 000
Add Balance brought forward from last year					10 000

Profit and Loss Appropn

		£	£
	PROFIT AVAILABLE FOR DISTRIBUTION		34 000
	Appropriated as follows:		
	Preference dividend 10%	2 000	
	Provision for taxation	6 000	
	Goodwill written off	1 000	
	General reserve	5 000	
	Debenture redemption reserve	3 000	
	Proposed ordinary share dividend (10%)	6 000	
			23 000
	BALANCE CARRIED FORWARD		11 000

Castle Industries Ltd
Balance sheet as at 31 December 19–2

	Cost	Depreciation to date	Present value	Total
Fixed assets	£	£	£	£
Intangible assets:				
Goodwill	3 000	1 000	2 000	
Tangible assets:				
Buildings	100 000	20 000	80 000	
Plant and machinery	40 000	10 000	30 000	
Fixtures and fittings	18 000	9 000	9 000	
Office equipment	2 000	1 000	1 000	
Vehicles	40 000	16 000	24 000	
	203 000	57 000	146 000	146 000

		£	
Trade investments:			
Shares in subsidiary at cost (directors' valuation £14 000)			12 000
			158 000

	£	£	
Current assets			
Other investments (market value £5 000)	4 000		
Stocks	20 000		
Trade debtors	30 000		
Bills receivable	2 000		
Cash at bank	7 000		
Cash in hand	750		
Prepayments	250		
		64 000	
Less Current Liabilities			
Creditors	10 000		
Bills payable	1 000		
Accruals	600		
Debenture interest due	400		
Proposed dividends	8 000		
		20 000	
Working capital (Net current assets)			44 000
TOTAL NET ASSETS			202 000

[cont. over

310 Preparation of internal final accounts and balance sheets

Financed by:
Ordinary share capital	Authorised £	Issued £	Total £
£1 ordinary shares fully paid	70 000	60 000	60 000

Reserves	£		
Debenture redemption reserve	37 000		
General reserve	8 000		
Profit and Loss Account	11 000		
			56 000
Ordinary shareholders' equity			116 000

	Authorised £	Issued £	Total £
10% preference shares £1 each fully paid	30 000	20 000	20 000

Long-term debt *(liabilities)*	£		
8% mortgage (buildings)	20 000		
6% debentures (redeemable 19–6)	40 000		
Reserve for Corporation Tax	6 000		
			66 000
CAPITAL EMPLOYED			202 000

DETAILED EXAMINATION

A detailed examination of the final accounts and balance sheet of Castle Industries Ltd is perhaps the best way to study the constituent parts and learn a little more about each.

The preparation of a Profit and Loss Account and balance sheet is required of all limited companies by law. Of course, manufacturing concerns will also prepare a Manufacturing Account.

Main function of final accounts

The main function of the final accounts is to compare the revenue of the period with the costs of the same period, so every item appearing in the final accounts will be either a revenue or a cost item. The overall result will show *an excess of revenue over cost (net profit)* or *an excess of cost over revenue (net loss)*. The trading revenue of the company will come from sales of either goods or services.

The most important figure, therefore, will be *sales*.

From this figure for sales will be subtracted the figure for *cost of sales*; the result will be *gross profit*. From gross profit, *selling expenses and trading losses* will be deducted to give *net profit* for the year.

Sales: All sales, cash or credit, of goods normally dealt in by the company are shown net (i.e. with returns deducted). The word 'turnover' is sometimes used instead of sales.

Cost of sales: This is the total cost of manufacture *plus* cost of finished goods which went to make up sales.

Main function of final accounts

Cost of manufacture = Cost of raw materials used + Direct labour + Direct expenses + Factory overheads + Cost of work in progress (See Manufacturing Account.)

\+

Cost of finished goods = Opening stock + Purchases (net) *less* Closing stock

= *Cost of sales*

GROSS PROFIT = Sales *less* Cost of sales

To gross profit are added revenue receipts obtained in the course of trading, such as discount received.

Selling expenses. For the sake of continuity and direct comparison of one year with the next, selling expenses can be grouped under five headings such as: (*a*) Administration; (*b*) Establishment; (*c*) Financial; (*d*) Selling and distribution; and (*e*) Research and development.

Castle Industries Ltd (See example, pages 307–9)
Manufacturing, Trading and Profit and Loss Accounts

	£		£
The Manufacturing Account shows the total cost of manufacture	160 000	*Components* Raw materials Direct labour Direct expenses Factory overheads	60 000 78 000 2 000 20 000
The Trading Account shows cost of finished goods	40 000		
Cost of sales is:	200 000		

GROSS PROFIT is the difference between Sales and Cost of sales
£400 000 − £200 000 = £200 000

			£
Profit and Loss Account To gross profit is added other revenue receipts (in this case discount received)			4 000
			204 000
		£	
From this figure, selling expenses and losses are deducted under five main headings	Administration Establishment Financial Selling and distribution Research and development	66 000 25 000 17 000 70 000 2 000	
	Total		180 000
leaving NET PROFIT for year:			24 000
to which is added balance brought forward from last year (last year's profit). Loss would be deducted making:			10 000
			34 000

	£
Out of this the directors recommend that a total appropriation be made amounting to:	23 000
leaving a balance to be carried forward of:	11 000

which will be shown under heading 'Revenue reserve' in balance sheet

Expenses are grouped under the headings listed above so that valid comparisons can be made between the totals spent under these headings and between individual items within each group.

In larger firms a manager or supervisor is usually responsible for each of the five main areas. They are called by various titles, e.g. the individuals responsible for the expenses of each department might be called:

For *establishment*: the establishment services manager.
For *administration*: the accountant or office manager.
For *financial expenses*: the accountant or financial controller.
For *selling and distribution*: the sales manager or sales supervisor.
For *research and development*: the research and development manager.

The titles and headings vary from company to company, but somebody is responsible for each area of expense. In a properly managed company, forecasts are made in the main areas of revenue and costs. Targets are set for sales; shares of the market and budgets are prepared in detail to anticipate as far as possible all likely costs.

The only justification for incurring extra expenses is to produce extra revenue, leading to increased profits. Regular checks are built into the system to monitor deviations from budgets or targets and to enable corrective action to be taken.

Some companies group expenses slightly differently, e.g. bad debts may be treated by one company as a financial expense and by another as a selling and distribution expense, arguing that bad debts arise as a result of sales. The most important thing is that the items grouped under each heading are consistent from year to year – the principle of consistency.

Some firms also amalgamate headings, e.g. administration and establishment.

Revenue receipts like discount receivable and rent receivable are added to gross profit before selling expenses and losses are deducted.

The following is an acceptable grouping of expenses:

Establishment
Rent
Rates
Insurance (other than National Insurance)
Heating
Lighting
Repairs to property
Depreciation of office buildings
Depreciation of office fixtures and fittings
Depreciation of office machines

Administration
Office salaries
Postage
Stationery and printing
Telephones and telex
Directors' fees
Directors' expenses
General expenses

Financial
Bad debts and provision for bad debts
Discounts allowed
Bank interest
Bank charges
Audit and accountancy fees
Legal fees
Debenture interest
Mortgage interest

Research and development
All expenses incurred in researching and developing new products and processes

Selling and distribution
Advertising and publicity
Showroom expenses
Salaries of sales staff
Commissions of sales staff
Expenses of sales staff
Carriage outwards
Packing materials
Delivery expenses
Repairs to sales cars, lorries and vans
Depreciation of delivery vehicles

A properly prepared Profit and Loss Account should show at a glance totals for each area of expense and a grand total for selling expenses and losses (see example, page 308).

Distribution of profits

We have now arrived at the net profit (or loss) for the year arising out of the normal trading of the company. The next question we must answer is what happens to the profit. The answer is that the directors propose to the annual general meeting of shareholders how they think the profits should be apportioned or distributed. It is most unusual for the proposals of the directors not to be accepted by the shareholders. The final accounts are presented to the shareholders on the assumption that they will be approved.

Non-discretionary items

Some items are outside the discretion of the directors, i.e. they must be paid if the company makes sufficient profit. Items like tax and preference share dividend come into this category.

Discretionary items

The other items are more discretionary, in that a variety of allocation options is open to the directors. As a general rule they will try to satisfy the ordinary shareholders by paying a reasonable dividend while at the same time improving the overall financial strength of the company by retaining part of the profits. The profits are the internal source of finance for future expansion. In good years they will provide for a write-off of intangible assets such as goodwill and patents and provide for the redemption of mortgages and other long-term liabilities.

Payments made to shareholders during the year in anticipation of profit (interim dividends) are accounted for in the appropriation section of the Profit and Loss Account. Only unpaid amounts will appear on the balance sheet.

Taking net profit for the year

Add   balance brought forward from last year (deduct if a loss in previous year)
Add   gains arising outside the normal operations of the company (see below)
Deduct   (a) the items that are legally payable out of the profit (e.g. preference dividend)
   (b) the allocations of profit recommended by the directors.

The difference is the 'Balance carried forward to next year' which will appear again in the balance sheet as Profit and Loss Account balance under the heading of 'Reserves'.

Additions to net profit (gains arising outside normal operations)

(a) Profit on sales of investments.
(b) Income from investment in subsidiary companies.
(c) Income from trade investments.
(d) Tax provision for previous years not used up.
(e) Any other abnormal gains.

Deductions from net profit (appropriations of profit)

(a) Provision for tax.
(b) Provision for dividends.
(c) Amounts written off intangible assets.
(d) Amounts put to general reserves.
(e) Amounts put to redemption of long-term liabilities (e.g. debentures or mortgages).
(f) Amounts put to special reserves (e.g. staff pension funds).
(g) Abnormal losses.

The balance sheet or position statement – three views

We can look at a balance sheet in three different ways:

1. A balance sheet is a list of balances taken from the ledger accounts on a particular date. The total debits will equal the total credits, because the books have been kept on double-entry principles. This is a rather narrow view of the balance sheet, but it has one advantage in that it highlights the fact that behind the figures on the balance sheet are ledger accounts.
2. The balance sheet is also a kind of snapshot taken on a particular date of the value of assets and liabilities of the business. This approach highlights the fact that the figures will of necessity change from day to day, particularly current assets and current liabilities.
3. The third and most productive way of looking at a balance sheet of a limited company is to see it as a statement showing on the one hand where the company has obtained its finance and on the other how this finance is being utilised. Each item appearing on a company balance sheet should be there as a result of a conscious decision of management. The size and composition

of the assets and liabilities should be under constant scrutiny and control. They should be adjusted to meet the changing needs of the company.

The basic make-up of any balance sheet is:
Fixed assets + Working capital (Net current assets) making TOTAL NET ASSETS

Financed by
Ordinary share capital + Reserves (which is equal to Ordinary shareholders' equity)
+Preference share capital (Preference shares)
+Long-term liabilities (not falling due within the year)

The total of these items will always be equal to the total for TOTAL NET ASSETS (sometimes called CAPITAL EMPLOYED).

Fixed assets can be subdivided into:
(a) Intangible assets
(b) Tangible fixed assets
(c) Trade investments
These are followed by:
(d) Current assets *less* Current liabilities (Working capital or Net current assets).
The total of all these amount to TOTAL NET ASSETS.

(a) *Intangible assets.* These assets will be valued at cost and shown separately less depreciation to date.
They are usually written off as quickly as possible.

Examples: Goodwill, Patents, Licences, Trademarks

(b) *Tangible fixed assets*
Land
Buildings
Plant and machinery
Fixtures and fittings
Lorries, cars, vans, etc.
These are shown on the balance sheet as follows under the headings:

Cost	Depreciation to date	Net

'Cost' will represent the balance on the particular Asset Account.
'Depreciation to date' will represent the balance on Provision for Depreciation Account for each class of asset.
'Net' will be the difference between the two.

(c) *Investments* are investments or shares in subsidiary companies. They must be shown at cost on the balance sheet with a note indicating their present value.

Working capital (net current assets). This is arrived at by subtracting the value of current liabilities from the value of current assets. It represents the finance available for the day-to-day running of the business.

This finance bridges the time gap from the time raw materials or finished goods are bought until the cycle is completed by the debtors paying for goods purchased on credit. This time period is called the 'operating cycle' of the business. It covers the time span during which

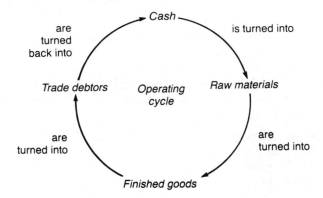

The length of time it takes to complete the operating cycle will vary from business to business. It will depend on:
(a) the type of business, e.g. a builder will need much more time than a baker
(b) the volume of business transacted
(c) the credit rating of the company
(d) the ability of the company to set and carry out policies in respect of stock levels, payments by trade debtors and payments to trade creditors.

Level of working capital

The level of its working capital is of vital concern to a company. Too little working capital relative to the size of the business means that the firm is *overtrading*. Too much working capital relative to the size of the business means that the firm is *undertrading*. It means that stocks and/or debtors are too high or that too much money is lying unused in the bank or in cash. Working capital levels will be investigated and quantified in greater detail in Chapter 22, 'Interpretation of financial statements'.

In this area of the balance sheet we set out the values of current assets and total them. Underneath we set out the values of current liabilities, total them and subtract the total from the total for current assets. (If current liabilities are greater, the figure is preceded by a minus sign or put into brackets to indicate the shortfall of working capital.)

Again it is important to list both assets and liabilities in the *same* order each year.

Current assets
(a) Other investments (i.e., temporary investments which can be easily converted to cash) shown at cost, but with a note indicating the directors' valuation.

(b) Stocks
    (i) Raw materials.
    (ii) Work in progress.
    (iii) Finished goods.
(c) Trade debtors, less provision for bad debts.
(d) Bills receivable.
(e) Bank balance.
(f) Cash.
(g) Prepayments.

Current liabilities
The usual items are:
(a) Trade creditors.
(b) Bills payable.
(c) Accruals.
(d) Bank overdraft.
(e) Provision for taxation due this year.
(f) Proposed dividends.

Now we have the full picture of how the finance is being used, i.e.

Total fixed assets + Working capital = Total net assets

We will now look at the sources of the finance.

Sources of long-term finance
(a) *The ordinary shareholders*: share capital + reserves.
(b) *Preference shareholders*.
(c) *Outsiders*: long-term liabilities (debts).

Share capital is the amount originally subscribed to the funds of the company by the ordinary shareholders. It can be shown under the following headings:

Type of shares   Authorised   Issued

Authorised capital is the amount the company is empowered to issue by its memorandum of association. *Issued capital* is the amount actually issued at the date of the balance sheet.

The most important type of share capital is ordinary shares, particularly ordinary shares that carry voting rights. These are the true owners of the company in that whoever holds over 50 per cent of these shares controls the company.

All reserves and retained profits belong to the ordinary or equity shareholders.

Reserves
1. *Capital reserves* are reserves which are not normally available for distribution as dividends. They have not been set aside out of profits like revenue reserves. They have been earned by the company in an unusual way such as:
    (a) Revaluation of assets – an increase in the value of assets such as land creates additional reserves.

(b) Share premiums – these arise when shares are issued at a price in excess of their face value.
(c) Profits prior to incorporation – these are profits that are made before the company receives its certificate of incorporation.
2. *Revenue reserves* are accumulated retained profits which are available, if necessary, for payment of dividends.
Examples: (a) General reserve, (b) Profit and Loss Account balance

Long-term debt (liabilities) is finance available to a company for a period of time longer than a year.
Examples: (a) Debentures, (b) Mortgages, (c) Bank term loans, (d) Reserve for Corporation Tax

Note
Fictitious assets include items relating to preliminary formation and issue expenses such as:
(a) Preliminary expenses
(b) Share issue expenses
(c) Debenture issue expenses
(d) Discounts on shares or debentures issued.

Balance on these accounts, if any, will be debit balances and might be expected to be seen in the assets section of the balance sheet. However, they should be deducted from shareholders' funds and written off as quickly as possible.

Balance sheet notes

Since the function of providing final accounts and balance sheets is to give a 'true and fair' picture of the affairs of the business, all relevant information should be supplied either on the face of the accounts or balance sheet or in notes attached to the balance sheet.

Castle Industries Ltd
Balance sheet

	£
How finance is being used	
Total for fixed assets is	146 000
Trade investments total	12 000
Working capital is	44 000
Total for net assets is	202 000
Where finance comes from	
Ordinary share capital provides	60 000
Reserves provide	56 000
Preference shareholders' provide	20 000
Long-term outside finance amounts to	66 000
(Total) Capital employed is	202 000

A More Difficult Example

Modern Plastics Ltd has an authorised capital of £450 000 divided into 300 000 £1 ordinary shares and 150 000 10% preference shares of £1 each. The following trial balance was extracted from its books on 31 December 19–1:

	Dr. £	Cr. £
Land (cost £245 000)	245 000	
Buildings (cost £200 000)	100 000	
Factory machines (cost £75 000)	50 000	
Office machines (cost £25 000)	15 000	
Delivery vans (cost £80 000)	40 000	
Goodwill	8 000	
Patents	6 000	
Investments in subsidiary	25 000	
Other investments	15 000	
Stocks at 1.1.19–1:		
Raw materials	75 000	
Finished goods	35 000	
Work in progress	25 000	
Packing materials	200	
Purchases of packing materials	1 900	
Trade debtors and creditors	66 500	60 000
Provision for bad debts		5 000
Sales		957 000
Bills receivable	3 000	
Bank	2 300	
Manufacturing wages	98 000	
10% debentures		50 000
10% preference shares		150 000
£1 ordinary shares		200 000
Interim dividend – ordinary shares	5 000	
Profit from sale of investments		8 000
Profit and Loss Account balance at 1.1.19–1	44 000	
Purchase of raw materials	215 000	
Purchase of finished goods	48 000	
Carriage on raw materials	5 000	
Customs duties on raw materials	1 000	
Royalties paid	5 000	
Hire of special equipment	7 000	
Rent (factory, £3 500; office, £700)	4 200	
Rates (factory, £1 500; office, £1 300)	2 800	
Light and heat (factory, £11 500; office, £7 700)	19 200	
Factory foreman's salary	10 000	
Office salaries	80 000	
Repairs to office machines	300	
Postage	4 000	
Audit fees	1 550	
Advertising	25 000	
Discount	5 900	
Carriage out	3 000	
Bank charges	450	
Mortgage interest	800	

Preparation of internal final accounts and balance sheets

	Dr. £	Cr. £
Salesmen's salaries	130 000	
Salesmen's commission	15 400	
Stationery	1 500	
Telephones	2 700	
Directors' fees	20 000	
General expenses	1 800	
General reserve		10 000
10% mortgage		8 000
Debenture redemption reserve		10 000
Suspense		3 000
Sale of scrap material		8 500
	1 469 500	1 469 500

The following information and instructions are to be taken into account:
1. Depreciation:
   Factory building   10% on cost
   Factory machinery   20% on cost
   Office machines   20% on cost
   Delivery vans   25% on cost
2. A debt of £1 500 is to be written off as bad and the provision for bad debts maintained at 10 per cent of debtors.
3. Goods costing £5 000 had been sent on a sale or return basis to a customer. These goods had been treated in the books as a credit sale of £7 000.
4. Manufacturing wages due amounted to £2 000.
5. Provide for a full year's debenture interest.
6. Purchase of finished goods – purchases book overcast by £3 000.
7. Raw materials costing £10 000 bought on credit from Forest Industries Ltd were in transit on 31 December but this transaction was not recorded in the books.
8. The directors recommend that:
   (a) preference dividend be paid in full
   (b) a final dividend of 10 per cent be paid on ordinary shares
   (c) £6 000 be put to general reserve
   (d) half the goodwill be written off.
9. The directors value investment in subsidiary at £20 000 at 31 December 19–1.
10. The other investments have a market value of £18 000.
11. Stocks at 31 December 19–1 are as follows:
    Raw materials   £86 000
    Finished goods   £40 000
    Work in progress   £20 000
    Packing materials   £500

SOLUTION

Modern Plastics Ltd
Manufacturing, Trading and Profit and Loss Accounts
for year ended December 31 19–1

	£	£	£	£
Sales (Note 1)				950 000
Less				
Cost of sales				
Raw materials:				
Stock of raw materials at				
1 January 19–1		75 000		
Add Purchases of raw				
materials (Note 2)		225 000		
Add Carriage in		5 000		
Add Customs duties		1 000		
		306 000		
Less Stock of raw materials at				
31 December 19–1		86 000		
Cost of raw materials used		220 000		
Add				
Direct costs:				
Manufacturing wages				
(Note 3)	100 000			
Royalties	5 000			
Hire of special equipment	7 000			
		112 000		
Add				
Factory overheads:				
Factory rent	3 500			
Factory rates	1 500			
Factory lighting and heating	11 500			
Factory foreman's salary	10 000			
Factory buildings deprecia-				
tion (10% of £200 000)	20 000			
Machinery depreciation (20%				
of £75 000)	15 000			
		61 500		
		393 500		
Add Work in progress				
at 1 January 19–1	25 000			
Less Work in progress at				
31 December 19–1	20 000			
		5 000		
		398 500		
Less Sale of scrap materials		8 500		
COST OF MANUFACTURE			390 000	

[*cont. over*

	£	£	£	£
Add				
Cost of finished goods:				
Stock at 1 January 19–1	35 000			
Add Purchases (Note 4)	45 000			
	80 000			
Less Stock at 31 December 19-1	40 000			
			40 000	
COST OF SALES				430 000
GROSS PROFIT TO PROFIT AND LOSS ACCOUNT				520 000
Less				
Selling expenses and losses				
Administration:				
Office salaries		80 000		
Directors' fees		20 000		
Postage		4 000		
Stationery		1 500		
Telephones		2 700		
General expenses		1 800		
			110 000	
Establishment:				
Office rent		700		
Office rates		1 300		
Heat and light		7 700		
Repairs to office machines		300		
Depreciation of office				
machines (20% of £25 000)		5 000		
			15 000	
Financial:				
Discounts allowed		5 900		
Bank charges		450		
Audit fees		1 550		
Debenture interest		5 000		
Mortgage interest		800		
Bad debts and provision for				
bad debts (Note 5)		2 300		
			16 000	
Selling and distribution:				
Advertising		25 000		
Salesmen's salaries		130 000		
Salesmen's commission		15 400		
Packing materials (Note 6)		1 600		
Carriage out		3 000		

	£	£	£	£
Depreciation:				
Delivery vans				
(25% of £80 000)		20 000		
			195 000	
TOTAL EXPENSES				336 000
PROFIT FOR YEAR				184 000
Balance b/f				(44 000)
				140 000
Add Profit from sale of investments				8 000
PROFIT AVAILABLE FOR DISTRIBUTION				148 000
Appropriated as follows:				
Yearly dividend on preference shares			15 000	
Interim dividend on ordinary shares	5 000			
Add Proposed final dividend	20 000		25 000	
Add General reserve			6 000	
Add Goodwill written off			4 000	
				50 000
BALANCE CARRIED FORWARD				98 000

Modern Plastics Ltd
Balance sheet as at 31 December 19–1

	Cost	Depreciation to date	Present value	Total
Fixed assets	£	£	£	£
Intangible assets:				
Goodwill	4 000	—	4 000	
Patents	6 000	—	6 000	
	10 000	—	10 000	
Tangible assets:				
Land	245 000	—	245 000	
Buildings	200 000	120 000	80 000	
Machinery	75 000	40 000	35 000	
Office machines	25 000	15 000	10 000	
Delivery vans	80 000	60 000	20 000	
	635 000	235 000	400 000	400 000
Trade investments:				
Share in subsidiary at cost (directors' valuation £20 000)				25 000
				425 000

[*cont. over*

	£	£	£
Current assets			
Other investments (market value £18 000)		15 000	
Stocks:			
Raw materials	86 000		
Finished goods	40 000		
Work in progress	20 000		
Packing materials	500		
		146 500	
Trade debtors (Note 5)	58 000		
Less Provision for bad debts	5 800		
		52 200	
Bills receivable		3 000	
Bank		2 300	
		219 000	
Less Current liabilities			
Trade creditors (Note 2)	70 000		
Accruals	2 000		
Debenture interest due	5 000		
Preference dividend	15 000		
Proposed ordinary dividend	20 000		
		112 000	
Working capital (Net current assets)			107 000
TOTAL NET ASSETS			532 000

Financed by:			
Ordinary share capital	Authorised	Issued	
	£	£	
£1 ordinary shares	300 000	200 000	200 000
Reserves	£		
Debenture redemption reserve	10 000		
General reserve	16 000		
Profit and Loss Account	98 000		
Ordinary shareholders' equity (funds)			124 000
			324 000
	Authorised	Issued	
	£	£	
10% preference shares £1 each fully paid	150 000	150 000	150 000
Long-term liabilities	£		
10% debentures	50 000		
10% mortgage	8 000		
		58 000	
CAPITAL EMPLOYED			532 000

Notes

		£
1.	Sales	957 000
	Less Goods on sale or return	7 000
		950 000

		£
2.	Purchases of raw materials	215 000
	Add Raw materials in transit	10 000
		225 000

		£
	Creditors	60 000
	Add Raw materials in transit	10 000
		70 000

		£
3.	Manfacturing wages	98 000
	Add Wages due	2 000
		100 000

		£
4.	Purchase of finished goods	48 000
	Less Error in purchases book	3 000
		45 000

5. Dr. **Bad Debts Provision Account** Cr.

19–1		£	19–1		£
31 Dec.	Bad debt w/o	1 500	1 Jan.	Balance b/d	5 000
	*Balance c/d	5 800	31 Dec.	Profit and Loss Account	2 300
		7 300			7 300
			31 Dec.	Balance b/d	5 800

		£
*Debtors		66 500
Less Goods on sale or return		7 000
		59 500
Less Bad debt written off		1 500
		58 000
Provision 10 per cent		5 800

		£
6.	Stock packing material 1.1.19–1	200
	Add Purchases	1 900
	Less Stock at 31.12.19–1	(500)
	Charge to Profit and Loss Account	1 600

Some more difficult adjustments

In examinations, additional testing of knowledge and understanding is done by means of requiring the student to adjust the given figures to take account of additional information available. These pieces of information must first be read very carefully and then analysed to see how many accounts are involved and for how much. Each account must then be altered accordingly.

Using Castle Industries Ltd as an example in all cases, study the following adjustments, taking each one as a separate item.

1. Bad debts written off after extraction of trial balance

EXAMPLE

A bad debt of £500 is to be written off and provision for bad debts to be retained at 5 per cent of debtors.
This item affects:
(a) Profit and Loss Account – an additional £500 has to be added to financial expenses.
(b) Trade Debtors Account – must be reduced by £500 to £31 500.
(c) Bad Debts Provision Account – must now be calculated at 5% of £31 500, i.e. £1 575.

2. Goods sent on sale or return, but included in figure for sales

EXAMPLE

Included in the figure for sales are goods on sale or return which cost £2 000 and were charged out at cost plus 25 per cent.

Goods on sale or return should *not* be included in sales until accepted by customers but must be included in stock figure.
This item affects:
(a) Sales Account – overstated by £2 500, i.e. cost + 25 per cent; figure must be reduced by £2 500 to £397 500.
(b) Closing Stock Account – finished goods understated by £2 000; figure must be increased to £8 000.
(c) Trade Debtors Account – overstated by £2 500; figure must be reduced by £2 500 to £29 500.

3. Goods purchased on credit in transit and not recorded

EXAMPLE

Goods purchased on credit from Dolan Ltd, valued at £1 000, were in transit and not recorded in the books.
This item affects:
(a) Trade Creditors Account – figure must be increased by £1 000 to £11 000.
(b) Credit Purchases Account – figure must be increased by £1 000 to £45 000.
(c) Closing Stock Account – figure must be increased by £1 000.

Some more difficult adjustments 327

4. Sale of assets (hidden loss or depreciation)

EXAMPLE

The figure for sales includes an error – the sale of a motor van for £700. This van originally cost £7 000 and had been written down in the books to £1 000.
This item affects:
(a) Sales Account – sale of fixed assets should not be included in the ordinary Sales Account.
£700 must be deducted from sales figure.
£400 000 − £700 = £399 300.
(b) Profit and Loss Account – there is a loss of £300 on sale of van.
Total cost, £7 000, less depreciation to date, £6 000.
∴ Present value, £1 000, sold for £700.
∴ Loss £300.
(c) Motor Vehicles Account – this figure must be reduced by £7 000 (cost of vehicle sold) to £33 000.

5. Use of firm's own workforce and/or materials

EXAMPLE

Castle Industries Ltd is a firm making concrete products. At present the workmen are employed in building an extension to the plant and no adjustment has been made in the cost of materials, £1 000, and in the cost of wages, £3 000. These sums have not been spent in making concrete products for resale, but in creating an additional fixed asset.
This item affects:
(a) Factory Wages Account – figure must be reduced by £3 000 to £75 000.
(b) Purchase of Raw Materials Account – figure must be reduced by £1 000 to £63 000 as this raw material was not resold.
(c) Buildings Account – figure must be increased by £4 000 to £104 000 as this was the cost of the extension.

6. Stock given as a bonus to employees

EXAMPLE

At Christmas the company gave out goods valued at £950 to its salesmen as a bonus.
This item affects:
(a) Purchases Account – these goods were bought for resale; figure must be reduced by £950.
(b) Bonuses must be put in as an expense under the heading 'Selling and distribution', £950.

7. Insurance claims granted by the court but not yet paid

EXAMPLE

A claim against an insurance company for van repairs, £460, and legal fees, £140, had been granted by the court on 30.12.19–2. The money had already been paid out but was not yet received from the insurers.

This item affects:
(a) Car repairs – figure must be reduced by £460 in the Profit and Loss Account (selling and distribution).
(b) Legal fees – figure must be reduced by £140 in the Profit and Loss Account (financial expenses).
(c) Claim against insurance company must be shown as current asset on balance sheet.

8. Suspense items explained

EXAMPLE

Suspense is shown as a debit balance of £300 in trial balance and the following note appears below: 'The suspense figure arises because rates were under-debited by £300.' Here £300 is added to rates in the Profit and Loss Account. The suspense figure is then ignored.

Exercises Set 21

1 From the following, prepare the Profit and Loss Account of Alex Ltd for the year ended 31 December 19–2, grouping expense items under appropriate headings.

	£
Gross profit from Trading Account	25 000
Discounts received	1 000
Dividends received	500
Office salaries	8 400
Advertising	1 600
Bad debts	400
Rates	440
Rent payable	960
Salesmen's salaries	5 600
Salesmen's commission	560
Depreciation:	
Premises	840
Fixtures and fittings	240
Delivery vans	460
Delivery vans: expenses	680
Insurance (fire)	160

2 From the following figures, prepare a properly presented Profit and Loss Account for Cider Sales Ltd for the year ended 31 December 19–2.

	£
Rent	1 280
Rates	640
Salaries	21 370
Postage and telephone	580
Bank interest (to 30 June)	1 250
Bank charges	50
Advertising	1 200
General expenses	480
Carriage outwards	3 200
Bad debts	956

	£
Showroom expenses	7 720
Audit fees	400
Trading profit for year	79 400
Rent receivable	740
Discount allowed	960
Discount received	260

Notes

1. Accruals:

	£
Rent	320
Salaries	480

2. Prepayments

	£
Rates	160
Advertising	600

3. Depreciation
   Buildings (£10 000) 2%
   Fixtures (£2 500) 5%
4. Provide a bad debts provision of 5 per cent of sundry debtors. Debtors stand at £16 800 on 31 December 19–2.

3 From the following figures taken from the books of Jones Ltd, prepare Profit and Loss Account (including appropriation) for year ended 31 December 19–1.

	£
Profit and Loss Account balance at 1 January 19–1	20 650
Trading profit for year	157 500
Rent payable	5 600
Discount received	2 500
Directors' fees	8 000
Salaries	49 000
Rates	2 960
Audit fees	3 720
Heating and lighting	880
Fire insurance	460
Travellers' salaries	16 928
Travellers' commission	4 232
Debenture interest (paid)	300
Depreciation:	
Buildings	4 000
Fixtures and fittings	1 140
Delivery vans	4 660
Delivery van expenses	3 340

The directors recommend that:
(a) £2 000 be written off goodwill; (b) £10 000 be transferred to general reserve; (c) preliminary expenses of £1 340 be written off; (d) preference shareholders should be paid; (e) ordinary shareholders should get a dividend of 10 per cent.

Note
The issue share capital of the company was:
40 000 5% preference shares of £1 each fully paid;
80 000 ordinary shares of £1 each fully paid.

4   Henry Smith Ltd has an authorised share capital of £240 000 divided into 80 000 5% preference shares of £1 each and 160 000 ordinary shares of £1 each. The net profits as shown by the Profit and Loss Accounts for the first three years of operation were: Year 1, £24 000; Year 2, £30 800; Year 3, £35 600.

Transfers to reserves were made as follows:
Year 1:   £2 000 to general reserve.
Year 2:   £4 000 to general reserve.
          £6 000 to redemption reserve.
Year 3:   £4 000 to debenture reserve.
          £4 000 to staff pension investment fund.

Proposed dividends	Preference	Ordinary
Year 1	5%	5%
Year 2	5%	7½%
Year 3	5%	10%

Show the Appropriation section of the Profit and Loss Account for each of the three years.

5   The accounts for Lobster Ltd, whose issued ordinary share capital is £400 000 in £1 shares, for year ended 31 March 19–5 showed available profits amounting to £268 800, including the unappropriated balance from the previous year. The general reserve stood at £72 000 and the plant replacement reserve at £48 000.

The directors recommend that: (a) the general reserve be decreased by £8 000; (b) plant replacement reserve be reduced to £28 000; (c) the preference dividend for the half year on 50 000 10% cumulative preference shares of £1 each be paid and a provision be made for the other half year; (d) a dividend on ordinary shares be proposed at the rate of 20 per cent; (e) the balance of unappropriated profits be carried forward.

You are required:
a   to show the Profit and Loss Appropriation Account
b   to give extracts from the balance sheet to show the relevant accounts after making all appropriations
c   to suggest five other items which are normally contained in an Appropriation Account.

6   The following figures are extracted from the books of Richards Ltd on 31 December 19–1:

Issued capital
50 000 ordinary shares of £1 each; 20 000 10% preference shares of £5 each.

	£		£
General reserve	60 000	Gross profit from trading	600 000
8% debentures	30 000	Profit and Loss balance	
Goodwill	20 000	at 1 Jan.	50 000
Debenture redemption reserve	11 400	Advertising	14 000
Preliminary expenses	2 400	Salaries (office)	80 000
Directors' fees	6 000	Salaries (salesmen)	120 000
Audit fees	9 000	Office heat and light	7 000
Rates (office)	4 000	Insurance (general)	4 600
Discount allowed	800	Showroom expenses	3 200

	£		£
Depreciation:		Legal fees	1 500
Fixtures and fittings	2 400	Salesmen's commission	19 200
Office machines	1 600	Repairs to vans	12 800
Cars and vans	12 000	Postage	1 460
Debenture interest	2 400	Carriage out	540
Printing	960	Bad debts provision	4 600
		Profit on sale of investments	22 000

The directors recommend:
(a) pay preference dividend;
(b) pay dividend of 15% on ordinary shares;
(c) write off goodwill of £4 000;
(d) reduce general reserve by £10 000;
(e) put £8 400 to debenture redemption reserve;
(f) appropriate £20 000 to a new staff pension fund;
(g) write off in full preliminary expenses;
(h) carry forward the balance.

a   Prepare Profit and Loss Account for year ended 31 December 19–1, grouping expenses under appropriate headings and showing clearly appropriations of profit.
b   Show the relevant extracts from the balance sheet after appropriations have been completed.

7   The net profit for the year 19–4 shown in the accounts of Mustard Ltd amounted to £93 000. The balance sheet dated 31 December 19–3 showed total net assets of £518 000 (which included goodwill of £30 000). Total net assets were financed by:

	£
Issued ordinary shares of £1 each	200 000
Issued 12% preference shares of £1 each	50 000
Plant replacement reserve	60 000
Debenture redemption reserve	10 000
General reserve	32 000
Profit and Loss Account balance	38 000
Mortgage (buildings)	34 000
11% debentures	44 000

The directors recommend that:
(a) the preference dividend be paid;
(b) a dividend of 15 per cent be paid on ordinary shares;
(c) goodwill be written off completely;
(d) £12 000 be transferred from general reserve to plant replacement reserve;
(e) debenture redemption reserve be increased to £42 000.

a   Show appropriation section of Profit and Loss Account for year ended 31 December 19–4.
b   What is the figure for total net assets on the balance sheet as at 31 December 19–4?
c   Show in detail how these assets have been financed after all appropriations have been made.

8 From the following figures prepare an 'outline' balance sheet using vertical layout for Fine Foods Ltd as at 31 December 19–2.

	£		£
Fixed assets	300 000	Capital reserves	40 000
Current liabilites	72 000	Current assets	112 000
Investments	80 000	Intangible assets	20 000
Share capital	200 000	Revenue reserves	80 000
Long-term liabilities	120 000		

9 Using the 'outline' balance sheet in Question 8, prepare in as much detail as possible a new balance sheet for Fine Foods Ltd, using your own figures and inserting as many items as possible within each sub-heading.

10 The following information pertains to Digby Ltd for the financial year ended 31.12.19–4:

	£
Plant and equipment at cost	84 000
Land and buildings at cost	63 000
Motor vehicles at cost	51 000
Profit and Loss Account (accumulated profits)	30 000
7% debentures	22 800
Authorised share capital:	
900 000 ordinary shares of 50p each	450 000
Profit for the year to 31.12.19–4	83 400
Issued share capital:	
300 000 ordinary shares of 50p each fully paid	150 000
Trade marks	3 300
Investments in subsidiary at cost	4 200
General reserve	12 000
Capital reserve	3 900
Provision for depreciation:	
Vehicles	6 900
Plant and equipment	5 400
Debtors	18 300
Creditors	14 100
Cash in hand	1 800
Stocks 31.12.19–4	18 000
Bank	6 600 cr.
Goodwill	91 500

Notes

1. The directors' valuation of investments is £3 000.
2. There exists a contingent liability of £20 000 in consequence of a legal action pending against the company.
3. Directors have approved capital expenditure for £24 000.

You are required to prepare the balance sheet using a vertical layout.

11 The following balances appeared in the books of Freeman Ltd on 31.12.19-7:

	Dr. £	Cr. £
Share capital:		
Authorised – 720 000 ordinary shares at £1 each		
Issued – 400 000 ordinary shares at £1 each fully paid		400 000
Plant and machinery (cost £150 000)	120 000	
Buildings at cost	288 000	
Office equipment (cost £4 000)	2 400	
12% debentures		16 000
Carriage inwards	1 180	
Stocks 1.1.19-7:		
Raw materials	11 720	
Work in progress (prime cost)	4 800	
Finished goods	17 000	
Purchases of raw materials	248 000	
Carriage out on finished goods	1 920	
Sales		320 000
Factory: direct wages	32 000	
Factory: direct expenses	4 360	
Discounts allowed	2 840	
Discounts received		3 240
Bad debts	680	
Directors' fees	12 000	
Rates of factory	2 440	
Rates of office	400	
Insurance of factory	580	
Advertising	2 480	
Repairs to plant and machinery	1 160	
Legal fees	240	
Printing and stationery	1 840	
Debtors and creditors	16 400	11 200
Bank		2 000
Bills receivable	1 960	
Profit and Loss Account 1.1.19-7		21 960
	774 400	774 400

You are given the following information and instructions:
(a) Stocks at 31.12.19-7:
    Raw materials   £15 900
    Work in progress (prime cost)   £3 160
    Finished goods   £20 580
(b) Provide for a year's debenture interest.
(c) Create a bad debts provision of 5 per cent of debtors.
(d) Stock of stationery on 31.12.19-7 was £2 400.
(e) Depreciation is to be provided as follows:
    Plant and machinery   5% of cost
    Office equipment   10% of cost

You are required to prepare:
a a Manufacturing Account for the year ended 31.12.19-7
b a Trading and Profit and Loss and Appropriation Accounts for the year ended 31.12.19-7
c a balance sheet as at 31.12.19-7.

12 From the following figures set out the balance sheet of Roma Industries Ltd as at 31 December 19–3:

	£		£
Land (cost)	900 000	Bills payable	7 000
Creditors	42 000	Unquoted investments (cost)	30 000
Quoted investments (cost)	50 000	Government grant	80 000
Share premium	6 000	Prepayments	2 000
Accrual	3 000	Buildings (cost)	260 000
Plant and machinery (cost)	140 000	Patents	22 000
Trade debtors	54 000	Cash at bank	9 400
Cash	2 600	Goodwill	12 000
Bills receivable	16 000	Temporary investments	18 000
Proposed dividend	6 500	Debenture interest due	3 500
Provision for taxation	16 000	General reserve	56 000
Profit and Loss Account balance	130 000	15% mortgage	66 000
11% debentures	42 000	Preference share redemption reserve	36 000
Fixtures and fittings	18 000		
Lorries, cars and vans	88 000		

Accumulated depreciation at 31 December 19–3:	£	Stocks at 31 December:	£
Buildings	90 000	Raw materials	14 000
Plant and machinery	68 000	Finished goods	8 000
Fixtures and fittings	14 000	Work in progress	6 000
Lorries, cars and vans	44 000		

Shares
600 000 ordinary shares of £1 each
 40 000 8% preference shares of £5 each
140 000 10% redeemable preference shares of £1 each

13 (*a*) Write a short note on what you understand by the following terms:
    (i) Prime costs;
    (ii) Gross profit.
(*b*) The following trial balance has been extracted by the book-keeper from the records of Appleby Ltd at the company's financial year end, i.e. 30 September 19–9.

	Dr. £	Cr. £
Advertising	1 740	
Audit and accountancy charges	1 050	
Bad debts	1 360	
Bad debts provision		2 000
Bank interest and charges	1 240	
Discount	1 150	940
Factory power	13 628	
Furniture (original cost £2 400)	1 800	
General expenses – factory	1 100	
General expenses – office	1 780	
Insurance	2 520	
Light and heat	1 320	
Plant and machinery (original cost £48 000)	38 000	

	Dr. £	Cr. £
Purchases of raw materials	127 376	
Packaging and transport	3 170	
Rent and rates	3 780	
Repairs and renewals	1 450	
Salaries – office	13 320	
Sales		229 340
Stocks (1 October 19–8):		
Raw materials	15 960	
Finished goods	23 800	
Work in progress (prime cost)	5 378	
Packaging materials	370	
Wages – factory	49 520	
Debtors and creditors	25 300	15 932
Balance at bank	7 952	
Cash in hand	336	
Share capital (authorised 100 000 ordinary shares of £1 each)		50 000
Capital reserve		6 000
General reserve		20 000
Profit and Loss Account		19 188
	343 400	343 400

You are given the following further information:
1. Stocks as on 30 September 19–9:

	£
Raw materials	9 336
Work in progress (prime cost)	7 398
Finished goods	47 320
Packaging materials	430

2. Provision is to be made for the following expenses incurred but unpaid at the year end:

	£
Factory power	1 372
Rent and rates	720
Light and heat	480
General expenses – factory	250
General expenses – office	70

3. Insurances are prepaid to the extent of £720.
4. Five-sixths of the rent and rates, light and heat and insurances are to be allocated to the factory, the balance to the office.
5. Depreciation is to be provided as follows:
  Plant and machinery   10% per annum on cost
  Furniture   5% per annum on cost
  Additional plant costing £8 000 was purchased on 1 April 19–9.
6. Included in the cost of repairs is £1 200 for repairs to plant and machinery.
7. Bad debts provision is to be increased to £3 000.
8. Provide for directors' fees in the sum of £4 000.
9. The directors recommend that:
  (a) £5 000 be transferred to general reserve.
  (b) 10 per cent be paid on the shares for the year (ignore taxation).

You are required to prepare a Manufacturing, Trading and Profit and Loss Account for the year and a balance sheet as on the year end.

14 The following trial balance was extracted from the books of Toffo Ltd, a manufacturing company, on 30 June 19–1:

	Dr. £	Cr. £
Advertising	1 500	
Audit and accountancy charges	1 800	
Bad debts written off	2 100	
Bad debts provision 1.7.19–0		5 000
Balance at bank	10 500	
Bank interest and charges	1 050	
Cash in hand	100	
Carriage inwards	1 450	
Carriage outwards	3 740	
Discounts allowed	3 350	
Discounts received		2 200
Factory power	3 440	
Factory wages	53 400	
Furniture and fittings (cost £5 000)	3 050	
General expenses – factory	3 200	
General expenses – office	7 000	
General reserve		100 000
Insurance	1 500	
Light and heat	2 400	
Motor vehicles (cost £14 000)	7 900	
Motor expenses	7 500	
Plant and machinery (cost £75 000)	51 100	
Premises	70 000	
Profit and Loss Account balance 1.7.19–0		70 000
Purchases – raw materials	116 000	
Rent and rates	2 400	
Repairs and renewals	1 600	
Salaries – office	15 000	
Sales		250 680
Share capital (authorised £200 000)		50 000
Stocks 1.7.19–0:		
Raw materials	13 000	
Finished goods	17 000	
Work in progress	7 500	
Telephone	1 300	
Trade creditors		24 000
Trade debtors	72 000	
	501 880	501 880

The following information is also furnished:
1. Stocks, 30 June 19–1:

	£
Raw materials	19 500
Work in progress (prime cost)	8 400
Finished goods	44 000

2. Provision is to be made for the following expenses accrued but unpaid at the financial year end:

	£
Factory power	800
Factory wages	1 100
General expenses – factory	500
General expenses – office	300
Light and heat	400
Insurance	300

3. Rates are paid up to 30 September 19–1. Annual charge, £1 600.
4. Three-quarters of the charges for insurance, light and heat and rent and rates are to be allocated to the factory.
5. Depreciation is to be provided as follows:
   Furniture and fittings   5% per annum on cost
   Motor vehicles   20% per annum on cost
   Plant and machinery   15% per annum on cost
6. Included in repairs and renewals is £1 000 for plant and machinery repairs.
7. Goods costing £6 000 were invoiced to a customer prior to the year's end at £8 000 on a sale or return basis. These had not been accepted at 30 June 19–1.
8. Bad debts provision to be increased to 10 per cent of the trade debtors.
9. Provide £5 000 for director's fees.
10. The directors recommend:
    (i) That £10 000 be transferred to general reserve.
    (ii) That a dividend of 5 per cent be paid on the ordinary shares.

You are required to prepare a Manufacturing, Trading and Profit and Loss Account for the year ended 30 June 19–1 and a balance sheet as on that date.

15 Old Castle Industries Ltd has an authorised share capital of £454 000 divided into 54 000 8% preference shares of £1 each and 1 600 000 ordinary shares of 25p each.

The following balances were extracted from the books on 30 June 19–7:

	Dr. £	Cr. £
Trade debtors and creditors	120 000	64 000
Discounts	5 500	4 000
Purchases and sales (finished goods)	64 000	1 152 000
Freehold land at cost	372 000	
General reserve		100 000
Profit and Loss Account balance 1.7.19–6		34 000
Investment in subsidiary at cost	28 000	
Plant and machinery (cost £220 000)	140 000	
Factory wages	104 000	
Purchase of raw materials	416 000	
Stocks at 1.7.19–6:		
Raw materials	24 000	
Finished goods	6 000	
Work in progress	8 000	
Carriage on raw materials	2 000	
Motor vehicles (cost £168 000)	112 000	
Factory foreman's wages	12 000	
14% debentures		64 000
Salesmen's salaries	52 000	

Preparation of internal final accounts and balance sheets

	Dr. £	Cr. £
Salesmen's commissions	18 000	
Rates – factory	3 000	
office	9 000	
10% loan from investment finance company		76 000
Office salaries	58 000	
Stationery and printing	5 000	
Suspense	1 000	
Office equipment (cost £36 000)	26 000	
Goodwill	24 000	
Interim dividend on ordinary shares	40 000	
Half-year dividend on preference shares	1 360	
Insurance (property)	3 500	
Bank overdraft		39 600
Payments to directors	28 500	
Bank charges	6 500	
Loan charges for year	7 600	
Advertising	17 500	
Investment in subsidiary	92 000	
Car repairs (sales staff)	1 150	
Packing materials	10 500	
Postage	1 500	
Bad debts provision (1.7.19–6)		16 460
Bad debts	460	
Bills receivable	22 000	
Patents	12 000	
Showroom expenses	13 050	
Telephone charges	11 200	
Bills payable		44 000
Debenture interest (½ year)	4 480	
Factory buildings (cost £128 000)	96 000	
Office buildings (cost £74 000)	40 000	
Share Premium Account		17 960
Factory light and power	11 000	
Direct factory expenses	1 000	
Cash	520	
Preliminary expenses	2 700	
Loan to directors (repayable 31.9.19–7)	12 000	
Issued capital (fully paid):		
8% preference shares £1 each		34 000
Ordinary shares 25p each		400 000
	2 046 020	2 046 020

The following information is relevant:
(a) Stock 30.6.19–7:
    Raw materials   £28 000
    Finished goods   £10 000
    Work in progress   £7 000
(b) Provide for depreciation as follows:
    Buildings   5%
    Motor vehicles   25%

Plant and machinery 20%
Office equipment 10%

(c) The figure for sales includes an item sent out on a sale or return basis which cost £20 000 and which has been charged at cost plus 25 per cent.
(d) The directors recommend:
  (i) payment of balance of preference dividend due and a final dividend on ordinary shares of 10 per cent
  (ii) the writing off of preliminary expenses over two years beginning this year
  (iii) £10 000 to be transferred to general reserve
  (iv) goodwill to be completely written off.
(e) An additional bad debt amounting to £4 000 has still to be written off and the bad debts provision maintained at 10 per cent of debtors on 30.6.19–7.
(f) The investment in subsidiary is valued by the directors at £35 000.
(g) The debenture interest due is to be paid.
(h) The suspense figure arises from an under-totalling of office salaries.

You are required to prepare Manufacturing, Trading, Profit and Loss and Profit and Loss Appropriation Accounts for the year ended 30 June 19–7 and a balance sheet at that date.

16 Moran Ltd has an authorised capital of £440 000 divided into 40 000 11% preference shares at £1 each and 400 000 ordinary shares at £1 each. The following trial balance was extracted from its books on 31.12.19–3:

	Dr. £	Cr. £
Issued capital:		
200 000 ordinary shares at £1 each		200 000
40 000 11% preference shares at £1 each		40 000
Calls in arrear (ordinary shares)	2 000	
Premises at cost	140 000	
Fixtures and fittings (cost £120 000)	62 000	
Goodwill at cost	60 000	
Delivery vans (cost £24 000)	16 000	
Interim dividend on ordinary shares	8 000	
Debentures 12%		70 000
Share premium		60 000
Debenture redemption reserve		30 000
Profit and Loss Account 1.1.19–3	10 000	
Investments (market value £140 000)	119 000	
Shares in subsidiary company at cost		
(directors' valuation £75 000)	71 000	
Profit from the sale of investments		29 600
Carriage inwards	3 000	
Purchases and sales	280 000	419 680
Bank		27 400
Bills receivable	2 800	
Debtors and creditors	32 960	23 260
Amount due by subsidiary company	19 200	
Stock 1.1.19–3	26 000	
Salaries and wages	36 240	
Light and heat	4 800	
Bills payable		920
Rent and rates	1 680	

	Dr. £	Cr. £
Audit and legal fees	1 520	
Delivery van expenses	3 600	
Showroom expenses	1 060	
	900 860	900 860

The following information and instructions are to be taken into account:
(a) Stock at 31.12.19–3 was valued at £24 720.
(b) The figure for light and heat includes £80 paid for fuel for delivery van.
(c) Provide for depreciation as follows:
    Fixtures and fittings   £16 000
    Delivery vans   10% of book value
(d) The figure for carriage inwards includes £460 paid for freight on fittings purchased during the year. The cost of installing the fittings, £940, is included in the figure for salaries and wages.
(e) Provide for debenture interest.
(f) Goods which cost £600 were sent on a sale or return basis to a customer. These goods had been treated in the books as a credit sale of £720.
(g) The directors recommend that:
    (i) A final dividend of 10 per cent be paid on ordinary shares.
    (ii) The preference dividend be paid.
    (iii) £10 000 be written off goodwill.
    (iv) The debenture redemption reserve be increased by £5 000.

You are required to prepare:
a Trading and Profit and Loss and Appropriation Accounts for the year ended 31.12.19–3
b a balance sheet at 31.12.19–3 in accordance with vertical format and layout.

17 Barnes Ltd has an authorised capital of £250 000 divided into 250 000 ordinary shares at £1 each. The following trial balance was extracted from its books on 31.12.19–5:

	Dr. £	Cr. £
Issued capital £248 800 ordinary shares of £1 each		248 800
Buildings and land at cost	190 000	
9% debentures		40 000
Delivery vans (cost £27 100)	16 600	
Investments (market value £162 000)	150 000	
Interim dividend	14 000	
Forfeited shares		1 200
Profit and loss balance at 1.1.19–5	32 600	
General reserve		56 000
Shares in subsidiary company (directors' valuation £55 000)	60 000	
Profit from the sale of investments		82 400
Carriage outwards	3 040	
Purchases and sales	360 000	480 000
Bank		2 580
Bills payable		3 600
Debtors and creditors	30 520	24 960
Amount due to subsidiary company		840

	Dr.	Cr.
	£	£
Stock 1.1.19–5	29 000	
Discount		3 180
Preliminary expenses	1 600	
Repairs to delivery vans	4 920	
Audit and legal fees	2 880	
Salaries and wages	44 400	
Rent and rates	1 200	
Insurance	2 800	
	943 560	943 560

The following information is to be taken into account:
- (a) Stock at 31.12.19–5 was valued at £30 200.
- (b) Provide for directors' fees, £20 000.
- (c) Provide for debenture interest.
- (d) On 1.1.19–5 Barnes Ltd sold for £400 a delivery van which cost £3 100. The £400 was treated in the books as a cash sale of goods (in error). The book value of the delivery van on 1.1.19–5 was £600.
- (e) Provide for depreciation as follows:
  Delivery vans   20% of book value
- (f) A claim against an insurance company for van repairs, £920, and legal fees, £280, was granted in the courts on 31.12.19–5. These expenses had already been paid and entered in the ledger.
- (g) Goods valued £4 200 received by Barnes Ltd during December on a sale or return basis were treated in the books as a credit purchase.
- (h) The directors recommend that:
   - (i) A final dividend of 10% be declared on ordinary shares.
   - (ii) £1 000 be written off preliminary expenses.
   - (iii) £8 000 be transferred to debenture redemption reserve.
   - (iv) General reserve be increased to £68 000.

Prepare:
a Trading and Profit and Loss and Appropriation Accounts for the year ended 31.12.19–5
b a balance sheet at 31.12.19–5.

342 Preparation of internal final accounts and balance sheets

18 Hume Ltd has an authorised capital of £700 000 divided into 400 000 ordinary shares of £1 each and 100 000 12% preference shares of £1 each. The following trial balance was extracted from its books on 31.12.19–9:

	Dr. £	Cr. £
Issued capital:		
400 000 ordinary shares of £1 each		400 000
100 000 12% preference shares of £1 each		100 000
10% debentures		80 000
Profit and Loss Account balance on 1 January 19–9	16 800	
Premises at cost	535 600	
Patents	40 000	
Investments at cost (market value £166 000)	110 000	
Delivery vans at cost	72 000	
Provision for bad debts		2 400
Patent royalties		9 000
Stock on 1 January 19–9	33 000	
Debtors and creditors	45 080	43 200
Accumulated depreciation – delivery vans		32 000
Purchases and sales	680 000	980 000
Bank		15 880
Motor expenses	6 640	
Salaries and general expenses	56 000	
Directors' fees	28 000	
Discounts	3 600	
Rates	1 760	
Interim dividend paid on ordinary shares	24 000	
Preference dividend paid for half year	7 000	
Debenture interest paid for half year	4 000	
Suspense Account		1 000
	1 663 480	1 663 480

The following information and instructions are to be taken into account:
(a) Stock at 31.12.19–9 was valued at £36 400 and included stock of fuel for motor vehicles, £400.
(b) Provide for depreciation as follows:
    Delivery vans   20% of book value
(c) Provide for royalties due, £360.
(d) Goods costing £2 800 had been purchased on credit. These had been included in stocks but no entry had been made in the books.
(e) A Christmas bonus of stock costing £1 200 was given to employees. No adjustment had been made in the books.
(f) The figure for suspense is as a result of the incorrect figure for the half year's preference dividend.
(g) The Rates Account includes a cheque for £1 520 paid in respect of rates for the year ended 31 March 19–0.
(h) Motor expenses include £800 paid for the collection of goods purchased for resale by Hume Ltd.
(i) A bad debt of £520 written off during 19–8 is now known to be recoverable in full. A further debt of £1 600 included in the debtors is to be written off and the provision is to be reduced to 5 per cent of debtors.
(j) Provide for debenture interest due.

(k) The directors recommend that:
  (i) a final dividend of 10 per cent be paid on ordinary shares
  (ii) the preference dividend due be paid
  (iii) patents be written off over five years commencing this year.

You are required to prepare:
a Trading and Profit and Loss and Appropriation Accounts for the year ended 31.12.19–9
b a balance sheet at 31.12.19–9.

19 Bilberg Ltd has an authorised capital of £360 000 divided into 360 000 ordinary shares of £1 each. The following trial balance was extracted from its books on 31.12.19–0:

	Dr. £	Cr. £
Issued capital:		
301 200 ordinary shares of £1 each		301 200
Buildings and land at cost	180 000	
Delivery vans at cost	31 600	
Profit and loss balance at 1.1.19–0	24 200	
Shares in subsidiary company (directors' valuation £165 000)	160 000	
Debtors and creditors	31 200	28 400
Investments (market value £140 000)	124 000	
Accumulated depreciation on delivery vans		11 600
16% debentures		100 000
Provision for bad debts		1 600
Discounts		2 680
Interim dividend paid	15 000	
Advertising	19 800	
General expenses	24 800	
Debenture interest	12 600	
Salaries and wages	31 200	
Suspense		600
Directors' fees	20 000	
Forfeited shares		400
Debenture redemption reserve		30 000
Stock at 1.1.19–0	24 500	
Bank		21 210
Purchases and sales	420 000	300 000
	1 118 900	1 118 900

The following information is to be taken into account:
(a) Trading stock at 31.12.19–0 was valued at £26 600.
(b) Included in the figure for sales is £720 received on 1.1.19–0 for a delivery van which had cost £3 600. The book value of the delivery van on 1.1.19–0 was £800. Provide for depreciation on the remaining delivery vans at the rate of 20 per cent of cost.
(c) The figure for suspense, £600, arises as a result of the incorrect debenture interest. The debenture loan was received by Bilberg Ltd on 1.4.19–0.
(d) Included in the figure for general expenses is a payment of £800 for fire insurance for the year ended 31.3.19–1.
(e) During the year an extension to the buildings was built by the firm's own

workmen. The cost of their labour, £5 400, is included in the figure for salaries and wages. The materials, costing £14 600, were taken from the firm's stocks. No entry had been made in the books.
(f) One-third of the advertising is chargeable to the current year and the balance to future years.
(g) During the year trading goods which had cost £1 600 were destroyed by fire. The insurance company has agreed to pay this amount in full, but no entry had been made in the books, and no payment has been received.
(h) The directors recommend that:
  (i) a final dividend of 10 per cent be paid on ordinary shares
  (ii) the debenture redemption reserve be increased by £10 000.

You are required to prepare:
a Trading and Profit and Loss and Appropriation Accounts for the year ended 31.12.19–0
b a balance sheet at 31.12.19–0.

20 Steel Ltd has an authorised capital of £1 100 000 divided into 800 000 ordinary shares of £1 each and 300 000 12% preference shares of £1 each. The following trial balance was extracted from its books on 31.12.19–3:

	Dr. £	Cr. £
Issued capital:		
600 000 ordinary shares of £1 each		600 000
100 000 12% preference shares of £1 each		100 000
Freehold premises at cost	500 000	
Delivery vans (cost £114 000)	93 600	
Machinery (cost £520 000)	400 000	
Debtors and creditors	81 000	64 000
15% debentures		160 000
Calls in arrear	400	
Stocks including stationery, £400, at 1.1.19–3	95 400	
Carriage on sales	5 200	
Salaries and general expenses	190 000	
Advertising	8 000	
Carriage on purchases	3 600	
Rent Account 1.1.19–3	200	
Rent		11 200
Debenture interest (for first 3 months) accrued		6 000
Debenture interest	6 000	
Purchases and sales	1 140 000	1 600 000
Provision for bad debts		2 200
Stationery	3 000	
Discounts	1 300	
Interim dividend on preference shares (quarter year)	3 000	
Profit and Loss Account balance	4 000	
Bank	8 700	
	2 543 400	2 543 400

The following information and instructions are to be taken into account:
(a) Stock at 31.12.19–3 was valued at £91 600 and included stock of stationery, £600.

(b) Provision is to be made for debenture interest due.
(c) Advertising includes an amount of £4 200 which is full payment for an advertising campaign which will not end until 30 April 19–4 and which commenced on 1 May 19–3.
(d) Goods with a sales value of £2 000 were sent to a customer during December 19–3 on a sale or return basis. These goods had been treated in the books as a credit sale at a mark-up on cost of 25 per cent.
(e) On 1 January 19–3 a delivery van, which had cost £9 600, was sold for £1 320 cash. At the date of sale the book value of the van was £1 000. This sale had been treated in the books as a sale of trading stock.
(f) A bad debt of £400 written off in 19–0 is now known to be recoverable in full. A further debt of £200 is to be written off and the provision for bad debts is to be adjusted to 4 per cent of debtors.
(g) The figure for bank in the trial balance has been taken from the firm's cash book. However, a bank statement dated 31.12.19–3 has subsequently arrived showing a balance of £13 400. A comparison of the cash book and bank statement has revealed the following discrepancies:
  (i) creditors' cheques not yet presented for payment, £1 600
  (ii) rent for three months ending 31.12.19–3 paid direct into firm's Bank Account, £3 200
  (iii) bank charges, £100.
(h) The directors recommend that:
  (i) depreciation be provided for as follows:
      Machinery   20% of cost
      Delivery vans   25% of cost
  (ii) the preference dividend due be provided for
  (iii) a final dividend of 10 per cent be provided for on ordinary shares.

You are required to prepare:
a a Trading, Profit and Loss and Appropriation Account for the year ended 31.12.19–3
b a balance sheet at 31.12.19–3.

21 The following trial balance as at 31 December 1983 has been extracted from the books of XYZ Ltd:

	£	£
Ordinary shares – 20 000 of £1 each		20 000
Profit and Loss Account		3 800
Sales		210 000
Purchases	160 000	
Rent and rates	9 000	
Light and heat	7 600	
Administrative expenses	11 300	
Motor vehicles: at cost	16 000	
Provision for depreciation		3 000
Stock at 1 January 1983	15 500	
Debtors	24 400	
Creditors		10 000
Balance at bank	3 000	
	246 800	246 800

Additional information relating to the year ended 31 December 1983:
1. Since preparing the above trial balance, a bill has been received for rates of £2 000 for the half year ending 31 March 1984.
2. The company has decided that a provision for doubtful debts be created of 2 per cent of debtors as at 31 December 1983.
3. Stock as at 31 December 1983 has been valued at £13 500.
4. Depreciation is provided annually on motor vehicles at the rate of 25 per cent of the cost of vehicles held at each accounting year end.
5. No entries have been made in the company's books for the sale on credit to Barry Dale of goods for £7 800 on 1 December 1983; payment for the goods was received on 20 January 1984.
6. It has been decided to transfer £5 000 to general reserve and to recommend that there be no dividends paid on the ordinary share capital for the year under review.

Prepare a Trading and Profit and Loss Account for the year ended 31 December 1983 and a balance sheet as at that date.

[*Association of Accounting Technicians, pilot, 1985*]

22 The following information is provided in respect of Shrub Ltd, a trading company, for 1983 and 1984.

Profit and Loss Account, year to 31 December	1983	1984
	£000	£000
Administration expenses	1 125	1 197
Selling costs	352	381
Distribution costs	81	98
Transfer to general reserve	—	250
Depreciation charge	156	182
Proposed dividend	65	130
Balance of profit	207	115
	1 986	2 353

Balance sheet at 31 December	1983	1984
	£000	£000
Assets		
Stock	486	508
Debtors	372	400
Plant and machinery at cost	1 208	1 740
Cash at bank	89	11
	2 155	2 659
Liabilities		
Trade creditors	320	312
Provision for depreciation	345	427
Dividend	65	130
Capital (£1 shares)	1 000	1 000
Profit and Loss Account	425	540
General reserve	—	250
	2 155	2 659

a   Re-draft the above accounts in order to show the gross profit, net profit and retained profits.
b   Re-draft the balance sheet in good style.
c   Comment on the view expressed by one of Shrub Ltd's directors that the company should not pay the proposed increased dividend because profits have declined.

[*Royal Society of Arts, II, March 1985*]

23 The trial balance extracted from the books of Flower Ltd, a wholesaling company, at 31 December 1983 was:

	£	£
Share capital		150 000
Share premium		50 000
10% debentures		150 000
Fixed assets at cost:		
Freehold land and buildings	290 000	
Plant and equipment	40 000	
Motor vehicles	150 000	
Provisions for depreciation at 1.1.83:		
Freehold land and buildings		20 000
Plant and equipment		16 000
Motor vehicles		20 000
Sales		526 500
Purchases	317 400	
Debtors and creditors	35 600	20 700
Bad debts	1 900	
Provision for doubtful debts at 1.1.83		1 600
Wages and salaries	46 200	
Rates	7 100	
Debenture interest	15 000	
Profit and Loss Account 1.1.83		75 100
Directors' salaries	36 000	
Motor expenses	16 800	
General expenses	1 200	
Stock in trade 1.1.83	74 500	
Balance at bank		1 800
	1 031 700	1 031 700

The following additional information is provided:
1. Share capital is divided into 150 000 shares of £1 each which are all issued and fully paid.
2. Stock in trade at 31 December 1983 was £81 200.
3. The provision for doubtful debts is to be increased to £1 800.
4. Motor expenses due but unpaid at 31 December 1983, £2 100.
5. Rates paid in advance at 31 December 1983, £1 500.
6. Provision is to be made for depreciation on:
    (*a*) plant at 10 per cent per annum of cost
    (*b*) motor vehicles at 20 per cent per annum of cost
    (*c*) freehold buildings are to be depreciated by £4 000.
7. A dividend is proposed for 1983 at the rate of 10p per share.

Required:
A Trading and Profit and Loss Account for 1983 and a balance sheet at 31 December 1983.

Note. Ignore taxation.

[*Royal Society of Arts, II, June 1984*]

24 The following trial balance was extracted from the books of Midland Ltd, a retail concern, at 31 December 1984:

	£	£
Share capital (ordinary shares of £1 each)		200 000
Share premium		50 000
Retained profit at 1 January 1984		194 500
10% debenture repayable 1990		120 000
Freehold land and buildings at cost	460 000	
Motor vans at cost	40 000	
Provision for depreciation on motor vans at 1 January 1984		22 600
Purchases and sales	1 350 800	1 720 500
Stock at 1 January 1984	227 100	
Rent and rates	10 350	
General expenses	75 150	
Wages	93 250	
Bad debts written off	1 600	
Provision for doubtful debts at 1 January 1984		2 100
Trade debtors and trade creditors	246 300	175 900
Bank overdraft		24 950
Debenture interest paid to 30 June 1984	6 000	
	2 510 550	2 510 550

The following additional information is provided:
1. During 1984, the company purchased a freehold building for £105 000. Legal costs of £2 500, relating to the acquisition, have been debited to general expenses.
2. The company depreciates its motor vans at 20 per cent on cost of vehicles owned at the year end.
3. Rates paid in advance at 31 December 1984 amounted to £1 350.
4. Wages outstanding at 31 December 1984 amounted to £900.
5. The provision for doubtful debts is to be increased to £2 450.
6. The directors propose to pay a dividend of £60 000 for 1984.
7. Stock at 31 December amounted to £235 350.

Required:
Trading and Profit and Loss and Appropriation Account for Midland Ltd for 1984 and balance sheet at 31 December 1984.

Ignore depreciation of freehold land and buildings.

[*Royal Society of Arts, II, May 1985*]

25 The following trial balance was extracted from the books of Printer Ltd at 31 December 1985:

	£	£
Share capital		300 000
Share premium		70 000
10% debentures		150 000
Freehold buildings at cost	350 000	
Plant at cost	300 000	
Vans at cost	24 000	
Provisions at 1 January:		
Depreciation of plant		130 000
Depreciation of vans		12 500
Doubtful debts		1 300
Sales		767 804
Purchases	490 084	
Debtors and creditors	55 750	32 196
Bad debts	2 532	
Wages	67 924	
Rates	7 812	
Debenture interest paid	7 500	
Profit and loss account at 1 January		33 184
Directors' salaries	50 000	
Motor expenses	7 101	
General expenses	12 841	
Stock at 1 January	102 150	
Balance at bank	19 290	
	1 496 984	1 496 984

The following additional information is provided:
1. Share capital is divided into 300 000 shares of £1 each which are all issued and fully paid.
2. Stock at 31 December 1985, £103 520.
3. The provision for doubtful debts is to be increased to £1 500.
4. Provisions for depreciation are to be made on plant at 10 per cent per annum of cost and on vans at 20 per cent per annum of cost.
5. At 31 December 1985 general expenses of £1 841 are prepaid.
6. Unpaid debenture interest for 1985 is to be provided.
7. A dividend of 10p per share is proposed for 1985.

Required:
Prepare the Trading and Profit and Loss Account of Printer Ltd for the year to 31 December 1985 and the balance sheet at that date.

Note. Ignore taxation.

[*Royal Society of Arts, II, March 1986*]

26 The following trial balance of Swift and Sure Ltd, wholesale electrical dealers, was extracted at 31 December 1985.

	£	£
Purchases	61 450	
Sales		75 210
Stock 1 January 1985	6 024	
Returns	320	410
Carriage inwards	630	
Carriage outwards	470	
Warehouse wages	1 716	
Heating and lighting	730	
Rates	1 200	
Repairs and maintenance	648	
Office salaries	972	
Premises at cost	15 000	
Other fixed assets	12 900	
Provision for depreciation – other fixed assets		5 250
Discounts	385	120
Directors' remuneration	2 400	
Debtors and creditors	8 050	5 120
Cash at bank	3 335	
Profit and loss balance – 1 January 1985		2 320
General reserve		4 000
Interim dividend ordinary shares	1 200	
Issued share capital		
Ordinary shares		20 000
8% preference shares		5 000
	117 430	117 430

Other matters to be considered are:
1. The stock of goods at 31 December 1985, valued at cost, was £7 434.
2. Heating and lighting, rates and repairs and maintenance are to be apportioned: seven-eighths warehouse and one-eighth office.
3. Accruals: warehouse wages £84; office salaries £28; electricity £70.
4. Prepayments: rates £240.
5. Provide for depreciation on 'other fixed assets', £1 390.
6. Transfer £1 000 to general reserve.
7. Provide for preference dividend £400 and for recommended ordinary dividend 14 per cent.

The authorised capital was 25 000 ordinary shares of £1 each and 10 000 8% preference shares of £1 each.

Prepare a Trading and Profit and Loss Account of Swift and Sure Ltd for the year 1985.

Note. A balance sheet is NOT required.

[*London Chamber of Commerce and Industry, Intermediate, summer 1986*]

27 The following draft balance sheet as at 30 September 1986 of Prime Products Ltd has been prepared by the company's assistant accountant:

	Cost £	Aggregate depreciation £	Net book value £
Fixed assets			
Plant and machinery	31 000	19 375	11 625
Motor vehicles	17 000	10 200	6 800
	48 000	29 575	18 425
Current assets		£	
Stock		12 400	
Trade debtors and prepayments		9 600	
Balance at bank		3 900	
		25 900	
Less Current liabilities			
Creditors and accrued charges		5 100	
			20 800
			39 225
Financed by:			
Share capital – ordinary shares of £1 each, fully paid			20 000
Share premium account			5 000
Reserves – General			10 000
Retained earnings			4 225
			39 225

The following discoveries were made after the preparation of the above balance sheet:
1. No entry has been made in the company's accounts for bank charges of £150 debited in the company's bank statements on 25 September 1986.
2. The draft accounts prepayments figure of £400 does not include insurance premiums of £300 prepaid at 30 September 1986.
3. A significant casting error has now been found in the stock valuation sheets of 30 September *1985*. As a result, the stock valuation at 30 September *1985* should have been £16 000 not £10 000 as included in the company's published accounts for the year ended 30 September *1985*.
4. On 1 September 1986, the company forwarded goods costing £1 200 to John Peters of Aberdeen on a sale or return basis. None of these goods was sold by John Peters until late October 1986. However, in preparing the draft accounts for the year ended 30 September 1986 of Prime Products Ltd it was assumed that all the goods sent to John Peters had been sold.
Note. Prime Products Ltd obtains a gross profit of 25 per cent on all sales.
5. No entries have been made in the company's accounts for a bonus (scrip) issue of ordinary shares on 10 September 1986 involving the issue of one ordinary share of £1 for every four ordinary shares previously held.
Note. It is the company's policy to maintain the maximum flexibility so far as the availability of reserves for the payment of dividends is concerned.

6. It has now been decided to introduce a provision for doubtful debts of $2\frac{1}{2}$ per cent of trade debtors at 30 September 1986.
7. A bonus of 1 per cent of gross profit is payable to the sales manager for all sales of the company on or after 1 October 1985; the bonus is payable annually on 30 November for the immediately preceding accounting year. Provision was made for this bonus in the preparation of the draft accounts for the year ended 30 September 1986.

Prepare a corrected balance sheet as at 30 September 1986 of Prime Products Ltd.
[*Association of Accounting Technicians, December 1986*]

22 Interpretation of financial statements

As we have already seen, a company balance sheet sets out on the one hand where a company gets its finance, and on the other hand it shows how this finance is currently being used. We assume that it is the aim of each company to make the most profitable use of all its resources without running any unnecessary risks.

The finance involved in the running of the business (capital employed) will be expected to earn the maximum return for its owners in the form of profits. The better organised and managed the resources of the business are, the greater will be the profits. So any analysis or interpretation of company final accounts and balance sheets amounts to an investigation of how successfully the company has used its resources when compared with its own performance in previous years and the performance of companies in the same line of business. Financial analysis and interpretation are investigative tools that, taken with the other non-financial information available, help to point out the degree of success (or failure) the company has achieved in the use of its resources.

This analysis will also point the way to improving performance in the future, i.e. it will indicate the areas where corrective action is necessary. In the ideal company the monetary size of each individual asset and liability will be a conscious decision of management. Norms for size and performance will be established and performance will be judged against these norms.

This is one of the main reasons why exactly the same layout of final accounts and balance sheets will be preserved from year to year, so that like can be compared with like and valid conclusions drawn from the figures.

In analysing a firm's performance, the more information one has the more valid are the conclusions one can draw.

We would suggest that a full set of accounts and balance sheets for at least three years should be available so that trends may be identified and corrective measures applied as necessary. In addition, other internal analysed information, such as the composition of sales and debtors, can be vital. For instance

(a) a company in which a few credit customers accounted for the bulk of its debtors would be in a serious position if the large debtors were unable to pay or if they were to delay payment;
(b) a company which sells a considerable proportion of its products in the

Middle East would not be as stable as it would be if sales were mainly on the home market.

The limitation of accounts and balance sheets as indicators of company performance

(a) Final accounts and balance sheets are limited because these statements are concerned only with factors that can be expressed in monetary terms. They are financial statements concerned with past events.
(b) The monetary values of some assets in the books are not and cannot be exact. For example, the value of stocks can be valued at either cost or market value. The values of fixed assets are shown at original cost which may not reflect the true *present* value of these assets.
(c) The accounts assume that the value of money remains constant. This is a very serious drawback as no allowance is made for inflation. Inflation distorts the whole picture and makes comparisons impossible unless allowance is made for its effects.
(d) The accounts give no indication of very important aspects of the company such as management/staff relations, staff morale, the activities of competitors or the economic climate of the country.

People interested in a company's performance

Various types of people will be interested in a company's performance and each will be more interested in a particular aspect of the firm's position. All will be anxious that the firm should continue in business and be profitable.

Internal management will analyse the figures to assess the efficiency of management and as an aid to further control. Management will be judged by the ability of the company to maintain or increase profits, ensure survival and carry out the directors' instructions.

Banks and other financial institutions will be interested mainly in the firm's ability to pay back borrowed money at the agreed times. They will be interested in the security available and the ability to repay interest charges and to repay loans. They will be interested in the break-up value of the company and the existence of any prior charges on the assets.

Trade creditors will be interested in the firm's ability to pay in a short space of time. They will also be interested in the number of other people who rank before them for payment.

Existing and potential shareholders will be interested mainly in the firm's ability to maintain and increase its dividends and reserves, making the holding of the company's shares more profitable. They will be interested in the dividend policy of the directors, the maintenance of dividends and the company's profitability. They will be interested also in the prior charges on the profits.

Employees and trade unions will be interested mainly in the firm's ability to retain or enlarge its workforce at acceptable levels of pay. Employees will also be interested in the profits earned by the firm, especially if the company operates a profit-sharing scheme.

Recently, employees are being appointed to the boards of directors in companies and, consequently, will be interested in all aspects of the firm's performance.

Inland Revenue will be interested in seeing that the company keeps proper records for tax purposes and discharges its tax liabilities when due.

Potential takeover bidders. Since the owners of the company's shares which carry voting rights, in essence, control the company, and since the shares of a quoted company can be freely bought and sold on the Stock Exchange, control of the company can be gained by buying up a majority of the voting shares. Having gained control of the company the new owners may, however, vary the operations of the company or indeed close it down altogether.

A takeover bid might arise (*a*) where the balance sheet figures for assets (e.g. land or buildings) are well below their current market value; (*b*) where the potential bidder sees that the assets are substantially under-utilised; (*c*) where the dividend policies of the directors may encourage the shareholders to sell their shares at a seemingly attractive price; or (*d*) where the potential bidder is interested in the realisation value of a particular asset, e.g. the value of the land in the area in which the business operates may far exceed its value in its present use.

Ratio analysis

Despite what has already been said about the limitations of final accounts and balance sheets taken in isolation, they can be most useful, when combined with other relevant data, in assessing the management's use of the resources entrusted to them.

They provide the basis for examining the firm's profitability, viability and liquidity as well as its capital gearing. In addition they provide the basis for examining the firm's success or failure in meeting predetermined norms; the ways or means available to the firm for improving overall performance, profitability and control; the firm's performance when compared to similar firms in the same industry; its dividend policy; and the value of its shares.

Ratio analysis is a tool which helps the commentator to see trends in the company's financial affairs. By comparing significant figures and totals, one set with the other, and from the results deducing the underlying patterns of strength and weakness, ratio analysis helps management pinpoint deviations from (*a*) established norms, (*b*) budget targets or (*c*) industry norms, and apportion responsibility for correction or improvement.

Profitability and activity

Profitability is the relationship between the profits earned and the resources used to earn those profits. The more actively and efficiently the resources are used the greater will be the profit.

In our analysis we will take profit to mean *net profit before interest and tax have been charged*. We relate this to the capital (assets) used in earning the net profit, i.e. *capital employed*, which we already know as share capital and reserves and long-term liabilities. It is also equal to total net assets (fixed assets and working capital). In ratio analysis it is common practice to deduct *intangible* assets such as goodwill, patents and trademarks from capital employed. Of course, fictitious assets like preliminary expenses are always deducted when arriving at a figure for capital employed.

So *capital employed* for us will mean:

(Share capital + Reserves + Long-term liabilities) − Intangible assets

or

Total net assets − Intangible assets

or

Total tangible assets

EXAMPLE

Scottish Industries Ltd
Trading and Profit and Loss Accounts for years ended 31 December 19–2 and 19–3

	19–2 £	19–2 £	19–3 £	19–3 £
Sales (credit)★		200 000		300 000
Less				
Cost of sales				
Stock at 1 January	7 000		10 000	
Add Purchases (credit)	103 000		190 000	
	110 000		200 000	
Less Stock at 31 December	10 000		20 000	
COST OF SALES		100 000		180 000
GROSS PROFIT		100 000		120 000
Less				
Expenses				
Administration	33 000		40 000	
Establishment	12 500		15 000	
Financial	8 500		12 000	
Selling and distribution	35 000		47 000	
Research and development	1 000		—	
TOTAL EXPENSES★		90 000		114 000
NET PROFIT★		10 000		6 000
Add Balance b/f		4 700		9 700
		14 700		15 700
Appropriated as follows:				
Proposed dividend 10%	4 000		4 000	
Provision for taxation	3 000		1 000	
		7 000		
Debenture redemption reserve			1 700	
				6 700
BALANCE C/F		7 700		9 000

★ Indicates the more important figures.

Scottish Industries Ltd
Balance sheet as at 31 December

	19–2 £	19–2 £	19–2 £	19–3 £	19–3 £	19–3 £
Fixed assets						
Buildings		31 000			38 500	
Plant		15 000			14 000	
Fixtures		5 000			4 000	
Delivery vehicles		12 000			10 500	
			63 000			67 000
Goodwill			9 000			9 000
			72 000			76 000
TOTAL FIXED ASSETS*						
Current assets						
Stocks	10 000			20 000		
Trade debtors	15 000			31 000		
Bank	4 500			2 500		
Cash	500			500		
Total*		30 000			54 000	
Less Current liabilities						
Trade creditors	6 000			35 000		
Proposed dividends	4 000			4 000		
Provision for tax	3 000			1 000		
		13 000			40 000	
Working capital			17 000			14 000
TOTAL NET ASSETS			89 000			90 000
Financed by:						
Ordinary shares		40 000			50 000	
Debenture redemption reserve		11 300			11 000	
Profit and Loss Account balance		7 700			9 000	
Shareholders' funds			59 000			70 000
Long-term debt (liabilities)						
6% debentures (Note 1)		20 000			20 000	
8% mortgage (Note 2)		10 000			—	
			30 000			
CAPITAL EMPLOYED*			89 000			90 000

* Indicates the more important figures.

Notes
1. 6% debentures are redeemable at par in 19–4.
2. Mortgage is on buildings and was taken out in 19–1.
3. Authorised share capital is 50 000 ordinary shares of £1 each.
4. Accumulated depreciation to date at 31 December 19–2:
   Buildings   £40 000
   Plant   £10 000

Fixtures £2 000
Delivery vehicles £8 000
5. Quoted price per share:
   19–2 90p
   19–3 60p

Step 1 First or primary test of profitability

This is the *return on investment*, which measures the efficiency with which management has used the resources invested to make profit.

Formula: $\dfrac{\text{Net profit (before interest and tax)}}{\text{Capital employed}} \times 100$

For Scottish Industries Ltd in 19–2 this works out at

$$\frac{10\,000 \times 100}{(89\,000 - 9\,000)} = \frac{10\,000 \times 100}{80\,000} = 12\tfrac{1}{2}\%$$

The formula for return on investment (RoI) can now be subdivided into two significant components.

Return on investment $= \dfrac{\text{Net profit} \times 100}{\text{Sales}} \times \dfrac{\text{Sales}}{\text{Capital employed}}$

Our $12\tfrac{1}{2}$ per cent return is a combination of percentage profit on sales (net profit %) and the volume of sales achieved by the use of the assets (asset turnover).

Step 2 Return on investment for 19–2

Scottish Industries Ltd:

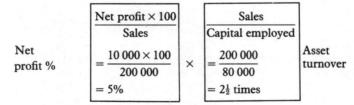

So $5\% \times 2\tfrac{1}{2} = 12\tfrac{1}{2}\%$ return on investment.

This return on investment could have been achieved by different combinations of net profit per cent and rate of asset turnover, e.g.
$2\tfrac{1}{2}\%$ Profit × 5 times Asset turnover = $12\tfrac{1}{2}\%$
or $1\tfrac{1}{4}\%$ Profit × 10 times Asset turnover = $12\tfrac{1}{2}\%$

The net profit per cent and rate of asset turnover will be affected mainly by the type of business, the mark-up or margin, the pricing policy and the efficiency of management and staff.

Step 3

We can now further investigate *return on investment* by examining the components that go to make up net profit per cent and asset turnover.

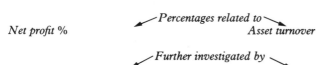

Net profit %   Asset turnover

1. Gross profit/sales
2. Total selling expenses/sales
   Broken up into:
   (a) Administration expenses/sales
   (b) Establishment expenses/sales
   (c) Financial expenses/sales
   (d) Selling and distribution expenses/sales
   (e) Research and development expenses/sales
3. In a manufacturing concern:
   (a) Raw materials/sales
   (b) Manufacturing wages/sales
   (c) Factory overheads/sales

1. Sales/current assets
2. Sales/fixed assets
3. Sales/working capital
   Broken up into:
   (a) Sales/debtors
   (b) Cost of sales/average stock

Net profit %

Scottish Industries Ltd 19–2:

1. Gross profit/sales $= \dfrac{100\,000}{200\,000} \times 100 = 50\%$

2. Total selling expenses/sales $= \dfrac{90\,000}{200\,000} \times 100 = 45\%$

   Broken up into:

   (a) Administration expenses/sales $= \dfrac{33\,000}{200\,000} \times 100 = 16\tfrac{1}{2}\%$

   (b) Establishment expenses/sales $= \dfrac{12\,500}{200\,000} \times 100 = 6\tfrac{1}{4}\%$

   (c) Financial expenses/sales $= \dfrac{8\,500}{200\,000} \times 100 = 4\tfrac{1}{4}\%$

   (d) Selling and distribution expenses/sales $= \dfrac{35\,000}{200\,000} \times 100 = 17\tfrac{1}{2}\%$

   (e) Research and development expenses/sales $= \dfrac{1\,000}{200\,000} \times 100 = \tfrac{1}{2}\%$

   Total = 45%

Step 4

For a manufacturing concern, net profit per cent can be further investigated by comparing:

Raw materials/sales $= \dfrac{\text{Cost of raw materials} \times 100}{\text{Sales}}$

360 Interpretation of financial statements

$$\text{Manufacturing wages/sales} = \frac{\text{Manufacturing wages} \times 100}{\text{Sales}}$$

$$\text{Factory overheads/sales} = \frac{\text{Factory overheads} \times 100}{\text{Sales}}$$

Step 5 Asset turnover

Scottish Industries Ltd 19–2:

1. *Current asset turnover* = sales/current assets (times)

   Formula: $\dfrac{\text{Sales}}{\text{Current assets}} = \dfrac{200\,000}{30\,000} = 6.67$ times per year

2. *Fixed asset turnover* = sales/fixed assets (times)

   Formula: $\dfrac{\text{Sales}}{\text{Fixed assets}} = \dfrac{200\,000}{63\,000} = 3.17$ times per year

3. *Working capital turnover* = sales/working capital (times)

   Formula: $\dfrac{\text{Sales}}{\text{Working capital}} = \dfrac{200\,000}{17\,000} = 11.7$ times per year

4. *Debtors' turnover* = credit sales/debtors (times)

   Formula: $\dfrac{\text{Credit sales}}{\text{Trade debtors}} = \dfrac{200\,000}{15\,000} = 13.3$ times per year

5. *Stock turnover* = cost of sales/average stock (times)

   Formula: $\dfrac{\text{Cost of sales}}{\text{Average stock}} = \dfrac{100\,000}{\frac{1}{2}(7\,000 + 10\,000)}$

   $= \dfrac{100\,000}{8\,500}$

   $= 11.7$ times per year or 31 days (365 ÷ 11.7)

Notes

Where the figures for both opening and closing stocks are not available, the figure for closing stock can be used in calculating stock turnover.

If monthly figures for stock are available the average monthly stock should be taken.

Solvency/liquidity

1. *Solvency.* Solvency is the measure of the ability of a firm to survive. A firm is technically solvent if its total assets exceed its outside liabilities, i.e. as long as the figure for shareholders' funds is positive, then the firm is solvent.

   The degree of solvency is measured by the extent that total assets exceed outside liabilities or, the bigger the figure for shareholders' funds the more

Solvency/liquidity 361

solvent is the company.
This can be expressed as a solvency ratio.

Formula: $\dfrac{\text{Shareholders' funds}}{\text{Total assets}} \times 100$

Scottish Industries Ltd 19–2: $\dfrac{59\,000}{93\,000} \times 100 = 63.4\%$

2. *Liquidity*. Liquidity ratios measure the ability of the firm to pay its short-term (current) liabilities out of its current assets.

The first measure of liquidity is the *current ratio*.

Formula: $\dfrac{\text{Current assets}}{\text{Current liabilities}}$

Scottish Industries Ltd 19–2: $\dfrac{30\,000}{13\,000} = 2.3:1$

3. *Liquid/quick asset or acid test ratio*. This ratio measures the ability of the firm to pay its current liabilities out of its liquid assets. Liquid assets are cash and assets that can be quickly turned into cash. For our purposes we will take it to mean *current assets less stock*. Stock is excluded when computing liquid assets as (*a*) its value is not certain and (*b*) it may take a long time to turn it into cash.

The question we are now asking is, if the firm were to cease trading immediately, whether it would be able to clear its immediate liabilities out of its liquid assets.

Formula: $\dfrac{\text{Current assets} - \text{stock}}{\text{Current liabilities}}$

Scottish Industries Ltd 19–2: $\dfrac{20\,000}{13\,000} = 1.54:1$

4. *Average period of credit given (days)*. This computation is a check on variations in the average period of time taken by trade debtors to settle their accounts. If the number of days varies significantly it can help to explain a deteriorating working capital or acid test ratio. It also indicates to management whether or not its credit policy is being carried out.

Formula: $\dfrac{\text{Trade debtors}}{\text{Credit sales}} \times 365$

Scottish Industries Ltd 19–2: $\dfrac{15\,000}{200\,000} \times 365 = 27 \text{ days}$

5. *Average period of credit taken (days)*. This calculation checks variations in the firm's record in paying its creditors. The firm may be able to take advantage of additional cash discounts by paying more promptly. An increase in the number of days' credit taken may be supporting evidence of a deteriorating working capital and acid test ratio. Inability to pay promptly may be an indication of over-trading, i.e. trying to carry on too large a volume of business with too little working capital.

Formula: $\dfrac{\text{Trade creditors}}{\text{Credit purchases}} \times 365$

Scottish Industries Ltd 19–2: $\dfrac{6\,000}{103\,000} \times 365 = 21$ days

Capital gearing

Capital to finance the activities of a company usually comes from two distinct sources:
1. The *ordinary shareholders* who do not receive a fixed rate of return.
2. *Fixed interest capital* which receives a fixed rate of return, e.g. debentures, bank term loans and preference share capital.

All these carry a fixed rate of interest, e.g. 10% debentures, 8% preference shares.

Capital gearing is the ratio of ordinary share capital to fixed interest capital. It is said to be low when a large percentage of the company's capital is in the form of ordinary shares.

Gearing is said to be high when a large percentage of the company's capital is in the form of fixed interest capital.

EXAMPLE

	Low geared company A £	High geared company B £
Ordinary shares	60 000	20 000
9% preference shares	30 000	35 000
10% debentures	10 000	45 000
Total	100 000	100 000

Company A is low geared because 60 per cent of its share capital comprises ordinary shares.

Company B is high geared because 80 per cent of its share capital comprises fixed interest capital. High gearing indicates a large proportion of debt capital.

Gearing is measured by the formula:
$$\dfrac{\text{Ordinary share capital}}{\text{Fixed interest capital}}$$

Company A
$= \dfrac{60\,000}{40\,000}$
$= 1.5:1$

Company B
$= \dfrac{20\,000}{80\,000}$
$= 1:4$

Capital gearing has a great effect on the distribution of company profits.

For company A £3 700 p.a. is needed to service fixed interest capital (9 per cent on £30 000 + 10 per cent on £10 000).

For company B £7 650 p.a. is needed to service fixed interest capital.

It is very important that a company's profit should cover its fixed interest charges. The

Dividend policy

ability to pay interest is measured by dividing net profit before interest and tax by fixed interest charges.

Formula: $\dfrac{\text{Net profit before interest and tax}}{\text{Fixed interest charges}}$

The answer is the number of times fixed interest is covered by net profit.

Shareholders/investors

Existing shareholders are interested in the returns received on their shareholdings (dividend) and on their increased market value (capital growth).

Investors will be examining the firm's performance with a view to buying the company's shares.

Shareholders will be interested in:

1. *Earnings per share* (EpS) (expressed in pence): This shows the return on the capital invested in the business by the ordinary shareholder, regardless of the dividends paid. It relates the profit attributable to the ordinary shareholders to the numbers of ordinary shares issued. Earnings per share is used to compare the performance of a company from year to year.

Formula: $\dfrac{\text{Net profit after tax and fixed interest and preference dividend}}{\text{Number of ordinary shares issued}} \times 100$

Scottish Industries Ltd 19-2: $\dfrac{10\,000 - 3\,000}{40\,000} = \dfrac{7\,000}{40\,000} \times 100 = 17.5\text{p per share}$

2. *Price/earnings ratio*. This indicates the number of years it would take a share to earn its cost at the present rate of earnings.

Formula: $\dfrac{\text{Market price per share}}{\text{Earnings per share}}$

Scottish Industries Ltd 19-2: $\dfrac{90}{17.5} = 5.14:1$

Dividend policy

The amount of dividend paid out is decided by the directors. They will strike a balance between the amount of profit paid to ordinary shareholders as dividend and the amount retained in the company. It is good policy to maintain a fairly steady rate of dividend from year to year. In a very good year the company will increase its rate of dividend but generally not in direct proportion to the increase in profits. In a bad year it will try to maintain the rate of dividend as near as possible to the rate of the previous year, using previously retained profits to do so if necessary.

Dividend per share (expressed in pence). This measures the actual amount received per share by the ordinary shareholder.

Formula: $\dfrac{\text{Dividend paid}}{\text{Number of ordinary shares issued}}$

Scottish Industries Ltd 19–2: $\dfrac{4\,000}{40\,000} \times 100 = 10\text{p per share}$

Dividend yield ratio. This compares dividend received per share and price of share.

Formula: $\dfrac{\text{Dividend per share} \times 100}{\text{Market price per share}}$

Scottish Industries Ltd 19–2: $\dfrac{10}{90} \times 100 = 11.1\%$

Dividend cover. This measures the number of times the dividend paid is covered by the net profit attributable to ordinary shares.

Formula: $\dfrac{\text{Net profit after tax, fixed interest and preference dividend}}{\text{Amount of dividend paid on ordinary shares}}$

Scottish Industries Ltd 19–2: $\dfrac{7\,000}{4\,000} = 1.75 \text{ times}$

Ratio analysis: problems and remedies

As we have already said, when using ratio analysis to investigate company final accounts and balance sheets the underlying trends are more important than the actual ratios and percentages. When the trends have been discovered, ways and means will suggest themselves for correcting undesirable patterns or accelerating beneficial ones.

Problems in the area of profitability/activity

As we saw in examining profitability the constituent elements are net profit per cent and asset turnover.
   Net profit is made up of gross profit less expenses.
   A falling net profit percentage could be due to:
(a)   a falling gross profit percentage;
(b)   a disproportionate increase in expenses to sales; or
(c)   a combination of both.
Falling gross profit can be seen from the gross profit ratio (gross profit/sales). Why is the ratio for Scottish Industries Ltd falling in 19–3 even though sales have increased by £100 000? In 19–3 gross profit has fallen to 40 per cent of sales.

Possible causes

(a)   *Theft of stock or cash* causes value of sales to drop, therefore less gross profit.
(b)   *Bad buying,* i.e. buying-in items that sell very slowly. Buyers may be out of touch with market trends. Prices may have to be reduced to clear stocks.

This is the reason why buyers in a department are very often paid a small salary but get a large bonus on sales above a certain figure.
(c) *Increased purchase price.* The cost of raw materials or transport may have gone up without the selling price being proportionately increased. This will lead to an increase in the cost of sales and reduced gross profit.
(d) *Overvalued closing stock* in one year reduces the cost of sales and inflates gross profit. But this same closing stock is the opening stock of the following year and so increases the cost of sales and reduces gross profit.
(e) *Falling volume of sales.* Sales are made up of volume multiplied by price. If prices rise but volume falls by a greater percentage, the overall sales figure will be reduced. It is usual to indicate volume on the internal accounts each year. This allows for comparison of total sales and enables cost per unit of sales to be calculated.

Disproportionate increase in selling expenses

The only valid reason for incurring additional selling expenses is proportionately greater sales.

As we have seen, totals for expenses can be expressed as a percentage of net profit and thereby be compared.

Each item within each expense group can be expressed as a percentage of sales and, by doing this, trends that might have been concealed by the group figure are discovered.

Possible remedies for falling profit percentage

(a) Increase selling price if possible.
(b) Tighten security on cash and stock.
(c) Check on slow-moving, shop-soiled and obsolete stock. See if slow-moving or obsolete stock is attributable to one particular buyer.
(d) Check stock valuation methods.
(e) Check on sales staff efficiency.
(f) Fire buyer or sales manager or both!

Of course, if gross or net profit percentages are rising it is indicative of increased efficiency which should be rewarded by increased remuneration.

Falling asset turnover

Current asset turnover

A rise or fall in profitability may also be due to a change in the rate of asset turnover.

A fall in the rate of current asset turnover indicates a problem in the area of sales or current assets. Sales may be falling without a corresponding decrease in working capital, i.e. under-trading.

A fall in the rate of stock turnover means a building up of stock, and a lengthening of the period of credit given to trade debtors which will be disclosed by a slower rate of debtors' turnover.

Fixed asset turnover

A fall in the rate of fixed asset turnover may be due to under-utilisation of capacity. The size of plant may be too big and expensive for the volume of sales being achieved. Expansion may have been too rapid. Outside economic circumstances may have slowed down the volume of demand for the product so that anticipated demand has not been achieved.

Problems in the area of liquidity

Over-trading. A firm is said to be over-trading when it is trying to carry on too high a volume of trading activity on too small a working capital. Over-trading occurs where there is a large expansion in *sales* which leads to a rapid build-up in *stocks* plus huge increases in *debtors*, with corresponding increases in *creditors*, i.e. trying to finance too much business from short-term resources.

Over-trading will *generate increasing profits* but because there is a delay (time-lag) between payments to suppliers and receipts from debtors on a rising market, serious cash shortages can lead to liquidation.

A firm which may appear to be thriving and profitable with full order books suddenly goes out of business because it is unable to meet its short-term liabilities out of its current assets.

Over-trading should always be suspected where:
(a) There is a falling *current (working capital) ratio*.
(b) A business is obtaining longer credit and/or allowing shorter credit than is customary in that particular trade – creditors' and debtors' turnover.
(c) A business is obtaining longer credit and/or allowing shorter credit than it used to do – compare balance sheets for three successive years.
(d) An increase in the ratio of sales to working capital is an indication that a business is over-trading.

Possible remedies for liquidity problems

1. See if it is absolutely essential to own each fixed asset. Can some of the fixed assets be sold (thus providing cash) and subsequently rented or leased?
2. Is there too high a level of stocks being maintained for the size of business, thus tying up liquid capital? Stock levels may have to be watched carefully so that only sufficient is on hand at any particular time.

If trade debtors are not paying in accordance with the firm's credit policy, money will not be available to pay creditors and day-to-day expenses. Credit policy may have to be strictly enforced even at the risk of losing marginal customers.

The credit rating of prospective credit customers may have to be more closely investigated to reduce the possibility of bad debts.

Additional sources of working capital may have to be investigated, for example
(a) The issue of un-issued share capital.
(b) A new issue of shares.
(c) Sale and leaseback of fixed assets.

A rising acid test ratio is not always a good sign of the optimum management of resources. If the ratio rises above 1:1 it may mean that too many resources are being held in liquid form and therefore not contributing to the profits of the firm. Finance held in the form of cash at bank or debtors does not earn any interest.

To sum up, a prudent balance must be kept between the firm's liquidity needs and the finance needed to expand its operations.

Additional working capital should be forthcoming when required so that the viability of the business is maintained.

By now the student will have grasped the uses and limitations of ratio analysis in the interpretation of accounts. The value of the analysis will be enhanced if taken in conjunction with all known non-financial information which enables a rational and accurate assessment to be made.

Exercises Set 22

1   From the final accounts and balance sheet of Scottish Industries Ltd for 19-3 calculate:
    a   return on investment (per cent)
    b   net profit/sales (per cent)
    c   sales/capital employed
    d   gross profit/sales (per cent)
    e   total selling expenses/sales
    f   administration expenses/sales
    g   establishment expenses/sales
    h   financial expenses/sales
    i   selling and distribution expenses/sales
    j   research and development expenses/sales
    k   fixed asset turnover
    l   current asset turnover
    m   working capital turnover
    n   debtors' turnover
    o   rate of stock turnover
    p   current asset ratio
    q   acid test ratio
    r   average period of credit given to debtors
    s   average period of credit received from creditors
    t   capital gearing – high or low?
    u   earnings per share
    v   price/earnings ratio
    w   dividend per share
    x   dividend yield
    y   dividend cover.

368 Interpretation of financial statements

2 Look at the following accounts of D Ltd, E Ltd and F Ltd and then answer questions **a–m**, showing the working.

Trading and Profit and Loss Accounts

	D £000	E £000	F £000
Stock at 1 January	20	40	60
Purchases	320	360	380
	340	400	440
Less Stock at 31 December	40	40	40
Cost of sales	300	360	400
Sales	560	600	560
Gross profit	260	240	160
Overhead expenses	120	120	80
	140	120	80

Balance sheets

	D £000	E £000	F £000
Fixed assets	240	400	140
Current assets			
Stock	40	40	40
Debtors	50	28	20
Bank	30	72	20
	360	540	220
Capital employed			
Ordinary shares £1	200	400	160
Reserves	80	100	40
Creditors	80	40	20
	360	540	220

a   Which firm has the highest average stock?
b   Which firm has the quickest stock turnover?
c   Which firm has the quickest debt collection?
d   Which firm obtained the longest period of credit from its suppliers?
e   Which firm has the highest current ratio?
f   Which firm has the highest acid test ratio?
g   Which firm has the best return on capital employed?
h   Which firm has the highest mark-up on cost?
i   Which firm is the most efficient in its expenditure on overheads when compared to sales?
j   Which firm has the highest fixed asset turnover?
k   Which firm has the highest current asset turnover?
l   Which firm has the highest working capital turnover?
m   Which firm has the highest earnings per share?

3 The following figures were taken from the final accounts of Cosgrave Ltd for the year ended 31.12.1980:

	£
Opening stock	36 000
Closing stock	24 000
Cost of sales	300 000
Sales	360 000
Net profit for year	20 000
Current assets	72 000
Liquid assets	48 000
Current liabilities	80 000
Long-term liabilities	40 000
Preference shares	140 000
Ordinary shares	200 000
Debtors	45 000
Creditors	48 000

You are required to:
a Calculate the following ratios, percentages and figures:
   (i) Stock turnover per annum.
   (ii) Gross profit percentage.
   (iii) Period of credit, in months, given to debtors.
   (iv) The purchases for the year if the period of credit received from creditors is two months.
   (v) Working capital ratio (net current assets ratio).
   (vi) Liquid assets ratio (acid test ratio).
   (vii) Return on capital employed.
b Indicate if you consider the above firm to be (i) liquid, (ii) profitable. Give reasons for your answer.

4 The following figures were taken from the final accounts of Coffee Ltd on 31.12.1984:

	£
Opening stock	30 000
Purchases	228 000
Closing stock	18 000
Sales – credit	320 000
Current liabilities	60 000
Liquid assets	34 000
Current assets	52 000
Creditors	38 000
Debtors	32 000
Shareholders' funds at 31.12.1984	260 000
Long-term liabilities	40 000
Net profit for year	20 000

a You are required to:
   (i) calculate the rate of stock turnover
   (ii) calculate the gross profit percentage
   (iii) calculate the return on capital employed
   (iv) calculate the total expenses of the firm for the year
   (v) explain what is meant by 'shareholders' funds'
   (vi) calculate the period of credit given to debtors
   (vii) calculate the quick (liquid) assets ratio.
b Would you as a shareholder be happy with the performance of the above firm? Give reasons for your answer.

370 Interpretation of financial statements

5   The following figures were taken from the final accounts of James Manton for the year ended 31.12.1982:

	£
Opening stock	40 000
Closing stock	44 000
Cost of sales	264 000
Sales	396 000
Total expenses	72 000
Current assets	80 000
Current liabilities	24 000
Liquid assets	36 000
Debtors	17 000
Shareholders' funds 31.12.1982	200 000
Long-term liabilities (secured)	40 000

a   You are required to:
   (i)   calculate the percentage mark-up on cost
   (ii) calculate the purchases for the year
   (iii) calculate the rate of stock turnover
   (iv) calculate the debtors' turnover
   (v)   calculate the return on capital employed.
b   Indicate if you consider the above firm to be:
   (i)   liquid
   (ii) profitable.

6   The following figures were taken from the final accounts of John Wade Ltd for the year ended 31.12.1983:

	£
Opening stock	56 000
Closing stock	48 000
Purchases	272 000
Gross profit	70 000
Total expenses	30 000
Fixed assets	184 000
Current assets	96 000
Liquid assets	48 000
Current liabilities	80 000
Creditors	34 000
Long-term liabilities (secured)	40 000
Shareholders' funds 31.12.1983	160 000

a   You are required to:
   (i)   calculate the sales for the year
   (ii) calculate the rate of stock turnover in the year
   (iii) calculate the percentage mark-up on cost
   (iv) calculate the return on capital employed
   (v)   calculate the period of credit received from creditors (in months)
   (vi) explain 'long-term liabilities (secured)'.
b   Would the above firm be able to pay its immediate liabilities at short notice? Use ratios to support your answer.

7   The final accounts and balance sheets for Spencer Products Ltd for the three years 19–1 to 19–3 are as follows:

Note that brackets indicate subtraction.

Final accounts

	19–1 £	19–2 £	19–3 £
Sales	300 000	360 000	500 000
Cost of sales	(140 000)	(200 000)	(380 000)
Gross profit	160 000	160 000	120 000
Selling expenses (incl. fixed interest charges £8 000)	(90 000)	(110 000)	(100 000)
Net profit	70 000	50 000	20 000
Tax	30 000	24 000	6 000

Balance sheets

	£	£	£
Assets			
Fixed assets (net)	600 000	560 000	500 000
Stock – 31 December	60 000	72 000	100 000
Trade debtors	30 000	40 000	62 500
Bank	10 000	6 000	9 500
Total assets	700 000	678 000	672 000
Liabilities			
Ordinary shares	400 000	400 000	400 000
10% debentures	160 000	160 000	160 000
Reserves	90 000	58 000	30 000
Creditors	40 000	60 000	80 000
Accruals	10 000	—	2 000
Total	700 000	678 000	672 000

Notes
1. Stock at 1 January   £20 000   £28 000   £90 000
2. Share price 31 December   50p   26p   12p
3. Dividends paid   £20 000   £12 000   £7 000

Calculate the key financial ratios for use of: **a** management, **b** shareholders, **c** creditors, **d** debenture holders.

372 Interpretation of financial statements

8 The following figures are extracted from the books of Engineering Products Ltd:

	19–1 £	19–2 £
Sales (all credit)	100 000	200 000
Total expenses	10 000	20 000
Fixed assets	120 000	180 000
Issued capital (£1 ordinary shares)	150 000	200 000
Reserves	30 000	50 000
Long-term liabilities	20 000	80 000
Stock 31.12	60 000	100 000
Trade debtors	50 000	90 000
Bank	24 000	9 000
Cash	6 000	1 000
Trade creditors	60 000	100 000
Dividends for year	10 000	15 000
Credit purchases	90 000	180 000
Stock 1.1	10 000	60 000
Quoted share price 31.12	£6.00	£5.00

Comment on the financial state of the company using relevant ratio analysis.

9 From the following figures taken from the accounts of Modern Millers Ltd calculate the significant ratios and comment on the financial position.

	19–1 £	19–2 £	19–3 £
Sales	200 000	300 000	400 000
Cost of sales	128 000	200 000	240 000
Administration expenses	6 000	10 000	12 000
Establishment expenses	4 000	8 000	6 000
Financial expenses	4 000	12 000	10 000
Selling expenses	8 000	10 000	12 000
Interest charges	2 000	2 000	2 000
Dividends ordinary	10 000	10 000	22 000
Fixed assets (net)	100 000	90 000	80 000
Stock 31 December	20 000	30 000	10 000
Stock 1 January	12 000	20 000	30 000
Trade debtors	40 000	75 000	50 000
Bank	8 000 (dr.)	3 000 (cr.)	20 000 (dr.)
Issued ordinary shares (£1 each)	100 000	110 000	110 000
Trade creditors	40 000	80 000	50 000
Price of ordinary shares	60p	50p	80p

10 You are supplied with the following figures in respect of two companies engaged in the same type of manufacturing business:

	Company A £	Company B £
Cost of raw materials	280 000	76 000
Manufacturing wages	60 000	32 000
Factory overheads	20 000	12 000
Sales – finished goods	540 000	200 000
Year end stocks	120 000	36 000
Cost of finished goods	40 000	10 000
Total selling expenses	30 000	20 000
Trade debtors at year end	67 500	20 000
Fixed assets	300 000	180 000
Current assets	520 000	60 000
Current liabilities	270 000	40 000
Paid-up ordinary shares	200 000	136 000
Reserves	50 000	24 000
Long-term debt (15% debentures)	102 000	40 000

Using relevant ratios, show which firm is in the better trading and financial position.

11 The following is a summary of the Trading and Profit and Loss Account of P. Butler, a wholesaler, for the year ended 31 December 19–4 and his balance sheet at that date:

Dr.	£		Cr. £
Stock at 1 January 19–4	15 200	Net sales	200 000
Net purchases	116 800		
	132 000		
Less			
Stock at 31 December 19–4	16 800		
Cost of sales	115 200		
Gross profit	84 800		
	200 000		200 000
		Gross profit	84 800
Administration expenses	21 600		
Selling and distribution expenses	5 200		
General and financial expenses	1 200		
Net profit	56 800		
	84 800		84 800

P. Butler
Balance sheet at 31 December 19-4

	Cost £	Depreciation to date £	Net £	Total £
Fixed assets				
Premises	112 000		112 000	
Fixtures and fittings	8 560		8 560	
Motor vehicles	12 480		12 480	
	133 040		133 040	133 040

	£
Current assets	
Stock	16 800
Debtors	20 000
Bank	9 920
	46 720
Less Current liabilities	
Trade creditors	23 360

	23 360
	156 400

TOTAL NET ASSETS

Represented by:
Capital
Balance at 1 January 19-4   113 400
Add Profit for year   56 800

    170 200
Deduct Drawings   13 800

CAPITAL EMPLOYED   156 400

a You are required to calculate:
    (i) rate of stock turnover
    (ii) gross profit as a percentage of sales
    (iii) each category of expense as a percentage of sales
    (iv) net profit as a percentage of sales
    (v) return on capital employed
    (vi) working capital
    (vii) working capital ratio
    (viii) ratio of fixed assets to total assets
    (ix) debtors' turnover
    (x) creditors' turnover
    (xi) one other important ratio which reflects the liquidity of the firm and name it.
b State what other figures you would require in order to comment on how well or otherwise the business has performed during the year.

12 The following is an abstract of the final accounts of a trading company:

Dr.			**Profit and Loss Appropriation Account**			Cr.
	19–3	19–4		19–3	19–4	
	£	£		£	£	
Proposed dividend	40 000	50 000	Net profit for year	75 000	80 000	
General reserve	29 000	24 000	Balance b/f	12 000	18 000	
Balance c/f	18 000	24 000				
	87 000	98 000		87 000	98 000	

Balance sheets

	19–3			19–4		
	£	£	£	£	£	£
Fixed assets						
Cost			726 200			941 000
Less Depreciation			370 200			462 000
			356 000			479 000
Investments: trade			12 000			14 000
Current assets						
Stock		105 000			125 000	
Debtors		120 000			115 000	
Bank		55 000			70 000	
		280 000			310 000	
Less Current liabilities						
Trade creditors	110 000			125 000		
Dividend	40 000			50 000		
		150 000			175 000	
Working capital			130 000			135 000
TOTAL NET ASSETS			498 000			628 000
Represented by:						
Share capital						
Authorised and issued ordinary shares of £1 each fully paid		400 000			500 000	
Surplus and reserve						
General reserve	80 000			104 000		
Profit and Loss Account	18 000			24 000		
		98 000			128 000	
CAPITAL EMPLOYED			498 000			628 000

Calculate the significant percentages, ratios and trends for each of the two years.

13 Prepare a company balance sheet for Hasett Ltd in as much detail as possible so that:
  a current asset ratio is 3:1
  b liquid asset ratio is 1:1
  c ratio of equity capital to debt capital is 12:1.

Suggest credit sales and net profit figures so that:

  (i) return on capital employed is 25 per cent
  (ii) average age of debts is 73 days.

14 The following is an abstract of the final accounts of a company:

Dr. **Profit and Loss Appropriation Account for the year ended 31.12.19–0** Cr.

	£		£
Profit and Loss Account			
(current year)	34 000	Balance b/d	46 000
Balance c/d	12 000		
	46 000		46 000
		Balance b/d	12 000

Balance sheet as at 31.12.19–0

	Cost	Depreciation to date	Net	Total
Fixed assets	£	£	£	£
	760 000	68 000	692 000	692 000
Goodwill				140 000
Investments				60 000
				892 000
Current assets	£	£		
Stock		220 000		
Debtors		52 000		
		272 000		
Less Current liabilities				
Creditors	124 000			
Bank	162 000			
Debenture interest	18 000			
Preference dividend	48 000			
	352 000			
Working capital				(80 000)
TOTAL NET ASSETS				812 000
Financed by:				
Authorised and issued capital				
400 000 ordinary shares at £1 each		400 000		
200 000 12% cumulative preference				
shares at £1 each		200 000		
Reserves				
Profit and Loss Account		12 000		
				612 000
Long-term liabilities				
9% debentures				200 000
CAPITAL EMPLOYED				812 000

a Select the relevant figures, ratios and other information (including omissions) from the above abstract of final accounts and discuss their implications from the point of view of:
  (i) the ordinary shareholders
  (ii) the debenture holders.
b What other information could be sought to assess more accurately the position of the company?

15 The following figures have been taken from the final accounts of Scott Ltd for the year ended 31.12.19–2:

	£
Purchases – cash	120 000
Purchases – credit	480 000
Stock 31.12.19–2	40 000
Cost of sales	580 000
Profit and Loss Account at 1 January 19–2	24 000
Net profit for the year	120 000
Dividend paid	20%
Fixed assets	460 000
Current assets	120 000
Current liabilities (creditors only)	60 000
Issued capital 300 000 ordinary shares at £1 each	300 000
General reserve at 1.1.19–2	36 000
12% debentures	100 000
Current market value of one share	£8

a You are required to calculate:
   (i) dividend cover
   (ii) price/earnings ratio
   (iii) interest cover
   (iv) period of credit received from creditors.
b If you were a bank manager would you consider giving a £100 000 loan to Scott Ltd? Give reasons for your answer.
c The gross profit percentage of the above firm fell from 25 per cent in 19–1 to 20 per cent in 19–2. Give five different possible causes for this decline.

16 The following figures have been taken from the final accounts for the year ended 31.12.19–3 of Bill Haley Ltd, a long-established manufacturing company whose authorised capital is 800 000 ordinary shares of £1 each and 200 000 12% preference shares of £3 each:

	£
Building (cost £440 000)	380 000
Stocks	330 000
Plant and machinery (cost £280 000)	240 000
Bank	220 000
Goodwill at cost	100 000
15% debentures	180 000
Patents	60 000
Investments (market value £320 000)	400 000
Debtors	110 000
Creditors	440 000
Issued capital:	
600 000 ordinary shares of £1 each, 80p paid	480 000
200 000 12% preference shares of £3 each	600 000
Profit and loss debit balance (including last year's debit balance £80 000)	300 000
Contingent liability	120 000
Capital employed (shareholders' funds + long-term liabilities)	960 000

a Select ratios, percentages and other information from the above figures and use them to explain the present state of affairs of the company.
b Suggest methods of overcoming any difficulties you note.

378 Interpretation of financial statements

17 The following balances were included in the trial balance extracted from the books of the Quality Trading Company at 31 December, the end of its trading year:

	£
Purchases	56 000
Stock at beginning of year	4 000
Sales	80 000
Expenses	10 000

Assume that:
Average trade debtors for the year were	£15 000
Stock at 31 December was valued at	£8 000
Average trade creditors for the year were	£21 000
Capital at beginning of year was	£150 000

Calculate:
a the percentage of gross profit to sales
b the percentage of net profit to capital
c the average collection period of trade debtors in months
d the average credit period taken by trade creditors.

[*Pitman, Intermediate*]

18 The following extracts relate to K. George's accounts for the year to 31 August 1984:

Trading, Profit and Loss Account for the year to 31 August 1984

	£	£
Sales (all credit)		100 000
Less Cost of goods sold:		
Opening stock	10 000	
Purchases	52 000	
	62 000	
Less Closing stock	12 000	
		50 000
Gross profit		50 000
Less Expenses		25 000
Net profit		25 000

Balance sheet at 31 August 1984

	£	£
Fixed assets		
Machinery at cost		30 000
Less Depreciation		12 000
		18 000
Current assets		
Stocks	12 000	
Trade debtors	7 000	
Bank	1 000	
	20 000	
Less Current liabilities		
Trade creditors	5 000	

	£	£
		15 000
		33 000
Financed by:		
Capital		18 000
Net profit for the year	25 000	
Less Drawings	10 000	
		15 000
		33 000

Calculate the following accounting ratios:
i gross profit; **ii** mark-up on cost of goods sold; **iii** net profit on sales; **iv** return on capital employed; **v** stock turnover; **vi** debtor collection period; **vii** current ratio; and **viii** quick (or acid test).

[*Association of Accounting Technicians, December 1984*]

19 Stephen House, the principal shareholder of Hilltown Traders Ltd, is very concerned that although the company's net profit has increased in the past year the bank is reluctant to continue the company's overdraft facility.

The summarised results of Hilltown Traders Ltd for the last three financial years are as follows:

Trading and Profit and Loss Accounts years ended 31 December

	1982 £000	1983 £000	1984 £000
Turnover	100	130	150
Less Costs of sales	80	110	125
Gross profit	20	20	25
Less Administrative expenditure	4	6	7
Distribution expenditure	6	5	5
	10	11	12
Net profit	10	9	13

Balance sheets as at 31 December

	1982 £000	1982 £000	1983 £000	1983 £000	1984 £000	1984 £000
Fixed assets		60		60		60
Current assets						
Stock	10		24		40	
Debtors	6		7		9	
Balance at bank	2		—		—	
	18		31		49	
Current liabilities						
Creditors	8		9		13	
Bank overdraft	—		3		4	
	8		12		17	

380 Interpretation of financial statements

	1982		1983		1984	
	£000	£000	£000	£000	£000	£000
Net current assets		10		19		32
Net capital employed		70		79		92
Capital						
Ordinary share capital		50		50		50
Reserves		20		29		42
		70		79		92

a Calculate five financial ratios of Hilltown Traders Ltd which will indicate to the company those aspects which have improved and those which have weakened in the past three years.
b Outline three significant and distinct limitations of financial ratios.
[Association of Accounting Technicians, pilot, 1985]

20 Cone is in business as a motor factor. His condensed financial accounts for the last three years are summarised below:

Profit and Loss Accounts for the year to 31 March

	1980		1981		1982	
	£000s	£000s	£000s	£000s	£000s	£000s
Sales (all on credit)		400		630		870
Less Cost of goods sold						
Opening stock	20		25		50	
Purchases	325		550		790	
	345		575		840	
Less Closing stock	25		50		100	
		320		525		740
Gross profit		80		105		130
Less Expenses	40		50		60	
Loan interest	—		—		10	
		40		50		70
NET PROFIT		40		55		60

Balance sheets as at 31 March

	1980		1981		1982	
	£000s	£000s	£000s	£000s	£000s	£000s
Fixed assets		89		93		101
Current assets						
Stocks	25		50		100	
Trade debtors	50		105		240	
Cash at bank	10		5		—	
		85		160		340
		174		253		441
Financed by:						
Capital		100		118		141
Add Net profit for the year	40		55		60	
Less Drawings (all on 31 March)	22		32		36	
		18		23		24
		118		141		165
Loan		—		—		100
Current liabilities						
Creditors	56		112		166	
Bank overdraft	—		—		10	
		56		112		176
		174		253		441

a Compute the following ratios for 1980, 1981 and 1982:
  (i) gross profit on sales;
  (ii) gross profit on cost of goods sold;
  (iii) stock turnover;
  (iv) return on capital employed;
  (v) current ratio;
  (vi) liquidity (or quick) ratio;
  (vii) debtor collection period.
b Comment briefly on the results of the business over the last three years using the ratios you have computed in answer to part **a** of the question.
[*Association of Accounting Technicians, June 1982*]

21 You are presented with the following summarised information concerning J. Free:

J. Free
Trading, Profit and Loss Account (extracts) for the year to 30 April 1982 and 30 April 1983

	1983	1982
	£	£
Sales (all on credit)	200 000	120 000
Cost of sales	150 000	80 000
Gross profit	50 000	40 000
Expenses	15 000	10 000
Net profit	35 000	30 000

J. Free
Balance sheet (extracts) at 30 April 1982 and 30 April 1983

	1983 £	1983 £	1982 £	1982 £
Fixed assets (net book value)		12 000		15 000
Current assets				
Stocks	18 000		7 000	
Trade debtors	36 000		12 000	
Cash at bank	—		1 000	
		54 000		20 000
		66 000		35 000
Capital account				
Balance at 1 April	29 000		12 000	
Net profit for the year	35 000		30 000	
	64 000		42 000	
Less Drawings	23 000		13 000	
		41 000		29 000
Current liabilities				
Trade creditors	15 000		6 000	
Bank overdraft	10 000		—	
		25 000		6 000
		66 000		35 000

Notes
1. There were no purchases or disposals of fixed assets during the year.
2. During 1982/83 Free reduced his selling prices in order to stimulate sales.
3. It may be assumed that price levels were stable.

a Calculate the following ratios for both 1982 and 1983:
   (i) percentage mark-up on sales;
   (ii) gross profit on sales;
   (iii) return on capital employed;
   (iv) debtor collection period;
   (v) current ratio;
   (iv) acid test (or quick) ratio.
b Comment upon the apparent effect that the increase in sales has had on profit and cash flow.

[*Association of Accounting Technicians, June 1983*]

22 The following information has been extracted from the accounts of Rock Ltd, a wholesale trading company:

At 31 December

	1981 £000	1982 £000
Fixed assets	300	275
Debtors	75	175
Cash at bank	25	—
Overdraft	—	10
Creditors	50	96

For the year to 31 December

	1981	1982
	£000	£000
Sales	1 000	1 500
Purchases	500	750
Net profit	100	125
Cost of sales	500	725
Average stock	100	125

Required:

a A statement showing the rate of stock turnover, the average number of days' credit taken and given, the percentage return on capital employed, and the working capital ratio. Your answer should be presented in the following form:

	1981	1982
Annual rate of stock turnover	___	___
Days' credit from creditors	___	___
Days' credit to debtors	___	___
Return on capital employed	___	___
Working capital ratio	___	___

b A brief discussion of the implication of the information calculated above for the working capital policy of Rock Ltd.

Notes
1. Work to the nearest whole number.
2. Assume that there are 360 days in the year.
3. Capital employed is defined as fixed assets plus net current assets.
4. Show all workings.

[*Royal Society of Arts, II, March 1983*]

23 The summarised final accounts of Sum PLC for the years 1983 and 1984 were as follows:

Profit and Loss Account for the year to 31 December

	1983	1984
	£000	£000
Sales	1 500	1 750
Cost of goods sold	1 000	1 100
Gross profit	500	650
Other expenses	200	250
Net profit	300	400

Balance sheet as at 31 December

	1983 £000	1983 £000	1984 £000	1984 £000
Fixed assets at cost *less* depreciation		900		1 100
Current assets				
Stock	90		110	
Debtors	150		160	
Cash	50		10	
		290		280
		1 190		1 380
Ordinary shares of £1 each		500		500
Retained profit		150		550
		650		1 050
Debentures repayable 1993		—		180
Current liabilities				
Trade creditors	130		150	
Short-term loan	410		—	
		540		150
		1 190		1 380

The following balances appeared in the company's balance sheet at 31 December 1982:

	£000
Stock	80
Debtors	130
Trade creditors	122

Calculate for 1983 and 1984 from the above accounts of Sum PLC the rate of stock turnover, the return on capital employed, the rate of debtor and creditor turnover (in days) and the working capital ratio. Your answer should be presented in the following format:

	1983	1984
Rate of stock turnover		
Return on capital employed (%)		
Rate of debtor turnover (days)		
Rate of creditor turnover (days)		
Working capital ratio		

Notes
1. Capital employed is to be measured as the company's long-term capital.
2. Answers should be calculated at one place of decimals.

[*Royal Society of Arts, II, March 1985*]

24 The summarised accounts of Brunel, a trader, for the years 1983 and 1984 are as follows:

Trading and Profit and Loss Account

	1983 £	1983 £	1984 £	1984 £
Sales		240 000		300 000
Less Opening stock	24 000		25 000	
Purchases	191 000		265 000	
Closing stock	(25 000)		(60 000)	
Cost of sales		190 000		230 000
Gross profit		50 000		70 000
Less Running expenses		28 000		30 000
Net profit		22 000		40 000

Balance sheet at 31 December

	1983 £	1984 £
Capital and liabilities		
Capital	99 500	100 500
Net profit	22 000	40 000
Drawings	(21 000)	(26 000)
	100 500	114 500
Trade creditors	25 500	37 000
Bank overdraft	—	11 000
	126 000	162 500
Assets		
Fixed assets at cost *less* depreciation	75 000	73 500
Stock	25 000	60 000
Trade debtors	21 000	29 000
Bank balance	5 000	—
	126 000	162 500

At 31 December 1982, trade debtors and trade creditors amounted to £19 000 and £23 500 respectively. All sales and purchases are on credit.

a Calculate the following ratios for 1983 and 1984.
  (i)   The rate of stock turnover.
  (ii) The rate of debtors turnover.
  (iii) The rate of creditors turnover.
  (iv) The working capital ratio.
  (v)   The percentage return on capital employed.
b Examine the progress and position of Brunel's business based on your calculations under **a**. You should indicate whether each ratio has improved or declined over the two years.

Note. Calculations to *one* decimal place.

[*Royal Society of Arts, II, May 1985*]

25 The following information relates to Osprey Ltd for the year 1985:

On 1 January 1985:	
Reserves brought forward	£62 500
On 31 December 1985:	
Working capital	£75 000
Stock	£50 000
Creditors	£100 000
Issued capital – ordinary shares of £1 each	£100 000
Fixed assets	£112 500
Average age of outstanding debts (based on a 50-week year)	9 weeks
For the year 1985:	
Net profit as a percentage of issued share capital	25%
Annual rate of turnover of stock – based on cost at 31 December	5 times
Gross profit as a percentage of sales	20%

Notes
1. The company's current assets consist of stock, debtors and cash.
2. The only liabilities are shareholders' funds and current liabilities.
3. There are no assets other than current assets and fixed assets.

Prepare in as much detail as possible:
a   Osprey's Trading and Profit and Loss Account for 1985
b   the balance sheet of Osprey Ltd at 31 December 1985.
[*Royal Society of Arts, II, March 1986*]

26 Bradwich PLC is a medium-sized engineering company whose shares are listed on a major stock exchange.

It has recently applied to its bankers for a 7-year loan of £500 000 to finance a modernisation and expansion programme.

Mr Whitehall, a recently retired Civil Servant, is contemplating investing £10 000 of his lump sum pension in the company's ordinary shares in order to provide both an income during his retirement and a legacy to his grandchildren after his death.

The bank and Mr Whitehall have each acquired copies of the company's most recent annual report and accounts.

a   State, separately for each of the two parties, those aspects of the company's performance and financial position which would be of particular interest and relevance to their respective interests.
b   State, separately for each of the two parties, the formula of four ratios which would assist in measuring or assessing the matters raised in your answer to a.
[*Association of Certified Accountants, Level 1, June 1984*]

27 Two companies, Quick Ltd and Lively Ltd, are in the same trade and both started trading on 1 April 1985. The summarised results of their first year of trading are:

Trading and Profit and Loss Account
for the year to 31 March 1986

	Quick Ltd £	Lively Ltd £
Sales	250 000	500 000
Less Cost of goods sold	150 000	300 000
Gross profit	100 000	200 000
Less Expenses	40 000	100 000
Net profit	60 000	100 000

Balance sheet at 31 March 1986

	Quick Ltd £	£	Lively Ltd £	£
Fixed assets at book value		150 000		200 000
Stock	50 000		75 000	
Debtors	25 000		125 000	
Cash	15 000		20 000	
	90 000		220 000	
Less Creditors	40 000		100 000	
		50 000		120 000
		200 000		320 000
Share capital		140 000		200 000
Profit and Loss Account		60 000		120 000
		200 000		320 000

Calculate appropriate ratios and state which company:
a turns over its stock more quickly
b pays its creditors more promptly
c collects the money owed by debtors more promptly
d makes a higher gross profit relative to sales
e has a better return on capital employed.

[*Royal Society of Arts, II, June 1986*]

28 Gordon Ray is currently reviewing his results for the year ended 31 December 1985 and comparing them with those of Smooth Dealers Ltd, a company engaged in the same trade.

The chairman of Smooth Dealers Ltd receives an annual salary of £12 000 for performing duties very similar to those performed by Gordon Ray in his business. The summarised final accounts for 1985 of Gordon Ray and Smooth Dealers Ltd are as follows:

Trading and Profit and Loss Accounts for the year ended 31 December 1985

Gordon Ray £000		Smooth Dealers Ltd £000
90	Turnover	150
48	Less Cost of sales	80
42	Gross profit	70
12	Administrative expenses	37
15	Sales and distribution expenses	25
—	Debenture interest	3
27		65
15	Net profit	5

Balance sheets as at 31 December 1985

Gordon Ray £000		Smooth Dealers Ltd £000
60	Fixed assets	50
28	Current assets: Stock	56
22	Debtors	69
6	Balance at bank	10
56		135
16	Current liabilities: Creditors	25
40	Net current assets	110
100	Net capital employed	160
100	Capital account	
	Ordinary share capital	80
	Retained earnings	50
	10% debenture stock	30
100		160

a Calculate five appropriate ratios comparing the results of Gordon Ray with those of Smooth Dealers Ltd and briefly comment on each ratio.

b Outline three distinct reasons why a comparison of the amount of profit earned by different businesses should be approached with great care.

[*Association of Accounting Technicians, June 1986*]

29 The following are the summarised Trading and Profit and Loss Accounts for the years ended 31 December 1983, 1984 and 1985 and balance sheets as at 31 December 1982, 1983, 1984 and 1985 of James Simpson, a retail trader.

Trading and Profit and Loss Accounts years ended 31 December 1983, 1984 and 1985

	1983 £000	1984 £000	1985 £000
Sales	100	120	140
Cost of sales	60	72	98
Gross profit	40	48	42
Expenses (including loan interest)	20	30	28
Net profit	20	18	14

Balance sheets as at 31 December 1982, 1983, 1984 and 1985

	1982 £000	1983 £000	1984 £000	1985 £000
Fixed assets	38	48	68	90
Current assets				
Stocks	14	16	20	29
Trade debtors	10	18	40	52
Balance at bank	9	13	39	16
	71	95	167	187
Financed by:				
Capital at 1 January	51	67	87	105
Add Net profit for the year	16	20	18	14
	67	87	105	119
Loan (received 31 December 1984)	—	—	50	50
Current liabilities – trade creditors	4	8	12	18
	71	95	167	187

Additional information:
1. James Simpson, a man of modest tastes, is the beneficiary of a small income from his grandfather and therefore has taken no drawings from his retail business.
2. Interest of 10 per cent per annum has been paid on the loan from 1 January 1985.
3. It is estimated that £12 000 per annum would have to be paid for the services rendered to the business by James Simpson.
4. All sales are on a 30 days' credit basis.
5. James Simpson is able to invest in a bank deposit account giving interest at the rate of 8 per cent per annum.

a Calculate for each of the years ended 31 December 1983, 1984 and 1985 the following financial ratios:
   return on gross capital employed;
   acid or quick;
   stock turnover;
   net profit to sales.

b Use two financial ratios (not referred to in **a** above) to draw attention to two aspects of the business which would appear to give cause for concern.
c Advise James Simpson whether, on financial grounds, he should continue his retail business.
   Note. Answers should include appropriate computations.
d Advise James Simpson as to whether it was a financially sound decision to borrow £50 000 on 31 December 1984.

[*Association of Accounting Technicians, December 1986*]

23 Accounts of non-commercial organisations

This chapter will deal with the methods and procedures adopted by non-trading organisations when 'accounting' for their financial activities. The description 'non-trading' embraces a very wide variety of organisations ranging from social and sporting clubs of all types to trade unions, political associations and firms providing professional services such as solicitors, doctors and accountants. We will deal in the main with the activity of clubs, bearing in mind that the principles apply equally to the other types of organisation. The type of accounts kept will vary with the type of organisation or with the type of service provided.

Each type of organisation will, however, prepare accounts so that a true and fair picture of the organisation is given. Indeed, it is the practice of clubs and societies to appoint auditors who give a written assurance that they have examined the books and other records of the organisation and are satisfied that the accounts and other pieces of information are true and accurate.

As in all other types of organisation, figures appearing in the final accounts are backed by ledger accounts.

Except in the case of clubs and societies whose financial activities involve the receipt and payment of money only, all non-trading organisations prepare final accounts (income and expenditure) and a statement of affairs (balance sheet) at the end of the period.

Where a club or society carries on an identifiable trading activity such as the running of a bar or restaurant on commercial lines, a separate Trading Account is prepared for this activity and the profit or loss on it is transferred to the Income and Expenditure Account proper.

Receipts and payments accounts

A Receipts and Payments Account is merely a summary of the cash book, showing under classified headings all cash received and all cash paid out over a given period (usually a year). It is normally kept by treasurers of small clubs and societies which possess little or no property.

Form

1. Receipts are entered on the debit side; payments on the credit side.
2. It contains only *actual cash receipts and payments received or made* during the period, whether such receipts and payments refer to the period covered or not, or whether they refer to capital or revenue items.
3. The balance on the account represents the balance of cash in hand or at bank.
4. The account usually opens with the balance brought forward, cash and bank, from a previous period, and the balance in hand at the end of the period is carried forward to the next period.

EXAMPLE

The Retired Seamen's Association had a balance at bank of £500 at 1 January 19–1. During the year the Association received and paid the following amounts:

Receipts: Members' subscriptions £700, Sale of raffle tickets £400, Sale of tea and refreshments £900, Sale of club ties £120.
Payments: Rent of hall £300, Postage £70, Stationery £40, Refreshments £600, Cleaner's wages £500, Club ties £80.

Prepare Receipts and Payments Account for the year 19–1.

SOLUTION

Retired Seamen's Association
Receipts and Payments Account

19–1	*Receipts*	£	19–1	*Payments*	£
1 Jan.	Balance b/d	500	31 Dec.	Rent of hall	300
31 Dec.	Members' subscriptions	700		Postage	70
	Sale of teas and refreshments	900		Stationery	40
	Sale of club ties	120		Refreshments	600
				Cleaner's wages	500
				Club ties	80
				Balance c/d	630
		2 220			2 220
31 Dec.	Balance b/d	630			

Disadvantages

The Receipts and Payments Account does not show the true financial position because:
(a) Amounts due but unpaid are omitted; amounts paid in advance to the organisation are included under receipts.
(b) Value of assets held and depreciation on them are not recorded.
(c) Outstanding liabilities at the end of the period are not provided for.
(d) Expenses covering more than one period are not apportioned.
(e) 'Balance in hand' represents only the cash or bank balance.
(f) It is not part of the double-entry system.

Income and expenditure accounts

1. This is another name for a Profit and Loss Account. This is a very important point to remember. If in doubt about any entry in an Income and Expenditure Account ask yourself the question: 'Would it appear on the Profit and Loss Account of a trading concern?' If it would, it belongs to the Income and Expenditure Account.

   An Income and Expenditure Account compares *all* the income and expenditure of a revenue nature for the year and the difference represents a profit or loss (called *excess*) on the club's activities for the year.

   To complete the picture a balance sheet is added, setting out the book value of the club's assets and liabilities at the end of the year. It takes the usual balance sheet format of fixed assets plus working capital (i.e. current assets minus current liabilities) which is equal to total net assets, financed by *accumulated fund* (another word for capital) plus long-term liabilities, which is equal to capital employed.
2. Expenditure is recorded on the debit side. Income is recorded on the credit side.
3. It must contain the whole of the revenue receipts and revenue expenditure applicable to the period, *whether received and paid or not.*
4. The balance on the account represents an excess of income over expenditure (profit) or an excess of expenditure over income (loss). This balance is not carried forward but is added to or deducted from the Capital Account (usually called the accumulated fund).
5. It is usually accompanied by a balance sheet.

Advantages

It shows the true financial position because:
(*a*) It includes all the revenue receipts and payments applicable to the period and not a penny more.
(*b*) Accruals and prepayments are clear.
(*c*) The balance sheet will show clearly the assets and liabilities at their true valuation.
(*d*) It forms part of the double-entry system.

Notes

1. Receipts and expenditure of a capital nature must not appear in the Income and Expenditure Account. These items will appear in the balance sheet (e.g., purchase of equipment or receipt of a legacy by the club).
2. The accumulated fund is the same as the Capital Account of the ordinary business. It is made up of the excess of income over expenditure (plus any capital receipts) accumulated over a number of years. It is equal to total assets less outside liabilities.
3. When a club or society carries on an activity designed to make a profit such as the running of a bar or restaurant, it is better to prepare a separate

Trading Account for this activity and transfer the profit or loss to the Income and Expenditure Account proper.

4. Many clubs and societies ignore subscriptions due when preparing Income and Expenditure Accounts and balance sheets. The reason is that clubs normally will not make the same efforts at collecting amounts due to them as would a commercial concern (e.g. they will not sue the member for subscriptions due). Therefore they maintain that unpaid subscriptions should not be shown as assets. This is called the 'convention of conservatism' by accountants. Convention of conservatism tends to understate assets rather than overstate them – hence the omission of subscriptions due. If subscriptions outstanding are subsequently paid they are regarded as receipts in the year they are received.

Note that in examinations, unless you get a clear indication that subscriptions due are to be ignored, they must be included in calculating accumulated fund, shown on Income and Expenditure Account and on balance sheet.

Procedure for tackling questions involving an Income and Expenditure Account and balance sheet

Step 1
Find the accumulated fund at the *beginning* of the year. Write down and total the value of all the assets on the first day of the financial year and *deduct* the value of all the liabilities on that date. Only assets and liabilities at the first day of the year are included (see examples below).

Step 2
(a) Prepare Trading Account if appropriate.
(b) Prepare an Income and Expenditure Account for the year, showing all the income and expenditure that relates to the year and that amount only. Items of a similar nature, e.g. receipts from sale of teas and cost of teas should be netted in the account so that a direct comparison of revenue and expenses can be seen at a glance. If necessary, show appropriate ledger accounts or explanations of figures as notes attached to the accounts. Pay particular attention to subscriptions, accruals, prepayments and depreciation. Purchase and sale of items of a capital nature are *never* included in the Income and Expenditure Account (see examples below).

Step 3
Prepare a balance sheet giving as much detail as possible on the last day of the financial year.

Remember that the Income and Expenditure Account and balance sheet of a club is dealt with in exactly the same manner as the Profit and Loss Account and balance sheet of a sole trader (see examples below).

A Simple Example

Included in the assets and liabilities of the Slimline Health Club on 1 January 19–1 were the following:

Bar stock, £800; Clubhouse, £30 000; Equipment, £1 800; Subscriptions due, £100; Wages due, £320. The following is a summary of the club's receipts and payments for the year ended 31.12.19–1:

Dr.	Receipts	£	Payments	Cr. £
Cash in hand 1.1.19–1		1 120	Wages	5 600
Bank balance 1.1.19–1		2 400	Prize bonds	100
Subscriptions		12 800	Purchase of equipment	1 400
Bar sales		11 000	Bar purchases	6 500
Competition receipts		520	Competition prizes	640
			Extension to clubhouse	10 000
			Cash 31.12.19–1	700
			Bank 31.12.19–1	2 900
		27 840		27 840

The treasurer also supplied the following information:
(a) Subscriptions in arrears at 31.12.19–1 amounted to £240.
(b) Bank interest receivable due to club on 31.12.19–1 was £300.
(c) Bar stock at 31.12.19–1 was valued at £1 000.
(d) Equipment (including addition) is to be depreciated by 25 per cent.

Prepare:
a a statement of accumulated fund on 1.1.19–1
b an Income and Expenditure Account for the year ended 31.12.19–1
c a balance sheet at 31.12.19–1.

SOLUTION

a *Step 1*

Accumulated fund on 1.1.19–1
Slimline Health Club

	£	£
Assets at 1.1.19–1		
Cash in hand	1 120	
Bank balance	2 400	
Bar stock	800	
Clubhouse	30 000	
Equipment	1 800	
Subscriptions due	100	
		36 220
Less Liabilities at 1.1.19–1		
Wages due		320
Accumulated fund at 1.1.19–1		35 900

b Step 2

(i)   **Bar Trading Account for year ended 31.12.19–1**

	£	£
Sales		11 000
Less		
Cost of sales		
Stock at 1.1.19–1	800	
Plus Purchases	6 500	
	7 300	
Less Stock at 31.12.19–1	1 000	
COST OF SALES		6 300
Bar profit to Income and Expenditure Account		4 700

(ii)   **Income and Expenditure Account for year ended 31.12.19–1**

Dr. *Expenditure*			*Income*	Cr.
19–1	£	£	19–1	£
Wages	5 600		Bar profit from Trading Account	4 700
Less Due at 1.1.19–1	320		Subscriptions (Note 3)	12 940
		5 280	Bank interest (due)	300
Competition prizes	640			
Less Competition receipts	520			
		120		
Depreciation of equipment (Note 4)		800		
Excess of income for year to accumulated fund		11 740		
		17 940		17 940

c Step 3

Slimline Health Club
Balance sheet as at 31 December 19–1

	Cost	Depreciation to date	Net	Total
Fixed assets	£	£	£	£
Clubhouse	30 000			
Add Extension	10 000			
	40 000		40 000	
Equipment (Note 4)	3 200	800	2 400	
			42 400	
Prize bonds			100	
	43 200	800	42 500	42 500

		£	£	£	£
Current assets					
Bar stock			1 000		
Subscriptions due			240		
Bank			2 900		
Cash			700		
Bank interest due			300		
				5 140	
Working capital					5 140
TOTAL NET ASSETS					47 640
Financed by:					
Accumulated fund					
Balance at 1.1.19–1			35 900		
Add Excess income for year			11 740		
Balance at 31.12.19–1				47 640	
CAPITAL EMPLOYED					47 640

Notes
1. There were no current liabilities at 31.12.19–1 in this question.
2. Prize bonds were treated as fixed assets.

3.
Dr.		**Subscriptions Account**			Cr.
19–1		£	19–1		£
1 Jan.	Balance b/d		31 Dec.	Bank	12 800
	(subs due)	1 100		Balance c/d	240
31 Dec.	Income and				
	Expenditure a/c	12 940			
		13 040			13 040
31 Dec.	Balance b/d	240			

4. *Depreciation of equipment* £
   Value at 1.1.19–1   1 800
   Add Equipment purchased   1 400

   Value at 31.12.19–1   3 200
   Depreciation – 25% of £3 200 = £800
   To Income and Expenditure a/c

A More Difficult Example

Included in the assets and liabilities of the Westfield Recreation Centre on 1.1.1984 were the following:

Buildings, £78 000; Equipment, £9 800; Bar and restaurant stock, £2 700; Bar debtors, £150; Bank Deposit Account, £3 800; Subscriptions due, £130; Bar creditors, £740; Life membership, £4 200; Secretary's expenses due, £60.

The club treasurer has supplied the following account of the club's activities during the year ended 31.12.1984:

Dr. Receipts		Payments	Cr.
1984	£	1984	£
Bank Current Account at 1.1.1984	530	Bar and restaurant purchases	34 200
Subscriptions	17 600	Sundry expenses	13 230
Bar and restaurant receipts	48 000	Transfer to Deposit Account	8 500
Life membership subscriptions	600	Repayment of £10 000 loan	
Donations	4 500	(with interest due)	12 750
Bank interest due	380	Purchase of equipment	2 400
Competition receipts	800	Competition costs	920
Sale of equipment	200	Balance at 31.12.1984	610
	72 610		72 610

You are given the following additional information:
(a) Bar and restaurant stock on 31.12.1984 was valued at £2 550.
(b) Bar and restaurant debtors and creditors on 31.12.1984 amounted to £90 and £670 respectively.
(c) Subscriptions prepaid on 31.12.1984 were £110.
(d) 10 per cent of life membership is to be treated as a revenue item.
(e) The interest payable on the £10 000 loan for the year 1984 amounted to £750.
(f) The value of equipment on 31.12.1984 was £10 800.

You are required to show:
a the club's accumulated fund (capital statement) on 1.1.1984
b the Income and Expenditure Account for the year ended 31.12.1984
c a balance sheet as at 31.12.1984.

SOLUTION
a *Step 1*   **Accumulated fund on 1.1.1984**

	£	£
Assets at 1.1.1984		
Bank Account	530	
Bank Deposit Account	3 800	
Buildings	78 000	
Equipment	9 800	
Bar and restaurant stock	2 700	
Bar debtors	150	
Subscriptions due	130	
		95 110
Less Liabilities on 1.1984		
Creditors	740	
Life memberships	4 200	
Loan	10 000	
Interest due on loan	2 000	
Secretary's expenses due	60	
		17 000
Accumulated fund on 1.1.1984		78 110

Explanatory notes
1. Loan due at 1.1.1984 was £10 000.
2. Interest on loan due at 1.1.1984 was £2 000, as £750 was the amount relating to year ending 31.12.1984.
3. Life memberships are a liability which are usually written off over a number of years, i.e. a certain amount is credited to the Income and Expenditure Account each year.

Step 2
(i)   **Bar and Restaurant Account for year ended 31.12.1984**

	£	£
Sales (Note 1)		47 940
Less		
Cost of sales		
Stock at 1.1.1984	2 700	
Add Purchases (£34 200 + £670 − £740)	34 130	
	36 830	
Less Stock 31.12.1984	2 550	
COST OF SALES		34 280
Profit on bar and restaurant to Income and Expenditure Account		13 660

Explanatory note
Cash sales and purchases must be adjusted for amounts due at both beginning and end of year.

b
(ii)

Westfield Recreation Centre
Income and Expenditure Account for year ended 31.12.1984

Dr. *Expenditure*			*Income*	Cr.
1984	£	£	1984	£
Sundry expenses (Note 4)		13 170	Profit on bar and restaurant	13 660
Competition costs	920		Subscriptions – ordinary members	
Less Receipts	800	120	(Note 2)	17 360
Depreciation of equipment			Life membership subscriptions	
(Note 5)		1 200	(Note 3)	480
Interest on loan		750	Bank interest	380
Excess income for year to accumulated fund		16 640		
		31 880		31 880

c *Step 3*

Westfield Recreation Centre
Balance sheet as at 31.12.1984

	Cost	Depreciation to date	Net	Total
Fixed assets	£	£	£	£
Buildings	78 000		78 000	
Equipment	12 000	1 200	10 800	
	90 000	1 200	88 800	88 800
Current assets	£		£	
Bar and restaurant stock	2 550			
Debtors	90			
Bank Current Account	610			
Bank Deposit Account (£3 800 + £8 500)	12 300			
			15 550	
Less Current liabilities				
Creditors	670			
Subscriptions in advance	110		780	
Working capital				14 770
TOTAL NET ASSETS				103 570
Financed by:				
Accumulated fund	78 110			
Add Excess income for year	16 640			
Add Donations received*	4 500			
	99 250			
Life memberships	4 320			
CAPITAL EMPLOYED				103 570

* Donations, unless for very small amounts, are regarded as capital receipts and added to accumulated fund. They are not generated by the activities of the club.

Notes

1. Bar and restaurant

receipts		£48 000
Add Amount due at 31.12.84		90
		£48 090
Less Amount due at 1.1.84		150
Total sales		£47 940

2.

Dr.		Subscriptions Account (ordinary members)				Cr.
1984		£	1984			£
1 Jan.	Balance b/d	130	31 Dec.	Bank		17 600
31 Dec.	Balance c/d (prepaid)	110				
	Income and Expenditure Account	17 360				
		17 600				17 600
			31 Dec.	Balance b/d		110

3.

Dr.		Life Membership Subscriptions Account				Cr.
1984		£	1984			£
31 Dec.	Income and Expenditure Account	480	1 Jan.	Balance b/d		4 200
	Balance c/d	4 320		Bank		600
		4 800				4 800
			31 Dec.	Balance b/d		4 320

4.

	£
Sundry expenses	
Payments	13 230
Less Amount due 1.1.84 (secretary)	60
Income and Expenditure Account	13 170

5.

	£
Depreciation of equipment	
Value at 1.1.1984	9 800
Add Equipment purchased	2 400
	12 200
Less Sale of equipment	200
	12 000
Value at 31.12.1984	10 800
Depreciation for year	1 200

Exercises Set 23

1 The Old Racquet Tennis Club had a balance at the bank of £900 on 1 January 19–1. During the year the club received and paid the following amounts:

Receipts: Members' subscriptions, £2 000; Sale of refreshments, £680; Sale of raffle tickets, £300; Sale of club badges, £230; Competition fees, £370.

Payments: Hire of hall, £520; Postage, £50; Stationery, £100; Cost of refreshments, £420; New tennis racquets, £250; Club emblems, £150; Competition prizes, £320.

Prepare the Receipts and Payments Account of the club for the year 19–1.

402   Accounts of non-commercial organisations

2   The Merry Widows' Association had the following assets and liabilities at 1 January 19–1:

Premises, £1 000; Furniture and fittings, £2 000; Stock of library books, £1 500; Cash at bank, £1 800; Subscriptions due from members, £300; Wages due to caretaker, £100.

During the year the following transactions took place:

Payments: Electricity, £450; Printing and stationery, £250; Purchase of new books for library, £500; Caretaker's wages, £5 100; Rates, £250; Annual subscription to National Widows' Association, £100.

Receipts: Members' subscriptions, £9 000; Profit on a raffle, £200.

At 31 December 19–1 the treasurer pointed out that:
(a) The figure for subscriptions included those in arrears at 1 January and subscriptions for 19–2 amounting to £450.
(b) The November/December electricity bill, £120, was still unpaid.

a   Calculate the accumulated fund at 1 January 19–1.
b   Prepare Receipts and Payments Account for the year 19–1.
c   Prepare Income and Expenditure Account for the year ended 31 December 19–1 and a balance sheet at that date.

3   The following is the balance sheet of the Piccadilly Dramatic Society at 31 December 19–3:

19–3	£	19–3	£
Accumulated fund	17 650	Stage equipment	10 500
Royalties due	100	Musical instruments	6 000
Subscriptions paid in advance	250	Subscriptions due	500
		Cash at bank	1 000
	18 000		18 000

The Receipts and Payments Account for the year 19–4 read:

Dr. Receipts		Payments	Cr.
19–4	£	19–4	£
Balance 1 January 19–4	1 000	Hire of costumes	1 040
Members' subscriptions	3 000	Royalties	620
Proceeds of raffle	2 500	Cost of new lighting	
Performance receipts	7 200	system for stage	4 400
Sale of old piano	550	Refreshments	500
Cash award at drama festival	250	Travelling expenses	950
		Sundry expenses	1 200
		Balance at 31 December 19–4	5 790
	14 500		14 500

The treasurer supplied the following additional information:
(a) Subscriptions in arrear at 31 December 19–4 amounted to £450 while subscriptions in advance at the same date were £550.
(b) Royalties in respect of a December performance, £150, were still unpaid at 31 December.
(c) The society's practice is to write off depreciation at a rate of 20 per cent on the

book value of stage equipment and 10 per cent on the book value of musical equipment at the end of each year.

Prepare an Income and Expenditure Account for the year ended 31 December 19–4 and a balance sheet at that date.

4 The West British Sports Club had the following assets and liabilities at 1 January 19–4:

Clubhouse, £15 000; Furniture and fittings, £3 200; Equipment, £680; Bank Deposit Account, £2 000; Subscriptions in arrears, £30; Subscriptions in advance, £20.

The following is a summary of the cash book for the year ended 31 December 19–4:

Dr.		Cr.	
19–4	£	19–4	£
Balance at 1 January 19–4:		Groundsman's wages	6 000
Cash	50	Cost of coffee mornings, etc.	350
Bank (Current Account)	1 000	Match expenses	920
Subscriptions:		Purchase of stop-watch	120
19–4	1 800	Postage and telephone	140
19–5	40	Printing and stationery	230
Donations	1 500	Bank charges	20
Gate receipts	2 800	Honoraria to officials	200
Sale of tickets for coffee		Transfer to Deposit Account	1 000
mornings, etc.	3 300	Insurance premiums	250
		Balance at 31 December:	
		Cash	50
		Bank (Current Account)	1 210
	10 490		10 490

The treasurer supplied further information as follows:
(a) During the year interest amounting to £70 has been credited to the Deposit Account at the bank.
(b) Subscriptions in arrears at 31 December 19–4 amounted to £60.
(c) Furniture and fittings are to be depreciated by 10 per cent and equipment (including additions) by 25 per cent.
(d) Insurance paid in advance at 31 December 19–4 amounted to £40.

Prepare the Income and Expenditure Account for the year ended 31 December 19–4 and the balance sheet at that date.

5 The following Receipts and Payments Account was presented by the treasurer of the Hawthorn Golf Club for the year ended 31 December 19–4:

Dr.	Receipts			Payments	Cr.
19–4		£	19–4		£
1 Jan.	Cash in hand	500	31 Dec.	Groundsmen's wages	26 500
	Cash at bank:			Secretary's expenses	750
	Current Account	2 500		Rent	3 600
	Deposit Account	6 000		Repairs to machinery	1 200
31 Dec.	Green fees	17 800		Purchase of new tractor	25 900
	Catering receipts	5 200		Competition prizes	7 200
	Interest on Deposit Account	180		Cost of catering	5 900
	Competition fees	7 800		Cash in hand	1 430
	Sale of old tractor	2 500		Cash at bank:	
	Subscriptions	37 000		Current Account	4 500
				Deposit Account	2 500
		79 480			79 480

The treasurer informed you that:

		1.1.19–4	31.12.19–4
		£	£
(a)	Subscriptions due	3 000	4 000
(b)	Subscriptions paid in advance	500	1 500
(c)	Wages outstanding	700	1 250
(d)	Estimated value of machinery	5 800	25 200

(e) Interest on Deposit Account, £140, for half year ended 31 December 19–4 was not credited by the bank until 5 January 19–5.

Prepare:
a a statement showing the accumulated fund at 1 January 19–4
b the Income and Expenditure Account for the year ended 31 December 19–4 and a balance sheet at that date.

6 The following figures were taken from the records of the Young Lions' Social Club for the year 19–5:

All receipts and payments are passed through the club's bank account.

Receipts		Payments	
	£		£
Members' subscriptions	27 500	Supplies for bar	22 000
Bar receipts	37 250	Barman's wages	8 500
Sundry receipts	1 000	Cleaner's wages	4 700
		Rates	2 400
		Purchase of new seating for bar	9 000
		Rent	3 500
		Repairs to club premises	800

The assets and liabilities of the club on 1 January 19–5 were: Cash at bank, £5 250; Freehold premises, £80 000; Furniture and fittings, £3 500; Bar stock, £8 000;

Subscriptions due for previous year, £500; Wages due, £250; Subscriptions in advance, £350.

At 31 December 19–5:
(a) Bar stock amounted to £9 500.
(b) Estimated depreciation of furniture and fittings (including additions), £1 250.
(c) Rates prepaid, £600.
(d) Subscriptions: due, £70; in advance, £450.
(e) Owing to brewery, £2 250.

Show:
a   accumulated fund at 1 January 19–5
b   Bar Trading Account
c   Income and Expenditure Account for year ended 31 December 19–5 and a balance sheet at that date.

7 This is the Receipts and Payments Account of the Old Soldiers' Social Club for the year ended 31 December 19–5:

Dr.	*Receipts*			*Payments*	Cr.
19–5		£	19–5		£
Bank balance 1 January 19–5		2 000	Telephone		580
Members' subscriptions		9 500	Steward's wages		7 500
Sales of drink		22 000	Light and heat		1 300
Billiard room receipts		2 300	Payments to suppliers		
Sale of bar fittings		250	for bar		19 000
			Cleaning		1 100
			Rates (1.4.19–5 to 30.9.19–5)		840
			Rates (1.10.19–5 to 31.3.19–6)		840
			New bar fittings		1 360
			Bank balance, 31 December		3 530
		36 050			36 050

The following facts are ascertained:
(a) The £19 000 paid to suppliers for bar during 19–5 included an amount of £750 due from 19–4.
(b) At 31 December 19–5 outstanding bills for drinks supplied to members amounted to £2 000.
(c) £150 of telephone charges relate to 19–4; £180 was due at 31 December 19–5.
(d) Rates for period 1.1.19–5 to 31.3.19–5 were paid in 19–4, £350.
(e) The amount received for members' subscriptions included £850 due from previous year; at 31 December 19–5 subscriptions outstanding were £550.
(f) Bar stock, 1 January 19–5, £5 000; 31 December 19–5, £7 500.
(g) Value of fixtures and fittings was £3 810 at 31 December as compared to £3 000 at 1 January.
(h) One-fifth of the steward's wages are to be charged to the bar.

Prepare:
a   Bar Trading Account for year ended 31 December 19–5
b   Income and Expenditure Account for the same period and a balance sheet at 31 December 19–5.

8 The following Receipts and Payments Account was prepared by the treasurer of the Greencourt Tennis Club for the year ended 31 December 1985:

Dr. Receipts			Payments	Cr.
1985		£	1985	£
1 Jan. Cash in hand		200	31 Dec. Groundsman's wages	2 300
Cash in bank:			Purchase of mowing	
Deposit Account	4 460		machine	3 000
Current Account	1 200		Rent	500
31 Dec. Interest on deposit			Cost of teas	500
to 30 June 1985		60	Travelling expenses	800
Subscriptions		5 200	Secretary's expenses	560
Receipts from teas		600	Repairs to machinery	
Contributions to			and equipment	1 000
travelling expenses		200	Cash in hand	500
Sale of equipment		160	Cash in bank:	
Net proceeds of socials		1 560	Deposit Account	2 180
			Current Account	2 300
		13 640		13 640

The honorary treasurer informed you of the following:

	1 Jan. 1985	31 Dec. 1985
	£	£
1. Subscriptions unpaid	300	200
2. Secretarial expenses outstanding	200	160
3. Estimated value of equipment	1 600	3 500

4. The groundsman is to receive a bonus of £1 100 in respect of the year 1985.
5. Interest on Deposit Account for six months ended 31 December 1985 was not credited until 2 January 1986, £120.

You are required to draw up:
a a computation showing the capital of the club on 1 January 1985
b an Income and Expenditure Account for the year ended 1985 and a balance sheet on that date.

9 The Downshire Social Club was formed on 1 January 1985. The following is the Receipts and Payments Account of the club for the year ended 31 December 1985:

Dr. Receipts			Payments	Cr.
		£		£
Subscriptions:			Purchase of premises	12 000
1985	£9 500		Purchase of bar and coffee	
1986	£300	9 800	supplies	8 000
Bar and coffee sales		12 000	Rates	3 000
Sale of raffle tickets		3 000	Raffle prizes	1 500
Donations		8 000	Heat and light	2 000
Prize bond prize		10 000	Cleaning	500
			Purchase of van (1.7.85)	8 000
			Purchase of prize bonds	250
			Dance expenses	3 000
			Outings expenses	2 500
			Balance at bank	
			31 December 1985	2 050
		42 800		42 800

The following information is relevant:
(a) At 31 December 1985 bar stock amounted to £900 and amounts owing to bar suppliers amounted to £500.
(b) Subscriptions due but not paid amounted to £250 at 31 December 1985.
(c) Cleaning expenses due amounted to £50 at 31 December 1985.
(d) Depreciation of the motor van is to be provided at 25 per cent of cost, per annum.

You are required to prepare an Income and Expenditure Account for the club for the year ended 31 December 1985 and a balance sheet as on that date.

10 The following cash summary was submitted by the treasurer to the committee of Helping Hands Social Club for year ended 31 October 19–5:

Dr.			Cr.
	£		£
Opening balances:		Wages and National	
Cash in hand	130	Insurance	7 720
Bank Current Account	6 380	Rent, rates and insurance	1 930
Bank Deposit Account	10 000	Repairs and renewals	1 380
Annual subscriptions	1 380	Mini-bus expenses	5 020
Sales of chocolates,		Annual outing expenses	960
papers, etc.	8 380	Purchases of chocolates, etc.	7 780
Bank deposit interest	400	Sundry expenses	950
Grant from government	12 000	Closing balances:	
Sundry receipts	320	Bank Current Account	1 130
Annual outing collection	880	Bank Deposit Account	13 000
	39 870		39 870

It is desired to obtain a larger government grant for running expenses but in order to do this an Income and Expenditure Account and balance sheet must be submitted.

The following data are available:

	31 Oct. 19–4	31 Oct. 19–5
	£	£
Mini-bus at cost	10 000	10 000
Stock of chocolates, etc. at cost	630	580
Annual subscriptions unpaid	90	140
Rent, rates and insurance paid in advance	1 030	910
Creditors for chocolates, etc.	510	480
Mini-bus expenses unpaid	180	590

The mini-bus was purchased on 31 August 19–4 and its market value on 31 October 19–5 was £7 200. Depreciation should be provided for accordingly.

You are required to prepare:
a a statement showing the capital of the club on 31 October 19–4
b Income and Expenditure Account for the year ended 31 October 19–5 and a balance sheet as on that date.

11 The following is a summary of the cash book of the Swanton Rugby Club for the year ended 30 November 19–3:

Dr. Receipts	£	Payments	Cr. £
Balance at bank (1 Dec. 19–2)	800	Equipment purchased	900
Annual outing	1 300	Captain's and secretary's	
Gate receipts	2 600	expenses	1 400
Members' subscriptions		Refreshments for visiting	
19–2/19–3	1 800	teams	1 200
19–3/19–4	300	Annual outing	950
		Printing and stationery	200
		Affiliation fees	250
		Balance 30 November 19–3	
		at bank	1 900
	6 800		6 800

The following information is available:

(a) On 1 December 19–2 the club's equipment was shown in the books at £1 200. Depreciation is to be provided at 20 per cent on all equipment in hand at 30.11.19–3.

(b) Subscriptions due to the club at 30 November 19–2: 19–1/19–2 £40
Subscriptions due to the club at 30 November 19–3: 19–1/19–2 £40
19–2/19–3 £20

(c) Amounts owing by the club:

	30.11.19–2 £	30.11.19–3 £
Printing and stationery	70	110
Captains' expenses	nil	80
Affiliation fees	120	nil

Prepare:
a the club's Income and Expenditure Account for the year ended 30.11.19–3
b the club's balance sheet as at 30.11.19–3.

*12 The treasurer of Hilltop Golf Club has submitted the following Receipts and Payments Account for the year ended 31 December 1985:

Dr. Receipts	£	Payments	Cr. £
Balance 1 January 1985	8 400	Social functions	8 750
Members' subscriptions	52 800	Repairs and renewals	2 150
Receipts from social		Light and heat	1 080
functions	9 600	Rent and rates	2 750
Sale of motor mower	2 400	Telephone	850
Bank deposit interest	600	New motor mower	6 000
Bar receipts	64 000	Extension to bar	12 000
Local council grant	5 000	Salaries and wages	44 600
		Secretary's expenses	600
		Bar purchases	41 000
		Sundry expenses	1 200
		Balance c/d:	
		Bank £21 180	
		Cash £640	
			21 820
	142 800		142 800

The treasurer has also supplied the following information:
1. Subscriptions received included £1 200 which had been in arrears on 31 December 1984 and £1 600 for year commencing 1 January 1986.
2. The motor mower sold had been purchased by the club on 1 January 1983 for £5 000. Provision for depreciation was at the rate of 20 per cent per annum on cost.
3. Accrued expenses:

	31 Dec. 1984 £	31 Dec. 1985 £
Light and heat	180	300
Rent and rates	250	500
Telephone	150	200
Salaries and wages	240	390
Bar creditors	6 500	7 700

4. Depreciation is to be charged on the original cost of assets appearing in the books on 31 December 1984 as follows:
   Fixtures and fittings 10%
   Machinery 20%
5. The valuation of bar stock on 31 December 1985 at cost was £4 620.
6. The following balances were shown in the club's books on 31 December 1984:

	£
Land at cost	48 000
Buildings at cost	33 000
Machinery at cost	25 000
Machinery, provision for depreciation	10 000
Fixtures and fittings at cost	22 000
Fixtures and fittings, provision for depreciation	8 600

* This question is more difficult than the others in this section and might be omitted at first reading.

	£
Subscriptions in arrears (including £200 due from lapsed member who had emigrated)	1 400
Subscriptions in advance	600
Bar stock	7 220
Bar creditors	6 500
Accrued expenses	820
Balance at bank	7 960
Cash in hand	440
Accumulated fund	118 500

You are required to prepare an Income and Expenditure Account for the year ended 31 December 1985 and a balance sheet on that date.

13 The treasurer of the Downtown Billiards Club has given you the following account of its activities during the year ended 30 June 19–4:

Dr. Receipts	£	Payments	Cr. £
Bank balance at 1 July 19–3 (including £75 received during the year ended 30 June 19–3 on the prize fund investment)	3 900	Additional billiard table with accessories bought 1 July 19–3	3 000
		Repairs to billiard tables	500
		Purchases for bar	36 800
		Stewards' wages and expenses	4 000
Annual subscriptions (including £20 relating to previous year)	3 400	Rates	1 400
		Lighting and heating	720
Life membership subscriptions (5 at £160)	800	Cleaning and laundry	1 380
		Sundry expenses	800
Sundry lettings	1 800	Prizes awarded for previous year from income available on 1 July 19–3	750
Bar receipts	45 900		
Receipts from billiards	2 750		
Gifts from members	35 000	Repayment of 5% mortgage on 30 June 19–4 with interest for two years	44 000
Income from £1 500 5% savings bonds set aside for a prize fund	750	Bank balance at 30 June 19–4	950
	94 300		94 300

You are also given the following information:
(a) The freehold building, owned and occupied by the club, was purchased for £60 000 many years ago.
(b) Six years ago the club acquired six billiard tables for which they paid £12 000 and it is considered that the billiard tables have a life of twelve years and will have no value at the end of that period.
(c) The bar stock at 1 July 19–3 was £1 500 and at 30 June 19–4 was £1 800.
(d) Annual subscriptions outstanding from members at 30 June 19–4 amounted to £100.
(e) On 1 July 19–3 there were twenty-five life members who had paid subscriptions of £160 each.

You are required to:
a briefly advise the club committee on how they should treat the subscriptions of life members
b set out your computation of the balance in the club's Capital Account (accumulated fund) on 1 July 19–3
c prepare an Income and Expenditure Account for the year ended 30 June 19–4
d prepare a balance sheet at that date.

14 The treasurer of the Mells Social Club has extracted the following information from records that he has kept for the year to 31 July 1984:
   1. Subscriptions received in cash from members during the year amounted to £9 700. At 31 July 1983, members had paid subscriptions in advance totalling £200 and £400 was in arrears. At 31 July 1984, £600 had been paid in cash for subscriptions in advance, whilst £300 of subscriptions was in arrears.
   2. The club had sent four cheques to the electricity board during the year, amounting to £2 400. However, at 31 July 1983, the club owed the board £700 and at 31 July 1984 there was an outstanding invoice for £500.
   3. Bar purchases amounted to £5 000 paid in cash during the year and £64 000 paid for by cheque. At 31 July 1983 £1 000 was owing to the brewery for bar purchases and £1 600 was owing at 31 July 1984. Bar stocks were valued at £4 500 at 31 July 1983 and at £6 600 at 31 July 1984.
   4. Cash sales at the bar were banked weekly and no cash payments were made out of them. For the year to 31 July 1984 the total amount banked was £101 270.
   5. Credit was very rarely allowed at the bar, but at 31 July 1983 the president owed £70 (which the club received on 31 August 1983), and at 31 July 1984 the new president owed £50.

Write up the following accounts in double-entry format for the Mells Social Club:
a Subscriptions; b Electricity; and c Bar Trading.
[*Association of Accounting Technicians, December 1984*]

15 The following is a summary of the receipts and payments for the year to 31 December 1983 of the Scott Social Club:

Receipts	£
Club subscriptions	17 000
Donations	1 500
Christmas dance	850
Bar takings	27 000
Payments	
Rates	900
General expenses	26 200
Bar purchases	18 500
Christmas dance expenses	150

Other relevant information at the beginning and end of the year is as follows:

	1 April 1982 £	31 March 1983 £
Subscriptions due	900	600
Subscriptions paid in advance	50	100
Rates owing	450	500
Bar stock	2 000	2 500
Club premises (cost £50 000)	20 000	18 000
Furniture (cost £10 000)	3 000	2 000
Bank and cash in hand	1 600	2 200

a Prepare the club's Bar Trading Account for the year to 31 March 1983.
b Prepare the club's Income and Expenditure Account for the year to 31 March 1983, and a balance sheet as at that date.
[*Association of Accounting Technicians, June 1983*]

16 As the accountant of the Swallow Bowling Club, you have been presented with the following information for the year to 30 September 1983:

Receipts	£	Payments	£
Cash in hand at 1.10.82	20	Club running expenses	770
Cash at bank at 1.10.82	1 200	Cost of refreshments	180
Subscriptions	2 050	Christmas dance expenses	500
Bar receipts	3 600	Bar purchases	1 750
Christmas dance ticket sales	650	Lawn mower	600
Refreshment sales	320	Cash in hand at 30.9.83	30
		Cash at bank at 30.9.83	4 010
	7 840		7 840

Notes

1. Subscriptions

	In arrears £	In advance £
At 1.10.82	100	50
At 30.9.83	200	75

2. Fixed assets

	At 1.10.82 £	At 30.9.83 £
Club premises at cost	50 000	50 000
Less Depreciation	35 000	37 500
	15 000	12 500

Depreciation is to be charged on the lawn mower at a rate of 15 per cent per annum on cost.

3. Bar stock at 30 September 1982 was valued at £150 and £200 at 30 September 1983.

4. Outstanding expenses

	At 1.10.82 £	At 30.9.83 £
Bar purchases	300	400
Club expenses	250	200

5. Rates paid in advance at 30 September 1982 and at 30 September 1983 amounted to £200 and £300 respectively.

Prepare the club's Income and Expenditure Account for the year to 30 September 1983, and a balance sheet as at that date.

[*Association of Accounting Technicians, December 1983*]

17 The following is the cash account of the Everard Social Club for the year to 31 December 1982:

	£		£
Balance at bank 1.1.82	450	Maintenance of premises	250
Subscriptions: 1981	50	Heat, light and power	700
1982	1 500	Bar purchases for resale	3 650
1983	75	Prizes for raffles	175
Receipts from raffles	270	Bar staff wages	800
Letting of club premises	200	Glasses and sundry bar costs	150
Bar takings	7 250	Printing, stationery and postage	175
		Purchase of new fixtures and fittings	850
		Transfer to deposit account	2 500
		Balance at bank 31.12.82	545
	9 795		9 795

You are given the following information:
(a) At 1 January 1982 the club owned, at the stated valuations:

	£
Premises	10 000
Cash in Deposit Account	1 000
Bar stock	1 250
Fixtures and fittings	2 250

(b) At 1 January 1982 the club had the following liabilities:

	£
Subscriptions for 1982 paid in advance	45
Bar purchases for resale	180
Electricity	125

(c) At 31 December 1982 the club owed £155 for electricity, £25 for stationery and £450 for bar purchases.
(d) For accounts purposes, the club's premises are to be valued at £9 500, the fixtures at £2 450 and bar stock at £950 on 31 December 1982.
(e) No credit is taken in respect of subscriptions in arrears when preparing each year's accounts on the ground of prudence.
(f) During 1982 the interest earned on the deposit account was £225.

Required:
a the Income and Expenditure Account for the Everard Social Club for the year to 31 December 1982, clearly identifying the results from the bar and the raffle
b the balance sheet of the Everard Social Club as at 31 December 1982 showing clearly, where necessary, calculations of items contained therein.

[*Royal Society of Arts, II, March 1983*]

18 The treasurer of the Pendiff Tennis Club has prepared the following Receipts and Payments Account for the year ended 31 December 1984:

	£		£
Balance 1 January 1984	162	Rates	263
Subscriptions	3 260	Refreshments	510
Sale of after-match		Maintenance	1 357
refreshments	526	Purchase of equipment for	
Sale of dance tickets	564	sale to members	422
Sale of equipment to		Dance expenses	411
members	621	Secretary's expenses	250
		Match expenses	500
		Furniture	1 100
		Balance 31 December 1984	320
	5 133		5 133

The following information is also available:

	At 1 January 1984 £	At 31 December 1984 £
Furniture	2 000	2 790
Stock of equipment for sale to members	250	300
Accrued maintenance expenses	97	113
Prepaid rates	62	70
Subscriptions in advance	88	36
Freehold property	25 000	25 000

Required:
a the Income and Expenditure Account of the Pendiff Tennis Club for the year to 31 December 1984. The profit on the dance, refreshments, and the sale of equipment to members should be identified separately
b the club's balance sheet at 31 December 1984.

[*Royal Society of Arts, II, March 1985*]

19 The secretary of the Fleetfoot Athletic Club submitted the following Receipts and Payments Account to club members, covering the year to 31 December:

Receipts and Payments Account

Receipts	£	Payments	£
Balance from previous year	54	Wages	300
Entrance fees	32	Purchase of new equipment	64
Subscriptions:		Printing and stationery	78
Current year	440	Sundry expenses	16
In advance	48	Heat and light	38
Profit on dance	106	Insurance	68
Locker rents	24	Repairs	40
Interest on deposit	4	Balance carried down	104
	708		708

Subscriptions due for the current year but unpaid total £42.
Printing bills unpaid total £10.
There is £200 on deposit at the bank.
Equipment at cost at 31 December totalled £192.

You are required to prepare:
a an Income and Expenditure Account for the year to 31 December
b the balance sheet of the club at the commencement of the year and the balance sheet at 31 December.

[*Pitman, Intermediate*]

20 The Lonsdale Boxing Club had the following assets and liabilities at 1 January:

Premises £7 500, Furniture £1 170, Equipment £1 500, Cash at bank £390, Subscriptions still owing £45, Subscriptions paid in advance £20, Stock of refreshments £37.

The summary of the cash book for the year to 31 December was as follows:

			£		£
1 Jan.	Balance		390	Repairs to premises	28
31 Dec.	Subscription receipts		1 455	Repairs to equipment	40
	Sales of refreshments		1 800	Purchase of new equipment	1 150
	Sundry revenue		200	Cleaning	72
				Heating and lighting	212
				Advertising	60
				Purchase of refreshments	1 350
				Balance	933
			3 845		3 845

At 31 December the secretary reported the following:
(a) Stock of refreshments was valued at £75.
(b) There was an outstanding account for advertising of £21.
(c) Subscriptions paid in advance totalled £60.
(d) Subscriptions still due amounted to £30.
(e) Equipment including additions to be depreciated by 6 per cent.

You are required to prepare an Income and Expenditure Account for the year to 31 December and a balance sheet at that date.

[*Pitman, Intermediate*]

21 The honorary secretary of the Hanford Social Club kept a cash book in which he recorded the day-to-day transactions of the club. An analysis of the transactions for the year 1985 produced the following information:

	£
Subscriptions: 136 members @ £20 per annum	2 720
Entrance fees: new members 20 × £15	300
Life membership subscriptions: 20×£100	2 000
Members' loans to New Pavilion Fund	140
Gaming machine licence (1 year)	500
Hire of gaming machine (1 year)	200
Secretarial costs including honorarium	240
Telephone	85
Repairs and maintenance: pavilion	1 680
Gas and electricity	850
Fire insurance	60
Wages: part-time caretaker	600
Sundry expenses	190
Gaming machine income	1 500
Net proceeds: fund-raising efforts	720

The following balances existed in the accounts named at the dates stated:

	31.12.84 £	31.12.85 £
Stoke Suburban Building Society (5½% ordinary shares)	1 000	1 055
National Bank: Current Account	40	
New Pavilion Fund: loans from members	850	510
Post Office Investment Account	—	940
Life Membership Suspense Account	1 400	1 500
(Life membership subscriptions were treated as subscriptions for five years)		2 250

There were the following prepayments and accruals:

Members' subscriptions in arrears	200	
Members' subscriptions prepaid	40	180
Telephone Account, received 25.12.85, not paid	—	30
		15

Provide for one year's depreciation of £1 000 on the pavilion.

Prepare an Income and Expenditure Account for the Hanford Social Club for the year 1985.

Note. In a horizontal account income should be on the credit side.

[*London Chamber of Commerce and Industry, Intermediate, autumn 1986*]

24 Preparation of accounts from incomplete records

So far we have been examining accounts kept on proper double-entry principles. However, not all traders follow this procedure. Some omit entries completely (*incomplete records*), while others post only one side of the transaction to the ledger (*single entry*). These traders are many in number and are to be found mainly among small shopkeepers and manufacturers who run their own businesses.

These people are concerned mainly about:
1. how much they have in the bank and in cash;
2. how much is owing to them and by whom;
3. how much they owe suppliers for goods and, possibly, how much they owe for large items such as rent, rates and wages.

They will probably keep a cash book and debtors ledger.

They will have no records for:
1. capital
2. creditors
3. assets other than debtors
4. expenses
5. total sales or purchases.

The difficulty now arises as to how to find net profit from the incomplete figures at our disposal.

The answer is that (*a*) by using the figures given, and (*b*) through our knowledge of accounting, we try to find the missing figures necessary to ascertain the profit or loss made by the business. The more information at our disposal the more complete and accurate accounts we can prepare.

There are *three* main ways of finding a trader's net profit from incomplete records:
I By comparing capital at the end of a period with capital at the beginning of the period (*the net worth method*).
II By finding the missing figures necessary to prepare the final accounts by means of *Control Accounts*.
III By finding the missing figures by means of *mark-up or margin*. A balance sheet can always be added if assets and liabilities at the end of the period are known.

Method I: By comparing capitals (the net worth method)

If we are given sufficient information to calculate capitals at the beginning and end of a period, and the capital at the end is greater than the capital at the beginning, we can assume that the difference is net profit. This figure may have to be adjusted for:
1. non-business receipts (money brought into the business which it has not earned, e.g. capital introduced, sale of personal items by owner the proceeds of which are put into the Business Account)
2. non-business expenditure (e.g. drawing of cash or goods by owner).

A SIMPLE EXAMPLE

Philip Oakes has not kept a full set of books but makes the following information available for the year 19–1:

	1 Jan. 19–1 £	31 Dec. 19–1 £
Cash in hand	40	20
Cash at bank	600	800
Premises	12 000	12 000
Fixtures and fittings	2 000	2 000
Stock	2 500	3 500
Debtors	3 500	3 800
Creditors	8 000	5 700
Accruals	140	120

During the year he took £50 per week out of the business as pocket money. He lodged £2 000 which he won in prize bonds to the business Bank Account.

Calculate his net profit for the year.

SOLUTION

Step 1: Find capitals at beginning and end of year

Comparison of capitals

	1 Jan. 19–1 £	£	31 Dec. 19–1 £	£
Assets				
Cash in hand	40		20	
Cash at bank	600		800	
Premises	12 000		12 000	
Fixtures and fittings	2 000		2 000	
Stock	2 500		3 500	
Debtors	3 500		3 800	
TOTAL ASSETS		20 640		22 120
Less Liabilities				
Creditors	8 000		5 700	
Accruals	140		120	
TOTAL LIABILITIES		8 140		5 820
CAPITALS		12 500		16 300

Step 2: Adjust for transactions which took place that affect the profit

Statement of profit or loss for year

	£
Capital at 31 December 19–1	16 300
Less Capital at 1 January 19–1	12 500
Difference – Increase for year	3 800
Add Cash drawings of owner (£50 × 52)	2 600
(Profit would be greater if drawings were not made)	
	6 400
Less Capital introduced (prize bonds win)	2 000
(This money was not earned in the normal run of the business)	
Net profit for year	4 400

A More Difficult Example

The following information is given to you in respect of the business of A. Mugg, who has asked you to prepare a statement of profit or loss for the year ended 31 December 19–2.

(a) On 1 January 19–2 his assets and liabilities were:
Cash, £144; Bank, £10 420; Debtors, £18 480; Stock, £38 640; Loan from D. Lock, £16 000; Creditors, £9 800; Motor vans, £19 240; Fixtures and fittings, £6 800.
(b) During the year he had drawings of £24 300.
(c) During the year he sold his private care for £6 000 and paid it into the business Bank Account.
(d) At 31 December 19–2 his assets and liabilities were: Cash, £820; Bank, £16 460; Debtors, £25 000; Stock, £39 660; Motor vans, £25 200; Fixtures and fittings, £6 800; Creditors, £10 240; Loan from D. Lock, £12 000.
(e) You are required to provide depreciation on fixtures at 5 per cent and on motor vans at 10 per cent and a bad debts' provision of 10 per cent on the balances at 31 December 19–2.

Solution

Comparison of capitals

	1 Jan. 19–2		31 Dec. 19–2	
	£	£	£	£
Assets				
Cash	1 440		820	
Bank	10 420		16 460	
Debtors	18 480		25 000	
Stock	38 640		39 660	
Motor vans	19 240		25 200	
Fixtures and fittings	6 800		6 800	
TOTAL ASSETS		95 020		113 940
Less Liabilities				
Creditors	9 800		10 240	
Loan	16 000		12 000	
TOTAL LIABILITIES		25 800		22 240
CAPITALS		69 220		91 700

Statement of profit or loss for year

	£	£
Capital at 31.12.19–2		91 700
Less Capital at 1.1.19–2		69 220
Difference – increase for year		22 480
Add Cash drawings during year		24 300
		46 780
Less Capital introduced (sale of car)	6 000	
Depreciation – Fixtures and fittings	340	
Motor vans	2 520	
Provision for bad debts (10% of £25 000)	2 500	
		11 360
Net profit for year		35 420

Method II: Finding missing figures by using control accounts

To prepare Trading Account we need to know or calculate at least opening stock, purchases, sales and closing stock.

To prepare Profit and Loss Account we need to know or calculate at least gross profit and expenses of running the business.

The first step is to identify the figures that are missing and set about calculating them.

A SIMPLE EXAMPLE

Alan Dukes started business on 1 January 19–3, but failed to keep proper books of account. You are asked to prepare his Trading and Profit and Loss Account for the year ended 31 December 19–3 and a balance sheet at that date. He has kept a cash record which is summarised as follows:

Cash received and lodged in bank

	£
Capital paid in by Dukes on 1 January	68 000
Cash received from debtors during the year	78 800
Loan from P. Considine	20 000

Cheque payments

	£
Purchase of premises	60 000
Purchase of fixtures and fittings	17 400
Payments to creditors for goods	61 600
Wages and administration expenses	23 200
Sundry expenses	5 800

Additional information

Debtors at 31 December 19–3	11 200
Creditors	4 800
Stock	6 400

In order to prepare a Trading Account we need figures for purchases and sales; to find these figures we prepare Creditors Control and Debtors Control Accounts.

(Note that missing figures found will be indicated by an asterisk (*).)

Preparation of accounts from incomplete records

Dr.	Creditors Control Account			Cr.
19–3		19–3		£
31 Dec. Payments to creditors	61 600	1 Jan. Balance		Nil
Amount due to creditors	4 800	31 Dec. Credit purchases*		66 400
	66 400			66 400
		31 Dec. Balance b/d		4 800

Dr.	Debtors Control Account			Cr.
19–3	£	19–3		£
1 Jan. Balance	Nil	31 Dec. Payments from debtors		78 800
31 Dec. Credit sales*	90 000	Amounts due by debtors		11 200
	90 000			90 000
31 Dec. Balance b/d	11 200			

Now we can compile the Trading and Profit and Loss Account.

Alan Dukes
Trading and Profit and Loss Account
for year ended 31 December 19–3

Dr.			Cr.
	£		£
Purchases	66 400	Sales	90 000
Less Closing stock	6 400		
Cost of sales	60 000		
Gross profit c/d	30 000		
	90 000		90 000
Wages and administration expenses	23 200	Gross profit b/d	30 000
Sundry expenses	5 800		
Net profit	1 000		
	30 000		30 000

Balance sheet

The only figure missing here is balance at bank. If we add up the receipts, £166 800, and payments, £168 000, there must be a bank overdraft of £1 200.

Alan Dukes
Balance sheet as at 31 December 19–3

	Cost	Depreciation to date	Net	Total
	£	£	£	£
Fixed assets				
Premises	60 000		60 000	
Fixtures and fittings	17 400		17 400	
	77 400		77 400	77 400
	£	£	£	
Add Current assets				
Stock	6 400			
Debtors	11 200			
		17 600		
Less Current liabilities				
Creditors	4 800			
Bank overdraft	1 200			
		6 000		
Working capital				11 600
TOTAL NET ASSETS				89 000
Financed by:				
Capital				
Balance at 1.1.19–3		68 000		
Add Net profit		1 000		
			69 000	
Loan – P. Considine			20 000	
CAPITAL EMPLOYED				89 000

A MORE DIFFICULT EXAMPLE

T. Doyle has not kept a full set of books. The following is a summary of his cash book for 19–4:

Dr.   Cr.

	£		£
Cash in hand, 1 January	100	Balance due to bank, 1 January	3 000
Cash sales	30 000	Cash purchases	22 000
Cash received from trade debtors	108 000	Payments to trade creditors	70 000
		Rent and rates	2 200
		Salaries	16 000
		Light and heat	2 000
		Drawings	8 000
		Sundry expenses	6 800
		Cash in hand, 31 December	1 000
		Balance at bank, 31 December	7 100
	138 100		138 100

422 Preparation of accounts from incomplete records

The following information is also available:

	1 Jan. 19–4 £	31 Dec. 19–4 £
Stock	25 000	25 200
Trade debtors	22 000	26 000
Trade creditors	16 000	17 500
Rates prepaid	200	300
Rent due	300	300
Fixtures and fittings	20 000	20 000
Motor van	8 000	8 000

Prepare a Trading and Profit and Loss Account for the year ended 31 December 19–4, taking the following matters into account:
1. Make a provision for bad debts, £1 000.
2. Depreciate fixtures and fittings by 10 per cent and motor van by 20 per cent.
3. Discounts allowed to trade debtors for the year were estimated at £3 000 and discounts received from trade creditors at £2 000.
4. The proprietor had withdrawn stock for his own use, £1 500.

SOLUTION

Step 1: Find opening capital

This can be done simply by listing the assets and liabilities at 1 January and totalling them. The difference between them is the opening capital.

Capital at 1 January 19–4

Assets	£	£
Cash	100	
Stock	25 000	
Debtors	22 000	
Rates prepaid	200	
Fixtures and fittings	20 000	
Motor van	8 000	
Total		75 300
Less Liabilities		
Bank overdraft	3 000	
Creditors	16 000	
Rent due	300	
Total		19 300
Capital at 1.1.19–4		56 000

Step 2: Find credit purchases

Dr.		Creditors Control Account			Cr.
19–4		£	19–4		£
31 Dec.	Payments to trade creditors	70 000	1 Jan.	Balance b/d	16 000
	Discounts received	2 000	31 Dec.	Credit purchases for year*	73 500
	Balance c/d	17 500			
		89 500			89 500
				Balance b/d	17 500

Therefore credit purchases = £73 500

Step 3

Add cash purchases   £22 000

Therefore total purchases = £95 500

Step 4: Find credit sales

Dr.		Debtors Control Account			Cr.
19–4		£	19–4		£
1 Jan.	Balance b/d	22 000	31 Dec.	Cash received from trade debtors	108 000
31 Dec.	Credit sales for year*	115 000		Discount allowed to trade debtors	3 000
				Balance c/d	26 000
		137 000			137 000
	Balance b/d	26 000			

Therefore credit sales = £115 000

Step 5

Add Cash sales   £30 000

Therefore total sales = £145 000

Step 6: Adjust for drawing of goods by proprietor

Purchases must be adjusted for goods taken by proprietor. If ledger accounts had been kept the journal entry would be:
Debit Drawings Account
Credit Purchases Account.

So correct figure for purchases for the Trading Account = £95 500 – £1 500 = £94 000.

Step 7: Prepare Trading and Profit and Loss Account and balance sheet

Trading and Profit and Loss Account for year ended 31 December 19–4

Dr.		£		Cr. £
Stock at 1 January 19–4		25 000	Sales	145 000
Add Purchases		94 000		
		119 000		
Less Stock at 31 Dec. 19–4		25 200		
Cost of sales		93 800		
Gross profit c/d		51 200		
		145 000		145 000
	£			
Rent and rates	2 200		Gross profit b/d	51 200
Add Rates prepaid			Discount received	2 000
1 January	200			
Add Rent due				
31 December	300			
	2 700			
Less Rates prepaid				
31 December	300			
Less Rent due				
1 January	300			
		2 100		
Salaries		16 000		
Light and heat		2 000		
Sundry expenses		6 800		
Bad debts provision		1 000		
Depreciation:				
Fixtures and fittings	2 000			
Motor van	1 600			
		3 600		
Discount allowed		3 000		
Net profit		18 700		
		53 200		53 200

T. Doyle
Balance sheet as at 31 December 19-4

	Cost	Depreciation to date	Net	Total
Fixed assets	£	£	£	£
Fixtures and fittings	20 000	2 000	18 000	
Motor van	8 000	1 600	6 400	
	28 000	3 600	24 400	24 400
	£	£	£	
Current assets				
Stock		25 200		
Debtors	26 000			
Less Provision for bad debts	1 000	25 000		
Bank		7 100		
Cash		1 000		
Rates prepaid		300		
			58 600	
Less Current liabilities				
Creditors		17 500		
Rent due		300		
			17 800	
Working capital				40 800
TOTAL NET ASSETS				65 200
Financed by:				
Capital				
Balance at 1.1.19-4	56 000			
Add Net profit	18 700			
	74 700			
Less Drawings				
(£8 000 + £1 500)	9 500			
CAPITAL EMPLOYED				65 200

Method III: Finding missing figures by means of mark-up or margin

The problem here is to deduce one or more of Trading or Profit and Loss Account figures by using a knowledge of the relationships between the various figures, given the fraction or percentage mark-up or margin.

Mark-up is the profit expressed as a fraction or percentage of *cost of goods sold (cost)*, e.g. mark-up of 25 per cent on cost.

Margin is the profit expressed as a fraction of the *selling price of the goods (sales)*, e.g. margin is 20 per cent of selling price.

So if we know the cost of goods sold and the mark-up, we can find the sales figure; or if we know the sales figures and the margin we can find the cost of sales.

Put another way,
     Cost of sales + Mark-up = Sales
or   Sales − Mark-up = Cost of sales
again, Cost of sales + Margin = Sales
or   Sales − Margin = Cost of sales.

Other relationships we should know:
1. Net profit = Gross profit − Expenses
   or
   Net profit + Expenses = Gross profit
2. Opening stock + Purchases − Closing stock = Cost of sales
   or
   Cost of sales + Closing stock − Purchases = Opening stock
3. Sales − Gross profit = Cost of sales.

Note

When answering questions of this nature, draft skeleton accounts, fill in the information given and deduce the other necessary figures.

A SIMPLE EXAMPLE

	£
Stock 1.1.19–1	8 000
Purchases	60 000
Stock 31.12.19–1	6 000
Mark-up 20%	

Prepare Trading Account.

Note. Missing figures indicated by a question mark (?).

Dr.		(Skeleton) Trading Account			Cr.
19–1		£	19–1		£
	Opening stock	8 000		Sales	?
	Add Purchases	60 000			
		68 000			
	Less Closing stock	6 000			
	Cost of sales	62 000			
	Gross profit	?			

Reasoning:
Gross profit = Mark-up = 20 per cent of Cost of sales = 20 per cent of £62 000 = £12 400
Cost of sales + Mark-up = Sales
Therefore £62 000 + £12 400 = £74 400 = Sales

Finding missing figures by means of mark-up or margin

Dr.		Trading Account			Cr.
19–1		£	19–1		£
	Opening stock	8 000		Sales	74 400
	Add Purchases	60 000			
		68 000			
	Less Closing stock	6 000			
	Cost of sales	62 000			
	Gross profit	12 400			
		74 400			74 400

ANOTHER EXAMPLE

	£
Stock 1.1.19–2	16 000
Sales	100 000
Stock 31.12.19–2	11 000

A uniform margin of 25 per cent is used in the business.

Prepare Trading Account.

Dr.	(Skeleton) Trading Account			Cr.
	£			£
Opening stock	16 000	Sales		100 000
Add Purchases	?			
Less Closing stock	11 000			
Cost of goods sold	?			
Gross profit	?			
	100 000			100 000

Reasoning:
1. Margin = Gross profit = 25 per cent of sales = 25 per cent of £100 000 = £25 000
2. Sales – Gross profit = Cost of goods sold = £100 000 – £25 000 = £75 000
3. Cost of goods sold + Closing stock = Opening stock + Purchases = £75 000 + £11 000 = £86 000
4. Opening stock + Purchases = £86 000
   £16 000 + Purchases = £86 000
   Therefore purchases = £70 000

Dr.	Trading Account			Cr.
	£			£
Opening stock	16 000	Sales		100 000
Add Purchases	70 000			
	86 000			
Less Closing stock	11 000			
Cost of sales	75 000			
Gross profit	25 000			
	100 000			100 000

A More Difficult Example

	£
Net profit for year	150 000
Margin 25% (on sales)	
Total selling expenses	10 000
Opening stock	12 000
Closing stock	14 000

Prepare Trading and Profit and Loss Account for year.

Dr.	(Skeleton) Trading and Profit and Loss Account			Cr.
	£			£
Opening stock	12 000	Sales		?
Add Purchases	?			
Less Closing stock	14 000			
Cost of sales	?			
Gross profit	?			
	?			?
Selling expenses	10 000	Gross profit b/d		?
Net profit	150 000			
	160 000			160 000

Steps

1. Find gross profit
   Gross profit = Net profit + Selling expenses = £150 000 + £10 000 = £160 000
2. Margin = Gross profit = 25 per cent of Sales
   Therefore Sales = £160 000 × 4 = £640 000
3. Cost of sales = Sales − Gross profit = £640 000 − £160 000 = £480 000
4. Cost of sales + Closing stock = Opening stock + Purchases
   £480 000 + £14 000 = £494 000 = £12 000 + Purchases
   Therefore Purchases = £482 000

Dr.	Trading and Profit and Loss Account			Cr.
	£			£
Opening stock	12 000	Sales		640 000
Add Purchases	482 000			
	494 000			
Less Closing stock	14 000			
Cost of sales	480 000			
Gross profit c/d	160 000			
	640 000			640 000
Selling expenses	10 000	Gross profit b/d		160 000
Net profit	150 000			
	160 000			160 000

Stock damaged by fire or flood

Another use for the technique learned in preparing accounts from incomplete records is that of finding the value of stock which has been destroyed by fire or flood.

The firms must use all available records. If all the financial books have been destroyed then the previous year's figures must be used as a guide, together with statements from suppliers and manufacturers. Copies of bank statements can also be obtained from the bank. The usual mark-up or margin on goods will also be known. Where some records are available the easiest way of finding the value of closing stock is to do a skeleton Trading Account, using all the figures given to find the figures missing either by use of control accounts or by deduction, using one's knowledge of the relationship between the figures in the Trading Account.

EXAMPLE

A. Spark's stock of goods was destroyed by fire on 31 July 19–1. The amount salvaged was estimated to be worth £700. You are asked to prepare his fire insurance claim.

The following figures were also available:

	At 1.1.19–1		At 31.7.19–1
	£	£	£
Stock at cost	4 800		
Trade debtors	15 000		13 500
Trade creditors	12 600		4 500
Discounts allowed		2 500	
Discounts received		1 100	
Cheques received from debtors		16 200	
Cash sales		1 800	
Cash purchases		4 400	
Cheques paid to creditors		14 900	
Gross profit on sales		30%	

Step 1: Prepare Debtor Ledger Control Account – to Find Credit Sales*

Debtors Ledger Control Account

19–1		£	19–1		£
1 Jan.	Balance b/d	15 000	31 July	Cheques from debtors	16 200
31 July*	Credit sales	17 200		Discount allowed	2 500
				Balance c/d	13 500
		32 200			32 200
31 July	Balance b/d	13 500			

Step 2

	£
Credit sales	17 200
Add Cash sales	1 800
Total sales	19 000

Step 3: Prepare Creditors Ledger Control Account – to Find Credit Purchases*

Creditors Ledger Control Account

19–1		£	19–1		£
1 July	Cheques paid to creditors	14 900	1 Jan.	Balance b/d	12 600
	Discount received	1 100	31 July*	Credit purchases	7 900
	Balance c/d	4 500			
		20 500			20 500
			31 July	Balance b/d	4 500

Step 4

	£
Credit purchases	7 900
Add Cash purchases	4 400
Total purchases	12 300

Step 5: Prepare Trading Control Account to Find Closing Stock

Trading Account

	£		£
Stock at 1.1.19–1	4 800	Sales	19 000
Add Purchases	12 300		
	17 100		
Less Stock at 31.7.19–1	3 800		
Cost of sales	13 300		
Gross profit (30% of Sales)	5 700		
	19 000		19 000

∴ Closing stock	= 3 800
Deduct Value of salvaged stock	700
Insurance claim	3 100

Single-entry conversion to double entry

Once we have prepared a balance sheet at the end of the financial period, it is a simple matter to convert the single-entry system to double entry.

Procedure

1. Verify as far as possible all assets and liabilities as shown on the balance sheet.
2. Open ledger accounts for each asset and liability. Debit all assets; credit all liabilities.
3. Set up appropriate subsidiary books for future use.
4. Apply double-entry principle of posting for all future transactions.

Exercises Set 24

1. On 1 January 19–1 J. Stokes commenced business with a capital of £100 000. On 31 December 19–1 his assets and liabilities were as follows:

	£		£
Premises	50 000	Cash at bank	8 000
Fixtures and fittings	12 500	Rates prepaid	1 000
Stock	27 000	Rent due	800
Trade debtors	28 000		
Trade creditors	14 500		

Prepare a statement showing his profit or loss for the year.

2. F. Barr, a sole trader, who does not keep proper books of account, supplies you with the following information and asks you to prepare a statement of profit or loss for the year ended 31 December 19–2.

His assets and liabilities were as follows:

	1 January 19–2 £	31 December 19–2 £
Freehold premises	30 000	30 000
Fixtures and fittings	5 600	7 200
Debtors	6 800	7 680
Stock	4 360	5 040
Creditors	5 300	3 960
Wages due	40	—
Balance at bank	—	1 500
Bank overdraft	660	—
Bank loan	—	2 000
Insurance prepaid	30	40

He also informs you that:
- (a) during the year he took out of the till £40 per week for household expenses;
- (b) he won £1 000 in a prize bond draw and lodged it to the business Bank Account;
- (c) he wishes to depreciate fixtures and fittings by 10 per cent on the balance at 31 December 19–2, and to provide a provision for bad debts of 5 per cent on debtors at 31 December 19–2.

3. M. Heath, a retailer, has not been keeping a full set of accounts. He supplies the following information for the year ended 31.12.1984:

	1 Jan. 19–4 £	31 Dec. 19–4 £
Premises	180 000	180 000
Equipment	—	3 000
Furniture	6 000	6 000
Stocks	14 000	15 500
Debtors	9 800	8 700
Creditors	12 200	10 600
Cash	1 800	400
Bank overdraft	—	2 800
Wages due	1 500	—
Rates prepaid	—	500

He also supplies the following additional information:
(a) Drawings for the year amounted to £36 000.
(b) He had transferred £6 000 from his private Bank Account to his business Bank Account.
(c) He had paid £1 500 for repairs to private house out of his business Bank Account.

From the above figures prepare:
a a statement of capital at 1.1.19–4
b a statement showing Heath's profit or loss for the year
c a balance sheet at 31.12.19–4.

4 Derek Ross, the proprietor of a small shop, keeps a cash book of which the following is a summary for the year 19–3. He pays all cash received into the bank and makes all payments by cheque.

Cash received and lodged	£
Balance at 1 January 19–3	15 200
Cash received from trade debtors	69 000

Cheque payments	£
Paid to creditors	35 700
Rent	800
Rates	1 200
Sundry expenses	2 500
Purchase of van	7 800
Drawings	15 000
Wages	14 500

The following additional information is also available:

	1.1.19–3 £	31.12.19–3 £
Trade debtors	87 000	95 000
Trade creditors	67 500	62 700
Stock	32 800	23 700
Premises	80 000	80 000
Fixtures and fittings	14 000	14 000

Prepare a Trading and Profit and Loss Account for the year ended 31 December 19–3 and a balance sheet at that date.

5 C. Ring operates a small business. He keeps a cash book of which the following is a summary. He lodges all cash received in the bank and makes all payments by cheque.

	£
Balance, 1 January 19–4	5 000
Cash sales	38 000
Receipts from trade debtors	17 500
Payments	
Trade creditors	29 250
Drawings	5 200
Wages	15 700
Rent	4 300
Rates	1 800

	£
Insurance	300
Cash purchases for resale	5 500

His assets and liabilities at 1 January 19–4 were:

	£
Premises	50 000
Fixtures and fittings	8 000
Stock	9 000
Trade creditors	17 000
Trade debtors	25 400
Rates prepaid	450
Rent due	2 150

At 31 December stock was valued at £7 500, trade debtors at £22 000 and trade creditors at £19 800. Further investigation reveals that discount of £1 250 had been allowed to debtors and discount of £900 received from creditors and that Ring had taken goods valued at £1 000 for his own use.

Prepare a Trading and Profit and Loss Account for the year ended 31 December 19–4 and a balance sheet at that date after taking into account depreciation on premises at 5 per cent and on fixtures and fittings at 10 per cent.

6 Patrick Moran did not keep a full set of books during the year ended 31.12.19–5. The following is a summary of his cash book for that period:

Cash receipts	£	£
Balance 1.1.19–5	1 000	
Cash sales	50 400	
Cash received from debtors	28 600	
		80 000
Cash payments		
Cash paid to creditors	39 200	
Purchases	6 600	
Drawings	4 800	
Sundry expenses of the business	14 400	
Delivery van	13 600	
		78 600

The following additional information is also available:

	1.1.19–5	31.12.19–5
	£	£
Premises	50 000	50 000
Furniture and fittings	5 000	5 000
Debtors	3 600	4 000
Stock	5 400	5 300
Creditors	4 400	4 900
Expenses due	—	600

You are required to:
a calculate Moran's total purchases and total sales
b prepare a Trading and Profit and Loss Account for the year ended 31.12.19–5
c prepare a balance sheet on 31.12.19–5.

7 Alan Cox, the owner of a small grocery, does not keep a full set of books. The following is a summary of his cash book for the year ended 31.12.19–3:

Cash received	£	£
Balance at 1.1.19–3	6 600	
Cash sales	102 000	
Cash received from debtors	17 400	
		126 000
Cash payments		
Drawings	8 000	
Total expenses	17 500	
Cash purchases	2 500	
Delivery van	15 000	
Cash paid to creditors	71 500	
		114 500

The following information is also available:

	1.1.19–3 £	31.12.19–3 £
Stock	14 000	15 800
Debtors	32 200	45 500
Furniture and fittings	3 600	3 600
Buildings	156 000	156 000
Creditors	62 500	71 900
Capital	149 900	

You are required to:
a calculate Cox's total purchases and total sales
b prepare a Trading and Profit and Loss Account for the year ended 31.12.19–3
c prepare a balance sheet on 31.12.19–3.

8 The following is the balance sheet of T. Roe as at 31 December 19–4:

Balance sheet as at 31 December 19–4

	£		£
Premises	37 000	Capital	75 000
Fixtures and fittings	10 000	Trade creditors	15 000
Trade debtors	25 000		
Stock	13 000		
Cash at bank	5 000		
	90 000		90 000

During the year 19–5 drawings were cash, £9 000; goods, £1 000. He also introduced additional capital of £5 000 on 1 April 19–5.

His mark-up on all goods is 20 per cent on cost.

His total selling expenses and losses for the year amounted to £7 500.

At 31 December 19–5 he had a favourable bank balance of £9 000, trade debtors owed him £32 000, he owed trade creditors £13 000 and he estimated his stock to be worth £15 000.

Prepare a Trading and Profit and Loss Account for the year ended 31 December 19–5 and a balance sheet at that date.

9   R. Dent does not keep a full set of records but you are given the following information:
   (a) Assets and liabilities at 1 January 19–6: Fixtures and fittings, £2 800; Stock, £5 600; Trade debtors, £2 900; Rent due, £200; Rates prepaid, £20; Trade creditors, £3 200; Bank overdraft, £100.
   (b) At 31 December 19–6 he had the following balances: Stock, £4 800; Creditors, £3 000; Bank overdraft, £500; Debtors, £2 500.
   (c) He wishes to make provision of 5 per cent on sundry debtors at 31 December and to write down the value of fixtures and fittings at 1 January by 5 per cent.
   (d) During the year his drawings were £520 cash.
   (e) His margin of gross profit is 25 per cent on all sales.
   (f) The total expenses to be charged to the Profit and Loss Account are £1 590 which includes bad debts provision and depreciation on fixtures and fittings.

   You are asked to:
   a   ascertain his net profit or loss for the year ended 31 December 19–6
   b   prepare Trading and Profit and Loss Account for that period
   c   prepare a balance sheet as at 31 December 19–6.

10 M. Day purchased a retail business on 1.1.19–2 for £40 000 consisting of:

	£
Premises	32 000
Equipment	2 200
Prize bonds	200
Stock	5 600

During 19–2 he did not keep a full set of accounts but he supplied the following information on 31.12.19–2:
1. Payments for the year were:

	£
Petty expenses	320
Drawings	4 160
Purchases	2 440

2. Bank lodgements for the year were:

Cash sales after cash payments had been made	77 320
Prize bonds	4 000
Cheques received from debtors	4 680

3. Bank payments for the year were:

Fixtures and fittings	1 600
Wages and general expenses	12 160
Cheques paid to suppliers	63 140
Motor car for his wife	3 200
Insurance	1 080
Electricity	720

4. During the year he received £260 discount from his suppliers and he took from stock, for personal use, goods costing £1 260.
5. One-quarter of insurance and electricity was in respect of Day's private house.
6. Included in his assets and liabilities on 31.12.19–2 were: Stock, £5 100; Debtors, £580; Creditors, £920; Cash, £100; Insurance prepaid, £120; Electricity due, £160.

Show with workings:
a   Trading and Profit and Loss Accounts for the year ended 31.12.19–2
b   balance sheet at that date.

436 Preparation of accounts from incomplete records

11 John Wilson commenced business on 1.1.19–4 when he lodged £12 000 to his business Current Account. On the same day he purchased premises for £50 000 with money all of which he borrowed from a finance company at 10 per cent interest per annum. The interest was to be paid on 31 December each year on the amount outstanding at the beginning of the year. During the year he failed to keep a full set of books but was able to provide the following details:
   (a) His gross profit was 25 per cent of total sales during the year.
   (b) During the year he purchased a delivery van for £7 000.
   (c) He paid light and heat, £1 200, and general expenses, £7 400.
   (d) On 1 October 19–4 he rented a neighbouring premises for £2 400 per year payable in advance. He moved into the private section of the rented premises and he estimated that one-third of the rent and £380 of the light and heat was in respect of this private residence.
   (e) During the year he took from stock goods to the value of £1 800 and he paid private expenses by cheque of £2 200.
   (f) During the year he lodged to his business Bank Account £3 000 which he won in a draw.
   (g) On 31 December 19–4 his stock was worth £10 000, his debtors owed him £1 600 and he had £5 200 in the bank.
   He owed £1 400 to his trade creditors and £42 000 to the finance company after the interest had been paid.

You are required to:
a compute Wilson's net profit or loss for the year ended 31.12.19–4
b prepare Wilson's Trading and Profit and Loss Account, in as much detail as possible, for the year ended 31.12.19–4.

12 T. Ward commenced business on 1.1.19–1 when he lodged £16 000 to his business Current Bank Account. On the same day he received a loan of £60 000 from Allied Bank PLC. The conditions attached to the loan were that it should be paid back in ten equal annual instalments together with interest at the rate of 10 per cent of the initial loan per annum. He did not keep a full set of books during the year but he was able to supply the following information on 31.12.19–1:

Cash payments: Drawings, £5 200; Purchases, £32 400; Lodgements to bank, £48 000; General expenses, £4 320.
Bank payments: Premises, £88 000; Furniture and equipment, £14 800; Wages and salaries, £17 200; Insurance, £1 200; Creditors, £18 920; Fur coat for wife, £1 800.
Bank lodgements: Cash, £48 000; Cheques from debtors, £4 200; Further capital introduced, £8 000.

During the year he took from stock £400 worth of household goods and one-fifth of the insurance was in respect of his wife's car.

Included in his assets and liabilities on 31.12.19–1 were: Debtors, £3 200; Creditors, £1 380; Cash, £480; Stock, £14 600; Insurance prepaid, £300.

Show with workings:
a Trading and Profit and Loss Accounts for the year ended 31.12.19–1
b a balance sheet on that date.

13 R. Roberts commenced business on 1 January 19–5 when he lodged £50 000 to his business Current Account. On the same day he paid £40 000 for a business which consisted of premises, £30 000, and stock, £10 000. During the year he did not keep a proper set of books but was able to provide the following details:
   (a) On 1 January he borrowed £80 000 from Allied Finance Ltd which he used to purchase a warehouse. This loan and interest was to be repaid in eight equal annual instalments on 31 December each year. The rate of interest was 12 per cent of the initial sum per annum.
   (b) During the year he purchased a delivery van for £12 000 and a car for his son's private use for £11 000.
   (c) On 1 September he rented a nearby premises for £3 000 payable yearly in advance. Roberts and his family moved immediately into the private section of the rented premises.
   (d) He estimated that he took each week from the business, for private use, goods costing £80 and cash, £50. He also paid light and heat, £1 800, and private expenses, £1 300, from the business Bank Account.
   (e) His wife received a legacy of £20 000 which she lodged to his business Bank Account.
   (f) His gross profit was 20 per cent of gross sales and he estimated that one-fifth of rent and light and heat was for private purposes.
   (g) On 31 December his stock was worth £11 600 and included £400 worth of heating fuel. His debtors owed him £900 and he had £3 900 in his Current Account. He owed £1 840 to his creditors and he had not yet made any payment to Allied Finance Ltd.

Prepare
a Roberts's balance sheet as at 31 December 19–5
b Roberts's Trading and Profit and Loss Account, in as much detail as possible, for the year ended 31.12.19–5.

14 A. Highton is in business as a general retailer. He does not keep a full set of accounting records; however it has been possible to extract the following details from the few records that are available:

Balances as at:	1 April 1981 £	31 March 1982 £
Freehold land and buildings, at cost	10 000	10 000
Motor vehicle (cost £3 000)	2 250	
Stock at cost	3 500	4 000
Trade debtors	500	1 000
Prepayment:		
Motor vehicle expenses	200	300
Property insurance	50	100
Cash at bank	550	950
Cash in hand	100	450
Loan from Highton's father	10 000	
Trade creditors	1 500	1 800
Accrual:		
Electricity	200	400
Motor vehicle expenses	200	100

Extract from a rough cash book for the year to 31 March 1982

	£
Receipts	
Cash sales	80 400
Payments	
Cash purchases	17 000
Drawings	7 000
General shop expenses	100
Telephone	100
Wages	3 000

Extract from the bank pass sheets for the year to 31 March 1982

	£
Receipts	
Cash banked	52 850
Cheques from trade debtors	8 750
Payments	
Cheques to suppliers	47 200
Loan repayment (including interest)	10 100
Electricity	400
Motor vehicle expenses	1 000
Property insurance	150
Rates	300
Telephone	300
Drawings	1 750

Note. Depreciation is to be provided on the motor vehicle at a rate of 25 per cent per annum on cost.

Prepare a Trading, and Profit and Loss Account for the year to 31 March 1982, and a balance sheet as at that date.

[*Association of Accounting Technicians, June 1982*]

15 J. Gregg operates an incomplete system of book-keeping, from which the following information has been extracted for the year to 31 March 1984:

Bank Account summary

	£		£
Bank balance at		Cash paid to trade	
1 April 1983	3 000	creditors	78 000
Cash received from		Electricity	900
trade debtors	76 000	Office expenses	1 500
Cash sales	4 900	Rates	2 500
Bank balance at		Telephone	400
31 March 1984	5 700	Wages	5 000
		Van expenses	1 300
	89 600		89 600

Additional information obtained was as follows:

Assets and liabilities at	1 April 1983	31 March 1984
	£	£
Furniture and fittings, at cost	2 000	2 000
Van, at cost	5 000	5 000
Stocks	10 000	12 000
Trade debtors	15 000	20 000
Prepayments:		
Rates	1 000	1 500
Van insurance	200	300
Cash in hand	100	200
Depreciation:		
Furniture and fittings	600	800
Van	2 000	3 200
Provision for bad debts	400	500
Trade creditors	14 000	12 000
Accruals:		
Electricity	300	400
Telephone	200	100

Notes
1. Gregg allowed his trade customers discounts of £9 000 and he also benefited from discounts received of £4 000.
2. Cash drawings from the till to pay for personal expenses amounted to £5 000, and goods withdrawn during the year for personal use were valued at £3 000.

Prepare:
a J. Gregg's Trading, Profit and Loss Account for the year to 31 March 1984
b a balance sheet at 31 March 1984.

[*Association of Accounting Technicians, June 1984*]

16 Wyre is in business as a sole trader. He does not keep a proper set of books of account, but the following details have been extracted from various sources for the year to 30 June 1985:

1. Cash transactions

Receipts	£	Payments	£
Cash sales	60 000	Cash purchases	68 000
Credit sales	300 000	Credit purchases	200 000
Cash from sale of van	2 500	Electricity	6 000
Rental income	5 000	Insurance	2 000
		Office expenses	26 000
		Proprietor's drawings	11 000
		Purchase of new van	8 000
		Rates	12 000
		Telephone	500
		Van expenses	4 000
		Wages and salaries	33 000

2. Opening and closing assets and liabilities

	At 1 July 1984 £	At 30 June 1985 £
Cash	4 000	1 000
Buildings at cost	50 000	50 000
Electricity (in arrears)	300	400
Insurance (in advance)	900	1 100
Office equipment at cost	8 000	8 000
Rates (in advance)	9 000	10 000
Stocks at cost	27 000	13 000
Telephone (in arrears)	150	100
Trade creditors	20 000	18 000
Trade debtors	30 000	35 000
Vans at cost	18 000*	24 000†

* including the van sold during the year to 30 June 1985.
† including the new van purchased during the year to 30 June 1985.

3. During the year to 30 June 1985, Wyre allowed his customers cash discounts amounting to £3 000 in total, but he was also able to claim cash discounts totalling £4 000 from his own suppliers during the same period.
4. Fixed assets are depreciated as follows:
Buildings: 2 per cent per annum on cost on a straight-line basis.
Office equipment: 10 per cent per annum on cost on a straight-line basis after allowing for an estimated scrap value of 10 per cent of the original cost.
Vans: 30 per cent per annum on a reducing balance basis, assuming a nil scrap value.
5. The buildings were purchased on 1 July 1980, the office equipment on 1 July 1982 and the old vans on 1 July 1983 (including the van sold during the year to 30 June 1985). The new van was purchased on 1 July 1984. No depreciation is charged in the year of disposal, but a full year's depreciation is charged in the year of acquisition.
6. Wyre's Capital Account at 1 July 1984 was £115 610.

Prepare:
a   Wyre's Trading, and Profit and Loss Account for the year to 30 June 1985
b   a balance sheet as at that date.
[*Association of Accounting Technicians, December 1985*]

17 Paul Peters commenced retail trading on 1 January 1983 with his capital consisting of stock in trade valued at £1 200 and a balance at bank of £4 800.

During his first year's trading, whilst all receipts and payments were passed through the business Bank Account, Paul Peters did not keep a full set of accounting records. However, the following information has been obtained relating to the year ended 31 December 1983:

1. Bank account: summarised transactions

	£
Receipts	
Loan from Paul Peters's father	4 000
Cash sales	17 000
Received from trade debtors	43 400
Payments	
Purchase of motor vehicle	5 000
Suppliers of goods	47 200
Rent and rates	3 400
Electricity	600
Motor vehicle running expenses	5 800
Sundry trading expenses	2 700
Drawings	4 100

2. Current assets, other than balance at bank, as at 31 December 1983

Stock in trade, at cost	5 100
Trade debtors	4 600
Amounts prepaid: Rent and rates	200

3. Current liabilities as at 31 December 1983

Trade creditors	3 200
Accrued charges:	
Electricity	100
Motor vehicle running expenses	250

4. Paul Peters obtains a gross profit of 30 per cent on all sales.

5. During the year, Paul Peters has taken a quantity of goods out of the business's stock for his own use. Unfortunately a record has not been kept of these goods.

The loan from Paul Peters's father is interest free until 1 January 1986.

It has been decided to provide for depreciation annually at the rate of 20 per cent of the original cost of motor vehicles held at each accounting year end.

Prepare a Trading and Profit and Loss Account for the year ended 31 December 1983 and a balance sheet as at that date.
[*Association of Accounting Technicians, pilot, 1985*]

18 The premises of James Card & Co. suffered a fire during the night of 18 February 1984 which destroyed a quantity of stock together with the stock records. The stock was insured against fire and the company wishes to submit a claim. The following information is available:
   (a) The company's accounting date is 31 December, and the balance sheet at that date in 1983 showed stock in trade of £33 000, debtors of £27 000 and creditors for purchases of £21 000.
   (b) During the period 1 January to 18 February 1984, the following transactions took place:

	£
Cash collected from debtors	48 500
Discounts allowed	500
Cash paid to creditors	34 000
Discounts received	200
Cash sales	18 000
Stock drawings by James Card at cost	300

   (c) The company's ledger shows that on 18 February 1984 debtors owed £28 500 and creditors were owed £19 500.
   (d) A stock take, carried out as soon as possible after the fire, showed the value of undamaged stock to be £9 000.
   (e) The company makes a gross profit of 25 per cent on the selling price of its goods.

A calculation is required of the cost of stock lost in the fire.

[*Royal Society of Arts, II, March 1984*]

19 During the night of 17 June 1983 the premises of Match Ltd were damaged by a fire which also destroyed a quantity of stock and all of the company's stock records. The destroyed stock was covered by insurance against loss by fire and the company wishes to calculate the amount to claim. The following information is available:
   (i)

	On 1 January 1983 £000	On 17 June 1983 £000
Stock at cost	132	
Trade creditors	45	53
Trade debtors	39	47

   (ii) The following transactions took place between 1 January and 17 June 1983:

	£000
Cash purchases	17
Payments to creditors	274
Cash received from debtors	314
Cash sales	80
Discounts received	10
Discounts allowed	8

   (iii) A physical stock take carried out first thing in the morning on 18 June 1983 showed the remaining stock to have a cost of £91 000.
   (iv) Match Ltd earns a gross profit of 30 per cent of selling price on all of its sales.

You are required to calculate the cost of the stock destroyed by the fire.

[*Royal Society of Arts, II, June 1983*]

20 The balance sheet of Huish Ltd, a wholesaling company, at 31 December 1984 was as follows:

Balance sheet at 31 December

	£	£		£	£
Share capital		100 000	Fixed assets at cost		
Retained profit		33 000	less depreciation		62 050
		133 000			
Current liabilities			*Current assets*		
Trade creditors	41 600		Stock	51 300	
General expenses	750	42 350	Trade debtors	54 650	
			Bank	7 350	113 300
		175 350			175 350

The company's premises were badly damaged by flood on the night of 23 January 1985 and some of the stock was destroyed. The following information is provided:
1. The stock salvaged from the flood was valued at £21 250.
2. Between 1 January 1985 and 23 January 1985 £43 500 was received from customers in respect of sales and £29 150 was paid to suppliers.
3. At 23 January 1985 trade debtors amounted to £61 270 and trade creditors amounted to £39 490.
4. The company earns a gross profit of 20 per cent on all sales.

A calculation is required of the cost price of stock destroyed by the flood.

[*Royal Society of Arts, II, May 1985*]

21 The following information relates to the business of C. Arbon, a sole trader:

Balance sheet at 31 December 1984

	£		£
Opening capital	27 500	Fixed assets	50 000
Profit for 1984	13 500	*Less* Depreciation	35 000
	41 000		15 000
Less Drawings	11 000	Stock	11 000
	30 000	Debtors	7 000
Trade creditors	5 000	Prepaid rent	500
Accrued expenses	1 000	Cash	2 500
	36 000		36 000

Trading and Profit and Loss Account
year to 31 December 1985

	£	£
Sales		88 700
Less Cost of goods sold		61 000
Gross profit		27 700
Rent and rates	1 200	
Depreciation	6 500	
Other expenses	7 500	
		15 200
Net profit		12 500

Notes
(a) All trading purchases and sales were made on credit.
(b) In addition to those related to trading, Arbon undertook the following cash transactions during 1985:

	£
Introduced capital	10 000
Purchased fixed assets	15 000
Drawings	12 000

(c) Balances at 31 December 1985:

	£
Stock	12 500
Debtors	8 000
Trade creditors	5 500
Prepaid rates	300
Accrued expenses	950

a Prepare the Cash Account of C. Arbon for the year to 31 December 1985.
b Prepare the balance sheet of C. Arbon at 31 December 1985.

All workings should be shown.

[*Royal Society of Arts, II, June 1986*]

22 A. Hamar is a retail grocer who does not keep complete records. However, he does keep his bank statements and a record of cash received and paid. A summary of his bank statement appears below:

Bank summary

	£		£
Balance at 1 November 1985	8 230	Rent and rates	6 250
Cash and cheques received		Trade creditors	100 750
from customers	140 150	Light and heat	4 600
Sale of old cash register	15	Vehicle expenses	4 800
Legacy paid into business		General expenses	12 900
account	14 000	Purchase of new cash	
		register	840
		Payment of private	
		electricity account	120
		Balance at 31 October 1986	32 395
	162 395		162 395

Hamar has withdrawn a total of £8 000 cash for his own use and paid £9 200 staff wages during the year. Both of these items were taken directly from the till.

His assets and liabilities on 1 November 1985 were as follows:

	£
Stock	18 750
Debtors	2 700
Creditors	6 500
Fixtures and fittings (at book value)	4 890
Motor vehicles (at book value)	6 800
Rates prepaid	250
Light and heat accrued	150
Bank	(as summary)

The following additional information is also available:
(i) On 31 October 1986 Hamar has trade debtors of £2 850. A debt of £50 included in this sum is deemed to be bad and this is written off.
(ii) The old cash register disposed of had a book value of £90. All fixed assets held on 31 October 1986 are to be depreciated by 25 per cent of their book value.
(iii) At 31 October 1986 trade creditors are £5 900, stock is valued at £14 250 and there is an account of £100 outstanding for heating.
(iv) During the year, Hamar took goods costing £750 for his own use.
(v) All payments except those for wages and Hamar's drawings are made through the bank.

Prepare Hamar's Trading and Profit and Loss Account for the year ended 31 October 1986 and a balance sheet as at that date.

[*Royal Society of Arts, II, December 1986*]

23 Jean Smith, who retails wooden ornaments, has been so busy since she commenced business on 1 April 1985 that she has neglected to keep adequate accounting records. Jean's opening capital consisted of her life savings of £15 000 which she used to open a business bank account. The transactions in this bank account during the year ended 31 March 1986 have been summarised from the bank accounts as follows:

	£
Receipts	
Loan from John Peacock, uncle	10 000
Takings	42 000
Payments	
Purchases of goods for resale	26 400
Electricity for period to 31 December 1985	760
Rent of premises for 15 months to 30 June 1986	3 500
Rates of premises for the year ended 31 March 1986	1 200
Wages of assistants	14 700
Purchase of van, 1 October 1985	7 600
Purchase of holiday caravan for Jean Smith's private use	8 500
Van licence and insurance, payments covering a year	250

According to the bank account, the balance in hand on 31 March 1986 was £4 090 in Jean Smith's favour.

Whilst the intention was to bank all takings intact, it now transpires that, in addition to cash drawings, the following payments were made out of takings before bankings:

	£
Van running expenses	890
Postages, stationery and other sundry expenses	355

On 31 March 1986, takings of £640 awaited banking; this was done on 1 April 1986. It has been discovered that amounts paid into the bank of £340 on 29 March 1986 were not credited to Jean's bank account until 2 April 1986 and a cheque of £120, drawn on 28 March 1986 for purchases, was not paid until 10 April 1986. The normal rate of gross profit on the goods sold by Jean Smith is 50 per cent on sales. However, during the year a purchase of ornamental gold fish costing £600 proved to be unpopular with customers and therefore the entire stock bought had to be sold at cost price.

Interest at the rate of 5 per cent per annum is payable on each anniversary of the loan from John Peacock on 1 January 1986.

Depreciation is to be provided on the van on the straight-line basis; it is estimated that the van will be disposed of after five years' use for £100.

The stock of goods for resale at 31 March 1986 has been valued at cost at £1 900.

Creditors for purchases at 31 March 1986 amounted to £880 and electricity charges accrued due at that date were £180.

Trade debtors at 31 March 1986 totalled £2 300.

Prepare a Trading and Profit and Loss Account for the year ended 31 March 1986 and a balance sheet as at that date.

[*Association of Accounting Technicians, June 1986*]

25 Treatment of stock and stock valuation

One figure that always appears on the balance sheet of a trading concern is stock, i.e. closing stock. The Companies Acts require that a balance sheet should give a 'true and fair view of the state of affairs of the company at the end of its financial year'. So it is reasonable to expect that the value placed on closing stock should be fair and reasonable. Firms normally (following the concept of conservatism) value stock at either the original cost price, the present cost price or the present selling price, whichever is the lowest. This would be an easy matter if all stock was bought at the same price at the same time. What happens, of course, is that stock is bought right through the year at varying prices. What price then should the stock be valued at?

Methods of stock valuation

There are many methods of stock valuation but the most common are:
1. FIFO (first in, first out).
2. LIFO (last in, first out).
3. Periodic simple average cost.
4. Periodic weighted average cost.
5. Continuous weighted average cost.

Before looking at the five methods it is important to remember three things:
(*a*) The word 'receipts' means the number of items bought into stock at various prices.
(*b*) The word 'issued' means the number of items issued by the storekeeper to the production side of the firm. It has *nothing* to do with sales. The sales figures in the example are given to show the effects of the different methods of stock valuation on gross profit.
(*c*) In practice, the storekeeper will issue the older stock first, particularly if it is of a perishable nature or would deteriorate with age.

Each of the five methods is presented using the information from the example below to show the different values for closing stock. Students should take the information and build up the examples for themselves.

448 Treatment of stock and stock valuation

A SIMPLE EXAMPLE
A manufacturing firm had the following transactions during its first year of operation:

19–1	Purchases (bought into stock)	Sales (to customers)
1 Jan.	100 items costing £5 each	2 Feb. 50 @ £8 each
5 Apr.	200 items costing £6 each	5 May 180 @ £9 each
9 Sept.	200 items costing £7 each	20 Dec. 250 @ £10 each

We can easily see that 500 items were bought costing £3 100 (total purchases) and that 480 items were sold realising £4 520 (total sales).

Therefore we know that 20 items are still held in stock. Our problem is the price at which we value these 20 items to arrive at a value for closing stock. The value will depend on the method used.

1. FIFO (first in, first out) method

In this method the goods received first are deemed to be the first to be used (first in, first out).

Advantages
(a) It is realistic – goods are issued in order of receipt.
(b) Closing stock valuation is realistic.

Disadvantage
It is awkward to calculate.

FIFO method of stock valuation

Date	Received (units and price)	Issued (units and price)	Stock in hand after each transaction	Value of stock in hand (£)
1 Jan.	100 @ £5	—	100 @ £5	500
2 Feb.	—	50 @ £5	50 @ £5	250
5 Apr.	200 @ £6	—	250 { 50 @ £5 200 @ £6	1 450
5 May	—	180 { 50 @ £5 130 @ £6	70 @ £6	420
9 Sept.	200 @ £7	—	270 { 70 @ £6 200 @ £7	1 820
20 Dec.	—	250 { 70 @ £6 180 @ £7	20 @ £7	140*

* The value of closing stock using the FIFO method is £140.

2. LIFO (last in, first out) method

In this method, each issue is deemed to be from the last lot of goods received before that date. When all units from that batch have been issued, the price of the previous batch is used.

Advantages
(a) It keeps the issue price close to current cost.
(b) Stock value is conservative.

Disadvantages
(a) It is awkward to calculate.
(b) It can result in issues being valued at out-of-date prices.
(c) It is not accepted for taxation purposes in the United Kingdom.

LIFO method of stock valuation

Date	Received (units and price)	Issued (units and price)	Stock in hand after each transaction	Value of stock in hand (£)
1 Jan.	100 @ £5	—	100 @ £5	500
2 Feb.	—	50 @ £5	50 @ £5	250
5 Apr.	200 @ £6	—	250 { 50 @ £5 / 200 @ £6	1 450
5 May	—	180 @ £6	70 { 50 @ £5 / 20 @ £6	370
9 Sept.	200 @ £7	—	270 { 50 @ £5 / 20 @ £6 / 200 @ £7	1 770
20 Dec.	—	250 { 200 @ £7 / 20 @ £6 / 30 @ £5	20 @ £5	100*

* The value of closing stock using the LIFO method is £100.

3. The periodic simple average cost method

In this method the average cost of goods held in stock is recalculated after each receipt of goods. Issues are then made at this price until further goods are taken into stock, when the average cost is again recalculated. The average price is found by adding the various prices and dividing by the number of different prices.

e.g. $\dfrac{£5 + £6}{2} = £5.50$

Periodic simple average cost method of stock valuation

Date	Received (units and price)	Issued (units and price)	Average cost of stock held	No. of units of stock held	Value of stock held (£)
1 Jan.	100 @ £5	—	£5	100	500
2 Feb.	—	50 @ £5	£5	50	250
5 Apr.	200 @ £6	—	£5.50	250	1 375
5 May	—	180 @ £5.50	£5.50	70	385
9 Sept.	200 @ £7	—	£6	270	1 620
20 Dec.	—	250 @ £6	£6	20	120*

* The value of closing stock using the simple average cost method is £120.

4. The periodic weighted average cost method

In this method the average cost of stock at a particular date is found by dividing the total value of receipts to that date by the total volume of receipts to that date, e.g. the value of stock on 5 April in the above example would be calculated as follows:

	Receipts (volume)	Value (£)
1 January	100	500
5 April	200	1 200
Total	300	1 700

Average $= \dfrac{1\,700}{300} = $ £5.66 per unit

Therefore value of stock on 5 April is $250 \times £5.66 = £1\,415$.

Periodic weighted average cost method of stock valuation

Date	Received (units and price)	Issued (units and price)	Average cost of stock held	No. of units of stock held	Value of stock held (£)
1 Jan.	100 @ £5	—	£5	100	500
2 Feb.	—	50 @ £5	£5	50	250
5 Apr.	200 @ £6	—	£5.66	250	1 415
5 May	—	180 @ £5.66	£5.66	70	396
9 Sept.	200 @ £7	—	£6.20	270	1 674
20 Dec.	—	250 @ £6.20	£6.20	20	124*

* The value of closing stock using the periodic weighted average cost method is £124.

5. The continuous weighted average cost method

In this method the average cost is calculated after each receipt and issues are made at this price until further receipts are obtained when the average cost is again calculated.

e.g. Value of stock on 5 April is calculated as follows:
  Balance: 50 units @ £5   = £   250
  + Receipts: 200 units @ £6 = £1 200
Total stock 250 units valued   £1 450

Therefore average cost is $\dfrac{£1\,450}{250} = $ £5.80 per unit

Therefore value of stock at 5 April is $250 \times £5.80 = £1\,450$.

The continuous weighted average cost method

Continuous weighted average cost method of stock valuation

Date	Received (units and price)	Issued (units and price)	Average cost of stock held	No. of units of stock held	Value of stock held (£)
1 Jan.	100 @ £5	—	£5	100	500
2 Feb.	—	50 @ £5	£5	50	250
5 Apr.	200 @ £6	—	£5.80	250	1 450
5 May	—	180 @ £5.80	£5.80	70	406
9 Sept.	200 @ £7	—	£6.69	270	1 806
20 Dec.	—	250 @ £6.69	£6.69	20	134*

* The value of closing stock using the continuous weighted average cost method is £134.

Advantages of using average cost methods
(a) They assume that identical items are of the same value.
(b) They overcome sharp fluctuations in price.

Disadvantage. They are cumbersome to calculate.

Effect on gross profit of using different methods of stock valuation

Trading Account for year ended 31 December 19–1

	FIFO	LIFO	Periodic simple av. cost		FIFO	LIFO	Periodic simple av. cost
	£	£	£		£	£	£
Opening stock	—	—	—	Sales	4 520	4 520	4 520
Purchases	3 100	3 100	3 100				
Less Closing stock	140	100	120				
Cost of sales	2 960	3 000	2 980				
Gross profit	1 560	1 520	1 540				
	4 520	4 520	4 520		4 520	4 520	4 520

The gross profit arrived at by the periodic weighted average and the continuous weighted average methods would be £1 544 and £1 554 respectively.

In the example given, all workings and calculations have been shown. In practice, the stock cards would be as shown below. Once students understand how the calculations are arrived at, they should have no problem in using this layout.

Method	Date	Receipts			Issues			Balance	
		Qty	Price	Value	Qty	Price	Value	Qty	Value
			£	£		£	£		£
FIFO	1 Jan.	100	5	500	—	—	—	100	500
	2 Feb.	—	—	—	50	5	250	50	250
	5 Apr.	200	6	1 200	—	—	—	250	1 450
	5 May	—	—	—	50	5	250	200	1 200
		—	—	—	130	6	780	70	420
	9 Sept.	200	7	1 400	—	—	—	270	1 820
	20 Dec.	—	—	—	70	6	420	200	1 400
		—	—	—	180	7	1 260	20	140

Method	Date	Receipts			Issues			Balance	
		Qty	Price	Value	Qty	Price	Value	Qty	Value
LIFO	1 Jan.	100	5	500	—	—	—	100	500
	2 Feb.	—	—	—	50	5	250	50	250
	5 Apr.	200	6	1 200	—	—	—	250	1 450
	5 May	—	—	—	180	6	1 080	70	370
	9 Sept.	200	7	1 400	—	—	—	270	1 770
	20 Dec.	—	—	—	200	7	1 400	70	370
		—	—	—	20	6	120	50	250
		—	—	—	30	5	150	20	100
Periodic simple average	1 Jan.	100	5	500	—	—	—	100	500
	2 Feb.	—	—	—	50	5	250	50	250
	5 Apr.	200	6	1 200	—	—	—	250	1 375
	5 May	—	—	—	180	5.50	990	70	385
	9 Sept.	200	7	1 400	—	—	—	270	1 620
	20 Dec.	—	—	—	250	6	1 500	20	120
Periodic weighted average	1 Jan.	100	5	500	—	—	—	100	500
	2 Feb.	—	—	—	50	5	250	50	250
	5 Apr.	200	6	1 200	—	—	—	250	1 415
	5 May	—	—	—	180	5.66	1 019	70	396
	9 Sept.	200	7	1 400	—	—	—	270	1 674
	20 Dec.	—	—	—	250	6.20	1 550	20	124
Continuous weighted average	1 Jan.	100	5	500	—	—	—	100	500
	2 Feb.	—	—	—	50	5	250	50	250
	5 Apr.	200	6	1 200	—	—	—	250	1 450
	5 May	—	—	—	180	5.80	1 044	70	406
	9 Sept.	200	7	1 400	—	—	—	270	1 806
	20 Dec.	—	—	—	250	6.69	1 672	20	134

Importance of stock valuation

Apart from helping in giving a 'true and fair view of the state of affairs of the company' as required by the Companies Acts, valuation of stock mainly affects net profit which in turn affects:

1. *Tax liability*
   Tax will be levied on net profit. A high value on closing stock will increase net profit, a low value will reduce it.
2. *The price of shares in the company*
   These are determined to some extent by the level of profits.
3. *The ability to borrow*
   Banks and other financial institutions take the level of profits into account when making decisions to loan money to firms.
4. *The accounting ratios*
   The value placed on stock will also affect the accounting ratios. Totals for stock will affect size of current assets which, in turn, will affect the working capital ratio and the liquid capital ratio. It will also affect the rate of stock turnover and any other calculation involving net profit.

All of these could have very significant effects on the perceived performance of a firm.

Exercises Set 25

1. **a** Why is stock valuation important to a particular firm?
    b Name and explain three methods of valuing stock.
    c State the advantages and disadvantages of each method.

2. From the following details, calculate the value of closing stock at 31 December 19–1 using: **a** the FIFO method, **b** the LIFO method and **c** the periodic simple average method.

19–1	Receipts	19–1	Issues
10 Jan.	20 items @ £20 each	10 Jan.	10 items
31 Mar.	40 items @ £25 each	1 Apr.	45 items
7 July	100 items @ £30 each	7 Aug.	70 items
30 Nov.	80 items @ £32 each	29 Dec.	100 items

3. The following figures were extracted from the stock records of Manufacturers Ltd at 31 December 19–3:

19–3	Receipts	19–3	Issues
3 Feb.	10 units @ £50 each	7 Apr.	25 units
1 Mar.	20 units @ £60 each	15 May	15 units
10 May	30 units @ £70 each	10 June	10 units
12 June	50 units @ £75 each	7 Aug.	35 units
1 Nov.	40 units @ £80 each	10 Dec.	45 units

    Total sales for the year were £20 000.

    a Show the value of stock in hand using (i) the FIFO method, (ii) the LIFO method, (iii) the periodic simple average cost method and (iv) the periodic weighted average cost method.
    b Show the Trading Account for the year ended 31 December 19–3 using the figures obtained by the four methods (i) to (iv) and assuming there was no stock in hand at 1 January 19–3.

4. Celtic Distributors Ltd started business on 1 January 19–5 as national distributors of machine parts.

    During the two years ended 31 December 19–6 the following transactions took place:

19–5	Purchases	19–5	Sales
1 Jan.	120 @ £50 each	4 Apr.	100 @ £75 each
7 Aug.	80 @ £60 each	13 Oct.	60 @ £90 each
19–6		19–6	
27 Feb.	160 @ £70 each	31 Mar.	20 @ £100 each
4 July	70 @ £75 each	5 Sept.	180 @ £105 each

    It is the company's policy to value stock in hand at the end of each year using the last in, first out method of stock valuation.

    a Prepare the Trading Accounts for Celtic Distributors Ltd for the years ended 31 December 19–5 and 19–6.
    b What effect would the use of the periodic weighted average cost method have on the gross profit/loss in each of the two years?
    c What effect would the use of the continuous weighted cost method have on the gross profit or loss in each of the two years.

5 Jock had 100 litres of foam liquid in stock as at 1 October 1982, purchased at £2 per litre. During the month to 31 October 1982, the following changes occurred in the stock position:

	Purchases			Issues
Date	Quantity (litres)	Cost per litre (£)	Date	Quantity (litres)
7.10.82	200	2.50	4.10.82	80
14.10.82	300	3.00	11.10.82	70
21.10.82	50	4.00	18.10.82	250
28.10.82	100	3.50	25.10.82	200

Calculate the value of the closing stock of foam liquid as at 31 October 1982 using each of the following three methods of pricing the issue of materials to production: **a** first in, first out (FIFO); **b** last in, first out (LIFO); **c** weighted average (note that the *periodic* weighted method is not required).

[*Association of Accounting Technicians, December 1982*]

6 The following information relates to the acquisition and issue of Material 2XA by Roe Ltd, a small manufacturing company, for the three months to 31 March 1983:

	Acquisitions		Issues
Date	Quantity (kg)	Price per kg (£)	Quantity (kg)
1.1.83	100	3.00	
15.1.83	200	4.00	
29.1.83			150
17.2.83	400	4.50	
5.3.83			450
16.3.83	100	5.00	
31.3.83			50

Note. There was no material in stock at 1 January 1983.

a Calculate the closing stock value of Material 2XA using each of the following methods of pricing the issue of stock to production:
   (i) first in, first out (FIFO)
   (ii) last in, first out (LIFO)
   (iii) periodic simple average
   (iv) periodic weighted average
   (v) weighted average.
b Examine the effect on gross profit of using the first in, first out (FIFO) and last in, first out (LIFO) methods of pricing the issue of stock to production assuming that price levels are rising.

[*Association of Accounting Technicians, June 1983*]

7   Big and Small keep a detailed stock record of all material purchases and of all issues of materials to production. The following information relates to the purchase and issue to production of Material MF for the month of October 1984:

Date	Receipts			Issues			Balance	
	Quantity (kg)	Price (£)	Value (£)	Quantity (kg)	Price (£)	Value (£)	Quantity (kg)	Value (£)
1.10.84							200	200
1.10.84				100				
5.10.84	700	3.00	2 100					
8.10.84				300				
12.10.84	400	5.00	2 000					
15.10.84				200				
19.10.84	800	2.00	1 600					
22.10.84				600				
26.10.84	1 100	4.00	4 400					
29.10.84				1 500				

a   Calculate the total charge to production of Material MF during October 1984 using the first in, first out (FIFO) method of pricing the issue of goods to production.
b   Calculate the closing stock value of Material MF as at 31 October 1984 using the last in, first out (LIFO) method of pricing the issue of goods to production.
c   Calculate the issue price per kilogram of Material MF on 29 October 1984 using the *continuous* weighted average method of pricing the issue of goods to production.
d   Calculate the issue price per kilogram of Material MF during the month of October 1984 using the *periodic* weighted average method of pricing the issue of goods to production.

[*Association of Accounting Technicians, December 1984*]

26 Hire purchase accounts and agreements to pay by instalments

Goods can usually be bought in five different ways:
1. by cash or cheque
2. on the seller's normal credit terms
3. by means of a bill of exchange
4. on a credit sale agreement
5. on a hire purchase agreement.

In the first method the goods are paid for immediately. In the second method the seller expects the buyer to pay in full for the goods not later than the last day of the seller's normal credit terms (e.g. one month). By paying by bill of exchange the debtor agrees to pay at an agreed later date. In the case of credit sale agreements and hire purchase agreements payments of capital and interest are spread over a number of regular intervals (e.g. month, quarter or year).

Credit sale agreement

A credit sale agreement provides for the payment for the goods over a period of time but unlike the goods supplied under a hire purchase contract the goods become the property of the buyer on payment of the first instalment. The seller cannot re-possess the goods but can sue for amounts remaining unpaid including interest.

Hire purchase accounts

In contrast to goods bought on credit sale agreements, with goods bought on hire purchase contract ownership does not pass to the buyer until after the last agreed instalment has been paid. Often after the final instalment has been paid the hirer (buyer) is required to exercise the option he has acquired to purchase the goods usually by payment of a small final payment. The goods are not legally his until this final payment has been made.

There are two elements to the payment of a hire purchase instalment:
(a) repayment of the (capital) sum borrowed
(b) repayment of interest on the sum borrowed.

The sum borrowed is known and the seller must inform the hirer (buyer) of (a) the cash price, (b) the 'true' rate of interest.

The main problem when drawing up accounts is one of deciding on how to split the amount actually paid between repayment of capital and repayment of interest each year.

There is no problem with the cost of the asset itself, it is the cash value. The real problem is one of spreading the interest element fairly over the accounting periods covered by the repayments. The Profit and Loss Account must be debited each year with the correct interest payment covering the financial year and no more; the accounts should not be concerned with interest that will accrue in future years. The correct amount for interest charges can only be ascertained if the 'true' running rate of interest is known.

The 'true' running rate of interest is the rate of interest that would have to be applied to each reducing balance so that the amount owed would come down to zero after the last instalment has been paid.

Methods of dealing with interest

In the buyer's books

There are two main methods of dealing with interest in the books of the buyer (or hirer). The first method is to credit the total interest to the account of the seller or hire purchase company at the beginning of the agreement. The second is to credit the appropriate amount of interest to the account of the seller at regular intervals as instalments are paid.

In each case the seller or hire purchase company is credited with the cash price of the asset purchased at the beginning of the agreement. The cash price plus the interest charges equals the purchase price.

The journal entries for each of the two methods are as follows:

Method I

Where interest is credited to the seller at the beginning:

(a) debit Asset Account } with cash price of the asset
credit Seller's Account

(b) debit Interest Suspense Account } with total value of the interest
credit Seller's Account

(c) debit Seller's Account } with the deposit and
credit Bank Account } instalments paid

(d) debit Profit and Loss Account annually } with the appropriate interest
credit Interest Suspense Account } for the accounting period.

Method II

Where interest is credited to the seller at regular intervals:

(a) debit Asset Account } with the cash price of the asset
credit Seller's Account

(b) debit Interest Account } with the appropriate interest for period
credit Seller's Account

(c) debit Seller's Account } with deposits and instalments paid
    credit Bank Account
(d) debit Profit and Loss Account } with the amount of interest
    credit Interest Account   payable during the accounting period.

You will notice that the only difference between the two methods is the use of the Interest Suspense Account in the first method. Here the total interest is debited with the total interest charges applicable for the entire period at the start of the agreement. The charge appropriate to each year is then transferred each year to the Profit and Loss Account.

In the second method the interest is credited to the seller as it arises and there is no need for an Interest Suspense Account.

EXAMPLE 1 (interest credited at beginning)
Peter Knowles, a trader, bought a lorry on 1 January 19–1 from Garages Ltd. The cash price of the lorry was £11 600. Knowles agreed to pay a deposit of £1 000 and three instalments of £4 000 each on 31 December in each year. Show the ledger entries in the books of Knowles for each of the three years and balance sheet extracts.

SOLUTION

Buyer's books

Garages Ltd (vendor)

19–1		£	19–1		£
1 Jan.	Bank – deposit	1 000	1 Jan.	Lorry Account	11 600
31 Dec.	Bank – instalment	4 000		Interest Suspense	
	Balance c/d	8 000		Account	1 400
		13 000			13 000
19–2			19–2		
31 Dec.	Bank – instalment	4 000	1 Jan.	Balance b/d	8 000
	Balance c/d	4 000			
		8 000			8 000
19–3			19–3		
31 Dec.	Bank – instalment	4 000	1 Jan.	Balance b/d	4 000
		4 000			4 000

Lorry Account

19–1		£			
1 Jan.	Garages Ltd	11 600			

Interest Suspense Account

19–1		£	19–1		£
1 Jan.	Garages Ltd	1 400	31 Dec.	Profit and Loss	
				Account	700
				Balance c/d	700
		1 400			1 400

19–2			19–2		
1 Jan.	Balance b/d	700	31 Dec.	Profit and Loss Account	467
				Balance c/d	233
		700			700
19–3			19–3		
1 Jan.	Balance b/d	233	31 Dec.	Profit and Loss Account	233
		233			233

Profit and Loss Account (extract) for year ended 31 December

			£
19–1	Hire purchase interest		700
19–2	Hire purchase interest		467
19–3	Hire purchase interest		233

Balance sheet (extracts) as at 31 December

	31.12.19–1	31.12.19–2	31.12.19–3
Fixed assets at cost	£	£	£
Lorry	11 600	11 600	11 600
Current liabilities			
Amount due to hire purchase company	8 000	4 000	Nil

Note
Up to 1981 it was acceptable to show the unpaid value of the hire purchase transaction (capital amount) off the fixed asset in the balance sheet. Since the 1981 Companies Act the amount owing on a hire purchase contract cannot be deducted from the value of the asset in the balance sheet.

Notes
1. The total interest payable £1 400 was arrived at by subtracting the cash price, £11 600, from the hire purchase price £13 000.
2. The charge to the Profit and Loss Account for each year was arrived at by using the 'sum of the digits' formula (sum of the number of instalments).
   e.g.   Instalment 1
          Instalment 2
          Instalment 3
          ―
          Sum of digits 6

   Interest would be apportioned as follows:
   $$\begin{aligned}&&£\\ \text{Instalment 1} & \quad \tfrac{3}{6} \times 1\,400 = 700 \\ \text{Instalment 2} & \quad \tfrac{2}{6} \times 1\,400 = 467 \\ \text{Instalment 3} & \quad \tfrac{1}{6} \times 1\,400 = 233 \\ \text{Total interest:} & \quad \phantom{\tfrac{1}{6} \times 1\,400 =\ } 1\,400\end{aligned}$$

460 Hire purchase accounts and agreements to pay by instalments

In the 'sum of digits' method more interest is written off in the first year, the reasoning being that as more is owed in the first year the interest charged in the accounts should be greater.

The interest carried forward in each year is treated as a prepayment in this method.

EXAMPLE 2 (interest credited as it arises)
On 2 February a trader bought a delivery van from Van Sales Ltd at a cost of £40 000 by means of a deposit of £4 000 and three annual repayments of £12 000. Interest was at the rate of 12 per cent on yearly balances outstanding. Payment of capital and interest to be made 31 December each year.

Show the ledger accounts in the books of the buyer for each of the three years.

SOLUTION

Delivery Van Account

		£
19–2		
1 Feb.	Van Sales Ltd	40 000

Van Sales Ltd

19–2			19–2		
1 Feb.	Bank deposit	4 000	1 Feb.	Delivery Van Account	40 000
31 Dec.	Bank – instalment	12 000	31 Dec.	Interest Account	4 320
	Balance b/d	28 320			
		44 320			44 320
19–3			19–3		
31 Dec.	Bank – instalment	12 000	1 Jan.	Balance b/d	28 320
	Balance c/d	19 200	31 Dec.	Interest Account	2 880
		31 200			31 200
19–4			19–4		
31 Dec.	Bank – instalment	12 000	1 Jan.	Balance b/d	19 200
	Balance c/d	8 640	31 Dec.	Interest Account	1 440
		20 640			20 640
				Balance b/d	8 640

Interest Account

19–2		£	19–2		£
31 Dec.	Van Sales Ltd (12% of 36 000)	4 320	31 Dec.	Profit and Loss Account	4 320
19–3			19–3		
31 Dec.	Van Sales Ltd (12% of 24 000)	2 880	31 Dec.	Profit and Loss Account	2 880
19–4			19–4		
31 Dec.	Van Sales Ltd (12% of £12 000)	1 440	31 Dec.	Profit and Loss Account	1 440

In the seller's books

There are many methods of dealing with hire purchase accounts in the seller's books. A particular method will be selected for its suitability for the type, number and frequency of transactions.

The one thing that will be common to all is that they will recognise that the interest element of hire purchase payments will be earned over a specific period of time and as such will be reflected in the profits of the firm over the same specific period of time.

The profits on hire purchase transactions can be treated in two ways:
1. The full profit could be taken into the accounting period in which the original sale was made or
2. A proportion of the profits could be brought into the accounts relative to the actual amounts received during a particular accounting period and to the total amount receivable.

It would be impossible in a book at this level to cover the details of the various approaches of different firms with different needs. We will confine the treatment to showing the interest suspense method.

The interest suspense method

The method is similar to that used in the books of the buyer. The purchaser (hirer) is debited with the total hire purchase price of the goods. Sales Account is credited with the cash price of the goods and Interest Suspense Account is credited with total interest. At the end of each financial period the appropriate interest is credited to the Profit and Loss Account and debited to the Interest Suspense Account.

Bank Account is debited with instalments paid and the Purchaser's Account is credited with these payments.

Journal entries:
(a) Debit   purchaser with total hire purchase price
    Credit   { Sales with cash price of the goods
             { Interest Suspense Account with total hire purchase charges
(b) Debit   Bank Account with instalments received
    Credit   Purchaser's Account
(c) Debit   Interest Suspense Account ⎫
    Credit   Profit and Loss Account   ⎬ with annual interest receivable

EXAMPLE (interest suspense method)
Taking Example 1 ('In the buyer's books', page 458) the ledger accounts would be as follows:

Books of Garages Ltd

Peter Knowles (purchaser/hirer)

19–1		£	19–1		£
1 Jan.	Lorry	13 000	1 Jan.	Bank – deposit	1 000
			31 Dec.	Bank – instalment	4 000
				Balance c/d	8 000
		13 000			13 000

19–2		£	19–2		£
1 Jan.	Balance b/d	8 000	31 Dec.	Bank – instalment	4 000
				Balance c/d	4 000
		8 000			8 000
19–3			19–3		
1 Jan.	Balance b/d	4 000	31 Dec.	Bank – instalment	4 000
		4 000			4 000

Interest (receivable) Suspense Account

19–1		£	19–1		£
31 Dec.	Profit and Loss Account	700	1 Jan.	P. Knowles interest charges	1 400
	Balance c/d	700			
		1 400			1 400
19–2			19–2		
31 Dec.	Profit and Loss Account	467	1 Jan.	Balance b/d	700
	Balance c/d	233			
		700			700
19–3			19–3		
31 Dec.	Profit and Loss Account	233	1 Jan.	Balance b/d	233

Sales

			19–1		£
			1 Jan.	P. Knowles (lorry)	11 600

Profit and Loss Account (extract) (credit)

			19–1		£
			31 Dec.	Interest Suspense Account	700
			19–2		
			31 Dec.	Interest Suspense Account	467
			19–3		
			31 Dec.	Interest Suspense Account	233

Hire purchase trading account

Some questions require the student to prepare a Hire Purchase Trading Account given certain information. The Hire Purchase Trading Account will be similar to the ordinary Trading Account in that the cost of sales will be subtracted from sales to arrive at the gross profit.

Cost of (hire purchase) sales will be composed of:
    Opening stock on hire purchase at cost plus
    Cost price of goods sent to customers on hire purchase.

The sales will comprise:
  Cash instalments paid
  Instalments due
  Closing hire purchase stock at cost.
The difference will be the gross profit.

Put in the form of a 'T' account it would look like this assuming the period covers a year:

Hire Purchase Trading Account for year ended 31 December 19–1

19–1			19–1		
1 Jan.	Stock on hire purchase at cost	___	31 Dec.	Cash instalments paid during year	___
31 Dec.	Cost price of hire purchase sales	___		Instalments due for year	___
(Balance)	Gross profit to Profit and Loss Account	___		Hire purchase stock at cost c/d	___
		___			___
19–2					
1 Jan.	Stock on hire purchase at cost				

The methods of computing the value of opening and closing hire purchase stock are beyond the level of this book and if a question is asked involving these two items the figures should be given for them.

Exercises Set 26

1 Explain the difference between credit sale agreements and hire purchase agreements.

2 James Joyce bought a delivery van on 1 January 19–1 from Transport Ltd on the following terms:
   (a) the cash price of the van was £29 000
   (b) deposit £2 000 and three annual payments of £10 000 to be made on 31 December each year.

   Assuming that the interest is credited in full at the beginning of the agreement and is written off each year in equal amounts show accounts for the following in the books of Joyce:
   1. Delivery Van
   2. Interest Suspense Account
   3. Transport Ltd.

3 Assuming that in Question 2 above interest charges are written off on the basis of the 'sum of the digits' formula, show the following:
   a Interest Suspense Account
   b Profit and Loss Accounts (extract).

4 James North bought a van from Motors Ltd with a cash price of £10 000 on the following terms on 1 January 19–1:
   (a) he must pay a cash deposit of £1 000 on 1 January
   (b) he must pay annual instalments of £1 500 on 31 December each year
   (c) interest is to be at the rate of 10 per cent on outstanding yearly balances.

Show the relevant ledger accounts in the books of James North for the first three years of the agreement and the relevant balance sheet extracts. Calculations to the nearest pound.

5 On 1 January 19–1 Trucks Ltd bought a lorry from Lorry Sales Ltd on a hire purchase instalment scheme. The cash value of the lorry was £25 000. The hire purchase agreement stipulated that the lorry was to be paid for in instalments of £6 000 each year.

Lorry Sales Ltd charges interest at the rate of 10 per cent per annum on yearly balances.

Show these transactions in the books of Trucks Ltd for 19–1, 19–2 and 19–3.

6 Show the books of Transport Ltd in Question **2** above.

7 Show the seller's books for Question **3** above.

8 Show the relevant ledger accounts for Motors Ltd in Question **4**.

9 Bromford Ltd sells office equipment and a number of its transactions are on hire purchase terms. The following information relates to a photocopier sold on hire purchase terms to Till and Co., a firm of accountants:
1. date of hire purchase sale – 30 June Year 6
2. terms of hire purchase sale:
       Deposit of £480
       Instalments: 24 of £95 each
3. instalments are payable at the end of each month, the first being due on 31 July Year 6
4. cash selling price £2 400 which gives Bromford Ltd a $33\frac{1}{3}$ per cent profit on the purchase cost of the photocopier.

Till and Co. decide to depreciate the photocopier over three years on a straight-line basis with no residual value, with monthly apportionments as necessary.

The respective financial year ends of the two businesses are:
   Bromford Ltd – 31 December
   Till and Co. – 31 March

On the assumption that all instalments are paid as due:
a prepare the Hire Purchase Trading Account for the photocopier in the books of Bromford Ltd for the year ended 31 December Year 6
b in the books of Till and Co.:
   (i) show the entries in the Profit and Loss Account in respect of the photocopier for the year ended 31 March Year 7
   (ii) show the entries on the balance sheet in respect of the photocopier as at 31 March Year 7.
       [*London Chamber of Commerce and Industry, Intermediate, March 1987*]

27 Sources and applications of funds

The profit and loss account and the balance sheet of a company show, *inter alia*, the amount of profit made during the year and the disposition of the company's resources at the beginning and the end of that year. However, for a fuller understanding of a company's affairs it is necessary also to identify the movements in assets, liabilities and capital which have taken place during the year and the resultant effect on net liquid funds. This information is not specifically disclosed by a profit and loss account and balance sheet but can be made available in the form of a statement of source and application of funds (a 'funds statement').   SSAP 10

The Trading and Profit and Loss Account shows the profit or loss at the end of a particular trading period. Let us suppose that the net profit shown in the accounts for a particular year amounts to £20 000. Does this mean that the company has increased its cash or cash at bank by £20 000? The answer is definitely No unless it is a cash business because the profit level for a particular period is not necessarily matched by a corresponding increase in cash and bank balances for the following reasons:
1. Some items charged to the Profit and Loss Accounts such as depreciation or provision for bad debts do not involve the movement of cash. They are not paid out; they are simply book entries.
2. Some items not charged to the Profit and Loss Account such as the purchase of fixed assets or the repayment of a loan do affect the movement of cash.

So while a firm can be shown to be making profits in the Profit and Loss Account this account does not indicate whether the funds and profit are being used wisely or not.

It is vital for any company which wishes to stay in business to monitor the effectiveness of management in controlling income and expenditure. In other words it must be able to indicate (by a statement) the level of funds generated during the period and explain how these funds have been utilised.

This statement is usually called the *statement of source and application of funds* for the period in question. It is a very useful link between the Profit and Loss Account on the one hand and the movement of liquid (cash) funds on the other. It helps the owners of the business to control the cash resources more effectively if it is known precisely where funds are coming from (source) and how they are being used (application). SSAP 10 explains clearly the object and the advantages of preparing a sources and application of funds statement:

> The funds statement is in no way a replacement for the profit and loss account and balance sheet although the information which it contains is a selection, reclassification and summarisation of information contained in those two statements. The objective of such a statement is to show the manner in which the operations of a company have been financed and in which its financial resources have been used and the format selected should be designed to achieve this objective. A funds statement does not purport to indicate the requirements of a business for capital nor the extent of seasonal peaks of stocks, debtors, etc.
>
> A funds statement should show the sources from which funds have flowed into the company and the way in which they have been used. It should show clearly the funds generated or absorbed by the operations of the business and the manner in which any resulting surplus of liquid assets has been applied or any deficiency of such assets has been financed, distinguishing the long term from the short term. The statement should distinguish the use of funds for the purchase of new fixed assets from funds used in increasing the working capital of the company.
>
> The funds statement will provide a link between the balance sheet at the beginning of the period, the profit and loss account for the period and the balance sheet at the end of the period. A minimum of 'netting off' should take place as this may tend to mask the significance of individually important figures; for example, the sale of one building and the purchase of another should generally be kept separate in a funds statement. The figures from which a funds statement is constructed should generally be identifiable in the profit and loss account, balance sheet and related notes. If adjustments to those published figures are necessary, details should be given to enable the related figures to be rapidly located.

The following lists indicate the various sources and application of funds:

Sources of funds

1. *Net profit from operations* — *Profit as shown in the Profit and Loss Account* adjusted for items that do not involve a movement of funds such as depreciation and profit and loss on the sale of fixed assets (these are book figures that do not increase or decrease the bank or cash balance)
2. *Capital introduced* — in the beginning and subsequently by the owners, partners and shareholders
3. *Borrowing of money* — on either a long- or short-term basis, e.g. loans or debentures, bank overdrafts
4. *Sale of fixed assets or sale of investments* — these provide additional funds

5. *Reduction in current assets*   e.g. debtors – a reduction in debtors accounts acts as a source of additional funds
6. *Increase in current liabilities*   e.g. an increase in creditors; this provides the company with an additional source of funds
7. *Issue of shares*   obviously increases the funds available.

Application of funds

1. *Net loss from operations* adjusted for items which are not a movement of funds, e.g. depreciation, profit or loss on sale of fixed assets.
2. *Repayment of money* borrowed on a long- or short-term basis – e.g. repayment of long-term loans, debentures or repayment of short-term loans.
3. *Purchase of fixed assets or investments.*
4. *Loans made to others.*
5. *Increase in current assets* – e.g. increase in stocks or debtors.
6. *Drawings of cash or profits* by proprietors – e.g. withdrawals of cash or payments of dividends.

Procedure for tackling a question

Step 1

Show *Sources of funds*.

Under the heading 'SOURCES OF FUNDS':
I   Take net profit before tax from Profit and Loss Account. Adjust this figure if necessary for *extraordinary* items such as preliminary expenses or goodwill written off.
II   To this figure under the heading 'ADJUSTMENTS FOR ITEMS NOT INVOLVING A MOVEMENT OF FUNDS', add back items such as depreciation and loss on the sale of fixed assets and *deduct* items like profit on the sale of fixed assets or reduction in provision for bad debts.

The total of these items is shown as TOTAL GENERATED FROM OPERATIONS.

Then under the heading 'FUNDS FROM OTHER SOURCES' add in any other items providing funds such as:
(a)   Loans received
(b)   Issue of shares
(c)   Amounts realised from the sale of fixed assets or investments.

Step 2

Show *Application of funds* (how money has been spent).

Show the amounts used for:
(a)   Purchase of fixed assets
(b)   Purchase of investments

(c) Repayment of loans, debentures and redemption of shares
(d) Actual dividend paid out (not the proposed one)
(e) Tax paid.

The total of these will be the total for application of funds.

Step 3

Subtract the figure for application of funds from the figure for sources of funds.

Note. The difference is the *change in working capital* which will represent a surplus or deficit of funds.

Step 4

To verify the overall changes in funds, find the difference between the working capital in the two balance sheets after deducting dividends and taxation.

Step 5

Analyse the increase or decrease in working capital including cash and bank. Show the increase or decrease in current assets and liabilities.

The resultant increase or decrease in current assets and liabilities must be the difference as shown by the sources and application of funds statement.

Note

SSAP 10 recommends that:

(a) enterprises with a turnover of more than £25 000 per annum should provide in addition to their audited financial accounts a statement of source and application of funds both for the period under review and for the corresponding previous period
(b) the statement should show the profit or loss for the period together with the adjustments required for items which did not use (or provide) funds in the period. The following other sources and applications of funds should, where material, also be shown:
  (i) dividends paid
  (ii) acquisitions and disposals of fixed and other non-current assets
  (iii) funds raised by increasing, or expended in repaying or redeeming, medium- or long-term loans or the issued capital of the company
  (iv) increase or decrease in working capital sub-divided into its components, and movements in net liquid funds.

Example

A summary of Joan's balance sheets as at 31 August 1985 and 1986 respectively is as follows:

	1985		1986	
	£	£	£	£
Fixed assets				
Equipment at cost	30 000		42 000	
Less Depreciation	20 000		28 400	
		10 000		13 600
Current assets				
Stocks	20 000		30 000	
Debtors	60 000		70 000	
Cash at bank	10 000		—	
	90 000		100 000	
Less Current liabilities				
Creditors	30 000		20 000	
Bank overdraft	—		23 600	
	30 000		43 600	
		60 000		56 400
		70 000		70 000
Financed by:				
Capital		20 000		30 000
Net profit for the year	14 000		30 000	
Less Drawings	4 000		10 000	
		10 000		20 000
		30 000		50 000
Loan		40 000		20 000
		70 000		70 000

Note. There were no disposals of fixed assets during the year.

Prepare a statement of sources and application of funds for the year to 31 August 1986.

Sources and applications of funds

SOLUTION

Note. This solution follows the format shown in the appendix to SSAP 10. (Brackets indicate minus figures.)

Joan
Statement of sources and application of funds for the year to 31 August 1986

	£	£
Source of funds		
Net profit		30 000
Adjustment for item not involving the movement of funds:		
Depreciation		8 400
Total generated from operations		38 400
Funds from other sources		—
		38 400
Application of funds		
(Money actually spent or withdrawn)		
Drawings	10 000	
Repayment of loan	20 000	
Purchase of equipment	12 000	
		42 000
Excess of application of funds		(3 600)
Financed by increase/decrease in working capital:		
Increase in stocks	10 000	
Increase in debtors	10 000	
Decrease in creditors	10 000	
Movement in net liquid funds:		
Decrease in cash balances	(33 600)	(3 600)

Explanatory note
In the above example:

Sources of funds (net profit + depreciation) show that the extra funds available from trading amounted to £38 400. (In this example there were no funds from other sources.)

These funds were spent (overspent) on drawings of cash + repayment of loan + purchase of additional equipment. The total amount actually paid out amounted to £42 000.

This excess application of £3 600 (£42 000 − £38 400) was financed by an overall decrease in working capital. (Stocks increased by £10 000, Debtors increased by £10 000, Creditors were reduced by £10 000). The total increase of £30 000 was offset by a change in cash at bank from +£10 000 to −£23 600 which resulted in a decrease in cash balance of £33 600 resulting in a net *decrease* in working capital of £3 600.

Exercises Set 27

1 From the following balance sheets of P. McKay for the years 19–1 and 19–2 prepare a source and application of funds statement for the year to 31 December 19–2:

P. McKay
Balance sheets

	19–1			19–2		
	£000	£000	£000	£000	£000	£000
Fixed assets						
Buildings at cost			60			100
Plant and machinery at cost		40			50	
Less Depreciation to date		10	30		14	36
TOTAL			90			136
Add						
Current assets						
Stock		16			19	
Trade debtors		24			28	
Cash at bank		15			6	
		55			53	
Less Current liabilities						
Trade creditors	19			21		
Accruals	2			2		
		21			23	
Working capital			34			30
TOTAL NET ASSETS			124			166
Financed by:						
Capital						
Balance at 1 January			88			100
Add Cash introduced			–			14
Add Net profit			18			40
			106			154
Less Drawings			6			8
			100			146
Long-term liability						
Mortgage loan			24			20
CAPITAL EMPLOYED			124			166

2   A summary of Alex Spain's balance sheets as at 31 December 19–2 and 19–3 respectively were as follows:

	19–2		19–3	
	£000	£000	£000	£000
Fixed assets				
Equipment at cost	75		105	
Less Depreciation to date	50	25	71	34
Current assets				
Stocks	50		75	
Trade debtors	150		175	
Cash at bank	25		—	
	225		250	
Current liabilities				
Trade creditors	75		50	
Bank overdraft	—		59	
	75	150	109	141
		175		175
Financed by:				
Capital				
Balance at 1 January		50		75
Add Net profit for year		35		75
		85		150
Less Drawings		10		25
		75		125
Term loan		100		50
		175		175

Prepare a sources and application of funds statement.

3 The balance sheets of Alan Walton for the years ended 31 December 19–3 and 19–4 were as follows:

	19–3			19–4		
Fixed assets	£	£	£	£	£	£
Premises		110 000			110 000	
Less Depreciation		41 250			44 000	
			68 750			66 000
Machinery		275 000			550 000	
Less Depreciation		165 000			220 000	
			110 000			330 000
			178 750			396 000
Investment at cost			70 000			110 000
TOTAL			248 750			506 000
Current assets						
Stock		60 500			93 500	
Trade debtors		49 500			82 500	
Cash at bank		22 000			—	
		132 000			176 000	
Less Current liabilities	38 500			60 500		
Creditors	—			71 500		
Bank overdraft		38 500			132 000	
Working capital			93 500			44 000
TOTAL NET ASSETS			342 250			550 000
Financed by			182 750			
Capital			110 000			342 250
Add Capital introduced			66 000			27 500
			358 750			102 750
Add Net profit for year			16 500			472 500
			342 250			56 500
Less Drawings						416 000
Long-term liability						
Loan			—			134 000
CAPITAL EMPLOYED			342 250			550 000

The investment at 31 December 19–3 was sold for £66 400 and was replaced by a new investment costing £110 000.

Prepare a sources and application of funds statement showing the changes in working capital.

4 The statement of sources and application of funds for C. Sohoe Ltd for the year ended 31 December 19–5 reads as follows:

	£000	£000
Sources of funds		
Net profit for year		204
Adjustment for items not involving a movement of funds		
Depreciation		230
Total generated from operations		434
Funds from other sources		
Issue of 10% preference shares	110	
Sales of fixed assets (book value)	64	174
TOTAL SOURCES		608
Applications		
Purchase of fixed assets		306
		302
Increase/decrease in working capital		
Increase in trade debtors	64	
Decrease in trade creditors	184	
Decrease in accruals	8	
Decrease in stock	(10)	
	246	
Movement in liquid funds		
Increase in cash at bank	56	302

The company's balance sheet as at 31.12.19–5 was as follows:

Balance sheet as at 31.12.19–5

	£000	£000	£000
Fixed assets at cost less depreciation		1 976	
Investments at cost		510	
TOTAL FIXED ASSETS			2 486
Add Current assets			
Stock	136		
Trade debtors	190		
Cash at bank	144		
		470	
Less Current liabilities			
Trade creditors	428		
Accruals	86		
		514	
Working capital			(44)
TOTAL NET ASSETS			2 442
Financed by:			
Ordinary share capital		930	
General reserve		510	
Profit and Loss Account balance		1 002	
			2 442

Prepare the company's balance sheet as at 31.12.19–6.

5 The following information has been extracted from the books of Context, a small trading company, for the two years to 31 October 1982 and 31 October 1983 respectively:

Trading, Profit and Loss Accounts (extracts)

	1982 £	1982 £	1983 £	1983 £
Sales (all on credit)		120 000		200 000
Less Cost of goods sold:				
Opening stock	15 000		16 000	
Purchases	96 000		196 000	
	111 000		212 000	
Less Closing stock	16 000		40 000	
		95 000		172 000
Gross profit		25 000		28 000
Less Expenses		20 000		20 000
Net profit		5 000		8 000

Balance sheet (extracts)

	1982 £	1982 £	1983 £	1983 £
Fixed assets				
Motor vehicles, at cost	25 000		25 000	
Less Depreciation	10 000		15 000	
		15 000		10 000
Current assets				
Stock	16 000		40 000	
Trade debtors	30 000		90 000	
Bank	2 000		—	
	48 000		130 000	
		63 000		140 000
Capital				
Opening balance		40 000		37 000
Profit	5 000		8 000	
Less Drawings	8 000		10 000	
		(3 000)		(2 000)
Long-term loan		37 000		35 000
Current liabilities		10 000		15 000
Trade creditors	16 000		72 000	
Bank overdraft	—		18 000	
		16 000		90 000
		63 000		140 000

Prepare a statement of sources and application of funds for the year to 31 October 1983.

[*Association of Accounting Technicians, December 1983 (part)*]

476 Sources and applications of funds

6 Alex is in business as a wholesale stationer. The following balance sheets have been extracted from his books of account for the two years to 31 May 1983 and 31 May 1984, respectively:

	1983				1984	
	£	£	£	£	£	£
Fixed assets						
Motor vehicles at cost			6 000			18 000
Less Depreciation			2 000			7 000
			4 000			11 000
Current assets						
Stocks		15 000			24 000	
Trade debtors	30 000			22 000		
Less Provision for doubtful debts	1 500			1 100		
		28 500			20 900	
Prepayments		500			1 000	
Cash at bank		1 300			—	
Cash in hand		100			400	
		45 400			46 300	
Less Current liabilities						
Trade creditors	6 000			3 000		
Accruals	400			800		
Bank overdraft	—			1 500		
	6 400			5 300		
			39 000			41 000
			43 000			52 000
Financed by:						
Capital			30 000			33 000
Net profit for year		15 000			18 000	
Less Drawings		12 000			14 000	
			3 000			4 000
			33 000			37 000
Loan			10 000			15 000
			43 000			52 000

Prepare a statement of sources and application of funds for the year to 31 May 1984.
[*Association of Accounting Technicians, June 1984*]

7 A summary of Thomas's balance sheets as at 31 August 1981 and 1982 respectively is as follows:

	1981 £	1981 £	1982 £	1982 £
Fixed assets				
Equipment, at cost	15 000		21 000	
Less Depreciation	10 000		14 200	
		5 000		6 800
Current assets				
Stocks	10 000		15 000	
Debtors	30 000		35 000	
Cash at bank	5 000		—	
	45 000		50 000	
Less Current liabilities				
Creditors	15 000		10 000	
Bank overdraft	—		11 800	
	15 000		21 800	
		30 000		28 200
		35 000		35 000
Financed by:				
Capital		10 000		15 000
Net profit for the year	7 000		15 000	
Less Drawings	2 000		5 000	
		5 000		10 000
		15 000		25 000
Loan		20 000		10 000
		35 000		35 000

Note. There were no disposals of fixed assets during the year.

a   Prepare a statement of sources and application of funds for the year to 31 August 1982.
b   By reference to the above example, explain briefly the main purpose of such a statement.

[*Association of Accounting Technicians, December 1982*]

8 James, a sole trader, has been in business for many years. The following series of balance sheets was prepared from his books at 31 December:

	1980 £	1981 £	1982 £
Assets			
Premises	10 000	10 000	20 000
Motor vans	15 500	11 500	18 000
Stocks	18 250	15 300	19 750
Cash at bank	6 600	9 850	650
	50 350	46 650	58 400
Sources of finance			
Capital	35 350	19 400	29 950
Creditors	15 000	27 250	19 450
Mortgage loan	—	—	9 000
	50 350	46 650	58 400

Notes
1. James's drawings for each of the last two years were:
   1981 £29 000
   1982 £27 500
2. On 1 January 1982 a motor van was purchased at a cost of £11 300 and new premises which cost £10 000 were acquired. The purchase of the premises was financed by a mortgage loan of £10 000, repayable at the rate of £1 000 per year. James complains that despite trading profitability the business is short of cash.

Required:
a statements of sources and applications of funds for each of the years 1981 and 1982
b a brief report to explain the decline in the cash balance to James.

[*Royal Society of Arts, II, March 1983*]

9   The following information relates to the affairs of South Western Engineering Ltd:

Balance sheets at 31 December

	1983 £000	1984 £000
Fixed assets		
Plant at cost less depreciation	806	931
Investments at cost	200	115
Current assets		
Stock	407	574
Trade debtors	316	329
Bank	25	140
	1 754	2 089
Capital and liabilities		
Share capital (ordinary shares of £1 each)	1 000	1 100
Share premium account	—	60
Retained profit	483	567
	1 483	1 727
12% debenture repayable 2000		80
Current liabilities		
Trade creditors	171	182
Proposed dividend	100	100
	1 754	2 089

Profit and Loss Account extracts, 1984	£000
Trading profit after charging all expenses including depreciation	139
Profit on sale of investments	45
	184
Less Proposed dividend	100
Retained profit for the year	84

Depreciation charged for the year was £87 000.

During the year, South Western Engineering Ltd purchased plant costing £212 000 and issued 100 000 ordinary shares to existing investors.

Required:
a   a funds flow statement for 1984 distinguishing between working capital changes and long-term financial changes
b   a discussion of the financial position of the company at 31 December 1984 as compared with one year earlier. You should base your discussion on calculations of working capital and the working capital ratios at each of these dates.

[*Royal Society of Arts, II, March 1983*]

10 The balance sheet of McGregor PLC as at 31 October 1986 (including comparative figures for the previous year) was as follows:

McGregor PLC
Balance sheet as at 31 October 1986

1985 £000		1986 £000
	Fixed assets	
250	Premises at cost	400
306	Plant at cost less depreciation	354
	Current assets	
180	Stock	230
106	Debtors	130
85	Bank	—
927		1 114
	Capital and liabilities	
500	Share capital (£1 ordinary shares)	600
—	Share premium account	20
162	Retained profit	224
—	10% debentures repayable 1996	50
	Current liabilities	
185	Trade creditors	120
80	Proposed dividend	90
—	Bank	10
927		1 114

The net trading profit for the year after charging depreciation of £38 000 was £152 000. During the year McGregor PLC made an issue of 100 000 ordinary shares to existing shareholders.

You are required to:
a   prepare a statement of sources and application of funds for the year ended 31 October 1986, distinguishing clearly between working capital changes and long-term financial changes.
b   comment on the liquidity position of the company at 31 October 1986, as compared with one year earlier. Your comments should include calculation of the working capital and working capital ratio at each of these dates. (Calculate ratios to two decimal places.)

[*Royal Society of Arts, II, November 1986*]

28 Computers in accounting

The development of commercial computing

The computer, as we know it today, was developed in military and university research laboratories. The early machines were built to calculate such things as the trajectory of shells fired from a battleship in stormy weather. However, it did not take long for the commercial applications of computers to be recognised.

In the initial stages only the largest companies could afford a computer. But over the last thirty years, great advances have been made in computer technology and companies such as IBM, Honeywell and Hewlett Packard have brought the development of business machines to a very advanced level. These advances in technology were accelerated by the invention of the microchip in 1975. This invention heralded what has been called the 'micro-revolution' which led to the dramatic increase in the use of home computers. This was mainly due to the fact that the invention of the microchip meant that computers could be made smaller but also cheaper.

The manufacturers of business machines took full advantage of the cheaper and smaller machines. IBM developed their PC series of computers (PC stands for personal computer) which were aimed at smaller businesses. With these new machines came the development of easier-to-use computer software. Furthermore, as computer technology reached the home, schools and every section of the office and factory, employee computer literacy has increased rapidly. It is now quite common for a person with limited computer experience to be using computer systems effectively after only a few hours of training. Even though the pace of technological advance has been rapid the performance projections for the 1990s indicate that these improvements are set to continue at an even faster rate.

Computerised business systems

With the advent of computers into the commercial environment it became obvious that manual accounting systems were not going to be able to keep pace with the speed at which business transactions were now taking place. It was necessary, however, to maintain the same procedure and conventions in computerised systems as existed in their manual predecessors – the purchase ledger, the sales ledger and the nominal ledger would remain intact.

Business packages

Early in the development of computerised business systems it became clear that it would be possible to develop an integrated business system which would monitor and control the financial situation within a company. As a result off-the-shelf business packages were developed. These provided an easy-to-use computerised accountancy system. They were developed in such a way as to assume no computer experience on the part of the user.

By their very nature business packages need to be flexible enough to be able to adjust to the needs of a wide variety of companies, for example, a textile company, an electronics company and a wholesale distributor. Each company would have its own rates of discount and different sources of income. And so these packages had to be flexible enough to cater for as many of these different features as possible.

Because of this need for flexibility these business packages consisted of a series of modules – each relating to a particular accounting function. Most of the modules can operate alone or will work together in a totally integrated system. The customer is able to choose how many accounting functions he or she wishes to computerise. Most computer systems consist of eight modules which make up the full accounting system:

Sales ledger
Purchase ledger
Nominal ledger
Invoicing/Sales order processing
Stock control
Payroll
Job costing.

The benefits of an integrated accounting system

At the centre of any accounting system is the nominal ledger. This is updated primarily by the computer from the information collated in the purchase, sales and payroll modules. Other items such as invoices, payments and salaries are only entered once into their respective modules. The transfer of data from the ledgers and payroll modules is computer controlled. Similarly the data regarding invoices and sales orders are passed from the relevant module to the sales ledger and to stock control if required.

All of this means that the data are entered only once and transferred to the other modules, thus avoiding duplication of effort as in the manual system, while at the same time ensuring that the double entry is maintained. When an invalid entry is made the computer will point it out to the user. Correction is simply a matter of rekeying the details.

Broadly speaking, it is true to say that, with computerised business systems, the greater the degree of integration that is achieved, the greater the speed, efficiency and business control that will be obtained.

The benefits of an integrated accounting system

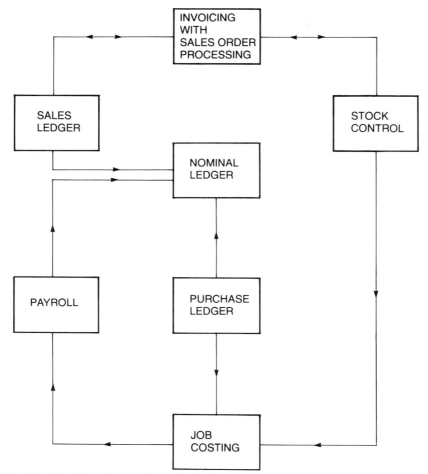

Fig. 1. Data flow diagram for typical computerised business system

Sales, purchases and stock control

Take the example of J. J. Nolan & Co. Ltd who sell business computers overseas. What actually happens within their accounting system when they buy and sell computers?

Sales

Nolans receive an order from Taylor and Taylor (Insurance Brokers) Ltd, for five of their Series 12 business computers. The invoice for this order is posted to the sales ledger module by the computer operator in the office where the data are put into the debtors file. The computer will then transfer this data to the nominal ledger module and to the invoicing and sales order processing module.

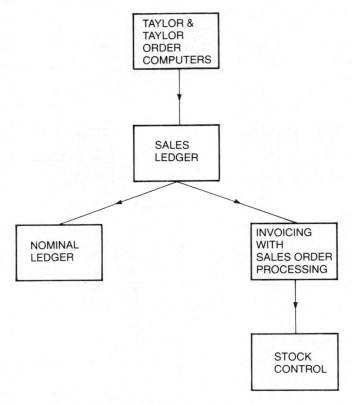

Fig. 2. Sequence of events following a sale of computers

Once the order has been processed and the invoice has been written the data regarding the sale are sent to the stock control module where the stock level is adjusted. Once all of this has been completed the computers are delivered to Taylor and Taylor (Insurance Brokers) Ltd. Within the sales ledger the order is posted to the debtors file until the account is settled. Remember that all of these changes within the system occur as the result of one entry.

Stock control

When Nolans sell any computers the stock level is adjusted within the stock control module from the data transferred from the invoicing and sales order processing module. After a number of sales the stock level would become low and the company would need to re-order more computers so that they do not run out of stock. How do they know when to re-order?

Within the stock control module there is what is known as the *re-order level* or *minimum stock level*. If the stock level of a certain item falls below this point the computer puts this item on the *re-order list*. Therefore, all that is required on the part of the user is to order the items on the re-order list and in so doing maintain the stock levels in the company.

The benefits of an integrated accounting system

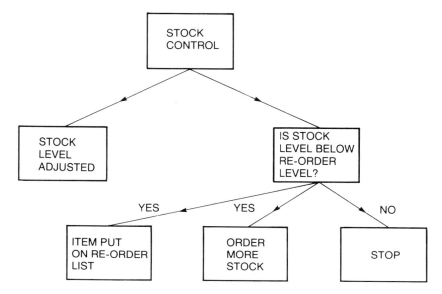

Fig. 3. Sequence of events within the stock control module following a sale

Purchases

Once more stock has been ordered, the invoices for those orders must be posted to the purchases ledger module by the computer operator in the office where the data are put into the creditor's file. The computer will then automatically transfer this data to the nominal ledger module. The stock level in the stock control module is not adjusted until the new stock has actually been delivered. Figure 4 shows the sequence of events.

Bar codes

In some businesses, like supermarkets and warehouses, stock is bought and sold very rapidly. Therefore, in order to keep the business running smoothly a fast and accurate method of stock control is essential. This can be done by using a *bar code* to identify each item of stock. A bar code consists of a series of black-and-white strips of various widths which encode a thirteen-digit number. The number itself is printed below the bars. These bar codes are printed on the packaging of goods, on cartons, or on labels. Each item has its own unique bar code. (See Figure 5.)

Bar codes are 'read' into the computer by bar code readers. These can be either in the form of a sort of pen which is moved across the bars or by means of a 'window' against which the bars are held.

Point of sale terminals

In businesses like supermarkets and superstores it is common to have the bar code readers located at the cash desk; in other words, at the point of sale. In many cases the bar code readers are now part of the cash register. This means

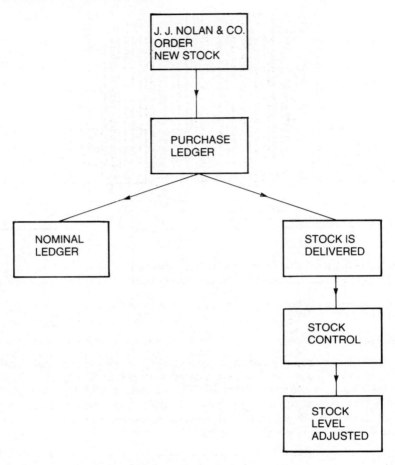

Fig. 4. Sequence of events following a purchase of new stock

that the stock levels are being automatically adjusted as each sale is made. Such cash registers are called *point-of-sale terminals*.

Spreadsheets

Managers are said to spend somewhere in the region of 30 per cent of their time preparing budgets. This is an activity that always calls for many 'what would happen if . . . ?' type of questions to be asked. Traditionally, a large sheet of paper was used for this. It was ruled vertically into a dozen or more columns; each column representing a separate month of the year. All of the different types of expenditure were entered down the left-hand side. The month's expenditure in the various categories was entered.

Using this method the sum of each column gives the total expenditure for each month and the sum of each row gives the total annual expenditure under each heading.

Fig. 5. A bar code

The problem with this method is that if you wanted to ask any of the 'what would happen if . . . ?' questions you would have to change a large number of

	JAN	FEB	MAR	APR	MAY	DEC	TOTAL
SALARIES	35791.63	35791.63	35791.63	35791.63	35791.63	35791.63	429499.56
NI	3891.28	3891.28	3891.28	3891.28	3891.28	3891.28	46695.36
INSURANCE	10116.00	10116.00	10116.00	10116.00	10116.00	10116.00	121392.00
HEAT	3012.71	2893.61	2789.25	1931.66	70.00	3321.99	35073.91
ELECTRICITY	1139.26	1071.89	1026.91	893.77	629.38	1204.05	10403.11
TELEPHONE							
CLEANING							
TOTAL							

Fig. 6. A spreadsheet

figures and having done that you would have to re-calculate each of the totals accordingly – a very tedious and very time-consuming process.

A spreadsheet program (which is basically a computerised version of the above method) is able to alter the entire set of figures and re-calculate all the totals every time a single element is altered. For example, if the cost of heating in January was changed this would cause the total expenditure for that month to be changed and the total annual expenditure for heating to be changed. This program has made the manager's life a lot easier.

The actual size of the spreadsheet is too big to fit on the screen all at once so what is seen is just a 'window' of the whole thing. That is to say, by using the appropriate keys on the keyboard you can cause the window to move to the specific part of the spreadsheet you require. If, for example, the window is located at the top of the January and February columns it can be moved further down the columns by pressing the [↓] key. Similarly, to move the window to the end of the year, November, for example, then the [→] key is pressed, and so on.

Each individual location of the spreadsheet, known as a *cell*, is addressed and located by its X and Y (across and down) coordinates. Horizontally they use the letters A–Z, AA–ZZ, and perhaps BA–BM to allow for the total possible width of the sheet – 65 cells in popular versions. Vertically, numbers 0–256 might be used. Each cell may contain a label (such as 'Sales' or 'Profit'), a value that is either entered or derived from a calculation or the formula for that calculation such as

B4 + B6*B5 (* means multiplication).

Most popular versions of spreadsheet software can split the window to display together parts of the sheet that are normally too far apart for the window to cover, and you can then scroll (move across) these windows separately.

Results can then be printed out. A sheet with a split window can also be printed. This is particularly useful when entering information, as one can refer back to any earlier entry.

Business-orientated spreadsheets all offer the user the ability to pass information from the spreadsheet to word-processing or database management packages, and there are many complementary programs available to allow output to be in a variety of graphic forms, e.g. pie charts or bar charts.

Packages for accounting and spreadsheets may cost hundreds of pounds but one should perhaps bear in mind the savings that their use can bring about. In the case of the spreadsheet, the fairly simple example used earlier of a manager compiling budgets can lead to savings of perhaps 15 or 20 per cent in a year. The cost of the software is a very insignificant part of such an economy, even before one starts to think about the savings in time and energy.

Customised business systems

It sometimes happens that none of the available 'off-the-shelf' business packages satisfies the requirements of a particular company. If this is the case they would have to have a business system specially developed to satisfy their particular requirements – that is, custom designed. Customised software is very expensive because of the time and expertise involved.

The system development process has three main stages:

1. systems analysis
2. systems design
3. systems implementation.

Broadly speaking, systems analysis involves the analysts going into the company and looking at the way things are done and suggesting any improvements that could be made to improve efficiency. Once the new system has been decided on the systems design people take over. These are essentially the computer programmers who will set about programming the new system. Having completed the program and tested it, the new system is then put into use or made 'live'. This is done in stages so that any errors can be easily identified and dealt with. Once all of the problems have been dealt with the system is ready for use.

Clearly, the cost of undertaking such preparatory work – which can take several months, even years – is very expensive. However, if the benefits which would result from having the system computerised are greater than the cost of having the system developed then it is generally regarded as worth while.

Abridged answers

Answers are provided here where appropriate. They aim, by giving key information, to help students check that they have followed the correct procedure.

Exercises Set 1

1   (a) See text, p. 1 (b) See text, p. 1
2   See text, pp. 4–5
3   See text, pp. 4–5
4   See text, pp. 2–4
5a 1. Money measurement 2. Going-concern 3. Realisation 4. Business entity 5. Accruals 6. Historic cost 7. Materiality 8. Consistency 9. Conservatism 10. Objectivity
5b See text, pp. 2–4
6a 1. Business entity 2. Money measurement 3. Going-concern 4. Consistency 5. Materiality 6. Accruals 7. Conservatism 8. Realisation
6b See text, pp. 4–5
7a 1. Consistency 2. Prudence 3. Accruals 4. Materiality 5. Going-concern 6. Money measurement 7. Capital/Revenue 8. Objectivity
7b See text, Chapter 6
8   Sales/VAT/cash discounts, stock valuation/profit, purchases/VAT/trade discount, wages/salaries, depreciation, unidentified difference.

Exercises Set 2A

1   (a) Sales (b) Sales Returns (c) Purchases (d) Cash (e) Purchases Returns (f) Cash (g) Purchases (h) Cash (i) Purchases Returns (j) Journal (k) Sales (l) Journal (m) Sales (n) Sales Returns (o) Cash (p) Purchases (q) Purchases Returns (r) Cash (s) Journal (t) Cash (u) Purchases (v) Purchases Returns (w) Cash

2

	Dr.	Cr.
(a)	E. Phelan	Sales
(b)	Sales Returns	E. Phelan
(c)	Purchases	T. Kite
(d)	Purchases	Cash
(e)	T. Kite	Purchases Returns
(f)	Office Equipment	Bank
(g)	Purchases	R. Green
(h)	R. Green	Bank
(i)	R. Green	Purchases Returns
(j)	Shop Fittings	New Fitters Ltd
(k)	P. Lawford	Sales
(l)	T. Hand	Lorries
(m)	M. Aspen	Sales
(n)	Sales Returns	M. Aspen
(o)	Purchases	Bank
(p)	Puchases	A. Green
(q)	A. Green	Purchases Returns
(r)	Cash	Sales
(s)	Lorries	Top Garages
(t)	Purchases	Cash
(u)	Purchases	A. Mann
(v)	A. Mann	Purchases Returns
(w)	Cash	Sales

3   1. b, 2. c, 3. a, 4. a, 5. a, 6. d, 7. a, 8. d, 9. c, 10. c

4   **Journal**

	Dr. £	Cr. £
Glyn	250	
Sales		250
Machinery	1 500	
Barlow		1 500
Cash	240	
Disc. All.	10	
Glyn		250
Loan	1 000	
McGregor		1 000
Investments	700	
Bank		700

Real: Machinery, Cash, Investments,
Nominal: Sales, Discount Allowed
Personal: Glyn, Barlow, McGregor, Loan

5a Balances: Capital £20 000 (cr.) Cash £1 900 (dr.) Bank £16 530 (dr.) Rent £500 (dr.) Shop Equipment £250 (dr.) Purchases £3 000 (dr.) Purchases Rets. £200 (cr.) Disc. Rec. £180 (cr.) Sales £2 500 (cr.) Sales Rets. £500 (dr.) Disc. All. £50 (dr.) Drawings £150 (dr.)

5b Trial balance total: £22 880

492 Abridged Answers

6a   Journal

	Dr. £	Cr. £
Equipment	36.70	
Sports Equipment (1978) Ltd		36.70
Match Fee	15.00	
Bank		15.00
Equipment	268.30	
Repairs	60.55	
Plumbing Services		328.85
Wages	11.21	
Groundsman		11.21
Depreciation	61.00	
Prov. for Depreciation		61.00
Income and Expenditure	132.76	
Repairs		60.55
Wages		11.21
Depreciation		61.00

6b Increase: Equipment £244.00, Prepayment £15.00, Creditors £36.70
Decrease: Bank £15.00, Accumulated Fund £132.76

Exercises Set 2B

		Total (net) (£)	Vat (£)	Purchases (£)
1	Sales Account	1 670	334	—
2	Sales Account	290	29	—
3	Purchases Account	2 740	274	—
4	Purchases Account	1 610	322	—
5	Sales Account	200 000	7 400	120 000
6	Purchases Account	3 270	327	—
7a	Sales Account	2 590	518	—
7b	Sales Returns Account	450	90	—

8a Purchases £181 590, Machinery £8 700, Motor Vehicles £18 700, VAT £30 000, Vehicle Exps. £410

		Total (net) (£)	VAT (£)	Purchases (£)
8b		—	30 000	—

9 Balances:

	£
T. King & Sons Ltd	660.24 (cr.)
XL Garages Ltd	9 200.00 (cr.)
G. Siddle Ltd	1 169.94 (dr.)
Purchases	576.00 (dr.)
Sales	1 020.00 (cr.)
HM Customs and Excise: VAT on Purchases	84.24 (dr.) ⎫
VAT on Sales	149.94 (cr.) ⎬ bal. £65.70 cr.
Motor Car	9 200 (dr.)

Exercises Set 3A

1

	Journal	Dr. £	Cr. £
R. Peters		900	
	Sales		900
G. Edwards		900	
	Sales		900
J. Long		100	
	P. Long		100
Machinery		50 000	
	Purchases		50 000
R. Strong		50	
	T. Lane		50
A. Wong		2 000	
	Purchases		2 000

2 Ledger balances: A. Client £830 (dr.) Sales £830 (cr.) T. Black £500 (cr.) Purchases £500 (dr.) B. White £700 (dr.) C. White nil Machinery £1 000 (dr.) Purchases £1 000 (cr.) Sales and Purchases reduced by £4 000; Bank £3 600 (dr.) P. Lane £3 600 (cr.)

3

		Journal	Dr. £	Cr. £
(a)	M. Hayes		300	
		T. Hayes		300
(b)	Computers		6 000	
		Purchases		6 000
(c)	B. Memory		500	
		Sales		500
(d)	Sales Rets.		200	
		B. Taaffe		200
(e)	Sales Rets.		200	
		Purchases Rets.		200
(f)	P. Dunne		640	
		Bank		640
(g)	J. Clarkin		180	
		Purchases		180
(h)	R. Day		290	
		R. Gray		290
(i)	Sales Rets.		580	
		J. Hayes		580
(j)	Sales		700	
		Office Machines		700
(k)	Disc. All.		600	
		T. Kenny		600
(l)	Purchases Rets.		100	
		Purchases		100

Exercises Set 3B

1. See text, p. 28
2. (a) No effect (b) Debit side by £1 000 (c) Credit side by £350
3. Trial balance total £87 000; Capital: Keenan £16 700
4. Trial balance total £273 550

5a

Journal	Dr. £	Cr. £
Suspense	8 200	
Downs		8 200
Suspense	800	
Disc. Rec.		800
Purchases	3 400	
Suspense		3 400

5. Suspense Account total £9 000
6. Suspense Account total £9 220

7a

Journal	Dr. £	Cr. £
Motor Cars	6 000	
Plant and Machinery		6 000
Suspense	18	
M. Walsh		18
Repairs	190	
Plant and Machinery		190
Suspense	1 400	
Disc.		1 400
Cash	2 000	
Suspense		2 000
Cash	400	
Suspense		400

7b. Original difference £982 (dr.)

8a

Journal	Dr. £	Cr. £
Suspense	1 680	
Interest		1 680
Bad Debts	1 200	
James Taylor		1 200
Equipment	2 500	
Suspense	5 000	
Purchases		2 500
J. Drake		5 000
R. Poole	1 760	
Suspense		1 760
Sales	890	
Suspense		890
Drawings	30 000	
Motor Expenses		30 000

8b Original difference £4 030 (cr.)

9a

Journal

	Dr. £	Cr. £
Interest	2 000	
Suspense		2 000
Bank Charges	150	
Suspense		150
Vehicle Repairs	1 400	
Vehicles		1 400
Suspense	270	
M. Grace		270
Sundry Debtors	1 800	
Sales		1 800
Suspense	250	
Purchases		250

9b Original difference £1 630 (cr.)

9c £96 500

10a

Journal

	Dr. £	Cr. £
A. Clott	2 400	
A. Clott Ltd		2 400
Suspense	1 000	
Purchases		1 000
Fixtures and Fittings	800	
Purchases		800
Sales	500	
Suspense		500
Suspense	250	
R. Shine		250
R. Bowen	4 000	
Suspense		4 000
Bank Charges	200	
Suspense		200
	—	—
Suspense		6 200

10b Original difference £9 650 (dr.)   **10c** £247 710

11a

Journal

	Dr. £	Cr. £
Bank Charges	200	
Suspense		200
Suspense	2 000	
Sales		2 000
Rates	100	
Suspense		100
Office Furniture	1 200	
Purchases		1 200

496 Abridged Answers

		Dr. £	Cr. £
	M. Malone	360	
	Suspense		360
	Disc. All.	1 940	
	Suspense		1 940
	Suspense	700	
	Disc. Rec.		700

11b £16 160   **11c** Balance sheet total £91 660

12a Original difference £16 150 (cr.)   **12b** £63 550   **12c** Balance sheet total £173 550

13a   **Journal**

	Dr. £	Cr. £
Suspense	360	
Sales		360
T. Dobson	1 760	
Suspense		1 760
Furniture and Fittings	350	
Purchases		350
Suspense	700	
R. Patton		700
Commission	400	
Drawings		400
Cash	60	
Furniture and Fittings		50
Profit and Loss		10
Suspense	85	
M. Edwards		85

13b Original difference £615 (dr.)   **13c** £20 320

14a Original difference £2 886 (cr.)   **14b** £29 510

15a   **Journal**

	Dr. £	Cr. £
A. Creditor	900	
Suspense		900
Sales	14 000	
Motor Vehicles		14 000
A. Debtor	28 000	
Suspense		28 000
Rent	600	
Suspense		600
Furniture and Equipment	580	
Suspense		580
Repairs to Equipment	850	
Suspense		850
Drawings	3 500	
Cash		1 500
Purchases		2 000

15b Original difference £30 930   **15c** £17 850   **15d** £124 350

16   **Journal**
		Dr. £	Cr. £
1.	Suspense	500	
	Sales		500
2.	Motor Van	5 000	
	Purchases		5 000
3.	Disc. All.	1 500	
	Sundry Debtors		1 500
4.	Purchases	3 000	
	Cook		3 000
6.	Electricity	400	
	Mercia Electricity Board		400
7.	Profit and Loss Account	500	
	Bad Debts Prov.		500
8.	Suspense	8 000	
	Bank		8 000
9.	Lee	200	
	Suspense		200
10.	Profit and Loss Account	4 000	
	Prov. for Depreciation on Workshop Tools		4 000

Item 5 will be added to the list of debtors' balances in the sales ledger. Will increase debit side of trial balance by £750

17a   **Journal**
		Dr. £	Cr. £
1.	Sundry Debtors	3 750	
	Sales		3 750
2.	Bank Charges	80	
	Bank		80
3.	Stock	4 500	
		—	—
4.	Insurance	100	
	Profit and Loss		100
5.	Machinery	10 000	
	A. Creditor		10 000

17b £35 170   **17c** Balance sheet total £272 670

18 Suspense Account total £211

19a   **Journal**
	Dr. £	Cr. £
Suspense	1 900	
Sales		950
Purchases		950

19b Trial balance total £145 666

20a   Journal

	Dr. £	Cr. £
Suspense	40	
Purchases		40
Sales	1 500	
Loan		1 500
Machinery	500	
A. Creditor		500
Disc. Rec.	80	
Suspense		80

20b Information given does not eliminate Suspense Account

20c £6 570

Exercises Set 4

	Corrected cash book balance (£)		Bank statement balance (£)	
1a	90 (dr.)	1b	150 (cr.)	
2a	5 348 (dr.)	2b	6 952 (cr.)	
3a	2 099.22 (dr.)	3b	2 568.98 (cr.)	
4	674 (dr.)	4	492 (cr.)	
5a	29 526 (dr.)	5b	42 628 (cr.)	
6a	3 660 (dr.)	6b	4 508 (cr.)	
7a	1 022 (dr.)	7b	798 (cr.)	
8b	788.86 (cr.)	8a	210.44 (cr.)	
9	2 481.98 (cr.)	9	1 782.22 (dr.)	
10a	3 022 (dr.)	10b	7 302 (cr.)	
11a	296 (cr.)	11b	374 (cr.)	
12a	32 300 (dr.)	12b	14 130 (cr.)	12c See text, pp. 49–50
13	410 (dr.)	13	470 (dr.)	
14a	705 (dr.)	14b	835 (dr.)	
15	223.35 (dr.)	15	1 012.09 (cr.)	
16	30 544 (dr.)	16	33 595 (cr.)	

17a Corrected cash book balance £151.85 (dr.)
Balance sheet entry £151.85 (current asset)

17b See text, pp. 49–52

Exercises Set 5

1 £9 500 (dr.)

2   £4 400 (cr.)
3a £15 660 (dr.)   3b £9 750 (cr.)
4   Bought £200 (dr.), £6 000 (cr.); Sold £2 440 (dr.), £420 (cr.)
5   Debtors £58 736 (dr.), £560 (cr.); Creditors £480 (dr.), £47 140 (cr.)
6   North £4 858 (dr.), nil (cr.); South £8 252 (dr.), £450 (cr.); West £7 852 (dr.), £178 (cr.)
7   £11 640 (dr.); List £11 640
8   Debtors £3 660 (dr.), £150 (cr.); Creditors £190 (dr.), £4 870 (cr.)
9   Debtors £6 450 (dr.), £110 (cr.); Creditors £140 (dr.), £4 310 (cr.)
10a £10 918 (dr.)   10b Original balance £10 650
11a £17 082 (cr.)   11b Original balance £16 860
12b Control Account and list £3 174 (dr.)   12c £3 174 (dr.)
13a £12 500 (dr.)   13b List (+£500 − £802) total £12 500
14a £73 700 (cr.) (i.e. £71 900 + £8 300 − £6 500)   14b £73 700
15a £22 000 (cr.)   15b (£23 800 + £4 850 − £6 650) total £22 000
16a £24 176 (dr.) £532 (cr.)   16b £25 716 (£24 176 + £7 000 − £5 460)
17 Sales ledger balances £65 026 (dr.), £384 (cr.); Purchases ledger balances £450 (dr.), £40 581 (cr.)
18 Debtors balance £44 144 (dr.); Creditors balance £55 152 (cr.)
19 Debtors balances £8 979 (dr.) £19 (cr.); Creditors balances £91 (dr.) £2 779 (cr.)
20 Sales Ledger Control Account and debtors' schedule £24 945.34 (dr.)
21 Creditors Ledger Control Account and creditors' schedule £87 125.35 (cr.)
22 £8 838 (dr.), £215 (cr.)
23a Debtors £19 000 (dr.), £670 (cr.); Creditors £365 (dr.), £7 187 (cr.)

23b
	£
Current assets	
Trade debtors (£19 000 − £475 − £365)	18 890
Current liabilities	
Trade creditors (£670 + £7 187)	7 857

24a £21 300 (dr.)   24b £639 (provision for 1986)

Exercises Set 6

1   See text, pp. 89–91
2   Capital (*c*), (*g*); Revenue (*a*), (*b*), (*d*), (*e*), (*f*)
3a Capital expenditure: (*b*), (*c*), (*d*); Revenue expenditure: (*a*), (*e*), (*g*); Revenue receipt: (*f*)
3b Understated by £41 790
3c Understated by £41 790

500 Abridged Answers

4 Capital expenditure: (*a*), (*b*), (*c*), (*e*); Revenue expenditure: (*d*), (*g*), (*i*), (*h*), (*k*); Capital receipt: (*f*); Revenue receipt: (*j*)

5 Capital balance sheet (*a*), (*b*), (*d*), (*h*)
Revenue, Trading Account (*c*), (*f*), (*i*)
Revenue, Profit and Loss Account (*e*), (*g*)

6b Understated by £62 500

7 See text, pp. 89–90

8 (*a*) Capital (*b*) Revenue (*c*) Capital (*d*) Revenue

9 (*a*) Revenue, Trading Account (*b*) Capital, balance sheet (*c*) Capital, balance sheet

Exercises Set 7A

1 (*a*) £1 000 (*b*) £1 410 (*c*) £1 500 (*d*) £104 250 (*e*) £60

	Transfer to Profit and Loss Account (£)	Balances/s b/d (£)
2	685	192.50
3	1 800	300 (cr.), accrual £300
4	945	240 (dr.)
5	480, 580	180 (dr.), 200 (dr.)
6	648, 798	168 (dr.), 210 (dr.)
7a	1 225	1 795 (dr.)
8	Rent 3 200	800 (dr.)
	Rates 1 320	360 (dr.)
9	Rent 240, 310, 310	20 (cr.), 30 (cr.), 60 (dr.)
	Insurance 120, 160, 240	80 (dr.), 160 (dr.), 160 (dr.)
10	D 150	25 (dr.)
	E 120	10 (cr.)
	F 180	15 (dr.)
11	Rent payable 8 000	666.66 (dr.)
	Rent receivable 1 200	100 (dr.)

12 1a Transfer to Profit and Loss Account:
      Year 6   £650
      Year 7   £710
  1b Prepayments:
      Year 6   £110
      Year 7   £120
  2a Transfer to Profit and Loss Account, Year 6:
      Rent   £1 800
      Rates   £554
  2b Rates prepaid   £128
      Rent due   £420

Exercises Set 7B

1a

Dr.		Bad Debts Account				Cr.
19–2		£	19–2			£
31 Dec.	A. Debtor	600	31 Dec.	Bad Debts Prov. Account or Profit and Loss Account		600

1b

Dr.		Bad Debts Prov. Account				Cr.
19–2		£	19–2			£
31 Dec.	Bad Debts Account	600 (or nil)	1 Jan.	Bal. b/d		2 000
31 Dec.	Bal c/d	3 000	31 Dec.	Profit and Loss Account		1 600 (or 1 000)

1c

Dr. Profit and Loss Account (extract) for year to 31 Dec. 19–2 Cr.

	£
Bad Debts Prov. Account	1 600 (or 1 000)
Bad Debts Account	nil (or 600)

Balance sheet (extract) as at 31 Dec. 19–2

	£	£
Debtors	60 000	
Less Prov.	3 000	
		57 000

2

Journal

	Dr. £	Cr. £
Bad Debts Account *or* Bad Debts Prov. Account	1 200	
Customer/s		1 200
Profit and Loss Account	1 400	
Bad Debts Prov. Account		1 400
or		
Bad Debts Account		1 200
Bad Debts Prov. Account		200

Dr.		Bad Debts Prov. Account				Cr.
19–2		£	19–2			£
31 Dec.	Sundry debtors	1 200	1 Jan.	Bal. b/d		1 800
	Bal. c/d	2 000	31 Dec.	Profit and Loss Account		1 400
		3 200				3 200
			19–3			
			1 Jan.	Bal. b/d		2 000

or

Dr.					Cr.
19–2		£	19–2		£
			1 Jan.	Bal. b/d	1 800
31 Dec.	Bal. c/d	2 000	31 Dec.	Profit and Loss Account	200
		2 000			2 000
			19–3		
			1 Jan.	Bal. b/d	2 000

Profit and Loss Account (extract) for year to 31 Dec. 19–2

Dr.		Cr.
	£	
Bad Debts Prov. Account	1 400	
or		
Bad Debts Account	1 200	
Bad Debts Prov. Account	200	

3

Journal

	Dr. £	Cr. £
Bad Debts Account *or* Bad Debts Prov. Account	1 620	
Customer/s		1 620
Profit and Loss Account	2 520	
Bad Debts Prov. Account		2 520
or		
Bad Debts Account		1 620
Bad Debts Prov. Account		900

Dr.		**Bad Debts Prov. Account**			Cr.
19–3		£	19–3		£
31 Dec.	Sundry debtors	1 620	1 Jan.	Bal. b/d	1 000
	Bal. c/d	1 900	31 Dec.	Profit and Loss Account	2 520
		3 520			3 520
			19–4		
			1 Jan.	Bal. b/d	1 900

or

19–3			19–3		
			1 Jan.	Bal. b/d	1 000
31 Dec.	Bal. c/d	1 900	31 Dec.	Profit and Loss Account	900
		1 900			1 900
			19–4		
			1 Jan.	Bal. b/d	1 900

	Profit and Loss Account (extract)	
Dr.	**for year to 31 Dec. 19–3**	Cr.
	£	
Bad Debts Prov. Account	2 520	
or		
Bad Debts Account	1 620	
Bad Debts Prov. Account	900	

Balance sheet (extract) as at 31 Dec. 19–3

	£	£
Debtors	38 000	
Less Prov.	1 900	
		36 100

4

Journal

	Dr.	Cr.
	£	£
Bad Debts Account *or* Bad Debts Prov. Account	590	
Debtor/s		590
Bad Debts Prov. Account	1 710	
Profit and Loss Account		1 710
or		
Profit and Loss Account	590	
Bad Debts Prov. Account	2 300	
Profit and Loss Account		2 300
Bad Debts Account		590

Dr.		**Bad Debts Prov. Account**			Cr.
19–4		£	19–4		£
31 Dec.	Sundry debtors	590	1 Jan.	Bal. b/d	5 000
	Profit and Loss Account	1 710			
	Bal. c/d	2 700			
		5 000			5 000
			19–5		
			1 Jan. Bal. b/d		2 700

or

19–4			19–4		
31 Dec.	Profit and Loss Account	2 300	1 Jan.	Bal. b/d	5 000
	Balance c/d	2 700			
		5 000			5 000
			19–5		
			1 Jan.	Bal. b/d	2 700

Abridged Answers

Profit and Loss Account (extract)
for year to 31 Dec. 19–4

Dr.			Cr.
			£
		Bad Debts Prov. Account	1 710

or

| Bad Debts Account | 590 | Bad Debts Prov. Account | 2 300 |

Balance sheet (extract) as at 31 Dec. 19–4

	£	£
Debtors	54 000	
Less Prov.	2 700	
		51 300

5
Dr. **Bad and Doubtful Debts Account** Cr.

19–7		£	19–7		£
30 Sept.	Bad Debts	1 870	1 July	Bal. b/d	3 500
19–8			19–8		
30 June	Bal. c/d	3 100	30 June	Bank	300
				Profit and Loss Account	1 170
		4 970			4 970
			1 July	Bal. b/d	3 100

6a J. Sweeney:
   Dr. Bal. b/d £3 000
   Cr. Bank £1 200, Bad Debts Account £1 800

6b Prov. for Bad Debts Account:
   Dr. Bal. c/d £4 300
   Cr. Bal. b/d £4 000, Profit and Loss Account £300

6c Bad Debts Account:
   Dr. J. Sweeney £1 800, P. Hickson £400
   Cr. Profit and Loss Account £2 200

7a A. Truck
   Dr. Bal. b/d £4 400
   Cr. Bank £1 100, Bad Debts Account £3 300

7b Bad Debts Account
   Dr. A. Truck £3 300, T. Owen £1 000
   Cr. Profit and Loss Account £4 300

7c Bad Debts Prov. Account:
   Dr. Bal c/d £7 000
   Cr. Bal b/d £6 200, Profit and Loss Account £800

8a Trade Debtors Account:
   1982 Bal. b/d £55 100
   1983 Bal. b/d £57 800
   1984 Bal. b/d £62 700

8b Bad Debts Account:
- 31.3.82 Dr. Trade Debtors £2 200
- Cr. Profit and Loss Account £2 200
- 31.3.83 Dr. Trade Debtors £4 900
- Cr. Profit and Loss Account £4 900
- 31.3.84 Dr. Trade Debtors £2 500
- Cr. Profit and Loss Account £2 500

8c Bad Debts Prov. Account:
- 31.3.83 Dr. Bal. c/d £5 780
- Cr. Profit and Loss Account £2 755
- Cr. Profit and Loss Account £3 025
- 31.3.84 Dr. Profit and Loss Account £1 077, Bal. c/d £4 703
- Cr. Bal. b/d £5 780
- 1.4.84 Cr. Bal. b/d £4 703

8d Disc. All. Prov. Account:
- 31.3.83 Dr. Bal. c/d £6 503
- 31.3.82 Cr. Profit and Loss Account £5 235
- 31.3.83 Cr. Profit and Loss Account £1 268
- 31.3.84 Dr. Bal. c/d £8 700
- 1.4.84 Cr. Bal. b/d £6 503
- 31.3.84 Cr. Profit and Loss Account £2 193
- 31.3.84 Dr. Bal. c/d £8 700
- 1.4.84 Cr. Bal. b/d £8 700

9a Bad Debts Prov. Account:
- 31.3.80 Dr. Bad Debts w/o £1 680, Bal. c/d £18 500
- 1.4.79 Cr. Bal. b/d £1 300
- 31.3.80 Cr. Profit and Loss Account £7 180
- 31.3.81 Dr. Bad Debts w/o £1 200, Bal. c/d £17 500
- 1.4.80 Cr. Bal. b/d £18 500
- 31.3.81 Cr. Profit and Loss Account £200
- 31.3.82 Dr. Bad Debts w/o £6 200, Bal. c/d £30 000
- 1.4.81 Cr. Bal. b/d £17 500
- 31.3.82 Cr. Profit and Loss Account £18 700
- 1.4.82 Cr. Bal. b/d £30 000

Balance sheets at 31 March:

	1980		*1981*		*1982*	
	£	£	£	£	£	£
Debtors	185 000		140 000		200 000	
Less Prov.	18 500		17 500		30 000	
		166 500		122 500		170 000

9b Reduced by £900
- Dr. Bank
- Cr. Bad Debts Recovered Account
- Dr. Bad Debts Recovered Account
- Cr. Profit and Loss Account

Exercises Set 8

	Transfers to Profit and Loss Account (£)	Profit/loss on disposal (£)	Final Asset Account balance (£)
1	2 000 for each year	—	2 000
2	450 for each year	—	3 650
3	2 000 for each year	—	nil
4	960 for each year	—	5 000
5a	6 000, 6 000, 6 000	—	18 000
6	2 280, 1 824, 1 460	—	11 400
7a	See text, p. 112		
7b	8 000, 4 800, 6 240	1 000 (L)	22 000
8	51 500	1 900 (P)	256 000
9	1 440, 3 240, 4 500		30 000
10	8 400, 8 400, 9 150	2 000 (P)	47 000
11	1 000, 1 750, 2 150, 2 720, 4 540	2 250 (L)	35 400
12	20 000, 17 000	1 000 (L)	170 000
13	278, 1 018, 1 261	B 420 (L), C 121 (P)	8 100
14	18 000, 23 400	1 000 (L), 600 (P)	216 000
15	17 066, 18 800	1 000 (L), 3 200 (P)	200 000
16	See text, p. 112		
17a	750, 750, 1 200	300 (L)	6 000
17b	1 125, 787.50, 1 417.50	162.50 (L)	6 000
18	17 000	14 000 (L) net	88 000
19a	3 600	300 (L)	18 000
20	20 100	5 400 (L)	100 500
21b	840, 4 000	1 100 (P) 400 (L)	20 000
22b	18 200		91 000
23b	26 800	300 (L)	134 000
24b	16 800	1 000 (L)	87 000

Exercises Set 9

1 1. **d**, 2. **b**, 3. **a**, 4. **b**, 5. **d**, 6. **c**, 7. **d**, 8. **c**, 9. **c**, 10. **c**, 11. **d**, 12. **c**, 13. **d**, 14. **d**, 15. **c**, 16. **d**, 17. **d**

2 Answers to **a** and **b** will depend on figures chosen

	Gross profit (£)	Net profit (£)	Balance sheet total (vertical presentation) (£)
3	27 998	10 964	16 534
4	128 800	46 300	234 100
5	33 466	19 660	18 300
6	44 000	11 726	15 050
7	14 620	4 990	10 970
8	12 080	6 552	12 852
9	17 500	10 400	15 400
10	40 000	19 000	15 400
11a	—	—	53 565
11b	24 250	10 825	53 640
12	—	63 500	78 500

Exercises Set 10

		Current account balances (£)	Share of residual profit/loss (£)	Balance sheet total (£)
1	Adam	52 500 (cr.)	50 000	
	Bob	31 500 (cr.)	30 000	
2	Carol	15 000 (cr.)	13 500	
	Dolores	15 000 (cr.)	9 000	
	Evelyn	7 000 (cr.)	4 500	
3	Tom	35 250 (cr.)	30 000	
	Dick	23 150 (cr.)	20 000	
	Harry	26 000 (cr.)	10 000	
4	Dermot	19 134 (dr.)	23 024 (L)	
	Erick	21 864 (dr.)	23 024 (L)	
	Frank	3 198 (cr.)	11 512 (L)	
5	Karl	28 032.50 (cr.)	28 770	
	Lester	20 055.00 (cr.)	19 180	
	Morgan	1 952.50 (cr.)	9 590	
6	Ann	16 262.50 (cr.)	11 962.50	
	Bill	18 850.00 (cr.)	20 000 (guaranteed)	
	Carl	5 887.50 (cr.)	3 987.50	
7	Pen	4 990 (cr.)	4 290	
	Ink	5 510 (cr.)	2 860	
8	Brief	670 (cr.)	7 000	
	Court	470 (dr.)	7 000	
	Deane	4 050 (cr.)	7 000	
9a	Smith	17 000 (cr.)	5 400	
	Jones	14 600 (cr.)	3 600	

Abridged Answers

		Current account balances (£)	Share of residual profit/loss (£)	Balance sheet total (£)
9b		Profit not sufficient		
10	Jack	2 865 (cr.)	3 385	
	Jill	3 485 (cr.)	3 385	26 350
11	Ben	16 500 (cr.)	18 000	
	Ken	9 700 (cr.)	12 000	
	Len	9 900 (cr.)	6 000	72 100
12	Ray	3 600 (cr.)	8 600	
	Mond	3 300 (cr.)	4 300	36 900
13	White	1 000 (dr.)	—	
	Green	3 000 (cr.)	—	—
14	Red	5 714 (cr.)	7 500	
	Amber	16 555 (cr.)	5 000	
	Green	2 534 (dr.)	2 500	63 735
15	Oak	4 640 (cr.)	2 570	
	Ash	3 042 (cr.)	1 542	
	Thorn	2 098 (cr.)	1 378	—
16	Dyo	11 240 (cr.)	9 510	
	Ull	9 410 (cr.)	6 340	
	Vez	8 920 (cr.)	3 170	154 570
17	Nail	—	8 686	
	Tack	—	4 343	
	Rivet	—	4 343	—
18a	Able	—	3 300	
	Baker	—	2 200	
	Charles	—	1 100	—
18b		—	10 000 each	—
19	James	5 480 (dr.)	2 610	
	Victor	3 940 (dr.)	2 610	40 220

Exercises Set 11

Note. Balance sheet totals are from a vertical presentation. For horizontal presentation, subtract total for current liabilities from total.

1a Dr. Bank £6 000, Goodwill £4 000
   Cr. Capital: Gary £6 000, Capital: Tom £2 000, Capital: James £2 000

1b Balance sheet total £34 000

2a Dr. Bank £10 000, Goodwill £6 000
   Cr. Capital: Clem £10 000, Capital: Ann £4 000, Capital: Brian £2 000

2b Ann £8 592, Brian £4 296, Clem £6 444

3 Journal:
   Dr. Premises £6 000, Bank £4 000, Bank £1 800, Capital: Acton £1 200, Capital: Bryant £600
   Cr. Capital: Crowe £10 000, Capital: Acton £1 200, Capital: Bryant £600, Bank £1 800
   Ledger: Post journal entries above
4 Journal:
   Dr. Premises £7 200, Bank (cash) £800, Bank £600
   Cr. Capital: E £8 000, Capital: C £450, Capital: D £150
   Balance sheet total £40 600
5a Ledger balances: Cash £400 (dr.), Bank £100 (dr.), Buildings £44 000 (dr.), Debtors £9 040 (dr.), Stock £8 200 (dr.), Furniture and Fittings £3 560 (dr.), Capital: Kate £33 500 (cr.), Capital: Susan £13 000 (cr.), Capital: Joan £12 000 (cr.), Creditors £6 800 (cr.).
5b Balance sheet total £58 500
6a Journal:
   Dr. Motor Vehicles £9 000, Stock £3 500, Bank (cash) £17 500, Goodwill £6 000
   Cr. Capital: Gray £30 000, Bank £6 000
   Ledger: Post journal entries above
6b Balance sheet total £130 000
6c $\frac{1}{4}, \frac{1}{2}, \frac{1}{4}$
7a Journal:
   Dr. Equipment £14 000, Stock £26 000, Bank £100 000, Bank £6 000, Revaluation £27 000, Premises £42 000, Revaluation £15 000
   Cr. Capital: Jacobs £140 000, Capital: Hale £4 000, Capital: Hearty £2 000, Equipment £12 000, Motor Vans £12 000, Stock £3 000, Capital: Hale £10 000, Capital: Hearty £5 000, Revaluation: £42 000
7b Ledger: Post journal entries above using existing accounts as appropriate
7c Balance sheet total £401 000
8a Journal:
   Dr. Stock £1 700, Bank (cash) £2 300, Bank £400, Bank £1 000
   Cr. Capital: Thomas £4 000, Capital: Eve £200, Capital: Patrick £200, Capital: Patrick £1 000
   Ledger: Post journal entries above using existing accounts as appropriate
8b Balance sheet total £20 000
9a Tim and Gerard are in partnership sharing profits and losses 3:1
9b Tim and Gerard agree to admit Jack as a partner on the following conditions:
   (a) Jack's capital is to be £30 000 comprising premises worth £28 000 and the balance (£2 000) in cash.
   (b) Jack is to pay a premium of £2 400 for his share of the goodwill. This cash is to be retained in the business.
   (c) Prior to the introduction of Jack, the following assets are to be revalued:
        Premises   £60 000
        Furniture and equipment £3 500
        Stock   £8 500

510　Abridged Answers

　　　(d)　The capital of the new business is to be £13 000 shared as follows:
　　　　　Tim　　　£60 000
　　　　　Gerard　£40 000
　　　　　Jack　　£30 000
　　　(e)　Tim and Gerard are to introduce or withdraw cash so that their capitals will be as agreed in (d) above.

10　Payment to Bull £10 500, Loan Account: Bull £3 745 (cr.), Capital: Bear £2 580 (cr.), Capital: Bison £4 050 (cr.).

11　Balance sheet total £102 400

12a　Net profit £26 550　　12b　Net loss £400　　12c　Balance sheet total £89 800

Exercises Set 12

Note. Balance sheet totals are from a vertical presentation. For horizontal presentation, subtract total for current liabilities from total.

1　Journal:
　　Dr.　Premises £30 000, Fixtures and Fittings £6 000, Motor Vehicles £2 500, Stock £4 400, Debtors £4 600, Bank £3 400
　　Cr.　Creditors £2 900, Capital: X £16 000, Capital: Y £32 000

　　Ledger: Post journal entries above
　　Partnership balance sheet total £48 000

2　Journal:
　　Dr.　Premises £9 000, Fixtures and Fittings £3 000, Stock £4 200, Debtors £1 600, Bank £900, Cash £300
　　Cr.　Creditors £4 000, Capital: Con £8 000, Capital: Dave £7 000

　　Ledger: Post journal entries above
　　Partnership balance sheet total £15 000

3　Journal:
　　Dr.　Premises £29 000, Equipment £1 600, Fixtures and Fittings £1 100, Vehicles £3 800, Stock £16 200, Debtors £5 000, Bank £2 000
　　Cr.　Creditors: £1 760, Wages £200, Capital: Early £28 540, Capital: Late £28 200

　　Partnership balance sheet total £56 740

4　Balance sheet totals: Morphy £34 400, Richards £24 300
　　Journal:
　　Dr.　Premises £26 000, Equipment £1 000, Goodwill £6 000, Motor Vans £6 800, Stock £5 600, Debtors £7 000, Bank £6 300
　　Cr.　Accruals £2 600, Creditors £12 100, Capital: Morphy £26 400, Capital: Richards £17 600

　　Partnership balance sheet total £44 000

5a　Journal:
　　Dr.　Premises £21 000, Equipment £1 180, Motor Vans £2 000, Fixtures and Fittings £1 780, Stock £6 200, Debtors £19 000, Bank £6 640, Goodwill £6 000
　　Cr.　Creditors £3 500, Accruals £300, Capital: A £36 000, Capital: B £24 000

　　Ledger: Post journal entries above

5b Partnership balance sheet total £60 000
6   Partnership balance sheet total £48 000
7   Partnership balance sheet total £52 000
8   Journal:
    Dr. Premises £8 125, Fixtures £9 610, Vehicles £100, Goodwill £5 000, Stock £12 974, Debtors £16 600, Bank £9 325
    Cr. Creditors £28 106, Bad Debts Prov. £1 328, Capital: A £6 982, Capital: B £25 318

Exercises Set 13

	Profit/loss on realisation (£)	Final cash settlement (£)
1	2 700 (L)	X 8 650, Y 8 650
2	9 000 (P)	Bonnie 34 000, Clyde 17 000
3	1 920 (L)	Dan 17 040, Erich 11 360, Frank 1 480
4	910 (L)	George 15 196, Harry 20 916, Irene 10 978
5a	3 600 (L)	Moran 6 480, Nelson 4 928
5b		Moran 6 454, Nelson 4 954
6a	1 140 (L)	A 4 660, B 4 850
6b	1 140 (L)	A 4 606, B 4 904
7	1 640 (L)	X 19 454, Y 9 454
8	11 040 (L)	Allen 7 600, Bond 4 020 (*Garner* v. *Murray*) or Allen 7 710, Bond 3 910

Exercises Set 14

	Net profit/loss (£)	Cash settlement (£)
1	3 660 (P)	280
2	4 000 (P)	800
3	3 750 (L)	150
4	26 400 (P)	13 800
5	3 000 (P)	2 800
6	4 640 (P)	880
7	1 200 (L)	1 170
8	9 080 (P)	12 820
9	16 500 (P)	100
10	52 700 (P)	57 150

Exercises Set 15

	Profit/loss on Consignment Account (£)	Bank draft/s (£)
1	1 700 (P)	7 300
2	25 645 (P)	36 270, 24 975
3	1 490 (P)	4 250, 3 020
4	22 185 (P)	35 800, 4 625

5a See text, p. 225

5b Profit on Consignment Account £11 640, bank draft £53 500

5d Bank Account bal. £50 700

	Profit/loss on Consignment Account (£)	Bank draft/s (£)
6	—	7 300
7	—	36 270, 24 975
8	—	4 250, 3 020
9	—	35 800, 4 625

10 (*a*) See text, pp. 225 and 228 (*b*) See text, p. 227 (*c*) Bank draft £18 100

11 Profits £11 340, £6 340

Exercises Set 16

Note. The ledger accounts are made up by posting journal entries.

1a Total, bills receivable book £3 670

1b Ledger balances: Bills Receivable £3 670 (dr.), Falls £400 (cr.), Hicks £800 (cr.), Fritz £300 (cr.), Heaney £1 000 (cr.), Call £450 (cr.), Orr £720 (cr.)

2 Total, bills payable book £2 910
Ledger balances: Bills Payable £2 910 (cr.), Michaels £600 (dr.), Scram £320 (dr.), Gospel £750 (dr.), Poole £1 000 (dr.), Price £240 (dr.)

3a

		Journal	Dr. £	Cr. £
19–1				
1 Jan.	J. Lannon		600	
	Sales			600
	Bills Receivable		600	
	J. Lannon			600
1 April	Bank		600	
	Bills Receivable			600

3b

			Dr.	Cr.
19–1				
1 Jan.	Purchases		600	
	Moss			600
	Moss		600	
	Bills Payable			600
1 April	Bills Payable		600	
	Bank			600

			Dr.	Cr.
			£	£

4a 19–5
			Dr. £	Cr. £
5 March	D. Grumley		1 600	
	Sales			1 600
	Bills Receivable		400	
	Bills Receivable		800	
	Bank		400	
		D. Grumley		1 600
5 June	Bank		800	
	Bills Receivable			800
5 Sept.	Bank		400	
	Bills Receivable			400

4b 19–5
			Dr. £	Cr. £
5 March	Purchases		1 600	
	D. Foster			1 600
	D. Foster		1 600	
	Bills Payable			1 200
	Bank			400
5 June	Bills Payable		800	
	Bank			800
5 Sept.	Bills Payable		400	
	Bank			400

5 *Kane's books*
19–5
			Dr. £	Cr. £
13 May	P. Doon		850	
	Sales			850
13 May	Bills Receivable		550	
	Bills Receivable		300	
	P. Doon			850
	Bank		539	
	Discount Charges		11	
	Bills Receivable			550
13 Nov.	Bank		300	
	Bills Receivable			300

Doon's books
19–5
			Dr. £	Cr. £
13 May	Purchases		850	
	T. Kane			850
	T. Kane		850	
	Bills Payable			550
	Bills Payable			300
13 Aug.	Bills Payable		550	
	Bank			550
13 Nov.	Bills Payable		300	
	Bank			300

Abridged Answers

6a

		Journal	Dr. £	Cr. £
19–6				
1 June	Purchases		200	
	J. Carr			200
	J. Carr		200	
	Bills Payable			200
1 Sept.	Bills Payable		200	
	J. Carr			200

6b

19–6				
1 June	T. Kelly		200	
	Sales			200
	Bills Receivable		200	
	T. Kelly			200
1 Oct.	T. Kelly		200	
	Bills Receivable			200

7a

19–7				
4 July	Bills Receivable		2 500	
	A. Peters			2 500
	S. Short		2 500	
	Bills Receivable			2 500

7b

19–7				
4 July	J. Dee		2 500	
	Bills Payable			2 500
4 Oct.	Bills Payable		2 500	
	Bank			2 500

7c

19–7				
4 July	Bills Receivable		2 500	
	J. Dee			2 500
4 Oct.	Bank		2 500	
	Bills Receivable			2 500

8 *Barnet's books*

19–7				
5 July	Purchases		400	
	J. Doakes			400
8 July	J. Doakes		400	
	Bills Payable			400
8 Nov.	Bills Payable		400	
	J. Doakes			400

Doakes's books

19–7				
5 July	T. Barnet		400	
	Sales			400
8 July	Bills Receivable		400	
	T. Barnet			400
	Bank		391	
	Discount Charges		9	
	Bills Receivable			400
8 Nov.	T. Barnet		400	
	Bank			400

9 *Collins's books* | Dr. | Cr.
19–7 | £ | £
1 Aug. Bills Receivable | 1 200 |
    Bills Receivable | 1 800 |
        J. Burke | | 3 000
    Bank | 1 193 |
    Discount Charges | 7 |
        Bills Receivable | | 1 200
    A. Creditor | 1 800 |
        Bills Receivable | | 1 800
1 Sept. J. Burke | 1 200 |
        Bank | | 1 200
1 Nov. J. Burke | 1 800 |
        A. Creditor | | 1 800

Burke's books
19–7
1 Aug. P. Collins | 1 200 |
        Bills Payable | | 1 200
    P. Collins | 1 800 |
        Bills Payable | | 1 800
1 Sept. Bills Payable | 1 200 |
        P. Collins | | 1 200
1 Nov. Bills Payable | 1 800 |
        P. Collins | | 1 800

10 *Hicks's books*
19–7
1 Sept. Bills Receivable | 800 |
        T. Monks | | 800
    Bank | 784 |
    Discount Charges | 16 |
        Bills Receivable | | 800
1 Dec. T. Monks | 800 |
        Bank | | 800
    T. Monks | 22 |
        Interest | | 20
        Bank | | 2
    Bills Receivable | 822 |
        T. Monks | | 822
19–8
4 Jan. Bank | 822 |
        Bills Receivable | | 822

Monks's books
19–7
1 Sept. N. Hicks | 800 |
        Bills Payable | | 800
1 Dec. Bills Payable | 800 |
        N. Hicks | | 800
    Interest and Noting Charges | 22 |
        N. Hicks | | 22
    N. Hicks | 822 |
        Bills Payable | | 822

516 Abridged Answers

			Dr. £	Cr. £
19–8				
4 Jan	Bills Payable		822	
	Bank			822

11 *Drennan's books*

			Dr. £	Cr. £
19–				
1 Oct.	Bills Receivable		200	
	D. Nestle			200
1 Nov.	Bank		195	
	Discount All.		5	
	Bills Receivable			200

Nestle's books

			Dr. £	Cr. £
19–				
1 Oct.	T. Drennan		200	
	Bills Payable			200
1 Nov.	Bills Payable		200	
	Bank			195
	Discount Rec.			5

12 Ledger balances:
    a Machinery £10 000 (dr.)   **b** British Engineering Ltd nil
    c Bills Payable nil   **d** Interest and Charges £50 (dr.)

13 Ledger balances: A. Green nil, D. Grey nil, H. Ford £600 (cr.), T. Cinders nil, Bills Receivable nil, Bills Payable £1 000 (cr.).

14a See text, p. 235   **14b** See text, p. 236

Journal

			Dr. £	Cr. £
19–1				
1 Jan.	Bills Receivable		7 500	
	Bills Receivable		10 000	
	White			17 500
	Green		7 500	
	Bills Receivable			7 500
11 Feb.	Bank		9 950	
	Discount Charges		50	
	Bills Receivable			10 000
1 Mar.	Bank		7 500	
	Bills Receivable			7 500
1 April	White		10 020	
	Bank			10 020
	Bank		2 020	
	Bills Receivable		8 160	
	White			10 020
	Interest Receivable			160
1 July	Bank		8 160	
	Bills Receivable			8 160

15a

		Dr. £	Cr. £
	A. Reardon	3 000	
	Promissory Note Account		3 000
	A. Reardon	80	
	Interest		80
	Promissory Note Account	3 000	
	A. Reardon		3 000

		Dr. £	Cr. £
15b	Bills Payable	3 000	
	T. Thumb		3 000
	Interest	400	
	T. Thumb		400
	T. Thumb	10 000	
	Bills Payable		10 000
15c	B. Hill	13 000	
	Bills Receivable		13 000
	Bank	7 135	
	Bills Receivable	6 000	
	B. Hill		13 000
	Interest		135
15d	Goldsmith	10 020	
	Bank		10 020
	Goldsmith	200	
	Interest Receivable		200
	Promissory Note Account	10 200	
	Bank	20	
	Goldsmith		10 220
15e	Promissory Note Account	6 000	
	A. Mastik		6 000
	Charges	20	
	A. Mastik		20
	A. Mastik	6 020	
	Bank		6 020

16   *A's ledger*
B's Account:
Dr.   £1 600, £60, £1 557
Cr.   £1 600, £1 600, £5, £12
Bills Payable Account:
Dr.   £1 600, £1 557
Cr.   £1 600, £1 557
B's ledger
A's Account:
Dr.   £1 600, £1 600, £5, £12
Cr.   £1 600, £60, £1 557
Bills Receivable Account:
Dr.   £1 600, £1 557
Cr.   £1 595, £5, £1 557

Exercises Set 17

	Gross profit/loss (£)	*Surplus/ deficiency* (£)	*Net profit/loss* (£)
1	180 000 (P)	—	—
2	135 960 (P)	—	—
3	23 000 (P)	—	—

	Gross profit/loss (£)	Surplus/deficiency (£)	Net profit/loss (£)
4	28 730 (P)	—	12 730
5	11 960 (P)	—	9 050
6	3 400 (P)	—	
7	37 200 (P)	2 000 (D)	—
8	5 500 (L)	27 500 (D)	
9	17 700 (P)	800 (D)	10 950
10a	19 760 (P) (Manchester) 38 150 (P) (Birmingham)		7 650 (Manchester) 21 400 (Birmingham)
10b	Balance sheet total £268 330		

Exercises Set 18

1. Ordinary Share Capital £50 000 (cr.), Bank £50 000 (dr.)
2. Ordinary Share Capital £60 000 (cr.), Preference Share Capital £200 000 (cr.), Bank £260 000 (dr.)
3. Ordinary Share Capital £50 000 (cr.), Bank £50 000 (dr.)
4. Ordinary Share Capital £50 000 (cr.), Bank £50 000 (dr.); Balance sheet total £150 000
5. Ordinary Share Capital £120 000 (cr.), Bank £120 000 (dr.); Balance sheet total £120 000
6. Ordinary Share Capital £120 000 (cr.), Bank £120 000 (dr.); Balance sheet total £120 000
7. Ordinary Share Capital £100 000 (cr.), Preference Share Capital £40 000 (cr.), Bank £139 880 (dr.), First and Final Call £120 (dr.); Balance sheet total £139 880
8. Ordinary Share Capital £400 000 (cr.), Preference Share Capital £50 000 (cr.), Share Premium £37 500 (cr), Bank £187 500 (dr.); Balance sheet total £487 500
9. Ordinary Share Capital £200 000 (cr.), Share Premium £28 000 (cr.), Bank £107 985 (dr.), First and Final Call £15 (dr.); Balance sheet total £227 985
10. Ordinary Share Capital £29 800 (cr.), Forfeited Shares £160 (cr.), Bank £29 960 (dr.); Balance sheet total £29 960
11.

Journal	Dr. £	Cr. £
Application	120	
Allotment	90	
First and Final Call	90	
Ordinary Share Capital		300
Bank	210	
Application		120
Allotment		90
Ordinary Share Capital	300	
First and Final Call		90
Forfeited Shares		210

12 *Ledger*
    A. Wren:
    Dr. £300
    Cr. £120, £180
    Forfeited Shares Account:
    Dr. £180
    Cr. £210
    Ordinary Share Capital Account:
    Dr. £300

Balance sheet (extract)

Current assets	£	£
Bank:		
Share capital	300	
Forefeited shares	30	
		330

13b Ordinary Share Capital £200 000 (cr.), Preference Share Capital £200 000, Share Premium £25 090 (cr.), Bank £125 090 (dr.); Balance sheet total £425 090
14   Balance sheet total £100 000
15   Balance sheet total £90 000
16   Balance sheet total £95 000
17b A charge

Exercises Set 19

	Balance sheet total (£)
1	80 000
2	115 000
3	90 000
4	320 000
5	570 000
6	420 000

Exercises Set 20

	Cost of manufacture (£)	Gross profit (£)	Net profit (£)	Balance sheet total (£)
1	73 000	—	—	—
2	112 970	—	—	—
3	525 800	—	—	—
4	393 940	35 340	—	—
5	76 540	11 900	39 260	—
6	64 974	35 906	20 018	—
7	316 000	170 800	100 000	—

8a (i) £180 000, (ii) £245 000, (iii) £270 000, (iv) £180 000, (v) £65 000   **8b** £9 000

		Cost of manufacture (£)	Gross profit (£)	Net profit (£)	Balance sheet total (£)
9a	1984	152 750	47 250	25 650	
9b	1985	285 500	114 500	42 550	
10		59 788	127 954	16 190	70 192
11		128 972	78 790	53 137	84 643
12		429 240	194 160	136 870	361 160
13		368 400	—	—	—
14		92 000	80 450		86 380
15		103 250	85 000	8 400	

Exercises Set 21

1   Net profit £6 160
2   Net profit £39 109
3   Net profit £55 780, bal. c/f £53 090
4   Bals c/f: Year 1 £10 000, Year 2 £14 800, Year 3 £22 400
5   Bal. c/f £206 800
6   Net profit £291 840, bal. c/f £304 140
7a Bal. c/f £27 000   7b £539 000   7c Capital Employed £539 000
8   Balance sheet total £420 000
9   Balance sheet total £420 000
10 Balance sheet total £302 100

	Gross profit (£)	Net profit (£)	Balance sheet total (£)
11	28 900	6 840	444 800
12	—	—	1 356 000
13	43 660	13 060	103 248
14	65 990	11 850	229 350
15	490 600	189 740	806 280
16	135 740	61 780	436 980
17	120 800	38 940	394 260
18	300 600	197 460	676 660
19	197 580	105 380	467 660
20	450 680	103 388	886 988
21	55 800	22 256	46 056

		Gross profit (£)	Net profit (£)	Balance sheet total (£)
22	1983	1 986 000	272 000	1 425 000
	1984	1 353 000	495 000	1 790 000
23		215 800	52 800	462 900
24		377 950	180 200	684 700
25		279 090	82 721	605 905
26		64 167	58 371	—
27		—	—	38 849

Exercises Set 22

1 (a) 6.6% (b) 2% (c) 3.3 times (d) 40% (e) 38% (f) 13.3% (g) 5% (h) 4% (i) 15.7% (j) nil (k) 4.5 times (l) 5.56 times (m) 21.4 times (n) 9.7 times (o) 12 times (p) 1.35:1 (q) 0.85:1 (r) 38 days (s) 67 days (t) 2.5:1 (u) 10p (v) 6:1 (w) 8p (x) 13.3% (y) 1.25 times

2 (a) F (b) D (c) F (d) D (e) F (f) E and F equal (g) D (h) D (i) F (j) F (k) F (l) D (m) D

3a (i) 10 times (ii) 16.67% (iii) 1.5 months (iv) £288 000 (v) 0.9:1 (vi) 0.6:1 (vii) 5%

4a (i) 10 times (ii) 25% (iii) 6.6% (iv) £60 000 (v) See text pp. 261–2 (vi) 1.2 months (vii) 0.57:1

5a (i) 50% (ii) £268 000 (iii) 6.3 times (iv) 12 times (v) 25%

5b (i) Yes (ii) Yes

6a (i) £350 000 (ii) 5.38 times (iii) 25% (iv) 20% (v) 1.5 months (vi) See text, p. 354

7	Ratio	19–1	19–2	19–3
	RoI (%)	10.8	7.8	3.4
	Net profit	25.3	13.9	4.0
	Sales/capital employed (times)	0.46	0.56	0.85
	Gross profit (%)	53.3	44.4	24.0
	Selling expenses/sales (%)	30.0	30.5	20.0
	Fixed assets turnover (times)	0.5	0.64	1.0
	Current assets turnover (times)	3.0	3.05	2.9
	Working capital turnover (times)	7.5	7.8	6.9
	Debtors turnover (times)	10	9	8
	Stock turnover (times)	3.5	4	4
	Current asset ratio	2:1	1.96:1	2.09:1
	Acid test ratio	0.8:1	0.77:1	0.88:1
	Credit given (days)	36.5	40.5	45.6
	EpS (pence)	10	6.5	3.5
	P/E ratio	2.5:1	2:1	0.58:1
	Dividend per share (pence)	5	3	1.75
	Dividend yield (%)	20	23	29
	Dividend cover (times)	2	2.2	2

Abridged Answers

	Ratio	19–1	19–2	19–3
8	RoI (%)	25	12.1	
	Net profit (%)	50	20	
	Sales/capital employed (times)	0.5	0.6	
	Gross profit (%)	60	30	
	Total expenses/sales (%)	10	10	
	Fixed asset turnover (times)	0.83	1.1	
	Current asset turnover (times)	0.71	1.0	
	Working capital turnover (times)	1.25	2.0	
	Debtors turnover (times)	2.0	2.2	
	Stock turnover (times)	1.14	1.75	
	Current asset ratio	2.33:1	2.0:1	
	Acid test ratio	1.33:1	1:1	
	Credit given (days)	182.5	164.25	
	Credit received (days)	243.3	203.8	
	EpS (pence)	33.3	20	
	P/E ratio	9:1	12.5:1	
	Dividend per share (pence)	6.6	7.5	
	Dividend yield (%)	2.2	3	
	Dividend cover (times)	5	2.66	
9	RoI (%)	37.5	52	107
	Net profit/sales (%)	24	19.3	29.5
	Gross profit/sales (%)	36	33.3	40
	Fixed asset turnover (times)	2	3.3	5
	Current asset turnover (times)	2.9	2.9	5
	Working capital turnover (times)	7	13.6	13.3
	Debtors turnover (times)	5	4	8
	Stock turnover (times)	8	8	12
	Current asset ratio	1.7:1	1.3:1	1.6:1
	Acid test ratio	1.2:1	0.9:1	1.4:1
	Credit given (days)	73	91	46
	EpS (pence)	48	52.7	107
	P/E ratio	0.6:1	0.47:1	0.37:1
	Dividend per share (pence)	10	9	20

		A	B
10	RoI (%)	20	25
	Sales/capital employed (times)	0.98	1.0
	Gross profit (%)	25.9	35
	Selling expenses/sales (%)	5.6	10
	Raw materials/sales (%)	51.85	38
	Manufacturing wages/sales (%)	11.1	16
	Factory overheads/sales (%)	3.7	6
	Working capital turnover (times)	2.16	10.0
	Debtors turnover (times)	8	10
	Stock turnover (times)	3.3	3.6
	Current asset ratio	1.92:1	1.5:1
	Acid test ratio	1.48:1	0.6:1
	Credit given (days)	45.6	36.5
	EpS (pence)	27.5	36.76

11a (i) 7.2 (ii) 42.4 (iii) Admin. 10.8, Selling & dist. 2.6, Gen. & fin. 0.6 (iv) 28.4 (v) 36.3 (vi) £23 360 (vii) 2:1 (viii) 0.74:1 (ix) 10 times (x) 5 times (xi) Acid test ratio 1.3:1

12		19–3	19–4
	RoI (%)	15.1	12.73
	Current asset ratio	1.86:1	1.77:1
	Acid test ratio	1.16:1	1.06:1
	EpS (pence)	18.75	16
	Dividend per share (pence)	10	10

13 Answer depends on figures used

14a (i) (a) Viability – yes (b) Profitable – no (loss £34 000) (c) Working capital ratio 0.77:1, Liquid capital ratio 0.15:1 (d) Prior charges
(ii) (a) Lack of profitability (b) Lack of liquidity

15a (i) 2 times (ii) 10:1 (iii) 11 times (iv) 1.5 months

15b Yes   **15c** See text, pp. 364–365

16a Company losses for year £220 000; Illiquid: working capital ratio 0.67:1, acid test ratio 0.167:1; No return on capital employed; Value of investment overstated

16b See text, pp. 364–367

17a 35%   **17b** 12%   **17c** 2¼ months   **17d** 4½ months

18 i 50% ii 100% iii 25% iv 75.8% v 4.54 times vi 26 days vii 4:1 viii 1.6:1

		1982	1983	1984
19a	Gross profit/sales (%)	20	15.38	16.67
	Net profit/sales (%)	10	6.92	8.62
	Return on capital employed (%)	14.29	11.39	14.13
	Working capital ratio	2.25:1	2.58:1	2.88:1
	Acid test ratio	1:1	0.58:1	0.53:1

19b See text, p. 354

		1980	1981	1982
20a	(i)	20%	16.7%	14.9%
	(ii)	25%	20.0%	17.6%
	(iii)	14.2 times	14 times	9.9 times
	(iv)	33.9%	35.5%	18.9%

20b See text, pp. 364–367

		1983	1982
21a	(i)	33.3%	50%
	(ii)	25%	33.3%
	(iii)	85.4%	103.4%
	(iv)	66 days	37 days
	(v)	2.2:1	3.3:1
	(vi)	1.4:1	2.2:1

21b See text, p. 361

		1981	1982
22a	Annual rate of stock turnover (times)	5	5.8
	Days credit from creditors	36.5	47
	Days credit to debtors	27	42
	Return on capital employed (%)	29	36
	Working capital ratio	2:1	1.7:1

22b See text, p. 361

Abridged Answers

		1983	1984
23	Rate of stock turnover (times)	11.8	5.5
	Return on capital employed (%)	46.2	32.5
	Rate of debtor turnover (days)	36.5	33.4
	Rate of creditor turnover (days)	46.5	49.8
	Working capital ratio	0.54:1	1.87:1

			1983	1984
24a	(i)	Rate of stock turnover (times)	7.76	5.41
	(ii)	Rate of debtors turnover (times)	11.42	10.34
	(iii)	Rate of creditors turnover (times)	7.49	7.16
	(iv)	Working capital ratio	2:1	1.85:1
	(v)	Return on capital employed (%)	46.15	32.5

25 Gross profit £62 500, net profit £25 000, balance sheet total £187 500

26b Bank: Operating profit/loan interest; outside liabilities/shareholders' funds; liquid assets/current liabilities; total assets/shareholders' funds
Mr Whitehall: Price per share; earnings per share; dividend per share; price/earnings ratio

27a Lively 4 times   27b Quick 73 days   27c Quick 36.5 days   27d Both 40%
27e Lively 33.3%

		Gordon Ray	Smooth Dealers
28a	Return on capital employed (%)	3	5
	Net profit/turnover (%)	3.33	5.33
	Gross profit/turnover (%)	46.67	46.67
	Current ratio	3.5:1	5.4:1
	Acid test ratio	1.75:1	3.16:1

28b See text, pp. 353 and 355

		1983	1984	1985
29a	Return on gross capital employed (%)	21.05	10.78	10.16
	Acid or quick ratio	3.87:1	6.58:1	3.78:1
	Stock turnover	4 times	4 times	4 times
	Net profit/sales (%)	20	15	13.6

29b Gross profit/sales, current assets/current liabilities

29c See text, pp. 364–367   29d See text, pp. 364–367

Exercises Set 23

1 Bal. b/d £2 670 (dr.)

2a £15 500   2b Bal. b/d £4 350 (dr.)   2c Excess of income £2 280, balance sheet total £17 780

3 Excess of income £4 715, balance sheet total £22 365

4 Accumulated fund £21 940, excess of income £930, balance sheet total £22 870

5 Accumulated fund £16 600, excess of income £18 420, balance sheet total £35 020

6 Accumulated fund £96 650, profit on bar £6 000, excess of income £22 800, balance sheet total £119 450

7   Accumulated fund £10 300, profit on bar £6 750, excess of income £7 330, balance sheet total £17 630

8   Accumulated fund £7 560, excess of expenditure £20, balance sheet total £7 540

9   Profit on bar & coffee £4 400, excess of income £2 600, balance sheet total £20 600

10   Accumulated fund £27 570, excess of expenditure £17 680, balance sheet total £21 980

11   Accumulated fund £2 010, excess of income £1 380, balance sheet total £3 390

12   Accumulated fund £118 500, excess of income £9 250, balance sheet total £132 750

13   Accumulated fund £40 850, excess of income £5 200, balance sheet total £86 600

14   Transfers to Income and Expenditure Account: Subscriptions £9 200, Electricity £2 200, Profit on bar £33 750

15   Accumulated fund £27 000, excess of expenditure £2 300, balance sheet total £24 700

16   Accumulated fund £16 070, excess of income £1 005, balance sheet total £17 075

17   Accumulated fund £14 600, excess of income £1 865, balance sheet total £16 465

18   Accumulated fund £27 289, excess of income £1 042, balance sheet total £28 331

19   Excess of income £98, balance sheet total at 31 December £480, balance sheet total at 1 January £382

20   Excess of income £1 496, balance sheet total £12 118

21   Excess of income £1 205

Exercises Set 24

1   Net profit £11 200

2   Net profit £4 686

3a   £197 900   3b Profit £34 300   3c Balance sheet total £200 700

4   Gross profit £22 500, net profit £18 000, balance sheet total £164 500

5   Gross profit £14 400, net loss £9 650, balance sheet total £62 850

6a   £46 300, £79 400   6b Net profit £18 000   6c Balance sheet total £77 800

7a   £83 400, £132 700   7b Net profit £33 600   7c Balance sheet total £175 500

8   Gross profit £27 500, net profit £20 000

9   Gross profit £625, net loss £965, balance sheet total £6 335

10   Gross profit £23 600, net profit £10 000, balance sheet total £44 920

11   Gross profit £35 400, net profit £21 780

12   Gross profit £60 100, net profit £31 860, balance sheet total £108 220

13   Gross profit £10 020, net loss £1 500, balance sheet total £118 960

14   Gross profit £25 650, net profit £19 500, balance sheet total £16 000

526 Abridged Answers

15 Gross profit £25 000, net profit £7 500, balance sheet total £18 300
16 Gross profit £84 000, net profit £850, balance sheet total £105 460
17 Gross profit £19 500, net profit £5 850, balance sheet total £10 750
18 Value of stock lost £4 025
19 Insurance claim £63 000
20 Cost of stock destroyed £17 394
21 Balance £2 650, balance sheet total £40 500
22 Gross profit £53 600, net profit £12 415, balance sheet total £52 515
23 Gross profit £24 900, net profit £3 015, balance sheet total £15 640

Exercises Set 25

1   See text, pp. 447–451
2a FIFO £480   2b LIFO £400   2c Periodic simple average £401.25
3a (i) FIFO £1 600 (ii) LIFO £1 350 (iii) Periodic simple average £1 340 (iv) Periodic weighted average £1 553
3b Gross profit: (i) £10 850 (ii) £10 600 (iii) £10 590 (iv) £10 803
4a Gross profit 19–5 £4 300, gross profit 19–6 £6 550
4b Periodic weighted average cost method:
    31.12.19–5   Value of closing stock £2 160, gross profit down by £40
    31.12.19–6   Value of closing stock £4 436, gross profit up by £176
4c Continuous weighted average cost method:
    31.12.19–5   Value of closing stock £2 320, gross profit up by £120
    31.12.19–6   Value of closing stock £4 877, gross profit up by £577
5a FIFO £550   5b LIFO £465   5c Weighted average £503
6a (i) FIFO £725 (ii) LIFO £550 (iii) Periodic simple weighted average £619 (iv) Periodic weighted average £638 (v) Weighted average £696
7a £2 000   7b £1 300   7c £1 457   7d £1 609

Exercises Set 26

1   See text, p. 456
2   1. Delivery Van Account:
       Dr.   £29 000
    2. Interest Suspense Account:
       Dr.   £3 000
       Cr.   £1 000, £1 000, £1 000
    3. Transport Ltd:
       Dr.   £2 000, £10 000, £10 000, £10 000
       Cr.   £29 000, £3 000
3a Interest Suspense Account:
    Dr.   £500, £1 000, £1 500
    Cr.   £500, £1 000, £1 500

3b Profit and Loss Account (extracts):
Dr. £500, £1 000, £1 500

4 Motor Vans Account:
Dr. £10 000
Interest Account:
Dr. £750, £676, £593
Cr. £750, £676, £593
Profit and Loss Account (extracts):
Dr. £750, £676, £593
Motors Ltd:
Dr. £1 000, £1 500, £1 500, £1 500
Cr. £10 000, £750, £676, £593
Bal. b/d £6 419 (cr.)

Balance sheet (extracts)

	19–1 £	19–2 £	19–3 £
Fixed assets at cost			
Motor van	10 000	10 000	10 000
Current liabilities			
Due to hire purchase co.	8 250	7 426	6 419

5 Lorries Account:
Dr. £25 000
Interest Account:
Dr. £1 900, £1 490, £1 093
Cr. £1 900, £1 490, £1 093
Profit and Loss Account (extracts):
Dr. £1 900, £1 490, £1 093
Lorry Sales Ltd:
Dr. £6 000, £6 000, £6 000
Cr. £25 000, £1 900, £1 490, £1 093
Bal. b/d £11 483 (cr.)

Balance sheet (extracts)

	19–1 £	19–2 £	19–3 £
Fixed assets at cost			
Lorry			
Current liabilities	25 000	25 000	25 000
Due to hire purchase co.	20 900	16 390	11 483

6 James Joyce:
Dr. £29 000, £3 000
Cr. £2 000, £10 000, £10 000, £10 000
Interest Receivable Account:
Dr. £1 000, £1 000, £1 000
Suspense Account:
Cr. £3 000
Sales Account:
Dr. £29 000
Cr. £29 000
Profit and Loss Account (extracts):
Cr. £1 000, £1 000, £1 000

528 Abridged Answers

7   James Joyce:
    Dr. £29 000, £3 000
    Cr.   £2 000, £10 000, £10 000, £10 000
    Interest Receivable Account:
    Dr. £1 000, £1 000, £1 000
    Suspense Account:
    Cr. £3 000
    Profit and Loss Account (extracts):
    Cr. £1 000, £1 000, £1 000
    Sales Account:
    Dr. £29 000
    Cr. £29 000

8   James North:
    Dr. £10 000, £750, £676, £593
    Cr.   £1 000, £1 500, £1 500, £1 500
    Bal. b/d £6 519 (dr.)
    Interest Receivable Account:
    Dr. £750, £676, £593
    Cr. £750, £676, £593
    Profit and Loss Account (extracts):
    Cr. £750, £676, £593
    Sales Account:
    Dr. £10 000
    Cr. £10 000

9a Gross profit £480

9b (i) Charge to Profit and Loss Account, Year 7: £2 135

9b (ii)

Balance sheet, end of Year 7 (extract)

	Cost	Depreciation to date	Net
	£	£	£
Fixed assets			
Photocopier	2 400	800	1 600
Current liabilities			
Due to hire purchase co.			1 425

Exercises Set 27

	Sources (£)	Applications (£)	Movement in net liquid funds (£)
1	58 000	62 000	− 4 000
2	96 000	105 000	− 9 000
3	392 000	441 500	−49 500
4	Balance sheet total £2 756 000		

	Sources (£)	Applications (£)	Movement in net liquid funds (£)
5	18 000	10 000	−20 000
6	27 600	26 000	− 2 500

		Sources (£)	Applications (£)	Movement in net liquid funds (£)
7a		19 200	21 000	− 16 800
8a	1981	17 050	29 000	+ 3 250
	1982	52 850	49 800	− 9 200
9a		596 000	312 000	+115 000
10a		270 000	236 000	− 95 000

Index

accounting: concepts and conventions 2–4; definition 1; policies 4; ratios 355–63
accounts: account sales 227; acid test 361, 367; classes of 11
accrual concept 3; accrued expenses 95, 96; accrued receipts 98
accumulated fund 393, 394, 395, 399
adjustments 326–8
agent, consignment accounts 225–8
appropriation accounts: companies 313–14; partnerships 154–7
articles of association 261
assets: appreciation of fixed 121; current 316; current asset turnover 360, 365; fixed 315; fixed asset turnover 360, 366; intangible 315; revaluation of 176; sale or disposal of 118, 119; tangible fixed 315

bad debts: definition 103; provision 104–5; recovered 106
balance sheets: composition of company 314–15, 317–18; interpretation of 353–67; notes 318; partnership 158; sole trader 133–41
bank: account 49; reconciliation statement 49–50, 54–6; statement 49–51
bar codes 485
bar trading account 393–4, 396
bills of exchange 232–43; bills payable 233, 238; bills receivable 232–3; discounting 235; dishonour 236; negotiation 235; noting charges 236; renewal 236; retiral 237
books of original entry 10, 14
bought ledger 71
branch accounts 247–55

branch stock account 251–2
business entity concept 2
business packages 482
business purchase 276–85

capital: authorised 261–2; called up 262; employed 356; expenditure 89–91; gearing 362; issued 262; liquid 361
capital and revenue expenditure 89–91
capitalisation of revenue expenditure 91
capital gearing 362
capital and revenue receipts 90
cash discounts on debtors and creditors 107–8
club accounts 393–401
company accounts: discretionary items 313; distribution of profits 313; main function of final accounts 310; non-discretionary items 313
company accounts, preparation and presentation of 306–28
compensating errors 29
computerised business systems 481
computers in accounting 481–9
conservatism concept 3, 394
consignee 225
consignor 225
consignment accounts 225–9
consistency concept 10, 312
continuous weighted average 451
contra accounts 71
contra entries 13
control accounts 69–75, 419–50
cost of manufacture 289–90
cost of sales 132
credit sale agreements 456

532 Index

creditors ledger control account 71, 419, 423
current assets 316–17
current liabilities 317
current ratio 361
customised business systems 489

debentures 266, 318
debtors control account 70, 419, 423
depreciation: causes 112; diminishing balance method 117–18; methods of calculating 114; of assets bought and sold 113; revaluation method 120–1; straight-line method 114–16, 118
direct costs 289
direct expenses 289
discretionary items 313
distribution of profits 313; cover 264; dividends 261; per share 363; policy 363; yield 364
double-entry concept 2–3
drawings 423

earnings per share (EpS) 363
errors: correction of 29–32; of commission 28; compensating 29; complete reversal of entries 29; effects on net profit 36; not disclosed by trial balance 28; of omission 28; of original entry 28; of principle 31
expenses: accruals 96; administration 311–12; direct 289; establishment 311–12; factory overhead 289; financial 311, 313; indirect (overhead) 289; ratio to sales 359; research and development 311, 313; selling and distribution 311, 313

final accounts: companies 328–52; partnerships 153–9; sole traders 131–41
FIFO 448
fire losses 429
fixed assets 133, 315
flow of funds statements 465–79

Garner v. *Murray* 210
general reserves 318
going-concern concept 3
goods in transit 326
goodwill 173–5

gross profit to sales % 359

hire purchase accounts 456–63
hire purchase interest, method of dealing with 457–62
hire purchase trading account 462–3

impersonal accounts 11
income and expenditure accounts 393–401
income statement 133
incomplete records 416–29
increased net worth method 417
insurance claims 327, 429
intangible assets 315, 356
interest on capital 154
interest on drawings 154
interest suspense method 461
interpretation of accounts 353–66
investments: other 316; trade 315

joint venture accounts 218–20
journal 10, 12–13; narration 29; uses 12, 14

liabilities: current 317; long-term 318
limitations of accounts and balance sheet 354
limited companies 306–52
LIFO 448–9
liquid ratio 361
liquidity 361
liquidity problems 366–7

manufacturing accounts 289–94
margin 425
mark-up 425
materiality concept 3
memorandum of association 261
memorandum joint venture account 218–20
money measurement concept 2
more difficult adjustments 326–8

net worth method of finding profit 417
nominal accounts 11
nominal ledger 69
nominal share capital 261–2
non-commercial organisations 391–401

omission, errors of 28, 30
operating cycle 316
order of liquidity 138

Index 533

order of permanence 137
ordinary shares 261
original entry: books of 13–14; errors in 28–9
overtrading 366

paid-up capital 262
partnership: accounts of 153–8; Act 1890 153; agreement deeds 153; amalgamation 196; appropriation accounts 154–7; balance sheets 158–9; capital accounts 153; current accounts 154; dissolution 208–17; drawing accounts 154; formation 173, 196–201; guaranteed share of profits 158; interest on capital 154; interest on drawings 155, 156; profit and loss accounts 154–6
periodic simple average 449
periodic weighted average 450
personal accounts 11
position statement 136–7, 314–18
preference shareholders 261
preference shares 261
preliminary expenses 318
prepaid receipts 99
prepayments 97–8
prime costs 289
principle, errors of 31
profit: effects of errors on 36; gross 132; increase in net worth as 417; manufacturing 291–2; net 133, 355; profitability and activity ratios 355–60; profit and loss accounts 132, 154, 311–13
provision for: bad debts 104–5; depreciation 113–18
prudence concept 3
purchase of business 276
purchases: book 10, 12–14; ledger control account 71; returns book 10, 12–14

rate of stock turnover 360
ratio analysis 355–66
real accounts 11
realisation concept 3
receipts and payments accounts 391–2
reconciliation statements 49–56
reserves 317–18
returns: inwards book 12–14; outward book 12–14
return on investment (RoI) 358–9

revaluation of assets 176
revaluation reserve 317
revenue expenditure 89–91
revenue reserves 318

sales: book 13–14; cost of 132; ledger control account 70; returns book 10, 12–14
self-balancing ledgers 71
shares: classes of 261; cumulative preference 261; equity shares 261; equity shareholders 317; forefeiture of shares 263; issue and redemption and purchase of 261–71; issued at premium 263; issue price of shares 262; ordinary 261; oversubscribed 263; payments for shares issued 262; preference 261; redeemable preference 261; redemption and purchase of company's own shares 267–71; re-issue of forfeited shares 263; types of share capital 261; undersubscribed 263; unpaid calls 263
single entry 416, 430
sole trader 131–41
solvency and liquidity 360–2
sources and application of funds 465–70
sources of long-term finance 317–18
spreadsheets 486
Statements of Standard Accounting Practice (SSAPs) 4–7, 10, 466, 468
stock: damaged by fire 429; turnover rate 360; valuation 447–52
straight-line method of depreciation 114
sum of digits 459–60
sum of digits formula 459
suspense accounts 33–5

trade investment 315
trading account 132
trial balance: definition 25; errors not revealed 28; failure to agree procedure 27; limitations of 25, 28

uncalled capital 262

Value Added Tax 18–24

working capital 133, 317
working capital level 316
work-in-progress 290